THE JEWS OF WARSAW, 1939-1943

THE JEWS OF WARSAW, 1939-1943

Ghetto, Underground, Revolt

BY YISRAEL GUTMAN

Translated from the Hebrew by Ina Friedman

Indiana University Press
BLOOMINGTON AND INDIANAPOLIS

First Midland Book Edition 1989

Manufactured in the United States of America

Library of Congress Cataloging in Publication Data

Gutman, Yisrael.
    The Jews of Warsaw, 1939–1943.

    Translation of: Yehude Varshah, 1939–1943.
    Bibliography: p.
    Includes index.
    1. Jews—Poland—Warsaw—Persecutions. 2. Holocaust,
Jewish (1939–1945)—Poland—Warsaw. 3. Warsaw (Poland)
—History—Uprising of 1943. 4. Warsaw (Poland)—
Ethnic relations. I. Title.
DS135.P62W27313   940.53′15′03924   81-47570
cl. ISBN 0-253-33174-9   AACR2
pa. ISBN 0-253-20511-5

3 4 5 6 7 93 92 91 90 89

The research for this book was conducted under the auspices of the
Institute of Contemporary Jewry of the Hebrew University of
Jerusalem.

To the memory of my son, Nimrod,
who fell while serving in the
Israel Defense Forces

Contents

ABBREVIATIONS

A.K.	Armia Krajowa
A.L.	Armia Ludowa
B.Ż.I.H.	Biuletyn Żydowskiego Instytutu Historycznego
Centos	Centrala Opieki nad Sierotami
C.K.U.	Centralna Komisja Uchodźców
CPR	Commission for Polish Relief
Dulag	Durchgangs-Lager
F.P.O.	Faraynigte Partisaner Organizatsye
Gestapo	Geheime Staatspolizei
G.L.	Gwardia Ludowa
HTO	Haupttreuhandstelle-Ost
JDC	Joint Distribution Committee
K.L.	Konzentrationslager
N.R.O.	Naczelna Rada Opiekuńcza
N.S.V.	Nationalsozialistische Volkswohlfart
O.B.W.	Ostdeutsche Bautischlerei Werkstätte
O.N.R.	Obóz Narodowo-Radykalny
ORT	Obshchestvo Razpostranienia Truda
Osti	SS-Ostindustrie
PLAN	Polska Ludowa Akcja Niepodległościowa
P.P.R.	Polska Partia Robotnicza
P.P.S.	Polska Partia Socjalistyczna
R.G.O.	Rada Główna Opiekuńcza
R.K.F.	Reichskommissar fur die Festigung des deutschen Volkstums
R.S.H.A.	Reichssicherheitshauptamt
S.D.	Sicherheitsdienst
SS	Schutzstaffel der NSDAP
Toporol	Towarzystwo Popierania Rolnictwa
TOZ	Towarzystwo Ochrony Zdrowia
W.V.H.A.	Wirtschaftsverwaltungshauptamt
Yikor	Yidishe Kultur Organizatsye
YIVO	Yiddish Scientific Institute–Yivo
Z.W.Z.	Związek Walki Zbrojnej
Ż.K.N.	Żydowski Komitet Narodowy
Ż.O.B.	Żydowska Organizacja Bojowa
Ż.S.S.	Żydowska Samopomoc Społeczna
Ż.T.O.S.	Żydowskie Towarzystwo Opieki Społecznej
Ż.Z.W.	Żydowski Związek Wojskowy

PREFACE

The purpose of this work is to examine the character and conduct of the Jewish community of Warsaw in face of the persecutive tactics of the Nazi occupation regime; to throw light on the means that were adopted to cope, both intellectually and psychologically, with the grave problems of the period; and to analyze the development of the armed resistance movement and the armed struggle of the Jews of Warsaw. During the preliminary research for this book, it became clear that one cannot detach the acts of resistance and the armed uprising from the broader character of Jewish public life as it took shape during the periods of the occupation and the ghetto. I have therefore chosen to describe the growth and development of the resistance movement and the armed struggle against the wider background of ghetto life and the clandestine communal activities. It is impossible to understand the significance of the resistance and the uprising without appreciating the tensions and human and social conditions that existed during the Holocaust.

Most of the works written to date have related events from a single point of view: Jewish or German. I have attempted to make use of the variegated source material that is available from Jewish, German, and Polish sources and to throw light on critical events by analyzing the motivations and conduct of each side in the conflict. The assumptions of many Jews at the time proved incorrect, since the Jews were not able to check the accuracy of German claims and distinguish between deceptive tactics and other meanings. The Germans likewise knew very little about what was going on in the Jewish underground, while the behavior of the Poles toward the Jews was motivated primarily by considerations of self-interest. In writing this work I have attempted to assimilate the aims and viewpoints of all the sides, on the assumption that only by clarifying the positions and actions of all the factors involved (while obviously attempting to place each point that bears on the subject in its proper perspective) is it possible to reconstruct and understand developments and events.

The material at the disposal of the scholar who wishes to study the Jewish underground and the armed resistance movement in Warsaw is relatively extensive. Among the Jewish sources, the "Oneg Shabbat" Archive that was set up in the Warsaw underground by the historian Dr. Emmanuel Ringelblum is of cardinal importance. Both parts of the archive, which was discovered after the war, contain a rich collection of articles from the underground press, diaries, and documents. Very little of this material has been exploited until now, and I have attempted to make as much use of it as possible in this book. Important testimony was also preserved in other underground archives and in letters and announcements that activists of the clandestine Jewish National Committee smuggled out to the free world.

Among the German sources dealing with the Jewish uprising in Warsaw, there is special importance to the detailed report of the SS General Jürgen Stroop, who commanded the battle against the rebellious Warsaw ghetto. References to the uprising, impressions, and evidence of the ramifications of the Jewish resistance campaign can be found in correspondences and even in the diaries of senior Nazi officials.

The Polish material is very rich indeed, comprising the responses of the Polish underground press, the positions adopted by the political and military circles both in the country and in exile, and the feelings of both common men and members of the intelligentsia, recorded in diaries and a variety of memoirs.

The extensive literature published on the Warsaw ghetto and the Jewish resistance and fighting organization constitutes a complex problem. The number of works already extends to hundreds of volumes of diaries, memoirs, historical surveys, and other genres. A scholar cannot afford to ignore such diversified works, which contain extremely important authentic material. On the other hand, he cannot ignore the fact that a large portion of this literature suffers from a number of drawbacks. Many who recorded their memoirs wrote from a very personal and idiosyncratic viewpoint, meaning that they passed on only what was known to them and inevitably skipped over all the rest. There are also cases in which the writer let his imagination run free and presents as factual testimony evidence that was only rumored or even merely surmised by the author himself. It is likewise important to keep in mind that the resistance organizations in Warsaw were made up of various political factions, and it is only natural that in many works the role of one faction or another was given added weight. Indeed, some works were written for the express purpose of glorifying a specific body or faction, and in such cases the authors take recourse to testimonies and generalizations that must be carefully checked. Characteristic of this approach is the historical and historiographic research carried on in Warsaw after the war. On the one hand, it contributed to the discovery of original material on the subject, yet it was heavily influenced by a constellation of political interests and clearly bears the mark of the People's Republic of Poland.

The scholar assumes a great responsibility in appraising the value and accuracy of sources. In doing so, I have tried to maintain an objective and pragmatic approach, but I am not oblivious to the fact that even the scholar is affected by the events and material that make up the body of his work. So much the more so when one is dealing with a horrifying period of contemporary Jewish history that is laden with incalculable emotional impact.

I should like to express my gratitude to all those who helped me with their wise advice and in other ways during my years of work. I owe special thanks to Professor Yehuda Bauer, who proposed that this study be undertaken and followed it through the stages of crystallization and composition. I was also fortunate to benefit from the wide knowledge of Professors Shmuel Ettinger and the late Haim Hillel Ben-Sasson, my mentors at the Hebrew University of Jerusalem, who not only instructed me in Jewish history but taught me much about scholarly methodology. My gratitude also goes to the staffs of the various archives in which I worked, especially to my friends and colleagues at the Yad Vashem Archive, who were untiring in their efforts to supply me with material, and to the staff of the Yad Vashem Library for their unflagging patience and kindness. I also wish to thank the staff of the Institute of Contemporary Jewry of the Hebrew University for their focal role in the creative and publication stages of this work and to Dr. A. Berman, Stefan Grajek, David Hanegbi, Simcha Holtzberg, Hadassah Zlotnitzki-Talmon, and especially Yitzhak Zuckerman, who spent many hours with me and helped me to certify facts and clarify complex problems in this book.

Introduction

This work chronicles the struggle of Warsaw Jewry from the outbreak of World War II (September 1939) through the final and most tragic chapter in the history of the community—the armed Jewish uprising, the annihilation of the remnant Jewish community, and the destruction of the traditional Jewish sector of the city (April–May 1943). The close of this period is essentially the final chapter in the annals of the Jews of Warsaw, a long-established and magnificent community that blossomed into the largest Jewish center in Europe and the second largest in the world. Even after the destruction of the ghetto in May 1943, thousands of Warsaw Jews continued to hide out among the Polish population of the city, and following the war Jews again came together in the Polish capital to set about reconstructing community life in the city. But the small postwar Jewish community of Warsaw could not compare, either in size or character, to Jewish society in the city before the war. Even from the perspective of its make-up, one could not view the reconstructed community as an organic sequel to its predecessor.

The Polish writer Kazimierz Brandys devoted a book to Warsaw during the war entitled *The Invincible City*. At the opening of the work, Brandys stated: "Warsaw was the capital of that war,"[1] in the sense that the city symbolized all that was both sublime and tragic during World War II. Warsaw was the first city to be bombed at the outset of the war and the first city to be turned into a battlefront. During the Jewish uprising, the ghetto—a Jewish residential district in which the Jews had been enclosed—was razed, and near the end of the war, during the Polish uprising in the summer of 1944, the entire city was demolished and turned into a ghost town. Thus Warsaw was the first victim of the global hostilities; she resisted the enemy and refused to accept docilely the terms of the occupation; she was reduced to a pile of rubble in the waning days of the Third Reich and on the eve of its collapse. Yet, although the Polish citizens of Warsaw lost their homes and property, most of them survived the war and returned to rebuild their city and their lives. But the Jewish homes in Warsaw were wiped off the face of the city, and their inhabitants were blotted out in the course of the "Final Solution to the Jewish Question."

The first Jews are believed to have settled in Warsaw during the thirteenth to fourteenth century. There are no documents to confirm the presence of Jews in the city at that time, but since we do have proof that Jews had settled in other cities of the Principality of Mazovia by then, it may be assumed that they were already in Warsaw as well. The earliest documents that speak of Jews in Warsaw date from the fifteenth century. For centuries thereafter, the Jews struggled for the right to settle permanently and pursue their livelihoods in Warsaw, which was an important commercial center and the capital of the Kingdom of Poland.

The Jews were expelled from Warsaw twice during the life of the Principality of Mazovia. In 1527, when the principality (of which Warsaw was the capital) was annexed to the Kingdom of Poland, the residents of Warsaw were granted the privilege *de non tolerandis Judaeis*. For a long period of time, Jews were forbidden to live in Warsaw and were thus forced to settle in the independent jurisdictions surrounding the city and in the suburb of Praga. But their ties with Warsaw were not severed, and Jews continued to take part in the economic life of the city. Jewish residence in Warsaw was legalized by the Prussian authorities in 1801–1802, and the number of Jews in the city reached eight to ten thousand.

The energetic growth and consolidation of the Warsaw Jewish community extended over a century (1815–1915) during the era of Congress Poland, which was a satellite of czarist Russia. In 1816 there were 15,600 Jews in Warsaw (constituting 19.2 percent of the city's population), and by 1914 the figure had grown to 337,000 (38.1 percent of the total population). The Jews assumed a leading role in construction, industrialization, and credit and investment operations. A number of Jewish families were pioneers in trade, industry, and banking both in Warsaw and in Poland as a whole. In the 1860s all restrictions on Jewish residence in the city were abolished. The years 1860–64 witnessed a strengthening of relations between Jews and Poles that was especially apparent during the Polish national uprising in 1863. But at the end of the nineteenth and beginning of the twentieth century, politically motivated anti-Semitism grew increasingly virulent in Poland and exacerbated the economic competition between the Jews and the Poles.

The impressive growth of the Jewish community was not exclusively the result of natural increase or migration from other Polish cities. During the 1860s, and especially after the wave of pogroms in Russia in 1881, an influx of Jews made their way to Warsaw from Belorussia, Volhynia, and especially Lithuania. The veteran Jews of Warsaw called these newcomers "Litvaks." The Poles, who objected to any accelerated growth of the Warsaw Jewish community, were particularly outspoken in their opposition to the migration of the "Litvaks," whom they considered to be bearers of Russian culture and loyal to the alien Russian regime.

The overwhelming majority of the community's members were Orthodox Jews, but from the middle of the nineteenth century onward, the circle of assimilated and enlightened Jews grew in size. They never succeeded in winning over the Jewish masses to their credo, but they did leave their mark on Polish cultural life and the Polish intelligentsia. The Jewish community was headed, alternately or in peculiar collaboration, by both the Orthodox faction and the assimilationists. This alliance was made possible by a clear delineation of functions and responsibilities for separate interests. The assimilationists represented the community vis-à-vis the Poles and were responsible for welfare projects, while the Orthodox (and later the Hasidim) managed the internal affairs of the community and its religious life. At the beginning of the twentieth century the status of the assimilationists declined, and with the subsequent sociocultural "renaissance," fresh political forces appeared on the scene in the form of nationalist (Zionist) organizations, autonomists, and the socialist efforts at class organization of the Bund. The immigrants who arrived from the Russian provinces, bringing with them the sense of unrest and the new currents of thought that inevitably influenced Russian Jewry, played a pivotal role in this cultural and political ferment.

During World War I the Jewish community of Warsaw absorbed a good many refugees. As the city passed from hand to hand during the course of the war, its economy was severely damaged, the Jews being affected worst of all. At the end of the war, with the establishment of an independent Polish state, the Jewish community in Warsaw grew in importance. In the wake of the war and the October Revolution, Russian Jewry was cut off from the rest of the Jewish people, and the Jews of Poland were now regarded as a community "in its own right" — a large national concentration of Jews bustling with life. Warsaw was the guiding center of Polish Jewry and to some extent a leading and influential focal point of world Jewry. It was a center of Jewish studies, Hasidism, and modern Jewish culture and housed major literary, educational, and scholarly institutions (the Institute of Jewish Studies, teachers' seminaries, and Jewish theaters), as well as the bodies that directed the affairs of cultural societies and welfare institutions. It was the headquarters for the leadership and activities of the Jewish political parties and the Jewish representatives in the Polish Parliament. Some of the famous Hasidic *admorim* chose Warsaw as their seat, and most of the Jewish dailies, periodicals, and literature of all genres were published in the city.

A large constituency of Polish Jews was not satisfied with merely the equal civil rights supposedly granted to them by the Treaty for the Protection of Minorities drawn up by the Paris Peace Conference and guaranteed in the Polish constitution. The various political factions, the Zionists, the Bund, and the Volkists all called for recognition of the Jews as a separate national entity with autonomous rights in the spheres of organization, culture, and education. But the swift realization that the Treaty for the Protection of Minorities was only a weak prop dashed the naïve hopes that the war would usher in a new era of liberty and justice for all. As matters unfolded, the new states established in Central and Eastern Europe made every effort to concentrate control of all spheres of life in the hands of the majority populations, and Poland stood out among them for its aggressive and intolerant nationalism. These trends, together with the traditional laws that discriminated against the national minorities in Poland, primarily affected the Jews, who were at the same time the target of deep-seated anti-Semitism. The Jews were an urban element that the Poles had long wanted to undermine and deprive of a livelihood—all the more so in light of the persistent economic difficulties and severe depression that overtook Poland between the wars. The Polish government, which was both unwilling and unable to carry out basic reforms and cope with the country's complex problems, increasingly singled out the Jews as a factor that aggravated the deepening crisis plaguing Poland.

Between the two wars, the Jews accounted for 10 percent of the population of Poland. In the 1931 population census, 2,700,000 Polish Jews, including 215,048 Jews in Warsaw, declared Yiddish and Hebrew as their native languages. In 1921 there were 310,322 Jews in Warsaw, about one-third of the capital's population, and the 1931 census tallied 352,650 Jews. But despite the rise in the absolute figure, the proportion of Jews in the Warsaw population fell to 30.1 percent. According to the 1931 census, 47 percent of the Jews of Warsaw engaged in industry and crafts and 33 percent in various branches of commerce. Over 47 percent of the Jews in the labor force were registered as self-employed, while the corresponding ratio among non-Jews was only 17.5 percent. These self-employed Jews, most of whom were independent craftsmen and small shopkeepers, were a very vulnerable element of the Jewish population.

During the 1930s the overall status of Polish Jewry was in consistent decline, and signs of the deteriorating situation were particularly evident in Warsaw. It is possible to point to a few dominant trends that illustrate the gravity of the situation: (1) the government heightened the economic and fiscal pressure on the Jews in an attempt to accelerate the ruin of the Jewish community; (2) Jewish political influence—grounded in the Jewish political parties, independent Jewish representation in the Parliament (for a time as part of a parliamentary bloc with other national minorities), and the power of organized Jewry in Western Europe and the United States—was rapidly eroding; and (3) Polish anti-Semitism and the demand that Jews be removed from their positions was growing stronger and louder and reached dangerous proportions after the agreement signed between Poland and the Nazi Reich in February 1934 and the death of Marshal Jozef Pilsudski in 1935. The extreme nationalist wing was controlled by a fascist-influenced faction that attempted to import methods used in the Third Reich. The so-called moderate wing, backers of the regime that had adopted many fascist traits, mildly expressed its reservations about the violent campaign against the Jews but openly supported the anti-Jewish economic boycott and the demand for heightened emigration.

In view of the economic depression of the 1930s, the cultural and sociopolitical activities of the Jews of Warsaw take on added significance. The political parties representing different, and often opposing, schools of ideology, and the youth movements continued to operate among the Jewish population, right down to the poverty-stricken slums. Cultural societies and ideological movements carried on intensive activities, and their memberships shared a strong bond and deep identification with their causes. During the 1930s the Jewish public became radicalized. Among the Zionists, this trend found expression in the decline of the centrist General Zionists and the growth of the leftist Po'alei Zion and the right-wing Revisionists. Among the non-Zionist secular Jews, the Bund grew in strength and in 1936 emerged victorious in the elections to the *kehillah* (the institutionalized leadership of the Jewish community). However, the Polish regime did not accept the results of the elections, and the *kehillah* was consequently run by an appointed body until the outbreak of World War II.

From the middle of the 1920s, and especially during the distressing period of the 1930s, the option to escape by emigrating—the course chosen by the Jews of Eastern Europe since the bloody pogroms of the 1880s—was closed off. The strong urge to leave Poland was thwarted by the immigration restrictions legislated in the traditional countries of refuge overseas, particularly the United States. In 1926 over 26,000 Jews left Poland, but by 1931 the number had dropped to 8,632. Emigration to Palestine rose sharply in 1934–35, but after 1936 this flow was likewise stemmed by the immigration restrictions imposed by the British mandatory government. From the beginning of the century to World War I, the annual average of Jewish emigrants from Poland was about 50,000–60,000, but in the decade 1921–31 it stood at 26,000 —i.e., half the previous figure—and thereafter the decline was even steeper. In addition to the immigration laws mentioned above, the objective international situation, which dictated that preference be given to finding a solution for the refugees and émigrés from Nazi Germany, further impeded emigration from Poland.

The great irony is that at the very time when a strong and fanatical ideological movement and the regime of the Third Reich depicted the Jews as a mysteriously powerful ruling force of international might, the Jewish people was in fact in a structurally weak condition and at a political nadir. The Jews of Poland did not have the advantage of a transition period in which it was still possible to make a hasty exit, like that open to the Jews of Nazi Germany until the outbreak of war in September 1939. The war descended on Polish Jewry like a thunderbolt, leaving no chance to escape.

THE
JEWS OF
WARSAW,
1939-1943

The Warsaw Ghetto

1940 — 1943

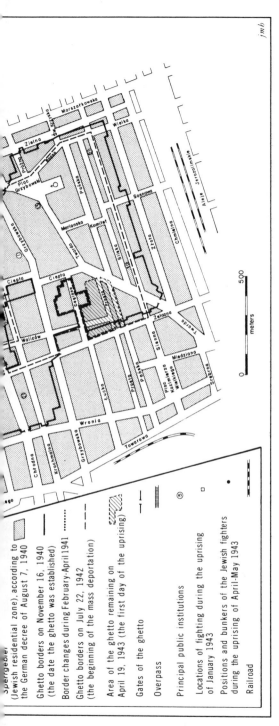

jmb

Principal Public Institutions

1. *Judenrat*
2. Order Authority (Jewish Police)
3. Jewish prison (Gęsiowka)
4. Pawiak Prison
5. Courts
6. Labor Department (*Arbeitsamt*)
7. Post office
8. Supply Authority
9. Office to Combat Usury and Profiteering
10: Berson and Bauman Hospital
11. Czyste Hospital
12. The Great Synagogue
13. Nozyk Sunagogue
14. Moriah Synagogue
15. Ż.T.O.S.
16. Centos
17. TOZ
18. ORT
19. Toporol
20. Center for Professional Studies
21. Orphanage (Janusz Korczak, director)
22. "Oneg Shabbat" Archive
23. Deportation center
24. *Umschlagplatz*

Redrawn by John Hollingsworth from a map by Yosef Ziemian.

Sperrgebiet (Jewish residential zone), according to the German decree of August 7, 1940

Ghetto borders on November 16, 1940 (the date the ghetto was established)

Border changes during February–April 1941

Ghetto borders on July 22, 1942 (the beginning of the mass deportation)

Area of the ghetto remaining on April 19, 1943 (the first day of the uprising)

Gates of the ghetto

Overpass

Principal public institutions

Locations of fighting during the uprising of January 1943

Positions and bunkers of the Jewish fighters during the uprising of April–May 1943

Railroad

PART ONE

Ghetto

Chapter One
The First Months
of the Nazi Occupation

Warsaw — A City at War   At dawn on September 1, 1939, German troops dressed in Polish-army uniforms attacked the broadcasting station in the German border town of Gleiwitz. This staged act of provocation served the Nazis as a pretext to initiate hostilities without a formal declaration of war.

Jews who had followed the political developments and mounting crisis that had preceded the outbreak of war realized that the conflict had immediately reached serious proportions. Nazi Germany had proved that it was not very particular about the means it used to achieve its ends. After the *Anschluss*, the Munich Pact, and the final dismemberment of Czechoslovakia, there was little room for illusions. The West European democracies, which had so long attempted to calm Hitler and defuse his rage by compromises and concessions, learned their lesson too late. The hastily signed Anglo-Polish mutual-assistance agreement did express a reversal in their policies, but the actual chances of Poland's receiving aid and support in an hour of crisis were slim. The Poles reacted to the immediate and sudden danger from Nazi Germany with patriotic fervor, rigidity, and a poor assessment of their true strength. The die had already been cast with the signing of the Molotov-Ribbentrop Agreement. Hitler was free to do as he pleased in Poland. The specter of a two-front war, which had haunted the Germans since their defeat in World War I, had been dispelled.

At the same time, frenzied developments during the last months preceding the war also aroused secret hopes. Many believed that Hitler, who had built his strength by virtue of threats and the creation of *faits accomplis*, would be sobered by the fact that the Powers were finally awakening from their lethargy and preparing themselves for armed defense. This outlook explains the reaction of the Jews to the news that war had become a fact: "War was expected, and had been expected for a long time, but when it actually broke out, it surprised everyone. . . ."[1] And Chaim Kaplan, a teacher in Warsaw, began his detailed diary of the war years with the sentence, "The German barbarian dared!"[2]

The events of the war unfolded with unimagined speed and consistency. By the second day of the fighting, Kaplan wrote in his diary: "Today there were four air raids in Warsaw. The inhabitants have already grown accustomed to them and know what they have to do."[3] On September 3, when news arrived of the French and British declarations of war, it was greeted with an outburst of enthusiasm. Few understood that at this stage of the war, the decisive move had only rhetorical value and would in no way alter the balance of forces in the field or aid beleaguered Poland.

The official bulletins issued by the Polish side during the first days of the war were evasive and confusing. In contrast, the frequent German broadcasts from the facilities at Breslau confidently reported swift advances and glorious victories. On the third day of the fighting, the Germans reported the capture of the important city of Częstochowa, about twenty miles from the German border. The residents of Warsaw were aware of the chaos that prevailed around them, and the clearest sign that the situation was critical came from the air—the intensity of the air raids and the feebleness of the Polish response. From the first days of the war, the Germans had already gained complete control of the skies of Poland.

The mass flight from Warsaw to the east began on September 7. It was a spontaneous, panicked escape of civilians with no clear destination in mind. Most of the refugees in this flood of hundreds of thousands were young men, who left parents, wives, and young children behind in the city. A strong urge to flee also gripped the helpless Polish government. Rumor spread that under cover of darkness, and without giving a hint of their intentions, the government and senior officials had abandoned the capital. There were also special motives to escape the city. Some of the refugees, especially the young people, among them Jews who were active in the youth movements, moved eastward on the assumption that the Polish retreat would be halted in the eastern provinces and the front would stabilize there. In addition, most of the Jews who fled assumed even then that they would be particularly vulnerable to harm under the Nazi occupation and must therefore escape.

Among those who escaped were many of the outstanding leaders of Polish Jewry, public figures and officials who ran the cultural and welfare institutions. They feared that their status and activities would cause them to be singled out as the first victims of the Nazi occupational regime. Since those who fled the city made their decision in haste, they naturally had no idea of what awaited them and had not made any contingency plans. Many of the refugees would find their way into the areas soon annexed by the Soviets. Others were the victims of bombings or the hail of bullets from planes strafing the roads to the east. Some of them were overcome by exhaustion or despair, changed their minds, and returned to Warsaw from somewhere along their road of escape or their first stop at a place of shelter. Only a few succeeded in making their way to safety in distant countries. Adam Czerniakow, who was to serve as head of the Warsaw *Judenrat*, described the flight in his diary in one sentence (September 7, 1939): "With only the shirts on their backs, some went off into the unknown."[4]

By the eighth day of the war, the Germans stood at the gates of Warsaw. The Poles decided to resist as long as possible, whatever the price, and refused to declare Warsaw a demilitarized city. Warsaw was transformed into an embattled fortress, and the population was called upon to dig trenches and set up barricades. Among those who volunteered to dig trenches were many Jews and intellectuals who had never tested their strength at physical labor. After a few days, however, the volunteers were sent home, for even the Polish command finally admitted that the last-minute shallow trenches were of little value against German armor. The barricades raised in the center of the city obstructed the movement of the civilian population, but they served no real defensive purpose. In general, all the improvised fortifications were worthless, just as there was no point, from a military outlook, in turning a heavily populated city into a fighting position. The residents of Warsaw were never asked whether they wanted their homes turned into army positions and their children enclosed in a beleaguered fortress. Yet at the beginning of the battle of Warsaw, the population was prepared to defend itself and fight with courage and dedication.

The Nazis were determined to break the spirit of Warsaw's defenders by any means necessary, and the German air command viewed the bombardment of the city as a useful experiment to test the destructive power of the air force and the effect of bombings on the morale of the civilian population. During the first days of the fighting, the Polish radio still broadcast air-raid warnings and all-clear signals, but afterward it ceased to give warning of attacks. The heavy bombers flew over Warsaw in waves and dropped their deadly loads on the heart of the city. Some bombs devastated an entire building in one blast, burying scores of people under the ruins. At first the blazes started by fire bombs were contained, but before long they raged out of control and spread to other buildings. Only a few shelters in the city were strong enough to stand up to the bombings. The natural response was for people to take shelter in their cellars, but in time it became clear that the heavy bombs were capable of destroying buildings down to their foundations, so that the cellars became mass graves. The crowded Jewish section in northern Warsaw suffered from heavy bombardments, especially on Rosh Hashanah and Yom Kippur. It is impossible to know for certain whether it was just by chance that the Jewish section was bombed during the "Days of Awe" or whether this was a premeditated act of vengeance. The experience under the Nazi occupation, however, tends to support the latter assumption. On September 14, 1939, Kaplan recorded in his diary: "Yesterday was a day of horror and destruction. Between five o'clock and seven o'clock on the eve of Rosh Hashanah there was an air raid on the Northern Quarter, which is predominantly Jewish. The day before there had been a respite in the bombing."[5] Another memoir relates: "On the two days of Rosh Hashanah, the planes bombed the Jewish section without mercy."[6]

In the meantime, refugees continued to stream into the besieged city. Warsaw was also flooded by individual stragglers and remnants of units that had lost their commanders and did not know where to turn or what to do. The Emergency Civil Guard established by Mayor Stefan Starzynski had to fulfill the regular functions of the police in addition to its own special tasks. Even at such a desperate hour, however, the Polish authorities did not abandon their prejudicial policy toward Jews, and, as Czerniakow and Ringelblum noted, no Jews were coopted onto the command of the Emergency Civil Guard.[7] There was, however, an attempt to form a "Jewish Council" or counterpart Jewish "Civilian Committee," which was eventually called the Jewish Civilian Committee of the Capital City of Warsaw.

On the first day of the war, the Polish authorities established the Metropolitan Committee of Mutual Social Aid (S.K.S.S.—*Stołeczny Komitet Samopomocy Społecznej*) and placed food storehouses, clothing, and substantial sums of money at its disposal. Jewish leaders met together and decided that they too would merge all the institutions and organizations dealing with aid and social welfare in a joint Coordinating Committee, which would establish contact with the S.K.S.S. The Coordinating Committee succeeded in acquiring funds from the Polish committee and organized a network of relief for refugees and the homeless. Soup kitchens were opened to provide nourishment for the needy, and refugees were housed in various hostels (*punkty*)—public clubs, schools, and synagogues. A group of activists, particularly from the ranks of the intelligentsia, were drawn to the Coordinating Committee, and the heads of the Joint Distribution Committee (JDC) placed funds, as well as the prestige and experience of this highly respected and dedicated American-backed institution, at the disposal of the committee. The Coordinating Committee was the first incarnation of the crucially important enterprise for Jewish self-help, which existed under a succession of names and functioned in a variety of ways throughout the struggle for Jewish survival in occupied Poland.

Despite all attempts to preserve order and discipline in the city, basic foodstuffs disappeared from the stores, prices soared, and bread lines began to form at the entrance to bakeries. At the end of the second week of September, the rumble of artillery from batteries surrounding the city joined the aerial bombardments. Even the relative respite of the nighttime hours now came to an end. Most depressing of all was the thought of people buried under the wreckage of buildings. During the fourth week of September, matters again took a turn for the worse when the Nazis intensified the shelling, and air and artillery bombardments continued without interruption. The number of homeless wandering the streets was substantial now, and people ceased to believe that caution increased one's chances of safety or that any hiding place or shelter was secure. The usually reticent Czerniakow recorded on September 24: "Shelling went on all night long. There is no gas, water, electricity, bread. A terrible day." In order to fill a pail with water, the residents of Warsaw had to reach the Vistula River or crowd around the few wells in the city.

By the last days of the siege, the morale of the public had been shattered. The citizens of Warsaw not only cursed the Germans but grumbled about their own government for stealing off and abandoning its citizens to their bitter fate. Once it had become painfully obvious that the defense of the surrounded city was a lost cause, people no longer found solace in the rumors that miraculous salvation was imminent and the Allies would finish off the Nazi forces in a few days. The Polish press, which had taken to publishing fictional reports in the hope of salvaging public morale, now ceased publication altogether. The consensus seemed to be that it was pointless to go on, for in a few more days the entire city would be swamped by destruction and death. It was also during that period of bitterness and despair that the short-lived phenomenon of Jewish-Polish brotherhood, which had been born out of the prewar political crisis and tension and reached its peak with the digging of the trenches, began to display signs of disintegration. Ringelblum noted that during the siege, relations between Polish and Jewish tenants living in the same building grew a little closer, but by the final days enmity was again revived.

On September 28 the guns fell silent. The German army had not yet entered the city, and Warsaw was in the grip of chaos and anxious expectation. As the citizens of Warsaw left their shelters and poured into the streets, the scene that spread out before them was shattering. About 25 percent of the city's buildings had been totally destroyed or badly damaged. It is estimated that about fifty thousand people had been killed or injured.[8] The streets were covered with dust, heaps of ruins, and the carcasses of horses. Diaries and memoirs of the period repeat over and over again the lament that arose when the full extent of the damage was finally assimilated: the beautiful Warsaw all had known was lost forever.

Two days after the city had fallen, the Nazi forces still had not entered Warsaw. Mobs broke into warehouses and made off with anything that came to hand. The homeless went out in search of shelter, and those fortunate enough to have a roof over their heads scrambled around in search of food for their families. The German troops who finally marched into the vanquished city exuded an aura of strength and self-confidence, not at all like men who had been sustained on "guns instead of butter," as the anti-Nazi propaganda organs had attempted to portray them. The demeanor of the well-fed Germans stood out in sharp contrast to the pitiful appearance of the remnants of the disgraced Polish army. On the day the Germans entered Warsaw, Kaplan wrote in his diary: "I studied Hitler's army . . . and I was amazed to see how well fed, sleek, and fat it was. . . . A doubt stole into my heart: perhaps it was I who had been deceived? Until now I had been certain that they were starving and we were well fed; now I see the exact opposite. . . ."[9]

The First Contact with the Occupation Regime

The refugees who flowed into Warsaw told of the torture and wanton murder perpetrated by the Germans in the captured cities and towns of Poland. Nonetheless, many of the Jews of Warsaw chose to underplay the gravity of the rumors and characterized the violence as the inevitable excesses of undisciplined soldiers at war. Many older and elderly Jews tried to muster hope by reminiscing about their experiences with the German occupation forces during World War I. They spoke of the Germans they had known then as refined and disciplined people who treated the Jews with politeness and sympathy. But the first real contact with the occupying troops served as a sobering lesson that the situation had changed.

With the entry of the Germans, supply trucks and field kitchens of the National-Socialist Welfare Association (N.S.V. —*National-sozialistische Volkswohlfahrt*) began doling out food at various points in the city. Many Jews and their children, who had not tasted any hot food for days, joined these food lines. But it wasn't long before Poles who did not know "a word of German learned how to say '*Ein Jude!*' in order to get the Jews removed from the lines."[10] The young German soldiers pulled Jews off the lines, kicked them, and, to the accompaniment of laughter from the many Poles looking on, drove them out of the area.

Then came the kidnapping of Jews for forced labor, which was a serious blow to the community. Soldiers would mount raids on Jewish neighborhoods and shanghai passersby for day labor. As a rule, these "conscripts" were forced to carry furniture, clean the apartments allocated to the occupying authorities, and work in the army camps that were in the process of being established. But the need for laborers was not the true *raison d'être* of the arbitrary abductions. For the most part, the soldiers treated their victims sadistically. They would often go out on a hunt for well-dressed women and force them to do cleaning jobs using their underwear as rags. It was not uncommon for them to confiscate a victim's papers, thus forcing him to appear for work for a number of days. The hunt for quarry in the open streets frightened the Jewish population, and many Jews, particularly the elderly, tried to avoid leaving their homes altogether. Another favorite sport of the German soldiers, as well as the "spruced-up officers," was to pluck out or cut off the beards of Orthodox Jews. Sometimes they didn't stop at beards and beat the Jews as they chopped off their hair as well in an orgy of derisive laughter.

It wasn't long before the Germans began confiscating Jewish property. Soldiers would turn up at relatively large Jewish apartments, present a signed warrant—or not even bother with such formalities—and make off with furniture, valuables, and cash. After household articles and money came the confiscation of salable goods. The Jews were at a loss to interpret whether these confiscations were according to official policy or were just random instances of individual pillage. "It's possible that the maltreatment of Jews is not the result of orders from above," Kaplan wrote on October 4, "but that individual soldiers who have been saturated with hatred of Jews since childhood carry out these revolting acts on their own, and their victims are too afraid to complain to the authorities lest something terrible happen to them."[11]

In memoirs written during the war, the engineer Henryk Brysker relates: "A few times, at the beginning, victims turned to the Germans and complained that property had been confiscated from them without legal process or written authorization. The Gestapo man to whom the complaint was addressed would respond with a blow of his revolver butt to clear the complainant's head of any notion that the German rulers might be pilferers or thieves. . . ."[12]

The fact that the Germans were in no hurry to impose order on the city, restore the supply of gas and electricity, or clean up the mounds of ruins and garbage that cluttered the streets nourished the stubborn rumors that the Nazi occupation was only transitory. The capricious pillage ran contrary to the accepted image of the Germans as disciplined and orderly people, and if German soldiers were allowed to run wild in the captured city, it must be a sign that their presence in Warsaw was only as a temporary occupation army.

Scores of people continued to flee eastward, while others placed credence in the rumors that the Russians were about to enter Warsaw, and even if the entire city was not turned over to them, they would establish their rule up to the Vistula line. These rumors were not at all unfounded. Today we know that the Molotov-Ribbentrop Pact signed in Moscow on August 23, 1939, contained a secret protocol that dealt with the division of the spoils between the two treaty partners in the event of the "territorial and political transformation" of the Polish state. The Baltic states, with the exception of Lithuania, were marked as a "sphere of Soviet influence," and a plan was drawn up to divide Poland four ways. According to the document, the Narew, Vistula, and San rivers were to be the borderline of the areas to be divided between Nazi Germany and the Soviet Union. It was decided to postpone the decision on whether to allow for the existence of a Polish state in any framework whatsoever until the necessary time had come and then to judge the question in the light of "forthcoming political developments."[13]

With the outbreak of war and the swift Nazi advance into Poland, the time for the "territorial and political transformation" had arrived. The Soviets attempted to find an excuse to justify the annexation of Polish territory, and on September 16 the German ambassador to Moscow, Friedrich Werner von Schulenburg, cabled Berlin that Molotov wanted to make a public declaration "that the Polish state has collapsed and ceased to exist, so that all treaties signed with it are null and void. . . . The Soviet Union therefore views itself obliged to intervene in defense of its Ukrainian and Belorussian brothers to enable these unfortunate peoples to labor in peace."[14] On September 28 Ribbentrop himself arrived in Moscow for an additional round of talks and the formal division of territory. The negotiators were presented with two options: (1) the division of Poland on topographic lines along the Pisa, Narew, Vistula, and San rivers and the inclusion of Lithuania in the German sphere of influence, i.e., the manifestation of the agreement more or less along its original lines; or (2) an alternative plan, preferred by Stalin, whereby the Vistula would not be the dividing line, the Germans would receive the entire district of Warsaw and Lublin up to the Bug River, and, in exchange for this "concession," the Soviet Union would receive Lithuania in its sphere of influence. It therefore appears that had the original version of the pact been carried out, with the Soviets moving up to the Vistula line, the eastern portions of Warsaw would indeed have fallen in the Soviet occupation zone.

It was in this fashion that about two million Polish Jews fell into the hands of the Nazis. The first question that arises is whether the Germans had already drawn up a defined policy to deal with the Jews of Poland. Hitler's orders and discussion prior to *Fall Weiss* (the code name for the invasion of Poland) make no mention whatsoever of the Jews. Though the Nazi Führer ranted that "Poland must not be spared," in the heat of the intense conflict on the eve of the war, the Jewish question did not receive special attention. Yet at the end of the "fateful year" (1938) and the beginning of 1939, Hitler turned his attention to the Jewish problem a number of times in discussions with statesmen and in public appearances. On November 24, 1938, in a talk with Oswald Perov, a pro-German South African minister, he stated that "one of these days the Jews will disappear from Europe" and that he "had exported one idea—not National Socialism . . . but anti-Semitism."[15] On January 21, 1939, Hitler told the Czechoslovakian foreign minister, František Chvalkovský, that "the Jews will be annihilated [*Die Juden würden bei uns vernichtet*] here,"[16] and his chilling threats are well known from his public address on January 30, 1939: "I wish to prophesy again today: 'If the international monied Jewry within Europe and beyond again succeeds in casting the peoples into a world war, the result will not be the Bolshevization of the globe and a victory for Jewry, but the annihilation of the Jewish race in Europe."[17]

The transition from peace to war and the invasion of Poland marked a new stage in Nazi policy and conduct toward the Jews. It appears that the change in approach was closely bound up with the very creation of a wartime mentality, since the war provided the Nazis with an opportunity to manifest their racist ideology and implement programs that were the antithesis of accepted mores and deep-rooted humane and cultural traditions. Under wartime conditions, Nazism was able to come to terms with itself and cast off the shackles of whatever internal or external restraints were still at play.

No less important was the fact that Hitler trapped the Jews of Poland at the very outset of the war. To the Nazis, the masses of Polish Jewry were the instrument for the biological increase of the Jewish people and the most tangible embodiment of the Jewish spirit. This attitude was also adopted by the young soldiers who had been raised in the ranks of the *Hitlerjugend*. Dr. Chaim Szoszkes, who was in Warsaw at the beginning of the German occupation, wrote in his memoirs: "The young soldiers, who had never seen Jews like these at home, shouted for joy. Here they had right before their very eyes the enemies of Germany, of humanity!"[18]

During the first weeks of the war, there were still signs that the outrageous behavior of the occupation forces was not completely in line with the official policy in the conquered territories. Rule of the occupied areas was in the hands of the *Wehrmacht*, and in the course of negotiations on Warsaw's conditions of surrender, the German representatives promised that no harm would befall the Jews. On September 4, 1939, the German chief of staff, Walther von Brauchitsch, declared in a radio broadcast that the Jews of Poland could feel secure about their fate; and General Johannes Blaskowitz, the commander of the German forces in Poland, stated in his September 30 appeal to the public that the Jews could return to their usual affairs.[19]

The *Wehrmacht*'s criticism of the harassment and persecution of the civilian population can be attributed in part to the rivalry between the regular army and the SS. Attached to the invasion forces were five, and later six, Special Operations Formations (*Einsatzgruppen*), comprising 1,600–2,400 men. Units of this type were placed in operation as far back as the period of the *Anschluss* and the dismemberment of the Czechoslovakian state. The *Einsatzgruppen* were supposedly needed to ensure security in the occupied areas and the army's rear and to deal with potential enemies of the Nazi Reich. It was therefore only natural that they would be engaged primarily in carrying out actions against the Jews. Formally, the *Einsatzgruppen* were attached to the General Staff, but in practice they took their orders from Heinrich Himmler and Reinhard Heydrich. It was not long before the *Einsatzgruppen* clashed with the army command and there was an increase in the number of complaints from senior *Wehrmacht* officers regarding acts of brutality and torture that were totally unrelated to security considerations or the hostile behavior of the population.[20]

Hitler put a stop to the discord between the army and the *Einsatzgruppen* in his November 25 decision abolishing the military government. The areas of Poland under German control were divided into two distinct political-administrative frameworks. A wide area in the west and north was annexed to the German Reich (Silesia, Warthegau, and part of eastern Prussia), while the rest of central Poland was proclaimed as the "Generalgouvernement of the conquered Polish territories."[21] The Generalgouvernement was divided into four districts —Cracow, Radom, Warsaw, and Lublin—each headed by a governor. Dr. Hans Frank, a well-known Nazi figure, was appointed head of the Generalgouvernement and was aided by a staff of senior officials, all loyal Nazis. No form of Polish administration was established in the area of the Generalgouvernement. Cracow, not Warsaw, was chosen as its capital and the seat of the governor-general. According to statistical data, there were 11,836,510 people in the area of the General-gouvernement at the time of its establishment in October 1939, including 1,457,376 Jews.[22] The original area of the Generalgouvernement was 95,000 square kilometers (36,600 square miles), i.e., less than a quarter of the size of prewar Poland.[23]

The principal authorities responsible for Jewish affairs in the Generalgouvernement were the SS and the Gestapo, on the one hand, and Frank and his administration, on the other. The Reich Main Security Office (R.S.H.A.—*Reichssicherheitshauptamt*), founded in September 1939 under the command of Heydrich, united under the auspices of the SS both the state police and the party police in one centralized body. The fourth division of the R.S.H.A. was the Gestapo (*Geheime Staatspolizei*), and a special branch of the Gestapo dealt mainly with Jewish affairs (Section IV B4). The Jewish Department of the Gestapo was the leading force responsible for carrying out the various phases of the "solution to the Jewish problem" in the spirit of Nazism. The SS gained broader authority to deal with Jewish affairs with the appointment in October 1939 of the *Reichsführer-S.S.*, Heinrich Himmler, as Reich Commissioner for the Consolidation of German Nationhood (R.K.F.—*Reichskommissar für die Festigung deutschen Volkstums*), an office that was established, *inter alia*, "to abolish the harmful influence of those alien national groups in the population that constitute a danger to the Reich and the German nation [*Volksgemeinschaft*]."[24] Himmler also exercised direct control in the area of the Generalgouvernement through the various arms of the police. The commander of the police forces in the Generalgouvernement and the man responsible for security affairs was the Higher SS and Police Leader (*Höherer S.S.- und Polizeiführer*), Friedrich Krieger. In the four districts of the General-gouvernement, SS and Police Leaders (*S.S.- und Polizeiführers*) were appointed as commanders of the police forces. The relations between Frank and Krieger were clearly influenced by rivalry. Frank, a jurist and veteran Nazi, was a *Reichsminister* and had direct access to Hitler. Ambitious and jealously possessive of his rule and anything related to his domain, he was unwilling to forfeit his authority over many matters related to the Jews. The rivalry and clashes between Frank and the SS sometimes affected the position of the Jews, though there were no substantial differences in principle between the two.

Heydrich was quick to set his plans and apparatus into motion even before Frank's administration was organized. On or about September 20, when the special train carrying Hitler and his entourage was stationed near Danzig for a few days, the basic lines of Nazi policy regarding the civilian population of occupied Poland were laid down in the first comprehensive talks on the subject. Heydrich and Himmler were among the small circle that attended Hitler during those days. The orders Heydrich received must have been both crucial and urgent, for by September 21 he had already returned to Berlin and convened a meeting of the heads of the R.S.H.A. and the commanders of the *Einsatzgruppen* stationed in Poland. Heydrich told his men that after the provinces that had formerly been part of Germany were detached from Poland, an enclave would be formed to incorporate the foreign-language-speaking population. The Jews would be sent into this as yet undefined area (*fremdsprachiger Gau*), and the entire process was scheduled to take a year. Within Poland, a line should be drawn between the political leadership and the intelligentsia, on one side, and the working classes, on the other. The Polish political leadership would be sent to concentration camps and the intelligentsia would be imprisoned. The Jews in the multilanguage area would be concentrated in ghettos in order to facilitate their supervision and hold them in a state that would abet their deportation at a later period. Any Jew living in a village or isolated in the countryside must be removed from his place of residence during the coming three or four weeks. In brief, Heydrich's orders regarding Poland were as follows:

1. Jews must be concentrated in the cities as quickly as possible.

2. Jews must be transferred from the Reich to Poland.

3. The 30,000 remaining gypsies must also be transferred into Poland.

4. Systematic transports of Jews were to be organized in the German provinces by means of freight trains.[25]

On the same day (September 21), following the meeting in Berlin, Heydrich sent his famous express letter to the commanders of the *Einsatzgruppen* concerning "the Jewish problem in the occupied areas."[26] The main points of the dispatch demanded:

1. Concentration of the Jews in the large cities.

2. The establishment of Jewish councils (*Judenräte*) in the Jewish communities. These councils would "be fully responsible, in the literal sense of the word, for the exact and punctual execution of all directives issued or yet to be issued." During the first stage, the councils would be required to take a census of the Jews, aid in the process of transferring Jews from small towns to the large cities, and absorb the Jews in these larger concentrations.

3. The required actions were to be carried out in coordination with the military authorities and the civilian administration. If military or economic interests dictated it, Jews would be allowed to remain in their places of residence for a time. At the same time, however, "prompt Aryanization of these enterprises is to be sought." In any case

of a clash of interests between the Security Police and the civilian administration, the question under dispute was to be referred to Heydrich for judgment.

4. Heydrich demanded detailed reports summarizing the actions that had been carried out and added that "for the attainment of the goals set, I expect total deployment of all forces of the Security Police and the Security Service."

The order cautioned that a distinction should be made between the final goal (*Endziel*) and the stages required to achieve that end, which should be carried out over defined periods of time. At the beginning of the dispatch, Heydrich emphasized that everything related to the program for reaching the final goal should be kept completely secret. Many who had access to this crucial document interpreted the term *Endziel* as identical with *Endlösung*, namely the total physical annihilation of the Jews. But a thorough analysis of the letter and the subsequent actions of the SS during this period does not substantiate this interpretation. The Nazi policy regarding the Jews and the means slated to achieve the "Solution of the Jewish Problem" underwent a number of changes and phases and had probably not crystallized completely at the beginning of the war. The branches of the police initially encouraged voluntary emigration, then moved on to enforced emigration, and during the stage under discussion here concentrated on the deportation and concentration of Jews in an undefined area within the Generalgouvernement. The fact is that during 1940—and within the Reich itself up to October 1941—it was still possible for Jews to emigrate legally, and the authorities within the S.D., the Gestapo, and the Foreign Ministry responsible for this sphere were searching for an area or country of refuge that would take in the émigrés.

In his first address to "Polish men and women" on October 26, Frank himself made mention of the Jews in a short paragraph stating that "under the just regime, every man will be able to earn his living by his labors. But there is no place for agitators, profiteers, or Jewish parasites in the area that has been placed under German sovereignty."[27]

The mass deportations from the areas annexed to the Reich, Austria, and the Protectorate into the Generalgouvernement began in October 1939. Eichmann and his aides marked out an area that extended southeast from Lublin, around the town of Nisko, with the intention of turning the region around Lublin into a mass reservation of Jews from the Reich and the annexed territories. The location of the reservation was chosen without any rational analysis of local conditions or the feasibility of implementing the plan. Crucial decisions regarding the Jews were left to members of the SS, who lacked the appropriate education or experience to handle such matters. These men had no use for critical analysis or a professional approach in conducting the affairs placed in their hands. Everything was subject to their arbitrary judgment. Their superiors demanded efficiency, decisiveness, and speed in carrying out orders. Any attention given to the humane aspects of a problem, fundamental legal considerations, or moral precepts was considered a sign of weak character, sentimentality, and inhibition that interfered with the work at hand.

The Lublin plan was accordingly an improvised move that came up in the course of the haphazard preparations to remove the Jews from the German Reich and concentrate them in a distant and isolated place. Almost one hundred thousand Jews and Poles were deported from the Reich and the annexed territories in a very short span of time. But strong opposition rose to the mass-deportation program in the person of Hans Frank, the governor-general. At the beginning of his term, Frank recognized the fact that the Generalgouvernement would have to absorb the Jews and Poles from the Reich. But as he grew more familiar with the local conditions and the food and health problems of his domain, he realized that the evacuation of Poles from the area around Lublin and the concentration of Jews in their place involved difficulties that were not even dreamed of in Berlin. As Frank saw it, the Generalgouvernement was already overcrowded with Jews, and as far as Lublin was concerned, "there are so many Jews there that the few Germans living in the area are almost swallowed up among them."[28] Frank also tried to contain the involvement of the SS in the Generalgouvernement. Alarmed by the growing daring of the SS and the Gestapo, he made for Berlin to present his complaints before Göring and Hitler. Frank clearly had the upper hand in the dispute. As a result of the meeting, the frequency of the deportations was cut down, and deportees could only be sent into the Generalgouvernement with Frank's approval. In 1940 the Lublin experiment was abandoned, but the deportations from small towns to larger centers within the Generalgouvernement not only went on but were even stepped up. Added to these deportations was the forced eviction of Jews from Cracow, which Frank wanted devoid of Jews, "because it is totally unbearable that thousands of Jews should be living in a city that, by the Führer's kindness, is honored to host the mighty authorities of the Reich."[29]

During the first stage of the war, the Soviet border was still open, and anyone who tried to cross into the Soviet zone could do so without great difficulty. But access to the border was fraught with obstacles. A Jew who traveled on the roads or through the fields was liable to be harassed or robbed of his belongings by German soldiers. Yet the Germans did not actually prevent people from crossing the frontier. The Jews of Poland were noted for their close family ties, and many made their leaving conditional upon the collective exit of their families. An elderly grandfather or an ailing relative was sufficient to prevent the movement of an entire extended family. The reports on the conditions prevailing in the annexed territories and the fate of the refugees in the border towns hardly encouraged a mass exodus. Those who chose to escape from Poland left with only a bundle of belongings in hand, abandoning their homes and property behind them. The severe winter was also an obstacle to movement, and many preferred to wait until spring and an improvement in the weather. In December the Soviet soldiers began to seal off the border, and it became necessary to steal across the frontier. At first the injunction against crossing the border was lax, but once the frontier became established, it was impassable. There are no certified statistics on the number of Polish Jews who passed from the German to the Soviet occupation zone during the first months of the war. It can be assumed, however, that the number reached hundreds of thousands (some estimate three hundred thousand), most of them young people.[30] A substantial portion of these refugees were destined to fall into the hands of the Nazis again at the beginning of the German invasion of the Soviet Union in June 1941. Others were dispersed far and wide and sent to detention camps deep inside the Soviet Union. The deportees suffered from hardship and isolation. But as matters turned out, for a number who survived, the cruel exile proved to be their salvation.

At the end of 1939 and the beginning of 1940, there was still a limited chance to emigrate to Palestine and other countries. Any Jew who bore a foreign passport or was issued an entry visa by a foreign country was permitted to leave Poland. Few Jews were so fortunate. The Palestine Office of the World Zionist Organization reached an agreement with the Lloyd Adriatic Company to handle the exit arrangements for those who had received an appropriate permit. The company also took upon itself responsibility for acquiring Italian visas and permits to travel through German territory. The acquisition of papers was a crucial element of the operation, since both a Jew's freedom of movement and his chances of getting through to the appropriate German authority to get the necessary documents were extremely limited. Apolinary Hartglas, one of the leading personalities among the Polish Jews, recorded in his memoirs how the first eighteen Jews, mostly Zionist leaders and their families, received exit permits and, at the end of December 1940, made their way from Warsaw to Trieste. Following them, successive groups were chosen as candidates for emigration to Palestine, and a waiting list of potential émigrés was composed.[31] When word of the agreement with Lloyd Adriatic spread, Jews streamed to the offices of the company and other travel agencies and offered large sums in exchange for the necessary papers. The travel agencies sensed that they were onto a bonanza, since the few who did succeed in acquiring exit permits were naturally among the wealthier Jews, and German officials, who were also in on the business, turned a blind eye in return for a fat bribe. But the crisis in relations between Italy and the Allies led to the closing of the Italian border around April of 1940 and thus ended the legal emigration of Jews.

A few thousand Jews are estimated to have left Poland on both recognized and forged exit visas. Among those who escaped by this means were community leaders and members of the first Warsaw *Judenrat*: Apolinary Hartglas, Shmuel Zygielbojm, Abraham Weiss, and Chaim Szoszkes. Rabbi Yitzhak Meir Levin and his son-in-law, the Gur Rebbe, together with the *rebbe*'s entourage, were saved by virtue of a special campaign to rescue them. The *rebbe* and his disciples left Warsaw on the eve of Passover 1940.[32] The last orders permitting Jews from the Generalgouvernement to leave the country were cancelled in the summer of 1940.

The Nazis' justification for preventing the emigration of Jews from the Generalgouvernement is expressed in a regulation issued by Frank's administration on November 23, 1940. According to orders circulated by the R.S.H.A., it was assumed that after the outbreak of hostilities, the number of countries willing to take in refugees had declined severely, and thus preference was to be given to Jews from the Reich, Austria, and the Protectorate. The memo goes on to state that the Jews in the Generalgouvernement had extraordinary powers of endurance and regeneration and were therefore dangerous from the National Socialist viewpoint. But for these very same reasons, their brothers in the United States wanted to take them in. Thus Jewish emigration from the Generalgouvernement was to be absolutely forbidden.

Daily Life during the First Months of the Occupation

One of the first orders the Nazis issued to the Warsaw *Judenrat* demanded that a census be taken of the city's Jewish population. The census was carried out with the aid of Jewish personnel on Saturday, September 28, 1939. According to the results, which were probably a close reflection of the actual situation, there were 359,827 Jews in Warsaw at the time. Even the fear spread by the German occupation regime from their very first contact with the Jews could not overshadow the most pressing concern of Warsaw Jewry: How would they continue to subsist? How would they be able to earn a living under the new conditions? According to the statistical data prepared by the Warsaw *Judenrat*, 95,000 of the 173,000 actively employed Jews in Warsaw were wage earners who worked in industrial plants and crafts workshops, commercial establishments, or as teachers and professionals. These people supported themselves and their families from fixed wages. Their savings were small, and loss of the jobs, or any drastic change in prices, would leave them without means of subsistence.

In April 1940 an economic survey was taken of both Jewish and Polish companies in Warsaw. The purpose of the survey was to evaluate the changes that had taken place in the city's economy as a result of the war and the occupation. It indicated that many of the industrial concerns that had been completely destroyed by the bombing and shelling had not been reconstructed and reactivated. Among the Polish population there were signs of adjustment to the new conditions. Many well-established enterprises reoriented their production objectives to the changes in demand, and a good portion of these companies began to fill orders for the occupation authorities. But these options were not open to the Jews. Their destroyed industrial plants were not reconstructed, and those which had survived the bombings decreased production or were closed down altogether.

The German plans for the Generalgouvernement exhibited a growing tendency to exploit the inherent capacities of the area. The territorial configuration of the Generalgouvernement had not been mapped out according to considerations of economic necessity and expediency. The Polish "enclave," for example, was cut off from access to the sea, and the areas richest in natural resources, such as coal and oil, were detached from it. At first the most salient feature of the German economic policy was the confiscation of existing resources, whether natural resources or machinery, to be transferred to Germany. During this initial stage, the occupied area served as a kind of trump card in the negotiations attempted with the Western Powers. The Nazis were willing to permit the existence of a dwarfed Polish state (*Reststaat*) congruent with the borders of the Generalgouvernement in exchange for Western recognition of the occupation of other parts of Poland and renunciation of the state of belligerency. But when it became clear that the Western democracies were unwilling to swallow the bait yet again, and especially after Germany's swift military victory in the West in the spring of 1940, other plans were drawn up for the future of the Generalgouvernement as an area to be exploited by the Reich. The remains of Poland were thought of as a kind of colony, part of the *Lebensraum* of the German nation. Field offices of the Four-Year Program began to operate within the boundaries of the Generalgouvernement, and large German concerns, especially companies involved in the war effort, opened branches in the area. Only 5 percent of the prewar work force was employed in the larger industrial plants in Warsaw in November 1939, but by February 1940 this number had risen to 27.4 percent.[33]

The Jews, however, were not allocated any role in the German program. On occasion German industrialists or enterprising men out in search of skilled workers came across Jews and passed on orders to Jewish manufacturers or merchants. Jews were active in the collection and retail trade of rags, scrap metal, and feathers; Jewish carpenters furnished the Brühl Palace (the headquarters of the German authorities in Warsaw); German suppliers who were attached to the military placed orders for brushes with Jewish manufacturers, and they were filled by Jews working at home in the crowded Jewish quarter of the city. But these are only examples of marginal branches of the Jewish economy, sporadic instances of employment or business carried out on the sly. There was no role for the Jews in the Nazis' comprehensive plan—or, to be more exact, the Jews were consciously deprived of any position in the economy or source of livelihood.

In their systematic campaign to confiscate Jewish property, the Nazis did not overlook art collections or even private libraries, and wholesale looting by soldiers and individual thieves went on alongside the "official" pillage. Jewish businesses were turned over to German "trustees" (*Treuhänder*), so that a Jew generally lost both his property and his source of livelihood at one and the same time. In some cases the *Kommissar* availed himself of a Jew's professional skills and left the actual management of the business in his hands. There were also instances in which a Jew managed to find an "Aryan" partner in time to transfer the business into his name. A memo (from the second part of the underground archive of the Warsaw ghetto) written at the end of July 1940 and entitled "The Ruin of the Jewish Economic Position in Poland" states:

> As early as the first stage of the new order in Poland, [the Germans issued] a new set of regulations that damaged the Jewish economy. At the beginning of last November, i.e., right after the end of the fighting in Poland, an order dated September 18 was published regarding the money in circulation. The regulation included the following severe restrictions on economic activities by Jews: (1) One could pay a Jew a maximum of 500 zlotys; the rest had to be deposited in a closed account in a financial institution. (2) Banks were allowed to pay out to Jews a maximum of 250 zlotys a week from their accounts. (3) A Jewish family was allowed to keep a maximum of 2,000 zlotys in cash outside of the banking institutions.

Further on, this document states that on January 31, 1940, an order was published by the Warsaw District permitting the establishment of new commercial enterprises only by permission of the district supervisor. But licenses were issued only to those who could prove that they were of pure "Aryan" extraction.

A regulation dated September 29 required that firms whose own-ers were abroad be turned over to the supervision of a "trustee." In practice, however, such "trustees" were appointed over Jewish busi-nesses whose owners were present in the country, and there was no way of objecting to the way in which these "trustees" managed the busi-nesses. One of the "trustees'" first moves was to fire Jewish employees from the firms under their control, and this aggravated the unemploy-ment problem among Jews. Jewish lawyers were stricken from the lists of professionals; retired Jews lost their pension rights; and Jewish peddlers were allowed to appear only on streets populated by Jews. According to the memorandum, a few weeks earlier all the Jewish "administrators" who ran the apartment buildings owned by Jews were removed from their posts. About five thousand Jewish "administrators" were "let go," and about twenty-five thousand landlords were deprived of their properties.[34]

In July 1940 the role of the Jews in the economy was defined in a report of the Generalgouvernement as follows:

> . . . The second question is to what degree will the active participa-
> tion of the Jews be allowed in the economy. There can be no doubt that
> Jews must not be given access to industry, wholesale operations in the
> sphere of import and export, real estate operations, banking, insurance
> companies, transport concerns, and warehouse management. We should
> examine—from a positive outlook—whether it is already necessary to
> remove the Jews from middle-level commerce altogether. It appears that it
> is still not possible to drive them entirely out of small-scale [commerce]
> and wholesale trade, and particularly from the supply of raw materials. The
> situation in the crafts resembles that in wholesale trade.[35]

Thus the aim of the German authorities was clear: The Jews were to be totally excluded from the main arteries of the economy. It was necessary to take into account considerations of efficiency or the harm that might result from the absolute displacement of the experienced Jewish elements. On the other hand, the necessity of allowing Jews to remain active in middle-level commerce required further consideration. It was clear, however, that the Germans ultimately intended to exclude the Jews from this arena of commerce as well. The authors of the report concluded that it was not yet efficacious to squeeze the Jews out of wholesale trade, especially as Jews were helpful to the Germans in the collection of scrap and left-over raw materials. But the general tone of the report indicates that these Jewish activities were a kind of evil that had to be tolerated until it was feasible to remove the Jews from these less important branches of the economy as well.

From the very start of the occupation, forced labor for the Germans assumed an important position in Jewish life. Although it did not make any substantial contribution to the subsistence of the Jewish masses, the whole question of slave labor became a salient motif in Jewish daily life and the activities of the *Judenrat*. The *Judenrat* became involved in the mobilization of forced laborers because, as noted earlier, German soldiers had taken to capriciously hunting down Jews for various jobs. Since the kidnapping of Jews off the streets was effectively paralyzing the community, the *Judenrat* believed that it was preferable to commit itself to a fixed quota of workers and put an end to the open manhunt. On the other hand, the Nazi authorities charged the *Judenrat* with implementing the regulations regarding forced labor. As early as October 26, Frank published an order making slave labor obligatory for the Jews under his jurisdiction.[36] The execution of the order and supervision of the work were turned over to the Reich Leader of the SS and Chief of Police in the Generalgouvernement; in effect, therefore, the organization and exploitation of Jewish slave labor were concentrated in the hands of the SS and the German police.

A labor battalion (*Batalion Pracy*) was established under the aegis of the *Judenrat*, and it quickly expanded in response to the growing demands and threats of the German authorities. In October 1939 the average number of workers supplied by the *Judenrat* was 381; by November the number had risen to 999; and by December it had reached 1,584. And this was just the beginning. In August 1940, which was undoubtedly a peak month, 9,000 Jews were working for the Germans daily in places of work called *palatzovka*. Their tasks included various services for the military units and work for German institutions and companies.

At first, when the *Judenrat* was obliged to supply only a few hundred workers per day, the work battalions were manned by Jews who had turned to the *Judenrat* for aid—usually refugees or people whose homes had been destroyed during the fighting. The *Judenrat* paid these workers 3 zlotys per day (later hiking the payment to 4 zlotys). Financing these wages was a difficult problem for the *Judenrat* from the outset, and Czerniakow's diary proves that the financial strain was the most serious problem he faced. As a result, in December 1939 the *Judenrat* decided to impose a special tax in order to cover the wages paid out to the forced laborers. Yet the number of volunteers that the *Judenrat* was able to mobilize failed to meet the escalating German demands. The *Judenrat* therefore demanded that various apartment buildings provide a set number of men for forced labor, but not all of the conscripts reported for duty. Since members of poorer families were willing to replace the conscripts for a price, a permanent class of "substitutes" came into being. About 107,000 people were required for forced labor in April 1940, and in August of that year the number was 105,000. Jews were required to work six and sometimes as many as nine days a month. The *Judenrat* was actually able to mobilize only about half of the conscripts demanded. It was at this time that a unit of stewards was organized to supervise the workers' assembly points and execute the mobilization of orders regarding truants. These stewards were the seeds of the Jewish police force that came into being when the Warsaw ghetto was later established.

The German authorities were eager to exploit Jewish labor, and in January 1940 they published an order requiring Jewish males aged twelve to sixty to register (for the first time) for forced labor. During the first half of February, 121,265 people signed up with the authorities. As soon as the registration was completed, new orders were issued by the head of the SS and the police in Cracow, and the registration was held over again. This time, in addition to giving personal data, it was necessary to report ownership of work tools, machinery, workshops, etc.[37]

Until April 1940 requests for Jewish workers were made to the S.D., which had a special department for Jewish labor headed by Karl Georg Brandt and Gerhardt Mende, who also supervised the *Judenrat* labor battalion. In April 1940, however, supervision was transferred to the Labor Office (*Arbeitsamt*) of the Warsaw District. By the middle of 1940 the Labor Office had established new rules regarding the Jews. It insisted that there were talented skilled laborers to be found among the Jews, and it was imperative to arrive at a level of general systematic benefit in the exploitation of Jewish labor. It therefore forbade the arbitrary shanghai of Jews off the streets or the submisson of requests for Jewish workers directly the *Judenrat*. Authorities and companies wishing to avail themselves of Jewish workers were required to address their requests to the office's Jewish Division, which would direct them to the Jewish labor battalion. In addition, the "employers" were obliged either to bear part of the costs of the operation or to keep the Jews in closed camps and provide for their needs.

Working conditions were abominable. The Jews were forced to clear away rubble, carry out various tasks in army barracks, serve as porters, load and unload supply trains, and clear snow off the streets. Most of them were not accustomed to strenuous physical labor, and they also suffered from malnutrition and the lack of proper clothing. Nonetheless, the long hours of work were not the most burdensome aspect of the *palatzovka*. It was much more difficult to bear the brutal acts of sadism. Many of the young German soldiers were not satisfied with merely humiliating the Jews. In some instances they forced Jews to remove their gloves and carry freezing lead pipes with their bare hands in the dead of winter. Some of the more sadistic supervisors devised intricate punishment exercises. Jews who appeared to be especially intelligent or those dressed in traditional garb were particularly sought out as victims. The supervisors would lie in wait for a Jew to display a moment of weakness, pull him out of line, and carry out a vicious scene for their own entertainment. Neither age, state of health, nor social status served as protection against the tortures.

In August 1940 young Jews began to be shipped off to distant labor camps. The first transports, which were sent to the Lublin area on August 16, 20, and 23, included 1,400 people, most of whom were volunteers. Thereafter the percentage of volunteers decreased, for two reasons. First, the early transports included the most destitute of the Jews—people without housing or means of support—but after a few transports had gone, the number of people in this category grew smaller. Second, and the main reason for the decline in volunteers, was the shocking reports that filtered back from the camps about the horrid living conditions, back-breaking work, and shortage of blankets, clothing, and food. The situation was so grave that the *Judenrat* had to organize a campaign to aid those who had been deported to the camps and help support their families, and volunteering came to an almost complete halt. The deportees were mainly refugees who had come to Warsaw to seek shelter and found themselves in untenable financial straits and completely helpless. Thus it was the weakest elements of the Jewish commuity that were sent to the labor camps. The *Judenrat* had chosen the path of least resistance. Yet the methods used to mobilize workers for the labor camps met with sharp criticism and led to a serious clash between the *Judenrat* and the Jewish community. This chapter in the *Judenrat*'s activities contributed to the alienation of the Jewish masses from its official leadership and a crisis of confidence in the council's representatives.[38]

After noting the distorted character of the Jewish economy during the first phase of the occupation and the forced exploitation of the Jewish labor force, the question still remains: How did the Jews manage to support themselves during the occupation? Leaving aside special sources of income, whose nature was bound up with war profiteering, black marketing, and smuggling, and whose importance was marginal, the overwhelming majority of the Jews did not engage in any productive work or wage-paying labor. Thus the welfare and self-help association organized with the aid of JDC funds—and, later on, the collection of donations from local Jews—was an important element in the fight for survival. But the main means of staying alive was by chipping away at savings and other resources of capital accumulated in the past. Most of the Jews were impoverished, and their property was of little value.

But as the war dragged on and shortages developed not only in food but also in clothing, shoes, housewares, and so on, farmers were willing to sell their produce in return for clothing and other types of goods found in the cities. One of the foundations of this barter was Jewish-owned goods—even junk that had accumulated over the years and the worn-out items found in every household. These used goods and possessions, which often underwent a metamorphosis in the hands of Jewish artisans, made their way into Polish hands in the villages or in the city, in exchange for food. That and more: every Jewish family—even one that sustained itself with great difficulty and found it a struggle to meet the needs of daily life—always managed to put something aside. They looked upon these small savings as "iron rations"—a dowry for a daughter, insurance in case of ill health or tragedy, or just something to have for a rainy day. Many families now turned to their emergency funds and lived off them for quite a while, zloty by zloty, in exchange for the bare necessities of life.

When Warsaw was under siege, prices on food were not fixed, and to keep up the supply of food required getting through on the roads and maintaining steady contact with the countryside. As early as November 1939, prices began to stabilize somewhat, but the cost of basic goods had already tripled or quadrupled in comparison with the prewar price levels. Most serious of all was the rise in the cost of bread. The wages earned by a man conscripted for forced labor sufficed to buy little more than a loaf of black bread. In February–March 1940 there was another hike in prices, bringing them up to five or even ten times the prewar level.[39] Two factors were especially influential upon the level of prices: the way in which the Germans counteracted the free market in food, and the distribution of food by means of ration cards. Food was supposedly supplied by means of official ration cards at the low prices set by the authorities. In practice, however, the food distributed through the ration system was far from sufficient—not only for the Jews, who were allocated smaller portions, but even for those whose ration was more generous and varied. Each time the German authorities declared a campaign of supervision and retaliation (including capital punishment) against the free market in food, goods would grow scarce and prices rise. On the other hand, every time the authorities began to distribute a wider selection of food—or merely announced their intention to do so—the price of food on the free market fell. On January 21, 1940, Kaplan wrote in his diary:

> Until now there was no shortage of bread. It was expensive (150 zlotys a kilo), but it was available in abundance all over. Besides its usual place in the food stores, it was also sold in the street. . . . As long as the conquerors took no notice of this, everything went smoothly. We got used

to the cost. . . . One fine morning notices were posted that profiteers and all those who sell their goods, including essential foods, above the fixed prices will be sentenced to death. Immediately afterward bread and baked goods disappeared, and we are doomed to deprivation and famine as though in a city besieged.[40]

The system of food distribution by means of ration cards was put into effect as early as January 1940. The colored cards were divided into small squares, each marked with types of quantities of food. The bearers were required to register at a grocery licensed to sell food. At first Jews received the same ration cards as Poles, and everyone was allowed to register at the grocery of his choice. But as early as February a change was instituted. Jews were allowed to register only at Jewish groceries, and Poles only at Polish ones. Before long the Jews were issued cards of a different color, stamped with a large Star of David, and following this change in form came one in content. Certain foods, especially variety items, were allowed only to Poles. There was even discrimination in the distribution of basic foodstuffs like brown sugar and potatoes. After a while a larger food ration was allocated to those engaged in strenuous forced labor. Jews who worked steadily for the Germans or in places of work supervised by the authorities also enjoyed a more ample ration.

The shortage of coal, and of fuel in general, also caused severe hardship, since the winter of 1939–40 was especially harsh (on some days the temperature dropped to −13 degrees Farenheit). The brutal cold was particularly burdensome because of the scarcity of warm clothing and insufficient nourishment. On January 6, Kaplan noted in his diary: "Aside from hunger, we also suffer from cold. For the hard, bitter winter has come, and there is not a piece of coal in any home to warm our miserable bodies. The coal mines are in the hands of the conqueror, and he is killing us with cold."[41]

The vicissitudes of war, the overcrowding, the hunger, and the cold brought in their wake an inevitable outbreak of contagious diseases. And once again the Jews, who had always lived in more crowded and less sanitary conditions, were the first victims of the epidemic, since the Jewish sections were a breeding ground for disease. The only effective way to fight such an epidemic was to remove the cause of the outbreak and provide proper medical aid. But the Germans chose a different course. Their propaganda machine branded the Jews as carriers of the disease germs and exploited the fear of contagion to widen the breach between Jews and non-Jews. The German authorities also instituted a special system to improve sanitation and fight the focal points of the disease. The ravaging malady that afflicted the Jews of Warsaw during the war and claimed countless victims was typhus.

In order to bring the epidemic under control, the authorities began to quarantine buildings, disinfect apartments and their contents, and send their occupants to the public showers. These measures were undoubtedly the most burdensome misery of the entire period. Moreover, according to the opinion of experts, not only were they totally useless in containing the epidemic, but their effect was exactly the opposite. The entire process added to the hardship of the population and caused the plague to spread.[42] On the instructions of the German doctors, any house in which a case of typhus was discovered was quarantined for a set period, the bed linens were sent out to be disinfected, a special sanitation unit was to go over the apartments and disinfect them, and all the tenants were collectively sent to the public showers. After a while, not only were the tenants of an infected building required to undergo this treatment, but the occupants of the buildings next door were subject to it as well. Furthermore, a supervising doctor could order these measures carried out in any building found to be unclean or dilapidated. The staff of the sanitation units, run by a department of the Municipality of Warsaw, were young Poles for whom the whole project meant nothing more than a chance to make a profit on the side. Many of them helped themselves to Jewish property that had been left unguarded while the Jews were at the public showers.

Relations between the Jews and the Poles

The relations between the Jews and the Poles during the first stage of the occupation were very complex and deserve thorough examination in and of themselves. The most blatant aspect of these relations was played out for months on the streets of Warsaw: the attacks by individuals and gangs of Poles on Jewish passersby and apartment houses, which took on the proportions of a wave of pogroms. The Jews did not organize a collective resistance to these attacks, as they had done many times during the outbreaks of violence in the interwar years. For the most part, the wild thugs were youngsters and underworld types, but even so the Jews did not dare to resist or strike back at them. It appears that the strain of the ever-mounting flow of German decrees, oppression, and brutality wore down the Jews' power of initiative and resistance and left them to concentrate only on ways to escape the danger that stalked them.

The Jews assumed that the wave of assaults was instigated and directed by the Nazis, and there was good reason for them to think so. The Germans described the outbursts of violence as an expression of the rage that had been seething among the Poles for generations and found its outlet only now, under German rule. On one occasion—the audience of a delegation of Jews, headed by Czerniakow, with Dr. Fritz

Arlt, head of the Department of Population and Welfare in the Generalgouvernement's Ministry of Interior—the Jews demanded, with some degree of insistence, that the Nazis put a stop to the violence. Arlt, who was an *Obersturmführer* in the SS, replied that the German authorities were helpless to deal with the Polish outbursts of rage. But when the members of the delegation continued to press him, claiming that they could not hold talks while Jews were being assaulted in the streets and the buildings of the *kehillah* were being vandalized, Arlt called Warsaw, and his intervention brought some relief.[43] Evidently one sharp word from a German official was sufficient to control the hooligans. That was reason enough to prove a connection—at the very least a tacit understanding—between the Germans and the Polish thugs.

On February 1, 1940, Kaplan noted in his diary: "In the past few days there has been no end to attacks upon Jews in public places in broad daylight. The conquerors' eyes look on, but they are struck with blindness.[44] And Ringelblum wrote on January 29: "Yesterday a gang of Poles was running around wild. . . ."[45] An eyewitness who managed to escape from Warsaw early in the spring of 1940 and reached Palestine told the United Jewish Committee for the Relief of Polish Jewry details of the events of March 1940:

> The pogrom committed against the Jews of Warsaw during the Passover holiday lasted for about eight days. It broke out suddenly, and ended just as suddenly. It was perpetrated by a bunch of hoodlums, about 1,000 of them, who spontaneously appeared on the streets of Warsaw. They hadn't been seen before and haven't been seen since. They were probably reckless and irresponsible youths who had come together for this purpose from all over the city. . . . For the most part the hoodlums acted on their own, but there were also instances in which German soldiers joined in on their assaults.[46]

The campaign of violence, which lasted for a few weeks, had a strong impact on the character of relations between the Jews and the Poles during the war. According to the testimony of various witnesses, the hoodlums received payment on the spot from the Nazis, who photographed the incidents and doctored prints to show German soldiers defending Jews against the Polish mob. Yet the impression that the Polish intelligentsia was supportive of the Jews comes up repeatedly in the testimonies of eyewitnesses. One such witness to the events of March–April 1940 who escaped and reached Palestine related: "The Polish intelligentsia was enraged by the pogrom in March, and especially by the fact that it was perpetrated by a mob of Poles, albeit under German direction. The Polish masses, on the other hand, were readily at the disposal of the Germans. They continued to assault the Jews, maltreat, beat, curse, and torment them . . . in German."[47]

Whenever a Jew tried to strike back at the Polish rabble, he met with intimidation from the Germans. One of the witnesses described the following scene: "There was one incident on Franciszkańska Street in Warsaw when just as a Polish youngster was about to beat a Jew, some Jewish youths came along, got a grip on him, and turned him over to a policeman. Germans immediately arrived and beat the Jews for daring to lay hands on the Pole."[48]

The Polish police ignored the rampages; the novice Polish underground did not respond at all; and the hoodlums learned that most of the Polish public, as well as the Germans, allowed them a free hand to attack Jews. The absence of a strong response from the Poles probably facilitated the emergence of the network of blackmailers and Jew-hunters, who would in time become the bane of Jews in hiding and those attempting to escape.

The measure that succeeded more than anything else in bringing about the isolation of the Jews was the order to wear an identifying emblem. On November 23, 1939, Frank published a regulation requiring that "as of December 1, 1939, all Jews ten years of age and up residing in the territory of the Generalgouvernement must wear on the right sleeves of their clothing and coats a white armband at least 10 centimeters wide with a Star of David on it."[49] The order also stated that the Jews must acquire the armbands on their own and that anyone disobeying the order would be subject to imprisonment or a fine. Following Frank's order came a regulation issued by Dr. Ludwig Fischer, the governor of the Warsaw District.[50] Fischer's order essentially repeated Frank's; the only difference was that Jews from the age of twelve, and not ten, were required to wear the armband. In addition, Fischer defined who, according to the regulation, "was considered a Jew."[51]

Neither of the two documents gives any indication of the purpose of the identifying bands or the motivation behind the issue of the regulations. But the reasons for the new measure are either implied or spelled out clearly in regulations dealing with other matters. Thus, for example, the second order to execute the conscription of forced laborers states that "the basic period of labor is two years. It will be extended in the event that, during that period, the essential goal of forced labor is not achieved."[52]

During the audience of Czerniakow's delegation with Dr. Arlt in Cracow, a discussion was held on the significance of the armbands and the identification of Jews. Dr. Arlt claimed that the purpose of the armbands was to enable a German to "tell from a distance whether a woman flirting with him was a Jewess; otherwise he might be beguiled into sinning against the purity of the race."[53] Naturally, this cynical claim that the stigmatization of Jews was intended to protect Germans against the seductive wiles of Jewish women was thoroughly refuted. Nonetheless, the branding led to a further deterioration in the status of the Jews. Since the Germans were not as a rule familiar with the external appearance of a Jew, before the institution of the armbands, a Jew whose dress did not give him away was able to walk about in the Polish districts and even some distance from the city. But once the regulation came into effect, any German could recognize a Jew in the street, and this obviously facilitated the daily kidnappings, thefts, and persecutions. The armbands also widened the breach between Poles and Jews. Hartglas noted in a report upon his arrival in Palestine: "The Jewish symbol on one's clothing was devised so that the Germans could distinguish a Jew easily and snatch him off the streets for forced labor, as well as to incite the Polish masses against the Jews."[54] And a Jewish doctor reported in his testimony that "during the first weeks [of the occupation], Jewish doctors enjoyed freedom of movement. But after the order on armbands was issued, the situation grew substantially worse for Jewish doctors, because the police and soldiers paid no attention to the medical insignia, and whenever they came upon a Jewish doctor they harassed him." Another eyewitness wrote: "At first the Poles tended to express support for the Jews forced to wear armbands, but in time this feeling cooled, and Poles apparently avoided encounters in the streets with their branded Jewish friends."[55]

The obligation to wear an armband extended even to converts who were alienated from the Jewish community, and they searched for a way out of the humiliating and insulting obligation to bear the mark of the Jews. The only official Polish representation in existence in the Generalgouvernement, the Welfare Council (R.G.O.—*Rada Główna Opiekuńcza*), drew up a list of converts who asked to be deferred from the obligation to wear an armband[56] and turned it over to the Germans. As later became clear, after the ghetto was founded, the Gestapo paid "a personal visit" to every name on the list and forced each of them to move into the ghetto.[57] The usual punishment for failing to wear an armband was imprisonment for terms of varying length. But there were also other consequences. Since the lives and property of Jews were not protected by any definitive law, the armbands also served as a pretext for acts of depravity.

In the collection of testimonies published as *Sefer ha-Zeva'ot* (*The Book of Atrocities*), a heartrending story unfolds in a few lines: "A child was ill in a Jewish house at 7 Miła Street. His father left the house to find some milk for the boy. In his distraught state, he forgot to put on the Jewish armband. A German soldier who was standing on the corner shot and wounded him." There were also some who objected to the armbands in principle and stubbornly refused to wear them, despite the danger to their lives and the prospect of imprisonment. Among them was the famous writer and educator Janusz Korczak, who preferred to spend a long period in prison (while his Polish friends worked to get him released) rather than concede to wearing the armband. (Korczak was finally released on the grounds that he was insane.) In the course of time, Jews with special privileges began to wear a colored armband with an appropriate emblem in addition to the white one bearing the Star of David. These colored bands distinguished rag collectors, doctors, and, later on, members of the Jewish police force and various other institutions in the ghetto.

The stigmatization was just one of the many measures designed to isolate the Jews and increase their vulnerability to the Germans and the Polish population. Other orders of this nature were the obligation to put up an eye-catching sign with a Star of David on it at the entrance to every Jewish shop; a curfew that remained in effect throughout the war; the limitation of freedom of movement for Jews, in contrast to the Poles; the prohibition against Jews' entering public gardens or walking on specified streets; and the regulation against Jews' traveling on trains (for a while there was a separate trolley for Jews).

The Germans wanted not only to isolate the Jews from the Poles in the city but also to erect a barrier between the Jews and the outside world at large. One of the most stringently enforced regulations was the confiscation of radios (which was also binding on the Polish population). The authorities also obstructed the delivery of mail to Jews, and at times the post office refused to serve them at all. Starting in June 1940, telegrams were accepted at the post office only under the aegis of the Judenrat, and only those cables classified by the Germans as urgent were transmitted. Within the territory of the Generalgouvernement, letters were permitted in only two languages: German and Polish. Letters sent to foreign countries were subject to the general regulations binding on all residents of the Third Reich, which forbade the sending abroad (obviously meaning only to those countries that were not at war with Germany) of letters written in the Hebrew alphabet.[58]

The Jews caught on quickly to the Nazi system of collective responsibility and punishment. There was more to this approach than the implication that if the Germans were after a specific individual and could not find him, they would take in his place a relative or anyone else who happened to be around. The wider ramifications of the system were demonstrated by two incidents that took place during the early months of the occupation.

On November 13 two Polish policemen entered the building on 9 Nalewki Street in search of a Jewish felon, Pinchas Ya'akov Zylberberg. A fight broke out, and it is believed that the clash was over dividing up the take from a robbery. During the fight, the Jew shot and killed one of the policemen, and in response the entire building was raided by the Gestapo. The Nazis went from apartment to apartment arresting all the men they found, fifty-three in all. "Among those arrested were people who didn't even live in the building but were just visiting acquaintances and decided to sleep over because the curfew for Jews had gone into effect during the course of their visits."[59] The wives of the detainees rushed to the headquarters of the *kehillah* and pleaded with the *Judenrat* to use its good offices to have their husbands released. At the same time, the Gestapo arrived and demanded a sum of 300,000 zlotys as ransom for the prisoners.[60]

Writing in his characteristic telegraphic style, Czerniakow first mentioned the prisoners and the punishment tax ("contribution") on November 21: "Representatives from the house at 9 Nalewki Street about the arrest of all the men in the building. In the evening I approached the Gestapo. The *Kommissar* said that we had to try our luck with the Polish police." And again, on the twenty-second of the month: "In the afternoon the SS. The mothers of 9 Nalewki." The *Judenrat*, which was in dire financial straits, tried to pull together the sum demanded for the "contribution" quickly. Czerniakow was told that "the *Kommissar* is not prepared to take checks but demands cash by 6 P.M. on Saturday." The members of the *Judenrat* and rabbis who took part in mobilizing the cash collected a substantial portion of the sum by appeal to the public. "I took 102,000 zlotys to the SS," Czerniakow recorded on November 25. "We need another 38,000 zlotys. A very difficult moment. . . . Finally an agreement about the remaining sum by Monday."

Once the ransom was paid, the Jews awaited the release of the hostages. But on November 28 the Nazis announced that the fifty-three men had been executed. It turned out that at the very time the Nazis were applying pressure for payment of a ransom, the men were already dead. Czerniakow described how he informed the poor families of the murder: "It's hard to describe the scene. Afterward one by one, a different victim each time. Then I was showered with abuse. At 1:30 I left the *kehillah*. The mourners held on to the cab. What could I do to help them?"[61] Kaplan recorded in his diary a rumor blaming Czerniakow's procrastination for the deaths of the Jews and placing responsibility squarely on his shoulders. A few days later Kaplan added that he had looked into the matter and it was slanderous to cast doubt on the *Judenrat* for its conduct in the affair. They had done everything in their power, while the Nazis had deceived them and slaughtered the hostages in their hands.[62]

The second case of collective punishment was related to the Andrzej Kott affair. On January 20, 1940, a poster was issued bearing the photograph of a young man and stating that "the Jew Andrzej Kott" was wanted for suspicion of murder, and whoever turned him in would receive a reward of 2,000 zlotys. Kott, the son of converts, had studied in a technical college in England, returned to Poland with the outbreak of war, and was among the founders of the underground movement PLAN, which was made up mostly of young members of the Polish intelligentsia and aspired to reconstitute an independent Polish state committed to the principles of social justice. Kott was head of the "Fighting Division" of this underground organization[63] and obviously had no connection whatsoever with Jews or any Jewish affairs. After the movement's first few actions, the most prominent of its members, including Kott, were caught. But Kott succeeded in escaping, and this drove the Nazis wild.

On January 20, the economist Ludwik Landau recorded in his diary: "Today a poster appeared promising a reward of 2,000 [zlotys] for aid in the capture of the Jew Andrzej Kott, who was born in 1919 (that is, twenty years old). Even though the Jewishness of the wanted man is only fictional, the Germans approached, as it were, the Jewish community for help in their search."[64] On the same date, Ringelblum wrote, "[The Germans] uncovered a group of terrorists headed by [Andrzej] Kott, and a hundred lawyers, doctors, and engineers (Brański, Wohl) were arrested. The *kehillah* must turn over the head of the group within forty-eight hours."[65] Czerniakow's diary also includes notes on the arrests and the relatives who turned to the *kehillah* requesting its intervention, followed by a number of entries reminiscent of the previous incident. But he does not mention the responsibility placed on the *kehillah* or the demand to turn Kott in.

Scores of people, Poles and Jews alike, mostly members of the intelligentsia, were arrested in the Kott affair. Only in the middle of August 1940 did the Gestapo give the *Judenrat* two lists of the prisoners involved. On one list, which included 165 names, the word "Dead" was scrawled in red pencil at the top of the first page. The word "Alive" was typewritten as an addition to the second list, which included ninety names. Both documents had the same heading: "A List of Those Arrested on January 18–25, 1940." Of the 208 people whose professions were cited, more than half were members of the professional intelligentsia, including lawyers, engineers, doctors, teachers, rabbis, and so on. Even though the Nazis tried to trick the hostages' families into believing that at least some of the prisoners were still alive, they were probably all executed in 1940. The murder of 225 Jews in the Kott affair, which was totally unrelated to the Jews, was the second lesson in the Nazis' system of collective responsibility and punishment.[66]

The sense of dread fostered by the Nazis through the mass executions and the murder of individuals—on any pretext or without pretext at all—made the Jews more circumspect about their conduct. A Jew knew that he was wise to keep his distance from anything that implied contact with the German authorities. Even if a serious injustice had been committed, it was best to ignore it. It was all the more imperative to avoid association with any act that truly involved breaking the law or could be interpreted as opposition to the regime, for not only were those actually involved in a suspicious act in danger, but their relatives and close acquaintances were equally liable to torture and death.

From the outbreak of the war until the establishment of the ghetto, there was also a noticeable change in the structure of the Jewish population of Warsaw. A decisive proportion of those who fled to the east were youngsters and men. Their escape therefore led not only to a quantitative decline in the population but also to a qualitative one. In contrast to those who left, the city was flooded by an influx of refugees and deportees from smaller towns. The first wave came from the areas in Western Poland annexed to the Reich. These refugees had been forced to leave their homes on a day's or few hours' notice, and they came destitute and broken to a city in the throes of anarchy. Later on, at the end of 1939 and the beginning of 1940, many Jews who had escaped from Lodz, Włocławek, Kalisz, and other cities west of Warsaw reached the capital. There were men of wealth and initiative among them, but the majority of the refugees were strangers to Warsaw and felt lost in their new home. In June and July, thirty-five hundred Jews evicted from Cracow arrived in Warsaw, and added to these large waves was a constant stream of individual families and small groups of Jews from the countryside and towns surrounding the capital. As usual in turbulent times, the Jews were afraid to live alone or in small groups within predominantly non-Jewish areas. Their sense of security disintegrated beyond the boundaries of the large Jewish centers, and it is estimated that up to the time the ghetto was closed off, ninety thousand Jewish refugees entered the city.[67] They were the weakest and most intimidated element of the Jewish population. Many of them required welfare assistance and lived in the "refugee stations" or temporary quarters.

The fact that the Jews tried as much as possible to avoid contact with the authorities and did not demonstrate active resistance does not mean that they had resigned themselves to accept their fate, come what may. Those who kept diaries and recorded the events of the time make a point of stating that if the Jews had obeyed every prohibition and regulation issued by the Nazis, they would have been eradicated within a few months' time. It seemed that everything was prohibited by the Nazi regulations: purchasing food, engaging in various types of commerce, keeping money, owning property, working without the knowledge of the authorities, changing one's place of residence. So the Jews cultivated shrewd methods of circumventing those laws that interfered with their means of existence. They were aided by means of the bribes that were welcomed by both low- and high-level German officials. As a rule, the Jewish community constituted a united front in its struggle to survive. On April 24, 1940, Kaplan recorded the following apostrophe in his diary:

> Dear God! How are all these people supporting themselves? Engaging in any trade or occupation is forbidden. All the businesses have been closed down; all the positions that provided prosperity or an income have been abolished; thousands of officials are wandering the streets of Warsaw unemployed; no shops other than groceries manage to stay open; everything is closed and shuttered; everything is broken and shattered; all the sources [of livelihood] have been blocked up . . . and yet, in spite of it all, the masses are living, the masses are sharp-witted, they treat all the decrees of the despots as meaningless and do everything possible to outwit them, to trick them behind their backs and under the table, and God provides for them.[68]

At the end of October 1939 Kaplan remarked on the uniqueness of the Polish Jews, a special character born of tradition and much experience:

> . . . The enemy erred in thinking he was in Berlin, dealing with his own "*Juden.*" After the prohibition forbidding a Jew to keep more than 2,000 zlotys in his home, the naïve Jews of Germany would probably have stood in line at the banks the next day by the tens of thousands to fulfill the *Führer's* commandments. But the Polish Jews said emphatically "No!" They didn't deposit a single penny, but you won't find a single Jew whose strongbox contains more than 2,000 zlotys! All these ridiculous decrees, which attest to low culture and sadistic wickedness, arouse laughter among the Jews of Poland.[69]

The entire period of the Nazi occupation was a chain of increasingly damaging measures and attacks against the Jews. There was no objective criterion of administration and conduct. During the first stage, when one prohibition followed on the heels of another and the Jews were the victims of severe shortages, disease, slave labor, and isolation from the world at large, they believed that the worst affliction possible had befallen them. As early as November 1939, two months into the occupation, Kaplan's tone seemed to run in complete contradiction to his earlier claim that the Jews of Poland succeeded in outwitting the enemy and continued to carry on in spite of everything:

> The Jews of Poland are faced with total extermination. If no sudden means of salvation appears, *force majeure* or otherwise (for in moments of despair such as these, one even begins to believe in miracles), we will witness a catastrophe unprecedented in Jewish history, overflowing with the torments of Hell—the total destruction and eradication of a Jewish community that played such a vital role in our history. It will vanish from the Jewish stage.[70]

To a man who makes no pretense of clairvoyance but is familiar with the course of events to come, the misfortunes of this first stage of the occupation of Warsaw (up to the establishment of the ghetto), which one historian has dubbed the period of the "little terror," appear to be relatively moderate compared to the future awaiting the Jews inside the ghetto and the almost two long years of terrible suffering that would pass until the beginning of the "Final Solution," namely the total annihilation of the Jews of Warsaw.

Jewish Institutions and the Organization of Public Life during the First Stage of the Occupation

The most important and most controversial institution that functioned during the period of the occupation was the *Judenrat*. We know already that the Nazis ordered its establishment. In addition to Heydrich's instructions in September, Frank issued an order on 28 November 1939 about setting up *Judenräte* in the Generalgouvernement. According to this directive, a *Judenrat* was to be established in each Jewish community. The councils would be composed of twenty-four members in communities with populations over ten thousand and of twelve members in those with populations under ten thousand. "The *Judenräte* are obliged through their heads or deputies to receive the orders of the German authorities." On the other hand, the *Judenrat* was also a direct extension of the prewar Jewish *kehillah*. Even its composition was similar to that of the *kehillah*, at least at the beginning of the occupation.

The Warsaw *Judenrat* is closely associated with the name of Adam Czerniakow, the engineer who headed the council from the time of its formation until the initiation of deportations to the death camps in July 1942. And just as the image and the activities of the *Judenrat* are the subject of sharp controversy, so has Czerniakow's personality been the focus of conflicting opinions and evaluations. A few years ago, Czerniakow's diary—which was believed to have been lost—was finally published, and this comprehensive and crucial document covering the period during which he headed the *Judenrat* cast light on his personal and public character, his inclinations, and the manner in which he handled his thankless task.

Hartglas depicts Czerniakow in his memoirs as an ambitious man who sought the German appointment as head of the *Judenrat*.[71] But the evidence available to us today casts doubt on this portrayal. When the war broke out, Czerniakow was a member of the council that directed the affairs of the *kehillah*. During the fighting and the siege of the city, Maurycy Mayzel, the nominated chairman of the *kehillah*, escaped from Warsaw, and Czerniakow was chosen as head of the civilian Jewish committee that was established during the siege.[72] On September 23 he wrote: "Mayor Starzyński appointed me head of the Jewish religious community in Warsaw. An historic task in a besieged city. I shall prove up to it." Thus he was not appointed head of the *kehillah* by the Germans at the onset of the occupation but by the mayor of the city at the height of the battle for Warsaw. Then, on October 4, Czerniakow recorded in his diary: "I was taken to Aleje Szucha [the headquarters of the Gestapo in Warsaw] and told that I must coopt twenty-four people to the community council and serve as its head." It therefore cannot be claimed that Czerniakow was a man who exploited the entry of the Germans to push his way to the top; but it is true that he was attracted to the leadership position and was not particularly reluctant to accept the appointment from the Germans. In the course of time, Czerniakow came to view his position as a heavy burden that must be borne with fortitude during a time of emergency and under extraordinary circumstances. He judged the leaders who fled the city harshly, describing them as captains deserting a sinking ship.

The original *Judenrat* included senior members of the different political parties, senior officials of the welfare institutions and public organizations, and members of the *kehillah* who had remained in Warsaw, among whom were Apolinary Hartglas of the General Zionists, Shmuel Zygielbojm of the Bund, Rabbi Yitzhak Meir Levin of Agudat Israel, and Dr. Abraham Weiss of Mizrachi. All these men were destined to leave the city during the first few months of the occupation. Hartglas claims in his memoirs that he was well aware that the *Judenrat* had been created to serve as a tool of the Germans. This purpose was not only clear from Frank's order to establish the council but was expressly stated in the letter of appointment itself.

Even after the veteran leaders left Poland, the *Judenrat* continued to be manned by a group of men whose reputation testified to responsible and loyal public service. The question therefore remains: How did the *Judenrat* bring so much animosity down upon itself? Why did a barrier of alienation and hostility rise up so quickly between the *Judenrat* and the common man? This sense of sharp opposition and enmity comes out not only in the publications of members of the underground but also in most of the diaries and journals kept during the period. Heinz Auerswald, the German *Kommissar* of the Warsaw ghetto, said in a letter sent to Berlin on November 24, 1941, that in the face of deficiencies, "the disappointment of the Jewish population is directed against the Jewish ghetto apparatus rather than against the German authorities."[73] Ringleblum believed that the *kehillah* did not know how to relate to the needs of the community and was "helpless." Kaplan, as usual, uses stronger language and is outspoken in his accusations: "The *kehillah* — or, as the conqueror calls it, the *Judenrat* — is a disgrace to the Warsaw community. Whenever the subject comes up, everyone's blood starts to boil."[74]

It is understandable that because the *Judenrat* unwillingly served as a kind of middleman between the Jewish community and the German authorities, and the public at large had no recourse to direct contact with the Germans, the community directed its rage against its own representatives. Yet Czerniakow's diary is an impressive testament to the fairness and courage of the man who was appointed to represent the largest Jewish community in Europe at a time of terror and supreme trial. Although he had displayed Zionist leanings in the past, Czerniakow was essentially an assimilated Jew who lacked confidence in the ability of the Jews to behave as a disciplined community. His conduct of affairs was inevitably influenced by this outlook, which had many ramifications for the climate that prevailed in the Jewish community. It is true that with the passing of time, Czerniakow grew increasingly sensitive to the suffering in the ghetto. He appealed to the community for its support and understanding, but by then it was too late: the *Judenrat* had become the object of total and universal hostility, and Czerniakow was singled out as the embodiment of all it stood for and the man personally responsible for its deeds.

It is clear in retrospect that even if the *Judenrat* had been faultless, the efforts of its members were doomed to bitter failure. As in a classical tragedy, the *Judenrat*'s fate was sealed from the outset, and its members were like fish caught in a net. A close reading of Czerniakow's diary reveals first of all that his major concerns and efforts came in response to German demands. The *Judenrat* was ordered to carry out a census, to supply workers for forced labor, to turn over large quantities of furniture and valuables, to assume responsibility for the payment of "contributions." Czerniakow and his colleagues desperately scrambled from office to office trying to get orders deferred or cancelled and were constantly haunted by financial crises. (A report delivered by the Department of Statistics included the main items of the budget of the *Judenrat* for the period January 1–April 30, 1940. The revenue side is composed of a few entries selected from a total of 3,082,101 zlotys: the regular community tax—206,000 zlotys; payments for labor battalion, exemptions from labor duty and labor registration fees—853,000 zlotys; cemetery payments—639,000 zlotys; various small revenues; and loans and borrowings of 764,000 zlotys. The column of expenditures is based primarily on what the head of the council called expenses "connected with the implementation of the authorities' instructions." These "instructions" included: direct payments to the authorities—238,000 zlotys; expenses for the labor battalion—816,000 zlotys; and expenditures for hospitals, health, and social help—1,146,000 zlotys. The budget for the the month of April 1940 is drafted as follows: revenue—498,500 zlotys; expenditures—910,050 zlotys; deficit—411,550 zlotys.)[75] For the most part, the efforts of Czerniakow and his colleagues were in vain, and even when they did succeed in achieving something—such as when they managed to put off the date for the sealing of the ghetto—their accomplishment was no more than a postponement of the inevitable, not a lasting victory.

The *Judenrat* was under the control of the arms of the police—the S.D. and the Gestapo. Junior officers—often primitive people—decided on matters that affected the fate of hundreds of thousands of people, and they bullied, intimidated, and punished the *Judenrat* representatives. It was clear to the SS and the Gestapo that the Jews had been assigned to their jurisdiction. But Frank and his administration wanted to contain the powers of the secret police, and, as noted earlier, the Jews became an object of rivalry and contention between the Nazi authorities. On rare occasions, the *Judenrat* succeeded in thwarting SS plans or gained the upper hand in a clash between the German bodies. More often, however, the Jews fell victim to the devices and whims of not only a single, centralized German authority but a whole patchwork of institutions and officials. Michael Weichert claims that the March 14 meeting with Arlt in Cracow had a profound impact on the status of the *Judenrat:*

> The direct result of that meeting was to have the *Judenrat* removed from the Gestapo's jurisdiction and turned over to the civilian administration—the mayors and district leaders. But the Gestapo had no intention of giving up a milk cow like the *Judenrat*. From then on, not only the Gestapo but all the mayors and district leaders could "legally" fleece the *Judenrat*, which had already been done before.[76]

An institution of a different character that functioned legally or semilegally during the occupation was the network of the Jewish self-help. Charity and philanthropy were two principles deeply rooted in Jewish communal life in Poland. Thus the efforts to provide relief to the needy and the attempts to foster mutual aid in the ghetto were first and foremost expressions of a desire to perpetuate long-standing imperatives.

As noted earlier, the creation of the Metropolitan Committee of Mutual Social Aid (S.K.S.S.) within the Polish sector of the population was immediately followed by the establishment of a similar Jewish body, the Coordinating Committee (K.K.), which united the various Jewish welfare and social aid institutions in the face of the new challenge. The committee's first efforts were directed toward the waves of refugees and the many Warsaw Jews who were victims of bombardments and fires. Because the organization lacked a firm legal basis, the entrance to the headquarters of the Jewish self-help in Warsaw, located in the building of the great Judaic Library, displayed the symbol of the JDC, on the assumption that the Germans would respect the American identity of the institution. The Poles broke off their ties with the Jewish Coordinating Committee soon after the Germans took over the city. They claimed that the German authorities disapproved of Polish aid to Jews. But from the very start, it was the resources of the JDC that served as the major financial support of the Jewish self-help.

Since the prewar *kehillah* had engaged in only a small portion of the functions that were assigned to the *Judenrat*, the latter found itself involved in unfamiliar areas and served by an inexperienced staff. Not so the social-welfare enterprise, which was essentially a comprehensive association of existing welfare organizations and institutions. Most of these organizations could draw on years of practical experience and were staffed by workers well tested in their roles and familiar with their field of operation. They included CENTOS (The National Society for the Care of Orphans), which had developed a network to care for hungry and neglected children; TOZ (Society for the Preservation of Health); and ORT (The Institute for Vocational Guidance and Training). These organizations attracted many public figures to their causes, and the militant management of the self-help enterprise was based on a strong foundation of public support. According to Abraham Berman, who was director of CENTOS in the Warsaw ghetto, three thousand volunteers worked with the Jewish self-help in Warsaw. The actor Yonas Turkow, active in the social-welfare program, noted: "All the cultured people in Warsaw at the time without exception, both social and political forces, devoted themselves unstintingly to all spheres of Jewish self-help."[77] Indeed, the Jewish self-help drew into its ranks members of the intelligentsia—teachers, writers, actors, journalists, and politicians. Michael Weichert, the representative of the Jewish craftsmen and a well-known figure in the Jewish theater, was the first chairman of the institution, and Emmanuel Ringelblum was its secretary-general.

In January 1940, in accordance with a German demand, the Coordinating Committee adopted a new name: Jewish Social Self-Help (Ż.S.S.). The Ż.S.S. was headed by a group of seven delegates from Warsaw, Cracow, and other cities, most of whom were members of *Judenräte*. Michael Weichert was appointed chairman, and Joseph Jaszunski, a veteran director of ORT and a member of the Warsaw *Judenrat*, served as vice-chairman.

Shortly after the establishment of the Ż.S.S., the German authorities in Cracow, represetned by F. Arlt, the head of the Department of Population and Welfare, asked to create a central body that would merge the existing social-welfare institutions of the various ethnic segments of the Generalgouvernement. By the end of May 1940, the status of the new institution, called the N.R.O. (*Naczelna Rada Opiekuńcza*—Central Council for Care), was confirmed. The N.R.O. included the Polish (R.G.O.), Ukrainian (U.R.O.), and Jewish aid organizations. The presidium of the N.R.O. was composed of seven members—five Poles, one Ukrainian, and one Jew. Michael Weichert became the Jewish representative and took up residence in Cracow.

It is pertinent to wonder what motivated the Germans to take an interest in the Jewish social-welfare program and allocate it legal status in a joint framework with the Polish and Ukrainian organizations. This move was completely contradictory to the overall Nazi policy toward the Jews, and especially to the tendency to isolate the Jews from other national groups. The Ż.S.S. was also the only Jewish institution allowed to function in the entire sphere of the Generalgouvernement. As it turns out, this same question troubled the people who were directly involved in the activities of the Ż.S.S. Weichert recorded the following doubts in his memoirs:

> It simply wasn't logical. On the one hand they persecute Jews to the utmost, and on the other they discuss a central organization for social aid with them. We didn't know that they were under pressure from the American Red Cross and the Commission for Polish Relief in America, which sent a few boatloads of food, medicine, and clothing for the civilian population of the Generalgouvernement and emphatically demanded that the distribution be handled by representatives of the population itself.[78]

Weichert's explanation goes a long way toward assuaging the sense of astonishment. American welfare institutions, such as the Commission for Polish Relief (C.P.R.) and the American Red Cross, were active in occupied Poland through the agency of the German Red Cross. Emissaries of the American institutions even visited Warsaw in 1940 and took part directly in the discussions about the distribution of goods, insisting that their aid reach Jews as well. At that time, the door was still open to negotiations with the Western powers—at any rate, the Nazis felt it was important to preserve the neutrality of the United States. In addition to these political considerations, however, the Nazis appreciated the value of the goods and dollars sent by the American relief organizations, which were traded at the normal rate of exchange.

Until the middle of 1942 the Ż.S.S. did receive a proportionate share of the donations delivered to the N.R.O. from the budget of the Generalgouvernement. A few of the most prominent Polish members of the board of N.R.O. were sensitive to Jewish demands. At early meetings of the N.R.O., the Ż.S.S. had argued that the Jewish population, in addition to its extraordinarily grave situation, lacked the regular social protection provided by the organs of the occupation authorities and the municipalities and therefore were entitled to a larger portion of the emergency relief. They requested 30 percent for the Jews in Warsaw and 25 percent for the Jews in other centers of the Generalgouvernement. This proposal was accepted by the Poles on the board of the N.R.O. but was categorically opposed by leading members of the Polish R.G.O. Finally, it was agreed that 17 percent of the relief provided from abroad and of the funds taken from taxes by the civilian administration would be allocated to the Jews.

Weichert maintained in his memoirs that the Ż.S.S. was different from the *Judenräte* in both structure and achievements. He claimed that in the eyes of the Jews the Ż.S.S. acquired resources from the Germans for the Jewish cause, while the *Judenrat* took money and valuables from the Jews and handed them over to the Germans. This way of presenting the functions of the two bodies is actually a far-fetched simplification of very complicated problems. As a matter of fact, many members of the *Judenräte* were active in the Ż.S.S., and in many places departments of the *Judenräte* constituted district and local branches of the institution. Thus the division between the *Judenräte* and the Ż.S.S. is in many cases misleading. On the other hand, the *Judenräte* were forced to deal with the German rulers both in order to try to prevent or moderate anti-Jewish decrees and to implement the Nazi policy among the Jews. Weichert's few attempts to abolish or postpone anti-Jewish measures by negotiations with the German authorities did not lead to any positive results. Nevertheless, the fact that the Ż.S.S. enjoyed, to a certain extent, freedom of action and dealt only with the sector of the German bureaucracy in charge of welfare, made their position and task easier in relation to the Germans as well as in respect to the Jewish population.

According to Weichert's data, the monthly allocation received through the N.R.O. from the German administration was about 450,000 zlotys, that is, between twenty-five and fifty thousand dollars. A slightly higher amount of money was provided by the organizations from abroad, especially the JDC. At least half of the total amount of money and goods was designated for Warsaw, the center of the Jewish population and, clearly, the city with the highest concentration of Jewish misery.

The Warsaw branch of the Ż.S.S. was in fact an independent body. From the first stages of the Coordinating Committee, the Warsaw relief program operated under the joint direction of two groups: a council of activists from the underground political factions, led by Emmanuel Ringelblum, and the board of JDC directors, led by Yitzhak Giterman. The board of directors was by no means simply a powerless body controlled by the policy of the American institution and expected to handle the local tasks according to decisions of the central management in New York. On the contrary, when their finances ran out, the Polish JDC did not hestitate to take independent initiative, sometimes in direct contradiction to the instructions and rules of the head offices abroad. They found a way to receive substantial funds from the JDC in Europe and appealed to wealthy Polish Jews to invest their money in social aid, promising that the JDC would reimburse them in dollars after the war. Since it was dangerous for individual Jews to keep cash and the Jews' fiscal freedom of maneuver was severely limited, some men of wealth hoped to insure their money and its value by "investing" it with the JDC, though in addition to the financial benefits they were undoubtedly moved by the desire to help Jews in need. This was only one of the stratagems employed by the organization. A voluntary tax was also collected during the occupation; special campaigns were initiated; and donations were collected at private celebrations and public assemblies. From the beginning of the occupation the leaders of the Polish JDC maintained close ties with the political underground, and to a great extent the institution was a focus of political activity up to the time of the revolt.

At the end of October 1940, the Ż.S.S. was ordered to change its name to Ż.T.O.S. (Żydowskie Towarzystwo Opieki Społecznej—Jewish Organization for Social Care). The name change was an attempt to abolish the independence of the Ż.S.S. in Warsaw and bring all the individual institutions under the control of the central body in Cracow. Some assumed that Weichert himself was interested in weakening the politically oriented independent center that had crystallized in Warsaw. Despite the fact that the Warsaw organization was forced to recognize the supremacy of Cracow and relinguish its separate administrative focus, the absorption of the Warsaw structure was only an official act. In reality, the independence and unique character of the Warsaw center were maintained until the end of the ghetto's existence.

The relief campaign in Warsaw extended to a number of spheres of life and assumed a variety of tasks. It organized hostels for refugees and a network of soup kitchens that distributed up to thirty thousand portions of soup at one stage. The character of these kitchens was not uniform. Most of them distributed watered-down soup that was not very nourishing, but anyone who was in need could receive a portion for a token price. At the same time there were also more exclusive relief kitchens that served as meeting places for members of various professions. A separate division of soup kitchens for children not only distributed food but secretly organized games and classes, and the hostels of the Jewish youth movements also doubled as relief kitchens and havens for meetings and activities of the underground. As a rule, the food offered by the exclusive kitchens was of a higher quality than in the regular relief outlets.

The self-help enterprise in Warsaw placed emphasis on aid to individuals. Relief was provided regardless of class or social standing, so that professionals, artists, public officials, and religious leaders who were left without means of support benefited from the program alongside the destitute refugees and chronically poor. The self-help program felt particularly obliged to stand by the intelligentsia and the organized sections of the public. This selective approach, whose aim was obvious, fell under sharp criticism. The heads of the program were accused of prejudice and preferential treatment of their own kind. Such criticism may have been inevitable, since the self-help framework was incapable of coping with the needs arising from a general shortage. It could not satisfy all the widespread legitimate demands and was therefore forced to establish criteria for distributing what little there was. Ringelblum wrote about "The Dilemma of Jewish Self-Help" in May 1942:

> . . . Relief work doesn't solve the problem; it only keeps people going a little while. The people have to die anyway. It lengthens suffering but cannot save them; if it [the Jewish Self-Help] really wanted to do anything, it would have to have millions of zloty at its disposal every month, and it does not have them. It remains a proven fact that the people fed in the soup-kitchens will all die if they eat nothing but the soup supplied and the dry rationed bread. The question thus arises whether it would not serve the purpose better to reserve the available money for selected individuals, for those who are socially productive, for the intellectual elite; etc. But the situation is such that, first of all, the numbers even of such select individuals is quite considerable, and there would not be sufficient even for them.

Secondly, the question arises why should one pronounce judgment on artisans, laborers and other useful persons, who were productive people back in their small towns, and only the ghetto and the war have turned them into non-people, into scrap, into human dregs, candidates for mass graves. There is left a tragic dilemma: What shall one do? Shall one [hand out the food] with little spoons to everybody, and then no one will live, or in generous handfuls to just a few . . . ?[79]

The fact that the enterprise provided monetary support for the remnants of the political parties and various underground bodies spurred competition among the potential recipients and aroused suspicions that the men who controlled the purse strings were allocating to their political allies and those close to them funds that were disproportionate to their true value in the spectrum of underground organizations. These accusations and distortions of the truth are an understandable phenomenon and probably did not exceed the usual rivalry that exists in similar institutions even under normal conditions.

The relief was not confined to material aid alone, for the self-help program initiated cultural and entertainment activities without official approval and even in defiance of a definite prohibition. The *Judenrat* warned that the enterprise had exceeded the limits of its jurisdiction and that people associated with the program for social aid were attempting to cull public support for their own causes. Yet it was thanks to the participation of political activists and the heads of public organizations, who viewed their roles in the self-help institutions as those of public servants, that the social-aid enterprise became, more than any other public framework during the occupation, a source of support for the clandestine movements and even the Jewish fighting organization, once it too came into being.

Another framework adopted and cultivated by the self-help endeavor was the network of building councils, which were organized both spontaneously and by public initiative during the early days of the war. The councils, which served as a kind of civil-defense authority and as representatives of the civilian government, were set up in every apartment house. Established to deal with the emergency situation, these frameworks continued to exist and even expanded during the occupation, though their character and functions changed. The building councils were cells of limited self-government in the apartment houses of the city; in addition to assuming responsibility for the upkeep of the buildings, they played a role in the mutual-aid program, especially by providing support for needy families. The councils also represented their constituents vis-à-vis the *Judenrat*, the relief organizations, and general municipal institutions.

Two factors that promoted the strengthening of the building councils were the curfew, which forced the Jews to be at home by an early hour and spend the long evenings with their families and neighbors, and the importance ascribed to the councils by the broader public institutions. The self-help program, and especially its Public Affairs Department under the direction of Dr. Emmanuel Ringelblum, immediately discerned the importance of the building councils as a grass-roots phenomenon and a reliable and efficient means of communication with the Jewish public. The Ż.S.S. therefore took the building councils under its wing, organized a kind of umbrella organization to direct and coordinate their activities, and tried to establish stable and permanent patterns for them to follow. A directive issued by the Center for the Building Councils, attached to the Public Affairs Department, stated that "Building councils should be established in all the apartment houses of Warsaw to represent the tenants. In buildings that have less than ten Jewish families, the councils should extend to include the tenants of a number of nearby apartment houses." According to the directive, building councils were to comprise three members in each building with less than twenty-five people; five members when the number of tenants was fifty; and seven members when the number of tenants exceeded fifty. At the end of April 1940, 788 building councils were functioning in 878 apartment houses; in May there were 1,518 councils in 2,014 buildings; and by September 2,000 building councils were in operation.[80] Among their other activities, the councils established youth groups and children's corners so that young people could meet for social gatherings and discussions over cups of tea (sometimes cultural or educational activities, or even programs of a political nature, were held during these gatherings) and children could play together and even receive allocations of food.

The building councils' operating funds came from several sources. First, the councils themselves imposed a standard tax on their tenants and exercised moral and practical pressure to exact the sum from anyone with the means to pay. They also appealed for special contributions from tenants who had formerly been well off and had kept part of their possessions. Parties were organized during the holidays and on other occasions, with the proceeds going into the councils' treasuries. Families in a relatively comfortable financial state would sometimes host hungry children from neighboring apartments. The building councils also engaged in collecting food, clothing, and blankets for tenants who had been sent to the labor camps. One side benefit of the building councils was the cultivation of local leaders who came to the fore by virtue of their natural leadership abilities and their talent at forging ties with diverse groups of tenants.

The Ż.S.S. tried to raise the stature of the building councils and turn them into an ubiquitous instrument of mutual aid. It attempted to place responsibility for impoverished families on the tenants of buildings in more affluent areas. One experiment was to have certain building councils adopt the inmates of an orphanage and take in refugees. This approach was only partially successful, since the mood in the apartment houses was characterized by strong "local patriotism," and the tenants worried first and foremost about matters closer to home.

At a certain stage the *Judenrat* intended to solicit the cooperation of the building councils in executing the orders issued by the occupation authorities. Indeed, there were instances in which the councils collected or donated funds by buy the furniture demanded of the *Judenrat* by the Germans. But the councils were not prepared to help the *Judenrat* mobilize conscripts for the labor camps. On the contrary, they were severely critical of the *Judenrat*'s methods of mobilization and the policemen who executed the conscription.[81] Czerniakow expressed his disappointment in the building councils, undoutedly because of their refusal to cooperate and their critical stance toward the *Judenrat*. It is also possible that Czerniakow misjudged the limits of what could be accomplished within a voluntary framework and asked of the councils more than they were able to deliver.[82]

Chapter Two
The Establishment
of the Ghetto

The Abortive Attempt to
Establish a Ghetto

The Warsaw ghetto was closed in the middle of November 1940, about fourteen months after the Nazis captured the city. But the actual sealing off of the ghetto was but the last step in a long process of systematically segregating the Jews, or "ghettoization."

The first attempt to create a ghetto was made soon after the Germans entered Warsaw. On Saturday, November 4, 1939,[1] the SS ordered a special session of the *Judenrat*. Because of the short notice and the fact that it was the Sabbath, not all the members of the *Judenrat* and their deputies appeared at the appointed hour. The SS men who showed up at the meeting insisted that all twenty-four members of the council, without exception, convene immediately, so that it was necessary to enlist a number of Jewish bystanders to fill the complement. Facing the Jewish representatives, who were all standing at attention, *Standartenführer-S.S.* Dr. Rudolf Batz read out an order in the name of the military commander of the city, General von Neuman-Neurode, stating that the Jews of Warsaw had three days to concentrate within certain streets in the Jewish section, i.e., in a ghetto. He then presented an improvised list of the streets involved.[2] The men who substituted for members of the *Judenrat*, and especially those who had been rounded up at the last moment, were taken as hostages until the order was executed.[3]

The grave implications of the edict to uproot and resettle 150,000 people in three days astonished the *Judenrat*. It was clear that even by

48

making a supreme effort, the order could not be executed by the deadline; in fact, the demand was totally unreasonable. Zygielbojm reported that:

> As a representative of the workers [in the *Judenrat*], I proposed that the community refuse to obey the order . . . [and] this suggestion was supported by a few members of the council. But the majority felt that they could not adopt this course, and some argued: What will happen if we ourselves do not carry out the order? Nazi soldiers will turn up at Jewish homes and evict the Jews from their apartments by force. What will they do to our women and children?[4]

The members of the *Judenrat* decided upon a daring step: they would bypass the SS and the Gestapo by sending a delegation directly to General von Neuman-Neurode. When the delegation, composed of Czerniakow, chairman of the *Judenrat*, A. Hartglas, and A. Weiss,[5] was received by the general, it turned out that Neuman-Neurode knew nothing about the order that was supposedly issued in his name. He promised to look into the matter, including the area delineated for the proposed ghetto, and ordered the *Judenrat* to await his decision. In the meantime, they were to ignore the order issued by the SS and the Gestapo. The general's attitude was undoubtedly a product of the discord that existed between the SS and the *Wehrmacht* in the confines of the Generalgouvernement.

News of the imminent formation of a ghetto spread quickly and created alarm and despair among the Jews, who were still recovering from the deep shock of the bombing, death, and destruction inflicted by the warfare in September. "Crowds under the windows of the *kehillah*," Czerniakow noted in his diary, and Kaplan recorded that "the order about the ghetto created an atmosphere of fright."

In negotiations that went on for several days, changes were made in the proposed map of the ghetto. Furious that the *Judenrat* dared to approach German authorities on their own, Batz threatened Czerniakow. According to Hartglas, Batz made off for Berlin to complain about Neuman-Neurode's conduct and drum up support from the power centers of the SS, "and in the meanwhile, Bischoff, who was Batz's superior in the SS but under him in the hierarchy of the [Nazi] party, exploited his absence and, in order to undermine him, cancelled the order to establish a ghetto."[6] Szoszkes claims that "late Tuesday night we learned that the order had been postponed as a result of the bitter struggle between the army and the Gestapo."[7] Czerniakow noted on November 10 that Bischoff ordered the release of the prisoners who were held hostage, and on November 14 he wrote, "Went to the SS. The idea of deportation is no longer being entertained."

This time the frantic efforts of the *Judenrat* produced results. The edict to establish a ghetto was shelved for about a year, and, according to Hartglas, the size of the ghetto was increased about 30 percent over the area delineated in 1939. But this accomplishment also gave rise to the belief—which in most cases proved to be only an illusion—that the discord between the various German authorities could be exploited, and there was a good probability that diabolical measures could be thwarted by Jewish intervention. However, the sabotage of the SS and Gestapo's improvised plan at this stage did not mean that the idea of creating a ghetto in Warsaw had been abandoned. Preparations to crowd the Jews into a ghetto and gradual implementation of the plan continued throughout 1940, until the dramatic step of sealing off the ghetto in November.

An item that appeared in the official German newspaper of the Generalgouvernement, *Krakauer Zeitung*, in November 1939 stated that the government of the Warsaw District had ordered the Jewish quarter to be blockaded by barricades and forbade soldiers to enter the area.[8] On January 18, 1940, the Nazi attorney Waldemar Schön arrived in Warsaw and was appointed by Ludwig Fischer, the governor of the Warsaw District, to supervise the population relocation program (*Abteilung Umsiedlung*) in the district.[9] Schön assumed responsibility for the various plans to establish a ghetto in Warsaw and played a principal role in turning these plans into a reality.

In March 1940 a new term was applied to the Jewish residential area in Warsaw—"A Plague-Infected Area" (*Seuchensperrgebiet*)—and on March 27 the *Judenrat* was ordered to build a wall around the "infected area." Czerniakow recorded on May 10, 1940, that he had received a sketch of the area to be cordoned off (*Skizze des Sperrgebietes Warschau*), and it covered 4 percent of the area of Warsaw.[10] From then onward the subject of the walls is a common theme in Czerniakow's entires. He approahced various officials and a number of authorities over the matter in an attempt to get the order cancelled. The Germans claimed that "the walls are being ordered to defend the Jews against [Polish] excesses,"[11] while they told the Poles that the hermetic isolation of the Jews was meant to protect the Polish population from the typhus epidemic.[12]

Once Czerniakow resigned himself to the fact that there would be no getting around the edict to build a wall, he became preoccupied with the question of who would bear the costs of the project. The *Judenrat* was constantly in the throes of a financial crisis. But in this matter as well, Czerniakow was dogged by failure, and on April 13, 1940, he wrote in his diary: "We are to pay for the walls."

By the beginning of June, twenty sections of the wall were already standing, but completion of the construction and the final alignment of the wall were not to come until the closing of the ghetto and were part and parcel of that act. Earlier, signs had been posted in a number of languages marking the boundary of the Jewish area and warning, "Danger. Epidemic."

In August 1940 came the official announcement that the city would be divided into three quarters: German, Polish, and Jewish. The Jews were required to abandon the German quarter completely, while Jews living in the area designated for Poles could remain in their places of residence. However, the Jewish refugees who entered Warsaw were not allowed to take up residence in the Polish quarter, and Jews changing their place of residence within the city were not allowed to settle there. In the course of time, the number and frequency of measures designed to bolster the distinction between the Jews and other sections of the population steadily increased. The curfew for Jews living outside the Jewish quarter was set back to an earlier hour; special trolley cars marked with a Jewish star were designated for Jews only; and Jews were required to make way for German soldiers passing in the street.

At the same time, Jews were gradually being evicted from apartment houses and sections of certain streets and were ordered to move into the Jewish quarter. In August 1940 Ludwik Landau began to record incidents of Jews being dislocated from certain streets and houses and crowded into the Jewish section. This gradual relocation continued until the final evacuation and the closing of the ghetto in Warsaw.

Planning the Establishment of the Ghetto

German documents provide us with insight into the Nazi policy of establishing a ghetto in Warsaw and clarify why the process of delimiting and closing the ghetto went on for so long—i.e., relative to the time it took the Germans to execute other orders related to the Jews. On January 20, 1941, Schön, who was appointed to supervise the relocation program and the organization of the ghetto, presented an extensive survey to the heads of the General-gouvernement.[13] His review contained two explanations for the delay in establishing the ghetto: (1) general reasons, meaning those bound up with broader political considerations; and (2) local problems, meaning difficulties that arose on the spot.

As early as February 1940, the Germans intended to locate the ghetto in eastern Warsaw, over the Vistula River in the suburb of Praga. This concept was based on the assumption that the ghetto had to be set apart from the body of the city. The traditional Jewish quarter of Warsaw, in the north of the city, was surrounded by Polish neighborhoods, and any attempt to isolate this area from the rest of the city would entail interfering with transportation and other municipal activities. According to Schön, the original plan met with oppostion from the Municipality, which claimed that since 80 percent of the craftsmen in the city were Jews and their products were essential commodities, the creation of a ghetto would harm the city's economy. It would also be impossible to sustain the Jews in a closed quarter. In March 1940, therefore, it was decided to postpone the establishment of a ghetto for the present. At the same time, Schön reported, a number of proposals were examined regarding the establishment of a reservation for the Jews in the province of Lublin, and only at the beginning of April did the authorities in Cracow announce that the idea of a reservation had been dropped. In the meantime, other ghettos had been set up in the Warsaw District and efforts were renewed to establish a ghetto in the capital.

By that stage, the Nazi conception called for the establishment of two ghettos in the suburbs of Warsaw. Schön explained that "this plan was based on the assumption that ghettos of this kind, located at the periphery of the city, would be a relatively minor obstacle and would be least harmful to the economy, industry, and transportation in Warsaw."[14] The operation was slated to begin on July 1 in order to ensure the completion of its most important phases before the winter set in. But further delays were caused by announcements from Cracow that any work pertaining to the establishment of a ghetto must take into account Hitler's plan to settle the Jews on the island of Madagascar at the end of the war. As a result, the activities of the Department of Relocation were halted.

At the end of August, the ghetto proposal was raised again, this time by the Health Department in view of the concentration of troops in the Warsaw District and the need to protect the health of the soldiers and the population at large. Since it was already the end of summer, and establishing ghettos in the suburbs would take at least four to five months, it was decided that the ghetto would be created in the crowded Jewish quarter ("the infected area"). November 15 was chosen as the date for completing the action.

On October 2 the Germans issued an official order regarding the establishment of the ghetto, accompanied by a list of streets to be included therein. The Jews were informed of the decree on October 12, 1940, by means of loudspeakers that had been set up in the streets. The *Judenrat* was officially informed of the directive on the same day. Describing the meeting, Czerniakow wrote in his diary: "It was thereupon proclaimed (Schön) that in the name of humanity and at the behest of the governor, the governor general, and in conformity with higher authority, a ghetto is to be established. I was given a map of the German quarter and the map of the ghetto separately. It turns out that the streets bordering on the ghetto have been allocated to the Poles."

It was obviously not by chance that the Jews were informed of the decision to establish the ghetto on October 12. That day was Yom Kippur. At the height of the holidays, the Germans had announced that public worship was forbidden. But the Jews ignored the warning and assembled in public halls and private prayer quorums (*minyanim*) to carry on their prayers and supplications. At the end of the day of fasting and prayer, Kaplan wrote:

> The Jewish community of Warsaw left nothing out in its prayers, but poured its supplications before its Father in Heaven in accordance with the ancient custom of Israel. To our great sorrow, as the day drew to a close, at a time when the gates of tears were still open, we learned that a new edict had been issued to us, a barbaric edict which by its weight and results is greater than all the other edicts made against us up to now, to which we have become accustomed.
>
> At last the ghetto edict has gone into effect. For the time being it will be an open ghetto, but there is no doubt that in short order it will be closed.[15]

Various and often conflicting versions of the map of the ghetto were circulated, and changes regarding the streets to be included in the closed area were made a few times in response to pressure from the Poles. The uncertainty regarding the exact boundaries of the ghetto added to the confusion and misery of those slated for relocation.

Schön's version of events, cited above, covers the general outline of developments and is certainly reliable about the facts. At best, however, it explains the delays and difficulties that contributed to extending the process of establishing the ghetto, but it fails to throw light on the Nazis' reasons for choosing this option. We know that the essential idea of creating a ghetto in Warsaw did not stem from local considerations, for the Warsaw ghetto was neither the first nor the last to be established in Poland. Yet if we examine the nature and significance of the Germans' reasons for establishing the ghetto in Warsaw, we find that Nazi claims on this subject are not consistent.

In September 1940 Frank declared that he approved the closing of the Warsaw ghetto because he was convinced that the five hundred thousand Jews constituted a great danger to the population at large and must be prevented from wandering around.[16] In consultations held with Frank's senior officials on April 3, most of the remarks centered on problems of economy, employment, and supply within the ghetto. Governor Fischer, however, addressed himself to the rationale behind the establishment of a ghetto. Like Schön, Fischer cited three reasons:

political, economic, and sanitary. The political goal of the move was to eliminate Jewish influence on the Poles. According to Fischer's description, the Jews were constantly undermining the efforts of the Municipality and served as a counterweight to German influences. From the economic viewpoint, Jewish activities had been damaging in two ways: Jews interfered with the planning and development of the economy, and they sabotaged the successful operation of price controls and the application of a standard and stable price structure. Finally, Fischer presented the most commonly cited justification for the establishment of a ghetto: the sequestration of the Jews was imperative to protect the health of the general population and fight the epidemic.[17]

Anyone who is even superficially familiar with the character of Jewish-Polish relations cannot seriously entertain the notion that Jews influenced Polish attitudes toward the Nazis, any more than one can accept Fischer's claims regarding the economy. The occupation regime had no intention of developing the economy of the Generalgouvernement. Its true design was to exploit to the utmost the existing natural resources, industrial plants, and the work force at its disposal, in the service of the Third Reich's war effort. The Jews had only a marginal role in these plans, and the prices of basic commodities, especially foodstuffs, were essentially determined by the supply of goods and agricultural produce, which was controlled by the occupation authorities themselves.

Naturally, it is important to relate to the repeated accusation that the Jews were a focus of contagious disease, and the free movement of Jews therefore constituted a threat to the environment. An examination of the fluctuations in the incidence of disease indicates that the ghetto was established at one of the low points of the epidemic, and, according to experts, had appropriate measures been adopted, it would have been possible to eradicate the disease altogether. *Gazeta Żydowska,* the only Polish-language Jewish newspaper published legally during the occupation, gave statistics on the epidemic in its issue of October 24, 1940:

> Typhoid began to spread in October–November 1939 and immediately reached alarming proportions—about 2,000 cases. From February [1940] there was a sharp decline in the epidemic, and in February and March only a few cases were reported. In the coming months the plague was contained, and only a dozen or so cases were detected each month. Typhus fever, whose first appearance was recorded in December 1939, reached its peak in April with 407 cases. As of June the epidemic had begun to decline, and it was contained by August, when only a dozen or so cases were recorded.[18]

The Germans claimed that a new outbreak of the epidemic was expected in the winter, and their efforts to complete the establishment of the ghetto before then were in order to avoid having the relocation operation run into the winter months, which were the peak season of the disease.

Professor Ludwik Hirszfeld, the baptized Jewish scientist who was coerced into the ghetto, wrote in his autobiography:

> The sensation of being locked in prison is reinforced by the fact that you can come up against walls and barbed wire at any turn. This is the way the authorities hoped to isolate the carriers of the deadly germs. People calling themselves doctors supported this theory. [But] science long ago abolished medieval quarantines, not only because they were inhumane but because they were inefficient. Inefficient? Why, their intention is not to wipe out an epidemic but to eradicate the Jews.[19]

Thus the claim that the Jews constituted a danger to the health of the population at large—which was not entirely unfounded—was consciously blown out of all proportion to serve as a convenient tool of the Nazi propaganda campaign to convince the Poles, as well as the Germans, that the Jews were being segregated out of concern for the non-Jewish masses of Warsaw. But the tone of this campaign belied the Germans' benevolence: posters appeared on the streets of Warsaw bearing a Nazi caricature of a Jew and the heading: "Jew—Louse—Typhus."

The Attitude of the Poles and Changes in the Borders of the Ghetto

As we have seen, the Poles initially opposed the plan to establish a ghetto and requested that it be abandoned. Such opposition on the part of the decisive majority of the population probably did not stem from a sense of identification with the Jews but from considerations of self-interest, for the establishment of a ghetto, in one form or another, required the relocation of a large number of Poles, as well as Jews, and a general upheaval that was bound to undermine the livelihoods of many Poles. Moreover, in the course of delineating the boundaries of the ghetto, the Nazis also proclaimed the exclusivity of the German quarter of the city. Polish pride was injured by the fact that the Germans treated the Polish capital as if it were their private property, and the creation of separate quarters was interpreted as the beginning of the "de-Polanization" of Warsaw.

The underground Polish press, which served as an organ for the major factions in the government-in-exile, viewed the ghetto as "discrimination against the citizens of the capital." One of these newspapers noted that according to official figures, 140,000 Poles and 104,000 Jews would be affected by the eviction orders.[20] The German quarter was also closed to Poles, so that the impoverished elements of the Polish population were particularly affected by hardship.[21] Another Polish paper protested the injustice to assimilated Jews or converts. "For the Jewish intelligentsia and people of Jewish extraction, who are rooted in Polish culture," the paper wrote, "[the requirement to live within the ghetto] means the imposition of an alien lifestyle and severance of all the ties treasured by these circles."[22] The newspaper of the Polish socialists reported on a handbill circulated by the party in protest against the establishment of the ghetto. The style of this appeal is characteristic of the class-oriented movement:

> The burden of all wars and subjugation forever falls on the working man, regardless of nationality. How degradingly cynical is the fact that the walls of the ghetto being raised by Polish and Jewish laborers deprived of other work are meant to become a barrier between them, as if different fates awaited them and their aims and purposes were not the same. That is a lie. The German oppression affects both of them alike.[23]

The contrast between Jews and Poles grew sharper when the plans to establish the ghetto were put into operation and a dispute broke out over the division of territory and the boundaries of the ghetto. Julian Kulski, the Polish mayor during the occupation, recalls in his memoirs (written after the war) that the municipal administration was asked to give its opinion about the ghetto. Kulski claims:

> The Municipality . . . considered how it should respond. On the one hand, [the very act of responding] might be construed as collaboration in the creation of the ghetto; yet this was nonetheless a matter of crucial importance to the non-Jewish population, since the magnitude of the relocations would undoubtedly be a hard blow to it. In the end, the opinion given was restricted to a "statistical" evaluation: proposals that based the size of the [ghetto] area on the quantitative ratio between the two sections of the population.[24]

This testimony, expressed with objective restraint, is not confirmed by the events recorded at the time. An article that appeared in the underground Polish paper *Wiadomości Polskie* notes:

> A serious threat also extends to the interests of the Municipality, which has been presented with a plan to dismantle or relocate a list of institutions and enterprises located in the area of the ghetto. When the borders of the future ghetto were announced in the press on October 10, the areas to be affected by the measure were plunged into despair. A series of delegations set out for Cracow to plead for changes in the boundaries, or at least postpone the creation of the ghetto until the spring. At the same time, a group of people who are known to carry weight with the

conqueror attempted to salvage their movable property from the area marked out for the ghetto. On October 19, when most of the relocation action had been completed, the population was informed of a change in the boundaries of the ghetto, which was constricted by 30 percent.[25]

An even more detailed description is found in the war journal of Ludwik Landau, an outstanding economist and statistician of Jewish extraction, who had cut himself off from the Jewish community. Landau's parents were later interned in the ghetto, but he and his family adopted a Polish-sounding name and continued to live openly among the Poles and be active in Polish underground circles. Landau wrote:

> It seems that there were some attempts at mediation by the Christian population. There's talk of a delegation to the German authorities. Intervention on behalf of the population is also being attempted by the Municipality, which, in the person of various councillors, sees itself—sometimes justifiably—as a representative of the Christian portion of the population, and in this role is struggling against the *kehillah*, as the representative of Jewish interests.[26]

Landau accused the municipal administration of following the German evacuation order to the letter. As he saw it, the Polish population should have delayed executing the order and pressured for postponements, whereas the Municipality actually helped to speed up the evacuation. In a number of instances, private interests intervened. Poles, and for the most part ethnic Germans (*Volksdeutsche*), appealed to have sections of streets, industrial plants, institutions, and certain buildings rezoned out of the area destined to become part of the ghetto. These pressures, which were exercised by men of influence, served to tighten the noose of the ghetto's perimeter. There is evidence that a well-known beer distiller, who transformed himself into a loyal German when the Nazis entered the city, received flowers from the Poles as a sign of their appreciation for his efforts to have various targets excluded from the area demarcated as the Jewish quarter. Some Poles even openly expressed their satisfaction that "the dream of Warsaw without Jews is coming true."[27]

And how did the Jews respond in light of these pressures and disputes over the boundaries of the ghetto? Czerniakow was not eager to haggle over the borders of the ghetto. On October 18, 1940, he recorded in his diary: "Today our own and city officials from the housing exchange are touring the ghetto. Bargaining for specific streets. The problem of the corner houses (Aryan shops), of the numerical ratio of the Jews to the Poles. I abhor this haggling, anyway I do not take part in it." Four days later he wrote: "Instructions from Cracow that the parties concerned should themselves come to an understanding on the question of the boundary adjustments." It is logical that the Germans would try to pass off the bargaining over streets to the two sides, thereby aggravating the tension between the Jews and the Poles. The ever-worsening situation evidently did not allow Czerniakow to remain aloof from the haggling. On October 25 he recorded in his diary: "In the afternoon, at the Office of the Plenipotentiary (Hanka)—winning back part of Żelazna, Skórzana, etc. streets."

Kaplan's entry of October 22 is indicative of the atmosphere that prevailed among the common men:

> When it came time to carry out the ghetto order, everything became chaotic. The Polish side began to haggle—in this suburb they have a church; another is mainly inhabited by Aryans; here is a beautiful school building; there is a factory employing thousands of Aryan workers. How can the rightful owners be driven from all these places? Thus they excised piece after piece, street after street, of the Jewish area, and the boundaries of the ghetto grew more and more constricted.[28]

Ringelblum notes: "Priests are collecting signatures on all the streets, because they will leave the mixed streets outside the confines of the ghetto. Even Nowolipie, a purely Jewish street, has been asked for because of the church [on the street]."[29] Few were the attempts to arrange collaborative action between Jews and Poles regarding the ghetto. We find only one mention of such a meeting in Ringelblum's entries: "Yesterday there was a consultation of Poles and Jews with [Adam] Ronikier [head of the Polish R.G.O.], who denounced the prevailing trend among Poles to salvage as much as possible from the area of the ghetto. He believes we should be waging a joint struggle against the ghetto in general, not a war between the two peoples.[30]

The question of converts and mixed marriages constituted a special problem in the context of events. This was not a very large sector of the public, but it was marked by its alienation and seclusion from the Jewish community and its affairs. The paradox was that the converts in Poland were even further removed from their Jewish roots than the parallel group in Germany, where it was common for large families to maintain close ties despite religious divisions that resulted from apostasy. The very structure of Jewish society in Germany allowed for various degrees of assimilation, but in each case the sense of being a part of the German nation was usually very strong. Not so in Poland, where conversion was an uncommon phenomenon during this period and the assimilationists constituted a distinct circle in the social landscape of the capital and were not particularly noted for their support of the Jews or concern for Jewish affairs.

In Poland, a staunchly Catholic country, even zealous anti-Semites had never dared to promote racist principles. But when the Nazis extended their racist legislation to the occupied areas of Poland, the requirement to wear a Jewish armband was binding on converts as well, though in most cases, if not all, the converts got out of having to display the mark of humiliation. Now the ghetto edict was also binding on them, and these same renegade Jews—some themselves even Jew-haters—faced a difficult choice.

The converts and mixed families turned to the Polish public for support and asylum. Many tried to blot out all evidence of their past and, with the help of Christian relatives and friends, re-create their identities. In a number of cases, like that of Landau, they fell victim to blackmailers or were arbitrarily turned over to the Gestapo. Julian Kulski relates that he was approached by people asking for his advice on the eve of the deadline to move into the ghetto and added that it was difficult to advise them. The Polish paper published under the auspices of the occupation regime recommended that the "Aryan" half of the mixed couples divorce their baptized partners to escape the misery of the ghetto.

As mentioned earlier, the Polish Welfare Council (R.G.O.), which to a large extent served as a representative of the Polish public vis-à-vis the occupation authorities, attempted to exempt a list of known converts who were "adapted to Polish culture" from the obligation to wear an armband with a Jewish symbol. The organization was asked to submit its list to the authorities, and, whether in innocence or through simple lack of foresight, it complied with the request. When the time came to seal off the ghetto, this list became a weapon against the converts. Inside the ghetto itself, the subcommunity of Christian converts, which encompassed about two thousand people, continued to preserve its insularity.

Continuous changes in the map of the ghetto added to the hardship. Often a man who had already moved once was forced to move again, and even his second apartment was not completely secure. "People are scurrying about like madmen because no one knows where to move to," Ringelblum commented. "No address is any more reliable than the next, because every street has something that places its fate in doubt." The Germans charged the Municipality and the *Judenrat* with effecting the relocation and arranging for the exchange of apartments. Ad hoc offices were established to maintain control over the evacuation procedure, but very few actually found apartments through such intermediaries. Czerniakow testifies that the members of the *Judenrat* were sensitive to how difficult conditions were for the Jews, but their ability to move or influence the Germans was negligible. Even Czerniakow himself had difficulty in finding a secure apartment for himself, and his concern over this problem finds expression in his diary.[31]

The Germans specified that the relocation process had to be completed by October 31; after that date, those who were subject to the edict would be evicted by force. A mad scramble began for apartments. Walls were papered over with notes announcing apartments for exchange. Many turned to relatives for help, and people who owned large apartments agreed to take in families of relatives and friends on the assumption that they would probably be forced to accommodate extra people anyway, without the advantage of being able to choose desirable boarders. The Jews of Praga put off their move as long as possible in response to rumors that they would be allowed to establish a separate ghetto in the suburb. Only during the last week of October did the frantic movement begin from Praga over the Vistula bridges to Jewish streets in the northern section of the city.

The convoys of evacuees moved without cease. Impoverished members of the population, who could not afford to hire wagons (the price of vehicles changed from day to day, and it was difficult to find one anyway), were generally forced to cart everything on their backs. Bundles of bedding and clothing moved along in exhausted convoys, with young children and the elderly trailing behind. The order to leave furniture behind in abandoned Jewish apartments was not obeyed, although there were cases in which Nazis confiscated furniture or Poles prevented it from being removed. Families deeply attached to their environment were forced to abandon homes and livelihoods and stumble off to a vague and threatening future. On November 1 the Jews were informed over the loudspeakers that the evacuation period had been extended until November 15.

According to German figures, 113,000 Poles and 138,000 Jews had to be relocated in the evacuation effort. The area of the ghetto was about 425 acres, of which about 375 acres were residential space. This meant that 30 percent of the population of Warsaw was cramped into only 2.4 percent of the city. However, the evacuation was just the first stage of the plan to concentrate the Jewish population in the ghetto. Afterward came evacuees from other cities and towns in the Warsaw District. The German figures speak of six to seven people per room, and according to calculations made after the war the density reached 9.2 people per room, while the population density of the ghetto as a whole reached 128,000 per square kilometer (over 200,000 per square mile).[32] Of the 1,800 streets in the city, only 73 were included in the ghetto, and of those only a few covered the entire length of the street and not just sections thereof. The boundaries of the ghetto were about 18 kilometers (11 miles) long; the walls were 3 meters (10 feet) high and were topped by barbed wire.

The Nazis were careful to call the ghetto the "Jewish quarter," in order to create the impression that it resembled the German and Polish quarters of the city, and they forbade others to use the term "ghetto." Even the official Jewish newspaper published under the auspices of the occupation regime used the term "Jewish quarter" rather than "ghetto."

The Jews of Warsaw assumed that the ghetto would remain open. The system of an open ghetto allowed Jews outside their quarter during specified hours, and food and other necessities could be brought into the area legally (Poles were granted free entrance to the ghetto for such purposes). Neither of these circumstances was permitted in a closed off and isolated ghetto, such as the one established in Lodz. The decisive question of whether the Germans intended to have the Warsaw ghetto open or closed was a standing topic of conversation among the city's Jews. For those who maintained shops outside the ghetto, as well as craftsmen and members of the intelligentsia who worked on Polish streets, the question affected their very existence. The Germans avoided any definitive comments on the subject, so that everyone relied on rumors and assumptions. Many Jews purposely left a good portion of their stocks outside the ghetto, since any attempt to move them would have meant risking the loss of their sources of income. The answer to the question that haunted the Jews was held back until the last day of the evacuation.

On November 16, 1940, the die was cast. Jews who gathered at the entrance to the ghetto in order to leave on their business found German and Polish police guards blocking the exit. The ghetto was sealed.

Chapter Three
The Warsaw Ghetto

General Background   The Warsaw ghetto existed in its
"normal" format from November
16, 1940, to July 22, 1942. The latter date does not mark the total
destruction of the ghetto but rather the start of the mass deportation of
Jews. During the seven weeks of the deportation, about 75 percent of
the Jews in the ghetto were driven out of their homes and transported
to the Treblinka death camp.

After the mass deportation, the ghetto continued to exist within
constricted borders and with a different internal structure. For all intents and purposes, during this last stage of its existence, the ghetto was
transformed into a labor camp, and the aim of the SS during that period
was to subject the Jews remaining in the ghetto to the harsh regime of a
concentration camp. The final extermination of Warsaw's Jewish quarter
began on April 19, 1943, when the Jews began their armed resistance, a
battle that has come to be known as the "Warsaw ghetto uprising."

As noted earlier, the ghetto covered 2.4 percent of the area of
Warsaw, and 30 percent of the city's population had been crowded into
it. The population crammed into a few streets was comparable to that of
a small city. According to the official Jewish newspaper, *Gazeta
Żydowska*, 380,740 people were living in the ghetto on January 1, 1941,
of whom 378,979 were Jews; 1,718 were Catholics, Protestants, and
Greek Orthodox; and 43 were of other religious sects.[1] The ghetto was
therefore a concentration of Jews defined by racist criteria.

Neither the area of the ghetto nor the size of the population concentrated in it was constant. As noted earlier, a number of changes had
been made in the map of the ghetto. Sections of streets with buildings

in good condition or containing large apartments were detached from it. Yet the principal changes were effected in order to tighten security along the walls and aid the Germans in their war against the smuggling of food from the "Aryan" side of the city. When the ghetto was established, there were twenty-two "gates" for entry and exit. By the time the mass deportation began, only four such gates remained.[2]

The fluctuations in the population of the ghetto and quantitative changes in its size were affected by two factors: (1) the eviction and transfer of people from smaller cities and towns in the Warsaw District to the ghetto; and (2) the phenomenal death rate of the ghetto's inhabitants. From January to March 1941, about 66,000 Jews from the Warsaw District were transferred to the ghetto, particularly from the western sector of the district. These refugees were one of the main sources of social tension in the enclosed area, and by April 1941 there were about 130,000 refugees there—meaning that one out of every three Jews in the ghetto was a refugee. Individual Jews and groups also penetrated the Warsaw ghetto from the ghetto in Lodz, because, despite the difficult conditions, the Warsaw ghetto was thought of as a place where supervision was more lax and people with means were able to acquire food.

In March 1941 the population of the Warsaw ghetto reached its peak at 445,000 people. From then on, a gradual decline can be seen, especially due to the high mortality rate throughout 1941 (see Tables 1 and 2).

TABLE 1
CHANGES IN THE SIZE OF THE
WARSAW GHETTO'S POPULATION,
JANUARY 1941–JULY 1942

1941	Population	1942	Population
January	380,740	February	368,902
March	445,000	May	400,000
May	442,337	July	335,514
June	439,309		
July	431,874		
August	420,116		
September	404,300		

SOURCE: "Materialn cu demografishn forshung vegn der yidisher bavelkerung in Warshe bees di hitleristishe ocupacye," *Bleter far Geshikhte*, VIII:3–4 (1955).

The high mortality in the ghetto—which can in no way be compared to that of a normal society—can best be described as a gradual extermination, meaning that while the inmates of the ghetto were not murdered outright, they were subjected to conditions that clearly accelerated the death rate. In the course of 1941, over 43,000 people—more than 10 percent of the ghetto's population—died in the Warsaw ghetto. At that fatal rate, it was possible to eliminate the ghetto within ten years even without recourse to extermination camps. There can be no doubt that this fact was likewise obvious to the Germans and well served their purposes. In August 1942, Frank stated: " . . . It is not necessary to dwell on the fact that we are sentencing 1.2 million Jews to death. That much is clear. And if the Jews do not die of starvation, it will be necessary to step up anti-Jewish measures, and let us hope that that too will come to pass."[3] At the same time, there is no evidence in 1941 of an ordered and consistent policy of general extermination by means of starvation and disease. On the contrary, there is proof that influential circles in the Generalgouvernement wanted to bolster the work and production capability of the Jews and demanded that the food ration in the ghetto be enlarged.

The historian Shaul Esh dubbed the period that preceded the initiation of the "Final Solution" in the occupied areas of Poland as "The Period of Indirect Extermination," and this description is nowhere more appropriate than in the Warsaw ghetto. For the most part, the high mortality rate in the ghetto was caused by starvation, endemic disease (primarily typhus and typhoid fever), deportation, and labor-camp conditions.

TABLE 2

MORTALITY RATES IN THE WARSAW GHETTO,
JANUARY 1941–MAY 1942

1941	Deaths	1942	Deaths
January	898	January	5,123
February	1,023	February	4,618
March	1,608	March	4,951
April	2,061	April	4,432
May	3,821	May	3,636
June	4,290		
July	5,550		
August	5,560		
September	4,545		
October	4,716		
November	4,801		
December	4,366		

SOURCE: T. Berenstein, A. Rutkowski, "Liczba ludności żydowskiej i obszar przez nią zamieszkany w Warszawie w latach okupacji hitlerowskiej," B.Ż.I.H., 26 (1958).

After the ghetto was sealed off, the mortality rate rose quickly due principally to starvation and endemic disease. It is important to compare the situation in 1940 with that during the first months of the ghetto's existence. Before the ghetto was formed, there was a relative stabilization in the incidence of disease, and the typhus epidemic even showed signs of abatement. As we have seen, the Germans claimed that the incarceration of the Jews behind the ghetto walls was meant to isolate the focal point of the disease. In reality, as might have been expected, the conditions in the ghetto caused a renewed flare-up of contagious disease, and the walls were hardly an effective barrier against it.

It is important to note that the mortality rate of the prewar Warsaw Jewish community—a good proportion of which lived in substandard housing and suffered from malnutrition—never reached a point comparable to that registered in the ghetto. Thus, for example, in August 1939, when there were 360,000 Jews in Warsaw, 360 deaths were recorded, while in August 1941, 5,560 deaths were reported within the ghetto walls.

The slight decrease in the death rate at the end of 1941 and during the spring of 1942 is indicative of demographic trends, and during this same period there was also a slight improvement in conditions; there were even signs of adjustment to the situation within the ghetto. But just as the Germans had neutralized the relative improvement and stabilization at an earlier period (right before the establishment of the ghetto), and the ghetto had not been created in order to cope with existing conditions but to serve the Nazis' political ends, so the elimination of the Warsaw ghetto was not motivated by the situation inherent in the ghetto itself. The population of the ghetto had actually managed to overcome the worst. The incidence of fatal disease began to decrease; the weaker elements of the population had already succumbed to death; more sources of employment and subsistence had been created; and the expectation grew that, in spite of everything, the majority would succeed in surviving the war. At that very time of growing immunity and adjustment to the appalling conditions, the Germans initiated the mass deportation and physical extermination of Warsaw Jewry. Thus the annihilation of the ghetto was not a corollary of the slow or rapid decline of the Jews. It was initiated as the manifestation of a comprehensive political and ideological creed and was not restricted to the Jews of Warsaw or the Generalgouvernement alone, but was part of the overall initiative to annihilate the Jewish people wherever the rule of Nazi Germany and its satellites had reached.

Food and Smuggling   The closed ghetto cut the Jews off
completely from the population at
large. This separation prevented Jews from coming into contact with
non-Jews and left them in a state of isolation, insulation, and choking
congestion. In one stroke the livelihoods of workers who had been integrated into the production processes of the city and self-employed
craftsmen whose businesses were outside the confines of the ghetto
were wiped out. Some members of the Jewish community understood
the implications of the ghetto and the rule imposed upon it. "Any comparison with the ghetto of the past is inappropriate," Ringelblum wrote
in his journal, "because the ghetto then was the product of historical
processes and corresponded to the general significance of such developments. But the ghetto today is a concentration camp whose inmates
must support themselves."[4]

There was supposedly also a positive side to the establishment of
the ghetto. Due to the segregation, Polish thugs were unable to carry
out pogroms within the Jewish quarter. Some even "rejoiced over the
autonomy" available to the Jews within the ghetto.[5] But it soon became
clear that the German pillage went on even within the ghetto, and the
other "advantages" were negligible in light of the apalling conditions
that existed inside the walls.

From the very beginning, the greatest concern and most damaging
factor was the shortage of food. Difficulty in acquiring food had been
evident in Warsaw even earlier, and it affected more than the Jews. The
entire population of the city was dependent on the supply of food from
the surrounding villages, and the German authorities imposed controls
on agricultural produce and raising animals in the countryside. Despite
the German intervention, however, the farmers and the city dwellers
developed a variety of means to ensure the supply of food to the city.
Obviously, however, the difficulties and dangers involved in acquiring
food contributed to the soaring increase in prices.

The establishment of the ghetto created a barrier between the Jews
and the channels by which food was supplied. The Germans established
the Transfer Authority (*Transferstelle*), an institution that had exclusive
authority to control the entry of food and other materials into the
ghetto and the delivery of materials, goods, and finished products from
the ghetto to the "Aryan" side. Thus, by means of the *Transferstelle*, the
Germans intended to supervise all movement to and from the ghetto.

According to a Polish source, the daily caloric content of food distributed to the various national groups in 1941 was as follows: Germans
—2,613 calories; Poles—699 calories; Jews—184 calories.[6] Thus the
Jews were victims of double hardship: they were the most discriminated
against under the system of rationing, and the nutritional value of the

ration apportioned to them was only 15 percent of the minimum daily requirement, so that there was little chance of surviving on the official ration alone. On the other hand, the Jews were prevented from acquiring food on the free market. According to one memoir, the official ration for an entire month was insufficient for three days.[7]

In such conditions, there was no option but to resort to smuggling, i.e., the transfer of food by means of clandestine channels. Throughout the existence of the ghetto, the Germans waged a war against such operations. Sometimes their efforts were more stringent, sometimes more lax, but the smuggling never stopped at any stage, and it can be stated with certainty that not a day passed in the ghetto when the smuggling operation did not supply a quantity of food through its channels. The chairman of the *Judenrat*, Czerniakow, told certain circles in the ghetto that 80 percent of the food entering the ghetto came by means of smuggling.[8]

At first the German sentries were lax and permitted the transfer of basic foodstuffs into the ghetto. The guard at the gates of the ghetto was made up of two German policemen, two Polish policemen, and two members of the Jewish Police. But the entry of food with the consent of the German sentries ceased very quickly when the German guards received strict orders not to allow any movement of goods without the express permission of the authorities.

Two types of smuggling went on during the lifetime of the ghetto. One was the work of individual smugglers, who attempted to sneak in small amounts of food to sustain themselves and their relatives; the other was organized and carried out by groups who engaged in smuggling as a profession and operated on a large scale. It was these groups who supplied most of the food to the ghetto. The smuggling was effected through various channels; in fact, the variety of methods was intentional, in order to ensure success. A single clandestine channel would not have sufficed to accommodate the vast quantities of essential goods and materials that reached the population of the ghetto.

In the course of the period under discussion, the smuggling operation took its toll of human life. Nevertheless, the rising number of victims did not prevent the operation from continuing. The discovery of a crack in the ghetto wall or a specific transfer point did not neutralize other means of transfer, just as the capture of a man or a gang in one place did not break the others involved in the operation.

A piece written by M. Passenstein on "Smuggling in the Warsaw Ghetto,"[9] uncovered in the Ringelblum Archive, enumerates the channels at the disposal of the smuggling operation and the techniques employed by the smugglers, in addition to providing portraits of the people and situations involved in the smuggling campaign. The most convenient method was to create a transfer point between two houses attached back to back, one facing on the Polish quarter and the other inside the ghetto. However, this relatively convenient system was thwarted by intentional changes in the ghetto's boundary. The *Kommissar* of the ghetto, Heinz Auerswald, who intensified the war against smuggling, ordered the borderline established in the middle of the street, so that attached houses were zoned out of the confines of the ghetto. After these boundary changes, improvised barbed-wire fences were used for a while to mark the border, and the smuggling continued through the barbed wire. "The work of the smugglers through the barbed wire was marked by incredible speed," Passenstein wrote. "The rate of the work was extraordinary, so that the transfer of 100 sacks of wheat or sugar took just a dozen or so minutes."[10]

The ghetto walls themselves served as a means of transfer for large items, and smuggling through the walls led to the development of sophisticated techniques. The smugglers would break through the wall and cover their opening with easily removable bricks, only to remove them again at an appointed hour after dark. For the most part, smuggling through the walls was resorted to for heavy items, such as sacks of food, furniture, disassembled machinery, and so forth.

Members of the various police forces played a key role in the smuggling carried out through the walls. The Jewish policemen found it to be a profitable business, while the Polish police were no less interested in making a profit off the ghetto, and the smuggling provided them with an opportunity. In time it became clear that even the German police were not immune to bribes, and no small number of them were eager to pocket easy money in return for looking the other way when wagons, or even trucks, passed through the gates. The Jewish policemen, who specialized in smuggling, were acquainted with the German guards and knew when, how, and to whom to propose a deal. Naturally, these attempts always involved risks. More than once German policemen shot down a Jew for so much as hinting at his intentions, and sometimes a patrol turned up at the very moment goods were being infiltrated into the ghetto. Poles who owned industries inside the ghetto smuggled in food together with the raw materials destined for their production lines. For a while deliveries were effected by means of the trolley cars that passed through the ghetto but did not stop inside it; afterward, however, the trolleys stopped running through the ghetto. Smuggling was also carried out by means of the wagons that carried the dead to cemeteries.

The "professional" smugglers in the ghetto became a new "elite" that flourished during the war. Only a small portion of these men had engaged in commerce before the war. The decisive majority came from the lower classes of the population and had been porters or even members of the true criminal class—thieves, agents in stolen goods, etc. These people were accustomed to a life of risk and adventure. The dictates of survival in the ghetto, so alien to conventional lifestyles and normalized relations between people, stimulated their daring and resourcefulness, and they adjusted more quickly to the abnormal conditions of life. Altogether, thousands of people were involved in smuggling, and they made their living—whether just barely or with profitability—from these operations.

The smugglers, and especially those at the top of the "profession," were also the patrons of the expensive restaurants and coffee houses of the ghetto. They would often appear with Germans and Jewish policemen, who were partners in their transactions. They sought after the good life and lived by the dictum "Eat, drink, and be merry, for tomorrow we die!" Nonetheless, even those who were sharply critical of the lifestyle and conduct of the smugglers were able to appreciate the vital role they filled in ghetto life. One memoir stated that "those same vulgar figures are deserving of mercy. Without them the ghetto would simply have been sentenced to starvation."[11] And Passenstein wrote: "The lives of the smugglers were filled with danger. Not a day passed when one of them was not cut down by machine-gun fire from the gendarmes, but the smuggling did not stop. After the corpse was removed, it continued with the same intensity and the same temptation of the fates, which placed the smugglers in the front line of the ghetto's struggle against Hitlerism."[12]

The isolated instances of small-scale smuggling assumed a different character. They were engaged in mostly by people who worked outside the ghetto in *palatzovkas* and individuals who sneaked past the wall or escaped from the ghetto. Such people would spend a day or two in the Polish zone and bring in some food when they returned to the ghetto. Those who worked outside the ghetto were frequently searched upon their return, and food hidden on their person was confiscated. Many women were among those who stole out of the ghetto to get food on the "Aryan" side. It was easier for a woman to conceal her Jewishness and, as the events of the period made clear, women were outstanding in their courage and self-possession.

Children, who proved to be particularly adept, made up a high proportion of this class of smugglers. They would find cracks or openings in the wall known only to them, and groups of starving and tattered youngsters would gather every day at the gates of the ghetto, exploiting any minor distraction of the German gendarmes and the Polish police to steal across to the other side. Sometimes a German sentry, moved by compassion or looking for a way to relieve his boredom with an entertaining sight, would let a gang of children pass through the gate. But it was not rare for a German guard to shoot and kill children who tried to steal across to the other side. For the most part, the children begged for their keep on the "Aryan" side. Even Poles who were hostile to the Jews were moved by the sight of the children—or, more accurately, the skeletons of starving children. On their way back to the ghetto, the children filched potatoes, vegetables, and even bread, which they hid in their sleeves.

This small-scale smuggling did not sustain a widespread commercial movement. For the most part, food smuggled in by this means sufficed only for the smuggler himself and members of his family. As a rule the children denied themselves and turned the food they had succeeded in acquiring over to their relatives. In many families young children, whose courage stemmed from a strong will to survive, provided the family's sole means of subsistence in the ghetto.[13] The famous Polish-Jewish lawyer Leon Berensohn, who built his reputation as a defense attorney in the political trials during the period of the independent Polish state, once proposed that it would be fitting one day to mark the area in which "there was once a ghetto" by a monument to the anonymous child-smugglers of the Warsaw ghetto.[14]

It is difficult to discern a definitive attitude on the part of the Poles toward the smuggling, which was a two-way operation and was carried out with the cooperation of many Poles. There were few direct references to the smuggling operation in the Polish press. After the war, in an attempt to magnify the scope of the aid and cooperation between Jews and Poles during the Holocaust, various Polish circles pointed to the smuggling operation as an example of such aid and credited its success to the support and cooperation rendered by the Poles. This claim has no basis in reality. While it is true that the food transferred into the ghetto was purchased in Polish areas and transported by Poles, the smuggling enterprise operated on the basis of middlemen's profits and must be seen as one of the facets of the black-marketeering that developed in wartime conditions. The simple truth is that the food smuggled into the ghetto was not only paid for in full at the going price, but goods originating in the ghetto—including clothing, furs, bedding, household items, furniture, etc.—were transferred to the Polish side in the course of the operation.

Much more complex was the German attitude toward the smuggling. The officially declared policy was perfectly clear: the illegal transfer of food was strictly forbidden. In fact, one of the primary and openly stated aims of establishing ghettos was to prevent the supply of food to the Jews. But the fundamental question is whether or not the Germans were capable of stopping the smuggling. Ringelblum wrote in

May 1942, "It's not for nought that the saying [making the rounds in the ghetto] goes that three things are invincible: the German army, the British Isles, and Jewish smuggling."[15] Yet an anonymous observer wrote in his memoirs during the ghetto period that the Germans could actually wipe out the smuggling operation in a few days. If they weren't doing so, it was a sign that they had ambivalent feelings about the phenomenon. The Germans were supposedly fighting against the smuggling, and sometimes they took stringent steps to stop it. But for the most part, smuggling was tolerated, and the measures taken against it were meant only to restrict its magnitude.[16]

Those who implemented the declared policy of preventing the smuggling were aware that carrying it out to the full would bring about the swift decimation of the ghetto, and in the course of time the ghetto had begun to play a role in the economy of the Generalgouvernement. It soon became evident to the Germans that they could not have it both ways: starve the Jews and annihilate the ghetto and at the same time take advantage of Jewish manpower. On another level, many Germans benefited from the hefty bribes offered in exchange for turning a blind eye to the smuggling, and they therefore had an interest in allowing it to continue. As noted earlier, in the second half of 1941 and during the months that preceded the major deportation of 1942, *Kommissar* Auerswald initiated steps to halt the smuggling. He ordered that smugglers be summarily executed, including women and children caught on the "Aryan" side, and that the German sentries intensify their guard. As a result of these measures, individual instances of smuggling were severely curtailed and the price of smuggled food began to soar, but the smuggling did not stop.[17]

The Jews, including all the various authorities in the ghetto, naturally supported the smuggling enterprise. The *Judenrat* made no attempt to stop it, and the fact that Czerniakow did not try to conceal its proportions from the Germans indicates his open belief that under the existing nutritional conditions, smuggling could not be avoided. Not only did the Jewish Police not interfere with smuggling, but as noted earlier, they took an active role in the operation, which was a major source of income for them. The position of the Jewish public at large was clear: it supported the smuggling and viewed it as a blessing in its state of isolation and deprivation.

Of course, even large-scale smuggling could not solve the food problem in the ghetto. The clandestine operations made it possible to acquire food, but prices were exorbitant. On December 5, 1940, Kaplan wrote: "And in spite of it all, the world continues to turn. Wherever there is a prohibition against supply, smuggling goes on; and it is thanks to this smuggling that we exist."[18] Hunger and death from starvation did not, therefore, result solely from a severe food shortage or the inability to get food into the ghetto. To a large degree they resulted from the absence of financial means and the rapid impoverishment of the Jewish masses.

It is estimated that during the occupation, wages in the General-gouvernement rose 100 percent, meaning that they doubled in comparison with their prewar level. At the same time, the price of food in the Warsaw markets increased twenty-seven-fold, according to the price index of May 1942. These prices reflected the situation on the "Aryan" side of the city, while in the ghetto they were even higher by 20 to 50 percent, and that additional percentage was the cost of the smuggling.

Economy and Employment   It is possible to summarize the German economic policy vis-à-vis the Jews under three major headings: (1) the confiscation of Jewish-owned businesses, commercial enterprises, and property in general; (2) the segregation of the Jews from the Polish population and the severance of economic ties between these two groups; and (3) the exploitation of Jewish labor for the benefit of the German economy and war effort.

The steps chosen to achieve the primary goal, namely the paralysis of Jewish economic initiative and the confiscation of Jewish property, were taken even before the establishment of the ghetto. As early as October 1939, the Germans issued orders that drastically curtailed the financial operations carried out by Jews, and these limitations forced the Jews out of the cycle of economic life. Furthermore, the following measures were intended to strip the Jews of their businesses. The Main Trustee Office East (*Haupttreuhandstelle Ost*—H.T.O.) established branch offices in the districts of the Generalgouvernement. These branches, known as *Treuhandstelle*, were authorized to appoint new managers (*Treuhänder*) over businesses and companies or confiscate enterprises if such a step was found to be consistent with "the public interest." If the owner of a business was absent from the country, the firm was automatically confiscated. In September 1940 Göring, in his role as the head of the Four-Year Program, issued the decisive order to confiscate all the property of the Jews residing in what had formerly been the state of Poland, with the exception of such personal belongings as clothing, furniture, and one thousand marks in cash.[19]

The forced move to the ghetto deprived the Jews—and especially the small shopkeepers and craftsmen with businesses throughout the city—of their income and property. In fact, one of the reasons for establishing a ghetto was to sever the economic ties between the Jews and the Poles. It is interesting to note that the German propaganda to the effect that the Jews had previously controlled the Polish economy and that the new German regime had liberated it from Jewish hegemony met with a sympathetic response from a good portion of the Polish public. Many Poles felt that the prewar sovereign Polish government had not been daring and decisive enough in its anti-Jewish measures, and the Germans had proved that it was possible to bring about the absolute neutralization of the Jews relatively quickly. Such feelings undoubtedly influenced circles in the Polish underground, which soon learned that defending the rights of the Jews was not a very popular stance among the Polish masses, and the general Polish opposition to the Germans did not extend to critcism of their measures against Jews. Leading figures in the Polish underground warned the government-in-exile in London that the German economic persecution was an accepted fact, and any future attempt to turn back the clock would probably meet with physical resistance on the part of the Poles, who had become the beneficiaries of Jewish property and jobs.[20] At the same time, the Polish enterprises could not do completely without the work of Jewish craftsmen.[21] In some of the crafts, Jews were the only artisans in the field.

The attempts to harness the Jews to the German war effort began during the first stages of the occupation, when one of Frank's first edicts, on October 26, 1939, instituted forced labor for Jews. The order stressed the concentration of Jews in labor camps in order to exploit them in paving roads, draining swamps, and building fortifications. The employment of Jews at physically strenuous jobs without proper nourishment and in abominable living conditions led to an appalling death rate among the laborers in the camps—and disappointing practical results.

Beginning in the middle of 1940, the Germans grew increasingly interested in exploiting Jewish labor in a more rational manner. Supervision of forced labor was transferred to branches of the civil administration. This new trend in German thinking was inspired by the pressures on the work force, for with Poles now being deported for forced labor in Germany, the authorities had to find manpower to replace the deportees. The Germans also became aware that there were many skilled workers among the Jews living in the Generalgouvernmement, and it would be in the interests of efficiency to employ them at their own vocations. In September 1940 Frank stated in an address before the heads of his administrative departments that the Jews were not just a worthless element; because of their vocational talents, they constituted an integral part of the Polish population within the Generalgouvernement. According to Frank, the Germans only became cognizant of this fact after they entered Poland. His attitude was expressed even more clearly in a speech delivered at the University of Berlin in November 1941: "Not all these Jews are useless from our point of view. It is astonishing, but there are Jews who fall into a different category, something which we discovered only on the spot. Difficult as it is to believe, there really are Jews there who work and are employed as transport and building workers or as craftsmen in tailoring, shoemaking, etc."[22]

The ghetto was faced with a difficult challenge. According to the December 13, 1940, issue of *Gazeta Żydowska*, the war had destroyed 75 percent of the enterprises under Jewish ownership. As a result, employment declined to about 12 percent of the prewar level in industry and 16 percent in commerce.[23] The *Judenrat* attempted to expand employment and viewed the increase in employees as the only way to pay for the food and goods apportioned to the ghetto by the German authorities. An article published in *Gazeta Żydowska* on July 21, 1941, explains this concept:

> The Jewish quarter of Warsaw lacks raw materials, sufficient capital, and significant industry. The only means at its disposal is labor. If labor is properly exploited, it can serve as the sole means of export capable of balancing import, at least to some degree. . . . Feeding the Jewish public consumes an average of 12,600,000 zlotys per month. How can the quarter—which, as we know, has no sources of capital—get its hands on this sum? Only by exporting labor.[24]

The *Judenrat* tried to attract German-owned and -supervised plants to the ghetto so that Jewish craftsmen could find employment. In August 1941 an incorporated company was set up for the purpose of expanding the scope of crafts in the ghetto by supplying financial support, tools, and production orders. But these efforts to attach workshops to the service of German companies did not yield the expected results. The August 11, 1941, issue of *Gazeta Żydowska* wrote: "The deputy chairman of the *Judenrat*'s Production Committee, Mr. Orlean, declared that the increase of communal workshops, and thereby the number of workers, has met with difficulties because the labor wages are too low in relation to the market price of food."[25]

As an incentive to attract workers, rations of soup were offered to laborers in the workshops. But this meager temptation failed to draw candidates to work. The principal reason for the failure of the initiative, despite the efforts invested in it by the *Judenrat*, can be found in the rigorous system of exploitation adopted by the Germans, who were eager to avail themselves of Jewish manpower but were unwilling to pay for it. The salaries earned by the craftsmen in the workshops ("shops") were a far cry from any standard of fair wages. After deductions, the "shop" workers received 3–5 zlotys per day, which was not even sufficient to buy half a loaf of bread.

The "shops" in the ghetto expanded to a limited degree only at the end of 1941 and in the spring of 1942, particularly in response to reports and rumors of the impending deportation and events in a number of other cities and ghettos. But even at this late stage, the number of "shop" workers only reached four thousand. The "shops" only became an attractive option on the eve of the deportation and during the *Aktion* itself, when having a place in a "shop" and the privileged document that went with it were believed to provide a chance to remain in the ghetto.

There were sharp fluctuations in the number of Jews working in German *palatzovkas* during the existence of the ghetto, but an average of two thousand men worked at various jobs, especially for the army. Beginning in the middle of 1941, there was a rise in the number of Jews employed in industrial plants outside the ghetto, and almost three thousand people found work in this sphere. Yet the legal economic activities managed by the *Judenrat* and Germans from the *Transferstelle* were only one aspect of the work and production effort of the Jews in the ghetto. Personal initiative, inventiveness, and resourcefulness were channeled in other directions.

The Ringelblum Archive contains a paper written by Jerzy Winkler, a Jewish economist living in the ghetto, on "The Struggle of the Ghetto against Total Subjugation."[26] Winkler makes clear that Jewish industrial enterprises and businessmen exhibited flexibility and initiative. The ghetto developed its own means of acquiring raw materials, distributed finished products as ordered, and developed a system that Winkler called "smuggled export." Orders for such "illegal export" were received not only from merchants who supplied the black market outside the ghetto, i.e., Polish wholesalers, but also from German sources and even the *Wehrmacht* itself. The *Transferstelle* tried to broaden the scope of production in the ghetto, but its efforts were impeded by both the shortage of raw materials and the refusal of the ghetto residents to become slaves working for the German war effort for next to nothing. On the other hand, the supply officers of the *Wehrmacht* learned that the ghetto was capable of overcoming the difficulties it faced and that they could get what they needed quickly by contacting Jewish manufacturers in the ghetto through Polish and Jewish middlemen.

The income from "smuggled export" was much greater than from exporting labor. Orders arrived directly at the workshops in the ghetto. The transport of goods was effected for the most part in army trucks or wagons equipped with permits from the district authorities, bypassing the *Transferstelle* altogether. Stanisław Adler wrote in his memoirs, composed during the war:

Before the war there were thousands of Jewish tailors, shoemakers, furriers, and hatters in Warsaw. These craftsmen slowly found work . . . and in the wake of such production small Jewish enterprises came into being whose products were channeled to the retail market. Thanks to initiative, inventiveness that overcame technical obstacles, and sheer hard work, there was actually no sphere in which excellent results were not achieved. It is sufficient to note that there were metal industries, electronic and chemical industries, and—without local heating—even factories for the production of sugar and chocolate products that directed a good portion of their finished products to the "Aryan" market. The Jewish worker, craftsman, engineer, and industrial pioneer met the test that life placed before them.

Later in the same work, Adler wrote:

As a rule, Jewish industry operated clandestinely and therefore avoided any planning. It [also] totally ignored German plans and did not submit to them. Moreover, to its great fortune, the masses of German troops were in urgent need of various supplies and equipment. Thus, with the support of the German authorities, there sprouted up plants to manufacture brushes, mattresses, beds, clothing, furs, shoes.[27]

This economic struggle consumed much energy and was fraught with risks, but it provided a partial, meager income to a certain proportion of the ghetto's population. Only a tiny portion of that population, ten to twenty thousand people (3 to 5 percent at most), was not under severe economic strain. This stratum included the smugglers and their relatives as well as wealthy people who kept their property in the form of cash or goods, thus providing a means of support even under ghetto conditions. All the others, including those employed in industrial workshops, the *Judenrat*, and the "shops," were unable to subsist on their wages and were forced to supplement their primary source of income by selling off personal belongings and effects. And these people were considered fortunate, because their jobs—especially the skilled jobs in private workshops—provided a minimal basis for existence. Far more serious was the condition of those who for one reason or another did not work and subsisted off the sale of personal and family belongings. Their reserves were limited, and their prospect for the future was to be counted, sooner or later, among the indigent, those in need of welfare aid and essentially doomed to starvation. Most of the refugees who arrived in Warsaw and the improverished class of day laborers fell into this category from the start.

The heads of families made desperate efforts to find work, and the decline of professionals in the ghetto led to tragicomic situations. As Henryk Brysker wrote in his journal:

> People who were engineers yesterday are happy to get a job as a
> doorman today; a lawyer—a peddler of candies; one who was a rich mer-
> chant a little while ago stands on line to receive a free portion of soup
> from the low-class charity kitchen; a professor of music plays in the streets;
> a lawyer—a prison guard; and a street peddler who stuck with his
> vocation—that is the gallery of the reshuffled classes.[28]

According to calculations of the Self-Help enterprise, in December
1941, sixty-five thousand people were employed in the ghetto, including fifty-five thousand salaried workers and ten thousand self-employed.
The same source testifies that the number of destitute people during
the same period was over two hundred thousand.

Stefan Ernest, a senior official in the *Judenrat*, described the situation in his memoirs written during the war:

> Perhaps twenty, perhaps thirty thousand properly nourished people,
> members of the "social elite." In contrast are the masses of a quarter of a
> million beggars and totally destitute who struggle just to postpone the
> hour of death from starvation. . . . And in the middle, between these two
> ends of the spectrum, a mass of about 200,000 "average people" who
> make do, more or less, but they are considered "personalities," still surviv-
> ing, decently dressed, their bodies not swollen by hunger.[29]

These different groups did not remain stable, for they existed in a situation that changed constantly. But the change was always in the same
direction: from deterioration to starvation.

In July 1942, the month in which the mass deportation began, the
Labor Corps (*Arbeitsamt "Ju"*)—which was a department of the *Judenrat*
but functioned under the direct supervision of the Germans—
conducted a registration of people working in the ghetto. According to
the results, sixty thousand men and ten thousand women, for a total of
seventy thousand people, were employed in the ghetto.[30]

**The Internal Administration
of the Ghetto**

Paradoxically, the *Judenrat*, which
the Germans established as an instrument to execute their orders
and implement their policy regarding the Jews, had broader authority
and dealt with more areas of activity than the prewar *kehillah* had. This
situation was already apparent at the beginning of the occupation, but it
developed even further during the existence of the ghetto.

Before the war, a Jew was rarely in need of the *kehillah*'s services,
and the institution's influence was limited mostly to the sphere of general religious services and welfare aid to the poorer classes. During the

era of the ghetto, however, the *Judenrat* directed all essential affairs, both as the executor of orders issued by the Nazi regime and as the authority that distributed food, allocated apartments, work, and public services, and collected taxes. With this rise in the *Judenrat*'s importance, tasks, and authority, the public's interest in the institution and its tactics naturally grew. Evaluations of the *Judenrat*'s policy and comments on the people who headed it are among the most frequently developed subjects in the chronicles and diaries written in the ghetto; they are also subjects that preoccupied the ghetto's underground press. For the most part, the opinions offered in these sources are sharply critical. Many of the accusations made against the *Judenrat* are the product of the incessant pressure placed on the population of the ghetto. Under conditions of deprivation and despair, it is natural for bitterness and rage to be directed at the institution that supposedly represented the occupation regime within the walls. Czerniakow writes of this attitude with a heavy heart: "I have to suffer in a stuffy room which looks like a prison cell. . . . Besides, all these Jewish complaints."[31]

Even if we discount the criticism and grumbling as a natural outgrowth of the climate in the ghetto, there still remain a few points of criticism that indicate serious failings. One consistently repeated claim is that the *Judenrat* was composed of men who were unfit as public leaders, did not represent the people, and were incapable of filling responsible positions at a time of trial. Abraham Levin, who was usually restrained in his criticism, wrote in his diary shortly before the annihilation of the ghetto: "In our small and isolated world, men who are unqualified and were never meant to head a Jewish community—the largest community in Europe—in these terrible times pushed their way to the top. That is one of the insipid consequences of war: the tragedy of 'the elite sinking and the rabble rising'; the tragedy of leaders who were not anointed to their thrones."[32]

The strongest indictment of all, however—one shared by all sides and even expressed in the official *Gazeta Żydowska*, which was published under the auspices of the Germans—was against the *Judenrat*'s social policy: the distribution of the tax burden among the various classes and the methods of mobilizing conscripts for the labor camps.

The essence of the metamorphosis that took place in the structure of the *Judenrat* (in comparison with the prewar *kehillah*) and in the scope of its tasks and authority was very clear to the men who headed the institution. In December 1940, i.e., about the time the ghetto was closed, *Gazeta Żydowska* wrote:

> The *kehillah* has now taken on the character of an *Office for the Jews* in all matters pertaining to the Jewish population. With the creation of the

Jewish quarter, this character has been reinforced. The *kehillah* must be careful to fulfill the obligations imposed on the Jewish population by the authorities while simultaneously representing the needs of the public before those same authorities. Thus the *kehillah* [*Judenrat*] has become the *only representative and agency mediating between the Jewish public and the regime.*

Moreover, in March 1941, a short announcement appeared in *Gazeta Żydowska* informing the public that "in accordance with instructions from the authorities, Jews in Warsaw may turn to a representative of the regime only through the auspices of the *Judenrat*. Direct approaches in writing will be left unanswered."[33]

The *Judenrat* was therefore the sole channel between hundreds of thousands of Jews and the authorities and the outside world at large. But this does not necessarily mean that we can view it as a legally recognized institution representing the Jews not as individuals but as a community. In reality, as indicated by the entries in Czerniakow's diary, the Germans charged the *Judenrat* with obligations and missions on behalf of all the Jews in the ghetto, but Czerniakow's efforts to mediate with the Germans on behalf of the same comprehensive public, or individuals in severe distress, were met by indifference and obstinacy. We can therefore say that the population of the ghetto was in limbo insofar as its legal status was concerned; at least it did not possess any rights that stemmed from a recognized status. Clearly the Germans had deprived the Jews of responsibility for their affairs and attempted to run the ghetto by means of edicts and forcible control.

In February 1941 *Gazeta Żydowska* published an article on the *Judenrat* and its authority:

> The legal basis of the *Judenrat* derives from the Generalgouvernement's order of November 28, 1939, which established the *Judenräte* and defined their tasks: execution of German orders. These orders, especially in cities with Jewish quarters, and so much the more so in Warsaw, endowed and endow the *Judenrat* with such a broad scope of different tasks that it becomes an institution managing and directing all affairs pertaining to the Jews. It is a Jewish Office, a Department for Jews in the broadest sense of the term.[34]

It is important to note that the very sphere of religious services, which was the focal point of the former *kehillah*'s activities, was severely downgraded during the era of the *Judenrat*. The German authorities forbade the observance of many religious laws, and pious Jews had to carry out their rituals in secret. For a certain period public worship was outlawed, with the authorities claiming that this step was taken to combat the epidemic.[35] Even community services that were clearly religious in nature and had formerly been in the jurisdiction of the *kehillah*, such as burials, were to a large degree stripped of their religious character. For a long time the *Judenrat* functioned without an official rabbinate, and only at a late stage of the ghetto was a recognized Rabbinical Department established within its framework.

In May 1941 a Berlin attorney named Heinz Auerswald was appointed *Kommissar* of the "Jewish quarter" on behalf of the German authorities. Auerswald's appointment over the "Jewish quarter" was parallel to that of Ludwig Leist, who was the commander of the entire city, and Czerniakow similarly became the head of the quarter, i.e., a kind of mayor within the confines of the ghetto walls (*Obmann des Judenrates*). Auerswald's office also assumed control of the *Transferstelle* and supervised the ghetto at close quarters. To the extent that the civil administration's appointment of a *Kommissar* over the ghetto was an attempt to prevent various authorities, and especially the SS and the police, from interfering in ghetto affairs, the effort was only partially successful. Nevertheless, when Auerswald's office began to operate, the management of Jewish affairs became more centralized and the *Judenrat* had a single address for its appeals. But the police and the SS continued to intervene in ghetto affairs.

Let us attempt to examine the personal composition of the *Judenrat*, its aims, and the scope of its activities. The *Judenrat* was not a representative body in the sense of an institution chosen by democratic elections or given a mandate by public bodies. Yet the question that deserves our attention is whether or not the men who worked within the *Judenrat* were respected figures with experience in public affairs. We must likewise examine to what degree the *Judenrat*'s conduct of affairs reflected concern for the welfare of the public and responsibility for the entire community.

Czerniakow's personality has already been discussed in these pages. The aforementioned document—Czerniakow's personal diary—reveals to us the ongoing activities of the *Judenrat*'s chairman and to some degree his attitude toward people and problems and even his innermost thoughts. It is impossible to cast doubt on the man's sincerity and good intentions. Yet we are obligated to examine how far he succeeded in turning his personal intentions into a guideline for the activities of the *Judenrat* and whether or not Czerniakow (who was characterized by critics as a weak man incapable of imposing his authority) was a figure who stood out among the other personalities in the *Judenrat*.

As it turns out, the *Judenrat* included quite a few figures who were renowned for their authority and experience in public affairs. In fact, as noted earlier, representatives of the Jewish political parties and senior officials of respected institutions who joined the *Judenrat* upon its establishment were among the few who escaped from Warsaw and the occupied areas before the spring of 1940. Of those who remained in the *Judenrat*, the most outstanding were respected public figures, such as Abraham Gepner (chairman of the Union of Jewish Merchants in Poland and a member of the prewar Warsaw City Council), Joseph Jaszuński (the chairman of ORT in Poland and a member of the board of YIVO), Dr. Gustav Wielikowski (a well-known attorney and member of the board of the Ż.S.S. during the occupation), Stanisław Szereszewski (before the war, chairman of the Toporol Corporation, an organization to encourage agriculture among the Jews), Dr. Joseph Milejkowski (a doctor and renowned activist), Shmuel Winter (from Włocławek, active in YIVO, and during the occupation and the era of the ghetto close to the underground and Jewish fighting organization), and Meshulam Kaminer (a former member of the board of the *kehillah* and one of the leaders of Agudat Israel, who died in the ghetto). There were also some members who had served on the appointed board of the *kehillah* before the war, including Czerniakow and Marc Lichtenbaum, acting chairman of the *Judenrat* during Czerniakow's term of office and, after Czerniakow's suicide, chairman of the *Judenrat* during the final dissolution of the ghetto.

Yet the background, talents, and fields of specialization of the *Judenrat*'s members were still no guarantee of proper administration, integrity, and dedication to the public weal. The unpopular and negative image that stuck to the *Judenrat* stemmed principally from other factors. The *Judenrat*'s efforts and the odds of achieving anything whatsoever were wholly dependent upon the whim of any one officer or official. Czerniakow adopted a system of mediation by appealing to logic and humane feelings, but his approach succeeded only rarely. On the other hand, strategies that centered on bribery, illegal business dealings, and pandering to the personal "style" or idiosyncrasies of the officials and policemen who served in the area proved far more efficient. The influence of the *Judenrat*'s top man steadily declined, while those who were close to the Germans grew more and more powerful. Czerniakow understood what was happening and believed that under the circumstances it was imperative to turn to people of dubious reputation who knew how to get what they wanted from the Germans. In January 1942 he quoted in his diary an introduction from the works of one of Poland's literary masters, Stefan Żeromski: "Don't I, indeed, have under my command all manner of thugs, cutthroats, and murderers, and yet I spare them and prize them; for it is they who know best. . . . They are the very ones who will lead you safely out of an ambush."[36] Beyond that, the *Judenrat* had been infiltrated by men who were controlled by the Germans and had been hired by express order of the authorities. Among these was Dr. Alfred Nossig, who was an informer for the Germans and had been appointed to a senior position in the *Judenrat* by German demand.

In a number of ghettos, the *Judenräte* pursued a more or less crystallized policy and claimed that it would ease the situation of the Jews and even ensure their physical survival. An elder of the Lodz ghetto, Mordecai Chaim Rumkowski, vigorously promoted the philosophy that productivity, i.e., turning the ghetto into a source of good vital to the Germans, would ensure the preservation of the ghetto and the survival of its inhabitants. Ephraim Barash in Bialystok and Jacob Gens in Vilna differed from Rumkowski in their personal approach to the public and their style of operation, but they also placed stock in this conception.

The question is whether the Warsaw *Judenrat* subscribed to the notion of productivity as a systematic approach to survival or whether, indeed, it had any clear-cut policy dealing with long-range interests. One gets the impression that the Warsaw *Judenrat* lacked any definitive or consistent policy. On the other hand, there were indications of trends that reflected the personality and outlook of Czerniakow and other *Judenrat* leaders. Czerniakow wanted both to meet the stringent demands of the Germans and to prevent, as much as possible, their intervention in the internal affairs of the ghetto. Within the ghetto, according to Ernest's testimony, Czerniakow tried "to preserve the status quo at any price,"[37] i.e., allowing the Jews a free hand in the management of their economic affairs and other spheres of life. "The *Judenrat*'s economic liberalism," Stanisław Adler wrote in his memoirs, "was expressed by not placing obstacles in the path of private initiative in the economic sphere."[38]

This laissez-faire attitude regarding internal affairs continued throughout the existence of the ghetto. The economic initiatives taken by the *Judenrat* during the later stages of the ghetto were in response to German demands, particularly Auerswald's pressure to develop a network of German-owned workshops and plants. But the *Judenrat*'s tolerance in internal affairs also had consequences that burdened the ghetto and aroused sharp criticism. A good example was its system of taxation.[39] As we know, the *Judenrat* suffered from a chronic shortage of financial resources. One of the means it adopted to acquire capital was the system of indirect taxation. Thus *Gazeta Żydowska* noted on September 10, 1940, that "instead of imposing taxes on those who are able to pay and should therefore bear responsibility for the community, the burden is now distributed evenly among the entire population."[40]

A similar, though even more serious, issue was the mobilization of conscripts for the forced-labor camps. When it was no longer possible to thwart the German demands and the *Judenrat* was forced to supply men for the camps, it was not the physically strong and less vulnerable who were taken but the weak and starving inhabitants of the ghetto population. The *Judenrat* and the Jewish Police avoided causing injury to men of means and influence, so that the *Judenrat* in essence filled the obligation imposed on the community as a whole at the expense of its weakest and poorest members. This selective system of conscription for the labor camps aroused deep bitterness and further alienated the ghetto's masses from the *Judenrat*.

The *Judenrat*'s approach also brought about a general resignation to the wide social and economic gaps in the ghetto. The *Judenrat* was not opposed to placing pressure on the men of means, or at least using a small portion of the private capital to try to sustain those doomed to hunger and death from starvation. Of course, even such measures could not solve the problem entirely, because hunger spread quickly, while the number of relatively wealthy people decreased over time. According to the *Judenrat*'s critics, however, such measures should have been adopted at least as a braking mechanism, and every means within Jewish society should have been exhausted for this purpose.

The administrative apparatus of the *Judenrat* expanded to encompass 6,000 employees during the era of the ghetto, whereas the prewar *kehillah* had employed about 530 workers. The nucleus of veteran *kehillah* employees was literally swallowed up in the mass of new officials and workers. At one point there were almost thirty departments in the *Judenrat*, the most important ones being the Economic Department, the Budget Department, the Labor Department, the Health Department, the Self-Help Department, and the Burial Department. The Jewish Police was also essentially a division of the *Judenrat*. The members of the *Judenrat* appointed to the various departments devoted most of their time to general public activities, while practical day-to-day work was given over to the chairmen or directors of the departments. Swamped with work, these divisions of the *Judenrat* had to develop patterns of effective administration in the course of their ongoing operations. Despite the extraordinary difficulties, however, in the course of time substantial progress was made in a number of areas. For example, notable success was achieved in the fields of sanitation and health. When the Self-Help was no longer able to finance relief activities from its own resources, the divisions of the *Judenrat* dealing with welfare were integrated into the general relief program, and progress was made in this area as well. The *Judenrat* developed a broad network of activities in the field of vocational training. In this case the council did not hesitate to deceive the Germans and ran a comprehensive program of classes, including even university-level courses, under the guise of vocational training.

Czerniakow himself, with the active aid and encouragement of his wife, was particularly concerned with protecting the interests of children. And although his efforts yielded only limited results, considering the grave state of affairs, the opening of community-financed kindergartens and children's corners in the ghetto should not be discounted. As a result of Czerniakow's strenuous efforts, in the summer of 1941 elementary schools were permitted to reopen in the ghetto, and the *Judenrat* initiated a program of educational activities in cooperation with the various political and religious groups that had supported independent school networks before the war.

At the end of 1940, when it had become clear that the authorities would not issue a permit to reopen the schools, studies were held secretly in some of the soup kitchens established specifically for children. Experienced teachers, aided by volunteers from the ranks of the youth movements, were drawn to this clandestine program. The classes run in these relief kitchens were on an elementary level, but secondary-school classes were taught to small study groups held in private homes (*komplety*). Pupils were given exams and received grades; textbooks passed from hand to hand so that typewritten copies could be made of them. Books from many underground libraries and private collections also circulated among the students as well as the general ghetto population. The children were enthusiastic about their studies, which were a kind of link with the great and free world outside.

In October 1941 the schools were reopened by official permission, and at first six schools operated in the children's shelters. Thus, for all intents and purposes, the clandestine classes were granted the status of open and recognized institutions. The number of schools increased during the first (and last) official school year in the ghetto, and at the end of the 1941/42 school year, nineteen schools were fully or partially operational with 6,700 pupils enrolled. The schools were divided among the various educational trends: four Tarbut schools, three CISO (Central Jewish School Organization) schools, six religious schools, five schools of various other trends, and one for the children of converts. In all, about 7,000 of the 50,000 children of school age were engaged in studying in the ghetto.[41]

There was an attempt to establish public watchdog committees attached to the *Judenrat* to monitor and correct the flaws that cropped up in the administrative bureaucracy and to improve the quality of relations between the *Judenrat* and the general public in the ghetto. Men like the historian Yitzhak (Ignacy) Schipper and evidently even distinguished activists in the underground like Menachem Kirschenbaum and Shakhne Zagan agreed to serve on these committees for a while. But the watchdog committees were short-lived and were not very influential. Underground activists demanded extensive reforms, to which the *Judenrat* did not agree, while the bureaucracy held on tenaciously to its powers, and it was impossible to effect much change from within.

It was primarily during the months prior to the final deportation—or, to be more exact, from the spring of 1942 onward—that the work of the *Judenrat* began to show signs of improvement, just as there was a general easing of conditions in the ghetto during this period. The standard contacts between Czerniakow and Auerswald had become all but routine and were sometimes graced with true communication. The financial state of the *Judenrat* improved, and signs of proficiency began to be evident in its work. As already noted, in the summer of 1941 the authorities finally permitted the reopening of schools, an aim toward which Czerniakow had worked since the beginning of his term as chairman.[42] The economic initiatives of the *Judenrat* never reached great proportions, but the council's modest achievements came primarily during this period. From the middle of 1941, the *Judenrat*'s efforts in the field of welfare were also intensified. For a time Czerniakow invested much time and effort in securing the release of prisoners who were in danger of dying. On March 17, 1942, he wrote in his diary: "I received some photographs of the release of the detainees from the Jewish prison. One can sense in these photographs the joy of the waiting crowd. It is the first time I see the ghetto smile." It is appropriate to add that this is one of the few instances in which emotion bubbles forth from Czerniakow's generally restrained prose. Yet, as we know in retrospect, at the same time the signs of change for the better were appearing, the date of the deportation and mass liquidation was drawing near.

Two other crucial institutions that functioned in the ghetto within the framework of the *Judenrat* were the Supply Authority (*Zakład Zaopatrywania*), which handled the distribution of ration cards to the Jewish population, the supply of food, and the problems of sustenance in the ghetto, as well as the obtainment of other essential needs, such as coal; and the Order Authority (*Ordnungsdienst*), or, in the language of the ghetto, the Jewish Police. In the course of time, the Supply Authority expanded its capacities and established enterprises in the ghetto to manufacture products and aid in distribution. Grains were ground into flour in the ghetto, and there were "factories" for the production of jam and synthetic honey. As time passed, in addition to supplying basic foodstuffs, the Supply Authority dealt with providing food to orphanages, hospitals, soup kitchens, and refugee hostels.

Since the Supply Authority was responsible for the most crucial aspect of life in the ghetto, it was naturally incapable of completely fulfilling its task, namely, feeding the population of the ghetto. Nonetheless, this institution enjoyed a greater measure of public confidence than any other division of the *Judenrat*. The stature of the Supply Authority is to be credited primarily to the man who stood at its head and exercised firm control over its operations, Abraham Gepner. Gepner was a well-known and wealthy merchant and industrialist, a self-made man who was respected by Poles and Jews alike. By the time the ghetto was established, he was already advanced in years and had accumulated a wealth of experience in commerce and public affairs, yet he still exuded energy, optimism, and charisma. Gepner not only devoted a great deal of time to welfare projects in the ghetto but also maintained contact with the underground.

The Jewish Police assumed an important position in the history of the ghetto and played a central role during the most tragic era in the annals of Warsaw Jewry—the period of the mass deportation and extermination. The stigmatized image of the Jewish Police as an alien force that collaborated with the enemy regime is rooted in this period.[43] Yet in order to comprehend the nature of the Jewish Police, it is necessary to go back to the origin of this institution and examine the course of its development.

The Jewish Police was established simultaneously with the ghetto itself. Of all the frameworks and services for which the *Judenrat* assumed responsibility, the police force was the institution most remote from and alien to the traditions of Jewish communal life in the Diaspora. It was an instrument with which the organized Jewish public had absolutely no previous experience. The percentage of well-educated and upper-class young men in the ranks of the police was high—especially among the men who had been enlisted during the early organizational stage—and the command level of the Jewish Police was composed mostly of men from the free professions, officers in the Polish army, and an extraordinarily large number of lawyers. When the Jewish Police was first organized, its members were not offered a salary and candidates were enlisted on a voluntary basis. Nonetheless, there was a flood of applications to join the ranks, many more than the number of openings appropriated for the ghetto. The volunteers were drawn to the police for a number of reasons. First of all, other sources of employment were not available, and many regarded the organization of the police in the "autonomous" framework of the ghetto as an enticing challenge. Second, the candidates evidently presumed that the voluntary nature of the force would be short-lived, and in the course of time some way would be found to remunerate the policemen. Third, membership in the police ensured immunity to deportation to labor camps or abduction off the streets.

On December 6, 1941, *Gazeta Żydowska* reported that 1,000 men were serving full-time in the police. The same article stated that the rush of volunteers was so overwhelming that applications were no longer being considered, and on December 24 the paper reported that by the middle of November the police had signed on 1,635 members.[44] Thus, in light of the profusion of applications and the backing that the candidates evidently received from various parties, the *Judenrat* did not limit the force to the intended number of 1,000 policemen but set its size at 1,600 men and upward.

Stanisław Adler, a senior officer in the police, related in his memoirs that "according to the German conception, the principal task of the police was to prevent people from gathering near the boundaries of the ghetto. The object of this mission could have been identical with the war against smuggling."[45] An anonymous police officer expressed a similar opinion in his memoirs in writing that "The major and most important task of the units on the front line was stationing sentries. These guards stood by the gates, the walls, and the boundary fences. The task of these units: checking people and wagons, preventing access to the walls and fences, the fight against smuggling."

As described earlier, however, not only did the Jewish Police fail to prevent smuggling but, quite to the contrary, the police force—or, to be more exact, many of the policemen—became an integral part of the structure and organization of the smuggling operation in Warsaw. According to the testimony of the anonymous police officer, the entire police force—not only those directly involved in the smuggling campaign—benefited from the clandestine transfer of goods and viewed itself as a partner to the operation. Usually the policemen looked for ways "to facilitate the smuggling in the best way possible, ensure it against discovery by the Germans, and exploit the gate, the fence, or the wall to the best advantage."[46]

The tasks assigned to the police in the ghetto were varied. They included: (1) directing traffic in the streets; (2) supervising garbage collection and clearing snow and dirt off the streets; (3) supervising sanitation in the buildings (special units were attached to apartment blocks and some of them kept an eye on the affairs of the tenants); (4) preventing crime and operating a kind of court that served as an "arbiter" in disputes that arose in the ghetto.

The dependence of the police on outside factors was complex. Established by the *Judenrat*, the force was formally subject to that institution. The head of the Jewish Police, like other *Judenrat* department chairmen, was a public figure and a member of the council's executive. Bernard Zundelewicz, who was regarded as an honest and well-intentioned man, headed the police on behalf of the *Judenrat* for a long period. But the degree of public control over the police was less than that over any other department of the *Judenrat*; in fact, it was negligible.

The Jewish Police evolved as an independent force in which the police chief and his officers set the tone.

At the same time, the policemen in the ghetto were subject to the supervision of the Polish Police (called the "Blue Police" because of the color of their uniforms),[47] which refused to relinquish control over the ghetto because it proved to be so responsive to extortion and was such a good source of income on the side. The ghetto was divided into six Jewish Police districts that were formally subject to the Polish Police. The Jewish force lacked the authority to deal with criminal infractions and was obliged to turn such cases and suspects over to the Poles. The Jewish officers, and especially Police Chief Szeryński, tried to cultivate close relations with the Polish Police.

The third factor and highest authority that controlled the Jewish Police was, naturally, the various arms of the German police. Szeryński would often accompany Czerniakow to meetings with the authorities; at least he participated in all sessions dealing with the Jewish Police and its activities. It was by means of these meetings that direct contact was established between the Germans and the command of the Jewish Police, and the Germans, especially the Gestapo and the S.D., passed orders directly on to the chief of the Jewish force. This direct tie grew stronger with time, and during the mass deportation the *Judenrat* was bypassed altogether, and "control" of Jewish affairs in the ghetto was given over almost entirely to the police force, which became the sole channel of communication with the Germans.

More than any other man, Józef Szeryński (whose name had been Sheinkman before his conversion to Catholicism) left his imprint on the police and its image in the ghetto. Szeryński had been colonel in the Polish Police until the outbreak of the war and had severed all his ties with Judaism, but the racial laws defined him as a Jew and forced him into the ghetto. His appointment as chief of the Jewish Police was not at the initiative of the Germans. Czerniakow himself choose Szeryński for a number of reasons, the most important of which was his intention to place this responsible position—which was essentially alien to the Jews—in the hands of an expert professional. Szeryński was also an attractive candidate because of his close and sympathetic relations with the commanders of the Polish Police. According to people who knew Szeryński and followed his career, he did not initially aspire to a position of control in the ghetto, and in accepting the appointment he fully intended to fulfill the obligations of a professional police officer responsible to a civilian authority. In the course of time, however, he came to realize that his subordinates in the ghetto viewed him as the man largely responsible for maintaining order and the status of the area.

Szeryński surrounded himself with a cadre of aides who regarded themselves as superior to the common masses in the ghetto and exploited the opportunity to enjoy special privileges, pursue a lifestyle that contrasted sharply with the grim realities of life in the ghetto, and cast their shadow of terror over all. The personal example set by Szeryński and his closest aides influenced the rest of the force as well. In the beginning, the attitude of the ghetto population toward the police was neither hostile nor reserved. In the middle of December 1940, Ringelblum wrote in his journal that "the Jewish Police is composed of experienced and sympathetic men" and on February 19, 1941, he wrote, "The public stands behind the Jewish policeman: 'would you obey a Pole and not a Jew?' There are intelligent men among the police who prefer persuasion to giving orders."[48] Yet in a review of the police written in December 1942, Ringelblum commented: "The Jewish Police had a bad reputation even before the deportation. Unlike the Polish Police, which did not take part in the abductions for the labor camps, the Jewish Police did engage in this dirty work. The police were also notorious for their shocking corruption and demoralization."[49]

Three stages can be distinguished in the development of the Jewish Police and its relationship with the ghetto population. First, from the formation of the police until the spring of 1941 (i.e., the beginning of the abductions for the labor camps), the image of the police and its relations with the public were, as a rule, respectable. Then, from the spring of 1941 until the initiation of the deportation in July 1942, there was a period of steady deterioration within the police force and in its relations with the public. Finally, during the period of the mass deportation, the Jewish Police sank to its nadir and was the most abhorred institution in the ghetto.

In the course of time, the gap between most of the Jewish policemen and the masses in the ghetto grew wider. Some of the tasks assumed by the police, such as guarding houses that were quarantined because of contagious disease and, especially, carrying out the forced conscription for the labor camps, aroused public enmity for them even before the period of the deportation. The police were not outfitted in full uniform, but their distinguishing marks—an armband, starred caps, and especially the shiny high boots and rubber clubs—became hated symbols of power.

In one sphere, however, the Jewish Police did faithfully serve the interests of the public. According to regulations, they were obliged to turn over cases of criminal offense, together with the lawbreaker, to the Polish Police. In practice, however, the Jewish Police created an internal system of justice that extended to include criminal offenders and thereby obviated the extradition of a good many people into hostile and alien hands. Both the criminals and those who requested legal arbitration knew that falling into the hands of non-Jews was a dangerous venture and therefore accepted the decision pronounced by the Jewish Police, even though its authority in such matters was dubious.

The prison in the Warsaw ghetto, which was opened in June 1941, fell under the jurisdiction of the Jewish Police. It consisted of a number of structures on Gęsia Street that had previously served as a Polish military prison. The decision to establish a Jewish prison was prompted by the growing number of Jewish prisoners held in jails outside the ghetto. In addition, reported cases of contamination in jails outside the ghetto probably bolstered the decision to create a prison within the walls. In the early stages of determining the prison's requirements, the planners spoke in terms of 150 prisoners, but in May 1942 there were about 1,300 Jewish detainees in the jail (known as Gęsiówka), all of them suffering from starvation and close to total collapse. Most of the inmates of Gęsiówka were amateur smugglers who had been caught on the "Aryan" side of the city, so that they included a high proportion of children (about 500 of the 1,300 prisoners in May 1942 were indeed children).[50]

Szeryński himself was arrested by the Germans a few months before the mass deportation. He was accused of smuggling furs that were supposed to have been confiscated, with the intention of concealing them in the Polish quarter. Jacob Lejkin, a diminutive lawyer who was known for his zeal and solemn attitude toward his police duties, was appointed in his stead. Lejkin was to become a disciplined and dynamic instrument of the Germans during the mass deportation. It was in anticipation of that move against the ghetto that the Germans also released Szeryński, on the understanding that he would serve them loyally, and his freedom increased his dependence upon them.

Another focal point of authority and power in the Warsaw ghetto that was fundamentally different from the *Judenrat* and the Jewish Police was the agency known as the "Thirteen" (*Trzynastka* in Polish and *Das Draitzental* in Yiddish), which took its name from the address of its headquarters on Leszno Street. It was neither an administrative-organizational framework like the *Judenrat* nor a kind of gendarmerie to maintain law and order, but it shared characteristics of both these institutions. The "Thirteen" network was closely identified with the name of its founder and moving spirit, Abraham Gancwajch, and the group of men who surrounded him. Gancwajch's "Thirteen" was not an extension or metamorphosis of any existing Jewish authority; neither had it been established by an active Jewish group in response to conditions and needs in the ghetto. Furthermore, Gancwajch and most of his senior aides were not even veteran residents of Warsaw but had come to the city as refugees. Their rise to power in the ghetto was due solely to the sanction they received from key figures in the occupation regime and the influence and power these same officials placed in their hands. It may therefore be stated with certainty that the "Thirteen" network was imposed on the ghetto by the Germans, and the status and fortunes of this group of men were probably a product of the rivalry and clashes between various parties within the German bureaucracy and the police.

The principal division of the "Thirteen" network, which was founded in December 1940, was the Office to Combat Usury and Profiteering in the Jewish Quarter of Warsaw, and a supervisory unit established within the framework of this office was parallel to the Jewish Police. Its personnel also sported polished boots, caps (with a green band rather than the blue one worn by the regular police), epaulets, and stars to denote rank. The ranks of the "Thirteen" encompassed three to four hundred men. In May 1941 Gancwajch's agency set up "First Aid," a kind of Red Cross emergency station. Gancwajch also inspired the establishment of a department to supervise weights and measures in the ghetto, an organization of disabled veterans of the 1939 fighting, and cultural and religious societies.

There were many who thought Gancwajch was a Nazi agent and a treacherous informer. (We now know that he provided the Germans with running accounts of developments inside the ghetto.) Others were impressed by him and believed he was trying to help, so that the facilities and connections at his disposal should be exploited. The man's past is shrouded in mystery. Some claim that he was already operating as a Nazi agent before the war broke out, but there is no proof to substantiate this allegation. Gancwajch himself claimed that his privileged position grew out of his recommendation to the Germans by a relative, Moshe Merin, who was chairman of the district *Judenrat* in Zagłębie. But other rumors spread in the ghetto. It was said that his rise to power was due to the recommendation of Dr. Olenbusch, a German whom Gancwajch had met and befriended during the time he worked as a journalist. Olenbusch was first in charge of propaganda in the Warsaw District and later ran the Propaganda Department of Frank's administration in Cracow. In any event, it is clear that Gancwajch's patrons were S.D. men in Warsaw.

The "Thirteen" and the *Judenrat* were locked in a long and bitter struggle. Gancwajch, who steadily built up and extended his influence, had his eye on the *Judenrat* and hoped to usurp Czerniakow's position or at least infiltrate the institution and pull strings behind the scenes. There was also a parallel struggle going on between the Jewish Police and the formations wearing the "uniform" of the "Thirteen." Gancwajch failed in his attempts to win the loyalty of the Jewish public, and it was his ambitious contest with the *Judenrat* that was largely responsible for the eventual decline of his power in the ghetto. He took great pains to demonstrate the public spirit behind his deeds and activities and tried to win the support of intellectuals and public figures by founding cultural societies, supporting struggling writers, and ostentatiously handing out food in the streets of the ghetto. At first he succeeded in angling in men whose powerful stature was beyond question, although there were cases in which men who were summoned by Gancwajch preferred to pretend that they were indisposed in order to avoid having to see him. At any rate, the name Gancwajch cast a net of dread over the ghetto. We cannot know whether his public-spirited activities were only a cover for the darker side of his affairs related to his links with the Germans or whether they were a sincere expression of one aspect of his complex personality. It is more probable that Gancwajch tried to develop an image of respectability in order to gain the upper hand in his struggle for control of the ghetto and to justify in the eyes of both Germans and Jews the appointment to which he aspired.

The actual work carried out by the various agencies in Gancwajch's network also raised doubts. The Office to Combat Usury and Profiteering had broadly defined powers. It was supposedly established to supervise weights and measures in the ghetto bakeries and to prevent the production of goods that were considered luxuries (rolls made from white flour, etc.). Thus his men may occasionally have intervened in affairs that required attention, but as a rule the purpose of his operation was to bully people into paying fines and blackmail. Since Gancwajch was subject directly to the Germans and operated as their representative, he did not need the consent of the Polish Police to establish a judicial body and prison of his own.

Other projects run by the "Thirteen" operated under the guise of constructive contributions to the ghetto's welfare. The First Aid Station, for example, rarely dealt with emergency cases, while its apparatus and ambulance were used for smuggling and other commercial operations. Gancwajch and his men received various leases and permits to establish economic enterprises, which they turned into sources of easy profit at the expense of the ghetto. During a certain period, two refugees from Lodz, Kohn and Heller, were counted among Gancwajch's associates. In time they broke with him and began operating on their own, but they did not give up their German patronage and found protectors among the Gestapo men. Kohn and Heller built up various commercial operations, one being the horse-drawn wooden trolleys that transported passengers in the ghetto. Though less concerned than Gancwajch about a respectable public image, they also donated some of their profits—albeit not without fraud and self-aggrandizement—to philanthropic causes, especially aid to rabbis and other religious officials. Kohn and Heller maintained their power longer than Gancwajch and his men, and their demise came only during the mass deportation.[51]

These men had another major source of influence and income. From the time of his debut in the ghetto, Gancwajch was known as a man with influence in German circles and the power to get prisoners released, obtain necessary permits, send telegrams, move in and out of the ghetto, transfer people to the ghetto from distant places, and so on. Considering the circumstances of isolation, sudden calamity, and the absence of binding laws, the services that Gancwajch offered were in great demand. Naturally, his intervention had its price — and it was high (he claimed that his activities required the outlay of large expenses, especially in gifts to the Germans). Although Gancwajch rarely kept his promises as an intermediary with the Germans, every successful venture was lavishly publicized to his advantage. The harrowing situation in the ghetto drove many to turn to Gancwajch, undoubtedly including members of the *Judenrat* itself.[52]

Was the appearance of a man like Gancwajch in the ghetto to be understood as an expression of cooperation with the Nazis that can be equated with the concept of collaboration in the occupied countries? The term "collaboration" is usually used to describe men and organizations that identified with the principles and ideological creed of National Socialism and Fascism and strived to become part of the "New Order" that Hitler promised to establish in Europe. According to Gancwajch's personal testimony and that of his deeds, we can see that he attempted to bring about a change in the ghetto by making it more responsive to the Germans' demands and more productive from their point of view. Seen from this perspective, there is a measure of identity between Gancwajch and the heads of the *Judenräte* in many of Poland's ghettos. In practice, however, this alternative goal was lost among the pressures of crude self-interest and extortion. From his earliest days in the ghetto, Gancwajch's opportunistic outlook in appraising the state of affairs and the prospects for the Jews under Nazi rule was readily evident. Gancwajch was a talented orator whose speeches were clothed in the rhetoric of public spirit, and his pronouncements were therefore the object of widespread attention. He contended that since the Germans were destined to win the war, it was best that the Jews forget the past, come to terms with the new reality, and arrive at a *modus vivendi* with their new rulers. Even though this posture did not imply identification with Nazism and its regime, but merely expressed recognition of the inevitable, it was met with astonishment and rage.[53] Gancwajch's pessimistic perspective was diametrically opposed to the outlook shared by all circles and classes in the ghetto. Even during the period of Germany's most glorious military victories, the Jews never abandoned their faith and confidence that the Nazis would ultimately suffer military defeat and bear responsibility for their crimes. This unequivocable confidence was common not only to religious Jews, who believed in divine protection, but to all those who clung to a deterministic philosophy and for whom it was inconceivable that the forces of evil and injustice would ultimately triumph and rule over mankind.

In July 1941 Auerswald closed down Gancwajch's principal bastion of power, the Office to Combat Usury and Profiteering. It is impossible to pinpoint the exact cause of Gancwajch's defeat in his contest with the *Judenrat*. Auerswald probably manipulated his downfall because he viewed Gancwajch as a lackey of the S.D., and the *Kommissar*'s civilian authority was interested in curbing the S.D.'s influence. Half of the office's "supervisors" were absorbed into the regular ghetto police, bringing the number of policemen up from 2,000 to 2,200. The dismantling of the Office to Combat Usury and Profiteering retarded the growth of Gancwajch's power, but it did not neutralize him altogether, for Gancwajch and his aides were undaunted by their setback. The focus of the "Thirteen" moved to "First Aid," which now became the base of the network, and as time went on, more attention was given to various commercial enterprises. On the night of April 18, 1942, when scores of Jews were murdered by the Germans according to a predetermined list, a number of the leaders of Gancwajch's network were counted among the victims. The two top men, Gancwajch and Sternfeld, were apparently on the list of targets, but they succeeded in escaping from their apartments in time. The reasons for Gancwajch's downfall are as obscure as the means by which he established himself in the ghetto and succeeded in building his power. Yet it is almost certain that the liquidation of Gancwajch's gang was related to the friction between factions in the German administration and the police. After the night of slaughter, Gancwajch withdrew from the arena of ghetto affairs, but this was still not the end of his career. During and following the mass deportation, he appeared again, and rumor had it that he was working, *inter alia*, as an informer on the "Aryan" side of the city.[54] When and how he met his end is unknown to us.

The German Authorities in the Ghetto

As a rule, the Jews were at the mercy of the whims and ambitions of two separate powers: the SS and the police, on the one hand, and Hans Frank's civilian administration, on the other. The SS, particularly the Gestapo, took it for granted that the Jews fell within their jurisdiction, based on the assumption that the

Jews were the archetypal ideological enemy against which the SS and its offshoots were fighting a war of their own. Since this position was generally accepted in Germany and in some of the countries annexed to the Reich, it was naturally presumed valid within the Generalgouvernement.

For a while after the disbandment of the *Wehrmacht*'s military government, the Gestapo and the SS determined policy regarding the Jews. The commanders of the Police and Security Service (KdS) and the Gestapo in Warsaw were Dr. Josef Meisinger and Johannes Müller (followed by Dr. Ludwig Hahn), respectively. The Jews had practically no means of access to this echelon; Hahn, at any rate, refused to have any contact with Jews, so their affairs were handled by the lower-rank officers of the Jewish section of the Gestapo—Brandt and Mende. At first Frank delegated responsibility for Jewish forced labor to Higher SS and Police Leader Friedrich Krieger. But when it became apparent that the SS could not cope with this operation, and especially when the need to exploit the reserves of Jewish skilled labor and manpower gained the upper hand, the supervision of the Jewish labor force was turned over to the Labor Department and the civilian administration.

In May 1940 the question of authority over the *Judenräte* was raised in the first consultation between senior police officers and Frank and his district governors. In the course of this discussion, the head of the Lublin District, Governor Zörner, who was embroiled in an open feud with Odilo Globocnik, the chief of the SS and the police in his district, commented that "The question of the *Judenräte* remains to be settled. No one knows under whose charge they come." This question had already been decided regarding sparsely populated areas, but it remained open in the case of large cities. The commander of the SS and Security Police (*S.S. Gruppenführer*), Bruno Streckenbach, replied to Zörner:

> The Security Police, for understandable reasons, is very interested in the Jewish problem, and it therefore created the institution of the *Judenräte*. After the *Judenräte* were established, officials of the civilian administration appeared on the scene and created a muddle in which every agency attempts—on its own authority and without any order—to take advantage of the *Judenräte*. An important decision must be made on this matter. First of all, we must decide the question of which authority should control the *Judenräte*—the *Starosta* [in prewar Poland, the representative of the regime in a defined administrative area], the district governor, or the Security Police.[55]

It was obvious to Streckenbach that this responsibility had to be delegated to the Security Police.

In his summary of the situation, Frank attempted to sidestep a clear-cut decision. On the one hand, he portrayed the police as the armed formation charged with maintaining order, which was likewise its task within the Generalgouvernement. Since the police had no aims of its own, the question of controlling the *Judenräte* should be weighed from the point of view of efficiency. But Frank could not ignore the senstive issue raised by Streckenbach, namely that the Jewish question was also a political matter that had been placed under the jurisdiction of the S.D. and the Security Police. Thus, as he continued his remarks, Frank began to contradict his own earlier generalization: "In Germany, the monitoring of political affairs lies in the hands of the political police, so that control of the *Judenräte* must likewise be handled by an appropriately invested authority—namely, the Security Police and the S.D. Any other answer to the question of control is illogical. The use of the *Judenräte* to obtain manpower, however, is an altogether different matter."[56]

This dichotomy remained a trademark of German policy toward the Jews in the Generalgouvernement up until the initiation of the "Final Solution." There were ups and downs in the power play between the two camps. As noted above, during the first phase, directly following the abrogation of the military government, the intervention of the Gestapo and the S.D. in Jewish affairs was particularly prominent. After May 1940, with the ascendancy of the aim to transform the Generalgouvernement into an area of permanent occupation over the impulse to confiscate and plunder everything within reach, the Germans began to direct their sights on long-range economic planning, and the civilian regime became more aggressive in imposing its hegemony on various spheres of life. Among the ramifications of this change was a heightened interest in the Jews, which was boosted by the deepening awareness of the Jews' professional caliber as a valuable asset. This new line of thinking also influenced the inherent competition between the SS and the police and Frank's administration.

A perusal of Czerniakow's diary reveals that during the first months of the occupation, the chairman of the *Judenrat* was summoned primarily by the SS and the Gestapo, while his contacts with the municipal authorities and the civilian administration were sporadic. The SS dealt with questions of labor, taxes and special levies, confiscations, arrests, emigration, etc. Czerniakow turned to the municipal authorities to find a solution to the *Judenrat*'s financial problems and to ease the food shortage. This system of subordinating the Jewish community to the civilian administration and managing its affairs in a systematic fashion was fully realized on May 15, 1941, when Heinz Auerswald took up his duties as *Kommissar* of the Jewish quarter. But the Gestapo and the

S.D. nonetheless continued to intervene in the affairs of the *Judenrat* and the ghetto. The various arms of the police made their presence felt in the ghetto by means of both pressures and direct demands upon the *Judenrat* and by infiltrating the *Judenrat* with their lackeys and supporting factions in the Jewish Police and the "Thirteen." Again, Czerniakow's diary entries indicate that approaching the date of the mass deportation, the intervention of the Gestapo and the S.D. was on the rise again, as was the dependence of the ghetto on these forces.

The question remains whether there was really any difference, from the viewpoint of both policy and personal attitudes, between the rigid officials (who were, after all, members of various party cadres) and the members of the Gestapo and the SS. An examination of the evidence available to us indicates that there was indeed a distinction. The civilian bureaucracy tended to act in a more rational manner and sometimes even moved to ease the distress of the Jews somewhat. From time to time Czerniakow permitted himself to address administration officials, including Auerswald himself, in a personal fashion and appealed to their reason or sentiment. Sometimes the response was a humane gesture, from which Czerniakow drew encouragement. Such exchanges hardly ever took place with the SS or the police.

The tense relations between the civilian bureaucracy and the SS were not the only overt friction within the German regime. The exaggerated fragmentation of authority and the tension it bred also left their mark on the individual departments. The bureaucracy suffered from the absence of clearly defined borders of authority, and there was no coordination among the officials who bore responsibility for deciding crucial issues. During Auerswald's term of office, when affairs were supposedly concentrated in the hands of a single authority, there was still friction within the bureaucracy, primarily because of the rivalry between Bischoff, the head of the *Transferstelle*, and Auerswald, who was formally his superior. The polyarchic system of rule was one of the trademarks of the Nazi regime throughout Europe, but the absence of definitive divisions between the jurisdictions of various authorities was especially prominent in the occupied areas, particularly in affairs related to the Jews.

From the viewpoint of the SS, the internment of the Jews in the ghetto was a step toward the comprehensive solution of the Jewish question, while the civilian bureaucracy probably gave some degree of serious thought to other considerations, such as limiting the spread of contagious diseases to the confines of the ghetto and striking out at the black market. The political rationale prevalent among the officials of the German regime was that by closing the Jews in the ghetto, they had achieved the total segregation of the Polish and Jewish populations.

Although Frank spoke of the ghetto as a phenomenon that would lead to the gradual annihilation of the Jews, in consultations with the senior echelon of his administration he participated in long-range planning for the ghetto, which projected years into the future and laid down some of the fundamental aims to be met. In a consultation of this kind dealing exclusively with the Warsaw ghetto in April 1941, one of the participants commented that "it must be assumed that finding an appropriate way to employ 65,000 to 70,000 Jews in the ghetto will be of benefit to the interested authorities. If this succeeds, the creation of the Jewish quarter will have been a positive step."

As for the governor-general himself, Frank's hostility toward the Jews was usually emphatic and uncompromising. His dominant aim was to eliminate the Jews from the Generalgouvernement. On July 22, 1941, exactly one year before the mass deportation from the Warsaw ghetto began, Frank stated at a meeting of the Generalgouvernement administration:

> During the conversation that I was able to hold with the Führer in the Reich Office three days before the invasion [of the Soviet Union], the Führer told me, among other things, that the Jews will be the first to leave the Generalgouvernement. In the coming days I shall issue an order regarding the evacuation of the Warsaw ghetto. We must make every effort to remove the Jews from the Generalgouvernement as quickly as possible.[57]

When the state of total liquidation arrived, Frank assumed his task with enthusiasm. He made no attempt to protect the Jews, not even the productive elements of the population. On the contrary, Frank's greatest concern, which was shared by his closest aides, was that the Jews be the first to be transported to their deaths.[58] By that point Frank had given the SS a free hand in all matters related to the Jews. While it is true that at the end of 1942, following the phase of mass extermination in the Generalgouvernement, Frank expressed cynical remorse over the loss of an important source of labor, these sentiments were undoubtedly no more than ammunition in his war with the SS—on which he placed responsibility for the extermination—when the friction between the two parties reached the boiling point.

Two other agencies of the German bureaucracy's control of and intervention in the ghetto are worthy of examination: the Office of the *Kommissar* and the *Transferstelle*. The first man placed in charge of the Jewish residential quarter in Warsaw was Waldemar Schön, mentioned earlier as the one who planned the creation of the ghetto. Schön did not make much of an impression as *Kommissar*. In the middle of March 1941 he was relieved of his duties, and in the middle of May the post was turned over to another official in the administration of the Warsaw District, Heinz Auerswald, who continued to serve as *Kommissar* until the beginning of the deportation and liquidation of the Warsaw Jewish community and, formally speaking, until the beginning of 1943.

Auerswald was a member of the Nazi Party. From the outset of his term as *Kommissar*, he met with Czerniakow almost daily. On May 12, 1941, just before the ceremony installing him in the post, Auerswald told Czerniakow that his treatment of the community would be "objective, reasonable, without feelings of hostility." For whatever reason, the Nazi *Kommissar* felt it appropriate to declare these intentions to the representative of the Jews in the ghetto. As noted earlier, we have evidence that on occasion Czerniakow approached Auerswald on a personal basis and spoke to him in a way that deviated from the accepted manner of behavior between a Nazi official and a Jew. Thus, for example, on November 1, 1941, Czerniakow recorded in his diary:

> Auerswald maintains that a worker should labor at extracting bricks from the ruins all day for a bowl of soup. I remarked that he could also have a wife and children. Auerswald retorted that two bowls of soup might be made available. And how is he going to have his shoes repaired? "As for myself, although I could afford it, I purchased only one pair of late." I then permitted myself to observe that as a recently married man, Auerswald could not understand what it means to have a family.

When Czerniakow was fighting to save the detainees in the Jewish prison, he accepted Auerswald's proposal to release the prisoners in exchange for a ransom of furs. But when it turned out that the matter involved a good deal of bother, Auerswald commented "that he wouldn't have taken it upon himself had he known it would be so complicated. I told him," Czerniakow wrote, "that more than anything else, he should make his account with God."[59]

Auerswald brought about improvements in a number of spheres of ghetto life, though in some he actually made matters worse. The *Kommissar* was fanatic about having the ghetto sealed off from the "Aryan" side. He tried to smash the smuggling networks and effected changes in the map of the ghetto that forced thousands of people to abandon their apartments just to impede the smuggling. But even more than that, he fought against the seepage of Jews into the "Aryan" side of the city. Auerswald attempted to improve nutritional conditions in the ghetto, but he was concerned primarily with the workers and coordinated his efforts with the need to step up the mobilization of laborers and increase production. He demanded that the Jews be divided into categories according to the value of their labor and services on behalf of the Germans. He also cancelled the regulations limiting financial operations, thereby contributing somewhat to the revival of economic activity in the ghetto, and he instigated and fostered the program of the "shops."

There can be no doubt that Auerswald's industriousness and involvement in ghetto affairs earned him the reputation of an outstanding expert in Jewish affairs in Warsaw, and his firm hold on his position substantially hindered the access of the police and other particularistic forces to the ghetto. Auerswald was not an ambitious man who hoped to prove himself through his control over the ghetto. He probably understood that he could not perform his duty properly without a minimum of contact with Czerniakow and his aides.

One incident in the history of the ghetto is particularly revealing of Auerswald's personality and attitude toward ghetto affairs. On January 21, 1941, the Germans issued an order enumerating the punishments that would be meted out to a Jew caught on the "Aryan" side of the city without a permit: a fine of 1,000 zlotys and/or three months' imprisonment. Later that year, on October 15, Frank issued an order threatening the death sentence for illegal exit from the ghetto to the "Aryan" side of the city.[60] The Jews assumed that Auerswald had instigated the change to bolster his incessant war against smuggling. After two Jews had been shot while attempting to steal across the ghetto border, the death sentence was pronounced on eight other Jews, including six women. Auerswald demanded that the Jewish Police carry out the sentence, but in light of their refusal to serve as executioners, the task was turned over to the Polish Police.

The execution, which took place on November 17, 1941, within the ghetto prison, was a traumatic shock to the ghetto. The underground press angrily denounced the "barbaric murder,"[61] and Ringelblum wrote on November 22 that during the occupation the Jewish population had undergone various trials, but "all that pales before the fact that eight people were shot for crossing the threshold of the ghetto." The chronicler of the ghetto added that Auerswald was assumed to have inspired the idea of shooting people for committing the sin of leaving the ghetto, the same Auerswald "whom the Jews initially viewed as a friend and believed to be a fair man." Incidentally, as stated earlier, these drastic steps did not put an end to the smuggling. But the sobering sanctions and executions did curtail the smuggling carried out by individuals and the poor; i.e., they affected the most destitute class of the ghetto population.

Two days before the start of the mass deportation, Auerswald pretended to be totally ignorant of impending events, and in a conversation with Czerniakow he dealt with the usual agenda of the day. After more than a year of daily contact with the chairman of the *Judenrat*, he did not even see fit to warn Czerniakow for his personal safety or so much as hint at what awaited the Jews of Warsaw. The ghetto was afloat with rumors that Auerswald, and even local Gestapo men, wanted the ghetto to remain intact. It is likely that this was the *Kommissar*'s personal desire, and he had good reasons of self-interest for adopting such a position. But it is obvious that Auerswald's intervention—if, indeed, such an act occurred—had little effect on matters related to the "Final Solution."

The other German institution dealing exclusively with the ghetto was the *Transferstelle*,which was founded in December 1940, soon after the ghetto was closed. Its first director was Alexander Palfinger, a German official who had previously served in the German administration of the Lodz ghetto. Palfinger wanted affairs managed along the lines adopted in Lodz, preserving the hermetic segregation of the ghetto and smothering independent economic initiative. But experts in the Generalgouvernement evidently realized that his methods impeded the economic growth desired by the Germans and contradicted the aim of raising the level of employment and exploiting the professional work force in the ghetto. Therefore, Palfinger was replaced by Max Bischoff, an economist who had been involved in the field of banking in the Generalgouvernement. Bischoff took up his post at the same time as Auerswald and was officially subordinate to the *Kommissar*. He managed the *Transferstelle* in his own fashion, striving toward increased industrial development in the ghetto and displaying more moderation and flexibility than his predecessor. Yet the German and Polish firms that operated within or maintained commercial ties with the ghetto preferred not to work through the *Transferstelle*, evidently because its supervision of the nature and scope of their business deals was not to their advantage. Moreover, the *Transferstelle* charged a commission fee, which raised the cost of the enterprise in the ghetto. Instead, the companies did their best to forge direct links with economic circles in the ghetto, and it appears that Bischoff did not actively oppose such ties.

Bischoff employed about 120 people in the *Transferstelle*. He tried to have the food ration for the Jews increased, and one gets the impression that his actions were motivated more by rational thinking than by blind ideological hatred. It is possible that this was the reason for the rise in denunciations against Bischoff by informers, who accused him of maintaining unnaturally close relations with Jews.[62] (Nonetheless, Bischoff once commented to Czerniakow that, "like all Jews," he wasn't precise.)[63] As a rule, he was more pragmatic and open-minded than Auerswald, who became obsessed with minor details and the finer points of things. Bischoff continued to head the *Transferstelle* until the liquidation of the ghetto at the beginning of 1943.

**Welfare and Mutual Aid
in the Ghetto**

Many regarded the Ż.T.O.S. as a responsible public alternative to the *Judenrat*. Despite the fact that certain groups in the population received preferential treatment (e.g., party members and political activists, members of the youth movements and the intelligentsia, and religious officials), the Self-Help was renowned for its sensitivity to those elements of the population that were particularly vulnerable and severely deprived: refugees, children, and the starving. The Social Welfare Department of the *Judenrat* was supposed to be dealing with these same elements, but in practice the *Judenrat* channeled its aid primarily to other recipients: conscripts sent to labor camps, workers in the "shops," orphans, etc. For quite a while, the Self-Help and the *Judenrat* operated on separate and conflicting planes, because, with the growing impoverishment of the population, the monetary resources of the JDC steadily dwindled until they ran out, while the status and maneuverability of the *Judenrat* increased during the later stages of the ghetto. The result was that at the height of need in the ghetto, the soup kitchens and social-welfare facilities were heavily dependent upon the *Judenrat*, while the latter was not entirely free to define relief policy, since Auerswald intervened to dictate the recipients of aid. As noted earlier, Auerswald tended to write off the weakest elements of the population and argued that support should be given to the workers, especially those with the best chances of survival.

The Ż.T.O.S. operated on two levels—one legal and recognized, the other illegal. This dichotomy was also an accurate reflection of the general structure of the enterprise. Even the leaders of the Ż.T.O.S. simultaneously engaged in approved routine activities and outlawed clandestine work. Some of Ringelblum's aides were employed managing the network of building councils, which were legally recognized, while others, working beside them in the same office, were busy preparing material for the underground archive in the ghetto.[64] The directors of the JDC obtained a portion of their resources from legal sources, while, as we have seen, other funds were drummed up by secret manipulations, like taking loans from wealthy Jews on the promise that the money would be returned to them by the JDC after the war. The ghetto's relief kitchens provided portions of soup to the hungry, a service approved by the authorities. But clandestine classes were held in the same buildings that housed the soup kitchens for children, and the relief outlets maintained by the political parties were used for illegal assemblies and to operate the underground press. The headquarters of the youth movements and urban training communes were also camouflaged as soup kitchens, and the symbol of the Ż.T.O.S. was a very effective protective device. With the knowledge and consent of the authorities, the Toporol, a society to encourage agriculture among Jews, took charge of organizing groups of Jewish youngsters to do seasonal work on Polish farms. What the authorities did not know, however, was that these young workers included organized members of Socialist-Zionist youth movements who constituted substantial cells of the Jewish underground. Certain cultural performances were given in the ghetto with official sanction, but the Ż.T.O.S. also organized events on an illegal basis. Even mass rallies were held under the guise of such performances, and Ringelblum told of how he turned over the large hall in the Ż.T.O.S. building to Mordecai Anielewicz to convene five hundred members of his movement for a classic underground meeting.[65] Thus the image of the Ż.T.O.S. merged both the known and the secret, and as far as this "double life" was concerned, the institution was true to itself to the end. Giterman, one of the directors of the JDC in Poland and a central figure in the Ż.T.O.S., did not hesitate to appropriate funds to the Jewish Fighting Organization for the purpose of self-defense and arms procurement, and the public council of the Ż.T.O.S. would in time become the foundation of the Jewish National Council and the Coordinating Committee, the institutions that were the supreme public bodies of the armed resistance movement in the Warsaw ghetto.

A systematic description of the campaigns and daily activities of the Self-Help is beyond the scope of this book. As Ringelblum notes, at the outbreak of the war the JDC had a relatively small amount of money at its disposal—about 40,000 dollars. Its staff quickly obtained funds and material from abroad—from the Polish Food Commission, the Red Cross, and JDC centers in Europe, all of which contributed substantial amounts. During the first stage of the occupation, the activities of the Self-Help were of cardinal importance. The JDC report covering September 1939–October 1940 states that the relief campaign for the Passover holiday in the spring of 1940 extended aid to 250,000 people in Warsaw. This same report enumerates spheres of activity in which the JDC participated: (1) feeding the hungry; (2) housing the homeless; (3) clothing the poor; (4) fighting the epidemic and disease; (5) protecting children; (6) aid to the intelligentsia, religious officials, craftsmen, and workers; (7) constructive aid, individual aid, and family aid; (8) emigration; (9) ties with relatives abroad; (10) the organization of mutual aid among the Jews of Poland.

Most of the resources in the ghetto were devoted to coping with the widespread hunger. In April 1940, seventy-two soup kitchens were operational in Warsaw, but by August–September of that year the number had decreased to thirty-three or thirty-four. This process of decline continued throughout the existence of the ghetto, and it stemmed from the financial inadequacy of the JDC. The problem was that as the deprivation grew worse, the financial reserves of the JDC were steadily exhausted, as were the sources from which the organization had previously drawn funds. The directors of the JDC continued to run their race against mass starvation, but their role in solving the problems of hunger, disease, and neglect waned.[66]

According to the data in our possession, during 1940 the JDC spent a total of 7,500,000 zlotys in cash in aid to the Jews of Poland and another 7,235,000 on food and other necessities for a total of 14,735,000 zlotys. In the course of the first eight months of 1941, it put out a sum of 5,800,000 zlotys, and, according to estimates, it spent another 2,650,000 zlotys up to the end of that year for a total of about 8,000,000 zlotys in 1941. Thus in the year of the greatest hardship—1941—there was a decline in the financial aid passed on to the Jews of Poland. The attempts to drum up capital from internal Jewish sources likewise met with increasing difficulties because the swift impoverishment soon depleted the number of men of means as well.

The funds that were transferred to the JDC came from the organization's central office in Lisbon and through the *Reichsvereinigung der Juden in Deutschland* in Berlin, the Jewish community of Vienna, and the Jewish community of Prague. The accounts were operated by the clearing system, whereby 10 zlotys were given in exchange for every dollar. Foodstuffs were also transferred by means of the Polish Food Commission, the Polish Red Cross, and institutions for the relief of Polish Jewry operating abroad. The JDC purchased products in bulk in the neighboring states and had them sent to the Generalgouvernement. As a rule, the quantity transferred in 1941, the year of severe starvation in the Warsaw ghetto and alarming hunger in most of the ghettos of the Generalgouvernement, was less than in 1940. Until the declaration of war against the United States in December 1941, the JDC was able to benefit from its recognized status. Thus the question remains why the aid provided and distributed by means of the JDC did not reach much greater proportions in 1941. If the aid provided in that year had been more effective, a substantial number of deaths from starvation and the serious crisis that plagued the refugee hostels and soup kitchens might have been prevented, and the Jewish population might have reached a much higher level of physical and psychological immunity as it approached the period of the ultimate trial—the "Final Solution."[67]

During the later phases of the ghetto's existence, the *Judenrat* became increasingly influential in the field of social relief. The *Judenrat* placed emphasis on vocational training and, indeed, scored impressive achievements in this area. As *Gazeta Żydowska* reported on August 25,

1941, four hundred people were studying in vocational-training courses organized by the *Judenrat*.[68] The German regime not only authorized these courses but viewed them as a contribution to the creation of a much-desired reserve of skilled workers. Many youths, especially young men, enrolled in the courses not only to acquire a skill but as a form of official protection against conscription for forced labor. As noted earlier, the courses conducted under the aegis of the *Judenrat* were also vehicles for a form and level of education that contradicted the aims of the Nazi regime. They included a course in medicine by Professor Hirszfeld geared to the level of a professional school of medicine and a university-level course in chemistry.[69]

The Ż.T.O.S. was forced to foster the cooperation of the *Judenrat*, because it could no longer respond to the urgent needs of the community on its own. When the Ż.T.O.S. was effecting drastic cutbacks in the scope of its operation, an opportunity opened for the *Judenrat* to infiltrate the aid enterprise. On June 20, 1941, the official newspaper announced in prominent type that thanks to the aid of the *Kommissar*, a large quantity of products had been obtained to serve as the basic ingredients for one hundred thousand portions of soup to be distributed over a number of months' time.[70] A committee headed by Czerniakow and composed of Wielikowski and Winter, among others, was to handle the logistics of the campaign. Some of the Ż.T.O.S. soup kitchens that had been closed because of the severe shortage of ingredients were reopened under the patronage of the *Judenrat*. In July 1941 it was reported that fifty-six soup kitchens for adults and thirty-five for children were in operation.

The contrast between the Ż.T.O.S. and the *Judenrat* was not limited to their different criteria in determining the recipients of aid and how to use the limited funds available. It was also reflected in their very outlooks toward their respective means of operation. The *Judenrat* looked upon relief as essentially a philanthropic and public-relations activity, while the Ż.T.O.S. placed its emphasis on the aspect of mutual responsibility and making the public an equal partner in the relief scheme. Among the organs united in the framework of the *Judenrat's* Public Affairs Department, special importance was ascribed to the building councils, which were discussed earlier. Another body founded and operated by the Public Affairs Department comprised the societies of émigrés from other cities and towns who had settled in Warsaw, similar to *Landsmanschaften* (C.K.U.—*Centralna Komisja Uchodźców*), whose role was to "keep the faith," as it were, with the most desperate of the refugees. These forms of grass-roots or popularly oriented frameworks, especially the building councils, played a central role in the voluntary public-welfare program directed by the Ż.T.O.S. Through its initiative a corps of volunteers was organized to take part in the care, organization, and maintenance of the refugee hostels and other institutions established for the needy. The aid, financial and otherwise, provided to the most desperate cases by selected apartment houses fell off in the course of time, until it ceased altogether. Jewish apartment buildings that had been capable of contributing some of the little they had before the establishment of the ghetto or during the first few months of its existence eventually found themselves unable to cope with the poverty that had overtaken them.

The Ż.T.O.S. enterprise run by the JDC and other broad-based public institutions was a daring and industrious operation. Its personnel did not limit themselves to the conventional systems employed in the past but displayed resourcefulness and diligence in obtaining funds and food despite the ghetto's state of isolation. And just as the means of acquiring resources were tailored to the unprecedented conditions, the programs of distribution and aid were marked by originality and imagination. It goes without saying that even the combined activities of the Ż.T.O.S. and the *Judenrat* were unable to cope with the desperate deprivation. Nonetheless, to focus exclusively on the magnitude of the hunger and death and ignore the stubborn and incessant struggle against them would be a distortion of history. It would not be an exaggeration to state that in Jewish Warsaw, where almost one hundred thousand victims succumbed to death, mostly from starvation and disease, from the beginning of the war until July 1942, a similar or perhaps even greater number prevailed until that fatal date, owing largely or decisively to the dedicated aid of the corps of relief workers fielded by the various branches of the Ż.T.O.S., the building councils, and the *Judenrat*. The occupation regime, which was rife with competition between opposing forces, was outwitted by the Jews, who used wisdom and guile to filter a modicum of relief through the cracks in the bureaucracy.

We are not aware of any Polish relief organization that aided the Jews during the period of starvation, disease, and the struggle against them. Polish aid was administered through the Caritas Society (a Catholic relief agency), which only catered to those Christians forced into the ghetto by the Nazi racial laws. There were also sporadic instances of Polish aid to personal friends and loyalists, but one cannot cite a massive and organized campaign of Polish aid to the persecuted and starving Jewish masses or to particularly vulnerable elements—members of the intelligentsia, refugees, or children.

**Daily Life in the
Warsaw Ghetto**

The ghetto's narrow streets offered no relief from the incredible overcrowding in the apartment buildings. Kaplan's diary contains a description of the traffic on Karmelicka Street, an artery that connected two sections of the ghetto: "A sea of thousands of heads floods the entire street from end to end. Pushing one's way through the great throng that flows by like the waves in a tempest is like trying to part the waters of the Red Sea."[71] Accompanying the crush of mobile blocks of humanity was the tumult of the crowd.

There were only a few lonely trees on the ghetto's caged-in streets. All the parks and gardens had been zoned out of the confines of the area, including those which had formerly been considered part of the Jewish quarter. The authorities had repeatedly promised Czerniakow that Krasinskich Park, a garden bordering on the streets of the ghetto, would be included within the Jewish quarter, but the commitments (which were made on various occasions) were never fulfilled. Writings that have survived from the ghetto contain parents' attempts to illustrate for their toddlers the meaning of a broad expanse, wide-open skies, and a forest.

On some of the ghetto's streets, open trade of anything that came to hand was carried on (this kind of barter did not take place in stores or special locations). People of all ages stood on the sidewalks hawking the belongings they held in their hands: clothing, housewares, books—anything that could be exchanged for a crust of bread. The barter added noise and tension to the throbbing pulse of the streets. Added to the hucksters who hauled out their remaining belongings in the hope of converting them into enough food for a day or so were the thousands of beggars who stood in the streets or lay propped up against the houses. For the most part the community of beggars consisted of whole families, parents and children alike, wrapped in worn blankets, each bawling out his entreaty in a different pitch of voice. The appearance of refugees and the indigent on the streets was evidently motivated by an impulse to bring their outcry into the open in the dim hope that in public, support and salvation might come out of the crowd. The number of beggars decreased in time, as only a few members remained of entire families. At a later stage corpses covered with newspapers began to appear beside the reclining beggars. These victims of starvation and disease had collapsed on the streets or had been cast onto the sidewalk by people who feared that the building in which they had died would be marked as a breeding ground of contagious disease. The sight of the corpses lying in the streets evidently affected the Germans, for Governor Fischer commented to Czerniakow that "the corpses lying in the streets create a very bad impression," and "the corpses must be cleared away quickly."[72] Thereafter, members of the *Hevre Kaddisha* (Burial Society) and the police would patrol each morning and remove the bodies that had piled up overnight.

Even though the ghetto adopted the slogan "all are equal," some people were "more equal" than others, and this imbalance could be felt on the streets as well. Some streets, such as Sienna and Chłodna, were considered well-to-do sections. The apartments there were larger, the congestion lighter, and, above all, the people relatively well fed. These streets were the address of the assimilated Jews who had been uprooted from the more exclusive neighborhoods of the capital and rich Jews who had managed to hold on to a portion of their wealth. As noted earlier, the most abhorrent and provocative inequality was apparent in the leisure and entertainment spots—cafés, nightclubs, restaurants, buffets—where the members of the new elite indulged themselves to the point of stupor. The "aristocracy" of smugglers, members of the "Thirteen" and the police, certain members of the *Judenrat*, and sometimes even Poles and Germans were counted among these bands. In April 1941 Ringelblum wrote that there were sixty-one such places of entertainment in the ghetto.[73] The April 11, 1941, issue of *Gazeta Żydowska* carried an advertisement for a café called Tira that promised "a concert every day," "tasty luncheons and portions of lamb," and "a garden by the café," while the very same issue reported drily that "seven people were lost [read: died of starvation]."[74] Grumblings of protest and bitterness over these manifestations of "dancing among the corpses" can be found in the ghetto diaries and in the underground press.

After the war, various writers who tried to come to terms with the disparities and contrasts within Jewish society in the ghetto resorted to such phrases as "class conflicts in the Warsaw ghetto," "social oppression by the *Judenrat*," or "class roots."[75] It is understandable that these concepts were proposed by people who had lived through the nightmare of the ghetto and whose rage and deprivation had clouded their retrospective vision. But it is difficult to understand how supposedly objective authors of historical works can employ terminology and categories borrowed from the life of a normal society to illustrate the experience of a deformed society suffering under relentless stress.

It is pertinent to ask why the starved masses resigned themselves to the demonstrations of debauchery and blatant waste and did not rebel. Emmanuel Ringelblum attempts to provide a rationale for this astonishing situation:

> One of the questions that arouses much interest is the passivity of the Jewish masses who succumb to death with a hushed sigh. Why do they all

remain silent? Why do fathers, mothers, all the children die without any protest? Why hasn't the prospect that threatened the public a year ago [i.e., rampant theft and plunder, which, incidentally, motivated the building councils to purchase food for their impoverished tenants] come to pass? There are many answers to this question: the occupation regime has cast such a heavy shadow of dread that people are afraid to lift their heads for fear of mass terror in response to any outburst by the starving masses. And that is why some of those who are conscious and alert remain silent and passive and do not create an uproar in the ghetto. There is also another reason: a goodly number of the poor who exercised initiative managed to get by somehow. The smuggling provides a means of subsistence for thousands of porters. The "shops" and the orders from the German authorities provide job opportunities for a substantial portion of the laborers and craftsmen. A section of the active proletarian element engages in street trade (the sale of bread brings in a profit of 25 pennies per kilo). So there remains the passive and hopeless portion that goes to its death in silence.[76]

Ringelblum also cites the fact that the Jewish Police had begun to beat people, which was a further restraining force. But one nonetheless has the impression that the principal reason for the passivity is to be found in another quarter, which Ringelblum does not sufficiently explore. Death from starvation was a gradual process. Those who were doomed to starve to death constituted about half of the ghetto's total population. But at no time during the existence of the ghetto did the entire public find itself in the same situation. Some had died, another sector was already starving, while a larger portion was destined to die within a month or two but cherished the hope that in the time left to them the coveted salvation would would arrive. Moreover, that portion of the population already in the grip of death had sunk below the ability to organize, act, or even bring itself to the point of a spontaneous outburst.

The truth is that there was a way for people in the ghetto to let out their feelings, a kind of "outburst" that was rather common. I am referring to the phenomenon of the "snatchers," usually young people dressed in rags who would ambush women leaving stores with baskets of food in their hands, especially bread. The moment such a "snatcher" saw the bread, he would accost the woman, grab the bread out of the basket or bag, and dig his teeth into it before the woman even had a chance to react. The crowd that gathered around might try to wrench the food out of his grip or beat him, but the "snatcher" was oblivious to what was going on around him and went on wolfing down the food. The nature of these individual outbursts is proof, perhaps, that the starving were unable to organize and operate in a broader and more effective fashion.

Crime was hardly a widespread phenomenon in the ghetto, however. Throughout the existence of the ghetto, until the mass deportation, there was not a single case of murder inside the walls. The author of one memoir, S. Szymkowicz, wrote that "it should be noted and stressed to the credit of the Jews that despite the starvation, cold, absence of law, and total anarchy, during [the ghetto's] entire existence there were no murders or serious crimes."[77] There were, however, instances of cannibalism in the ghetto, such as the case of the mother who fed off her daughter's corpse, and this is further testimony to the insanity caused by the extreme hunger.

As to the character of the ghetto family and the nature of relations within the family unit, it is difficult to trace any one trend. The Jewish family was renowned for its close ties and the devotion of parents to their offspring, and this trait continued to be prominent in the ghetto. Many memoirs testify to the devotion of mothers and fathers who deprived themselves in order to feed their children. But the opposite was also true. The hunger and incessant stress also induced the undermining and disintegration of the family. There is evidence of slackening ties within the framework of the extended family. As already described, many children became the sole supporters of an entire family. Sometimes a child who had not yet reached adolescence was responsible for feeding his younger brothers and sisters. But there were also examples of youngsters organizing into wild street gangs, abandoning their parents' homes, and attempting to obtain food and subsist in any way they could.

Together with starvation, infectious diseases—especially typhus fever—were the bane of the ghetto. Beginning in April 1941 there was a serious recurrence of typhus. In the course of that year, 14,661 cases were reported, but for all practical purposes even this official figure is far from exact, and it is assumed to have represented only 25 to 30 percent of the actual number of cases (some estimates go as high as over 100,000 cases). The victims and their relatives were reluctant to report the illness for fear of the sanctions that were likely to descend on the entire apartment building. In 1940, 10 percent of those infected with typhus fever died of the disease; in 1941 it is estimated that the death rate reached 20 percent. The main obstacle to fighting the epidemic was not a shortage of doctors, however. There were more doctors per capita in the ghetto than on the "Aryan" side of the city, and it is believed that their number was as high as 800. But the shortage of injections, drugs, and soap and the lack of proper hospitalization facilities made effective medical treatment impossible. The *Judenrat* established a Public Health Department, which quickly trained a cadre of workers who fought with dedication against some of the causes of the disease. For the most part, the results were negligible because of the conditions in the ghetto and the absence of proper facilities. But around June 1942, not long before the mass deportation began, the curve declined and there were indications that the epidemic was being contained.[78]

The population was also burdened by other diseases related to conditions in the ghetto. Noteworthy among them was a rise in the incidence of tuberculosis and intestinal diseases. Even hunger manifested itself as a kind of mass disease that could be distinguished by clinical symptoms. On the initiative of Dr. Joseph Milejkowski, a group of ghetto doctors began scientific research into the clinical aspects of starvation. The external symptoms of the illness were complete emaciation, which left only dry skin stretched over a skeleton, or, on the other hand, a diseased tumescence, characterized by a kind of doughiness of the face and legs.

The lifestyle of the ghetto gave rise to a number of phenomena that were new to the area and unique to the atmosphere within the walls. For example, there was a "promenade" in the ghetto that attracted groups of young strollers, and special courtyards were outfitted with chairs and established as spots for sun-bathing. Skits and satires on daily life were performed in the ghetto's theaters, and there was also a kind of folklore of the ghetto—popular heroes, special mottoes, jokes about the state of affairs, and even a special ghetto slang. "Ghetto" songs were sung, and a substantial corpus of prose and poetry (much of which has been preserved) was written by veteran artists and novices alike. The social gatherings of tenants of all ages, set up by the building councils, also contributed to the special atmosphere of life in the ghetto. During a later period, this atmosphere penetrated the "shops" as well.

The residents of the ghetto tried to maintain contact with relatives and friends abroad by various means. As stated earlier, letters sent abroad could be written only in Polish or German, and the Nazis forbade the dispatch of photographs, crossword puzzles, and the like. In spite of these restrictions, those people who sent postcards (which were permitted) succeeded in incorporating hints about their condition. One method was to mention the names of relatives and friends who were long dead to report the death of loved ones, while suggesting that a similar fate awaited all. The correspondents also developed a kind of code by using forms of Hebrew or Yiddish words as names, e.g., L. Elefowitz to denote thirty thousand Jews (*L* standing for the Hebrew letter *lamed*, which is equal to thirty; *elef* being the Hebrew word for "thousand"), or using the names of well-known people or mutual acquaintances living in various places to signify geographic areas. More generalized information was also transmitted, although it was necessary to forsake exactitude as well as explanations. Such information was included in letters sent by representatives of the political parties and youth movements, and it even found its way into personal letters. As a rule, Jews were allowed to send letters within the Generalgouvernement, to states under the control and political influence of the Reich, and to neutral countries. In December 1940–January 1941 the postal services within the ghetto were turned over to the *Judenrat*, and from January to July 1942, between 10,000 and 13,000 letters were mailed out of the ghetto every month.

The parcels that arrived from abroad were of special importance to the residents of the ghetto, since these packages were one of their means of survival.[79] It can be assumed, however, that the majority of the packages that reached the ghetto were not tailored to aid people in severe distress. Packages containing up to four and a half pounds of food arrived through the mails from locations both within the Generalgouvernement and abroad. The small parcels sent from locations within the occupied territories usually contained flour, bread, cooking fats, grains, etc., while packages that came from abroad, particularly from neutral countries, were filled with coffee, chocolate, rice, sardines, condensed milk, etc. The latter were items of great value in the ghetto and were usually bartered for quantities of more basic foodstuffs. Until June 1941 an abundance of such food parcels was sent from the eastern territories of Poland annexed by the Soviet Union, but after the outbreak of the Soviet-German war, this source of relief was blocked. It is estimated that from December 1940 to March 1941 the parcels sent from Soviet-occupied territory constituted about 84 percent of all the parcels that arrived from abroad. The other countries from which substantial amounts of food were sent were Switzerland, Sweden, Portugal, and Rumania. The parcels sent to the Warsaw ghetto from other locations within the Generalgouvernement were considered smuggled goods, and the post office was ordered not to accept packages from Jews in the Generalgouvernement addressed to the ghetto. Yet this regulation did not substantially reduce the number of parcels. The Germans kept track of the flow of parcels into the ghetto, and the *Kommissar* issued an order to take note of whether a particularly large number of parcels was being sent to any one person or persons at a specific address. An abundance of packages sent to a specific address served as a pretext for the authorities to confiscate the goods, and during certain months literally thousands of packages were indeed seized.[80] Overall, the flow of parcels into the ghetto was qualitatively significant, and in the peak month—June 1941—113,006 parcels were delivered to ghetto residents.

There were only a few telephones in the ghetto, mostly in the headquarters of various institutions and industrial plants, although people holding important positions and certain professionals, such as doctors, were allowed to have phones in their apartments. The telephone was valuable as an instrument of communication with Poles on the "Aryan" side of the city and later with Jews who had secretly crossed to the "Aryan" side and gone into hiding there.

The ghetto landscape boasted one building that, up until a certain point, served as a meeting place for Poles and Jews. This was the large courthouse with one entrance on Leszno Street, on the ghetto's border, and another within the Polish quarter. With some effort it was possible to get permission to enter the building, and in its corridors one could confer briefly with a Polish acquaintance. This system provided one opportunity to negotiate smuggling deals and maintain liaisons with interested Polish parties.

The ghetto received its water and electricity supply from the Central Municipal Service. Jews were also obliged to pay certain taxes, which were collected by Polish assessors. Thus a number of Polish officials and technicians were permitted to enter the ghetto on behalf of the Polish agencies and departments that operated within the walls. No small number of them behaved in a capricious and despicable manner. For example, the Jews were compelled to pay long-standing debts that had been incurred on apartments long before they had moved into them. The electricity supply was cut off from buildings in the ghetto for extended periods of time. It operated only during certain hours, and special payments were demanded of the Jews for the right to electric lighting. On the other hand, many of the Poles who entered the ghetto in their official capacities engaged in smuggling, and there were some who helped ghetto residents maintain communication with their friends on the "Aryan" side of the city.

Alongside the hunger and disease, cold was a formidable hardship in the ghetto, since an emaciated body requires a warmer environment and is particularly vulnerable to frostbite. Coal and coal dust were evidently distributed in the ghetto, but the cost of these fuels on the free market was so prohibitive that few were able to buy them. Only the privileged and well connected regularly benefited from the meager and sporadic distribution of coal and coal dust, and heating fuels practically never reached those who needed them the most. Cold and weakness forced indigent families to wrap themselves in quilts and blankets day and night, sleep in their clothing, and otherwise try to protect themselves from the bitter weather. As a result, infection spread, and the lice that carried the deadly typhus fever flourished.

On December 24, 1941, the commander of the Security Police and Security Services in the Generalgouvernement, Karl A. Schöngart, issued an order in Himmler's name to the commander of the SS and the police in the Warsaw District requiring all the furs belonging to Jews to be confiscated immediately.[81] Schöngart did not give any explanation for the confiscations, but his order detailed how to carry out the fumigation process to ensure that the furs were free of lice. The reason for the order was related to the situation on the Russian front and the urgent need to outfit the troops with warm clothing (a problem that had not been properly anticipated by the *Wehrmacht*). The Germans demanded not only whole furs and fur coats but neck pieces and hats — i.e., any piece of fur in Jewish hands. The edict regarding the fur pieces was issued at the height of winter and thus aggravated the hardship of the Jews.

Fur was also the object of a lively trade in the ghetto, and Poles could acquire fur goods for pennies. There were distinct trends in the dress of the ghetto residents. Most people were shabbily dressed, and many, having sold their valuable items of clothing, were left with only rags. Common among the outfits were clothes made out of blankets. The wealthy Jews, especially those who had amassed fortunes during the war, wore shiny boots. Boots, as Ringelblum pointed out, had become a symbol of power in the ghetto.[82] Another sign of privilege was the special armband. In addition and in distinction to the regular "Jewish armband," colored armbands with appropriate emblems were worn not only by the Jewish Police and the "Thirteen" but by various categories of people: doctors, *Judenrat* staff, personnel of the distribution network, first-aid workers, and social-welfare staff. The double armbands served as a measure of protection against assault in the streets. Moreover, under a regime in which everything was based upon hierarchy and anyone who boasted any status whatsoever appeared in uniform, the additional armband was taken as a sign of privileged position and special rights.[83]

Just before the mass deportation began, a group of German scriptwriters and cameramen arrived in the ghetto and began preparing a film on the life of the Jews there. In addition to capturing scenes of street life, they staged situations that were compatible with the ideological tenets of National Socialism and their propaganda goals. The nature of these faked scenes is elaborated in an entry in Abraham Levin's diary dated May 13, 1942:

> Yesterday, with the help of Jewish policemen, the Germans abducted off the streets, and especially from 38 Dzielna Street, Jewish girls, young and old women, and bearded and clean-shaven men. Two large cars drew up to the entrance to the building carrying Germans — pilots, S.S. men, and members of other units — alongside a smaller car with officers inside.

First the girls were photographed. By the way, they were particularly interested in well or even elegantly dressed girls and women. Then they
moved all the Jews to the bathhouse located in the same courtyard. They
photographed the women inside. Afterward they forced all the men and
women to strip naked and German officers arranged the Jews in couples,
but they paired off a young girl with a bearded man and a young man with
an elderly woman. Then they forced the couples to come into sexual contact. This scene (one must assume that the Jews were only posing) was
filmed by special cameras brought along and set up for the purpose. There
were about 200 Hitlerites present.[84]

As we know, the film that was made by using these tactics was locked
away in an archive and never presented to the public. In spite of their
ruse in staging the scene, the Germans presumably felt that this portrayal of the ghetto was too shocking to screen before any viewer at all.
The filmed material, or perhaps only part of it, was found after the war
and is now in our hands.

No catalog of emphatic descriptions and generalizations can summarize life in the ghetto. It is clear that the Jewish public was subject to
conditions of unprecedented stress, conditions that were the antithesis
of values, concepts, and mores generally accepted in the past. The
hermetic isolation from human society at large also influenced the quality of life. The Jews of Warsaw felt segregated and abandoned, and the
motivations that usually direct a group that strives to be counted among
the components of a standard human society disintegrated completely
in the ghetto. There is deep significance to the fact that the Jews were
uncertain of what awaited them at the hands of the Nazis. Their sense
of distress and despair had two aspects. The edicts followed one after
the other and left the public in a state of continuous anxiety, which left
no time or strength to concentrate on or analyze affairs from a broad
and forward-looking perspective. Faced with the hail of regulations and
prohibitions, the Jews were preoccupied with only one thought: Where
will it all end? Will the Jews have the strength to bear up under the
shortages and pressures for an extended period? How long will the war
last, and what are the Germans ultimately intending to do?

The portrait of Jewish public life is likewise not uniform.
Alongside the work of welfare organizations and donations of charity
were the phenomena of apathy and hedonism. A strong underground
coexisted with the cancer of the "Thirteen." Stanisław Adler attempted
to find a common denominator to define the character of the Jewish
public by citing unique traits that came to the fore in the ghetto. It
cannot be stated unequivocally that his characterization is accurate in all
respects, but it does illuminate important features of ghetto society:
"The Jews know how to complain, make themselves miserable, and

grow angrier than any other people; but that is only during normal times. In times of cataclysm, they generate impressive inner resources of tranquility, faith, and self-possession. From generation to generation, Jewish families foster the strength to prevail in times of communal tragedy."[85]

PART TWO

Underground

Chapter Four
The Political Underground in the Warsaw Ghetto

Fundamental Changes at the Beginning of the Occupation During the interwar years, the Jewish community of Poland held a focal position among the dispersed Jewish people. Polish Jewry had achieved this status for a number of reasons. With the advent of World War I and the Russian Revolution, the masses of Russian Jewry had been cut off from the Jewish people at large, leaving Polish Jewry as the largest community of its kind in Europe. It was also a community at once anchored in Jewish tradition and experiencing the throes of increasingly intense sociopolitical ferment. During this period Polish Jewry stood out for both its nationalist-Jewish activities and its struggle for political and cultural rights in the Polish state.

The question before us here is what actually happened to the social-organizational framework or skeleton of Polish Jewry during the Holocaust. What became of the various political parties, the cultural and athletic organizations, the youth movements, and the institutions that were bubbling with life and activity during the interwar period? This question relates first and foremost to the Jews of Warsaw, for it was in the capital that the headquarters of the political organizations and cultural institutions were located and the leaders of the various divisions of the Jewish community made their homes.

The German occupation regime did not issue special regulations forbidding the Jews to organize politically. In fact, the legislative situation in the Generalgovernment as a whole remained vague throughout its existence.[1] The official edict closing down societies and organizations of a political, military, or academic nature was published only on July 23, 1940.[2] But before this date, the occupation regime had already established an atmosphere of repression and terror, in which no independent political or social body dared to exist openly. Neither freedom of the press nor nationalist-oriented education was permitted.

The first guidelines regarding the national status of the Poles in the Generalgouvernement were established during a conversation between Hitler and the Commander in Chief of the *Wehrmacht* (Chief OKW): "It is imperative to prevent the Polish intelligentsia from rising to the echelon of leadership. Only a low standard of living must be allowed there. We only wish to draw manpower from there. Poles must be mobilized to aid in managing the affairs of the country, but the creation of nationalist cells must not be allowed."[3]

On October 31, 1939, a high-ranking consultation, in which Goebbels and Hans Frank took part, was held in Lodz in order to outline a policy regarding the cultural and spiritual life of the Poles. At the opening of the meeting, Frank made it clear that "the Poles must be allowed to study, but only to the extent that they prove to themselves that as a nation they have no prospects whatsoever."[4] Goebbels countered that "all Polish systems of transmitting information must be destroyed. They don't need radios. We must permit them only newspapers of an informative nature, in no case a press that represents points of view." According to Frank, "it is necessary constantly to keep an eye out for the direction in which Polish nationalism seeks an outlet. Any expression of nationalism must be smothered in its own hostility."[5]

The trends in Nazi thinking regarding the national image of the Poles and the development of their cultural life in occupied Poland are important to our study, because the Jews assumed that if the German policy toward the Poles was oppressive, it stood to reason that any activity in the realm of politics and culture among the Jews would be suppressed all the more stringently. For wherever the German regime was strict with the Poles, it was countless times more severe with the Jews.

The intentions and terrorist methods of the occupation regime were the dominant factor that paralyzed open and widespread political and propaganda activity among the Jewish public. But there were also other factors, which stemmed from developments and trends within the Jewish community itself. The leading factor from this perspective was the disappearance of the group of men who led the Polish Jewish community. At the outbreak of the war, during the fighting, and in the first months of the occupation, the top echelon of Jewish public and political leaders left Warsaw and German-occupied Poland altogether. Among those who departed were Moshe Kleinbaum (Sneh), Apolinary

Hartglas, Moshe Kerner, all of the General Zionists; Henryk Ehrlich and Victor Alter, Bund leaders; Anshel Reiss and Abraham Bialopolski of Po'alei Zion Z.S.; Zerah Warhaftig and Aaron Weiss of Mizrachi; Yitzhak Leib and Nathan Buksbaum of Left Po'alei Zion; Yitzhak Meir Levin of Agudat Israel; and Menahem Begin, who was at that time the young leader of Betar but already stood out as a rising star in the Revisionist camp. In addition, among those who left during the fighting around Warsaw were the heads and older members of the youth movements. However, in contrast to the party activists, who never returned to Warsaw or German-occupied Poland and sought refuge in the Soviet Union or the free world or immigrated to Palestine, some of the leaders of the youth movements were sent back to Poland by their movements' central leadership, out of the irrepressible conviction that members of these movements, and Jewish youth as a whole, must not be abandoned without direction at a time of trial.[6] Among those who returned on orders from the youth movements were Mordecai Anielewicz, Yitzhak Zuckerman, Yosef Kaplan, and Zivia Lubetkin, all of whom were destined to stand at the head of the armed resistance movement and the uprising in Warsaw.

There can be no doubt that the departure of the elite leadership of Polish Jewry, which included communal leaders and the representatives of the Jewish public in Polish institutions, left its mark on the image and bearing of the Polish Jewish community throughout the period. In the course of time, political activists in the underground and heads of the youth movements were to cite this retreat as a cause of confusion and weakness. In his memoirs, composed while in hiding on the "Aryan" side of Warsaw, Hirsch Berlinski, a member of Left Po'alei Zion, described the community's loss of direction and asked: "And the Jewish political parties? The best elements left for distant lands. Second- and third-echelon leaders remained, and to our regret the war has also left its mark on them."[7] At the end of 1941, Ringelblum recorded that "the departure of the leaders of institutions and enterprises who left during a difficult hour and abandoned everything behind them is often a subject of debate."[8]

Another cause of the isolation and weakness in political life was bound up with the surprise, shock, and disintegration that came in the wake of the new situation. Such astonishment and loss of balance were not peculiar to the Jews. We have already noted that the members of the Polish government and state institutions fled like thieves in the night without leaving anyone to lead and direct the public. It is therefore understandable that the swift defeat of the Polish forces surprised the Jewish bodies as well, and there was no actual preparation or contingency plan or consideration of who would be charged with responsibility for conducting affairs in the event that Poland were conquered. It is likely that the very dread of such a somber prospect triggered a psychological denial of its likelihood and prevented those in responsible positions from considering its consequences soon enough.

The departure of the recognized Jewish leadership affected another sphere, whose importance was felt when the various elements in the Jewish underground sought to establish communication with the Polish underground. Among the leaders who fled were a number of prominent representatives of Polish Jewry in the *Sejm* and other state bodies. The absence of these experienced and legitimate representatives made the initiation and maintenance of contact with the Poles all the more difficult. In addition, with the loss of their legal status, the political parties and organizations were deprived of the instruments that enable public bodies to function in a modern society — newspapers, meeting halls, ties with other centers within the country and abroad.

The Political Underground in the Ghetto

Despite this situation, the activity of the existing political bodies and organizations was not halted entirely or for long. The first impetus toward renewed organization on a broader scale came from the Self-Help. As early as the end of October or the beginning of November 1939, Emmanuel Ringelblum convened a meeting of party activists in his office. His intent was not to hold a political meeting—i.e., an assembly to exchange views on the political situation—but rather to rouse and mobilize previously organized and responsible sectors of the public in order to activate the welfare campaigns so urgently needed for the refugees and homeless in Warsaw.

The first *Judenrat* also contained a good number of members who were former party activists, and at a later stage the composition of the *Judenrat* still included past representatives of political parties. Yet the majority of the party representatives invited to constitute the *Judenrat* at the time of its establishment were not mandated by any authoritative body or framework. When Czerniakow began to compose the *Judenrat*, he turned to a group of people known to him as representative figures of party establishments. It appears that most of them did not request a mandate from any authority whatsoever, and the decision on whether or not they should join the *Judenrat* was entirely a personal one. As a result, those *Judenrat* members who were chosen because of their association with a political party (with the exception of the member from the Bund) no longer viewed themselves as representatives of the parties, would not have to activate their former colleagues in connection with their work for the *Judenrat*, and were not required to report to a forum of superiors or to a consituency on their plans and decisions.

From the very first meeting initiated by Ringelblum, the close relationship continued between the JDC, the Self-Help, and the political
parties. In November–December 1939, the political cells of the various
bodies began to consolidate. In addition to caring for an inner circle of
their own party members, the party activists participated in the general
welfare operation directed by the Coordinating Committee of the welfare institutions and the JDC. Shmuel Zygielbojm noted in his journal
covering the early period of occupation: "People suddenly turned up in
thousands of Jewish apartments in Warsaw and explained that they had
been sent by the 'underground council.' They asked every family
whether any tragedy had befallen its members, whether any special help
is needed, like a doctor or drugs, and the like. They left behind finan-
cail aid in every apartment. The sum depended upon the size and condition of the family. . . ."9

Throughout the phases of the occupation and the ghetto, up until
the mass deportations, mutual aid and social welfare were the central
task of the parties in the underground. They extended aid to and cared
first and foremost for their own comrades, yet they also tried to formulate an aid policy that would provide relief to the most vulnerable
elements of the population. The establishment of guidelines and management of this activity were left in the hands of the council that consolidated alongside the Self-Help and included the party representatives, a group that should be viewed as the leadership of the parties in
the underground.

Ringelblum explained the nature of the change in relations and
cooperation among the various people charged with political tasks:

> The war confronted Jewish public circles with crucial questions. It was
> imperative to abandon the prewar political relationships and forge a united
> front from left to right: Hitler's campaign against the Jewish population
> bore the stamp of annihilation. It was directed against all strata and classes
> of Jewish society. For Hitlerism, there was no difference between a
> Zionist and a Bundist; both were hated to the same degree. It wanted to
> destroy them both. Thus it was necessary to define the course of struggle
> for the Jewish public. . . . The institution of consultation by all the parties
> across the political spectrum was not defined by name, but it became a
> permanent body whose opinion was solicited by the *Judenrat*, the Self-
> Help, and more than once by the community as well.10

The involvement of the party representatives in the relief and welfare operations placed the Self-Help on a broad public footing. At the
same time, the work of the party activists was marked by a blatant flaw,
which aroused disgruntlement and bitterness: the parties and their representatives were a classic example of an interest group, and they gave
priority to the needs of their own members and supporters.

In the course of time, a debate arose within the parties over whether it was sufficient to organize relief and welfare campaigns or whether the parties in the underground were not indeed charged with missions of another nature. In an issue published at the end of 1940, the underground newspaper of Po'alei Zion Z.S., *Bafrayung* (*Liberation*), described the dilemma and debate that had arisen within that party:

> The course of our work has often aroused debate among the comrades. In one discussion, the question under consideration was: What are our tasks at this time? What must our role be during this war? And there were two answers. Some members believed that we must confine our attention to economic problems, providing welfare to the majority of the members, who are in difficult straits, seeking out means to aid them, and often ensuring that a slice of bread and a bowl of soup will be available to those in need. In their opinion, all our efforts must be channeled in that direction, and no other activities should be initiated. Another sector claimed that the goal of a movement like ours is not to become a charity institution catering to the welfare of individuals. In their opinion, such a role was never delegated to us or to movements like ours, and neither must we deal with such matters today, even though circumstances have changed. We must concentrate on cultural activities, establishing organized cells, holding frequent meetings, expanding our propaganda activities, and taking advantage of this period to reinforce from within.
>
> If, a few months ago, this kind of discussion was pertinent, today, in light of the present situation and after the experience of more than a year, it is once again totally irrelevant. Life has stricken this question off the agenda. All the comrades were right: Activity is going on in both directions simultaneously, and the two viewpoints have been fused into one.[11]

It is clear, therefore, that a portion of the party members were not prepared to view aid and welfare as the be all and end all of their activities, despite the circumstances of the times. In addition to material aid, the parties in the underground concentrated on: (1) meetings and propaganda activities among groups associated with a specific faction; (2) the clandestine publication of newspapers; and (3) a broader scope of cultural activities, usually in conjunction with other parties and bodies of a similar nature, and aimed at the general public.

The nature of the relief and the means of distributing the meager amounts of food—namely, the popular soup kitchens—provided convenient meeting places for the parties, like underground clubhouses, all with their own kitchens. The custodial sign at the entrance was always the same: Self-Help. Watered-down soup was portioned out in all the soup kitchens, without distinction, and in the beginning a slice of bread was added. But people in the know were aware of differences. Each of the party-sponsored relief kitchens was run by stalwarts of a specific party, and alongside the usual patrons was a strikingly large number of needy party members and followers. Assemblies and meetings of party cells were held in these kitchens in the evenings. The place was relatively safe, and it was always possible to disguise a meeting as an innocent meal or a gathering to discuss the affairs of the kitchen. There was a standing prohibition against mass assemblies, but it was obviously not binding on the relief kitchens.

The clandestine publication of newspapers assumed a place of primary importance among the party activities. Further on we shall deal with the role and structure of this press in detail. Here it is sufficient to note that most of the parties in the underground engaged in publishing newspapers. In addition to providing important and accurate information on developments on the fronts and in the international political arena, these papers also placed emphasis on advancing their individual political positions and ideologies. Yet the political differences between them were of little relevance to the realities of life for the Jews in the occupied territories. One has the impression that in most cases the writers of the articles constantly reiterated the party line, mechanically repeating old ideological formulas without seriously attempting to examine whether and how such tenets were relevant to the present.

We can discern two principal subjects that preoccupied the clandestine press: (1) an attempt to define the essence of the war and the position of the Jewish people therein; and (2) an evaluation of the posture and status of the Soviet Union in the war and its policy and intentions in light of the Molotov-Ribbentrop Pact. Centered on these subjects were ideological articles, polemics, and exchanges between the various political factions. In addition to their presentation of principles and debates, each faction pointed to the distant example of the free world, in which it found a model to emulate, an object of yearning, and the hope of the future. The various constituents of the Zionist press published many articles, news items, and reminiscences about Palestine. The Bund publications emphasized the socialist underground in Poland and the free countries of the West. The communist press, which began to wield influence over the Jewish public in the spring of 1942, concentrated its attention almost exclusively on the communist movement, the Soviet Union, and the war on the eastern front.

The standard and dogmatic positions promoted by the parties made it difficult to arrive at realistic appraisals of the essence of the war, Nazi racist anti-Semitism and its objectives, the fabric of relations between the Jews and the Poles, and other essential issues. Thus, for example, Left Po'alei Zion and many members of the radical youth movements—such as Ha-shomer ha-Za'ir and to a lesser degree Dror He-

Halutz—refused to perceive Fascism and National Socialism as other than the phenomenon defined as a "capitalist regime." Moreover, in line with the dogmatic communist approach, they defined Fascism and National Socialism as the most degenerate and brutal stage of the "era of the decline of capitalism." The war itself was in the nature of an "imperialist war," a conflict between two kinds of imperialism—the "sated" and established vs. the "hungry" and ambitious. "A struggle over material interests is going on between these two world forces, and the objective of their plunder is camouflaged in 'social' or 'democratic' phraseology."[12]

The organ of the youth division of Left Po'alei Zion, *Yugntruf* (*The Call to Youth*), wrote in January 1941:

> The [First] World War has returned in a stronger and more repulsive form. Then as now, the battle cries and "ideological" motivations of the two warring camps are nothing but a complete fraud, a disguise designed to camouflage the true capitalist-imperialist motives and objectives. . . . And must the working class rely upon one of the two fighting forces, aspire to the victory of one of the capitalist blocs as the endeavor of international Social Democracy?[13]

The newspaper's reply is that the hour of the working class will come only after the two warring forces "wear each other down." This belief is also the source of its position vis-à-vis the Soviet Union, which must also wait until an appropriate revolutionary situation is created and then enter the world arena at the head of an "independent revolutionary proletarian force."[14]

The members of the Bund refuted these rigid positions. *Yugnt-Shtime* (*The Voice of Youth*) claimed in the "Letter to a Comrade" column of its January-February 1941 issue:

> Let us imagine a situation in which the proletariat says to itself: "Since the imperialists are beating one another, and none of them intends to protect the interests of the working class, as far as we are concerend they can all bang their heads against the wall. For us, the workers, this entire affair is about as meaningful as last year's snow." What would be the consequences of such a stand? Germany, armed to the teeth, would launch an attack on England. The British working class, believing it has nothing worth fighting for, would bring this attitude with it into the army (since most of the troops are workers), with the probable result that the people would lay down their arms—in a moral sense—and at any rate allow Germany a swift victory over England. (The fall of France is living proof of this. The unfortunate role assumed by the Communists and the pacifist position of a few of the Socialists contributed without doubt to Hitler's swift victory.) It is true that British imperialism would be destroyed

thereby, but it would be replaced by another imperialism, Hitlerite, brutal and more domineering than the British version. And with that the freedom and rights of the working people of Europe would be destroyed.[15]

Yet the Bund, which held a more sober view of the significance of the war, had no realistic insight into the fate awaiting the Jews in that conflict. As far as the Bund was concerned, there was no basic difference between the situation in which the Jews found themselves and that of other subjugated peoples. Thus the alliance between the Jewish working class and the Polish workers was more important than general Jewish solidarity. For a long time the members of the Bund attempted to nurture the belief that the regime's campaign of persecution against the Jews was part of a policy of repression directed against Poland. We find in the July 1, 1941, issue of *Yunge Gwardye* (*Young Guard*), published by the Bund's youth division, an article under the headline "The War and the Jews," which includes the following evaluation:

> Every time the Jewish community falls upon hard times, whenever the reactionaries launch an attack on the freedom of the workers' movement accompanied by expressions of anti-Semitism, Jewish nationalism stirs beneath the surface, begins to sow a loss of confidence in all we have here, and tries to dampen the fighting spirit of the masses of Jews who have integrated into the general struggle against reactionism and for liberty. Jewish nationalism claims that we are in exile, and for as long as it lasts we must endure it. All the peoples that Hitler has subjugated are in Hitler's exile. The Austrians, Czechs, Poles, and Dutch are persecuted and oppressed. They have all been dealt a fate similar to that of the Jews, even though they have a country of their own.[16]

Therefore the suffering of the Jews is once again a side effect of the class struggle, and Jewish interests dictate the unification of the struggle in a class framework common to Jews and Poles, for "as long as capitalism survives, there will be room for anti-Semitism in other international struggles."[17]

The December 1940 issue of the Zionist *Bafrayung* defined the state of the Jewish people during the war as follows:

> It is true that wherever Jews reside, they are counted among the opponents of Germany. . . . We could say that the entire Jewish people is a party to the war today, even though it has no army of its own. Yet it is clear to all that there is no proportion between the importance of the Jews as a "party to the war" and the damage they cause to the Germans. . . . The whole world openly accepts the fact that *the standard employed toward the Jews differs completely from the standard toward others.*[18]

Only two issues of Revisionist publications have reached our hands. One is devoted entirely to Vladimir Jabotinsky; the other, *Magen David* (*The Shield of David*), evidently from February 1942, dates from the period immediately prior to the liquidation of the ghetto. An ideological article in this paper states:

> There is no point in explaining to the Jews that emigration and even evacuation from the countries of Eastern Europe was a kind of rescue. And again, there is no point in persuading the peoples of the world that the Jewish problem, among others, played no small role *before* this war, at the time of its outbreak, and while it is going on, and it demands a comprehensive solution if only for the sake of tranquility in the world. . . . The Jewish people has reached the status of a partner, at the very least, in the general struggle of the Powers, a partner that does not have to remind and convince the world of its existence; and it must be active in all the areas together with the others and in the name of self-evident common interests.[19]

Despite the fact that Ringelblum stresses the existence of a sense of unity in the face of the challenges of the day, which was particularly evident in the field of welfare, these obvious differences of outlook influenced the parties, largely dulling their perception of the impending dangers and, as we shall see, retarding somewhat the general organization of armed resistance.

The political underground shared a generally negative attitude toward the *Judenrat,* and, although there were differences of emphasis in their expressions of condemnation, dissociation from and denunciation of the *Judenrat* were common to all factions in the underground. On the other hand, the criticism and sharp accusations hurled against the *Judenrat* were never translated into any concrete action, i.e., an organized move against the institution. Obviously, it was impossible to instigate open resistance to the occupation regime itself. Yet even those instances of active opposition to the *Judenrat* that characterized other ghettos were lacking in Warsaw. (Even in the Lodz ghetto, which had a particularly firm internal regime, the hungry held protest demonstrations). We get the impression that the participation of the party activists in leading the Self-Help—a kind of alternative to the *Judenrat* but simultaneously a partner with it in the relief activities—stood in the way of any pragmatic opposition on the part of the political bodies. Logic dictates that the party activists and members of the dynamic cells belonged to a social stratum that was hardly at the bottom of the scale of poverty and hunger in the ghetto. We may assume that this situation contributed to the fact that although the political parties in the underground expressed unequivocal criticism in the clandestine press, they did not actually reach the point of a confrontation or open clash with the *Judenrat.*

In addition to producing underground newspapers, the parties engaged in cultural and propaganda activities in another framework. There were two cultural societies in the ghetto: Yikor (*Yiddishe Kultur Organizatsye*) and *Tekumah* ("Revival"). The very existence of two competing societies, one adopting Yiddish as a language and culture and the other dedicated to the renewed Hebrew language, suggests that although the groups had their ideological differences, the primary conflict between them was a language rivalry, which did indeed exist in the ghetto. *Tekumah* was headed by the historian Menachem Stein; Lipa Bloch, an official of the Jewish National Fund in Poland; Menachem Kirschenbaum, a leader of the General Zionists in the ghetto; and the poet Yitzhak Katzenelson, among others. The founder and moving spirit of Yikor was Menachem Linder, an economist and demographer by profession and a student of the sociologist Jacob Lestchinsky. The society's main membership came from the ranks of Left Po'alei Zion and the Bund. It held literary evenings devoted to the Jewish classics and gatherings at which Jewish artists living in the ghetto read from their works and stage artists participated as readers and performers. The building councils were drawn into this activity, and hundreds of cultural evenings were held for the tenants after curfew. In February 1941 Ringelblum recorded in his journal that more than ninety meetings devoted to the literary works of Mendele Mokher Seforim had been held in the apartment houses.[20] He also noted that Yikor carried on illegal activities under the auspices of the Self-Help and the building councils established by it.[21]

Of the hard-core underground remnant of the former mass parties, the most outstanding—from the perspective of their activities and relative stability—were the Bund and Left Po'alei Zion. In contrast, there is scant written testimony on the organized underground activities of such large and influential parties as the Revisionists and Mizrachi. One explanation for this seeming discrepancy may be that even before the war, association with radical leftist factions implied swimming against the current, and the leftist parties had already forged a basis for illegal activities during their clandestine campaigns and rallies in the last years of the Polish republic.

We must also examine the special conditions and circumstances that aided the active factions in their work. The Bund undoubtedly drew encouragement from the ties that its activists succeeded in maintaining with socialist factions in the Polish underground. Until a relatively late stage, the Bund continued to regard itself as an integral part of the general Polish underground. This sense of belonging or affiliation with a strong underground movement with access to substantial resources and constant contact with the free world certainly contributed to the solidarity of the Bund activists. Nonetheless, it is important to note that the Bund had been a mass party in Poland between the wars, and its membership was constantly on the increase during the last years of that period. It is therefore understandable that it succeeded in holding together a nucleus of stalwarts at various levels, as well as a broad public following.

Between the wars Left Po'alei Zion had not been as strong as the Bund or some of the other parties, but it was led by a core of devoted activists. Some of them, such as Emmanuel Ringelblum and Adolf Berman, assumed key positions in the Self-Help and the institutions under its aegis. These men helped their comrades obtain the instruments and means to direct the clandestine work, and this direct aid in turn bolstered the solidarity of the party's membership. In the past, Left Po'alei Zion had fostered personal ties that went deeper than shared ideological affiliation, and many of its members were united by feelings of intimate friendship.

Paradoxically enough, and in contrast to expectations, for most of the ghetto period the illegal economic activities—particularly smuggling—involved far greater risks than the clandestine political enterprise. Until April 18, 1942, a night of slaughter in the Warsaw ghetto whose target was chiefly the political underground, the work of the clandestine organizations went on almost without interference. Ringelblum called it a "legal conspiracy." The fact that clandestine political activism did not attract German reprisal or take its toll of lives helped to bolster such activity. Ringelblum wrote in a disgruntled tone that the Germans' seeming indifference toward the ghetto's political underground led to a slackening of vigilance.

> All the political parties in the ghetto conducted activities that were practically semi-legal. Political publications sprouted like mushrooms after rain. If *you* publish your paper once a month, *I'll* publish mine twice a month; if *you* print twice a month, *I'll* print weekly; it finally reached the point where the bulletin of one of the parties was appearing twice a week. These publications were distributed openly, "in full view of the people and the congregation." The political leaflets and communiqués used to be read in offices, factories, and similar public places.
>
> The various parties used to hold their meetings practically in the open in public halls. They even had big public celebrations. At one such meeting, a speaker addressing an audience of 150 preached active resistance. I myself was present at a celebration along with 500 young people who all belonged to the same party. The names of the authors of anonymous articles that appeared in the party newspapers were common knowledge.
>
> We had begun to debate and insult one another, as in the good old prewar days. We imagined that anything went.[22]

The apathy displayed by the Germans toward clandestine political activities in the ghetto and the Jews' outlook on political and social affairs contrasted sharply with the fears that had prevailed during the early period of the occupation and were a far cry from the regime's vigilance, aggressiveness, and rigidity regarding cases of clandestine political and nationalist activity on the part of the Poles. While the Jews were subject to brutal physical attacks, hunger, disease, deportation to labor camps, and a drastic mortality rate, there were no persecutions on political grounds. The Poles, on the other hand, were not subject to severe deprivation, yet the full force of the regime's iron fist came down on the focal points of the Polish underground and nationalist movement. Officials of the Polish government-in-exile in London claimed for a time that the Poles were doomed to national destruction, while the Jews were only slated to be driven out of Europe.

What explanation can there be for the apathy of the police and the civil administration toward the diverse activity of the Jewish political underground? Does the answer lie in the assumption that the Germans were simply unaware of this political activity or its scope? It is possible that the Germans did not know of the breadth and variety of Jewish political activity, but if so, their ignorance stemmed from lack of interest, or only peripheral interst, in this realm. There can be no doubt that the Germans had access to sources of information. These channels, which provided reports on smuggling and developments in the economic sphere, could also have been used to obtain information on political activities. A thorough and consistent examination of subsequent events shows that even at the later stages of the ghetto, the Germans never related seriously to the Jewish underground and its potential. In retrospect we can see that because of their shortsightedness, the Germans failed to discern the secret organizational activities in the ghetto, preparations for the uprising, and the crystallization of the resistance forces.

As to the fundamental question of why the Germans ignored the views and political actions of the Jews, while they consistently suppressed any hint of independent political thought or expression of nationalism among the Poles, we lack the advantage of documentation that would supply an authoritative explanation of this astonishing lapse. It is clear that the Germans were determined to destroy the Polish elitist leadership class and sustain the Poles as a nation of lowly and defeated woodcutters and water-drawers. Their objective was therefore to wipe out the Polish intelligentsia, or bring it to its knees, paralyze the Polish nationalist movement, and turn the masses of the Polish people into stooges of the master race. This goal could only be accomplished by treating the various classes in the Polish population differently, educating toward loyalty, and instituting a regime of terror that smashed any potential leadership or national-political faction that was roused to action.

The same was not true in regard to the Jews. It was not necessary to differentiate between classes, since the Jews as a whole comprised an independent category for which a comprehensive policy had been prepared. From the standpoint of the Germans, the Jews' outlook or political posture was simply irrelevant. The occupation regime had provided for the hermetic isolation of the Jews from the rest of the Polish population and the supervision of their economic activities. Having done so, the Germans viewed Jewish spiritual or ideological involvement as inconsequential, as long as it was limited to the confines of the ghetto and could not influence the outside world. The Jews were in any case slated to be dealt with by means of a special "solution" that would encompass every single Jew or everyone defined as a Jew by the Nazis' racialistic principles.

This outlook shares a certain common trait with the policy adopted toward the Jewish community in Germany in the 1930s. The Nazi Party and the Third Reich had embraced a policy of *Gleichschaltung* regarding all strata of the German nation. But the Jews, who were set apart from the whole, were permitted a limited degree of autonomous cultural and spiritual activity. During a certain period, the Jews were actually given the right to maintain political organizations and express relatively bold views in print, but only in an internal Jewish framework.

We are not able to present statistics on the size of the organizations in occupied Poland or the dimensions of the underground parties' activities, since no authoritative and accurate material has come into our hands, not even numerical estimates, and the sources we do have at our disposal do not supply detailed data on the internal organizational structure of these bodies or their routine activities.

Youth Movements in the Underground

The youth movements and youth divisions of the parties were the moving spirit behind the organization of the armed resistance movements and the nucleus of the fighting force that was formed in 1942–43. But even before the idea of armed resistance had taken hold in these movements, their role and influence in the underground were outstanding.

The status achieved by the youth movements was not commonly expected or taken for granted, since before the war they had not played an active role in Polish-Jewish affairs. It might well have been presumed, therefore, that during the era of the occupation and the underground, the youth movements would operate in the shadow of the political parties and not stand as a force in their own right. But matters turned out quite differently. The development of the youth movements' role was gradual, and, as we shall see, the key members of these movements at first believed that the leadership and direction of underground political activities should be left in the hands of the parties. It was only later that the youth movements overcame the hegemony of the parties, began to operate on their own, and launched daring campaigns and projects quite different from the standard activities of the political parties in the underground. During the stage of the "Final Solution," there was a rift between the youth movements and the veteran parties, and for a while the movements built up armed forces of resistance without the cooperation, and even against the will, of the parties and some of the prominent public figures in the underground.[23]

There are objective factors of time and circumstances that provided opportunities for new and younger people to come to the fore. The sharp reversals of the war and the occupation created a vacuum and a demand for people capable of coping with the changed circumstances and adjusting to needs that differed radically from those of the past. Likewise, the characteristics of youth—daring, sensitivity to social injustice, and a willingness to sacrifice—were important requirements that advanced the young into the roles they were destined to assume.

Between the two wars, the Jewish youth movements had fashioned a special image of youth and woven a network of intimate and stable relations with their organizational frameworks. In addition to their devotion to ideology, some of the movements placed emphasis on education toward communal living at some future time. Thus a causal relationship developed between ideological identification and personal comradeship. The leaders of the youth movements, who were graced with strong powers of persuasion, were also young; in fact, many had not yet left their teens. Political education in the youth movements did not consummate with commitment only to an ideological line; the dominant foundation of this education was a yearning for radical change—in the existing state of affairs, the nature of the Jew as a human being, and the fate of the Jewish people. Beyond differences of outlook, although each one of the movements had a character unique to itself, these basic qualities were shared by all the youth organizations.

The major youth movements survived the storm of war in September 1939, though they were not immune to the shock, and thus to some degree of dissolution, and their leaders were swept away in the mass flight to the east. Indeed, the wide-scale reconstruction of the movements and the upswing they experienced in the underground were directly related to the return of movement leaders from the east for exactly those purposes. The leaders' decision to return from the areas under Soviet rule or embraced by "Free Lithuania" was not an easy one, for it meant leaving areas where they were not likely to be bothered as

Jews—places from which it might be possible to escape to other countries or reach Palestine—and cutting themselves off from their comrades and peers. But as stated earlier, in taking this step they were obeying the decisions of their central leadership bodies, which had charged them with this mission.

In the middle of 1942, the fourth issue of *Internal Correspondence*, a review for members of Dror He-Halutz designed to pass on internal information to provincial towns, defined the movement's activities by chronological phases as follows:

1. September 1939–April 1940: the period of searching out movement members.
2. April 1940–November 1940 [until the ghetto was closed]: renewed organization of the training farms and the youth movement. The work reaches its peak.
3. November 1940–June 1941: concentration in the large cities.
4. June 1941 [from the outbreak of war between Germany and the Soviet Union]–the present: the movement's great struggle to find a way out.[24]

This sequence of organization, the nature of the tasks, and, to a large degree, the chronological order reflect the developments in other movements as well.

The initial period was characterized by the mustering of forces, that is, the search for youngsters who had belonged to movement frameworks before the outbreak of war. Added to these veteran members were the newly arrived refugees who had joined the various movements. At the same time, meeting places, the structure of the basic cells, the system of contact between members, and the agenda of activities were all decided upon. For the most part, the meetings of the small cells were held in private homes, while larger assemblies took place in the soup kitchens. At the beginning of the reorganization stage, the movements set exacting rules of conspiracy, but they were not followed strictly, and this aspect of movement discipline soon grew lax. The reason for the lack of attention to the strict rules of caution derives from the atmosphere cultivated in the youth movements and the ways in which they operated. Boisterous behavior in the streets, singing, stormy debates—these were the trademarks of the movements, and, despite the warnings and indoctrination in the rules of the underground, many of the old habits returned, including assembling at standard meeting places in the street. One factor that undoubtedly encouraged the renewal of such uninhibited behavior was the Germans' obvious lack of interest in and response to the political activity of the Jews, as described above.

During the peak period, which ran parallel to the establishment of the ghetto, the membership of the underground youth movements reached its prewar level and may even have surpassed it. According to membership figures of Dror He-Halutz, during the four stages listed above, about one thousand members, including about three hundred fifty "Warsawites, together with deportees from the nearby towns," passed through the movement's training facilities in occupied Poland (mostly summer camps for agricultural work on Polish farms). Members of Ha-Shomer ha-Za'ir reported that their membership in Warsaw was eight hundred youngsters,[25] while Ha-No'ar ha-Ziyyoni reported that "during the early days of the occupation, the [Warsaw] group numbered 160 members, including builders of the movement from throughout the country."[26] One source testifies to a meeting of eighty members of the North Warsaw Betar group—one of eight Betar groups in the city; unfortunately, it does not mention the other groups or the size of their memberships.[27]

The various movements established their headquarters in Warsaw and managed both the activities in the city and the ties with provincial centers. Dror He-Halutz maintained its den in a popular soup kitchen on Dzielna Street, which served as both a residence for the urban commune and the site of diversified movement activities. During the existence of the ghetto, Ha-Shomer ha-Za'ir established its den in a heavily populated house with a number of courtyards at 23 Nalewki Street. It too served as a soup kitchen and residence for the urban commune, and it included a library and meeting rooms. In the same house, under the Ha-Shomer ha-Za'ir headquarters, was the Gordonia den, which was likewise a composite soup kitchen, residence for the urban commune, and center of activities. The members of Ha-No'ar ha-Ziyyoni established their first commune for refugee members of their movement on Nowolipki Street.

The various centers functioned under the patronage of the Self-Help. Such patronage was not limited to granting the headquarters recognition as soup kitchens, which, as we have seen, provided a convenient cover for semilegal operation. The Self-Help also extended financial support to cover the costs of movement programs and set aside sums for minimal aid, which the movements passed on to their needy members—primarily refugees—in the form of rations of soup.

A program of aid to the needy was also organized within the movements. In some instances joint treasuries ("financial communes") were established by small groups, and in other cases it was common for a member whose family had not yet been afflicted by poverty to invite a comrade—usually someone from his troop who was suffering from hunger or a refugee—home for lunch each day. This custom was not only an innovation born of wartime conditions but actually ran counter to the accepted rule during normal times, since the youth movements usually drew a sharp dividing line between the spheres of home and movement. Marek Edelman relates that the council of Tsukunft ("Future"), the Bund's youth movement, cooperated with the parents' committee of the children's organization (Skif) in setting up workshops and cooperative enterprises in barbering, tailoring, and shoemaking, whose sites also served as meeting places for movement members.[28]

From the time they assumed their roles in the underground, the leaders of the youth movements viewed themselves as responsible for the branches of their membership throughout the occupied areas. Tosia Altman, a leader of Ha-Shomer ha-Za'ir, wrote an impressionistic piece on an underground emissary who makes his way from town to town in order to rebuild the branches of the movement in the provinces:

> . . . And someone began to bounce along in a wagon on dark nights, over rain-swept roads, to the towns of Zagłębie and to the furthest corners of Podlasie. Someone would secretly knock in the evening on dark windows . . . the tapping on the windowpane would become more and more frequent, more and more doors and hearts opened. And the next day — the glowing faces during the discussions, full of faith, holding on to faith. And not everywhere was the knocking on a dark window. Sometimes there was a lighted room with a circle of heads around a lamp. And afterward there were words of pride: "It's not necessary to rouse us, we have begun ourselves. While you were still in the midst of burning houses and collapsing walls, we had already begun again. Believe in us; we shall prevail." And a wave of warmth billows in the heart. He flooded the distant cities in the Reich, he penetrated into the Lodz ghetto, which was sealed for destruction, he aroused, encouraged. And afterward the letters poured in — Kielce today, tomorrow Staszów, the next day Międzyrzec and Szydłowiec and many more: "The family feels fine, is working, and making profits."[29]

The work of maintaining contact and reviving the distant branches was carried out by means of movement liaisons, mostly girls. If clandestine activity in the ghetto did not involve risks or take a toll of lives, the work of the emissaries was a brazen courtship of danger, for they assumed a double risk. First, they were emissaries of a political underground, and although they knew that the Germans and their agents were on the lookout for any suspicious types in train stations and railroad cars, the emissaries nonetheless carried with them secret newspapers, letters, and cash — the kind of material that would incriminate them if anything went wrong. Second, they were Jews, and as such they were forbidden to travel at all. Moreover, besides being dogged by the threat of being exposed by the Germans, they were equally likely to be turned in by Polish blackmailers and anti-Semites. Indeed, many of the best liaisons were lost en route, but the mishaps did not discourage the rest from continuing their work. Some of the emissaries even had classic Jewish facial features, like Yosef Kaplan and, later, Mordecai Tennenbaum, who passed himself off as a Tartar after equipping himself with the appropriate papers.

The liaisons began their journeys as emissaries in the traditional sense, carrying out the work of the individual movements. But as the isolation of the Jews grew, the liaisons became links between the insulated communities, serving as bearers of information and instruments of coordination between them. Some who took on the task of liaison for the movements were Poles, loyal friends of Ha-Shomer ha-Za'ir from the ranks of the Catholic scouts. Outstanding among them was Irena Adamowicz, who volunteered for a series of dangerous missions and maintained uninterrupted contact with the Jewish movements in the underground. Later on, starting with the outbreak of war between Germany and the Soviet Union, the emissary-liaisons were responsible for renewing the link between the occupied areas in the west and the eastern territories newly conquered by the Germans, and it was they who carried the first terrifying word of the mass-murder campaigns. There were many traveling liaisons, since each movement fielded a number of people who specialized in this activity. Naturally, the risks grew as time passed and the prohibitions, edicts, and Jew-hunters multiplied.

It is only natural that the desire to open a route to Palestine or forge other means of escape preoccupied the members of the youth movements. Letters that reached the free world (via the He-Halutz office in Geneva) included the understandable outcry: "We all long for our relative Aliyah [Hebrew for "ascent to the Land of Israel]."[30] As described in chapter 1, during the first months of the occupation, efforts to reach Palestine still appeared to be realistic. The members of the Vilna community, under Soviet rule, wrote that perhaps because the members of the movements under the German occupation were humiliated and oppressed to the extreme, they would be the first to be saved. At the beginning of 1940, He-Halutz members signaled from Berlin that a center of activity had been established in the city of Oś-więcim (Auschwitz), where they had succeeded in bribing the Slovakian border police, and there was a chance of crossing over to Slovakia.[31] The small group that left Warsaw crossed into the territory that had been annexed to the Reich and arrived at the appointed place only to find that the breach in the border had been blocked. Meanwhile, the "Two Hundred Plan" had been devised, whereby two hundred members of the pioneering youth movements were to cross into Slovakia, whence passage to their destination was assured by the emissaries in

Switzerland. News spread quickly, letters flowed from the outlying cities to Warsaw, and in veiled language the leadership was repeatedly asked about the chances of being included among the candidates for escape. As time went on, however, and the details of the plan were thoroughly examined, it turned out that the suggestions proposed abroad were unrealistic.

In addition to the "Two Hundred Plan," for a while the youth movements concentrated on the proposal of exploiting a chance to escape legally. Contact was established with the German and Italian Emigration Departments in Warsaw, and until the end of 1940, correspondence was maintained with Switzerland in the hope of receiving assistance in arranging the necessary permits. There was talk of negotiations toward an agreement with Nord-Lloyd Company, but mention of the subject gradually petered out in the exchange of letters, and this effort also came to naught.

In July 1940 two members of Dror He-Halutz were dispatched to check out the possibility of stealing across the Slovakian border, but they were lost along the way. Following an October 1940 decision of the He-Halutz plenary to renew attempts to emigrate illegally to Palestine, Shlomo Cygielnik volunteered to try his hand. He succeeded in reaching Slovakia and, with the help of movement members there, established a kind of bridgehead and way station on the Slovakian side of the border at Bardejov. News of the achievement was passed on to comrades in Turkey, Yugoslavia, Switzerland, and Greece, and within the occupied territory a network of safe houses was established as way stations for those moving in the direction of the border. Members of the various movements joined in setting up the safe houses and the transport arrangements, and the project continued until June 22, 1941 — the day war broke out between Germany and the Soviet Union. Great care was taken in moving a comrade from ghetto to ghetto, including smuggling him across borders and "securing the route." Since the ban on the movement of Jews was strictly enforced in the border areas, it was particularly difficult to operate there. Altogether, about forty people were transferred within the framework of this operation, eight of whom fell into German hands on the Polish side of the border and six on the Slovakian side. One, a member of the Akiva movement, was shot down in the process of crossing the border. Some of those who succeeded in crossing into Slovakia remained there, while another group reached Hungary. Even though they all had immigration certificates, only one of the forty-odd people succeeded in reaching Palestine during the war.

Another project of the Zionist youth movements was to renew their agricultural-training activities and adjust them to wartime conditions. The first to demonstrate initiative in this sphere were members of Dror He-Halutz. With the help of the JDC and the *Judenrat*, in April 1940 they obtained permission to return to their training farm in Grochów on the outskirts of Warsaw. The group that resided at Grochów was joined by smaller bands of members from other movements. With the establishment of the ghetto, the Grochów group was forced to abandon the farm, but its members would not reconcile themselves to the edict, kept watch over the farm, and returned to it thereafter. Difficulties arose when a German *Kommissar* was appointed to supervise the farm, for he seized control of the farm's produce and allocated insufficient portions of food to the workers. At the end of 1941, the farm at Grochów was liquidated, and the group was forced to abandon the place for good.[32]

In the summer of 1941, members of Ha-Shomer ha-Za'ir attempted to return to their movement training farm in Częstochowa. When they failed in the attempt, they decided to establish an agricultural-training farm on land belonging to a Jew from the town of Zawiercie in the Częstochowa area. The permit was obtained, and small groups moved from the urban commune to the Żarki farm. Gordonia sent a group of older comrades from Warsaw to the city of Opoczno and to other places.

Organizing groups for seasonal work on farms opened a way for hundreds of youngsters, the overwhelming majority of them youth movement members, to escape the city for the countryside. During the war there was a shortage of work hands in the Polish villages. One reason, and perhaps the most pertinent, for this severe shortage was the mass deportation of Poles for forced labor in Germany. Owners of large farms were desperate for laborers, and they were enamored of the idea of taking on Jews, because they did not have to pay them any wages and could get away with providing only food and crowded living quarters. The arrangements for such groups to go out to the countryside in the summer of 1940, and in even greater numbers in the summer of 1941, were handled by Toporol (The Society to Encourage Agriculture among the Jews), which was devoted to training skilled workers in the field of agriculture, working small parcels of land as green areas in the ghetto, and supplying groups of Jews at the request of the owners of Polish and German farms. The Germans were willing officially to recognize organized agricultural labor as a work camp, while the youth movements viewed it as a desirable combination of acquiring experience in agriculture and keeping groups of members together. The German farm owners naturally did not know the identity of these Jews who came to work in the villages and behaved as remarkably well-organized and disciplined groups. In 1940 only a few groups were engaged in seasonal agricultural work in the "training camps" (a designation distinguishing this work from the agricultural training carried out on farms owned by the youth movements). In 1941 the number rose to hundreds of youth movement members. Not every instance was successful, and there were cases where severe work regimes were imposed without benefit of even minimal living conditions or nourishment. Moreoever, there were differences of opinion on this subject within the organized Jewish underground. While the Zionist bodies supported and promoted this kind of training, the Bund violently opposed it, claiming that it was a form of "volunteerism" on the part of the Jews that made it easier for the Germans to draft Poles for forced labor in Germany.[33]

Let us go into deeper detail regarding two training camps, since they have been credited with far-reaching influence upon the consolidation of power in the underground and, at a later stage, upon the armed resistance movement. The first was located on a farm near the city of Hrubieszów in the Lublin district, where many Betar members from Warsaw found refuge. From the beginning of the occupation, Betar had been attempting to consolidate its membership. The movement's leaders fled the city at the beginning of the war, but individual members of the command (Salek Hasenszprung, Haim Haus, Moshe Shapshik) returned and were mobilized to work in the underground. For a while Betar maintained a soup kitchen, although it did not serve as a multipurpose underground headquarters as the kitchens of the other movements did. In the spring of 1941, Betar received information that a Jewish farmer—a Betar supporter who commanded a certain degree of influence over his holding—was prepared to employ a large number of Betar members, and throughout the summer a substantial number, including the heads of the movement, left for the farm.[34] The Betar contingent at Hrubieszów found comfortable conditions for maintaining the movement framework, and it was even allowed to remain on the farm during the winter. At the same time, the departure from Warsaw of so many Betar members, including the echelon of activists, naturally weakened the movement's influence in the ghetto underground. During the deportations from Hrubieszów, close to the time of the mass deportations from Warsaw, most of the Betar members were lost, but those who returned to Warsaw became the nucleus of the Jewish Fighters' Union (Ż.Z.W.), which played an important role in the battles of the April 1943 uprising.

The second farm, which differed from the usual training camp and employed members of Dror He-Halutz, was in Czerniakow, a suburb of Warsaw. The farm was privately owned, and, like the farm at Hrubieszów, was not a seasonal camp only, since the Dror group remained there year round. At the peak period, in the spring of 1942, between

140 and 170 pioneers were concentrated there. Since Czerniakow was in the vicinity of the ghetto, it was exploited as a base for underground work. The farm served as a safe house for liaisons who entered or left the ghetto and as a meeting place for discussions between Poles and Jews on underground affairs.[35] When the Germans closed down the farm at Czerniakow in November 1942 and ordered the pioneers to return to Warsaw, the ghetto underground was reinforced by a united group of youngsters who had not suffered the terror of months of systematic deportations and who overwhelmingly joined the Jewish Fighting Organization.

Within the ghetto itself, the youth movements carried on a variety of organizational and cultural activities. After the initial reconstruction stage, when prewar members were located and returned to the fold, the movements went on to recruit additional members who had entered adolescence since the outbreak of war. While attracting new members, the movements also held seminars to train leaders for educational work. Ringelblum, who lectured before the seminars run by Ha-Shomer ha-Za'ir, described his experience in his journal: "When I looked into the glowing faces of youth thirsty for knowledge, I altogether forgot the war [ravaging] the world. The seminars were held directly opposite the [post of the] German sentry who guarded the ghetto gate. The Ha-Shomer comrades felt good in their home, to the point where more than once they would turn their attention away from the fact that there is a war going on in the world."[36]

The underground youth movements ran their own study circles and schools, and Dror He-Halutz even established a Hebrew secondary school in the ghetto. In addition to carrying on independent cultural activities, such as parties and literary debates (Ha-No'ar ha-Ziyyoni, for example, had a forty-member choir), they took an active part in the general cultural institutions of the ghetto, such as the Ringelblum Archive, Yikor, and *Tekumah*. The movement members were also active as counselors in the children's soup kitchens and youth and children's corners organized by the building councils. Some of the meetings and conventions held by the movements extended to include members from outside Warsaw, with delegates from provincial cities secretly making their way to Warsaw to participate in these general councils.

Until reports began to arrive on the mass murder of Jews, no concrete plans for armed resistance to the German forces were drawn up by the youth movements. Here and there, the possibility of such action was raised in the wake of specific developments in the war, but the strong stimulus to arm came only with the outbreak of the German-Soviet war. Thus until the end of 1941 and the beginning of 1942, the dominant task of the youth movements was not in the field of self-defense and armed struggle. Like their elders, the youth were struggling to secure their physical existence. Yet emphasis was placed on their obligation to preserve their spiritual world as well. The September 1941 issue of *Yugnt-Shtime* (*The Voice of Youth*), published by the Bund's youth division, warned:

> Our rulers are mistaken in thinking that a draconian prohibition, an official stamp, can nullify cultural values that have been acquired over tens and hundreds of years. . . . We, the working youth of the people, must assume the task of initiating and directing the cultural and educational endeavor among children and youth . . . otherwise our cultural movement among the youth is in danger of spiritual decline. . . . The hour of the political struggle against the enemy has not yet arrived. We must exploit the period of calm to prepare for missions that are sure to come.[37]

And the organ of Ha-Shomer ha-Za'ir, *Neged ha-Zerem* (*Against the Current*), wrote in its May 1941 issue: "The poverty and total economic deprivation will pass when political conditions change, but the people will not recover from their decline if our youth are blemished and decadent; for only we, youngsters aged thirteen to eighteen today, are destined to lead the Jewish masses to a different, better future."[38]

There were two reasons for the emphasis placed on the spiritual-cultural aspect of the movement's role: (1) fear that the poverty and other ghetto conditions would permanently damage the psyche of the youth—which the movements assumed was precisely the aim of the Nazis; and (2) the assumption that in the near future the movement youth would be called upon to lead the people, so that they must prepare themselves for the task under the difficult conditions of the Nazi occupation.

The heads of the youth movements were aware that events necessitated their penetration into the broader arena of public life. Yet this change in their status did not take place suddenly, at a definitive turning point, but was a complex and extended process. The youth movements did not compete with the political parties and public institutions or intentionally usurp control over certain spheres of activity in the underground. Together with the extension of their influence and their accumulation of achievements, their self-confidence and self-awareness grew stronger. In a letter dated September 1941, Zivia Lubetkin, one of the leaders of He-Halutz, explained to comrades in the United States: "In addition to our educational work, we must give our attention to things we never dreamed of. We have established elementary and secondary schools. We travel on visits, even though this is by no means a simple matter. . . . We were never recognized as we are recognized and appreciated now. . . . [39] And in *Neged ha-Zerem* we read: "The task of the movement, as a public force in the ghetto, has grown, not as a result of intentional action in that direction but rather because of (1) tension and an upsurge in internal activities; and (2) the collapse of all the Jewish political parties."[40]

During the war and the Holocaust the youth movements succeeded in functioning as a kind of existential enclave, the spirit of which contrasted markedly with the reality around them. The question that naturally arises is, what was the deeper resource that nurtured the youth movement members? Why was this sector of the Jewish public immune to disintegration and the individual obsession with self-preservation, in total disregard of the next man or the common good? What are the factors that united these groups of youth and lent content and meaning to ideas and values so far removed from the reality of the times and the mores of the ruling power? These questions deserve consideration, even if the answers to them can only be in the nature of broad generalizations.

Probably the most important force behind this transcendent phenomenon was the character of the youth movements between the wars. The sense of comradeship had been so firmly established that it was able to withstand the unprecedented conditions that now arose. Because they belonged to organizations that extended beyond the borders of the occupation, members of the youth movements were able to preserve their consciousness of being part of human society and thus to remain undefeated by the general sense of isolation. The newspapers, coded letters, and conversations that have reached us attest to a devotion to the Land of Israel or socialism, or both, which reinforced the feeling of belonging and the belief in the future.

In his biographical sketch of Mordecai Anielewicz, Ringelblum wrote that the resistance leader eventually came to the conclusion that the years of educational work in the underground were more or less "wasted time," for he and his comrades were not quick enough to grasp the cruel nature of the changed circumstances, which from the very start called for the forging of fighters trained in the use of weapons and equipped for battle.[41] It is probable that Anielewicz complained at one time or another of not beginning to prepare cadres for an armed struggle early enough. It is also likely that such a thought haunted him during the last months of the ghetto, when he struggled to build a fighting organization in a race against time.

Similar words of regret were to be expressed by Yitzhak Zuckerman before the council of Kibbutz Ha-Meuchad when he arrived in Palestine in May 1947: "If we had foreseen, if we had understood, if I could turn the wheel of history back to 1939, I would say: 'An immediate uprising!'—because then we had much more strength, many more youth; because we had much more pride, a greater store of human feeling; because we had much more energy . . . many more arms . . . many more soldiers; because then we also had much more hope."[42] But such regret is not the same as viewing the years in the underground and the investment in clandestine education as a total waste. From our standpoint, these efforts played a decisive role in the struggle by keeping together a united cadre of people who maintained and cultivated social norms and values during a desperate time. Thanks to the protracted existence of the movements in the underground and the creation of the "underground man," when the time came, a consolidated and reliable nucleus stood at the disposal of the Jewish Fighting Organization.

The Ringelblum Archive and the Underground Press

Special value is placed upon the underground archive established in Warsaw and known by the secret name "Oneg Shabbat." The historian Emmanuel Ringelblum was motivated by the feeling that during the period of the occupation and the ghetto, the Jews were being exposed to a situation unprecedented in history, and "it is imperative that future historians receive material on the past written with precision."[43] Thus the idea of an underground archive was born. But in reality the "Oneg Shabbat" was far more than a repository for documents and other material at hand. Its major value was its far more active role as a motivator, proposer of ideas, and stimulus to creativity. Ringelblum laid the foundations of the "Oneg Shabbat" Archive as early as October 1939. His position as head of the Social Welfare Department of the Coordinating Committee enhanced his ability to interview Jews coming to Warsaw from provincial cities and towns and to concentrate material on what was happening throughout occupied Poland during the first months of the war. In the first stage, the work of the "Oneg Shabbat" Archive was carried out within modest limits, but this did not satisfy the energy or aspirations of Ringelblum and his assistants. In May 1940 the archive was established on a broader public foundation, and in the course of time its board of directors expanded to include a host of prominent personalities and representatives of the various political factions and the youth movements: Emmanuel Ringelblum, M. Kahan, Eliyahu Gutkowski, Rabbi Szymon Huberband, Hirsh Wasser, Abraham Levin, Shakhne Sagan, Yitzhak Giterman, Alexander Landau, David Guzik, and Shmuel Breslaw. The "Oneg Shabbat" Archive employed a small full-time staff and commissioned works on a number of specific subjects from experts and well-informed people in various fields. It adopted the aim of giving as broad a coverage as possible to the changes that had taken place during the period of the occupation and the ghetto in Warsaw as well as in many other Jewish centers throughout the country.

A large quantity of documents, surveys on specific topics, partial monographs, and literary works were concentrated in the archive. At an advanced stage of the work, which was supported by JDC funds, the idea arose to write summary works entitled "Two and a Half Years," that is, covering the two and a half years of Jewish life in Warsaw since the outbreak of the war. However, in the midst of this endeavor, the mass deportations from Warsaw began, and they put an end to the routine work of the "Oneg Shabbat" Archive, just as they halted all underground public activity.

The "Oneg Shabbat" Archive also published an informative newsletter, which first appeared at the beginning of 1942, when news began to arrive of the deportations and mass-murder campaigns. Wasser relates:

> In addition to that, the leadership of the underground in the ghetto charged the "Oneg Shabbat" with the task of preparing various memoranda for consumption abroad, e.g., on the death camp at Chelmno (March 1942), on the *Aktion* in Lublin (April 1942), on the state of the Jewish population in the Nazi-occupied areas (July 1942), and later on, in November 1942, the first exhaustive description of the initial stage of the liquidation of Warsaw Jewry. The editing of these works was placed in the hands of Dr. E. Ringelblum, A. Gutkowski, and H. Wasser.[44]

During the deportations, which continued from July 1942 until April 1943, the small staff of devoted workers took pains to hide the invaluable material in a secure place. The archive included, *inter alia*, a representative section of the underground press, packets of letters and internal material belonging to the political organizations, and documentary material on the Jewish Fighting Organization. Ringelblum and some of his associates continued the task of writing and documentation while in hiding on the "Aryan" side. It would not be an exaggeration to say that Ringelblum remained faithful to his goal right up until his tragic death, when the bunker in which he, his wife, his son, and a group of Jews were hiding was discovered on the "Aryan" side on March 7, 1944. Miraculously, with the help of Hirsch Wasser, two parts of the "Oneg Shabbat" Archive that were hidden within the confines of the ghetto were subsequently found, while the third part, which included vital material on the organization and activities of the fighting underground and the Jewish Fighting Organization, has evidently been lost forever. The sections of the archive in our hands are an unsurpassable tool for understanding both the internal life of the Jewish community during the time of the occupation and the ghetto, and the emergence of the political underground and the armed struggle in the Warsaw ghetto.

A classic expression of the upsurge of the political underground in Warsaw was the diversified and widely distributed clandestine press. Thanks to underground archives—most especially the "Oneg Shabbat" Archive—this body of material has reached us almost intact, and we are able to apprehend its quality and scope. The periodical press in Warsaw filled a role as a molder of public opinion in the ghetto. The Germans deprived the Jews of their radio sets; the foreign free press did not penetrate the occupied territories; and after a while the Jews were forbidden even to read the German press. In Cracow a weekly Polish-language newspaper, *Gazeta Żydowska*, was published expressly for the Jews in the Generalgouvernement from July 1940 until the beginning of 1942. Since its publication was supervised by the Chief of Propaganda in the Generalgouvernement, the paper usually served as an instrument of Nazi policy and a channel to disseminate official political and military communiqués of the German administration. The alert Jewish reader, accustomed to a forum of thoughts and opinions, was revolted by this legal newspaper, whose tone was hostile and style strictly uniform. The September 1940 issue of the Bund's clandestine newspaper, *Biuletyn*, claimed that "You won't find a single self-respecting person who will pick up that filthy rag, that so-called Jewish newspaper."[45] There was a thirst for reliable news and commentary in the ghetto, and not only for the sake of preserving the alertness of the population and the standards of the intelligentsia. Developments in the political and military arenas directly affected the fate of the incarcerated Jews, and the yearning for encouraging news went hand in hand with the hope of being liberated.

The underground newspapers began to appear at the beginning of 1940 and continued to be published with increasing intensity until the fatal deportation on July 22, 1942. They did not cease publication after the political terror on the night of April 18, 1942, despite the explicit warnings given to the *Judenrat*, and after the mass deportations, during the period of the armed struggle, issues of the standard underground press and single-edition publications continued to come out. Even after the final liquidation of the ghetto, Jewish underground bodies in hiding and on the "Aryan" side brought out isolated publications that can be considered an extension of the underground Jewish press in Warsaw. But the heyday of the clandestine Jewish press essentially came to an end with the mass deportations.

The collection in our hands comprises forty-seven papers in Yiddish, Polish, and Hebrew. They were published at various intervals—biweekly, monthly, irregularly and in single editions—and with one exception, to which we shall devote greater attention later on, all the newspapers were printed on duplicating machines. When it was impossible to obtain proper newsprint in the ghetto, they were printed on coarse, bulky paper. The length of the publications also varied, ranging from a few pages to collections of over one hundred pages. We lack definitive data on the number of copies for each issue, but we do know that some of the papers were duplicated in three to five hundred copies. Yet these figures do not indicate the true scope of distribution. As a rule, a paper passed from hand to hand down a chain of readers, and we can assume that each copy reached twenty people or more. Edelman claims, for example, that a survey taken by the Bund revealed that each copy was read by twenty people.[46] Moreover, the contents of the papers—especially political items and news from the fronts—were then passed on by word of mouth and spread throughout the entire ghetto. At a later date, duplicated news summaries were instituted in addition to the regular periodical press. Some of the youth movements distributed these summaries to a standard list of people in the ghetto. At a set hour a pair of youngsters would turn up at an appointed address, turn the summary over to the resident, wait until he had finished reading it, and then go on to the next address.

The preparation and printing of the copy was carried out under difficult conditions. Since most of the hectographs were outdated, the work was slow and time-consuming. In some cases the typewriters and other instruments were hidden in popular soup kitchens, and work began after they had closed for the night. The secret location of hidden radios was closely guarded, for they supplied material indispensable to the papers. Whoever was appointed to monitor news broadcasts and commentary from the Western countries and Moscow would take down any news and pass it on for editing and publication.[47]

The clandestine newspapers published in Warsaw were not meant for residents of the city alone, since the Jewish political organizations saw themselves as centers of activity and therefore responsible for Jewish communities throughout occupied Poland. Great efforts were expended in smuggling the prohibited material out of the ghetto and over dangerous routes to their final destination. This was one of the heaviest responsibilities and most daring missions of the liaisons, for in addition to the risk involved in camouflaging their identities as Jews, they carried identifying and politically incriminating material. The very shape of the newspapers, which were often bulky, made them quite difficult to conceal. A Polish socialist who was asked to help the Bund distribute its papers related that he was astonished when he laid eyes on the piles of eye-catching paper. Indeed, the Polish liaison who was charged with managing the distribution of the Bund newspaper was caught on her first or second foray, and the mishap had disastrous consequences.[48]

It has already been noted that the political activities in the underground were not countered by repressive measures, though this does not mean that there were no snags or mishaps in the process of disseminating the newspapers.[49] Yet the relative freedom and the limited number of breakdowns did not deceive those engaged in the publishing endeavor. They were acutely aware that they were tempting fate, and it was impossible to know when and how the beast would spring from its lair. The papers repeatedly warned their readers of the risks inherent in the operation and demanded increased vigilance and avoidance of suspicious people; yet caution was not to impede the efficient distribution of the newspapers, which had an important role to fulfill. In the Bund's *Yugnt-Shtime* of December 1940, we find a list of instructions on how to treat the newspaper and the permissible means of distributing it. The first point exhorts: "Who is eligible to be a reader? Not everyone is worthy of receiving the *Yugnt-Shtime*. The recipient must be someone known and trusted. He must not be mentally unstable, a blabbermouth, or confused. Disseminating the paper left and right is a foolish and criminal act."[50]

In the course of time, the warnings became more strident. The readership was told that the "Gestapo is lurking at every turn," or "After reading—pass it on! Beware of *provacateurs* and the Gestapo."[51] For the most part, the articles in the underground press were not signed with the authors' full names, and the mastheads did not make mention of the publisher or editor. But the identity of the political faction that published any one paper was nonetheless common knowledge, and, as Ringelblum testified, the authors of the ideological articles were also known. The phenomenon of the underground press was too widespread to conceal from the enemy.

We may assume that the forty-seven names included in Table 3 cover almost all the papers, with the exception of exclusively internal organs or publications in commemoration of specific events. Although it is almost certain that various issues of these newspapers are missing, we may presume that this factor is more or less evenly distributed over the list, so that the issues in our hands are probably a representative sample from a qualitative point of view. We have not indicated the number of pages for each publication, and, as stated, the fluctuations in this area are extremely wide.

The party that issued the most publications was the Bund, together with its youth division, which published eleven different organs, sixty issues of which are in our hands. It is important to note that sometimes a publication would change its name for security reasons and continue

TABLE 3

UNDERGROUND PUBLICATIONS OF THE WARSAW GHETTO

Masthead	Published by	Period of Publication	Language	Number of Extant Copies
1. Awangarda	Left Po'alei Zion	1942	Yiddish	2
2. Awangarda Młodzieży	Left Po'alei Zion	1941	Polish	4
3. Bafrayung	Po'alei Zion Z.S.	1940	Yiddish	1
4. Biuletyn	Bund	1940–41	Yiddish	18
5. Das Frei Wort	Bund	1942	Yiddish	1
6. Der Głok	Bund	1942	Yiddish	1
7. Der Ruf	Anti-Fascist Bloc	1942	Yiddish	1
8. Der Veker	Bund	1942	Yiddish	12
9. Dror	Dror He-Halutz	1940–41	Yiddish-Polish	6
10. El Al	Ha-Shomer ha-Za'ir	1941–42	Polish	5
11. Getto Podziemne	Polish Socialists in the ghetto	1941–42	Polish	1
12. Hamedinah	Betar	1940	Yiddish	1
13. Iton Ha-Tnua	Ha-Shomer ha-Za'ir	1942	Polish	2
14. Jutrznia	Ha-Shomer ha-Za'ir	1942	Polish	10
15. Kol Bamidbar	Agudat Yisrael	1941	Yiddish	1
16. Magen David	Betar	1942	Yiddish	1
17. Mitteylungen	Oneg Shabbat	1942	Hebrew-Yiddish	1
18. Morgen-Fraybayt	Communists	1942		news briefs

(*Table 3 continued*)

	Masthead	Published by	Period of Publication	Language	Number of Extant Copies
19.	*Nasze Hasła*	Left Po'alei Zion	1941	Polish	2
20.	*Neged ha-Zerem*	Ha-Shomer ha-Za'ir	1941–42	Hebrew-Yiddish-Polish	8
21.	*Nowa Młodziez*	Bund	1942	Polish	1
22.	*Nowe Tory*	Po'alei Zion Z.S.	1942	Polish	1
23.	*Oyfbroyz*	Ha-Shomer ha-Za'ir	1942	Yiddish	4
24.	*Oyf der vakh*	Bund	1942	Yiddish	3
25.	*Oysdoyer*	Gordonia	1941	Yiddish	1
26.	*Payn und Gvure*	Dror He-Halutz	1940	Yiddish	1
27.	*Płomienie*	Ha-Shomer ha-Za'ir	1940	Polish	2
28.	*Proletarisher Gedank*	Left Po'alei Zion	1941–42	Yiddish	4
29.	*Proletarishe Radyokamunikaten — Morgen-Fraybayt*	Communists	1942		news briefs

30. *Przedwiośnie*	Ha-Shomer ha-Zaïr	1942	Polish	4
31. *Przegląd Marksistowski*	Communists			
32. *Sheviv*	Ha-No'ar ha-Ziyyoni	1940–41	Hebrew	3
33. *Shturm*	Bund	1942	Yiddish	1
34. *Słowo Młodych*	Gordonia	1941–42	Polish	5
35. *Tsayt Fragn*	Bund	1941	Yiddish	2
36. *Underzer Hafenung*	Ha-No'ar ha-Ziyyoni	1942	Yiddish	2
37. *Underzer Veg*	Po'alei Zion Z.S.	1941–42	Yiddish	2
38. *Wiadomości*	Oneg Shabbat	1942	Polish	6
39. *Wiadomości Żydowskie*	Oneg Shabbat	1941	Polish	1
40. *Yediot*	Dror He-Halutz	1942	Yiddish	8
41. *Yunge Gwardye*	Bund	1941	Yiddish	1
42. *Yungtruf*	Left Po'alei Zion	1941–42	Yiddish	5
43. *Yugnt-Shtime*	Bund	1940–42	Yiddish	13
44. *Żagiew*	Assimilated Jews	1942	Polish	1
45. *Za Nasza I Wasza Wolność*	Bund	1941–42	Polish	7
46. *Zarzewie*	Ha-Shomer ha-Zaïr	1942	Polish	1
47. *Z Problematyki Ruchu W. Sbwili Obecnej*	Gordonia	1942	Polish	1

to appear in an identical format but with a new masthead. Thus, for example, in 1940 and 1941 the Bund published the *Biuletyn*, while in 1942 the same organ appeared under the name *Der Veker* (*The Wakener*). Ha-Shomer ha-Za'ir also changed the name of its biweekly, which appeared in 1942 and included news items, political commentary, and appeals to the Jewish public. In all, Ha-Shomer ha-Za'ir brought out eight publications, thirty-six issues of which are in our hands. Left Po'alei Zion—both the party and its youth movement—published five newspapers, seventeen issues of which have reached us. Dror He-Halutz published three, of which we have fifteen issues. If we add to the Dror He-Halutz list the publications of its mother party, Po'alei Zion Z.S., we arrive at a total of six publications and nineteen issues. It is appropriate to point out that Betar was the only movement to publish a printed newspaper during the occupation, a feat accomplished by using the only legal press in the ghetto, which was at the disposal of the *Judenrat*. The collection *Hamedinah* (*The State*), published in five hundred copies to commemorate the death of Vladimir Jabotinsky, included articles of appreciation and eulogies, as well as directives to Betar members on how to express their mourning over the demise of their leader.

All in all, of the forty-seven newspapers listed in Table 3, twenty-six were published by Zionist bodies of various orientations, while seventeen were brought out by the other underground factions. Four publications can be classified as "independent," three of them being the newsletter published by the "Oneg Shabbat" Archive and one the organ of the Anti-Fascist Bloc (which we shall discuss at length in a later chapter). If we do not count the Bund newspapers, we find that two-thirds of the publications belonged to the youth movements and youth divisions of the parties. In terms of the number of issues produced, the proportional contribution of the youngsters is even greater. When we add in the publications of the Bund's youth movement, the young people's decisive share in the underground press is all the more conspicuous.

As to the content and internal structure of the newspapers, the choice of subjects and emphasis on certain topics naturally derived from the publishers' philosophies and political stances. But incidents that agitated the ghetto and specific critical situations in which the ghetto found itself were also faithfully reflected in most of the papers. The Zionist-oriented press devoted much space to the history of the *Yishuv* (Jewish community in Palestine), articles on its leaders and those of the Zionist movement as a whole, commemorating holidays, and presenting news on topical developments in Palestine. The Zionist-Socialist parties, which were particularly prolific, emphasized the pioneering venture in

Palestine, analyzed problems in the history of the international workers' movement, debated their relationship to the Soviet Union, and presented their outlook on the factors behind the outbreak of World War II and the forces at work in international politics.

The Bund offered much material on the Social-Democratic parties in the West and detailed information on happenings in the Polish sector of the population throughout the occupied country. The communist press gave priority of place to the Soviet Union and the ideological fabric of the international communist movement. None of the papers refrained from attacking what others had written or criticizing others' modes of presentation.

All the underground newspapers adopted a more or less standard format. Each issue opened with an ideological article that reflected the particular party's position on events of the day in the international arena or the ghetto. The major portion of the paper was devoted to news from the fronts and political developments, as well as articles and polemics on ideological issues. The publications of the youth divisions presented surveys of innovations in science, book reviews, and profiles of famous personalities. The youth movements' papers also featured columns devoted to educational issues raised by the war. Sometimes an issue closed with a short chronicle, including brief items on the activities and campaigns of the movement, or the initials of those who had made financial donations to the paper. There was also a list of subjects common to all the clandestine newspapers. In addition to news, they all published largely identical analyses of ghetto affairs that were of concern to all, namely their sharp criticism of the *Judenrat* and denunciation of the police.

During various periods the papers devoted space to subjects that attracted particular attention or aroused curiosity or fear. While the Polish underground press received the news of the German-Soviet hostilities with mixed feelings and undisguised vexation, the whole of the Jewish press viewed this development as a step toward a turning point in the war and clung to its optimistic view even in the face of the shattering Soviet defeats during the summer and autumn of 1941.

The first items on the slaughter of Jews in the east appeared in the underground press in the autumn of 1941. Emissaries of the movements and Warsaw residents who had returned from Vilna brought with them detailed descriptions of the bloodcurdling murder recently perpetrated in the newly occupied areas. Soon thereafter, the clandestine press of the youth movements began to ponder the implications of the murders in the east—whether they were a localized, random phenomenon, a consequence of the anarchy of war, or rather an ominous sign of a concrete change in the Nazi policy toward the Jews. Although the

full scope of the plan for the "Nazi Final Solution" was not yet perceived, the cry for revenge, the demand for alertness, and the imperative to prepare for the events ahead became prominent themes in the
underground papers.

In 1942, with the initiation of deportations in the Lublin area, the
character of the Jewish underground press in Warsaw changed. The
broad-based theoretical debates and the intermovement and interparty
polemics were laid aside, and the papers concentrated on political
items, news on the progress of the fighting, and a flood of items and
warnings from the Jewish front. The press resoundingly called for an
armed uprising. It praised news of resistance that filtered through from
the east, and the message to the masses of Jews that was repeated without end was a warning and a call to revolt. In Dror He-Halutz's *Yediot*
of June 9, 1942, this position is expressed clearly:

> The Warsaw ghetto lives in the shadow of constant danger. Indeed, it
> must live like a besieged fortress. All means [must be prepared] to defend
> it, for its final battle. All the energy [must be preserved for] the great act
> that we must carry out and shall carry out. The spirit of our daily actions
> must be that of Masada. All other questions must be placed aside in the
> shadow of the eternal problem: life or death. And not just at a time of
> stock-taking but objectively, out of systematic self-defense, daily, with
> precision, and in the despairing spirit of a Polish Jew in a German ghetto
> in the month of June 1942.[52]

Chapter Five
Prelude to the Mass Deportation

The German-Soviet War and the Onset of the Extermination Campaign

On June 22, 1941, war broke out between Germany and the Soviet Union, with the Germans initiating a surprise attack. The actual outbreak of hostilities between the two sides did not come as a complete surprise to the Jews of Warsaw, most of whom—supporters and opponents of the Soviet regime alike—believed that the existing alliance between Stalin and Hitler was artificial and would not stand up to the test of the world war. In addition, as the date of the German attack approached, signs of both heightened political tension and concrete preparations for a military operation in the east were readily evident. On the day the war broke out, Chaim Kaplan recorded in his diary:

> Our political instinct has not misled us. Even when the cruel reality, the Stalinist reality, was against us, we felt that [the German-Soviet alliance] was a circumstantial friendship, and therefore merely a charade, and the ideological clash would eventually generate contention and strife between the "lovers." Little by little we began to see unmistakable signs that a war would break out between the "friends." A few days back, after we had already caught wind of the preparations for an eastern front and could all but see it with our own eyes, Tass feigned innocence and published an announcement that nothing was happening between the two sides; but we were not discouraged. They persist in their diplomatic denials full of lies and deceit; and we go on living in a reality that, despite all the denials, is concrete. . . .[1]

The reaction to the opening of the new front was not unequivocal, since the extension of the war meant an aggravation of the food shortages, a rise in the cost of essential goods, an earlier curfew, and strict blackout regulations—all of which revived fearful memories of the days of fighting in September 1939. Nevertheless, such fears could not overshadow the predominant feeling, and most of the Jews of Warsaw greeted the news of the latest turn of events with exultation. Whereas the general mood of the Polish public indicated a degree of vexation and division over the sharp, manifest change that had taken place with the Soviet adherence to the anti-Nazi alliance,[2] the Jews tended to welcome and place great hopes upon the new developments. The Poles looked forward to the war concluding with both Germany and the Soviet Union on the defeated side. To achieve that end, they were prepared for a long war, so long as it ensured the undoing of Poland's traditional enemies and the resurrection of the independent greater Polish state. Not so the Jews, whose salvation was dependent upon the war's ending quickly. And since the Jews in the occupied territories waited impatiently for the deadlock on the fronts to be broken, the renewal of fighting in the east raised new hopes.

At first, news of the Germans' swift advance and the brisk conquest of cities in the areas annexed to the Soviet Union and beyond the annexation line created an atmosphere of depression. A gnawing fear set in that the Soviet Union might not be able to withstand the driving force of the victorious, well-trained, and heavily armed German troops. In a few weeks, however, the mood changed, and the underground press wrote of the "bankruptcy of the [Nazi] *Blitzkrieg.*" For the first time since the outbreak of World War II, the spectacle of a lightning victory and unchallenged conquest was not played out repeatedly. The war shifted into a static state, and in a conflict of that nature, time and conditions were on the side of the Soviet Union. The Jews frequently cited the lesson of Napoleon's defeat in the depths of Russia, and it was the Napoleonic campaign against Russia that preoccupied the Warsaw ghetto at the close of 1941.

Jewish sources contain no hint of a presentiment that the campaign taking place in the Soviet Union might generate another radical turn for the worse in the Nazi policy toward the Jews or that the threat of deliberate mass extermination hovered over the Jews of Europe. Early into the German-Soviet war, the underground press wrote at length about "waves of pogroms" taking place in the newly conquered areas, but they attributed this campaign of violence primarily to the Lithuanian, Ukrainian, and Polish populations. In an article headlined "A New Napoleon on the Old Road," Gordonia's newspaper *Słowo Młodych* (*The Word of Youth*) stated:

We Jews are now paying our heavy toll. No sooner have the German forces crossed the Bug River than the blood of thousands of innocent victims has stained the streets of Bialystok, Lvov, Brześć [Brest Litovsk], and many other cities. Exactly who is responsible for these pogroms against the Jews in the cities of Poland is unknown. We would like to believe that the Poles have not been caught in the web of German propaganda and have not soiled their hands with this blood.[3]

We do not possess official documents or unequivocal testimony as to exactly when, where, and under what circumstances the total destruction of the Jewish people was decided upon. One version, which has been confirmed by several scholars, has it that when the guidelines and orders for "Operation Barbarossa" (the German attack on the Soviet Union) and the tactics to be adopted in the fighting within Russia were being formulated, Hitler wanted to bestow upon the war against the Soviet Union more of an ideological character than the struggle and conquests to date. The battle in the east was portrayed as the consummate confrontation between two world views, a war of life or death, and a mission assumed by the German people to liberate the world from the Bolshevik regime. In the war against Bolshevism, which took on the character of a war of annihilation (*Vernichtungs Kampf*), Hitler ordered his armies to ignore the accepted ground rules of war that were dictated by various international conventions. In justifying these unprecedented orders, Hitler contended that since the Russians would fight the war using barbaric tactics, in total disregard of binding conventions, the Germans must from the very start resort to the same methods that the enemy was likely to adopt. And before all else, the nucleus of the Communist leadership—the political commissars and the Communist intelligentsia—must be utterly wiped out.[4]

As usual, any ideological attack on the part of the Nazis was accompanied by a reinforcement of their anti-Jewish policy. This was especially true in regard to their assault on Bolshevism—or, in Nazi terminology, the "Jewish Bolshevik enemy," which strived to impose the control of Judaism on the entire world. It was not merely fortuitous that in a speech delivered on January 30, 1941, Hitler cited the words of "prophecy" that he had spat out two years earlier in threatening "international monied Jewry" that if it cast the world into a new war, "the result will not be the Bolshevization of the globe and a victory for Jewry, but the annihilation of the Jewish race in Europe." The coming months and years, Hitler claimed in January 1941, would prove how right he had been. It is therefore clear that in the outbreak of war in the east and the proclamation of the anti-Bolshevik campaign, Hitler saw an opportune moment to harshen his anti-Jewish policy and embark upon the "Final Solution of the Jewish Problem" by means of outright mass murder. For example, Frank's comments following a meeting with Hitler shortly before the inception of fighting in the east clearly imply that the Führer regarded the invasion of the Soviet Union as the start of the extermination campaign against the Jews of Europe.

The German scholar U.D. Adam believes that after the abandonment of the plan to concentrate the Jews in Nisko or Madagascar, another plan was devised on the eve of the attack on the Soviet Union that called for evacuating the Jews from the Reich and the occupied countries to areas deep inside Russia.[5] But the halt of the advance on the eastern front and the frustration of German expectations for a swift victory over the Soviet Union caused Hitler and the SS to shelve this plan as well. Adam claims that no decision had been arrived at regarding the total physical extermination of the Jews until the end of 1941, and both the senior echelon of the political administration and the arms of the SS were examining and evaluating various plans for dealing with the Jews. Moreover, even the ban on Jews emigrating from the original boundaries of the Reich did not go into effect until October 1941, over three months after the attack on Russia.

Adam's assumptions and claims, however, do not accord with the established fact that during the first months of the fighting on the eastern front — that is, before the end of 1941 — hundreds of thousands of Jews in the areas originally annexed to the Soviet Union had already been slaughtered during the mass-murder campaign of the *Einsatzgruppen*. Adam tries to skirt this crucial fact by portraying the activities of the *Einsatzgruppen* on the Russian front as an extension of the murder methods that had already been employed in Poland.[6] But the attempt to group together the tactics and outcome of the *Einsatzgruppen*'s activities in both Poland and the Soviet Union essentially serves to underscore the weakness of Adam's claims.

At the beginning of the occupation of Poland, there were signs of friction between the *Wehrmacht* and the *Einsatzgruppen* over the increase in assaults on the civilian population that were totally unrelated to the concern for the security of the occupying troops. In the east, however, not only did the *Wehrmacht* reconcile itself to giving the *Einsatzgruppen* a free hand, but in some areas the regular troops even aided the *Einsatzgruppen* in carrying out their mission. The Polish-Jewish historian Szymon Datner concluded in his book *Fifty-five Days of Wehrmacht [Rule] in Poland* (September 1, 1939–October 25, 1939) that during this period various branches of the army and police carried out 714 execution operations and the total number of victims reached 16,336. In his summary, Datner states that "Jews and Poles fell victim to these 'executions,' and in comparing the statistics on the 'executions,' it turns out that during the first fifty-five days, the major blow in the extermination wave was directed against the Poles."[7] Czesław Madajczyk, in his comprehensive work on *The Policy of the Third Reich in Occupied Poland*, comments that in the districts of Cracow, Warsaw, and Rzeszów, the number of Jewish victims in September 1939 was greater than the number of Poles, while in the rest of the districts the proportion was reversed.[8]

In order to illustrate the manifest change in policy that found expression in the newly occupied areas in the east—in both the number of victims and the main target of the renewed wave of terror—we shall quote figures from a report on *Einsatzgruppe A*, one of the four *Einsatzgruppen* that operated along the extended front from north to south. *Einsatzgruppe A*, which was assigned to the Baltic states and the Leningrad area, reported in a summarizing communiqué that in its extermination operations up to February 1, 1942 (actually until November 25, 1941), 1,064 Communists, 56 partisans, 653 mentally ill people, 44 Poles, 28 Russian prisoners of war, 5 gypsies, 1 Armenian, and 136,421 Jews had been killed by *Einsatzkommando 3* (a section of *Einsatzgruppe A*).[9]

In many cases, the killing in the east began by instigating pogroms against the Jews among the local population. These were usually not spontaneous outbursts but campaigns staged and coordinated by the German occupation authorities, while the host populations— Lithuanians, Latvians, and Ukrainians—readily provided mobs of enthusiastic murderers and looters. In the wake of this "groundwork" came the four *Einsatzgruppen*, about three thousand regular troops who had been collected together from the various branches of the police and the SS. The command of the *Einsatzgruppen* comprised officers of the S.D. and the Security Police, and among the heads of these murder formations were "true academics with two doctorates." According to the testimony of *Einsatzgruppen* commanders, during the stage of their deployment Heydrich informed them that Hitler had ordered the wholesale murder of the Jews in the areas to which the *Einsatzgruppen* were assigned, that is, the territory conquered during the course of the war against the Soviet Union.[10] It stands to reason that the message was related as an order from Hitler. The planning that went into the operations of these special units and the fact that the organized murder was carried out systematically and according to identical techniques in various places can only be explained as the result of an explicit and authoritative order.

After the initial wave of slaughter by the *Einsatzgruppen*, units of the police and security forces attached to the newly established administrative regime were integrated into the extermination campaign. In most places the murder operations continued until the end of 1941, with the surviving Jews concentrated in ghettos in the occupied areas.

In a few sectors there was an intermission in the mass murders, which were not renewed until the summer of 1942 or even 1943. During the early stages of the campaign, the murders were carried out by firing squads at the edge of open trenches, a method that forces the murderer to confront his victim directly and puts even the most cold-blooded killer to a severe test. As time went on, however, the gassing method was introduced into operation, exploiting the experience and skill of the teams that had conducted the euthanasia program in the Third Reich. The murder was effected inside sealed railway cars injected with gas while they were in motion.

The mass-murder campaigns were accompanied by a barrage of propaganda, and in each case an accusing finger was pointed at the Jews, who were themselves allegedly responsible for the deportations and killing. The Jews were portrayed as the focus of contagious diseases and were charged with incitement against the Germans. The most common charge of all, however, was that the Jews were responsible for the acts of resistance on the part of "partisans and bandits." This method of accusation is substantially similar to the line that would later be adopted in the Generalgouvernement.

At the beginning of 1942 there was a slowdown in the extermination campaign. The murder squads found it difficult to continue their work at the height of the winter, since trenches could not be dug in the frozen ground at the rate and to the dimensions that had been planned. In terms of the overall process, however, the establishment of the civil administration in the eastern territories, with interests of its own to protect, was of even greater importance. Under these new circumstances, the Jewish work force—and especially craftsmen—was a factor that the administration was loath to relinquish. Moreover, circles in the *Wehrmacht* that likewise benefited from Jewish labor insisted on their right to employ readily available Jews. Part of the western Ukraine, with its large concentration of Jews in the city of Lvov, was annexed to the Generalgouvernement and was subsequently administered by an extension of the regime headed by Frank. Thus the need of the civil administration and branches of the *Wehrmacht* for Jewish manpower and skilled workers acted as a brake on the murder campaign. The surviving Jews concentrated in ghettos were exploited as vital manpower, and the extermination process was temporarily halted.

In December 1941 an extermination camp began to operate in the town of Chełmno, some thirty-five miles northwest of Lodz. Far from being at the distant reaches of the eastern front, Chełmno was in the Warthegau District of western Poland, which had officially been annexed to the Reich. The construction of the camp, which centered around an abandoned castle in an isolated and heavily wooded area, had begun in November 1941, and SS murder squads commanded by *Hauptsturmführer* Lange—and thereafter by SS *Hauptsturmführer* Bothmann—were transferred to the site. The camp was used primarily as a site for the extermination of Jews from the towns in the Lodz area. Here too, the murder was effected inside sealed freight cars that had been transferred specifically for this purpose from the Minsk sector of operations.

Chełmno was the first camp for mass extermination to be established outside the occupied territory in the Soviet areas. The moving forces behind this operation were Arthur Greiser, the *Gauleiter* (Major District Party Leader) of Warthegau and Lodz, and the Gestapo in Lodz. There were two innovations in the murder installations at Chełmno. In the east the killing squads would move from town to town, and the site chosen for the executions was somewhere in the immediate vicinity of each settlement. Chełmno, however, was established as a permanent camp, and victims from the entire area were transported to it. Second, Chełmno was the first place in which the Germans employed a permanent Jewish *Sonderkommando*, namely a group of Jews selected from the transports, isolated, and used to bury corpses and sort the belongings that the victims had brought with them.[11]

Although we lack definitive proof, there is reason to believe that the order regarding the wholesale murder of Jews issued together with the instructions to prepare for the invasion of the Soviet Union related exclusively to the Jews living in the eastern territory about to be invaded and should not be regarded as a general license to exterminate all the Jews within the reach of the Third Reich. If so, the application of the Nazi plan to all the Jews of Europe in effect extended the scope of an order or decision after it had been successfully implemented on a limited scale without encountering difficulties or opposition in the occupied territories, among the German people itself, from the native population, or in the free world. From the internal Jewish viewpoint, however, the outright mass murder began with the German invasion of the Soviet Union and continued without interruption until close to the end of World War II. It is likely that the order issued in the spring of 1941 was a limited one whose scope was later extended to embrace comprehensive proportions. On the other hand, it is a fact that as early as the end of 1941, Jews from the Reich and the Protectorate were transported to the eastern territories, where they too were overtaken by the killing operations. As a general rule, the advent of the *Einsatzgruppen* in the east should be viewed as the turning point that marked the escalation from a policy of assault and destruction short of outright mass murder to the opening phase of the Nazi "Final Solution."

Renewed Contact with the Eastern Districts and News of the Extermination Campaigns The first attempts to send emissaries from Warsaw to the east were grounded in the understandable desire to renew ties with communities that had been an integral part of Polish Jewry until September 1939 and those who had sought refuge in the areas annexed to the Soviet Union at the beginning of the war. Once these areas were conquered by the Germans, the border that had divided Polish Jewry was dissolved, and plans were made to forge direct contact.

The first envoy that we know of was Heniek Grabowski, a member of the Polish Scout movement, who left Warsaw for Vilna, met with the heads of the pioneering youth movements, and received detailed information on developments there. Grabowski returned with authoritative news on the situation in the eastern territories, and for the first time the truth about the dimensions of the slaughter became painfully clear to the members of the Warsaw underground.

In the latter part of October 1941, the first youth movement members began to reach Warsaw from Vilna, including two outstanding underground figures: Tema Shneiderman of Dror He-Halutz and Arie Wilner of Ha-Shomer ha-Za'ir. Soon afterward Ha-Shomer ha-Za'ir's underground monthly, *Neged ha-Zerem*, published an article headlined "The Days of Blood in Vilna," which opened by stating:

> On October 16 one of our members arrived here from Vilna [probably Arie Wilner] and brought news of the events that have taken place there. . . . The Jewish population is in the grip of terrible shock and depression. All are convinced that they are about to die, and they await their turn. Whoever can tries to escape and make his way to White Russia, where the situation is less horrifying. . . . In many towns in the Vilna District, every last Jew was murdered. . . .[12]

Neither the article itself, however, nor the rest of the description gleaned from the witness suggests that the events in Vilna are symptomatic of the danger hovering over all the Jews trapped within the Nazi occupation.

In December 1941 two female liaisons of Dror He-Halutz—Tema Shneiderman (for the second time) and Lonka Kozibrodzka—reached Vilna after spending some time in Warsaw. At about the same time, Tosia Altman also appeared in Vilna and during her stay attended a meeting of youth movement members convened on the eve of January 1, 1942. About 150 youngsters were present when a manifesto written by Abba Kovner and addressed to the bodies in the underground of the Vilna ghetto was read out in Yiddish and Hebrew. This appeal, voiced three weeks before the representatives of the underground

political bodies moved to establish a united fighting organization
(F.P.O.—*Fareynigte Partizaner Organizatsye*), unequivocally stated that
"Hitler is plotting to annihilate all the Jews of Europe. It is the fate of
the Jews of Lithuania to be the first in line. . . . It is true that we are
weak and defenseless, but the only answer to the murder is self-
defense." The state of affairs in Vilna did not in itself prove that a plot
was afoot to exterminate all the Jews of Europe, and Kovner's bold
assessment was essentially intuitive. Yet it was accepted by many elements in the Vilna underground, and the unified fighting organization
established on January 21, 1942, gave priority to "laying the ground for
mass armed resistance in the event of any attempt to liquidate the
ghetto."[13]

A delegation of youth movement members—composed of Shlomo
Entin of Ha-No'ar ha-Ziyyoni, Edek Boraks of Ha-Shomer ha-Za'ir,
and Yisrael Kempner and Yehuda Pinczowski of Betar—had left Vilna
for Warsaw at the beginning of December 1941. They were charged
with reporting on the slaughter in Vilna and, according to the Jewish
Fighting Organization report of 1944, with obtaining financial aid and
arms from Warsaw. Kempner and Pinczowski remained in Warsaw and
were integrated into Betar's underground activities there. According to
another source, Entin and Boraks returned to Vilna in January, bringing
money they had received from the JDC, "and they said that not a single
person believed their stories about the outright extermination of Jews,
and no one wants a war or a revolt against the Germans."[14] At the
beginning of the following spring, evidently in March 1942, Mordecai
Tenenbaum-Tamarof, one of the leading members of Dror He-Halutz
in the underground, also reached Warsaw, and he too warned against
the "complacency" that still prevailed there and challenged the belief
that Warsaw was immune to the upheavals that had affected the communities in the east.

A month later Chaika Grossman reached Warsaw. Born in Bialystok, she too had left Vilna at the beginning of 1942 and returned to
the city of her birth, together with a small group of Ha-Shomer ha-Za'ir
pioneers. After they had established themselves in Bialystok, she left
for Warsaw to report on developments in Vilna and Bialystok and
mobilize funds for the force that was crystallizing in Bialystok. Her
mission was successful. Yitzhak Giterman of the JDC came to her aid,
and by her own testimony she was delighted with this achievement "not
only because I obtained money, but because Giterman gave it for the
purpose of self-defense, in order to purchase arms."

In addition to the envoys and delegations sent by the movements,
hundreds of people who had fled to the east at the beginning of the war
began to return to their families in Warsaw at the end of 1941 and the

beginning of 1942. For the most part, the returnees made their one-way journey alone, disguised as Poles and equipped with forged papers.

The documentary material at our disposal suggests that the first reports arriving from Vilna and the areas where slaughter had been perpetrated in the east did in fact cause deep shock, but very few seemed to grasp that these grave events had direct implications for the safety of the Jews of Warsaw. Moreover, only after confirmed reports had flooded into Warsaw from many Jewish communities, and the movement of the emissaries had made it possible to reconstruct the picture of the slaughters, did the realization begin to dawn that the events taking place in the east were not just a replay of the kinds of pogroms familiar to the Jews from previous wars. This time the dimensions of the blow were overwhelming, and its consequences were countless times more devastating.

The Jews of Warsaw had been subject to the vicissitudes of war and the occupation for two years by then. Disease and starvation had taken a high toll in human life. The bitter struggle to survive consumed material resources and physical strength as well. But, with the exception of the murder of individuals in the streets and at the gates of the ghetto and a few large-scale terror operations, Jewish Warsaw had not experienced a relentless campaign of mindless slaughter. That the Jews had not "grown accustomed" to the indiscriminate murder of innocent victims is clear from the public's response to the execution of eight people on November 17, 1941, for the "crime" of illegal presence on the "Aryan" side of the city. As noted earlier, this incident left the ghetto in an uproar, and the underground press described it as "a nightmare" and an unprecedented "abomination." Moreover, at the end of 1941—the year of severe distress and heavy loss of life—there were, or appeared to be, indications that the situation in the ghetto was stabilizing, and diary entries from that period expressed a burgeoning hope that, despite all, the inured population of Jewish Warsaw would survive the war.

In his introduction to *Pages from the Conflagration*, the literary legacy of Mordecai Tenenbaum-Tamarof, Yitzhak Zuckerman stated that once the horrifying news arrived from Vilna, "all the education work, which aspired to preserve the humanity of the younger generation and arouse in it the spirit of battle, would have been meaningless . . . unless together with it, and by virtue of its power, an armed Jewish self-defense force would come into being."[15] In this statement, Zuckerman puts his finger on the turning point between the stage of underground activity that placed emphasis on mutual aid and educational-ideological work and the stage devoted primarily to forging a spirit of resistance and preparing for an armed struggle. Yet this transition process was in reality both gradual and complex. We shall try to trace its course and the various factors that contributed to it.

The outbreak of the German-Soviet war seemed to mark a let-up in the ideological competition between the various movements in the Jewish underground. According to *Neged ha-Zerem*, "as of June 22 — or to be more precise, with the signing of the Anglo-Soviet alliance— differences of opinion have lost all significance."[16] Yet in November– December 1941, intensive educational-ideological work was still going on. Then, at the end of December and the beginning of January, a change took place. The last ideological seminar of Ha-Shomer ha-Za'ir was being held in Warsaw at the time. Ringelblum relates:

> . . . Once, during a break between classes in the Ha-Shomer seminar (I lectured on the history of the Jewish labor movement), Mordecai [Anielewicz] and Yosef Kaplan called me down into the yard of the building at 23 Nalewki Street. They let me into a special room and showed me two revolvers. These revolvers, the members of the central leadership explained to me, were to be employed to train youth in the use of arms. This was the first step taken by Ha-Shomer Ha-Za'ir even before the Fighting Organization was founded.[17]

According to Marek Edelman, it was the Bund that established "the first fighting organization," in coordination with the Polish Socialists, headed by Bernard Goldstein, Abrasza Blum, and Berek Szajndmil. "The acute shortage of arms prevents the expansion of the operation," Edelman explained. "Thus the work is restricted to trailing members of the Gestapo and warning people of a possible 'debacle.'" Obviously Edelman is talking about the organization of a group whose missions were in the nature of security operations and not the "first fighting organization." Elsewhere he states that after April 19, 1942, all the underground work of the Bund "was channeled exclusively toward organizing a resistance movement."[18]

Thus at that stage, the organization of resistance forces was still being carried out on a separate party or movement basis. Before long, however, new circumstances and developments forced the various bodies in the underground to move toward agreement and the establishment of a broad-based self-defense organization. The need for arms was an important motive, since each body found it difficult to obtain weapons on its own, and logic dictated that unifying their forces would facilitate access to the sources of arms in the Polish underground and on the "Aryan" side of Warsaw.

The most important impetus to organize a resistance force, however, came from events that pointed to a further deterioration in the situation and the spread of the systematic slaughter. In January 1942

Ya'akov Grojanowski, a young Jew from the town of Izbica, escaped from the ranks of the *Sonderkommando* in the Chełmno extermination camp and gave detailed testimony on the installation.[19] The news about Chełmno had far-reaching implications for the Jews of Warsaw. Even if events in the east could be discounted as a campaign of revenge and unbridled frenzy in an area close to the front that was allegedly infected by Communism, Chełmno was, after all, in one of the provinces of western Poland that had been annexed to the Reich! The very location of the camp proved that the murders in the east were not just short, localized sprees of violence but a systematic venture of as yet unknown scope, which bode ill precisely because of the uncertainty and threat it carried. The experienced instinct that demanded these phenomena be viewed in their proper context found expression in an article headlined "Nowogródek"[20] published in the March 28, 1942, issue of *Jutrznia*:

> . . . We know that Hitler's system of murder, slaughter, and plunder relentlessly leads to a *cul-de-sac* and the destruction of Jewry. The fate of the Jews in the areas of the Soviet Union conquered by the Germans and in Warthegau signifies a new phase in the complete annihilation of the Jewish population. The gigantic killing apparatus has turned against masses of weak, unarmed, hunger-stricken Jews in the form of camps and deportations. . . . There can be no doubt that Hitler, sensing that the downfall of his regime is approaching, intends to drown the Jews in a sea of blood. Jewish youth must prepare itself for such difficult days. Mobilization of the vitality of the Jews will therefore begin. Many such vital forces still exist, despite the destruction. From generation to generation, we are troubled by the burden of passivity and lack of faith in our own strength; but our history also contains glorious and shining pages of heroism and struggle. We are obliged to join these eras of heroism. . . .[21]

When news of what was taking place in the east began to arrive in Warsaw, the youth movements in the underground took pains to pass the information on to public figures and the heads of the political parties in the ghetto and even arranged for them to meet with the emissaries who reached Warsaw. As noted earlier, the envoys came away with the impression that no one in Warsaw truly understood what was happening in the east, and the ghetto's leaders were unswervingly sure that "nothing like that will happen in Warsaw." Only the nucleus of the political underground—that is, the public leadership that centered around the Self-Help and the directors of the JDC—participated in these consultations and were let in on the secret. The Jewish public at large picked up only echoes of rumors and bits and pieces of news through the underground press.

Even the leaders of the Warsaw community were at a loss to cope

with the news. Their consciousness, forged by a classic European education, dismissed out of hand the possibility of a calculated system to
murder masses of innocent and helpless victims. Like many an ordinary
citizen in the ghetto, they tended to hold fast to the assurances or vague
statements offered by representatives of the Nazi regime, which were
for the most part threads in a sophisticated web of camouflage and
deception.

David Wdowiński, a leader of the Revisionists in the Warsaw underground relates in his memoirs that a fairly late stage—the end of
April 1942—two Betar members, the brothers Zvi and Moshe Zilber-
berg, reached the Warsaw ghetto from Lublin. They told of the mass
deportation from the Lublin ghetto during the latter half of March
1942. More than any other operation to date, the *Aktion* in Lublin, a
large city and the capital of one of the districts of the Generalgouvernement, suggested ominous implications about the overall policy
and aims of the Nazis. The Lublin *Aktion* was effected by methods that
were later repeated in place after place and became a routine system of
dealing a terrorizing blow and then deporting the population of Jewish
communities throughout the Generalgouvernement. Moreover, in Lublin the Nazis set up the headquarters and organized the units of the
"Einsatz Reinhardt," commanded by *S.S.- und Polizeiführer* Globocnik,
which served as a special SS force for deportation and liquidation operations. Wdowiński relates that he broke the news of the Lublin deportation to Adam Czerniakow, the chairman of the *Judenrat*:

> He—Czerniakow—considered the report an exaggeration. He also
> said that General Governor Frank had given assurances that three ghettos
> will remain [intact]—Warsaw, Radom, and Cracow. . . . [22] And then I went
> to the Zionist leaders, including Dr. [Ignacy] Schipper, a former member
> of the Polish *Sejm*; the head of the Jewish National Fund, Mr. Bloch; and
> the director of the JDC, David Guzik. I told them what happened in Lub-
> lin. Meanwhile, other refugees from Lublin—the few who had managed to
> escape—reached Warsaw, including Yosele Kestenberg, the head of the
> Orthodox Jews of that city. They confirmed the story told by the Zilber-
> berg brothers. I suggested that we organize for self-defense. Dr. Schipper,
> a very intelligent and enlightened man, looked at me as if I were suffering
> from a high fever and babbling out of delirium. "You Revisionists are al-
> ways hot-headed," he said with a friendly smile. "It's impossible to wipe
> out a population of half a million people." The Germans wouldn't dare
> annihilate the largest community in Europe. They would have to consider
> world public opinion. And finally, there is the assurance of General Gov-
> ernor Frank that Warsaw, Radom, and Cracow will be left intact.[23]

A month earlier, sometime in the latter half of March 1942, the
He-Halutz movement had invited representatives of political bodies in

the Warsaw underground to a meeting. Since prior consultations had already been held, it was evidently not necessary to debate the seriousness of the threat to the Warsaw community in this framework, so that the discussion centered on the questions of organization, response, and unification of forces in light of the recent developments. The main item on the agenda was the organization of a common defense force by the political parties and youth movements in the Warsaw underground.

We have in our hands a number of versions of that meeting, each written under different circumstances and at different times, so that each undoubtedly represents the individual writer's memory and impressions of the consultation. Two of the authors of these accounts, Yitzhak Zuckerman and Hirsch Berlinski, were present at the meeting and took an active part in the deliberations; the third, Marek Edelman, was not himself present but heard a detailed report of the discussion from people who had been there. We shall first present the report written by Yitzhak Zuckerman:

> In mid-March He-Halutz, after appropriate preparations, convened a preliminary consultation of the political parties with the following taking part: Lazer Levin, Shalom Grajek of Po'alei Zion Z.S.; Melech Feinkind, Hirsch Berlinski of Left Po'alei Zion; [Maurycy] Orzech, Abrasza Blum of the Bund; and Yitzhak Zuckerman of He-Halutz. The He-Halutz representative presented a report on the latest news received from the eastern and western provinces, appraised the situation as the beginning of an operation designed to completely annihilate Polish Jewry, and presented the following concrete proposals:
>
> 1. Establishing an overall Jewish fighting organization.
> 2. Collective representation of all the Jewish political parties and youth organizations vis-à-vis the Polish military authorities.
> 3. The establishment of an apparatus in the "Aryan" residential area for the purpose of obtaining arms and organizing workshops to manufacture arms in the ghetto.
>
> Po'alei Zion Z.S. and Left Po'alei Zion supported this proposal. Orzech stated on behalf of the Bund that talk of a united fighting organization was still premature. Each party and organization must establish its own combat troops independently. The idea of collective representation is out of the question. The Bund engages in socialist, not collective Jewish, politics. The meeting did not produce any positive results.[24]

Berlinski noted in his memoirs, written in 1944, that there was only one item on the agenda of that meeting—the defense of the Warsaw ghetto—while the second item was listed as "miscellaneous." He elaborates upon Orzech's argument:

> The Bund has always been in favor of self-defense. Its history is proof of that. Were it not for the disruptive conditions of the ghetto, we would

not be sitting around the same table in the present political composition. What is happening before our very eyes could only happen in the ghetto! [Yet] the ghetto is not a world unto itself. The liquidation of the ghetto depends upon external political factors. The Bund is linked to international political forces whose decisions are firmly binding upon it. Therefore the Bund will not join a union whose course and tactics might contradict its general policy. The Bund has its own combat squads, as do other parties [the reference being to the Anti-Fascist Bloc]. For the reasons detailed above, [the Bund] will not take part in the overall fighting organization.[25]

According to Berlinski, the other Bund representative at the meeting, Abrasza Blum, tried to soften his party's stand and phrase his arguments more tactfully. But his concluding statement essentially echoed Orzech's: "The Bund will not take part in the overall fighting organization." Po'alei Zion Z.S. and Left Po'alei Zion supported Zuckerman's initiative, but in the final analysis Melech Feinkind stated on behalf of Left Po'alei Zion that "to our great regret, because of the Bund's opposition, the committee cannot be established now. We proclaim [however] that if a self-defense committee does come into being in the Warsaw ghetto, we shall participate in it without reservation."[26]

The March consultation is described in Marek Edelman's memoirs as well. Edelman was to become a member of the command of the Jewish Fighting Organization, and he survived the war. In his book, *The Ghetto is Burning: The Participation of the Bund in the Defense of the Warsaw Ghetto*, which appeared in 1945, he stated:

> In January [as opposed to March] 1942 there was an intra-party meeting. All the bodies adopted the position that the only appropriate response is to fight. For the first time, the [Labor-Zionist] "Shomrim" and "Halutzim" organizations came forward with a concrete proposal to create a fighting organization. M. Orzech and A. Blum spoke on our behalf. They took the position that a combat approach can succeed only through coordination and cooperation with the Polish underground movement. The time had not yet arrived to establish a common fighting organization.[27]

In light of these testimonies, we can assume that the establishment of a common fighting organization in March 1942 was thwarted by the separatist policy of the Bund. Clearly, the Bund was not prepared to cooperate with forces from the "bourgeois-Zionist" camp. But its fundamental objection derived from a reluctance to recognize and accept the pressing need to organize on an independent Jewish basis within the ghetto. Its ties with the Polish Socialists and membership in broader frameworks meant more to the Bund than a cooperative Jewish effort.

The question therefore arises: Why was so much effort invested in convincing the Bund to join the proposed common organizations, and why did its refusal to do so prevent the proclamation of a common front? To understand the problem, we shall return to Zuckerman's report. In addition to the central clause on the establishment of a common Jewish fighting organization, two other propositions were raised for discussion: "2. Collective representation of all the Jewish political parties and youth organizations vis-à-vis the Polish military authorities"; and "3. The establishment of an apparatus in the 'Aryan' residential area for the purpose of obtaining arms and organizing workshops to manufacture arms in the ghetto." These clauses make it clear that the object of the meeting was to establish a Jewish force that would be recognized by the Polish underground as an authorized representative of the Jews and thus pave the way for obtaining both arms and help in weapon's training from a Polish source. "We placed great hopes on the Bund's capability," Zivia Lubetkin comments in her memoirs, "since the Poles were acquainted with [the Bund], and it even had ties with the P.P.S. [the Polish Socialists]."[28] Thus the Bund was an indispensable channel of contact with circles in the Polish underground, and while it was true that the Poles were not then engaged in outright combat operations against the Germans, it was common knowledge that they commanded a wealth of arms, benefited from a network of ties throughout the country and with the Allies, and had professional training forces within their ranks. Thus the Bund held the trump card in the March meeting, and its voice determined the fate of the entire plan at this early stage.

The Anti-Fascist Bloc   Two months before the He-Halutz–sponsored meeting, another political event took place on the "Aryan" side of Warsaw that was to have a major impact upon the eventual organization of a fighting underground in the ghetto and the political future of Poland as a whole. In January 1942 the Polish Workers' Party (P.P.R.) was established in the Polish sector of Warsaw. The P.P.R. was essentially a revival of the defunct Polish Communist Party, which had been disbanded before World War II. Among those who were called upon to take part in the renewed party activity in Warsaw was Joseph Lewartowski-Finkelstein (known as the "Old Man"), who was living in Bialystok at the time. A veteran and renowned Communist stalwart, Lewartowski answered his party's call, left his wife, in the last months of a pregnancy, in Bialystok, and rushed off to report to Warsaw, evidently arriving in January 1942. He remained on the "Aryan" side of the city for a few days or weeks and was then sent to head a branch of the Communist Party that was crystallizing in the ghetto.

The P.P.R. intentionally adopted a name that played down its membership in the world Communist movement. Its objective was to rouse various strata of Polish society to take up arms in a struggle against Nazi Germany, thereby diverting some of the pressure from the Soviet front. While the Polish underground had decided that it must build up strength and train cadres but the moment had not yet come for an outright struggle (the timing of which would be dictated by political and military developments and Polish political interests), the P.P.R. proclaimed that it was interested in forming a "National Front" and "would go along with anyone who was in favor of a struggle against the Nazi occupier."[29] But the P.P.R. essentially failed to make inroads among the Polish public, at least during this early period, so it decided to try its hand within the ghetto and forge a common front within the Jewish realm.

At about the time of the abortive attempt to found a common fighting organization in the ghetto, Joseph Lewartowski began to search around for allies. He turned to members of Left Po'alei Zion, the radical left wing of the ghetto underground. According to the account of Adolf Abraham Berman, one of the leaders of Left Po'alei Zion in Warsaw and a founder of the Anti-Fascist Bloc:

> In March 1942 the Polish Workers' Party [P.P.R.] in the ghetto reached an understanding with Left Po'alei Zion. The two parties founded a common front—the Anti-Fascist Bloc—on the basis of an agreed program to fight against Fascism and the Nazi occupying power. Ha-Shomer ha-Za'ir joined the common front. A common political council was elected, and a common fighting organization began to be established. . . . After a while, He-Halutz, Dror, and the political party ideologically associated with these movements, Po'alei Zion Z.S., joined the Anti-Fascist Bloc.[30]

The bloc's platform, as given in Yitzhak Zuckerman's report on the Jewish Fighting Organization, does not indicate that emphasis was placed on independent Jewish combat or on concentrating all efforts upon active self-defense in the ghetto. Zuckerman defines the bloc's aims as:

1. To organize joint forces for a political and propaganda war against Fascism and reactionary forces within the ghetto.
2. To organize anti-Fascist combat divisions.
3. To organize a relief enterprise for the victims of the war against Fascism.[31]

There can be no doubt about the fact that the originators of the bloc, the Communists, wanted to place emphasis on participation in the

Soviet Union's comprehensive war effort. Zivia Lubetkin notes that "the aim of the council [the bloc] was to join in the wider anti-Nazi war by [carrying out] assaults in the rear and thereby aiding Soviet Russia." He-Halutz evidently had reservations about joining the bloc under such conditions but finally decided to do so, although "we made it an explicit condition that combat groups must be left in the ghetto as well." Obviously the aims of the Communists and the various Zionist factions in the bloc were not identical. The decision to join the broad framework was based upon the expectation that it would subsequently be possible to obtain arms ("and the most important thing is that they will help us get weapons"[32]), train combatants, and make contact with an organized political and military force in the "Aryan" sector. As would later become clear, however, the Zionist camp miscalculated the true strength of the Communists in assuming that the Polish Communists were backed by the power of the Soviet Union with respect to organization and arms supply.

Zuckerman states that the elected council of the bloc was composed of one representative from each faction, for a total of five members: Joseph Lewartowski of the Communists, Shakhne Sagan of Left Po'alei Zion, Joseph Sak of Po'alei Zion Z.S., Zivia Lubetkin of Dror He-Halutz, and Mordecai Anielewicz of Ha-Shomer ha-Za'ir. During its existence, the bloc published a joint periodical, *Der Ruf (The Order)*, but its basic activity was training cadres for combat and preparing groups for partisan warfare in the forests.

The bloc's combat squads were composed of "fivesomes," each faction organizing its own members. Transforming groups of people who had operated in a relatively open political framework into a coalescent brigade under conditions of complete secrecy was not at all easy. It is estimated that the combat units of the bloc numbered about five hundred people.[33] Not all members of the underground political parties and youth movements that comprised the bloc were automatically organized in its battle units, since membership in the combat squads was on an individual basis, and each candidate had to declare his readiness to join a "fivesome." As a rule, the younger party comrades and older youth movement members enlisted in the combat units. The bloc also announced that enlistment in the squads was open to people who were not members of the underground organizations, as long as they were completely reliable and physically fit for combat. But the number of nonparty or nonmovement people who joined was infinitesimal. The combat units, known as the bloc's Military Division, were headed by Joseph Kaplan of Ha-Shomer ha-Za'ir, Mordecai Tenenbaum-Tamarof of Dror He-Halutz, Abram Fiszelson of Po'alei Zion Z.S., and Hirsch Lent of Left Po'alei Zion, but the moving spirit behind the battalions was Andrzej Szmidt, a veteran Communist activist with combat experience.

Andrzej Szmidt was the underground name of the Jewish Communist Pinkus Kartin, a colorful personality whose very appearance in the ghetto undoubtedly impressed the Jewish underground. Kartin was born in the city of Lutsk in the western Ukraine, which had been part of the Polish state between the two wars. While still a youth he joined the Communist movement, and in the Spanish Civil War he was an officer in the Polish Dombrovski Brigade. When World War II broke out, Kartin was in France working for the Comintern. He was recognized as a citizen of the Soviet Union and repatriated to the USSR under the terms of the German-Soviet exchange of citizens agreement (which was honored until the outbreak of war between the two countries). In the Soviet Union he joined the circle of Polish Communist émigrés, underwent special military training, and was counted among the elite "Enterprising Group" that was chosen to penetrate into Poland, lead the underground Communist Party, and organize an armed force backed by the Communists. After a number of abortive attempts to reach Poland, the first squad, including Szmidt, parachuted into the Warsaw area at the end of 1941.

Kartin could not participate in the enlistment campaign in the Polish sector, since his appearance would immediately betray his Jewish origins. For a while he hid out in the home of a Polish shoemaker, suffering severely from a lack of sufficient nourishment and warm clothing. Finally his comrades decided, "without taking the original plans and the predetermined division of responsibilities into account, to charge Kartin with the mission of organizing the party and the combat units in the ghetto."[34]

Although it provoked friction within the bloc, the question of whether the combat units would operate in the ghetto or go out to the forests was essentially a theoretical one. Because the Zionist components of the bloc grossly overestimated the actual strength of the Communists, they assumed that the bloc would immediately be called upon to send its forces to join partisan units. "We said that if we receive an order to go beyond the walls of the ghetto," Zuckerman wrote in his memoirs, "we shall not go, we shall not obey that order, we shall remain in the ghetto."[35] Yet the conflicting aims and the discord over both objectives and courses of action never reached a crisis point, because the bloc's expectations were never realized in the form of actual combat. The yawning gap between the expectations and readiness, on the one hand, and the severe inertia, on the other, was due to the state of the Communist camp. While they did believe in and preach that combat operations should be undertaken forthwith, at that stage the Communists were too weak to translate their intentions into action. They were just beginning to organize and lacked financial resources, trained manpower, and stores of weapons. The Polish underground Home Army (A.K.), which controlled arms stores from the September 1939 fighting and had access to plentiful sources of funds, charged that the "agents of Moscow" were being supplied with money and arms by the Soviet Union. But the fact of the matter is that the handful of Communists did not even maintain uninterrupted contact with the Soviet Union at that time, and they certainly did not receive aid in the form of funds or equipment. Henryk Kotlicki, a Communist activist who smuggled the first revolver into the ghetto for the bloc, states in his memoirs: "The organization had no weapons. The better part of our arms was located in the provincial cities. Nevertheless, we decided to turn one of the two revolvers in our hands over to the ghetto. I smuggled the gun in my sleeve and turned it over to members of CENTOS. . . ."[36] That revolver was the common weapon of all the members of the bloc. It served as an instrument for training, and all the pretentious plans were supposed to be based on that single gun.

In May 1942 the Communists began to organize the first group slated to go out to the forests, and mobilization extended throughout the ghetto. For weeks meetings of the bloc's "fivesomes" were devoted to instruction on the character of partisan warfare and combat tactics in city and forest. At the last moment, however, this campaign, which was supposed to be the bloc's first actual combat operation, was cancelled, and the reasons for its suspension led to the total disintegration of the bloc. On May 30 three of the P.P.R.'s principal activists, including Andrzej Szmidt himself, were arrested just as they were about to meet with liaisons of the Communist Party from the "Aryan" side in a ghetto café. It later became clear that a Gestapo agent who had infiltrated the ranks of the Polish Communists was responsible for the arrest, and the setback in the ghetto was part of a campaign of arrests and persecutions directed against the Communist Party on the "Aryan" side of Warsaw, which effectively paralyzed its activities for months.

Szmidt's arrest sent a tremor of shock and fear through all the component elements of the bloc. The Communist leader was on close terms with some of the heads of the ghetto underground, knew many addresses, and was familiar with the location of secret clubhouses and meeting places. At the time, the reasons for the arrest were unknown, so there were grounds to fear that the Nazis knew about Szmidt's role in the bloc, they were on the organization's trail, and the incident in the café was just the first sign of impending collapse. The movements organized in the bloc tightened up their rules of conspiracy, declared a temporary cessation of routine activities, and continued to meet only in small cells. The mobilization campaign was discounted, the "fivesomes" disbanded, and for all intents and purposes the bloc ceased to function. The greatest blow, however, fell on the Communist Party in the ghetto: some of its leading personalities had been lost, its status was undermined, and, more than any other body, its members were gripped by a fear of events to come.

We can find no trace of any bloc operations after the arrest of Szmidt and his associates. Probably no formal decision was ever taken to disband the bloc, but its disintegration had become a fact: the bloc effectively ceased to exist in June 1942. When the Jewish Fighting Organization was founded on July 28, 1942, at the end of the first week of deportations from Warsaw, it was not simply a direct continuation of the bloc with a new name. The Communists, for example, were not among the founders, but members of the Zionist youth movement Akiva, which had not been associated with the bloc, took part in the formation of the new body. The bloc never attained any real achievements in the military sphere, nor did it even make much progress in effectively training its members for combat. Yet its importance lies in the fact that it united various underground political bodies whose primary common goal was to organize a fighting force and embark upon combat operations. In this way, just as by its failures, the bloc contributed to the maturation of the frame of mind and decisions that subsequently led to the founding of the Jewish Fighting Organization.

Before leaving the subject of the budding Jewish resistance movement, we must also examine the position of the Revisionists and Betar on the organization of an armed force in the ghetto. David Wdowiński, who was considered the political leader of the Betar fighting organization later established in the ghetto, described his efforts to warn the Jewish public leaders of the impending danger and goes on to state:

> . . . In April–May 1942 the better part of the Revisionist youth was living outside the Warsaw ghetto. But even if they had been in the ghetto, we Revisionist party members could not have taken upon ourselves the organization of resistance. Resistance of that kind must have the backing of the decisive majority of the population. We did not have [such support]. It is clear that the only conceivable German response to even the least evidence of resistance in the ghetto would be a blood bath. We could not assume responsibility for that.[37]

The question of public responsibility and the dread of collective punishment, which weighed so heavily on the Revisionists, were indeed among the factors that restrained the resistance operation. Yet these considerations had not yet been raised in internal-party and collective political consultations or at the time that the Anti-Fascist Bloc was founded. The full gravity of these questions had to be faced during the stage of the mass deportation, when not merely the problem of organization but the actual question of whether or not to act was under consideration. In any event, Wdowiński makes it clear that the Revisionists had no fighting organization of their own prior to the mass deportation. He also notes that the organization of his comrades into a fighting formation began after the Betar members returned from Hrubieszów.

The Significance of "The Night of Blood"— April 18, 1942

On the eve of the Sabbath, April 18, 1942, the Nazis perpetrated a massacre in the Warsaw ghetto, and the date has come to be known as the "Night of Blood" or the "Bartholomew's Night" of the Warsaw ghetto. For a day or two before the operation, a rumor made the rounds of the ghetto that a uniformed German had been killed in the no-man's-land between the ghetto wall and the "Aryan" side. The ghetto residents whispered of a possible reprisal raid or terrorist act, but no one knew what might happen. German trucks entered the ghetto after dark and spewed forth armed SS troops. The small squads of uniformed men, accompanied by Jewish policemen acting as guides, then made for the homes of dozens of people. Those on the wanted list were dragged out of their beds into the street fronting their houses or somewhere nearby and murdered by a shot in the back. Of the sixty people on the wanted list, fifty-two were killed,[38] a few were wounded, and some had been warned in time and were not at home when the SS troops arrived for them. Sometimes others were taken in their place or the relatives who refused to turn the wanted man in to the Nazis were summarily shot.

After the operation the ghetto was haunted by questions. What did the Nazis hope to achieve by murdering dozens of ghetto residents? And what was the common denominator that established the victims of such calculated murder? The enigma was not easy to solve. Kaplan wrote in his diary:

> When the initial shock began to wear off and the panic had subsided a bit, we began to wonder about the episode. Why that particular kind of selectivity? What was the key to the list they had drawn up? The victims came from every level of our ghetto society: Well-to-do merchants like Blajman, the baker, former officials, small shopkeepers, even some from the very poor.[39]

Some of the victims were involved in the ghetto underground; others were known to have grown wealthy during the war; and some even belonged to Gancwajch's inner circle. The dead included Menachem Linder, a talented economist and demographer who was Ringelblum's friend and colleague and the moving spirit behind Yikor, and members of the Bund who had been printshop workers and were active in the ghetto underground.

None of the leaders of the underground political movements were murdered on the "Night of Blood," which is not to say that none were wanted by the Gestapo. Yitzhak Zuckerman and Lonka Kozibrodzka of Dror He-Halutz, for example, were definitely on the Nazis' list. Germans had asked about them at one of the *Judenrat*'s Registration Offices, and some Dror members who were temporarily employed there immediately warned the two, who absented themselves from the movement's communal living quarters that night.[40] Also on the list were two prominent Bund activists, Sonya Nowogrodzka and Lezer Klog. Sonya was warned of her impending arrest by an anonymous caller, and she in turn warned Klog, so that both of them were out of their apartments that night.[41]

The residents of the ghetto interpreted the night of terror as a blow directed against the political underground. Kaplan believed that the illegal publications were the reason for the slaughter.[42] Indeed, the Nazis themselves claimed that the slaughter was in retaliation for the publication of underground newspapers, as evidenced by Czerniakow's entry on April 19, 1942, a day after the incident: "Apropos recent occurrences they [the Germans] claim that underground papers may bring about untold harm to the Jewish population."[43]

Czerniakow accepted the German claim and took their warning very seriously. But he preferred to handle the matter through judicious intervention, without involving the Germans or even making them aware of his own efforts. Zuckerman writes: "The next day Czerniakow, the chairman of the *Judenrat*, summoned Dr. Emmanuel Ringelblum and ordered him to speak to the representatives of the underground on his behalf and pass on his demand that they cease publication of illegal newspapers and refrain from any illegal activity. The underground is responsible for the fate of the victims."[44] Ringelblum does not explicitly confirm having had such a meeting with Czerniakow in any of his writings, but he does make mention of warnings from "*Judenrat* people."[45] Czerniakow's diary does not mention such a meeting either. Then again, Bernard Goldstein of the Bund tells in his memoirs of another summons by Czerniakow: "The chairman of the *Judenrat*, Adam Czerniakow, summoned Maurycy Orzech and told him that Gestapo circles had explicitly informed him that the executions would not stop as long as the secret press continues to appear. He therefore demanded of the Bund, through Orzech, that it stop disseminating illegal publications and not provoke additional punitive actions."[46] And Czerniakow's diary does not mention this meeting either.

As to the response of the underground bodies to the German threats and appeals from Czerniakow, as well as the conclusions that the "Night of Blood" prompted them to draw about the future, Yitzhak Zuckerman wrote that after receiving Czerniakow's message, "We convened as a council, and as a response to the Germans and the *Judenrat* chairman we decided to publish the weekly *Yediot* exactly on time and in an expanded edition. The paper must expose the barbaric actions of the Germans [for what they are] and destroy any belief in their assurances that the Jewish population may harbor."[47]

A glance at future events proves that the underground press was not suppressed. Quite to the contrary, the short period from the "Night of Blood" until the mass deportation (about three months in all) was actually the golden age of the clandestine press—both from the standpoint of the abundance of publications and their aggressive political tone—though more cautious methods were stringently enforced in preparing and distributing the papers following the April massacre.

At the same time, April 18, 1942, was a turning point for the Warsaw ghetto. The political leadership went deeper underground, moved out of their apartments, and met together less frequently. Large public assemblies were not even considered. Some of the youth movements confined their underground activity exclusively to groups of older members, disbanding frameworks that had been organized during the war. And all the cultural activities that had taken place fairly openly were evidently dropped altogether.

The underground bodies could not avoid facing up to two critical facts. First, the terror operation on the "Night of Blood" was undoubtedly intended, among other things, to harm the underground, which meant that the Germans—who had until then been largely indifferent to the existence of Jewish political organizations—had now decided to embark on a campaign against clandestine political activity. Furthermore, the Nazis must have been receiving information on the political underground from agents planted in the ghetto. These two conclusions demanded the exercise of extreme caution in choosing means of organization and operation. Second, the consensus in the ghetto was that the entire ghetto had been punished because of the relative few who were operating in the underground. The *Judenrat* even published a statement to that effect, calling for the cessation of clandestine activity. There is no doubt that the majority of the ghetto's residents, preoccupied with the struggle against hunger, disease, and overcrowding, were hardly sympathetic to those who were "playing around" with outlawed politics and thereby invited further persecution and risks.

Yet the underground organizations were convinced that the strike of "political terror" was not motivated by the Germans' resolve to muzzle the underground press but was part of a broader strategy, some far more pervasive Nazi plan. They soon discovered that sudden murderous attacks were also taking place in other ghettos where there was no clandestine press and secret political activities were not at all in evidence. Thus the "Night of Blood" was actually the prologue to a more comprehensive action, a campaign of deportations to camps. It was designed to heighten the sense of psychological stress, instigate internal conflict, and thus further weaken the ghetto from within. Furthermore, by murdering a wide selection of people in the ghetto, the Germans evidently intended to smother any leadership that might come forward to guide the masses of Jews. That was one possible explanation of the otherwise inexplicable fact that people of such widely diverse backgrounds were singled out for elimination. Many were evidently included on the wanted list for their capabilities, initiative, and resourcefulness in spheres that bore no relation to secret political activity. But faced with extreme circumstances — i.e., deportation to the camps — they might nonetheless become the focus of Jewish resistance.

The July 1942 issue of Gordonia's newspaper *Słowo Młodych* wrote under the headline "The Secret Courts":

> There are various ways of wiping out Jewry. Acts of mass murder carried out before the eyes of thousands of people in broad daylight and the deportations to "unknown" destinations have now been added to by acts of murder perpetrated on the basis of what are called "the secret courts." This wave of killing began in Warsaw on the night of April 18, when Gestapo men moved through the city and, following a list that included the names and address of specific Jews, hauled them out of their apartments and shot them dead in the street. Shortly afterward, prewar and present-day Jewish political officials were murdered in many cities throughout the Generalgouvernement in the very same way. . . .[48]

In the coming months, the execution of specific individuals was repeated a number of times, and usually on Friday night — the eve of the Sabbath. Moreover, the Nazis adopted a strategy of brutal and widespread punishment for the least act of resistance in which Jews were involved. In June 1942, 110 Jews incarcerated in the ghetto prison were executed. According to *Kommissar* Auerswald's public statement, the execution was a retaliatory act, since "in the last few days, the Jews have repeatedly disobeyed the instructions of the German police. In many cases, matters reached the point where the Jews physically attacked the police."[49] A source in the *Delegatura* (the representation of the Polish regime in the underground) reported that the execution of 110 Jews (10 policemen and 100 civilians) was carried out because of "disobedience to the authorities. The reason given for this act was the fist fight that allegedly broke out in the eastern railway station between Jewish workers, headed by the student Robak, and a Polish engineer who called the "Blue Police." Shots rang out. The Jews resisted. Robak fell during the battle."[50]

Instances of resistance did indeed occur, and the newsletter *Yediot* of July 1, 1942, notes with vehemence:

> The ghetto has been punished for "disobedience" and "resistance" to the German police. And that is a mark of praise for the ghetto. We have no desire whatsoever to obey. On the contrary, our desire is to skirt the law of the wild beasts as often as possible, while taking care to incur a minimum of casualties; [we want] to break the draconian rules. Thus the most recent punishment is also something of a blood-stained achievement for us.[51]

Nonetheless, it is clear that after the "Night of Blood," the Nazis took advantage of every act of resistance—or, indeed, any pretext whatsoever—to strike a blow of terror. Such violence bore no relation to the alleged provocation, for its real purpose was to pave the way for the incredible slaughter that the Nazis were planning. The terror that began in April continued relentlessly. As Abraham Levin wrote in his journal on May 12, 1942, "Hardly a day passes without Jewish blood being spilled on the cobblestones and sidewalks of the Warsaw ghetto."[52]

Ghetto inmates

Dealer in the ghetto

Young boy in the ghetto

A meal in the ghetto

Ghetto inmates

In the streets of the ghetto

Warming up on the ghetto streets

Waiting in line for potatoes, under an announcement
of a ballet performance in the ghetto

Hungry Jewish children

Trading in the streets of the ghetto

Jews on their way to daily forced labor

Deportation from the ghetto

During the uprising

Ruins of the Warsaw ghetto during the revolt

Ruins of the Warsaw ghetto during the revolt

Ruins of the Warsaw ghetto during the revolt

The ghetto after the uprising

Adam Czerniakow

Yitzhak Katzenelson

Janusz Korczak

Mordecai Anielewicz

Emmanuel Ringelblum

Chapter Six
The Fateful Deportation

The Background to the
Deportation from Warsaw

The mass deportation, or "resettlement," of the Jews of Warsaw
began on Wednesday, July 22,
1942—the eve of the Ninth of Av[1]—and continued, with occasional
short pauses, until September 12, 1942. During those seven weeks,
some 265,000 Jews were uprooted from Warsaw, transported to the
Treblinka death camp, and murdered in the gas chambers.

The deportation from Warsaw was part of "The Final Solution of
the Jewish Problem"—a comprehensive plan to annihilate the Jews of
Europe. In the spring of 1942, forces of the SS and the police initiated
a campaign of sudden roundups and mass deportations to the death
camps within the Generalgouvernement. These deportations and kill-
ings were implemented in the framework of *Aktion Reinhardt* ("Operation Reinhardt") by the units of the *Einsatz Reinhardt*, which were
under the command of the *S.S.- und Polizeiführer* of the Lublin District,
General Odilo Globocnik. The operation shifted into high gear on July
19, 1942, when Himmler informed the Higher SS and Police Leader of
the Generalgouvernement, Friedrich Krieger, that the evacuation of the
entire Jewish population of the Generalgouvernement must be completed by December 31, 1942 ("Ich ordne an, dass die Umsiedlung der
gesamten jüdischen Bevölkerung des Generalgouvernements bis 31
Dezember durchgeführt und beendet ist").[2]

Globocnik tried to carry out his mission with speed and decisiveness, for he believed that as time went on there was a chance that
difficulties might slow down the extermination process.[3] Methodical

197

preparations were made for implementing the extermination program, and during the first half of 1942 the Bełzec, Sobibor, and Treblinka death camps were put into operation. All the deportees to these camps—with the exception of a small staff that was maintained for handling necessary skilled jobs and unloading and sorting the belongings left behind by the victims—were murdered in the gas chambers that had been installed in permanent buildings. In the summer of 1942, construction of the Majdanek camp near Lublin was completed. Like Auschwitz, Majdanek served as both a concentration and extermination camp. Most of the Jews transported there—and particularly children, women, and the elderly—were immediately sent to the gas chambers, while a certain percentage that met the standards of the *Selektion* were assigned to the concentration camp.

In the course of time, Operation Reinhardt was extended to include: (1) siege operations within the ghettos and deportations to extermination camps; (2) supervising the means and rate of extermination in the death camps; (3) exploiting the labor of Jewish prisoners in the forced-labor and concentration camps run by the SS; and (4) the confiscation of Jewish property, be it in the form of money, jewelry, movables, or immovables.[4]

Himmler's above-mentioned order of July 19 stated that at the end of 1942 no Jews were to be left in the Generalgouvernement, other than laborers who had been concentrated in assembly camps in Warsaw, Cracow, Częstochowa, Radom, and Lublin.[5] The civilian authorities of the Generalgouvernement not only supported the extermination campaign but encouraged and abetted the liquidation process. Dr. Josef Bühler, a representative of Frank's regime at the Wannsee Conference, promised the administration's full support in implementing the "Final Solution" and proclaimed that "the Generalgouvernement will be delighted if the solution to this question will commence in the Generalgouvernement" ("das Generalgouvernement es begrüssen würde, wenn mit der Endlösung dieser Frage im Generalgouvernement begonnen würde . . .").

On December 16, 1941, shortly before the Wannsee Conference, Frank stated at a meeting of the Generalgouvernement administration:

> As a veteran National Socialist, I must state that if the Jewish tribe were to survive this war while we sacrifice our finest blood to save Europe, the victory in this war would only be a partial achievement. For that reason, my outlook toward the Jews is based on the hope that they will cease to exist. It is necessary to remove them . . . but what should be done with them? Do you suppose we will resettle them in settlers' villages in Ostland? In Berlin they said to us: What is all the great fuss about? There is nothing to be done with them in Ostland or in the *Reichskommissariat*. Do away with them yourselves.[6]

On the same occasion, Frank announced that a broad-based consultation on the question of the Jews would be held in Heydrich's headquarters in January 1942, namely the forthcoming Wannsee Conference. At a later stage, on July 3, 1942, the governor-general issued an order extending the authority of the security forces in the Generalgouvernement and placing Jewish affairs within the jurisdiction of the Security Police (*Sicherheitspolizei*), that is, the SS.[7]

As related in chapter 3, rumor was rife in the Warsaw ghetto that the local administrative apparatus, and particularly Auerswald himself, were trying to prevent the "evacuation" and liquidation of the ghetto.[8] It is quite possible that Auerswald and other parties involved in Jewish affairs in Warsaw were interested in preserving the ghetto, since control over a large Jewish population reinforced their sense of authority and provided them with substantial material benefits, not to mention the fact that it insured the members of the bureaucracy against reassignment to the front. Nevertheless, we have no authoritative confirmation that these parties actually demurred on the question of the ghetto's future. On the other hand, we know for a fact—as the matter has been verified—that these local officials, including Auerswald, took part in a campaign designed to deceive the Jews about their future up until the very last moment.

The main parties with a vested interest in preserving a Jewish work force, and thus preventing the liquidation of the ghettos and Jewish settlements, were the officials and arms of the *Wehrmacht* responsible for armament, supply, and equipment. Beginning in 1942, as a result of the difficulties encountered on the eastern front, the authorities of the German Reich announced a build-up in the arms industry and a heightened mobilization of manpower. In contrast to the increasing shortage of manpower in Germany, the Generalgouvernement embraced a substantial reserve of underexploited Jewish labor. The area was also a fitting place to concentrate war industries because it was not expected to be a target of aerial bombardment. Therefore the *Wehrmacht*'s armaments and supply authorities planned to establish new factories in the Generalgouvernement, as well as transfer some of their factories there from the Reich proper. Their idea was to have Jews replace the Poles conscripted for forced labor inside Germany. There was also talk of vocational training for Jews in critical branches of industry. All these plans were wrecked, however, by the mass-extermination program. As matters turned out, the deportations were not coordinated in advance with the *Wehrmacht* authorities responsible for armament and supply, and in a number of factories the Jewish workers were taken off without any prior warning or consideration for supplying replacements.

This development led to the initiation of complex negotiations between the SS and the concerned parties in the *Wehrmacht*. As a rule the SS had the upper hand in this confrontation, for, as Himmler put it, the annihilation of the Jews was "imperative to achieve ethnic separation between the races and nationalities in the spirit of the New Order in Europe."[9] Moreover, even in cases where a compromise was arrived at between the two sides and Himmler appeared to be yielding (and in one case, a concession was wrung out of the SS by Hitler's personal intervention), the retreat on the part of the SS was only temporary, and Himmler repeatedly emphasized that in the final analysis—and in accordance with Hitler's wishes—it was crucial that the Jews employed by the *Wehrmacht* be consumed by the process of total annihilation.[10]

As we shall see, the position of the concerned *Wehrmacht* parties in Warsaw was particularly weak, while Himmler closely monitored events in the ghetto and prodded his commanders to liquidate its Jews with greater speed and by resorting to the most drastic methods. The veteran Jewish leadership in Warsaw believed that the Germans would not dare to inflict serious harm on the largest Jewish community in Europe in a city that had been the capital of Poland and was still a focus of world attention. But exactly the opposite was in fact about to happen: Himmler devoted special attention to ensuring that the annihilation of the Jews of Warsaw was carried out in full. The reason for his special interest in Warsaw was evidently twofold: (1) Warsaw was a focal point of Polish national resistance, and Himmler looked upon the liquidation of the Jewish quarter and its residents as part of a general campaign designed to reduce the size and importance of the city; (2) since the Jewish community of Warsaw was the largest urban concentration of Jews in all of Europe, he viewed the total annihilation of that community as an important step toward reaching the "Final Solution." In the course of time, these aims were augmented by the complications that arose in Warsaw and reinforced Himmler's decision to uproot and destroy the city's Jewish community as quickly as possible.

The extermination campaign moved steadily westward, in the direction of Warsaw and the heart of the Generalgouvernement, and 1942 was indeed the decisive year of achieving the "Final Solution" within the Generalgouvernement. According to German figures, at the end of 1942 only 297,914 Jews remained in the Generalgouvernement, 161,514 of whom were located in the Galicia District. That left a total of 136,400 Jews in all the other provinces of the Generalgouvernement, or about 10 percent of the Jewish population of the area at the outbreak of the war. About 50,000 Jews remained in the Warsaw District, that is, less than 10 percent of the district's Jewish population during various periods of the war.[11]

The Jews knew nothing certain about the German plans and events awaiting them. With the initiation of the "Final Solution," the Jewish leaders were deprived of even the limited maneuverability left to them as long as they maintained contact with officials of the civil regime. The forces assigned to implement the "Final Solution" disguised and concealed their intentions in a calculated and cynical fashion, so that a thick fog of nescience and uncertainty blanketed the Jewish communities.

As the wave of terror that first struck the ghetto on April 18, 1942, continued unrelentlessly, ominous signs began to mount. Grave news arrived of developments in distant communities (e.g., the deportations from Lublin and Lvov), and rumors burgeoned about the impending evacuation from Warsaw. On May 16, 1942, Abraham Levin recorded in his diary that upon hearing the news of murders in the night, ". . . my throat constricts and a stone weighs on my heart. A dark fear strangles and overcomes [me]."[12] During the spring of 1942, Jews from the towns around Warsaw were concentrated in the ghetto and an additional 3,872 Jews were transported there from the territory of the Reich and the Protectorate. In May gypsies caught in Warsaw and its vicinity were incarcerated in the ghetto.[13] In the following month, Jews of foreign citizenship were ordered to register with the authorities, and about 700 people who fell into this category were jailed in the Pawiak prison. Chaim Kaplan wrote on April 30, 1942: "Terrible rumors about Warsaw are flying thick and fast among the ghetto dwellers. A non-Jew from outside the ghetto has brought the news that a quarter of a million Germans living in Lübeck, Rostock, Köln, and Kiel, whose homes were destroyed by the English bombardments, were marching toward Warsaw in order to take over the Jews' homes."[14]

Naturally, the flood of rumors about the impending deportation did not escape the attention of the chairman of the *Judenrat*. As early as January 19, 1942, Adam Czerniakow had expressed his fears of such an eventuality in his journal: "I have heard that Auerswald had been summoned to Berlin. I cannot shake off the fearful suspicion that the Jews of Warsaw may be threatened by mass resettlement." On May 6 he noted: "In the city alarming rumors about deportations continue." On May 15, the chairman of the *Judenrat* wrote: "The city is full of rumors about deportations. Tens of thousands are being mentioned. Work as usual under such conditions is indeed worthy of admiration. And yet we are doing it every day. Tears will not help us. I must repeat Dickens' words once more: 'You cannot wind your watch with your tears.'" And again, on May 18, Czerniakow noted in his daily entry: "Besides all this, persistent rumors about deportations. It appears that they are not without foundation."[15]

Czerniakow's diary testifies to more than just the uneasiness that permeated the ghetto in anticipation of a fateful upheaval. It also provides us with insight into the tactics of deception that were part and parcel of the preparations for the deportation operation and were used to even greater effect during the course of the *Aktion* itself. On the other hand, taking note of only the heightened terror and the rise in incidents that portended the deportation does not provide a full picture of developments in the ghetto during this period. At one and the same time, regulations were issued and acts were committed that seemingly contradicted one another. A report about the last weeks before the deportation, sent to London by the underground Jewish bodies in Warsaw on November 15, 1942, states:

> . . . On the other hand, positive orders were issued; for example: the Jewish Council [*Judenrat*] received permission to operate new elementary schools. The Department of Technical Training for Jews was allowed to run new courses. A play was put on for children; kindergartens were opened in the ghetto. Here and there positive things were said about the work done by Jews. It was even commented that the Jews of Warsaw, by virtue of their professional ability, constitute a different type of Jew.[16]

Czerniakow's diary shows that three days before his suicide—two days before the inception of the deportation—the chairman of the *Judenrat* tried to clarify exactly what lay behind the growing rumors about the impending deportation. He turned to the German officials and Gestapo men with whom he had been dealing throughout his difficult term of office. The preparations for the operation had just been completed, and the unit brought in from Lublin to execute the deportation was already deployed in Warsaw when Czerniakow recorded in his diary on July 20, 1942:

> In the morning at 7:30 at the Gestapo. I asked Mende how much truth there was in the rumors. He replied that he had heard nothing. I turned to Brandt; he also knew nothing. When asked whether it *could* happen, he replied that he knew of no such scheme. Uncertain, I left his office. I proceeded to his chief, Kommissar Böhm. He told me that this was not his department but Hoeheman [Höhmann] might say something about the rumors. I mentioned that according to rumor, the deportation is to start tonight at 7:30. He replied that he would be bound to know something if it were about to happen. Not seeing any other way out, I went to the deputy chief of Section III, Scherer. He expressed his surprise hearing the rumor and informed me that he too knew nothing about it. Finally, I asked whether I could tell the population that their fears were groundless. He replied that I could and that all talk was *Quatsch* and *Unsinn* [utter nonsense].
>
> I ordered Lejkin to make the public announcement through the precinct police stations. I drove to Auerswald. He informed me that he re-

ported everything to the SS *Polizeiführer*. Meanwhile, First went to see Jesuiter and Schlederer, who expressed their indignation that the rumors were being spread and promised an investigation.

On that same day, Czerniakow was still negotiating for the release of children held in the ghetto prison, and Auerswald was leaning toward freeing the youngsters—most of them food smugglers—if some agency could be found to assume responsibility for mending the children's ways. "It appears that about 2,000 children will qualify for reformatories," Czerniakow recorded with relief. Thus the *Kommissar* of the ghetto, who had met with Czerniakow almost daily for over a year, not only failed to warn him of what was about to happen, but actually made a fool of him on the very eve of the impending tragedy.

The Course of the *Aktion*   About a week before the deportation from Warsaw began, Hermann Höfle arrived in the city at the head of a company from the *Einsatz Reinhardt*. On July 21, hostages were arrested in the ghetto, including many members of the *Judenrat*, and people were shot down in the streets; that night, others were also shot in their homes. Early on the morning of Wednesday, July 22, the walls and gates of the ghetto were placed under the guard of special forces of the Polish "Blue Police" and Ukrainian, Lithuanian, and Latvian support troops. (According to Ringelblum, fifty SS, two hundred Ukrainians, and two hundred Latvians took part in the *Aktion*.) At 10:00 A.M. Höfle and his aides appeared at the *Judenrat* headquarters. Czerniakow recorded: "We were told that all the Jews, irrespective of sex and age, with certain exceptions, will be deported to the East. By 4 P.M. today a contingent of 6,000 people must be provided. And this (at the minimum) will be the daily quota." Czerniakow closed his diary entry for that day—the last full day of his life—with a comment written in his characteristically restrained and businesslike manner: "*Sturmbahnführer* Höfle (*Beauftragter* in charge of deportation) asked me into his office and informed me that for the time being my wife was free, but if the deportation were impeded in any way, she would be the first one to be shot as a hostage."[17]

At midday official wall posters appeared in the streets of the ghetto announcing the deportation and the means by which it was to be effected. The announcement had been dictated by the Germans, according to detailed data provided by Höfle and his men, and the *Judenrat* was forced to sign it. Contrary to custom, however, the signature was not of the "chairman of the *Judenrat* in Warsaw" but rather "the Jewish

Council in Warsaw." The decree opened with the statement that "By order of the German authorities, all the Jews living in Warsaw, irrespective of sex and age, will be evacuated." It then went on to list in detail categories of people exempt from the deportation, which included "the Jews employed by the authorities or in German enterprises," "Jews working in German-owned factories," "all the Jews who are members of the *Judenrat* or who work for the *Judenrat*," members of the Jewish Police, the staffs of Jewish hospitals, and the sanitation squads. This exemption also covered the immediate families of those included in the listed categories, but for the purposes of the order only wives and children would be considered family members. In addition, the announcement stated that "all Jews fit for work who have not yet been integrated into the labor process" would not be included in the deportation but would be concentrated in barracks within the ghetto and put to work. Likewise, the final paragraph of the list exempted "those Jews who were hospitalized in one of the Jewish hospitals on the first day of the evacuation and were not in condition to be moved."

Thereafter the announcement stated that any Jew slated for evacuation was permitted to take along up to fifteen kilograms (seven pounds) of personal belongings, including such valuables as gold, jewelry, cash, and so forth. Responsibility for the orderly conduct of the evacuation lay with the *Judenrat* and its chairman, while the actual task of executing the order was assigned to the Jewish Police.[18]

This wall poster was the sole official document available on the subject of the deportation. After recovering from their shock, the Jews of the ghetto began to seek clarification of a number of critical questions regarding the extent of the evacuation and the categories of workers exempt. But they could refer only to this public statement, which apparently left many loopholes and thus encouraged people to find a legal sanction for remaining in the ghetto. According to calculations worked out in the ghetto, the deportation would encompass about 70,000 of the 350,000 Jews confined within the walls at that time.[19] In addition, the decree apparently provided a way out for anyone physically fit for labor who agreed to serve as a conscript within the ghetto and thus be covered against expulsion. The paragraph stating that hospitalized persons would not be moved nurtured the illusion that the ghetto dwellers would not be treated unreasonably, so that there were no grounds to fear that the deportees were being sent to their deaths.

During the first days of terrible tension, which continued to grip the ghetto throughout the deportation, everyone tried to find an admissible job and obtain papers that proved he was employed so that he could cover himself and his family. The result was a mass assault on the workshops in the ghetto, since a place in a "shop" meant having a job, the minimum amount of food allocated to laborers and their families, and a place to live in one of the apartment blocks (the equivalent of barracks for "shop" employees). The "shop" workers were not even paid for their labor (although their employers had to compensate the SS by paying a fixed sum for each Jewish worker, since the Jews were considered to be the equivalent of SS property).[20] The German "shop" owners, among the many who exploited the constellation of circumstances created by the war and the ghetto conditions, behaved as if they had the power to decide men's lives and made fortunes off the panic in the ghetto.

A prominent example was Walter C. Többens, the giant among these German businessmen, who had begun to expand the network of "shops" in his empire even before the deportation order was published and had already reached the point of employing 4,500 Jewish workers. Többens was part of the *Deutsche Firmengemeinschaft Warschau m.b.H.*, which, starting in the second half of 1941, dealt with the exploitation of Jewish property and labor. He controlled and finally inherited the Jewish production undertaking in the ghetto (*Jüdische Produktiongesellschaft m.b.H.*), which operated under the auspices of the *Judenrat*. Többens received orders from the *Wehrmacht* and supervised production accomplished with Jewish labor and Jewish-owned tools.

Többens truly came to the fore in the ghetto during the period of the deportations, when the number of workers in his charge reached about twelve thousand.[21] This precipitate rise in the number of employees necessarily had negative consequences. The workshops and factories were not prepared for such rapid expansion. Managers could not get their hands on enough mechanical equipment or orders to be filled, and raw materials were at a premium. Furthermore, many of the workers absorbed by the "shops" were not only unskilled in the specific branch of production but, due to their advanced age and poor physical condition, were not even fit for unskilled physical labor. With no productive outlet for the suffocating glut of workers, the various ghetto enterprises in the fields of tailoring, fur making, leather goods, carpentry, and metalwork were left semiparalyzed. Workers were provided with documents and they usually turned up at the workshop or factory every morning, but because of the phenomenal featherbedding, the enterprises had become largely fictional. As a result, there was sharp friction within the "shops" between the skilled workers actually engaged on the job and the scores of people who merely sought refuge, since the true workers believed that the increase of unskilled people in the "shop" endangered its very existence.[22]

Alongside the enterprises directly owned by Germans, an assortment of "branches" began to crop up under the management of Jews.

Jewish-owned workshops would get in touch with recognized German firms and, in exchange for a bribe or partnership in the business, were taken under their wing. In this way a Jewish workshop turned into a branch of an officially recognized "shop" and, as such, could accept workers and issue proper documents. In fact, the commerce in documents was the essence of all these machinations, and it flourished beyond description. A Jew who owned a sewing machine could easily find a place in one of the German "shops," and sewing machines in private homes were transferred to workshops. In addition, there was a thriving trade in such machines, and gigantic sums were paid out for secondhand sewing machines smuggled in from the "Aryan" side. The authority to endorse work documents with the stamp of the SS-S.D., which was believed to be a strong safeguard against deportation, was limited to the Gestapo, since it directed the overall operation. At first the Gestapo men stamped papers generously, with hardly a glance at the documents presented to them, and the abundance of papers graced with the coveted stamp further reinforced the belief that the deportation would embrace only those who lacked even the minimal economic means, in ghetto terms—beggars, refugees, and the infirm.

With the initiation of the deportation, there was an important change in the authority that controlled affairs in the ghetto. The administrative regime, including Auerswald and his aides, ceased to fulfill any function whatsoever in the Jewish quarter of Warsaw, and exclusive control over the ghetto was transferred to the Gestapo and the deportation division. Moreover, the role of the *Judenrat* was also reduced to almost nought, and the Jewish Police became the only Jewish agency that was recognized in the ghetto. In essence, no agent of the Jewish public was allowed access to those in charge of the deportation. The *Judenrat* personnel were ordered to take an active role in the operation and were even equipped with armbands to identify their function. But their contribution was insignificant and was phased out completely during the first days of the *Aktion*. Even the commanders of the police were not allowed to discuss the operation or be briefed in advance about what was going on. They merely served as a channel to convey directives, a tool that was ordered to play an active role in the course of the operation.

On July 23, the second day of the operation, the chairman of the *Judenrat* took his own life. Adam Czerniakow's suicide had repercussions throughout the ghetto and was interpreted in various ways. Those close to Czerniakow, who valued his efforts as the chairman of the *Judenrat*, believed that his final act was testimony to his personal courage and sense of public responsibility. Others—and particularly circles in the underground who had resolutely denounced the policy of the

Judenrat —claimed that Czerniakow's act of self-destruction at a time of supreme trial was evidence of his weakness, and some charged that he had not even summoned up the courage to warn the ghetto before taking his own life or at least warn his close associates and issue a call for resistance.[23] Today we can emphatically state that the denunciation of Czerniakow at the time of his death was neither just nor pertinent. As we shall see, during this initial phase of the deportation, even the various underground factions were unable to concur in an appraisal of the situation, address the masses of Jews with a common appeal, or call for resistance as a means of response.

The SS directed the progress of the deportation from two centers in the ghetto. The command of the *Einsatz Reinhardt*, which comprised about a dozen SS officers, sergeants, and soldiers, set up its headquarters at 103 Leszno Street, after evicting the Jews from the building. The second command post was established in the headquarters of the Jewish Police on Ogrodowa Street and was manned mainly by SS and Gestapo men who had been stationed in Warsaw for some time. These men had maintained contacts with the ghetto and supervised its affairs, and their names were often mentioned in Czerniakow's diary. The most prominent members of this group were Höhmann, Witosek, Jesuiter, and Stabenow. But those most involved in the *Aktion* itself were the two men responsible for Jewish affairs in the Warsaw branch of the Gestapo's Department IV B: Karl Georg Brandt and his aide, Gerhardt Mende. Though there were higher-ranking officers in the *Aktion* unit, it was said that *Hauptsturmführer* Brandt "was the true lord of the ghetto." In the course of time, Brandt and Mende became the real directors of the deportation operation, its character, and its tempo. Brandt was indefatigable and seemed to be omnipresent. He is remembered for the fact that during the *Selektionen* he never even bothered so much as to glance at the victims' documents but decided men's fates by his visual impression of them and his mood. He was reputed to be mercurial, and his fits of rage wrought destruction on countless numbers of people. Mende, on the other hand, was a quiet man, self-possessed, and highly diligent in his work. He was among the officers who freely graced documents with the SS-S.D. stamp, which gave their bearers a false sense of security; yet a few days later he would lead his men in an *Aktion* and totally ignore those very same documents.

The Jewish Police played an important, though different, role during the early stages of the *Aktion*. As noted in chapter 3, the commander of the Jewish Police, Józef Szeryński, had been arrested by the Germans on May 1, 1942, on charges of smuggling furs from the ghetto to the "Aryan" side of the city. During the first days of the *Aktion*, however, he was released from prison and reinstated in his position in order to command the Jewish police during the operation. Yet it was the man who had taken over during Szeryński's imprisonment, Jakób Lejkin, who stood out for his diligence and initiative in commanding the strategy of the deportation. It is important to examine why Lejkin and his men were so devoted to their task that the poet Yitzhak Katzenelson described them as "a product of Germany and the spirit of that murderous nation."[24] According to the testimony and writings of Jewish policemen, we can conclude that many of them believed that the participation of Jews in the *Aktion* would make it possible to limit its scope, prevent harm from befalling people who "deserved to be protected," and, above all, avoid the prospect of the Germans' taking direct action, which might result in infinitely greater harm. During the opening days of the *Aktion*, when they still believed that the Germans intended to deport only the unemployed and destitute elements, the Jewish Police were even aided by *Judenrat* personnel, but, as stated earlier, the operations carried out jointly with the *Judenrat* staff only lasted a few days.[25]

The approximately two thousand policemen who were mobilized for the *Aktion* were faced with a complex dilemma. The Germans had promised total immunity to them and their relatives and purposely emphasized the alleged difference between them and the common Jews of the ghetto. At the same time, a good portion of the Jewish public made no attempt to conceal the hatred it felt for the policemen—"Jews outfitted in boots and caps"—who played a role in the deportation. As the *Aktion* progressed, the policemen began to understand that they were no more than a pliant tool of the Germans, and their future, like that of every other Jew, was clouded by doubt. When it became obvious to the police that their own inviolable documents were not being honored, they began to desert the ranks, and many went to work in the "shops" and were employed as internal guards (*Werkschutz*) in the factories, while others simply failed to appear at morning roll call, when daily orders were issued for assaults and roundups in the streets of the ghetto. According to various sources, a certain number of policemen avoided taking part in the *Aktion*.[26] In response, strong measures were adopted to force them to continue their work. When the roundups met with difficulties and fell short of the quotas set by the Germans, each policeman was personally ordered to bring in "five heads" a day, and those "who did not fulfill their mission" were threatened with having their relatives taken off to make up the difference.

The crowds of Jews trapped in the dragnets were herded to an assembly point—a lot that had formerly been used by the *Transferstelle* as a corridor of transport to and from the ghetto. In the adjoining yard, which was surrounded by a high fence, was an abandoned building (formerly a hospital), into which the victims were crowded until the freight cars arrived to carry them off. The *Umschlagplatz*, as this area was called, was guarded by contingents of SS troops, support troops, and the Jewish Police and was under the command of a Jewish Police officer named Schmerling, who had won the Germans' confidence for his stern and cruel treatment of the deportees. In order to ensure the regularized transport of deportees during the *Aktion*, SS General Karl Wolff of Himmler's headquarters took special pains to obtain freight trains through Dr. Theodor Ganzenmüller of the Reich Transport Ministry, and in a letter dated July 28, 1942, Ganzenmüller confirmed that "since July 22, each day a train carrying 5,000 Jews has left Warsaw for Treblinka via Malkinia."[27]

As noted earlier, certain branches of the *Wehrmacht*, particularly the *Rüstungs Kommando* in Warsaw, attempted to protect those Jews employed in factories and workshops associated with the army. But they lacked official authority in their dealings with the SS. Even the limited arrangements between the two sides regarding the employment of a restricted number of Jews were reached only at a later date, and they could not serve as a basis for negotiations during the mass deportation from Warsaw. The businessman Walter Többens related in a statement addressed to a German court that the *Wehrmacht* officials could get nowhere with the SS soldiers responsible for the deporation, and even his own position was stronger than that of the *Wehrmacht* people.[28] And the memoirs of Jewish policemen confirm that high-ranking *Wehrmacht* officers were forced to "stand [waiting] in the corridor" and devise all kinds of schemes to obtain the release of Jews employed in military camps and firms that supplied army units.[29] German enterprises maintained their own representatives in the *Umschlagplatz* to try and save individuals who were needed by specific firms or by the *Judenrat*. During the first stage of the deportation, their demands did receive some consideration. Nachum Remba, for example, a representative of the *Judenrat*, fought valiantly to extricate *Judenrat* employees and public figures who turned up in the *Umschlagplatz*. At a later stage, however, all channels of protest were cut off, and the chances of rescuing people from the *Umschlagplatz* were reduced to almost nil.

The deportation can be divided into four phases, and although the exact demarcation between them is difficult to determine, each phase can be clearly identified by the methods used in executing the *Aktion* and the tactics employed to deceive the Jews.

1. During the first phase, July 22–30, the implementation of the "evacuation" in the streets of the ghetto was assigned primarily to the Jewish Police. The SS men responsible for the *Aktion* confined their

role to devising a plan, establishing a quota of deportees, issuing orders, leading surprise sorties to check progress, and increasing the guard over the walls and gates of the "Jewish quarter." In addition, the SS directly supervised the concentration and embarkation of the deportees at the *Umschlagplatz*. At this stage they still honored the work papers of those who fell into one of the exempt categories listed in the public announcement on the deportation procedures.

2. The second phase began on July 31 and continued until August 14. During the previous phase there were occasional instances in which a band of SS men, bolstered by other forces, would spill into the streets of the ghetto and snatch up people in order to fill the quota that the Nazis had set for that day. With the initiation of the second phase, however, the SS forces assumed full responsibility for the methodical performance of the *Aktion* in the streets of the ghetto. They were joined by support troops of the German gendarmerie and Ukrainian, Latvian, and Lithuanian soldiers. This combined force, comprising about two hundred men, handled the dragnets supervised by the SS and systematically laid siege to blocks of buildings and streets. Jewish Police units were added to the operational forces, and mixed squads were used during the *Aktion* itself. The exemption papers were still honored during this stage as well, yet when pressed to fill the quota of deportees, the soldiers and police no longer bothered with the finer points of such formalities, and even people carrying documents that supposedly assured them immunity were crammed into the freight cars.

3. The third phase extended from August 15 to September 6, including a few days' intermission at the end of August, when the *Einsatz Reinhardt* left Warsaw to execute deportations from smaller ghettos in the district. During this stage the SS and their support units heightened the effect of terror, and hardly any attention was paid to documents of any kind. In addition to "blockades"—sealing off and searching blocks of streets and buildings—they placed the "shops" under siege. The *Selektion* in the factories and workshops screened out all but the real workers—and Jews who paid a king's ransom—while most of those who had recently sought refuge in the "shops" were herded off to the *Umschlagplatz*. Neither did the *Aktion* commando take care to spare the skilled workers in the "shops," since its only concern was to fill the quota of the day and keep the operation going according to plan. It was during this phase that a growing number of people lost faith in the value of the "documents" and began to go into hiding. The dragnet troops found it increasingly difficult to meet the demands made upon them, so that the tactics used to surprise their victims became more and more sophisticated.

4. The fourth phase opened on September 6, and its main feature

was the comprehensive *Selektion* that went on until September 10. All the Jews left in the ghetto on September 6 were ordered to leave their apartments and assemble in a block of streets adjoining the *Umschlagplatz*. The "shops" and other recognized places of work were allocated quotas of workers, and all those who did not receive a numbered tag were doomed to be sent to the *Umschlagplatz* — and from there to the extermination camp. This lethal *Selektion*, carried out among the throng concentrated in the small area, was dubbed the "cauldron" (*kesl* in Yiddish; *kociol* in Polish). The German quotas allowed for about 35,000 Jews to remain in the ghetto after the deportation. In addition, about 20,000 to 25,000 Jews remained in hiding and were classified as "wildcats" — people whose existence was not officially recognized. The final act of the deportation took place on the Day of Atonement, September 21, 1942, and its victims were the Jewish policemen and their families. The number of *Ordungsdienst* (the ghetto police) was reduced to 380.

There are no exact or consistent statistics as to the final number of Jews sent to the Treblinka death camp in the course of the *Aktion*. According to testimony, in April–May 1942 the ghetto contained about 350,000 people. Various sources cite that as the number of ration cards allocated in the ghetto during the same period.[30] We know that the overall number of ration cards included a certain percentage of "departed souls," whose relatives continued to use the cards on their own behalf. The source quoted here assumes that there were about 20,000 "fictitious" ration cards of this kind in circulation; on the other hand, the ghetto also contained about 2,000 to 3,000 people who, for various reasons, were not registered and did not carry ration cards. According to other sources, 370,000 people were incarcerated in the ghetto in April–May 1942, and that is also the pertinent statistic at the beginning of the deportation.[31] There is also reason to believe that on the eve of the deportation, the Warsaw ghetto contained refugees who had escaped from other ghettos decimated by deportation operations, and since these escapees did not hold ration cards, the number of Jews in the ghetto was actually greater than the number of ration cards. We also lack exact data on the number of people deported to the death camp. German figures state that 253,741 Jews were sent to their death, according to the breakdown in Table 4.

The authors of the Jewish underground report sent to London in November 1942 concluded that the numbers quoted by the Germans were intentionally reduced, and the total number of deportees must be set at approximately 300,000. This is the figure usually quoted by various memoir writers and other chroniclers, and some speak of as many as 320,000 or 350,000 Jews being deported to Treblinka during the

TABLE 4
GERMAN STATISTICS ON THE DEPORTATIONS

Date	No. of "Evacuees"	Date	No. of "Evacuees"
July 22	6,250	August 13	4,313
July 23	7,300	August 14	5,168
July 24	7,400	August 15	3,633
July 25	7,530	August 16	4,095
July 26	6,400	August 17	4,160
July 27	6,320	August 18	3,926
July 28	5,020	August 19-24	20,000 (estimate)
July 29	5,480	August 25	3,002
July 30	6,430	August 26	3,000 (estimate)
July 31	6,756	August 27	2,454
August 1	6,220	August 28–September 2	intermission
August 2	6,276	September 3	4,609
August 3	6,458	September 4	1,669
August 4	6,568	September 5	intermission
August 5	6,623	September 6	3,634
August 6	10,085	September 7	6,840
August 7	10,672	September 8	13,596
August 8	7,304	September 9	6,616
August 9	6,292	September 10	5,199
August 10	2,158	September 11	5,000 (estimate)
August 11	7,725	September 12	4,806
August 12	4,688	September 21	2,196

Total: 253,741

SOURCE: *B.Ż.I.H.* 1 (1951), 81, 86, 90.

massive *Aktion* of the summer of 1942. The numbers calculated by the Germans are a sum total of the people shoved into the freight cars. These figures were scrawled on the doors of the cars in chalk, and some believe that the Jewish policemen deliberately inflated figures to convince the Germans that the greatest possible number of people had already been extracted from the ghetto—which would mean that the German figures represent more than the actual number of people deported.[32]

In addition to those transported directly from the *Umschlagplatz* to Treblinka, 11,580 people were sent to a *"Dulag"* (*Durchgangslager*— Transit Camp), where they were transferred to forced-labor camps. The

Selektionen for the *Dulag* took place as the Jews passed from the *Umschlagplatz* to the plaza adjacent to the train. The assignment of people to a *Dulag*, where they were placed at the disposal of the German *Arbeitsamt* (Labor Office), ceased on August 19 and was renewed for just one day, September 12. Evidently once the *Arbeitsamt* had met the urgent demand for temporary workers, the *Selektionen* were no longer carried out at the *Umschlagplatz*. It is clear that at the closing stage of this final mass *Selektion*, that is, from the last weeks of August to September 12, the ratio of fit young people was higher than during the initial weeks of the operation. The manner in which the *Selektionen* for the *Dulag* were handled proves that the Germans did not intend to deduct a fixed percentage of employable people from the transports but were merely responding to the pressures exercised by parties urgently in need of Jewish labor.

If we assume that there were 350,000 Jews in the ghetto on the day the *Aktion* began and we deduct from this figure the various categories that were not deported to the death camp, we obtain the following picture: assumed to be living in the ghetto — 350,000; died or were killed during the course of the *Aktion* — 10,380; deported to a *Dulag* — 11,580; assumed to have illegally crossed to the "Aryan" side of the city — 8,000; exempt workers and "wildcats" — 55,000; deported to the death camp — 265,040; total — 350,000.

The original plan of the *Einsatz Reinhardt* apparently was to have 35,000 Jews left in the ghetto at the conclusion of the "Grand *Aktion*" — 10 percent of the predeportation population — as a temporary work force subject to concentration-camp conditions. The other 90 percent of the Jews were to be exterminated in Treblinka. As the statistics indicate, during the forty-six-day *Aktion*, about 75 percent of the ghetto's Jews were sent to Treblinka or murdered on the spot, while about 73,000 of them — over 20 percent — survived the *Aktion* to face an uncertain future.

The Jewish Public during the Mass Deportation

The ghetto public at large neither understood the true significance of the deportation that began on July 22, 1942, nor knew the destination of the transports. Confirmed reports on the slaughter at Ponary filtered down to the general public as vague snatches of information, usually in the form of contradictory rumors. Moreover, these rumors seemed to run counter to the cumulative experience of the ghetto population during almost three years of living under the occupation regime. The Jews of Warsaw had encountered many deportees and evacuees — both people who had

been forcibly uprooted from their homes in the compulsory resettlement operations and had turned into pitiful refugees, and transients
who had chosen to leave their homes and clandestinely move to Warsaw
for reasons of their own. Thus the phenomenon of expulsion and root-
lessness was rather common during the era of Nazi rule. "Władka"
(Feigel Peltel), a member of the Bund in the Warsaw ghetto and a
liaison on behalf of the Jewish Fighting Organization, gave the following description of the first days of the deportation from Warsaw in her
memoirs:

> Many Jews believed that the displacement meant no more than mov-
> ing on to a strange city. They couldn't have imagined anything else. For
> months upon months the residents of the Warsaw ghetto had seen packed
> trucks bringing in Jews who had been expelled from the surrounding
> towns, so they believed that the same fate awaited us. My mother quickly
> resigned herself to whatever might happen. As she always did when over-
> come by anxiety, she tried to comfort herself and adapt her thinking to the
> inevitable.[33]

The tactics used by the Germans during the first days of the *Aktion*
presumably reinforced the assumptions of the man in the street. First to
be evacuated were the refugees, prisoners in the ghetto jail, those who
had recently been transferred to the ghetto from the Reich, and
thieves—all of whom lacked a stable source of support in the ghetto.
Some of the people deported during those first days accepted their fate
with equanimity. The German Jews who had been "resettled" in Warsaw and found themselves in a strange place and subject to abominable
conditions assumed that their next destination could not possibly be any
worse. Their concern was primarily about conditions during the journey
and not at all about what awaited them at its end. An eyewitness related
in his memoirs: "The tenants of two hostels [that housed Jewish refugees from Germany and Czechoslovakia] received a day's notice that
they must leave on the morrow. They had already undergone so many
moves from city to city and country to country that they showed no
signs of despair or fear. Warsaw or Vilna, Smolensk or Kiev —it was all
the same to them."[34]

The German plan called for keeping the Jews in a state of suspense
about their fate, thereby wearing on their nerves and causing a sense of
disintegration, in something like a strategy of "divide and kill." At each
stage of the operation, they landed a blow to one section of the population while reinforcing the illusions of the rest that they were among the
privileged and immune from harm. Furthermore, these same "privileged" sectors of the population were explicitly warned that their status
was secure only as long as the deportation operation ran along

smoothly; i.e., the uncontested removal of one portion of the population was a condition for the stability and security of the rest. The first to be taken were therefore the weakest elements of the ghetto public. Then came the turn of those who lacked papers and permanent jobs, followed by the relatives of people who did have exemption papers (relatives had originally been as immune as the document bearers themselves). Finally even the workers outfitted with supposedly protective papers were sent to the *Umschlagplatz*. Even at this stage the strategy of divide and discriminate was still in force. First, some of the workshops considered less vital to the German war effort were liquidated; then came the turn of large enterprises that worked for the army; and finally *Selektionen* were carried out in the remaining factories, and increasing numbers of workers were removed from the shop floor. Toward the end the ultimate *Selektion* took place to ensure that only 10 percent of the original population remained in the ghetto.

From time to time news and rumors were circulated about the closing date of the *Aktion*. As noted earlier, the official announcement of the deportation had itself set limits upon the scope of the expulsion. The illusions about this matter are clearly reflected in Abraham Levin's diary. On Thursday, July 31, he wrote: " . . . At 4 they suddenly unloaded the people off the [roundup] wagon and said that the *Aktion* was over. The joy and hopes that were raised! At 6 the blockades began again." Four days later he wrote: "Again there's talk that the wild manhunt will end today. But they've said that before, and nothing came of it. . . ." His entry for Monday, August 24, reads: "There are rumors that the G[ermans] have permitted the preparation and distribution of 120,000 ration cards for the month of September. That was a sign that they want to have an equivalent number of Jews remain [in the ghetto]. But it's only a rumor and no more. On the other hand, there are even more pessimistic rumors. Again there's talk that the operation [deportation] will go on for another week."[35] The truth was obviously far worse than Levin's pessimistic forecast. Mira Piżyc speaks in her memoirs of "rumors about 80,000 deportees, then 100,000, then 150,000, and at any rate 50 percent."[36]

At the beginning of the deportation, people were still prepared to help one another and attempt to get around the edicts by deceiving the Germans. For example, there was an upsurge of fictitious weddings, by means of which men equipped with recognized documents tried to extend protection to women close to them. There were even cases in which men fraudulently married their own sisters. Considering the grave circumstances, rabbis did not place obstacles in the path of such applicants. In fact, according to Ringelblum, "they issued *ketubot* [marriage licenses] without even laying eyes on the couple."[37] We have already seen how Jews who managed workshops transformed their businesses into officially recognized "shops" and proceeded to employ their relatives and acquaintances. The Self-Help provided papers not only to its permanent staff but also to public figures and people in the arts in the hope of saving them from the clutches of the SS. Some of the large "shops"—particularly those owned by A. Landau and R. Hallmann—absorbed party and youth movement activists even though they were neither skilled workers nor men of means (i.e., able to pay a ransom). A few of these businessmen were involved in the underground and remained faithful to the cause even during the deportation.

The most difficult situation of all, however, was that of the ghetto's children. German regulations called for every Jew employed in a "shop" to be found in his place of work. Since it was unthinkable to leave children alone and exposed to danger, they remained with their parents. The large enterprises kept the children occupied in a kind of kindergarten attached to the workshop or factory. Thus the children were protected as long as the "blockades" did not affect the "shops." In the second week of August, with the initiation of *Selektionen* in the "shops," the children concentrated together in one spot became easy prey. On Friday, August 14, 1942, Levin wrote in his diary that "yesterday 3–4,000 people were taken from Többens's 'shops' in the ghetto, mostly women and children." Individuals were torn away from their families, and as the deportation proceeded apace the ghetto was emptied of old people, women, and children. Here and there groups of filthy, ragged, and starving children were left to wander the streets of the ghetto. No one paid any attention to these pitiful orphans, whose parents had been taken off during the *Aktion*.[38]

The case was different for the children living in orphanages and completely dependent upon the housemothers and teachers in these institutions. In most cases these workers refused to abandon their charges, and many of them accompanied the children to the *Umschlagplatz* and into the freight cars. The most renowned, though certainly not the only example of such devotion was the conduct of the prominent author and educator Janusz Korczak (the pen name of Dr. Henryk Goldszmidt) and his staff. Korczak ignored the pleas and attempts of his friends and colleagues, Jews and Poles alike, to save his life by concealing him on the "Aryan" side of Warsaw. Having made a superhuman effort to overcome the material shortages that plagued the orphanage and to protect the children in his care from the sufferings of war, he remained committed to his charges to the last. The parade of the orderly and outwardly calm children, accompanied by "the old doctor," his long-time assistant, Stefania Wilczyńska, and the rest of the staff, is a scene etched in the memory of many who witnessed it and had already become a legend at the height of the *Aktion*. Ringelblum wrote: "Korczak created the feeling that it was easy to go to the *Umschlagplatz*. There were heads of orphanages who knew full well what awaited them in the *Umschlagplatz*, but they believed that they could not leave the children alone at that dreadful moment and must go with them to their deaths."[39]

In the second week of August, faith in the value of "documents" began to fail, and many channeled their energies toward finding a place to hide. But mothers with infants were barred from the hideouts for a time because the wailing of a child or loud talk might give the fugitives away. Thus by the time of the final *Selektion*, few children remained in the ghetto, despite the desperate efforts of parents to smuggle their children through the *Selektion*. Mira Piżyc related in her memoirs:

> ... And another sight that freezes the blood in your veins: Behind me marches a young woman. She has a pack on her back. The German smiles a satanic grin, walks up to her, raises the whip, and lands a blow to the pack. A terrible scream erupts from the concealed child. The German grabs the pack and, together with its living contents, smashes it up against the wall. The stricken mother wants to go after her child; the executioner explodes with laughter—the scene amuses him. With a blow of the [whip's] handle, he pushes the woman, blue with agony, back into line.[40]

During the deportation, hunger reached proportions undreamed of even during the worst periods of starvation in the ghetto. Against this background, it is easy to understand the step taken by the Germans early on in the operation. On July 29 an "appeal" to the population of the ghetto was published over the signature of the commander of the Jewish Police: "I hereby inform the residents subject to expulsion that in accordance with the orders of the authorities, anyone who voluntarily reports for evacuation on July 29, 30, and 31 will be provided with food, namely: 3 kilos [6.6 pounds] of bread and a kilo [2.2 pounds] of jam. The assembly point and distribution of food—Stawki Square, corner of Dzika."

Many were lured by the offer and reported to the area adjacent to the railway siding. They had despaired of continuing the struggle, and the temptation of the bread drew them like a magnet. The above-cited report submitted to London by the Jewish underground explains this phenomenon in the following way:

> If we also take into consideration the fact that some family members had already been "resettled" and the rest, without being sure of the situation, hoped to be reunited with [them], it is possible to understand the initial phenomenon of hundreds, and later on thousands, coming to the

assembly point daily, individually or in groups, in wagons or in rickshaws, carrying their bundles for the long journey in their hands or on their backs. Every day you could see little children—eight, ten, twelve years old—going to the *Umschlagplatz* to travel on to their parents. In order to supply food to the "volunteers," the German authorities allocated 180,000 kilos [396,000 pounds] of bread and 36,000 kilos [79,000 pounds] of jam. On August 1, further appeals to the population appeared in the ghetto stating that the "resettlement" operation was not over and urging those who had not succeeded in getting into safe "shops" to report to the *Umschlagplatz* willingly.[41]

Jews who were disqualified as workers during the *Selektionen* in the "shops" but nonetheless escaped the SS dragnets lost the "legal" basis for their existence within the ghetto. Deprived of a job, food, and living quarters, these "wildcats"—whole families or what remained of families—scrambled from one hiding place to another in an effort to escape the "blockades." One memoir of the period described them as "thousands staggering back and forth out of despair and fear, as if seeking shelter from the fire and lava spewing forth from a volcano that shook the earth and the city."[42] As the *Aktion* continued, the staying power of these fugitives steadily deteriorated until it broke altogether, and they emerged from their hiding places to become easy prey of the roundups or decided to "volunteer" so that at least they could go off to the unknown together. Jonas Turkow wrote of his sisters:

> When my two sisters came to see us in the office after they had decided to go voluntarily, my wife and I couldn't stop them. Rachel and Sarah, twins, loved one another so dearly that they couldn't imagine living without each other. This way, at least, they had an opportunity to go together and "chose" a place in the east where they would work—albeit at hard labor—but they could survive the storm of the war without quaking [with fear] all the time that they might be caught.[43]

There was another, no less tragic, option open to the Jews of the ghetto. Many diarists had commented that the Jews of Poland differed from their German and Austrian counterparts in that they did not break down and take their own lives but kept up a long, stubborn struggle to survive despite everything.[44] This was indeed true from the beginning of the occupation until July 1942. But during the period of the mass deportation, many people surrendered, and, as Levin put it, there were "scores of suicides."[45] Ringelblum put the number of suicides at hundreds, particularly among the intelligentsia.[46] "The ghetto doesn't cry anymore," Stefan Ernest wrote. "A kind of stiff determination has been aroused, but unfortunately it expresses itself not in active resistance but in the courage to die a sufferable death."[47]

Letters and Evidence about Treblinka

The uncertainty and delusions of the remaining ghetto population were further heightened by the letters that had allegedly been sent to Warsaw by "resettled" Jews. The ghetto was rife with rumors about such messages. As the underground later reported to London:

> Mysterious letters written by the deportees and dispatched from the vicinity of Bialystok, Pińsk, Brześć on the Bug River cropped up [in the ghetto]. They were supposedly brought to the ghetto by policemen and railroad workers. As later became clear, these were either poor forgeries or letters that were indeed written by the "evacuees" as dictated by the Germans at the site of [their] death in Treblinka.[48]

Levin's diary also contains references to letters received from the deportees. On Thursday, July 30, 1942, he wrote about "a letter written by a woman to her husband that arrived from Bialystok by means of a Polish policeman. She and her children are together with some other family and work hard in the fields, but they receive food." On Tuesday, August 4, Levin noted that "a letter [was received] from Baranowicze. She is working in the fields, asks for underwear. . . . The letter came by mail." On Sunday, August 16, he recorded: "Again news reached me that letters were supposedly received from deportees working in the vicinity of Siedlce, and their condition is more or less good. Lifschitz (a school friend of Walk's) said that his own daughter read such a letter from an aging couple."[49] The testimony of Tokar-Warszawski, who was in the Warsaw ghetto at the time of the deportation and managed to reach London at the height of the war, mentions that "three postcards that arrived from people who had been deported were passed around in Többens's ['shop']."[50]

The issue of the Bund's *Oyf der vakh (On Guard)* dated September 20, 1942 — that is, a week after the *Aktion* ended — contained an article headlined "The Jews of Warsaw Are Murdered in Treblinka":

> During the first weeks of the "Evacuation *Aktion*," Warsaw was swamped by postcards written by Jews deported from the city. Greetings supposedly arrived from Bialystok, Brześć, Kosów, Malkinia, Pińsk, Smolensk. It was all a lie! All the trains [filled] with Jews from Warsaw went to Treblinka, where the Jews were exterminated in a horrifying way. The letters and the postcards come from people who managed to escape from the [freight] cars or the camp itself. It is also possible that a few Jews included in the first deportations . . . were intentionally sent to Brześć or to Pińsk so that their postcards would deceive, mislead, and create false illusions in the Warsaw Jewish community.[51]

We have no evidence to the effect that the transports were deliberately sent to a place that would abet the deception of Warsaw's Jews. It is likewise doubtful that the Germans had to bother with any such special circuitous action, since it was much simpler to compel the deportees to copy down dictated letters immediately upon their arrival at Treblinka. This system was used at a number of camps. In fact, it was a customary tactic of deception employed throughout the course of the "Final Solution." But it is also true that many escaped from the trains on the way to Treblinka. Youth movement members, for example, repeatedly escaped from the freight cars ánd returned to the ghetto.[52] Thus it is highly probable that there were escapees who did not return to the ghetto and that they too wrote letters but consciously failed to state that they had escaped from the train on the way to Treblinka and were living someplace illegally. It is logical that such letters would be deliberately vague, just as there were good reasons why they might be misunderstood or the true location of the sender might easily be misinterpreted. Yet in many cases the tales of greetings and letters were no more than hearsay, and the more one tried to track down the person who had actually seen the letter with his own eyes, or had received the letter himself, the clearer it became that the so-called source had only heard about such a letter from someone else, who had in turn heard about it. The true source of the rumors was evidently the Germans and their Jewish agents, though we can also presume that in a community starved for hope and trying to block out the horrible truth, rumors of this kind come into being even without an instigator at work. In addition, Polish swindlers operated in the ghetto in the hope of turning an easy profit from the misery of the Jews. Ringelblum's insights on the subject of self-deception were as follows:

> . . . A legend began to grow up about letters from the deportees, particularly from certain places—Brześć, Kowel, Pińsk, etc. Hard as you might try, you could never get to anyone who had actually read a letter with his own eyes. It was always a third person who had heard from someone else that so-and-so had read the letter. These letters were always phrased in exactly the same way and appeared in the same form: a few words scrawled on a chit torn from a paper bag saying that we arrived safely to wherever. A letter like this never contained details about the living conditions of the deportees or how they occupied their time. But they always requested money and belongings and always mentioned that other deportees had asked to pass on their regards—and these others always happened to be wealthy people.
> Such letters were always delivered by Polish Christians who "managed to reach [the proper address] after overcoming various difficulties." The amicable Poles were willing to take money and clothing back for the de-

portees. They were also prepared to aid in the search for others who had been deported—naturally, in return for the payment of hundreds or thousands of zlotys. And there were people who paid out tens of thousands of zlotys to find their closest relatives; and only after protracted and costly efforts were they persuaded that it was all a lie and not a trace remained of their loved ones. But even though such news from relatives was exposed as a swindle time and time again, others could always be found who were willing to pay a high price for the slightest news of their loved ones. When people became fed up with the letters and stopped believing in them, the swindlers worked out a new strategy. Lately they have been bringing information about camps in which women, children, or elderly people are being held. These camps are supposedly located somewhere near Lublin or, of all places, in Galicia (Sokol, Lemberg), the eastern border region, etc. And if the same tales of letters from individuals or even whole camps start again, it's not just because of the crooks and swindlers who know how to exploit every situation for the good of their dirty business. These swindlers play on the popular imagination, which constantly dreams—and will not stop dreaming—that the hundreds of thousands and millions of deportees are alive, are working, and will even return. . . . [53]

But even as people clung to their delusions, the truth about Treblinka slowly penetrated the ghetto and became incontestible. Ernest wrote in his memoirs that "in time, not only were the numbers of the engines identified, but the same freight cars returned the next day, and that inspired gruesome thoughts." Yet actual certified information reached Warsaw only when fugitives from Treblinka returned to the city. According to Ernest, "The destination was discovered at the beginning of the second half of August."[54] Levin's entry for Friday, August 7, contains an unexplained reference to "the crematorium near Malkinia and Sokolov." Levin was undoubtedly referring to the extermination camp near both these places, and it is true that these towns were close to Treblinka. But this sentence fragment does not indicate what Levin knew about Treblinka by that date or whether he had made any connection between the deportees and the extermination camp. On Tuesday, August 11, he wrote about Treblinka in more detail:

Smolar phoned Sokolov. He told him that those going—if they are going—to Tre[blinka] are destined for "death." The news brought by K——n. There is a Jew in Warsaw by the name of Slava who passed on information about Tre[blinka]. Fifteen kilometers before the Tre[blinka] station, the G[ermans] meet the train. During the disembarkation from the cars, they brutally beat [the people]. Then they put [them] into gigantic barracks. For five minutes you can hear terrible screams. Then everything is quiet. They remove the dead, who are grotesquely swollen—a single man cannot get his arms around a body of that size, it's so gross. Grave diggers are selected among the victims, and the next day they too are among the corpses. It's dreadful.

Levin, who worked for the underground archive and had found refuge in Landau's "shop" (the most important center of the ghetto underground during the deportation), met with David Nowodworski, a member of Ha-Shomer ha-Za'ir who escaped from Treblinka and went on to become the leader of a combat squad in the Jewish Fighting Organization. On Friday, August 28, Levin wrote of that meeting: "[David Nowodworski] told us in detail the whole story of his suffering from the moment he was caught until he escaped from the site of the killing and returned to Warsaw. His words again confirm in a way that can leave no doubt that all the deportees—whether they were trapped or went willingly—are killed; not one is spared."[55]

Letters and rumors notwithstanding, the truth of the matter is that all those deported in the *Aktion* of July–September 1942—with the exception of groups of elderly people shot near the cemetery as far back as the first days of the operation and the thousands sent to transit camps—were transported to the Treblinka extermination camp. The Bund assigned Zalman (Zigmunt) Friedrich, one of its members who could readily pass for a Pole (and later became a liaison for the Jewish Fighting Organization on the "Aryan" side of Warsaw), to follow the trail of the deportees. Friedrich started out at the beginning of August (the exact date is unknown). On the "Aryan" side of the city, he established contact with a Polish member of the Socialist Party who was a railroad worker and was familiar with the route taken by the transports that left Warsaw. Overcoming obstacles, Friedrich reached Sokolov and learned that there was a side track to the village of Treblinka, an isolated and elevated area surrounded by a thicket. Two camps had been established there: Treblinka A and Treblinka B. The first was a punishment camp primarily for Poles, while only Jews were taken to the second. Polish residents of the area told terrible tales of what went on at Treblinka. In Sokolov Friedrich met with a member of the Bund named Uziel Wallach (a nephew of the former Soviet foreign minister, Maxim Litvinov). Wallach had escaped from Treblinka and passed on to Friedrich the details that he had recorded on the camp. The description of the Treblinka camp published in the *Oyf der vakh* article quoted above was evidently based on the information that Friedrich brought back with him. The article also noted that: "Even within the camp itself, the Nazis try to deceive the Jews up to the very last moment. Not just in their speeches, but also by signs [put up in the camp] and the [general] outward appearance. They create the impression that Treblinka is just a stop on the way to [something] else, [a stop] on the ongoing journey to work—at any rate, to a continuation of life.[56]

Even toward the end of the lethal *Aktion*, the illusions remained steadfast and the pointless rumors continued. Ringelblum explains this phenomenon in a piece that was written after the deportation:

> I am deeply convinced that even today, when the meager remnant of the Jews of Warsaw know about Treblinka, there are still hundreds and perhaps even thousands of people who nevertheless believe in the bogus reports about an alleged children's camp. Thus just a few days ago, rumors circulated about 2,000 children who had returned from Treblinka. I believe that years after this war ends, when all the secrets about the death camps have long been exposed, wretched mothers will continue to dream that the children torn from them are still alive somewhere in the depths of Russia. . . . [57]

Thus by the middle of August, the truth about Treblinka was known to the Jews of Warsaw. Even though it was not proven that all the Jews deported from Warsaw were taken there, the threat of Treblinka had become real for the deportees and those destined to follow them.

During the final stages of the deportation, the ghetto resembled a camp divided into separate factories and housing blocks. Its residents were not allowed into the streets during work hours, and the ties between relatives and friends were severed completely. A man attached to a "shop" had no idea of what was happening to his counterpart in another enterprise. Events occurred with dizzying speed, and it was impossible to know from one day to the next whether any one particular person was still in the ghetto.

Toward the end of August, the belief began to set in that the Germans had no intention of halting the deportation and the entire Jewish community was condemned to death. Nevertheless, we have no concrete information on spontaneous acts of resistance. All in all, only a few such incidents took place throughout the entire *Aktion*. On Sunday, August 9, 1942, Levin recorded in his diary: "Today, the nineteenth day of an 'operation' unprecedented in the history of mankind . . . one can speak of only a few isolated incidents of resistance. A Jew defended himself against a G[erman] and was shot on the spot; another struggled with a Ukrainian and got away after being wounded; and a few other facts of this kind."[58]

The Question of Response and Resistance during the *Aktion* Statistics compiled by the *Judenrat* show that 6,687 people were shot in the ghetto during the months of the *Aktion*: 1,224 in July, 2,305 in August, and 3,158 in September. It is therefore clear that the number of casualties rose at the height of the deportation and was especially high toward its conclusion. In order to understand the significance of the slaughter in the streets during the *Aktion*, these figures should be compared with the corresponding number of murders committed during the months that preceded the *Aktion*. The *Judenrat* statistics show that 81 people were shot in the ghetto in April 1942, 54 in May, and 90 in June, making a total of 225 people over a three-month period of constantly rising terror.[59] A number of writers have therefore come to the conclusion that the increased rate of murder during the *Aktion* indicates a rise in the incidence of resistance, and the massive slaughter was in reaction to more assertive opposition. Yitzhak Zuckerman, for example, stated in the report on the Jewish Fighting Organization: "We were witness to the courageous stand of the incalculable number of Jews who displayed resistance to the Germans. These anonymous heroes are included in the category of the '5,394 who were shot,' according to the German report on the 'resettlement campaign.'"

Nevertheless, the resistance implied by these figures was not equivalent to an active struggle against the Germans and their associates. Such acts were only isolated incidents, and although some of them may not have been reported in the testimonies and memoirs in our hands, we can confidently assume that demonstrations of assertive resistance were the exception rather than the rule. The killing in the streets was directed primarily against the "wildcats" and those who attempted to escape from the ranks on the way to the *Umschlagplatz*. We know that the number of people who opted to go into hiding rose dramatically during the later stages of the *Aktion*, and, indeed, the figures on those felled by bullets also rose sharply during that period. We may therefore conclude that as the operation progressed, instances of physical resistance became more prevalent, while the murderous response undoubtedly quelled the urge to fight back against the Germans and their accomplices with force.

Even so, the extravagant German response to demonstrations of physical resistance still does not explain why people who knew what awaited the deportees at Treblinka did not revolt or even put up a struggle. After the *Aktion* Ringelblum commented that the Jews left in the ghetto were overcome by feelings of remorse and reproach, not only because they had failed to rise up against the armed Germans, but because they had not even put up a struggle against the Jewish policemen, who were not armed with guns.

Historians have tried to explain this enigmatic phenomenon, which not only relates to Warsaw but was characteristic of the Jews throughout Nazi-occupied Europe. Some believe that a profound faith in the Divine Will of God and a long-standing tradition of fatalism and submission prevented the Jews from resisting and made for a situation in which people being slaughtered by the thousands not only failed to respond but did not even think to take revenge on their murderers. Philip Friedman, a Jewish historian who was intimately familiar with the Jewish communities of Eastern Europe, attempted to explain this complex phenomenon as follows:

> Jewish traditions differed [from those of other nations] and had their own uniqueness. At the same time they were not uniform because of the cultural and social pluralism of the Jewish public. The intelligentsia, the educated portion of the middle class, and the working class adopted the traditions and values of the peoples among whom they lived. But the broad masses of pious Jews, especially in eastern and southeastern Europe, took a different approach to these questions. Other peoples cultivated a tradition of heroism in the sense of physical and martial strength. But in the heritage of Orthodox Jewry, the concept of heroism was synonymous with spiritual courage, self-sacrifice for the sake of religion—*Kiddush Hashem.* And this was the only possible form of resistance considered by Orthodox Jewry: resistance derived from religious conviction; resistance based upon a deep-rooted heritage summed up in the saying "Not with power, and not with force, but with the spirit." The essence of this creed, to which the Jews remained faithful over many generations of religious persecution, was reduced to the idea that one must not fight the evil in the world or defeat it by physical force, for it is the Divine Protector who will decide the struggle between good and evil.[60]

It cannot be denied that the Jewish population of Warsaw embraced a community whose faith and devotion to tradition largely dictated its conduct during the Holocaust period. But the Orthodox sector of Warsaw's Jewish population comprised only a part of the larger Jewish community, which likewise embraced a substantial population of ideologically committed people devoted to a Jewish and human tradition laden with examples of rebellion despite overwhelming odds, the obligation to defend oneself, and revolt against an oppressive power.

All this is to say that the unique aspects of tradition and character do not resolve the enigma, or at least do not explain it fully, and we must look for the answer elsewhere. As we have seen, the entire subject of "information" is a complex one. It is true that a few weeks into the deportation operation, word began to circulate about what was really happening in Treblinka. But at no stage did this information fully penetrate the ghetto's consciousness. The gap between the concepts, values, and environment of the Jewish victims and the Nazi reality created at Treblinka was so vast that the truth simply could not be fully apprehended. Logic, emotion, and deep-seated convictions about man's basic humanity all dictated that what was going on at Treblinka was simply not possible. So-called information was largely related to as a bad dream, a nightmare that was destined to end—that must stop at some point! These psychological blocks and emotional defense mechanisms were as characteristic of public figures as of the average man in the street. The fact that information reached the ghetto and was circulated did not necessarily mean the creation of a whole new dimension that was perceived as reality. But if we ignore the fact that the truth was simply not assimilated by the people of the ghetto, we will fail to grasp the complexity of the situation. This breakdown in perception, for example, is the source of the sharp swings from total despair to unfounded hope, arbitrary declarations about the unavoidable end, and the clinging to optimistic rumors that we find jumbled together in diaries and journals of the period.

Another factor is bound up with the essential willingness and daring to resist. From a psychological viewpoint, it has repeatedly been proved that people who are overtaken by conditions of severe stress or find themselves in a calamitous situation suffer from shock and do not function according to the standard expectations of one who views the situation from a distance, whether of space or time. It is a fact that in situations of acute oppression, which apparently create a motivation for spontaneous resistance and revolt, people are not always capable of rebelling. This phenomenon is true not only of Jews. Professor Henri Michel, a French historian of the resistance movement in the Nazi-occupied countries, draws attention to three categories of severely oppressed people that came into being as a consequence of the war: (1) forced laborers who were transferred to Germany from various countries; (2) prisoners of war; and (3) inmates of concentration camps. These three groups suffered the brunt of the Nazi regime's repression and were thus presumably the most strongly motivated toward spontaneous resistance and revolt. Yet they were, for the most part, conspicuously resigned to their fate.[61] Indeed, an examination of these categories of subjects reveals that groups subjected to severe stress by totalitarian regimes display an astonishing degree of tolerance and submission. Any inquiry into the reasons behind such behavior is obviously beyond the limitations of this book and requires multifaceted scientific experimentation. Professor Michel's work has been cited here to suggest that a full understanding of why the Jews behaved as they did during the mass deportation from Warsaw—and from other places, as well—requires us to take a broad view of human problems and behavior under conditions of acute stress.

The concrete factors that influenced the response and behavior of the Jews during the extended *Aktion* in Warsaw can be summarized as follows:

1. Perpetual uncertainty and ignorance of what awaited the deportees.

2. The assumption that the Germans intended to uproot only part of the ghetto population — primarily refugees and those without a stable means of support.

3. Persistent rumors about the date on which the *Aktion* was scheduled to end — the hearsay that was a deliberate aspect of what Ringelblum termed the "German perfidy."

4. The assumption that resistance would only make matters even worse, while resignation to the dispossession of part of the population might secure the safety of the remainder of the ghetto.

5. To cope with the stress created by the *Aktion*, individuals (or the nuclear family) had to draw upon all their physical and emotional strength, which left no room for organization or action in a broader framework.

6. The steadily deteriorating circumstances — isolation from those who had already been caught, hunger, and fear — paralyzed the will to live and with it the ability to resist.

7. Even after reports about Treblinka had been circulated, they could not counterbalance the influence of the letters and rumors about deportees who had been "resettled" somewhere and were supposedly healthy enough to be working. Despite daily evidence of Nazi brutality on the streets of the ghetto, the truth about Treblinka could not break through the psychological barriers that the ghetto population had erected.

If we can indeed speak of the uniqueness of the Jewish experience, its existential basis is to be sought in the condition of the Jews as a minority dispersed among a hostile majority, cut off from the free world, and unable to avail itself of sources of aid. The paradox is that the Jews, who were defined as the foremost racial and political enemy of the National-Socialist regime — an enemy against which a program of total annihilation was planned and executed with the help of armed forces — were actually the embodiment of weakness and helplessness.

Chapter Seven
The Ghetto Underground during the Deportation and the Establishment of the Jewish Fighting Organization (Ż.O.B.)

Attempts to Establish a Comprehensive Resistance Organization During the first days of the *Aktion* (according to some sources, on July 23, 1942, i.e., the day after the operation began), representatives of the organized forces in the underground convened in an effort to appraise the significance of the latest events and decide upon immediate measures. The following description of that meeting is taken from notes and reports written by participants in the consultation and by others who heard about it firsthand from those who took part.

In the Jewish Fighting Organization report sent to London in November 1943, Yitzhak Zuckerman mentions a body he called the Public Council, by which he meant the institution whose composition was identical to that of the advisory board attached to the Self-Help. According to Zuckerman, the following people were present at the above-mentioned meeting: Lipa Bloch (General Zionists), Shmuel Breslaw (Ha-Shomer ha-Za'ir), Adolf Berman (Left Po'alei Zion), Yitzhak Zuckerman (Dror He-Halutz), Zisha Frydman (Agudat Yisrael), Joseph Lewartowski-Finkelstein (Communists), David Guzik, Yitzhak Giterman (JDC), Joseph Kaplan (Ha-Shomer ha-Za'ir), Menahem Kirschenbaum (General Zionists), Alexander Landau, Maurycy Orzech (Bund), Emmanuel Ringelblum (Left Po'alei Zion), Joseph Sak (Po'alei Zion Z.S.), Shakhne Sagan (Left Po'alei Zion), and Ignacy Schipper (General Zionists). These sixteen people represented a broad public and political constituency, from the Orthodox Agudat Yisrael to the Communists, and included both heads of the youth movements and men whose authority derived not from their political or party affiliation but from their indisputable public stature. Conspicuous in their absence from this meeting were representatives of Mizrachi and the Revisionists. Zuckerman states in his report:

> The representatives of the leftist Zionist parties and He-Halutz, as well as some of the public figures present, called for some form of energetic action. The majority [however] demanded that [we] wait. How long? Until the situation became clear, for rumors were rampant that only 50,000–70,000 people would be deported from Warsaw (the elderly, sick, prisoners, beggars, and the like), and with that the *Aktion* would end. All the rest would remain.

Another version of the discussion at that meeting can be found in the memoirs of Hirsch Berlinski, who was not personally present at the consultation but, as one of the prominent activists in Left Po'alei Zion, undoubtedly heard a detailed report from the representatives of his party who did participate. Berlinski described the discussion as follows:

> . . . The agenda: the situation that has arisen in the Warsaw ghetto. . . . The conclave was impressed by the statements of Zisha Frydman and Schipper. Z. Frydman placed his trust in faith: "I believe in God and in miracles. God will not allow his people, Israel, to be destroyed. We must wait, and the miracle will happen. Resistance is hopeless. The Germans are capable of finishing us off in a few days (as in Lublin). But if things are handled [as I suggest], everything may continue for quite a while, and a miracle is bound to happen. . . ." Schipper was not in favor of resistance. Self-defense would mean the total destruction of the Warsaw ghetto! "I believe that we will be able to preserve the essence of the ghetto in Warsaw. We are in the midst of a war. Every nation sacrifices victims; we too are paying the price in order to salvage the core of the people. Were I not convinced that we can succeed in saving that core, I, too, would come to a different conclusion. . . ." The meeting dispersed with the intention of convening a second time. [However,] the course of events put to rest the possibility of any further gathering.[1]

We also find echoes of this meeting in the writings of Bund members. Marek Edelman's report, which was published in 1945, stated that: "On the second day of the *Aktion*, July 23, there was a meeting of what is called the Workers' Committee—on which all the political factions are represented—and with the support of only the 'Halutzim' and the 'Shomrim,' we called for active resistance." Bernard Goldstein, among the foremost activists in the underground Bund, relates in his memoirs that before the meeting convened on July 23, the Bund held an internal consultation and a directive was given to the party's representatives that "active resistance and sabotage of the deportation is the only possible approach." Goldstein also reiterates Edelman's claim that during the broad-based consultation of July 23, the majority opposed the Bund's position, with only He-Halutz and Ha-Shomer ha-Za'ir supporting the demand for active resistance.[2]

The notes and reports written by members of the various factions allow us to reconstruct a reliable account of the meeting and its results. First, it is clear that the participants represented the major public bodies and political factions and that the consultation took place close to the inception of the *Aktion*, evidently on July 23, 1942. During the course of the meeting, the demand for active resistance—namely, armed resistance—was put forth. This proposal was vehemently rejected by two very influential personalities within the circle of participants: Zisha Frydman of Agudat Yisrael and the historian and veteran Zionist activist Dr. Ignacy Schipper. Frydman claimed that resistance was futile and it was best to place faith in Divine Providence and wait for the turning point that would bring salvation. Schipper invited the assembled leaders to study the lessons of Jewish history: more than once the Jewish people had been forced to resign itself to cruel bloodletting in order to save the core of the nation and perpetuate Jewish existence. Physical resistance is no solution in the present situation, he claimed, and it would only accelerate and expand the dimensions of the tragedy. Frydman and Schipper's emphatic statements left a strong impression on other representatives and ruled out the acceptance of a decision in favor of active resistance.

Among the proponents of armed opposition to the Germans were the representatives of Dror He-Halutz and Ha-Shomer ha-Za'ir, who for the first time were considered as having an equal say in matters alongside the veteran circle of public activists. The view of these younger representatives was essentially supported by the Bund and the factions that had formerly been organized in the Anti-Fascist Bloc. According to most of the reports, the meeting ended without reaching any concrete decisions, on the assumption that it was best to await the course of further developments. Thereafter, a few of the bodies issued appeals to the public at large, not as a result of any decision adopted during the meeting but on their own initiative.

Still, the fruitless July 23 consultation did not put an end to further attempts to found a broad-based, operative public framework dedicated to resisting the deportation. Zuckerman relates that after the abortive consultation:

> The more activist elements—the leftist factions that had been united in the Anti-Fascist Bloc—established an Actions Committee together with

Bund. The members of this committee were Breslaw, Zuckerman, Finkelstein-Lewartowski, Kaplan, Orzech, Sak, and Sagan. [Yet] this body was likewise unable to carry out its tasks properly, since . . . any imprudent step brought death in its wake. The mere act of crossing the street was like crossing through the front between two warring countries. In addition, the number of [the committee's] members declined a few days after its establishment. . . .

Phrased in other words, the tension and risks that pervaded the entire ghetto left no room for ongoing contact and joint activity. Each individual had to look after his own safety and that of his family. Thus the committee lasted only a few days.

Unable to organize into a comprehensive framework, the various parties and public bodies individually closed ranks in an effort to save their own followers. Berlinski relates in his memoirs, for example, that on July 28 a meeting of the Warsaw board of Left Po'alei Zion was held in a soup kitchen on Elekteralna Street. Shakhne Sagan reported on the efforts of CENTOS to extend legal recognition to a few thousand people over and above its permanent staff. At the same meeting, Sagan spoke of "two SS officers who swore on their honor as officers that no Jewish deportee had been killed [and] all of them were transported to places of work," which goes to prove that even this relatively radical circle still did not see through the Germans' deceptive tactics. A "stormy debate" took place at the meeting over the question of self-defense. At its conclusion, the board decided to publish an appeal to the population, and Sagan was charged with preparing the draft of the manifesto.

The greater part of the discussion during the meeting was devoted to the problem of finding legal accommodations for the party's members. Sagan's report suggests that despite its ferverish efforts, CENTOS was standing on "thin ice," and the Germans were not interested in the *Judenrat* or its staff either, for the reality of the situation was that they would only give in on the "shop" workers. At the conclusion of the meeting, the committee "decided to take appropriate steps to ensure its members legal status in the 'shops.'"[3] A large group of Left Po'alei Zion members concentrated together in Landau's "shop," O.B.W. (*Ostdeutsche Bautischlerei Werkstätte* —East German Carpenters Workshop), which became a headquarters for members of the underground and the hub of clandestine activity during the deportation. On August 1, before he completed the composition of his party's manifesto, Sagan was caught during a "blockade," and all attempts to get him released from the *Umschlagplatz* were in vain.

According to Marek Edelman, during the first days of the *Aktion*, the Bund's central committee held extended discussions. Among the participants were Orzech, Blum, Sonya Nowogrodzka, Goldstein, and Edelman. "Any moment now we expect to receive arms from the 'Aryan' side of Warsaw," Edelman recorded. "All the youth are mobilized. For three days, so long as the last chance of receiving arms has not been dispelled, the state of tense alert has continued." Bernard Goldstein's memoirs also mention the state of alert in the ranks of the Bund and the vain expectation that arms would arrive. He adds, however, that after the call for resistance had been rejected by the July 23 interparty consultation, "it was clear to all of us that we were incapable of rebelling and calling for active resistance now on our own, against the will of the overwhelming majority of the ghetto."

The Bund lost many members during the assaults of the *Aktion*. As Edelman described it:

> We remain a tiny remnant. We do what we can, but that's not very much. We want to save whatever possible at any price. We arrange for people to work in German enterprises, which—it was believed at the time—were the best. Slowly we lost contact with almost everyone. There remained only one fairly large group of members (about twenty to twenty-five people) at the "Brushmakers" on Franciszkańska Street.[4]

Among the outstanding Bund activists who were swept away by the *Aktion* was Sonya Nowogrodzka, while the party's recognized leader, Maurycy Orzech, smuggled his family out of the ghetto at the height of the *Aktion* and went into hiding on the "Aryan"side of the city.

The situation in which the Jewish Communists found themselves was particularly onerous. Even before they had managed to crystallize into a stable framework in the underground, the Communists were overtaken by the crisis precipitated by the arrest of Andrzej Szmidt and his colleagues. As stated earlier, the Communist Party in the ghetto was the only division of the Jewish underground attached to a political framework whose members were both Polish and Jewish and whose headquarters were outside the ghetto.[5] Its routine activities were therefore dependent upon steady contact with the headquarters on the "Aryan" side. Shortly before the beginning of the *Aktion*, the meager foundations of the party in the Polish political arena were undermined by arrests, the work of informers, and suspicions. Yet the arrest of Szmidt and his colleagues in the ghetto was only one manifestation of the crisis that plagued the party. The demoralized state of the Communist Party on the "Aryan" side exacerbated the isolation of the Jewish comrades within the walls. Anna Duracz, a member of the party, elaborated in her testimony:

We couldn't explain to ourselves how come the party outside couldn't find any means or tactic whatsoever to reach us—or at least pass on information or orders to us. After all, some telephones were still working in the ghetto; Joseph Lewartowski could have put through a call. Some people on the outside maintained means of contact. We had the feeling that the party wasn't making the effort, wasn't exercising all its ability to help us, to save its people, or provide us with the means to act.

Unlike other organizations, the Communists in the ghetto did not assemble together in any one "shop." Lewartowski himself, a veteran revolutionary figure, found refuge in Landau's "shop" and was taken off in one of the roundups. Duracz wrote of the incident:

> I also know that faced with the immediate threat of deportation, when Joseph Lewartowski phoned the party's Central Committee for the last time, asked those responsible what he should do in his situation—after all courses of action had been blocked—and requested urgent aid and help in escaping (he was an invalid), he was told, according to what I heard: "You have to make your own way through personal contacts. . . ." The next day Joseph Lewartowski was taken to the *Umschlagplatz*.[6]

As to the Revisionists and members of Betar, we have no information on these organizations or their activities during the *Aktion*, other than the fact that a substantial number of Betar members were living in the vicinity of Hrubieszów. Thus the question remains: How did the members of the Revisionist Party and those Betar youngsters who remained in the ghetto respond during that period? The Revisionists were not represented at the broad-based consultation during the early days of the *Aktion*, and no reason is given for their absence. Neither can an explanation be found in the memoirs of David Wdowiński, the leader of the Revisionists in the ghetto. In the section of his book that describes the *Aktion*, Wdowiński details his personal suffering and that of his family at great length, but he does not write a word about organized efforts to rescue his political colleagues—not to mention the fact that there is no hint in these passages of any initiative to organize and respond to the challenge posed by the mass deportation.[7]

The leaders of the other youth movements, however, invested tremendous effort in attempts to save their members from deportation by arranging "documents" and places in the "shops" for them. As mentioned earlier, throughout the *Aktion* Dror He-Halutz maintained a large group of youngsters on an agricultural farm in Czerniakow, a suburb of Warsaw. According to Dror figures, 140 youngsters were living on the farm in the spring of 1942 and additional youngsters from the ghetto joined them during the months of the deportation. While it is true that the comrades living on the farm also faced risks, since the Germans could easily have trapped them inside, leaving no place to hide or route of escape, the fact of the matter is that the Dror group at Czerniakow was left unharmed during the *Aktion*. The farm served as a haven for a substantial number of youngsters, an island untouched by the oppressive atmosphere of desperation and helplessness that pervaded the ghetto. Thereafter, it continued to serve as a base for envoys and liaisons sent to the "Aryan" side by the Jewish Fighting Organization in order to obtain aid. The heads of Dror He-Halutz—Zivia Lubetkin and Yitzhak Zuckerman—remained in the ghetto throughout the deportation and played an active role in the initiative of building the resistance movement.

Most of the Ha-Shomer ha-Za'ir activists were concentrated in the ghetto during the deportation (one exception being Mordecai Anielewicz, who was on a mission to the cities of Zagłębie when the *Aktion* began). During the first week of the operation, the movement's members were called upon to move out of their parents' homes and concentrate together in communal groups. A good number of them were caught in the roundups and deported during the first days of the *Aktion*, but after the first week a group of "Shomrim" succeeded in escaping from a transport, and thereafter such escapes were undertaken repeatedly. The "shop" in which most of the Ha-Shomer comrades were concentrated was the O.B.W.—or "Landau's shop," as it was most commonly known—which had taken in so many members of the underground that Ringelblum described it as having a "civic character." Alexander Landau, one of the partners who owned the "shop," was close to leftist Zionist circles in the ghetto, and his daughter, Margalit, was a member of Ha-Shomer ha-Za'ir. Thanks to the relationship of trust and loyalty between Landau and the Ha-Shomer activists— particularly Joseph Kaplan—the "shop's" office was placed at the disposal of the underground for telephoning secret contacts outside the ghetto, stamping forged documents, and obtaining helpful information on the planned course of the *Aktion*.

Before the *Aktion* began, Gordonia had managed to transfer many of its members from Warsaw to a number of provincial cities— Częstochowa, Opoczno, and afterward Będzin—that were still relatively tranquil. The members of Gordonia did not harbor any illusions (as did many Jews in these remote regions) that these cities, unlike the eastern and central provinces of occupied Poland, would escape the fate of deportation. But they hoped to gain time, on the assumption that a change in objective conditions might come about, or they could at least plan some kind of rescue operation. They may also have wanted to concentrate in cities where their movement was stronger and better known to the public. At any rate, their departure from Warsaw continued right into the period of the deportation, and among those who abandoned the city at the time was the movement's most prominent and energetic activist, Eliezer Geller. According to Natan Eck, a close friend of Geller's in Warsaw, at that early stage of the deportation Geller did not believe that there was any real chance of mobilizing into a fighting force and demonstrating resistance, so he decided to save himself and his comrades from the trap. Geller later regretted this move, and in January 1943 wrote to his friends:

> On the threshold of death, I must state that although certain tactical and technical considerations forced us to adopt the course we have taken during the past half year, they were fundamentally erroneous. It is now beyond any doubt that all the forces and the energy invested by the comrades on the training farm in feverish rescue [efforts], so that action could be initiated at a later date, should have been directed toward preparing for self-defense and resistance. I personally cannot forgive myself for allowing myself to be persuaded and moved by the activists in Warsaw to abandon Warsaw four months ago.[8]

There were two fundamental differences between the rescue efforts staged by the political parties in the underground and the methods adopted by the youth movements. First, the veteran party stalwarts were concerned with saving noted individuals, members of the public and cultural elite, while the youngsters, although they generally displayed admiration for these "privileged" people, felt that during the period of the ghetto's decline there was little point in struggling to save the elite and leadership of the people when the people themselves were doomed to death. Second, the parties tried to provide arrangements that would protect their members and their families from deportation, while the members of the youth movements took the personally painful step of detaching themselves from the familial framework and throwing in their lot with their comrades. This difference in means derived from an *a priori* difference in objectives, for the youth movements had set their sights on more than rescue alone. The purpose of restructuring the movements under the new circumstances was to maintain organized units as a reservoir of strength for future action.

This restructuring operation was the turning point in the movements' conception of their status and role in the new situation that had come into being in the ghetto. The failure of the broad-based July 23 consultation convinced their leaders that there was no hope of building a common front dedicated to the cause of immediate armed resistance, while a more limited union of forces, comprising the groups that had been organized in the Anti-Fascist Bloc plus the Bund, would not be capable of realizing the idea of armed resistance. Thus from the beginning of the deportation, the heads of the youth movements despaired of convincing the majority of party and public leaders to support the notion of resistance and join in the struggle. They therefore came to the conclusion that they were left with no choice but to establish a fighting organization that would draw its forces exclusively from the youth movements. As Yitzhak Zuckerman put it, "the Jewish Fighting Organization was formed without the parties, in opposition to the parties."

The Establishment of the Jewish Fighting Organization (Ż.O.B.) On July 28, 1942, at the close of the first week of the *Aktion*, representatives of three pioneering youth movements — Ha-Shomer ha-Za'ir, Dror He-Halutz, and Akiva — met at the Dror He-Halutz commune on Dzielna Street and founded the Jewish Fighting Organization. The organization bore the Polish name *Żydowska Organizacja Bojowa*, but in the course of time both its members and many residents of the ghetto commonly referred to it by its initials, Ż.O.B.

According to Zuckerman's 1943 report to London, the command of the newly established organization consisted of Shmuel Breslaw, Yitzhak Zuckerman, Zivia Lubetkin, Mordecai Tenenbaum, and Joseph Kaplan, and a delegation was appointed to operate on the Polish side of Warsaw, making contact with the underground and combat organizations and obtaining the necessary arms and equipment in any way possible. The members of the first delegation were Tosia Altman, Frumka Plotnicka, Leah Perlszejn, and Arie Wilner ("Jurek"), who soon became the Ż.O.B.'s official representative vis-à-vis the Polish underground bodies.[9]

The founders of the Ż.O.B. viewed the organization not as an instrument limited to the Warsaw ghetto alone but as a nationwide enterprise. Their approach was a natural corollary of the fact that the component movements of the Ż.O.B. operated throughout the country; thus their very transformation into a combat organization meant the creation of a nationwide fighting force. In addition, by the time the Ż.O.B. was established, it had become incontestably obvious that the Nazi extermination program was not a localized phenomenon but a design to wipe out the Jews wherever they were found. The contact between the movements' headquarters in Warsaw and their branches in outlying cities and towns continued and to some degree even intensified, with the aim of establishing cells of the Ż.O.B. and preparing the organized youth throughout the country for the ultimate trial. Among the Ż.O.B.'s tasks, cited by Zuckerman in his report, was "To dispatch envoys to all the large cities in order to organize the defense of those ghettos that still exist." Thus the flurry of organizational activity and uprising in a number of places—Cracow, Będzin, Sosnowiec, Częstochowa, and to some degree Bialystok—should be viewed as expressions of a dynamic that was set in motion in Warsaw in July 1942.

During the first days of the *Aktion*, the Bund published a special edition of its newspaper, calling on the population of the ghetto to resist the deportation in the following way: not to report to the *Umschlagplatz*, not to allow the Germans to catch them, to struggle with the Jewish Police, and the like.[10] The appeal also warned that the Germans were liars and that the transports were carrying the deportees not to places of work but to death. According to Goldstein, the special issue was so widely distributed that it was necessary to mimeograph it three times.

The members of Ha-Shomer ha-Za'ir also addressed the residents of the ghetto by means of a handbill that was pasted up at the entrances to buildings and placed in mailboxes. According to the testimony of Arie Najberg, this handbill appeared on the third day of the *Aktion* and called upon the people "to revolt, disobey the German orders, explain to people that the way to the *Umschlagplatz* leads to death."[11] Yet Najberg noted that the ghetto residents reacted to these demands skeptically, suspecting that German provocation lay behind the call to resist. Many believed the Germans had a vested interest in inciting the Jews to rash acts of resistance; that is, the Nazis intended to exploit any opposition as a pretext to adopt more ruthless methods in carrying out the *Aktion* and to extend its scope.

Zuckerman's report states that with its establishment, the Ż.O.B. anticipated receipt of a shipment of arms. Until it arrived, the command decided:

> (1) To publish a manifesto addressed to the Jewish public and explain that "the 'resettlement' meant Treblinka, and Treblinka meant death." The Jews must hide their women and children and forcefully resist the German commands. (2) To forge German "livelihood cards" [i.e., work documents] and distribute them among the sector of the population that was not "privileged" to work in German workshops and be counted among the "productive element"; we distributed thousands of documents of this kind. (3) Since members of the *Ordungsdienst* [the Jewish Police] in the ghetto and the "Jewish Council" [*Judenrat*], along with the Ukrainians and Latvians, are carrying out the Germans' orders, their contemptible work must be actively resisted. A death sentence was issued against the commander of the Jewish Police, Józef Szeryński. To our astonishment and bitterness, our appeal fell on deaf ears then. They still didn't believe.

When the Ż.O.B. was established on July 28, it was clear to its founding members that they were obligated to take up arms in resistance to the "resettlement *Aktion*," which they understood to be a massive and perhaps wholesale extermination operation. Yet the Ż.O.B. command had not worked out a plan for an uprising and, most significant of all, had no arms or other fundamental instruments of combat. Immediately following its description of the organization's establishment, structure, and institutions, Zuckerman's report comments that "the fighting organization was established, but the entire store of arms in the ghetto at that time consisted of one revolver!"

The new fighting organization was divided by differences of approach regarding the means and timing of the uprising. The younger members of the Ż.O.B., eighteen- and nineteen-year-olds, were impatient and demanded the initiation of acts of resistance without delay. There was neither time nor reason, they claimed, to be fussy about means or to make the proposed action contingent upon systematic preparation. The point was to instigate a spontaneous insurrection, in which the fighters would use knives, clubs, poisonous acids—in short, whatever came to hand. Overruling them, however, the leaders and older members of the organization resolved to initiate the armed struggle only after weapons had been obtained and appropriate means of action had been decided upon. Their decision was based upon the assumption that an angry outburst, rather than a well-planned and extended struggle, would blow over quickly without leaving any lasting impression or causing any real damage to the Germans. The Nazis could easily quell an uprising of that sort, and the bold fighters would be relegated to the obscure category of "people shot during the course of the evacuation." The younger comrades countered that the acquisition of equipment and long-range planning would merely postpone the action to an unknown date and, in the final analysis, as the lethal pace of the *Aktion* proved, the Germans would be able to complete the extermination operation before the fighting organization had even prepared its resistance campaign. This conflict grew increasingly sharp as the *Aktion* proceeded apace and the German tactics grew increasingly ruthless.

The first measure agreed upon during the period of the *Aktion* was the implementation of the death sentence pronounced on Józef Szeryński, the commander of the Jewish Police. A small circle of Ż.O.B. members debated the merits of various candidates for the mission and finally chose Yisrael Kanał, a member of Akiva. Kanał, who had been a member of the Jewish Police for a time, placed himself at the disposal of the underground and had been active in the Ż.O.B. from its inception. Arie Grzybowski and Yehuda Engelman, who were still serving in the ranks of the Jewish Police during the deportation, regularly passed on information about developments within the force, participated in getting members of the Ż.O.B. released from the

Umschlagplatz, and fulfilled a string of assignments that only men in uniform could have carried out in the midst of the *Aktion*. A description of the assassination attempt, carried out on August 20, 1942, has been preserved in the memoirs of a Jewish Police officer:

> During the second half of August, the attempt on Szeryński's life was carried out. A man dressed in a policeman's cap rang [the bell of] his private apartment. He told the woman who opened the door that he had a letter for Szeryński. When Szeryński walked out toward him, his head slightly turned to the side, the man shot at him and wounded him in the face. In a rare fluke, the bullet penetrated his left cheek, a bit high, and exited through his right cheek without touching the tongue, teeth, or palate.

The writer goes on to state that not only did the members of the Jewish Police fail to denounce the assassination attempt, they even expressed their delight over Szeryński's misfortune and the fact that he had felt the hand of "Jewish retribution." (The addition of this comment was undoubtedly influenced by the writer's generally apologetic stance toward matters concerning the Jewish Police.) Further on, the same officer states that the developments over the summer soon overshadowed the assassination attempt, and the incident ceased to be a sensation. "The only sensation," he comments, "was what lay behind the scenes of the incident, the implication that political cells of one sort or another actually existed, that political life was organized in some way. . . ."12

An entry from Abraham Levin's diary is instructive in this context. On August 21, 1942, he recorded: "There's talk of an assassination attempt against the head of the police, Szeryński. He was wounded in the cheek. According to the rumors, he was hit by someone from the P.P.S. [the Polish Socialist Party] disguised in the uniform of a Jewish policeman."13 Levin, who was a member of the "Oneg Shabbat" staff in the underground, had taken shelter in Landau's "shop" on Miła Street— i.e., the place where the members of the Ż.O.B. were concentrated— and personally came into contact with a number of the organization's leaders. Yet it never occurred to him that a clandestine armed body existed in the ghetto or that it was a Jew who had shot at Szeryński.

The rumor that a Polish Socialist was responsible for shooting Szeryński was evidently not haphazard. Adolf Berman related in an article written in May 1943:

> . . . It was on August 20 that the organization [Ż.O.B.] also fired its first shot. A fighter seriously wounded the commander of the Jewish

Police, Józef Szeryński. . . . The public generally reacted to the news of the assassination attempt with admiration, since the police force was the object of hatred. *Judenrat* circles spread the rumor that the assassin was a Polish Socialist. It is interesting that no German retaliation followed the assassination attempt. The ghetto's internal settling of accounts no longer concerned them. . . . [14]

Levin wrote on August 21: "Leaflets were distributed today against the Jewish Police, which aided in the execution of 200,000 Jews. The death sentence was pronounced on the entire police force." The leaflet cited by Levin had been distributed even before the assassination attempt, on August 17, and was a kind of forewarning of the action. After the incident the Ż.O.B. posted another handbill stating that the commander of the Jewish Police, officers, and rank and file members alike had been tried and found guilty, and as a result the assassination was directed against Józef Szeryński, adding that similar acts would reflect the full gravity of the sentence. Levin recorded in his diary on August 25: "In the morning I read a typewritten announcement on Lubecka Street (in Polish) to the following effect: 'Since the head of the police, the officers, and the rank and file policemen are judged guilty, an assassination has been carried out against Szeryński, Józef. Further sentences of this nature (repression) will be enacted with the full weight of the judgment."[15]

In the latter half of August, the Ż.O.B. perpetrated a number of acts of arson in apartments in the housing blocks that had been requisitioned by the Germans and still contained the property of the deportees, as well as in the warehouses of "shops" whose legitimate status had been cancelled and whose employees had lost their right to remain in the ghetto. This series of arson attacks reached its climax on August 19, a day before the attempt on Szeryński's life. Then, at dawn on August 21, Soviet planes appeared over Warsaw and bombed the heart of the city. Despite the peril and the losses, the Jews drew encouragement from the bombardment, and those who still anticipated that the free world would somehow respond to the Nazi murders viewed the bombing as an act of retaliation for the deportation from the ghetto. Obviously, however, this concurrence of events was merely coincidental, and the Soviet aerial attack was in no way related to the Jews or the ghetto.

Another operation initiated by the underground organizations and camps within the Ż.O.B. during the deportation was related to the dispatch of youngsters to join the partisans. This campaign was worked out in coordination with the Communists outside the ghetto, who promised to absorb the youths who managed to get out of the ghetto into units under their command. The organizations that had made up the defunct

Anti-Fascist Bloc were particularly active in forming these groups. Berlinski related in his memoirs:

> During the first half of August, a meeting was held at the O.B.W. between Pola Elster, Lewartowski, and Kaplan—representatives of Left Po'alei Zion, the Communists, and Ha-Shomer [respectively]. They examined the possibility of transferring comrades to the partisans [and] . . . reached the conclusion that the candidates for joining the partisans must look like "Aryans" and know the Polish language perfectly. The partisan leadership demands that the candidates be males only; no details on the structure of the hideouts [in the forest] and the transportation system are known as yet. The conferees decided to train people for the partisans.[16]

Anna Duracz wrote about the dispatch of members of the Communist Party to join the partisans at the height of the deportation: "Our previous belief was that people should be brought out of the ghetto and integrated into the partisan groups of the P.P.R., and a few bands of our people did indeed leave for the *'partizanka.'* This was in August 1942."[17]

Mordecai Tenenbaum also wrote of the campaign to join the partisans in *A Letter to Friends:*

> An *Aktion* in the ghetto. Five to seven thousand victims each day. And on the other side of the wall—searching for a way out, seeking out the possibilities of obtaining arms, of ties with the partisans. The slogans and mottoes of the P.P.R. were meaningless. They weren't waiting, they didn't know, they didn't want to know. All the attempts to dispatch people to groups in the Lublin District—the center of partisan activity—ended in arrest and death. Other attempts—in worse than death.[18]

In *The Book of the Wars of the Ghettos,* edited by Yitzhak Zuckerman and Moshe Basok, a footnote to the report on the Ż.O.B. elaborates that during the mass deportation from Warsaw:

> A group of twenty-five to thirty members of Ha-Shomer ha-Za'ir and Dror was also sent from Warsaw to the Międzyrzecz forests. They succeeded in making contact with partisan bands in the Red Army [i.e., the P.P.R.], were tested in many incidents, and suffered quite a bit from their non-Jewish comrades in arms. They obtained their weapons by attacking Germans. The first revolver was obtained in a literally bare-handed raid. While still inexperienced and hardly armed, they fell in battle, to the last man, in one mass attack by the Germans.[19]

As the broad lines of the above description indicate, we lack details on the experiences and fate of the Jewish fighters who left the ghetto bound for the forests and the partisan struggle. Polish sources do not cite the names of Jewish fighters. However, we do know of a number of Communist youths who left the ghetto to join the partisans and later turned up in the Communist advance units that operated in Warsaw.

There was a glaring discrepancy between the hopes that the Jews placed on the partisan struggle under the aegis of the Communists and the Communists' true strength and ability to operate. The ghetto had visions of a Communist front digging in throughout the forests and carrying on an increasingly aggressive struggle against the enemy. This image, which was fostered by the Communists in the underground, was intentionally embellished for propaganda purposes, while the true state of affairs was quite different. The truth of the matter is that until May 1942 the Communists cannot be said to have had a real fighting force at all. It was only in May that the first small cells began to crystallize, and even then the partisans lacked training, arms, and combat experience. During the months of the *Aktion* in the Warsaw ghetto, the first units took shape in the forests, but they were far from a stable force that dominated the area in which they operated. The crisis that overtook the P.P.R. affected the partisan units as well, and many of them disbanded before they had even become firmly established. As a result, the Jews who were promised a place in the partisan movement failed to find units in the areas where they were supposed to be stationed, did not receive weapons or necessary aid, and were for the most part abandoned to their fate. For lack of choice, they tried to establish themselves in the forest on their own. But without knowledge of the area or aid from beyond the forest, they were doomed to fail before long. Only a few survived this brutal trial and returned to Warsaw.

As stated earlier, the bodies that had formerly made up the Anti-Fascist Bloc were active in the attempt to organize candidates for the partisans. The bands made their way out of the ghetto via the Jewish cemetery. The graveyard was not included within the boundaries of the ghetto, but a group of youngsters—mostly members of Ha-Shomer ha-Za'ir from Landau's "shop"—cultivated a small vegetable garden nearby, and those who were chosen to leave the ghetto were integrated into this group, which made its way out to work each morning. In addition, the Jewish cemetery bordered on the Christian cemetery and the Polish suburb of Powązki, and meetings between members of the Jewish underground and organizations on the "Aryan" side took place within its bounds.

One group of Dror comrades that left Warsaw during the deportation was trapped under unique circumstances, and it was evidently to this incident that Mordecai Tenenbaum was referring in his comment "Other attempts—in worse than death." The entire incident is described in a footnote to the Ż.O.B. report in *The Book of the Wars of the Ghettos:*

> Since 1941 a group of forty Dror pioneers had been living in a saw-mill in the vicinity of Hrubieszów (in the village of Werbkowice) under the leadership of Moshe Rubenczyk. . . . In August 1942, during the fatal deportation, another thirty comrades were sent there and charged, to-gether with their predecessors, with initiating partisan activities in the area. A short time afterward a third group of eighteen members was sent (the three groups numbered a total of about sixty people) . . . and it was caught during an inspection of documents on the way to Hrubieszów. Only one young comrade, Moniek Stengel, managed to make his way back to War-saw. The rest were murdered on the spot, with the exception of Yisrael Zeltzer, who for some reason was brought by the Gestapo to the Pawiak prison in Warsaw and murdered there. The capture of this group also led to the murder of all the comrades who were concentrated in the sawmill near Hrubieszów.[20]

As we shall see, the incident did not end here and had further grave consequences for the Ż.O.B. in Warsaw.

On August 21 the first shipment of arms acquired by the representatives of the Ż.O.B. on the "Aryan" side was smuggled into the ghetto. It included five revolvers and eight hand grenades and was purchased under the aegis of the P.P.R., which aided Arie Wilner in reaching the agents and arms dealers. The weapons were transferred to a "cell" of Ż.O.B. members in the housing block of the O.B.W. "shop" on Miła Street. According to Berman, Arie Wilner and Tosia Altman obtained "the first five revolvers and eight hand grenades for the ghetto thanks to the help of the [Communist] People's Guard." The quantity of arms was pitifully small, but the fighters in Warsaw, who had waited so long for these weapons, regarded them as a treasure.

September 3 and Its Aftermath

September 3, 1942, a day that spelled disaster for the Ż.O.B., brought the downfall that quashed all of the plans "to defend the honor of Warsaw Jewry." To describe the events of that date, we must begin with the group of Dror comrades that was trapped on its way to Werbkowice. The captured youngsters bore forged documents that had been prepared in the O.B.W. office by Joseph Kaplan. As noted earlier, the entire group was executed immediately, with the exception of one member who succeeded in escaping, and Yisrael Zeltzer, who was transferred to the Pawiak prison in Warsaw.

Yisrael Zeltzer was one of the leading activists in Gordonia, but unlike most members of his movement he did not leave Warsaw before or during the *Aktion*. In the course of the deportation, after his wife had been sent to Treblinka, he turned up at the He-Halutz commune on Dzielna Street in a state of despair, declaring that he had nothing left in life and was prepared to take on even the most perilous mission. Thus on the last day of August or the first of September, he was assigned to the group bound for Werbkowice.

On September 3 a group of Gestapo men, accompanied by the German "shop" supervisor, entered the O.B.W. "shop" and demanded the list of workers employed there. After going over the names, they ordered Joseph Kaplan to be brought before them. The demand did not arouse any particular suspicions, since Kaplan was officially listed as a worker in the office. When he was brought into the "shop," Kaplan was arrested and taken off to an unknown destination.

Shmuel Breslaw immediately turned to a number of parties in the ghetto, asking them to make every effort to save Kaplan. During that period Jews were not allowed to be out in the streets during working hours unless they had a special permit. Breslaw, who had no such permit, was arrested by uniformed Germans who were riding down Gęsia Street in a car. He tried to pull a jackknife out of his pocket but was shot on the spot.[21] Ringelblum commented in his record, under the heading "Resistance": "Shmuel could not bear the tragedy of the ghetto."[22]

When the events of that day became known, the Ż.O.B. decided to transfer the weapons from the Ha-Shomer ha-Za'ir "cell" in the O.B.W. area on Miła Street to a new cache on Dzielna Street. Zuckerman described the operation and the reasoning behind it:

> At first we believed that there was a connection between Shmuel's death and Joseph's arrest. At any rate, definitive clues led to the housing block on Miła, where the small cache of arms belonging to the Ż.O.B., which had been acquired at the cost of such great effort, was hidden behind a wall in a top-floor apartment. It was imperative to save the arms for a last stand. We therefore ordered that as soon as dusk falls, when the workers are returning from the "Aryan" side and the streets are full of movement and activity, we would transfer the arms and the secret radio to our safe house at 34 Dzielna Street. In the meantime, we worked in one of the cellars on Dzielna Street, moving piles of coal and creating a temporary hiding place for our treasure. The hideout was completed by sunset. At the appointed hour one of the comrades brought the radio wrapped in

a sack. That radio was important to us, but the grenades and the revolvers were vital.[23]

The revolvers and grenades never made it to the new haven. Reginka Justman, a member of Ha-Shomer ha-Za'ir who had been integrated into the O.B.W. "shop," carried the arms hidden in a sack of vegetables. On her way from Miła to Dzielna Street, she was stopped by a sentry, and the precious arms fell into the hands of the Germans.[24]

The Ż.O.B. had suffered a mortal blow. In a single day, two members of its command had fallen and the weapons upon which all its plans depended had been lost. Immediate efforts were launched to clarify the reasons behind Kaplan's arrest, which was followed by the downfall of September 3. Zuckerman explained:

> The details became known to us later. [When] the Gestapo men left the car and entered the factory's office, some workers, who just happened to be standing in the street, noticed that in addition to the driver, a man wrapped in a coat remained seated in the car. At first we didn't attribute any importance to the mystery of the anonymous man in the car. Only much later did it become clear that he held the key to the tragic events in Warsaw, at one of the way stations before Lublin, and at the sawmill in Werbkowice.[25]

Adam [Zylberstejn], who was then a member of the nucleus at Częstochowa and heard about the incidents from envoys who later arrived from Warsaw, related:

> During the first days of September, ten comrades who produced suspicious documents during an inspection were arrested in front of the railroad station at Ostrowiec [Werbkowice]. After a two-hour interrogation, everything was revealed—the detainees were immediately executed. But first the Germans tried to get information out of them by promising to release them on condition that they revealed who had prepared the papers for them. One of the group, Y.Z. [Yisrael Zeltzer—the "anonymous man in the car"], was taken in by the temptation and revealed Joseph Kaplan's name and address. Joseph was arrested and sentenced to death.[26]

While efforts continued to secure Kaplan's release, Arie Grzybowski, a personal friend of Kaplan's and a Ż.O.B. loyalist working within the Jewish Police, kept a close watch on the case. He always tried to be somewhere near the route leading from the Pawiak prison to the *Umschlagplatz* in the hope of being able to identify Kaplan and perhaps even succeed in getting him released from the railroad yard.

Finally, Kaplan was led to the *Umschlagplatz* together with a group of Jews from the Pawiak prison, but the plan to rescue him never came to fruition: on the way to the *Umschlagplatz,* one of the German escorts pulled two of the prisoners out of line, marched them over to the entrance of a building, and shot them. The two were Joseph Kaplan and Yisrael Zeltzer. Grzybowski and Yehuda Engelman were sent to identify their bodies in a pile of corpses that were delivered to the cemetery.[27]

The disaster of September 3 and its brutal aftermath left the command and membership of the Ż.O.B. in a state of confusion and despair. The situation is described in a memoir of the period:

> In our naïveté, we saw ourselves as fighters combating the armed Nazis face to face. What a devilish farce. The devil is omnipotent. He is totally unrestrained. We debate, deliberate, discuss. And by the time we've arrived at something, they come along and slap our faces. A single gentle slap. For what actually happened? They came to arrest a man in one of the "shops," shot a pedestrian on Gęsia Street, and arrested a girl wandering around the streets with a sack during the deportation. All quite routine acts that neither surprise nor particularly disturb anyone in the ghetto. But for us—it's the end. Nothing's left but to go out into the streets and fight with our fists . . . while we're still together; while we still have the will.[28]

After the debacle of September 3, the O.B.W. "shop" became a repeated target of German raids. While the rest of the "shops" enjoyed relative peace, the O.B.W. was subjected to stringent "blockades." The veteran workers of the "shop," who had stood by and watched with rising fury as public figures and people suspected of political activism flooded into their "shop," now reacted with demonstrative hostility and placed the blame for the heightened victimization of the O.B.W. and the revocation of its recognized status on the members of the underground who had gathered there.

Rumors that the end of the deportation was in sight revitalized the question of how to react to the new circumstances in the ghetto and exactly how to proceed. The Ż.O.B.'s undermined morale and sense of frustration were painfully obvious during the discussions on this subject. It was clear—to the member of the Ż.O.B., at any rate—that the cessation of the transports did not mean that the remaining Jews in the ghetto were safe. At best, the halt in the deportations was only a pause, of shorter or longer duration, in the Nazi operation. The truth about Treblinka and what that camp held for the Jews was already crystal clear to the Ż.O.B., especially since some of its members were themselves fugitives from the camp's death machine.

By the time of the final *Selektion* in the ghetto, the members of the Ż.O.B. were divided into two camps: the "extremists," who demanded immediate action without any further consideration of the significance or consequences of the battle, and the "moderates," who believed that the strong will to resist called for postponing action until a convenient time could be chosen and proper preparations undertaken and then dealing as effective a blow as possible. Yitzhak Zuckerman and Arie Wilner sided with the so-called moderates and tipped the scale in their favor. According to a witness, Arie Wilner told a gathering of Ż.O.B. members:

> . . . It would be best to sit tight and just pull through now, during this deportation. Not for the sake of our future or out of hope for a new life. The future and the new life will undoubtedly be built by others, who will come after us. We are no longer a creative *avant-garde*. Our creation can only be destruction and revenge. Our weapons have been taken from us. We should therefore vanish off the face of the earth, burrow down and hide, prepare and train there, and then reemerge once we have become a force that can assualt the enemy in a single [massive] attack.[29]

During the final days of the *Aktion,* the members of the Ha-Shomer ha-Za'ir "cell" in the O.B.W. "shop" were joined by remaining Dror He-Halutz comrades in the ghetto. Yitzhak Zuckerman described how a group of veterans of the two movements sat together reminiscing about Joseph Kaplan and speculating out loud about what the future held in store for them:

> We ate our meager meal in sorrow and silence. [Then] the younger members went into the other room and we remained. Well, we're alive. We must know today what we shall do tomorrow. I don't remember who spoke first—Arie Wilner or Zivia Lubetkin. The words were bitter; words of decision. Jewish resistance will never come into being again. After us. The nation is lost. If we couldn't organize a Jewish force while there were still hundreds of thousands in Warsaw, how can we do so when only a few thousand are left? The masses did not place their trust in us. We do not have—and probably never will have—weapons. We don't have the strength to start all over again. The nation has been destroyed; our honor trampled upon. This tiny group might yet save us. Let us go out into the streets tomorrow, set the ghetto aflame, and attack the Germans with knives. We will die. It is our duty to die. And the honor of Israel will be saved. In days to come, it will be said: The youth of that hapless people rose up to defend its honor while it still could.
> The comrades continued to speak out, each one in turn, and they

were all moved by a single idea. Despair was the dominant feeling, and that feeling demanded action. In such an atmosphere of despondency, it was impossible to speak otherwise. Nonetheless, one of the comrades gathered up his courage and said: The feeling is sincere; the conclusions erroneous. The disaster is overwhelming and the shame terrible. But what is being discussed here is an act of despair. It will be swallowed up without so much as an echo. It won't serve as revenge on the enemy in the least way. Our youth will be wiped out. We have failed countless times up to now, and we will yet fail again. What we must do is start all over again. The liquidation operation is coming to an end for the meantime. There may be some days of respite—perhaps weeks or even months—and with money we obtain in the ghetto, we shall try to buy arms. We must fight to the end against Jewish traitors. Were it not for Jewish treachery, the Germans would not have succeeded in dominating the ghetto so quickly and so easily. Perhaps the splendor is still not lost.

There was a great uproar, shouting down the comrade who wanted to postpone the last possible act. If we don't go out into the streets immediately, by tomorrow we won't have the strength to do so. He's trying to clip our wings. The discussion was heated, the atmosphere torrid. But gradually more tempered voices began to be heard. Concrete suggestions were raised. It was a fateful night for the remnants of the Jewish Fighting Organization. We took a vote and resolved to pluck up our courage and rebuild the armed Jewish force. Our remaining strength would be dedicated to that end. No effort would be spared. The fate of January and April 1943 was sealed on that night.[30]

Zuckerman does not explicitly state who was responsible for convincing the group to decide the issue in favor of waiting, but we may infer that the anonymous speaker was Zuckerman himself. Arie Wilner, who brought word from the "Aryan" side on an extended intermission in the deportation, leaving room to plan and prepare for an uprising, also supported the position of waiting and using the time to organize, obtain arms, and finally exercise the armed force effectively. The decision to postpone action in favor of building up and arming the resistance force was of decisive importance to the ultimate success of the uprising, since the nucleus of surviving Ż.O.B. members was the foundation on which the eventually broad-based Jewish Fighting Organization was built. There can be no doubt that future events justified the position of those who favored waiting.

To summarize the situation during the deportation, the general underground movement did not manage to reach a stage of broad unity or attain many concrete achievements. Many public figures and certain quarters in the underground rejected the idea of active resistance outright, while another sector of the underground supported such resistance in theory but for various reasons did not devote itself to such activity in practice, preferring to make do with appeals calling on the general public to display physical opposition to the deportation operation.

The Ż.O.B. was founded by a few of the pioneering Zionist youth movements after they had despaired of working in concert with the parties and had come to the pivotal conclusion that under the existing circumstances they could no longer subscribe to either the authority or the general objectives of the parties and were obligated to act on their own. The extent of the Ż.O.B.'s activity was not wide enough to make an impression on the ghetto. It carried out a few acts of sabotage and only one other more striking endeavor—an attempt on the life of Józef Szeryński, which was only partially successful and was not recognized by the masses in the ghetto as an act perpetrated by a Jewish organization. Before the Ż.O.B. had even formulated its course of action and obtained the minimum of arms necessary to operate effectively, it was struck by a disaster that demolished all its plans and divested it of the few weapons it had acquired with such difficulty.

Neither did the plans to join the partisans—which were discussed and implemented by the bodies that had been united in the defunct Anti-Fascist Bloc—yield impressive results. The only noteworthy achievement during the harrowing period of the fatal deportation from Warsaw was the very existence of a nucleus of Jews who regarded combat as their primary mission, the crowning contribution of their lives.

Chapter Eight
The Polish Response
to the Liquidation
of Warsaw Jewry

**Background Remarks on
Polish-Jewish Relations**
The Poles were not directly involved in the operation to liquidate
the Jews of Warsaw; that is, they
were not ordered to take an active part in the deportation campaign,
and the Polish ("Blue") Police were commanded only to increase the
guard on the ghetto walls and pursue Jews who succeeded in filtering
through to the Polish side of the city. Yet the question remains: How
did the Poles react to the tragedy that unfolded before their eyes and
what did they do—or fail to do—at a time when their response—or
failure to take action—had the power to determine the fate of many
Jews and the staying power of the ghetto underground?

The Poles as a nation, and the organized Polish underground in
particular, were the only potential ally that could have come to the aid
of the Jews imprisoned within the ghetto. The nature of such presumably available aid might have been threefold:

1. The Poles could have disrupted the process of the *Aktion* by
sabotaging the railroad track to Treblinka or even attacking the extermination camp itself.

2. They could have saved a substantial number of Jews by preparing appropriate hiding places, forged documents, and so forth.

3. The armed Polish underground could have bolstered the resistance movement in the ghetto by supplying it with arms and directing
many people to partisan units.

Before we analyze the position of the Poles and their response to
the mass extermination of the Jewish community, it is appropriate to

review, if only briefly, the situation in which the Polish population found itself and appraise its actual capacity to take action in the ways mentioned above. The Poles were subject to an oppressive regime and were deprived of an autonomous national administration. Any attempt to help the Jews was bound up with far greater difficulties and risks in Poland than in any other European country under Nazi domination. The Poles were liable to severe punishment—such as deportation to concentration camps and, from the close of 1942 onward, capital punishment—for concealing Jews. Yet there was a tremendous differ-ence between the oppression suffered by the Poles and that suffered by the Jews, for while the Poles were subject to restrictions on their liber-ties, conscription for forced labor, and devastating blows to specific classes of the population, the Jews were doomed to nothing less than total physical annihilation. The fact of the occupation notwithstanding, the Poles were a nation of over twenty million people living on their own soil and to a large degree united in their animosity toward the occupying power. And despite all the difficulties, they also benefited from supportive circumstances: Poland was rich in forested areas, which provided excellent cover for guerrilla warfare; a comprehensive and well-organized underground operated throughout the country; and monasteries and many welfare institutions under exclusively Polish supervision continued to exist during the occupation.

Moreover, one crucial fact must be established from the outset. While the population of the Allied countries did not know, as a rule, what became of the Jews deported to the east, the Poles themselves knew only too well—meaning that although the West was rife with rumors and suppositions that the deported Jews were engaged in forced labor somewhere in the eastern reaches of Nazi-occupied Europe, the Poles knew for a fact that the true meaning of the deportations was wholesale murder.

The conduct of the Poles and the reaction expressed by various classes and quarters of Polish society were a reflection of both the ter-ror implanted by the Germans and the innate attitude of the Poles that had crystallized both before and during the war. Ringelblum com-mented on the general Polish response to the deportation from Warsaw with bitterness:

> The "resettlement action" went on for 44 days, and not even an echo was heard from the Polish side. Complete silence—that was the response of the "Aryan" side to the drama which unfolded before the eyes of hun-dreds of thousands of Poles. No indication came from the Polish govern-ment that it would call for resistance; not a single word of encouragement was expressed; no assurance of support—even moral support—was of-

fered. Only the P.P.S. [Polish Socialist Party] published an appeal to the Jewish population, which was distributed in the area of the "Little [constricted] Ghetto," under the heading "Do Not Surrender!"[1]

Yet after the war, the Poles came out with a spate of publications supposedly proving that they had exerted great effort to rescue Jews and help them to defend themselves. If, nevertheless, no impressive gains were scored in the field of rescue and self-defense—at least at the time of the first mass deportation from Warsaw—responsibility lay with parties other than the Poles. This classically apologetic approach, which evades any self-criticism by pointing an accusing finger at others— including the victims themselves—was typical of both the ruling circles and spokesmen of Communist Poland and the loyalists of all the factions represented in the Polish government-in-exile who found refuge in Western Europe and America. In reality, however, the majority of the Polish population adhered to the view that the Jews were an alien body and that their fate neither concerned the Poles nor obliged special action on the part of Poland's political underground or clandestine armed force. Thus the mass deportation from Warsaw to the Treblinka death camp was carried out without a word of protest from the Polish public, while the underground did not even bother to adopt a position on the matter.

If any change can be said to have taken place in the Polish attitude toward the Jews, it was that the Poles' apathy and long-standing sense of hostility intensified during the course of the war. Two factors that came into being as a result of the war had a strong impact on the network of relations between the Jews and the Poles: (1) The Poles accused the Jewish community of Communist leanings, as evidenced by the enthusiastic welcome the Jews accorded to the Soviet forces that took over the country's eastern provinces in September 1939; and (2) the establishment of the ghetto and the eviction of Jews from their homes and positions in the economy benefited a broad class of people who moved in, both literally and figuratively, to fill the vacuum left by the removal of the Jews.

Spokesmen for the underground reported that the Nazis' anti-Jewish propaganda often met with a positive response, and the Poles particularly supported the fact that the Jews had been displaced from the Polish economy. Official representatives of the underground therefore insisted that the anti-Jewish measures promulgated by the Germans be accepted as the new and irrevocable reality in Poland and warned that if any future attempt were made to restore the Jews to their former positions, sharp opposition could be expected—even to the point of a general revolt.[2] The press in the Generalgouvernement, which was published by permission of the Germans and was tailored to the Polish readership, was filled with anti-Jewish sentiment and hammered away at the fact that in instituting the kind of "order regarding the Jews," the German regime had merely carried out what the Poles themselves demanded and the government of independent Poland had been incapable of doing.[3]

The Reaction from London to News of the Deportation and the Stance of the Underground

We shall now examine whether the Poles in London, who had lines of communication with the world at large, were aware of the events taking place in the Warsaw ghetto in the summer of 1942 and, if such information had indeed reached them, what their response was to these events.

A few days after the inception of the deportation, the Polish underground learned of what was taking place at Treblinka from a member of the Home Army (A.K.) who was employed at the Treblinka railway station. He reported in detail on the preparations being made in the camp, the number of railway cars, the transports, and their fate.

Among the most prominent activists in the Polish underground, Stefan Korboński, who was responsible for broadcasts from Poland and clandestine radio contact with London, wrote in his memoirs, *The Secret State*, that from the beginning of the deportation in July 1942, radiograms describing the course of events were sent to London regularly. Amazingly, and in contrast to custom, Korboński claims, the London Poles did not respond to the broadcasts and nothing was mentioned on the BBC. He further claims that the underground did not resign itself to London's disregard of such important information and insistently demanded a reply to the radiograms regarding the ghetto:

> This game went on for a few days, and evidently as a result of the alarms of the London station, the Polish government finally responded. The radiogram did not explain much. Its exact wording was: "Not all of your radiograms are deserving of publication." . . . It was only about a month later that the BBC reported an item based on our information, and only many months later that the entire matter was explained to me by an envoy of the government who was parachuted into the homeland. . . .[4]

The enduring silence of the Poles in London could not have derived from disbelief or lack of information, since the government-in-exile constantly received reports on developments within Poland, and a number of times, starting as early as July 1942, had reported the mur-

der of 700,000 Jews inside Poland. A section of an address delivered by
Władysław Sikorski, the head of the Polish government-in-exile, on May
4, 1943, deals with the final destruction of the Warsaw ghetto and the
armed struggle that had been carried out there. The speech was published on page 3 of the official Polish daily that appeared in England,
Dziennik polski. Yet for weeks before and after this speech, nowhere
did this paper, which published detailed, running accounts of events in
Poland, make any mention at all of what was taking place in the Warsaw
ghetto. According to the journal kept by Yitzhak Schwartzbart, the representative of the Zionist parties on the Polish National Council, the
Poles in London refrained from any explicit reference to or emphasis
on the suffering of the Jews and demanded that the Jewish tragedy be
mentioned only in the broad context of terror and assaults directed
against Poles and Jews alike. Shmuel Zygielbojm, the Bund's representative on the Polish National Council, evidently received news of
developments in Warsaw through the P.P.S., and he made that information public. But Schwartzbart was not informed of what was going
on, and in October 1944 he wrote in his diary: "I shall never forgive
[Prime Minister Stanisław] Mikołajczyk for remaining silent about the
news regarding the extermination of Jews during July 1942–September
1942. . . ."[5]

As to the underground in Poland itself, a number of published
sources testify to the Polish version of affairs during this period. One
published version is that of General Tadeusz Komorowski (known as
Bor), one of the leaders of the major armed organization in the Polish
underground (the Home Army—*Armia Krajowa*, or A.K.) and from
mid-May 1943 the commander of the A.K. (and of the Polish uprising
in August 1944). Komorowski wrote at length in his memoirs, *The Secret Army*, of the measures taken by the A.K. during the deportation of
Warsaw's Jews in the summer of 1942:

> As early as July 29th we had learned from the reports of railroad
> workers that the transports were being sent to the concentration camp at
> Treblinka and that there the Jews disappeared without trace. There could
> be no further doubt this time that the deportations were but a prelude to
> extermination.
>
> General Rowecki,[6] swift in his decisions as always, made up his mind
> that we could not remain passive, and that at all costs we must help the
> Jews so far as it lay in our power. He called a conference, at which, how-
> ever, some doubts were expressed. The argument ran: "If America and
> Great Britain, with powerful armies and air forces behind them and
> equipped with all the means of modern warfare, are not able to stop this
> crime and have to look on impotently while the Germans perpetrate every

kind of horror in the occupied countries, how can we hope to stop them?" Rowecki's opinion was that failure to show active resistance would only encourage the Germans to further mass exterminations on the same lines.

We had a department in our organisation which arranged protection and help for escaped Jews and the distribution of money to them which had been sent to us from London for the purpose. A certain "Wacław"[7] was chief of the department, and he was now instructed by Rowecki to get through to the Ghetto and establish contact with the Jewish leaders. He was to tell them that the Home Army was ready to come to the assistance of the Jews with supplies of arms and ammunition and to co-ordinate their attacks outside with Jewish resistance from within.

The Jewish leaders, however, rejected the offer, arguing that if they behaved quietly the Germans might deport and murder 20,000 or 30,000 and perhaps even 60,000 of them, but it was inconceivable that they should destroy the lot; while if they resisted, the Germans would certainly do so. When Wacław reported this to Rowecki, the General decided to intensify the sabotaging of German lines of communication in such a way as to hamper and delay the deportations.[8]

Not a single one of the details in Komorowski's description is based upon fact. Komorowski, who wrote his memoirs in exile from Poland, evidently wished to create a picture that would improve the image of the Poles' behavior during the war, regardless of whether or not it bore any resemblance to reality. The truth of the matter is that the alleged meeting and the decisions adopted on Rowecki's initiative are pure fiction. Moreover, the civil and military branches of the Polish underground did not make direct approaches to the Jews at that time, and neither was there any department to deal with providing aid to the Jews. It is true that an A.K. officer, Henryk Woliński, was assigned to handle "Jewish affairs." But during the period under discussion, Woliński's task was limited to gathering information on what was happening on the Jewish front, for the benefit of the A.K. and the Polish government's representation in occupied Poland. Indeed, Woliński wrote a detailed report on his work and his ties with the Jews, but it contains no reference to Rowecki's so-called order, or the negative reply allegedly received from the Jews, or any independent action decided upon by the Poles, as Komorowski claims.[9]

During the mass deportation from Warsaw, the A.K. emphatically did not provide any aid to the Jews or distribute a single zloty to those who had escaped the ghetto. Throughout that two-month period, Arie Wilner, the Ż.O.B. liaison on the "Aryan" side of Warsaw, made incessant attempts to reach authoritative circles in the A.K. and acquire urgent aid in the form of arms. Yet it was only in September 1942 that he succeeded in arranging to meet with the man he been trying to see, and even then the meeting yielded no results. Władysław Bartoszewski, whose later aim was to highlight the aid extended to the Jews by Polish circles, wrote of this meeting in his introduction to the book *Righteous Among Nations*:

> Aryeh Wilner ("Jurek"), an activist in Hashomer Hatz'air, was the official liaison officer between the Jewish Fighting Organization and the Polish underground. As early as September 1942, he made the first attempt to make contact with a representative of the Underground Army in order to obtain aid for the armed resistance movement in the ghetto. But he got through to cells in the A.K. that were not authorized to take decisions of this nature. Word of "Jurek's" mission did not reach the proper quarters in the A.K. Higher Command at the time.

Only at a later date, *after* the mass deportation, did Wilner succeed in getting through to Henryk Woliński. Strong ties developed between these two men, and the results of their meeting were crucial to the continued growth and strengthening of the Ż.O.B. Wilner and Woliński were brought together by Alexander Kamiński, the editor of the Polish underground's official organ, *Biuletyn Informacyjny,* and formerly a member of the Polish Scouts, which was known to be sympathetic toward the Jews. In his first discussion with Woliński, Wilner gave vent to his rage over the fact that his initial contact with the Polish underground, which had been achieved after exhausting efforts, had been broken off without explanation. It is therefore clear that during the deportation the Polish underground certainly did not initiate contact with the Jews of the ghetto. In fact, exactly the opposite is true—the A.K. actually ignored and thwarted every approach from the Jewish liaison.

In addition, the personal attitude of the then-commander of the A.K., General Stefan Rowecki (Grot), was evidently quite different from that described by his second-in-command and eventual successor, Komorowski. The text of a message sent by Rowecki to London on January 2, 1943 conclusively indicates the position adopted by the commander of the A.K. and his degree of willingness to aid the Jews. The radiogram states:

> . . . Jews from all kinds of groups, including Communists, have turned to us lately asking for arms, as if we had depots full of them. As an experiment, I took out a few revolvers. I have no assurance that they will use these weapons at all. I shall not give out any more weapons, for you know that we ourselves have none. I am awaiting another shipment. Apprise me of what contact our Jews have with London.[10]

Rowecki's message was sent approximately three months after the mass deportation, by which time not only the fate of the deportees but also what lay in store for the remnant within the diminished ghetto was common knowledge. Yet despite the obvious fact that the Jews were trapped, Rowecki's attitude was nothing short of hostile. Not only does he fail to mention any initiative of his own or attempt to coordinate action with the Jews; he actually implies that he opposes offering the least bit of help to the Ż.O.B. The few revolvers that Rowecki did turn over to the ghetto, after repeated requests from the Ż.O.B., were given half-heartedly, for like many other Poles, he did not believe that defending the Jews was any of his affair, nor did he have faith in their combat ability or desire to fight. In the context of having to deduct a small amount of arms for the Jews, Rowecki raises the objection that the A.K. itself is suffering from a shortage of weapons and is waiting for another shipment. One might easily deduce from this comment that the Jews' requests threatened to drain the A.K.'s stores and would have to be given serious weight in any account of the Home Army's strength. Up until January 1943, the Home Army provided the Ż.O.B. with a total of ten revolvers, while, according to an authorized representative of the Polish government stationed in the United States, in the spring of 1943 the A.K. had in its possession 25,000 rifles, 6,000 revolvers, 30,000 grenades, and other types of even heavier weapons.[11]

Finally, the A.K. never did—and never even attempted to—execute any act of sabotage that might have impeded the transports to Treblinka or caused damage to the camp itself.

The Polish Response during and as a Result of the Deportation

The first Polish declaration of any consequence was published in Warsaw in the name of the Directorate of the Civilian Struggle (*Kierownictwo Walki Cywilnej*), which represented the entire spectrum of underground political forces that backed the Polish government-in-exile, on September 17, 1942—meaning at the end of the extended deportation operation. This lengthy delay in speaking out undoubtedly points to reservations and differences of opinion over both the phrasing of the declaration and the very act of publishing it. The declaration stated that together with the tragedy that had overtaken the Poles, for a year the soil of Poland had been turned into the arena of the systematic murder of Jews. Such murder had no precedent in history, and its victims—people of all ages from infants to the elderly—were being exterminated just because they were Jews. The number of victims was reaching one million, and it grew higher with every passing day. "Unable to resist this actively, the Civil Struggle Directorate protests in the name of the entire Polish people against the crimes being committed against the Jews. All Polish political and social groupings join in this protest. As in the case of the Polish victims, the physical responsibility for the crimes will fall on the executioners and their accomplices."[12]

The declaration is phrased in such a way that denunciation of the crimes is expressed in general humanitarian terms; conspicuous in its absence is any indication of an activist Polish stance or an appeal that the masses of the Polish people take a concrete stand by helping Jews escape the ghetto and hiding them on the Polish side of the city. This evasive posture regarding any direct Polish involvement is also true of the paragraph that clarifies that Jews who have converted to the Catholic faith are also among the victims. Thus, although the declaration is literally a sharp protest, it simultaneously provides a stamp of approval to the total inertia of the Poles.

The Home Army likewise failed to issue any order to its troops regarding the adoption of a stand or the initiation of action to counter the mass extermination of the Jewish community. Its command related to the annihilation of the Jews only in an indirect manner, implying that after the Jews had been totally wiped out, the Germans might embark upon the methodical extermination of the Polish people. On November 10, 1942, Order Number 71 of the armed forces (A.K.) command in Poland stated:

> 1. As to the operation of annihilating the Jews [carried out] by the occupier, there are signs of disquiet among the Polish public lest after this operation is completed the Germans will begin the liquidation of the Poles in exactly the same manner. I order self-control and action to calm the public. . . . 2. However, if the Germans do indeed make any attempt of this sort, they will meet with active resistance on our part. Without consideration for the fact that the time for our uprising has not yet come, the units under my command will enter armed battle to defend the life of our people. In this battle, we will move over from defense to offense by cutting all the enemy's arteries of transport to the eastern front. My decision is to be passed on to the ranks within the underground armed forces. . . .

This order is signed "Grawica," the *nom de guerre* of General Rowecki.[13] It clearly indicates that the annihilation of Jews, in and of itself, did not concern the A.K. and was not a motive for action on the part of the Polish forces. It merely served as a portent of the fate that might befall the Poles as well.

Rowecki's clarification of how the A.K. would respond to any move by the Germans to extend their extermination program to the Polish population was deemed necessary in wake of the incessant claims voiced by the Communists that after the Jews, the Poles were next in line. It was on the basis of this assumption that the radical left demanded the immediate inception of an armed struggle, a move that the A.K. opposed on grounds of both principle and tactical considerations. The A.K. was preparing for a nationwide uprising at a time when political and military conditions would be propitious and the exercise of its forces would be able to determine the future status of the Polish state. Rowecki explicitly stated, however, that should the Germans move to begin the extermination of Poles, even if only on a limited scale, he would abandon his long-range political considerations and order his troops to enter an all-out struggle against the enemy. All this in the event that the victims were Poles, while vis-à-vis the extermination of Jews—no less citizens of Poland—the A.K. commander had no policy and did not see fit to propose any plan of action.

The ratio of Communists to the Polish public at large, and to the armed underground in particular, during the period under review was marginal, at best. It is therefore interesting to note that, as a rule, the Communists were moved more deeply by the Jewish tragedy than were the others factions of the Polish population. Among the reasons for this phenomenon was the fact that the Communists had already developed a history as a deviant and persecuted minority, and within the framework of the party it was not at all exceptional to find strong ties between Jews and Poles. We also cannot ignore the fact that the Communist credo of that period condemned anti-Semitism.

In August 1942 an article appeared in the P.P.R.'s clandestine newspaper *Trybuna Chłopska (The Farmers' Platform)* under the headline "45,000 People in Warsaw Await Death." It described the *Aktion* in the Warsaw ghetto and added:

> There are still among us scoundrels who accept this fact with an idiotic smile, or a shrug, saying: "Oh well, they're just Jews." We cannot leave it at that. We must remember that after the Jews will come the Poles' turn to be evacuated to the east. Thus even now, we are all obligated to oppose these murders. . . . The Polish population, including the farmers in the villages, must extend aid to those who escape, conceal them, and provide them with food. The Poles must see that the brisk rate at which Hitler is being allowed to destroy the Jews will [only] speed up the murder of our people, the Poles. Thus the Jews who are actively resisting are also fighting for the lives of the Polish population, because they are causing the disorganization and debilitation of the abominable murder machine.[14]

Thus even when the Communists appeal to the Poles to help the fugitive Jews—and this appeal must be duly appreciated—their real emphasis is on a different point. They do not focus on the fact that the

murder of Jews must be thwarted and aid extended to the victims because they are innocent, and humane and ideological values demand
helping one's fellow man during times of trial. The Communists' basic
claim is that the Nazis will not be satisfied with the murder of Jews and
will afterward begin exterminating Poles—perhaps on an even broader
scale. It is for this reason that armed action must be initiated without
delay. In brief, this outlook was the Communists' overall political line at
the time.

On November 27, 1942, the Polish National Council in London, a
kind of parliamentary authority-in-exile, passed a resolution regarding
the deportation and murder of the Jews of Warsaw. As stated earlier,
the long delay in arriving at this decision is bound up with the deliberate suppression of reports that reached London through underground
channels. The resolution, which was adopted after extended internal
discussion, opened with the following statement:

> The Government of the Polish Republic has brought the last news
> about the massacres of the Jewish population in Poland, carried out sys-
> tematically by the German occupying authorities, to the attention of the
> Allied Governments and of public opinion in Allied countries. The
> number of Jews who have been murdered by the Germans in Poland so
> far, since September, 1939, exceeds 1,000,000.
>
> From the beginning of the conquest of the territories of the Republic,
> the bestial occupying power has subjected the Polish nation to an appalling
> policy of extermination, to such an extent that by now the Polish popula-
> tion has been reduced by several millions. Now the occupying power has
> reached the summit of its murder-lust and sadism by organizing mass-
> murders of hundreds of thousands of Jews in Poland, not only the Polish
> Jews but also the Jews brought from other countries to Poland with the
> purpose of exterminating them. The German murderers have sent to their
> death hundreds of thousands of men, women, children and old people.
> Their purpose is to enfeeble the Polish nation and completely to extermi-
> nate the Jews in Poland before the end of this year. In the execution of
> this plan Adolf Hitler and his henchmen are using the most appalling
> tortures.
>
> The Polish Government and the Polish National Council, and the
> Polish Nation at home, have often protested against the German crimes,
> and announced that a just punishment would be meted out to these of-
> fenders against mankind. Lately the Polish Government has submitted to
> the Polish National Council the draft of a law providing for the punish-
> ment of the German criminals. . . .
>
> The Polish National Council appeals to all the Allied nations and to
> all the nations now suffering together with the Polish nation under the

German yoke, that they should at once start a common action against this trampling and profanation of all principles of morality and humanity by the Germans, and against the extermination of the Polish nation and other nations, an extermination the most appalling expression of which is provided by the mass-murders of the Jews in Poland and in the rest of Europe which Hitler has subjected.

To all those who are suffering and undergoing torture in Poland, both to Poles and to Jews, to all those who are taking part in the struggle for liberation and for the preparation of a just retribution on the German criminals, the Polish National Council sends words of hope and of unshakeable faith in the recovery of freedom for all. The day of victory and punishment is approaching.[15]

This declaration specifically relates to the mass extermination of the Jews; in fact, the harrowing fate of the Jews is the very reason behind its publication. Nonetheless, it is a sobering fact that the Polish state institutions appeal for help only rhetorically. They send words of encouragement to the Polish people, but do not ask them to take an active stand and extend aid to the Jewish victims.

The Polish Government-in-Exile, Contact with Jews outside of Poland, and the Organization of Aid

We shall now turn briefly to the activities and contacts of the commission representing Polish Jewry in Palestine and its branch in the United States. This body consisted of a group of veteran leaders drawn from the Zionist and Orthodox camps who had led the Polish Jewish community during the interwar years, some of whom had fled Poland during the early period of the war. They included officials of the Jewish Agency like Yitzhak Gruenbaum, Dr. Emil Szmurak, Elihu Dobkin, Moshe Shapira, Moshe Kleinbaum (Sneh), Apolinary Hartglas, Yitzhak Meir Levin, Leon Lewite, Benjamin Mintz, and others. Yitzhak Schwartzbart, a Jewish representative on the Polish National Council, was also a member of this representation and was considered its liaison with the council. The commission deemed itself authorized to appear in the name of Polish Jewry, for its members "still bear the mandate from the elections recently held for the various institutions of Polish Jewry."[16]

Until the latter half of 1942, the representatives of Polish Jewry in Palestine seem not to have known exactly what was taking place in Poland or comprehended the far-reaching implications of the German actions. But in the second half of that year, the first vague reports began to arrive, and they spoke of freight cars jammed with Jews making their way off to the unknown. It was only at the end of 1942 that official confirmation of widespread murder arrived from the Polish government. By this stage the Poles were taking care to publicize the information that was brought to their attention, and from then on alarming news filtered out without cease.

On Novermber 5, 1942, the Polish-Jewish representation in Palestine sent a letter to the Polish consul-general in Tel Aviv stating: "Today the press published reports from London and Geneva to the effect that the Germans have deported all the Jews from the Warsaw ghetto, so that only 100,000 remain, and there were, as you know, over half a million Jews in Warsaw."

The letter goes on to state that there is an urgent sense of alarm regarding the fate of the Jews, and the representatives ask the consul to cable on to London their request for detailed information on what the Polish government knows about this subject. "If London still does not have information on the situation," the letter closes, "we strongly request that the government be good enough to use all means at its disposal to clarify the matter immediately and inform us whether the above-mentioned reports are consistent with the truth." The consul-general in Tel Aviv replied to this letter on November 25, that is, two days before the Polish National Council issued its public appeal regarding the systematic murder of the Jews, in general, and the murders in the summer of 1942, in particular. His reply read:

> In regard to your letter of the 6th of this month, we wish to inform you that in response to a cable to the Polish government regarding the deportation of all the Jews from the Warsaw ghetto, I received the following telegraphic reply: "The report has not been confirmed to date. The government is making every effort to obtain accurate information. When it is received, I shall pass it on by cable. [Raczyński]. Foreign Minister."

The full scope of the disaster became known to the members of the Polish representation in Palestine only with the arrival of a few dozen Jews from Poland (nine men, thirty-four women, and twenty-six children) who were exchanged for German citizens by a special arrangement. This group, which arrived in Palestine on November 16, 1942, was held in the British coastal installation at Atlith for a few days. Thus it was only on November 25 that the members of the Polish representation were able to take detailed testimony from Ya'akov Hirsch Kurtz—a Palestinian Jew who had been trapped in Poland during the war—regarding the events taking place in occupied Poland.[17]

The detailed and accurate picture provided by witnesses caused profound shock. The members of the representation, who tried to activate every possible source of influence, immediately exploited the fact that a senior minister of the Polish government, Professor Stanisław Kot, was visiting Palestine at that time. The first of a series of extended and pointed meetings with Kot was held two days later, on November 27.

The secretary of the commission, Dr. Abraham Stoop, opened the meeting by noting that it had recently become known to the representation, beyond all doubt, that a systematic operation to liquidate Jewish communities in Poland was being carried out by regular units, and Jews were being uprooted from their homes and were disappearing without a trace. Kot replied heatedly that he did not see anything new in these facts; they had long been known, and it was the Polish government that had made them known. Furthermore, he claimed that the Polish government was doing everything in its power to warn the free world and stimulate action. But it was precisely the Jews, in these days of war — both Jews in Palestine and in the United States — who showed little inclination to act.

Stoop reiterated that the representatives of Polish Jewry had in no way been informed of these events by the Polish government in London. "We have just now received a reply from Minister Raczyński," he said, "stating that these reports have not been confirmed and that the government is making every effort to obtain accurate information."[18]

In the course of the discussion, Moshe Kleinbaum presented a list of concrete steps called for by the situation, about which explicit information was known. They included (1) a pronouncement by the government-in-exile and the National Council indicating the responsibility of every man participating in the extermination operation; (2) a request that the Polish government use its influence to encourage the Allies toward adopting appropriate measures against the Germans, and the neutral countries to extend aid to Jews who managed to escape from countries under German domination; (3) having the Polish radio broadcasts encourage the Polish public not to fall susceptible to the anti-Jewish propaganda and to resist the Nazis' barbaric acts; (4) encouraging the Polish clergy to make its voice heard in protest against the crimes, as the French clergy had.

In addition to four extensive discussions with Kot, the representation appealed by cable to the president of Poland, W. Raczkiewicz; the prime minister, General Sikorski; and the Polish government-in-exile. The replies to these various appeals were channeled through the Polish consul-general in Tel Aviv. The first of these, received on December 10, 1942, and signed by Professor Stanisław Stronski, stated: "The Information Ministry has taken care since June [1942] to distribute throughout the world information on the persecution of the Jews. The same was done at the end of November regarding the Warsaw ghetto.

An appeal to the Polish public is unnecessary, for it is from there that the information and the sharp protests come."[19]

The replies of Prime Minister Sikorski and Foreign Minister Ra-czyński related to appeals made to the Allied governments, the arousal of public opinion, and the stir that had taken place in church circles and among politicians. However, there was not a word in these replies regarding special action on the part of the Polish population or any plan to initiate action of this nature.[20]

In general, beginning in December 1942, there was a harsh awakening concerning the Jewish issue in the Nazi-occupied countries and the mass murder of Jews in Poland. On December 17, 1942, British Foreign Minister Eden issued a declaration in Parliament in the name of the Allies and the French National Council. It noted that the Jews in the German-occupied countries were being transported under abysmal conditions to Eastern Europe and Poland, which had been transformed into an arena of murder. The Jews in the ghettos were disappearing without a trace. In light of these facts, Eden proclaimed, the Allies had grown more firm in their resolve to destroy the Nazi regime and the Nazi threat. Likewise, they had become determined to punish those responsible for crimes and even now were taking necessary steps to achieve this goal.

Yet the world reaction, expressed both through the communications media and from official political platforms, failed to influence the Germans or bring about any change in the program for the "Final Solution." Other than the publication of reports, the organization of protest rallies, and the airing of official warnings that those responsible for the crimes would be punished, no concrete steps were taken to impede the Nazi program or cause damage to the German people while forcing them to realize that the moves against them were in retaliation for the unrestrained slaughter of Jews.

As already noted, the Polish underground and government-in-exile avoided appealing directly to the Polish masses or mobilizing their forces to counter the acts of murder. At the same time, the profound shock did not pass without yielding any results at all. We can presume that whatever concrete response did come forth in Poland derived from both the humanitarian sensibilities of those who were revolted by the means and scope of the murder of innocent people and from the wave of appeals to the Polish public emanating from Jews and non-Jews abroad. On the initiative of a group of Poles, at the end of 1942 the Council for Aid to Jews (Żegota) was established in Warsaw.[21] Some time later, this council acquired official patronage and was joined by representatives of the factions that composed the London-based government-in-exile. The council received funds from Polish-government sources and, through them, from general and Jewish relief agencies. It cared for thousands of fugitive Jews hiding out principally in Warsaw but in other cities as well. This development also left its mark on the posture taken by the military, which was expressed in more concrete terms after the demonstration of Jewish resistance in January 1943. A detailed description of negotiations over aid and the nature and scope of the Polish support that was eventually extended to the Jews will be presented in a later chapter.

Thousands of Jews escaped to the "Aryan" side of Warsaw and its vicinity at the time of the mass deportation, and it is estimated that between fifteen and twenty thousand Jews were in hiding beyond the ghetto during the period. Even if these figures account for only 5 percent of Warsaw's Jewish population at its height, they nonetheless represent a substantial number in absolute terms. Depsite the fact that the Polish public was rife with elements that exposed Jews and turned them in to the Nazis, and gangs of Polish extortionists (*szmalcownicy*) were the bane of Jews in hiding or living under false identities, it is obvious that the concentration of such a large number of fugitives in a single area could not have been possible without the active involvement of a good number of Poles.

There are many facets to this ardent involvement. One particular sector of the intelligentsia—comprising both men of progressive views and devout Catholics who worked with unrelenting devotion to rescue Jews—was of singular importance. At first these people attempted to help Jews with whom they were personally acquainted—primarily assimilated Jews—but in the course of time, the aid and rescue of Jews per se became an all-consuming mission. These circles were the seed that eventually blossomed into *Żegota*. However, a substantial number of common people took part in the rescue work as well, usually out of profound religious, ideological, or humanitarian convictions. These people, in many cases villagers and townsfolk, risked their lives to help Jews escape the jaws of the Nazi death machine.

Many, in fact almost certainly the majority, of those rescued were concealed by Poles in exchange for what amounted to a ransom. Some of these Poles behaved honorably, that is, they earned the payment by attempting to protect the Jews under their care. But a portion of them were eager to extort Jewish property as quickly as possible, and when these resources were exhausted, they did not hestitate to evict the Jews from their hiding places and even went as far as turning them directly over to the Germans. The clergy and members of certain religious institutions also engaged in the rescue and concealment of Jews, particularly children, though these efforts were not undertaken on a broad scale and were certainly not free of proselytical motives.[22]

Those fugitives, especially Jewish girls and women, whose features allowed them to pass for Poles and who therefore did not arouse suspicion were a class in themselves. Such people assumed a new identity, as it were, and worked wherever they could find a position. Their papers were obtained with the help of Polish friends or members of Żegota, or in return for a bribe. Obviously, however, these modern "Marranos" were neither free nor secure in their dissemblance. A keen-eyed extortionist could discern their Jewish characteristics, and past acquaintances could identify them. Indeed, these disguised Jews were in a state of constant pursuit, and most of them fell into the hands of the Germans.

In closing this chapter, we shall again address ourselves to the question of why the Poles in London suppressed reports on the mass deportation from Warsaw for so long. There is no unequivocal or authoritative explanation for this disturbing fact. In and of itself, this grave phenomenon was evidently a function of both fundamental policy and tactical considerations. As we have seen, the Poles tried to tone down their appraisals of the character and extent of the oppression and annihilation of the Jews in Poland for fear that an accurate description of the state of affairs might direct the free world's attention primarily to the Jewish problem. Thus the London government-in-exile preferred to speak of the persecution of the Polish population at large. A second reason for playing down the Jewish aspect of the tragedy was a sensitivity to the mood in Poland. Repeated hints reached London that the government need not go out of its way to defend the Jews and that, moreover, expressions of support for the Jews did nothing to enhance the popularity of the exiled government among the Polish people.[23] Finally, the delay in publishing the reports also derived from differences among the various factions that composed the government-in-exile.

In June 1942, when the Polish government disseminated reports on the murder of 700,000 Jews on Polish soil, the information related primarily to Jews living in the eastern territories that had been annexed by the Soviet Union in September 1939 and fell under Nazi domination in June–July 1941. The Poles did not consider themselves directly responsible for the fate of the Jews living in these territories and—to a great degree justly—highlighted the role played by the Lithuanians in the slaughter. These eastern border regions were populated primarily by other national groups—Ukrainians, Belorussians, Lithuanians—and had been subject to a period of foreign, and in the Polish view hostile, rule.

Quite different, however, was the situation ruling the extermination campaign in the Polish heartland, and particularly Warsaw. While it is true that both Warsaw and Lublin were in the area of full Nazi occupation, they were, after all, heavily populated by Poles and supported a strong Polish underground. It is therefore reasonable to assume that the Allies, the Jews, and world public opinion in general would expect and demand that the Poles take steps to aid the Jews in these areas.

It was exactly an appeal of this sort that the London government wished to avoid. At first it tried to suppress the reports and references to the subject. The official response came only months after the mass deportation from Warsaw had been completed—and even in these long-overdue statements, the Poles avoided an appeal to their countrymen demanding concrete action against the German operations and in support of the rescue of Jews. All the appeals from London were addressed to the Allies, or Jewish groups, and great pains were taken to evade the question of the Poles' responsibility or obligation to help.

Chapter Nine
The Remnant of the Ghetto
until January 1943

The Boundaries and Internal Structure of the New Ghetto

After the mass deportation, the remaining Jews in the ghetto did not resume their former way of life, which had been extraordinary from the very start and, over the years, had created definite patterns of its own. The administrative-governmental structure and mode of existence of the ghetto—or, as the Germans officially called it, the "Jewish residential quarter"—remained in force from mid-November 1940 until the end of July 1942. At the end of the mass deportation, namely the middle of September 1942, the Jews remaining in the ghetto were granted a respite of a few more months. However, the Germans did not intend and the Jews did not expect a mere continuation of the former ghetto in a constricted format. The situation after the mass deportation was perceived, rather, as a temporary phenomenon of a completely different character. During this last phase of its existence, the ghetto was essentially a mass labor camp, although—and in contradiction to the aims and intent of the Germans —it continued to be marked by certain features characteristic of the former ghetto.

The territorial area of the original ghetto was abrogated, and the remaining Jews were concentrated together in the following enclaves within the ghetto's former bounds:

1. The "Central Ghetto," which encompassed a number of streets and sections in the heart of what had traditionally been the Jewish section of Warsaw. Within this enclave lived the employees of the *Judenrat* and the diminished police force, as well as most of the laborers who were transported to work outside the ghetto. It also contained several

of the "shops," though not the largest and most important of them. A specific and closed off section within the Central Ghetto housed the *Werterfassung*, an SS enterprise devoted to collecting, classifying, and storing the movable Jewish property left behind in deserted buildings and apartments. In contrast to the other "shops" and ghetto enterprises, which had been pared down during the deportation, the *Werterfassung* expanded to immense proportions during the liquidation process. Most of the "wildcats"—more than twenty thousand people who were denied permission to remain in the ghetto during the final *Selektion* and had been stripped of their legal status—also lived in the Central Ghetto. Since this area contained both a diverse population and what remained of the ghetto's public institutions, the Central Ghetto continued to be viewed as the focal point of the Jewish remnant in Warsaw, and it was there that the nucleus of the underground and resistance organizations lived. In fact, more than half the Jews left in Warsaw were concentrated in the Central Ghetto.

2. The area of the large "shops," the most prominent of which were Többens (Leszno Street), K. G. Schultz (Leszno Street), and Fritz Schultz (Nowolipie Street), as well as some of the smaller "shops"— Oskar Schilling, Kurt Röhrich, Bernard Hallmann, and others. The boundary of this area extended along Leszno, Żelazna (with the exception of No. 88), Nowolipie, Smocza, Nowolipki, and Karmelicka streets, back to where the latter met Leszno Street. It housed almost twenty thousand Jews who lived in the housing blocks attached to their factories.

3. The area known as the "Brushmakers' Shop," which contained the brush factory and its employees, in addition to a number of other small "shops." Its boundary ran along the following streets and sections thereof: Swiętojerska, Bonifraterska, Wałowa, Franciszkańska. The area contained about four thousand Jews.

4. The enclave of "Little Többens," or one part of the enterprise of W. C. Többens, remained in fact in the former "little ghetto," which had been completely emptied of Jews. This area housed close to two thousand people.[1]

The various enclaves were not contiguous but were separated by areas that had been completely evacuated. Movement in these deserted areas was officially prohibited without special permission, so that Jews were not allowed to go from one enclave to another even for the purpose of visiting relatives and friends. Yet movement in the general area was not strictly supervised, and many took the risk of cautiously making their way through the streets alone or in small groups in order to go visiting or maintain contact between the fragmented sections of the ghetto.

The ghetto population had been not only drastically reduced but also fundamentally altered from the standpoint of its composition and age structure. Of the thirty-six thousand Jews officially reported to be in the ghetto at the end of November 1942, the outstanding majority were males; the abnormal composition of this population was also reflected in its age structure (see Table 5).

TABLE 5

POPULATION OF THE GHETTO BY AGE GROUPS AT THE END OF NOVEMBER 1942

Age	Males(%)	Females(%)
0–9	1.3	1.6
10–19	11.1	14.5
20–29	19.5	29.5
30–39	34.1	30.8
40–49	21.9	16.5
50–59	10.2	6.1
60–69	1.8	0.9
70–79	0.1	0.1

SOURCE: *Wiadomości* (newsletter published in the Warsaw ghetto), December 1942. Yad Vashem Archive, Underground Press Division.

At the beginning of 1942, there were more females in the ghetto than males, in a ratio of approximately 4 to 3. This imbalance in favor of women was particularly heavy in the age groups between twenty and fifty. After the deportation, however, the opposite situation prevailed, with the ratio running 4 to 3 in favor of males. Altogether, the percentage of males remaining in the ghetto was 12.6, while that of women was only 7.4. In the ten to thirty age group, however, the number of females was slightly higher, in absolute figures, than the number of males (see Table 6).

The demographic consequences of the deportation are even more startling when viewed from the perspective of age groups regardless of sex. Children under the age of ten and the elderly over the age of sixty all but totally disappeared from the ghetto. The picture gave cause for concern as far back as the beginning of 1942, since these two general age groups were particularly vulnerable throughout the years of the occupation, while the birth rate naturally declined considerably. The mass deportation was virtually a death sentence for the ghetto's children, and after the *Aktion* the total number of youngsters up to the age of ten and elderly over the age of sixty was less than one thousand in a population

TABLE 6

Deportation of the Population by Age Groups

Age	Before the deportation	Males, end of November	% of deportees	Before the deportation	Females, end of November	% of deportees
0–9	25,759	255	99.0	25,699	243	99.1
10–19	35,238	2,183	93.8	39,790	2,263	98.3
20–29	19,747	3,851	89.5	36,041	4,581	87.3
30–39	29,155	6,748	76.9	40,892	4,791	88.3
40–49	21,128	4,319	79.6	30,652	2,564	91.6
50–59	14,758	2,019	86.3	20,812	928	95.4
60–69	8,881	353	96.0	12,335	143	98.8
70–79	2,553	30	98.8	4,361	——	99.7
80 and over	287	——	100.0	603	——	100.0
Unknown	59	179	——	107	148	——
Total	157,610	19,937	87.4	211,292	15,696	92.6

SOURCE: *Wiadomości,* December 1942. Yad Vashem Archive, Underground Press Division.

of approximately thirty-six thousand. Although the statistics at our disposal relate only to those whose presence in the ghetto was recognized by the German authorities, and the percentage of children and the elderly may have been higher among the "wildcat" population, here, too, their absolute number could not have been very large.

The German administration, whose authority over the ghetto was manifested through the special *Kommissar* and his office, the *Transferstelle,* and the various departments of the administrative bureaucracy, was not revived after the deportation.[2] Instead, absolute, unchecked power, without regard for even the most basic of accepted administrative procedures, continued to be concentrated in the hands of the police and the Gestapo. The unit that had been transferred from Lublin to carry out the deportation now left Warsaw, and Jewish affairs were turned over to a handful of junior and noncommissioned officers commanded by Brandt and Mende, since they were considered to be the most familiar with local affairs. Fateful decisions, such as the scope of the deportation operation and the destination to which the deportees would be sent, were not left to this echelon, and one can sense the heavy hand of the senior ranks of the SS and even Himmler himself in the broader conception of the *Aktion*. But once the operation was completed, daily affairs in the ghetto and short-term policy were decided by these low-rank officers, who were free to behave like lords in their own castle.

The tactics of deception that had proven themselves during the *Aktion* in Warsaw (as well as many other places) continued to be employed in the postdeportation period. Immediately after the *Aktion* ended, the Germans published an official announcement promising the remaining Jews that they did not intend to carry out additional "resettlement" operations. The Jews were merely told to remain disciplined and to carry out their work properly. This same "liberal" line was also adopted toward the illegal residents of the ghetto. At first most of "wildcats" remained concealed in permanent hiding places, but it soon became evident that the Germans were not hunting down the illegals and were presumably resigned to their existence. Although no official amnesty was declared, many nonregistered inhabitants were accepted to *palatzovkas* outside the ghetto and by the *Werterfassung*.

In an attempt to cope with the illegals in another fashion, Krieger, the commander of the SS and the police in the Generalgouvernement, published an order on October 28 regarding the establishment of residential quarters for Jews in the Warsaw and Lublin districts.[3] On his roster of quarters designated for Jews, Krieger listed "Warsaw-city (ghetto)," and his order stated that all Jews living outside the residential areas marked out for Jews—i.e., those who had escaped and gone into hiding beyond the ghetto—were obligated to choose one of the areas in the vicinity of Warsaw or Lublin before November 30, 1942. Those who disobeyed the order were to be sentenced to death, which was also the punishment slated for anyone who "consciously provides refuge for a Jew, that is, whoever houses, feeds, or otherwise conceals a Jew outside of the residental area." Clearly the Germans were following a "carrot and stick" policy, hoping to tempt the fugitives by allowing them to come back to live in reconstituted ghettos while increasing the severity of the punishment meted out to those who remained in hiding and Poles who offered Jews sanctuary. We can estimate that the number of Jews roving around or in hiding outside the ghettos of the Generalgouvernement reached tens of thousands at the time, and Krieger's order was one means of trapping them, since the majority were homeless and on the brink of complete despair. Indeed, we know for a fact that hundreds of Jews were caught on the "Aryan" side of Warsaw and transferred back to the ghetto.

The following account testifies to both the Germans' intent to continue deceiving the Jews and the degree to which their cynicism had evolved. It comes from the memoirs of an officer in the Jewish Police and was written after the deportation:

The problem of abandoned children came into being. Despite the fact that the child was the most hunted of Jews, the most dangerous enemy, a few score abandoned and orphaned children remained in the area of the ghetto and in the "shops." What should be done with them? On the authority—and even the recommendation and initiative—of Brandt, the council [*Judenrat*] set up an orphanage for these children at 50 [or 52] Zamenhofa Street. Brandt arrived at the opening . . . and delivered a speech before the gathered officials and activists whose primary thesis was that everything possible must be done for the children; every sacrifice made; [every drop of] strength and resources [devoted to them]. No intervention [on their behalf] could be too strenuous, since the child is a treasure, the future of the nation.[4]

Another indication of supposed normalization in the ghetto's status was the conversation held at the end of October or beginning of November 1942 between the commander of the SS and the police in the Warsaw District, *Oberführer* von Sammern–Frankenegg, and the chairman of the *Judenrat*, Marc Lichtenbaum—an encounter that was unprecedented in the three preceding years of the occupation.

The economic life of the ghetto underwent no less of a radical change. During the first years of the occupation, despite all the prohibitions and limitations, the Jews of Warsaw fulfilled a necessary function in the economy of occupied Poland as a whole and the city of Warsaw in particular. In the course of the deportation, however, many of the Jewish artisans had been eliminated, and even those who remained in the ghetto were assigned to "shops" and thereby deprived of the conditions—and perhaps also the will—to engage in independent labor for the private economy and the civilian market in the General-gouvernement. The resultant effect upon the economy is reflected in a report submitted to the administration of the Generalgouvernement by the governor of the Warsaw District, Dr. Fischer. Dated October 15, 1942, it describes the situation in the ghetto during the months of August–September:

> Since a new change has taken place in the format of the Jewish residential area, we can no longer speak of independent economic life therein. In July the value of export from the Jewish quarter surpassed 15 million zlotys, while in August it declined to 1.9 million and in September to 1.1 million—and these [figures] still account for commercial transactions and services provided in the past. . . . Among the 3,500 workers in the clothing industry, formerly at least 3,000 were Jews. As a consequence of the resettlement, therefore, production has suffered a substantial decline. In August it fell from 4.4 million zlotys to 3.3 million, that is, 25%. For all practical purposes, production has decreased up to 50%. . . .[5]

Despite the ramifications of this analysis, the shortages and hunger suffered by the ghetto residents did not grow more severe following the deportation. On the contrary, there was a noticeable improvement in the situation. The paradox that the nutritional state of the remnant Jewish population improved precisely at a time when the economy and production in the ghetto were in the final stages of collapse can be explained by the temporary and improvised character of the ghetto's economic life. In the climate of living only for the here and now, which reached its peak during this period, the Jews lived almost exclusively off the sale of their property, in any conceivable form.[6] It is also true that there was a slight improvement in the food ration apportioned to Jews, and the laborers in the "shops" received their food allotments from their employers. But these sources of subsistence covered only a fraction of the need, and the workers were only one section of the remnant population.

Because of the revolution in the economic structure, transactions in currency and the use of cash ceased almost entirely in some areas of the ghetto. This was particularly true in the territory of the "shops," since instead of receiving wages, the "shop" workers were provided with coupons that could be cashed in for permissible goods. A German source elaborates upon this system:

> The supply and economic situation in the Jewish residential quarter of Warsaw have been placed on a new footing. In an order dated September 1, 1942, the commander of the S.S. and the police, who was in charge of directing the entire Jewish operation, has required the labor enterprises to pay 5 zlotys per day for each Jewish worker left in the factory. Of this sum, 3 zlotys must be turned over to the commander of the S.S. and the police, while 2 zlotys go for the upkeep of the Jewish workers. . . . [7]

A memoir writer described the situation in the "shops" from the viewpoint of the Jews:

> . . . Jews have no need to pay out money when an economy is run without capital. And what would they need money for? Food is received upon presentation of coupons: rations of soup and half a kilo of bread per day, jam from time to time, synthetic honey, and sometimes even three eggs per person. They receive kindling materials, sometimes matches; they get soap and washing powder—and that's enough for them.[8]

It must be remembered, however, that these descriptions reflect the situation only in the "shops" and the rations meted out to the *Judenrat* employees or the police. The majority of the remaining Jews did not receive such quantities of permissible items, and, most important of all, the ghetto contained over twenty thousand illegal Jewish residents, some of whom did not receive any ration whatsoever. Thus cash was superfluous only on the plane of relations between the Germans and the Jews or as a function of the official economic life in the ghetto. It did not cease to play a role in the clandestine commerce, smuggling operations, or the campaigns related to rescue efforts and preparations for an armed struggle. It is instructive, for example, that the only (reported) case of murder in the entire history of the ghetto occurred during this period, and the murderers were a group of *palatzokva* workers who fell out with one of their partners and intended to rob him of his money.[9]

Another aspect of the revision in the ghetto's internal structure was the fact that the importance of the *Judenrat* and its influence over the remnant Jewish population was in constant decline. And, in contrast to its position during the *Aktion* itself, the fate of the Jewish Police after the deportation was similarly grim. At the end of the *Aktion*, the Germans rewarded the Jewish Police in their own special way by drastically reducing the number of men on the force. At the same time, the Jewish public treated the police with open contempt and hatred, and the policemen themselves lost much of their self-confidence. Once the police were disabused of the illusion that the Germans were out to remove only specific categories of Jews while they themselves served to protect the rest of the population, their naïve belief in their own privileged and protected status disintegrated.

Yet the erosion in the status of the Jewish Police was not counterbalanced by a revival of the influence of the *Judenrat*. The simple fact is that most of the functions and activities of the *Judenrat* became superfluous in the various enclaves of the reconstituted ghetto. In practice, the employees of the *Judenrat* and its various organs never set foot in the area of the "shops," where affairs were managed exclusively by the German factory owners and their Jewish and non-Jewish assistants. In addition, the *Werkschutz* (Factory Police), composed mostly of Jews, was placed at the disposal of these managers to maintain order in the area of the "shops." The close to two thousand people who were certified as *Judenrat* employees were restricted to the Central Ghetto, and although many of the council's thirty-one departments became obsolete (there was no longer a role for the Education Department, tax collectors, legal advisers, social workers, etc.), they continued to show up at their offices and to keep up the pretense of being occupied. But the intimidated members of the *Judenrat* itself no longer even pretended to be public figures of any stature. Their greatest concern now was for themselves and the members of their families, as well as the many officials and workers who were supposedly employed under the aegis of the *Judenrat*. The only *Judenrat* department that remained functional, and even maintained a number of enterprises (for producing jam and synthetic honey), was the Supply Authority. In order to justify the continued existence of the *Judenrat*, hundreds of its employees were mobilized for temporary jobs, such as clearing the streets of the belongings that had been piled up during the deportation, building walls along the ghetto's new boundaries, helping the *Werterfassung*, and so forth. As a public institution, however, the *Judenrat* no longer fulfilled any concrete role.

Directly before the end of the mass deportation, on September 14, 1942, von Sammern, the commander of the SS and the police in the Warsaw District, issued a regulation regarding the status of the Jews concentrated in the "shops." The ordinance was addressed to "the owners of enterprises that employed Jews" and contained the following points:

1. All the certified enterprises in the Jewish quarter must ensure that the area of the factory and the housing block for the Jewish workers are adjacent and constitute a single, closed unit.
2. For this reason, the factories and housing blocks must be surrounded by walls or appropriate barriers.
3. The Jews are forbidden to leave the factories or housing blocks, and sentries of the *Werkschutz* should be posted on the boundaries of the area.
4. If the areas of the factory and the housing block are not adjacent, the Jewish workers are to be led [to work] in orderly formations. This is also binding on the Jews who work outside the ghetto.
5. The owners of the firms are personally responsible for carrying out these orders.
6. Jews found outside the factory or housing-block area without the express personal permission of the commander of the SS will be shot.[10]

During the first few weeks, the Jews obeyed these stringent regulations, and the ghetto — including those areas still populated after the deportation — resembled a ghost town. On October 1, 1942, Abraham Levin recorded in his diary that "it is prohibited to walk in the streets. Not a single Jew can be seen. Every *fabryka* ["shop"] is a locked prison. You walk to and from work in groups before seven in the morning and at six in the evening."[11] Peretz Opoczyński wrote in his diary on September 24 that "today a regulation has gone into effect whereby no one is to take a single step in the ghetto during the day. Everyone must be in the shops from morning until evening."[12]

Despite the ban on mobility between the enclaves and housing blocks, as well as the total prohibition on being outside the "shops" during work hours, in practice such movement did take place on a very limited scale. The attitude of the police and the SS toward this phenomenon was not consistent. On certain days, or for weeks at a stretch, no drastic steps were taken against Jews found in the streets, but there were days on which such Jewish offenders were summarily shot. In general, the number of shootings that took place in the streets during this period was high, in comparison with the period preceding the deportation, despite the sharp decline in the size of the population. Statistics compiled by the *Judenrat* spell out the number of Jews shot in the streets during the months of April 1942–January 1943 as follows: April—81; May—54; June—90; July—1,224; August—2,305; September—3,158; October—360; November—121; December—65; January—1,171.[13]

These figures accurately reflect the course of events and the security situation in the ghetto. The deaths recorded in the months of April, May, and June were primarily a function of the wave of terror that extended from the "Night of Blood" (April 18, 1942) until the inception of the deportation, and served to pave the way for the upheaval to come. The high figures for July, August, and September include people murdered during the course of the deportation. Yet from November onward, despite the attempts to create an atmosphere of normalization, the slaughter in the streets continued, and the figures for this period are relatively high in comparison with the situation prior to the deportation, though there was a decline from 360 murders in October to 65 in December. The upswing in January 1943 was related to the second deportation from Warsaw, beginning on January 18, 1943, meaning that the figure incorporates those who fell in the January phase of the campaign to liquidate the Jews of Warsaw.

German Plans for the Diminished Ghetto

The tactic of calming the ghetto's residents and distracting their attention was the essence of the German strategy of distorting the truth, and it was therefore an irrelevant gauge to their true intentions regarding the future. The primary question that arises in this context is why the Germans officially permitted 10 percent of the Jewish population to remain in Warsaw, instead of taking their liquidation operation through to the end in the summer of 1942. Perhaps the main reason behind this policy was that 1942, the year in which Himmler hoped to see the Generalgouvernement "almost cleansed of Jews," witnessed a steady exacerbation of the shortage of manpower harnessed to the German war effort. The *Rüstung* (Armament) authorities exerted great pressure and tried to protect the people working for them, and although the SS and the police disregarded most of their pleas, they could not be ignored altogether.

There were also two other, less important reasons for the Germans' leaving a certain percentage of Jews in Warsaw, as well as other places. First, they evidently feared that totally liquidating the Warsaw ghetto in one massive and continuous operation would lead to the destruction of existing assets in the ghetto, including enterprises that they wanted to transfer intact. Second, the SS intended to employ the remaining Jews—or at least a portion of them—in gathering up, storing, and guarding abandoned property.

The weight ascribed to the issue of property and the question of who would become the beneficiaries of the Jews' assets is indicated by a jurisdictional dispute that arose between the SS and the governor-general. As we have seen, Frank did not hesitate to give the commanders of the SS and the police a free hand in all that related to the removal and liquidation of the Jews, but he reversed his policy when it came to dividing up the spoils. In a meeting of the Generalgouvernement regime on January 26, 1943, Frank argued:

> . . . I do not recognize the injunction [issued by] the *Reichsführer-S.S.*, Himmler, to decide the issue of Jewish assets within the Generalgouvernement. It has no binding force, since the authority to promulgate regulations within the Generalgouvernement rests solely with the governor-general or the Council of Ministers for the Defense of the Reich. The issue of Jewish assets can only be settled by the governor-general publishing a regulation that all Jewish assets will be recognized as the *property of the state* within the Generalgouvernement.[14]

The reason behind the growing importance of confiscated Jewish property can be explained by the trend in thinking that developed during the final months of 1942. Globocnik and "Operation Reinhardt" had been responsible to two principal offices of the SS: the Main Reich Security Office (R.S.H.A., which encompassed the Gestapo), in all matters related to the physical annihilation of the Jews, and the Main Office of Economy and Administration (W.V.H.A.), under the command of SS *Obergruppenführer* Pohl, in matters related to the confiscation and exploitation of Jewish property. Toward the end of 1942, which was marked by a further deterioration of the manpower supply in the Reich, the efforts of Himmler and the SS to build an independent military and economic capacity that would have a major impact on the war gained further impetus. And the remnant of European Jewry was exploited in this power struggle as well. Himmler's motive was to remove the Jews entirely from the jurisdiction of the civilian bureaucracy and the *Rüstung* and place them at the exclusive disposal of the SS. His steps toward achieving this aim will be discussed at length in chapter 12.

It will serve our purposes here to note that in January, as the culmination of his strategy to reduce the influence of the *Wehrmacht* and the factory owners, Himmler ordered the liquidation of the Warsaw ghetto. But in this phase of the liquidation campaign, most of the ghetto's remaining residents—at all events, those working for the large German-owned firms—were to be sent not directly to extermination camps but rather to the camps established in the Lublin area as components of the comprehensive economic-industrial complex built by the SS. This complex, known as the "Osti" *(S.S.-Ostindustrie GmbH)*, was a constellation of enterprises based primarily on machinery, production tools, and materials confiscated from the Jews. Its organization and objectives will later be discussed in detail.

Despite his determination to transfer the Jews to the Lublin area, Himmler's plans did not in any way alter the Nazis' fundamental aim of totally annihilating the Jews. Testimony to this fact can be found in a directive dated October 9, 1942, addressed to the commanders of the SS and the Economic Command of the *Wehrmacht*. In clause 3, the concluding paragraph of the directive, Himmler stated: "Our aim is to replace this Jewish manpower with Poles while consolidating the many Jewish K.L. [*Konzentrationslager*] firms into a few large Jewish K.L. enterprises in the eastern Generalgouvernement. For whatever happens, the Jews will have to disappear from there, too, someday, in accordance with the Führer's will."[15]

The Early Stages of the Transfer to the Lublin Camps and the Danger That the Deportation Would Be Resumed

The Jews' heightened suspicions demanded that they follow the Germans' moves closely and learn how to interpret information coming from the "Aryan" side, the movement of military units, and visits by senior members of the Nazi hierarchy in order to forecast what awaited the ghetto. Rumors proved to be contradictory. For example, the dismantling of the *Umschlagplatz* (i.e., the release of children held there during the first weeks after the *Aktion*) was interpreted as a positive sign and perhaps an important indication of the "normalization" process.[16] But as early as November, the first attempt was made to uproot thousands of Jews from the ghetto. On Tuesday, November 10, 1942, Levin recorded in his diary:

> Another thing has fallen in our tiny world; half of Hoffmann's "shop" (in which tailors worked sewing coats for both the army and regular civilians) has been closed, meaning completely shut down. The number [of people] laid off or fired is as high as 500. It's said that the reason is the authorities' (SS) demand for 2,000 expert (or nonexpert) tailors to be sent to Lublin because they are needed in their workshops there.[17]

Beginning early in January, rumors spread that the *Aktion* would be resumed, and, as Levin noted in a generalization, the mood was "grim and very depressed." On Thursday, January 4, 1943, Levin noted:

> In the last few days, we have again been attacked by a sense of uneasiness and startling fear. The reason is the arrival of Ukrainians in Warsaw. There's talk of a brigade of 600 men . . . [and] all kinds of suppositions have been aired about it. The Jews walk around downcast and perplexed, afraid that they have come for us and we are about to witness a new deportation — this time total.[18]

A week later, on January 11, he continued:

> On Friday afternoon there was an uproar in some of the streets of the ghetto. The Jewish Police warned the population not to rove around outside. At 4:30 P.M. I was in Roosters Street. . . . The Policemen shouted: "Don't bring a calamity down on yourselves and on us." People were saying that Himmler is in Warsaw. Jews started to run for cover. After a few minutes, I made my way on to Muranowska [Street] . . . and three [limousines] passed by me. It well may be that the chief of the murderers passed through Warsaw to see for himself the fruit of his "labor" — the destruction of the largest [Jewish] community in Europe. He is undoubtedly satisfied with his work. . . . It's best that we face up to the awful, bitter truth: *The prospect of total annihilation constantly hangs over our heads.* "They" have evidently resolved thoroughly to wipe out European Jewry.[19]

Finally, on January 15, 1943, three days before the "January *Aktion*" began in the ghetto, Levin recorded:

> The Jews have been terrified of this day. Many never lay down to sleep till late at night, for terror of a sudden assault [as the start] of a new *Aktion* disturbed their rest and robbed them of their sleep.[20]

It is therefore clear that the tension in the ghetto rose considerably in January 1943, and the Jews were expecting another *Aktion*. The alert was particularly high on Mondays, for past experience indicated that it was usually on Mondays that the Germans initiated or renewed their deportation operations. But ironically enough, on Monday, January 18, no one expected an *Aktion* to begin. It seems that on the days preceding the eighteenth, the Germans had devoted their attention to hunting down Poles in the streets of Warsaw, with the intention of transporting them to Germany as slave laborers.[21] The Jews assumed that as long as the Germans were occupied with the Polish operation, the ghetto was not in immediate danger. Thus, although there was a general sense of tension in the ghetto and its residents anticipated the renewal of the *Aktion,* when troops penetrated the area on January 18, 1943, the move came as a surprise.

PART THREE

Revolt

Chapter Ten
The Movement toward
Combat: Mid-September 1942–
January 17, 1943

The Mood of the Jewish
Community after the
Deportation

Following the deportation, a profound change—far more pronounced than the revision in the ghetto's structure or its mode of daily life—occurred in the perceptions and psychological outlook of the remnant Jewish population. Conditions during the deportation required every individual to exhaust his physical stamina and strain all his senses in an unrelenting struggle merely to survive. The result was inevitably a state of benumbed emotions and apathy, so that each individual Jew had neither the strength nor the wherewithal to worry about anyone but himself. It was only after the deportation that the sense of realization and its shattering effects set in:

> And when Saturday, September 12 arrived, when the *Aktion* had been completed and the SS soldiers packed up and left, when the people emerged from their hiding places and came out into the streets . . . those who had been spared could not believe it [was true]. They simply couldn't believe their eyes; they were incapable of feeling any emotion. It was as if they had just come out of a long and terrible trance.[1]

Once the tension eased somewhat, the remaining Jews of the ghetto began to take stock of themselves, and the awful truth of the situation—that those who had been deported were dead and those who remained inevitably faced the same end—finally took root in their consciousness. The longing for relatives who had been torn away and the searing pain over their loss were truly felt only after the deportation had ended, and the bereaved Jews of the ghetto—who had lost parents, wives, and children—were now plagued by guilt for being alive while their relatives and friends had perished. Many were tortured by the fact that they—young men and women—had allowed helpless creatures wholly dependent upon their maturity and resourcefulness to be taken off. The all-consuming urge to survive, which had spawned an iron will and all kinds of schemes to outwit the Germans, subsided now, and many began to question the value and purpose of remaining alive. In any case, it became clear to all that the precarious lives they had managed to save were not secure for any appreciable length of time. All they had achieved in their exhausting struggle was at best a prolongation of their suffering without any guarantees of the future.

Out of this sobering change in the postdeportation period, a new mood arose, and two dominant patterns of response crystallized—with major implications for future events in the ghetto. The first was an implacable hatred of the Germans, which expressed itself in a refusal to believe any of their pronouncements—be they oral or written—and a deep desire for revenge. The second was the certainty that surrender would not guarantee survival, so that the only course left was to adopt initiatives that would foil the Germans' plans.

This mood, which embraced the majority of the ghetto's remaining population, was expressed in different ways. Some thought in terms of active resistance and searched for ways to manifest their anger. Others saw the only hope in escaping from the ghetto and finding a place to hide on the "Aryan" side of the city. And there were those who wanted to forget both the past and the probable future by living only for the moment and giving themselves up to food, drinking, and sexual abandon.[2]

Dr. Leński, one of the ghetto's physicians, explained the situation in the following way:

> If we compare the mood of the Jewish population before and after the operations of the summer, we can readily establish that there was a profound change in the Jews' state of mind. The sense of perplexity and impotence and the specious evaluations of the situation were all put behind them. Every man and woman, even every child, resolved not to give in to the German demands, to resist by all means possible, and not to go to Treblinka.[3]

According to Leński's description, the ghetto was psychologically ripe for an act of resistance. But in order to translate this desire into action, weapons were needed, and since even the armed underground was not able to guarantee arms and equipment of any consequence, the preparations for resistance were channeled in other directions, such as preparing hideouts for future need or means of escape to the "Aryan" side.

At this stage, the preparation of hideouts had not yet reached the scope and level of virtuosity it would later attain. Some people began searching out hiding places only for use in cases of emergency, while others devoted themselves to establishing more sophisticated hideouts with secret entrances and a method of covering their tracks in the area. Indeed, when the January deportation began, many sought refuge in these secret shelters.

Crossing to the "Aryan" side of the city was by nature limited to the few who could stand up to the test of "appearance": facial features that did not betray Jewish origins, a Polish accent, and no trace of the "foreigner"—traits that were unusual among the Jews of Poland. Those who had trusted Polish friends or had enough money to buy themselves a place of shelter for an extended period could also try their luck on the "Aryan" side. But few were so fortunate, and all who chose to leave the ghetto, including those Christians who had been classified as Jews by the Nazi racial laws, took a grave risk. As mentioned earlier, the last months of 1942 witnessed an important shift in the attitude of the Polish community, and the awakening of a number of men of conscience and goodwill led to the establishment of an underground movement to aid the converts and Jews. But just as this small measure of relief began to be extended, the Germans intensified their pursuit of fugitive Jews. As might have been expected during that period, the work of the hunters—which was carried out both in the open and with great zeal—was far easier and more effective than the path of those who chose flight. In the end, the overwhelming majority of the Jews who went into hiding or lived in disguise on the Polish side of Warsaw were either captured, by one means or another, or perished during the Polish revolt (which broke out in August 1944 and ended in collapse and ruin). Only about a quarter or a third of the Jews who smuggled past the ghetto wall survived to witness the liberation.

The Establishment of the Expanded Jewish Fighting Organization and the Jewish National Committee

The leaders of the Jewish Fighting Organization were well aware of the fact that the limited framework of the organization constrained the scope of their future actions. The Ż.O.B.'s narrow political base was a direct function of the conditions that prevailed at the beginning of the deportation. In all the discussions devoted to the timing and character of the inevitable uprising, broadening the framework and acquiring arms and other military equipment were repeatedly raised as vital concerns. Even during the deportation itself, the groups that constituted the Ż.O.B. continued to maintain contact with those sections of the underground that had not initially joined the combat organization.

Berlinski related that in October 1942 the members of Left Po'alei Zion met with a representative of Ha-Shomer ha-Za'ir, Arie Wilner, who informed them that "he had managed to establish contact with the military circles of the Polish government, and we will receive aid in our war against the conqueror." They decided "to meet more frequently and employ joint forces to undertake the difficult missions."[4]

Meanwhile, a number of youth-movement emissaries who had been on missions throughout occupied Poland began to return to Warsaw. Outstanding among them was Mordecai Anielewicz, who was engaged in underground work in Będzin-Sosnowiec in eastern Silesia (an area that had been annexed to the Reich) and made his way back to Warsaw upon receiving word of the deportation. Anielewicz's return was to have a major impact upon the organizational aspects of the Ż.O.B. and the eventual struggle in Warsaw. His first steps, however, were to clear the air and consolidate the nucleus of the Ż.O.B. Since Anielewicz had not been in the ghetto during the decisive days of the deportation, he was not directly familiar with the events that had overtaken the ghetto and the reactions of the people. Yet his absence during that time also gave him a certain advantage, in that he was free of the reluctance and indecisiveness that had eroded the spirit of the Ż.O.B. members when they realized that their failure to rally the masses to resistance during the deportation was as much a function of their own internal weakness as of the oppressive and paralyzing effect of the German terror operation.

Another key figure who returned to the constricted ghetto was Eliezer Geller, one of the leaders of the Gordonia movement. Geller had left the ghetto at the height of the deportation (together with the majority of the movement's members), in accordance with the decision of Gordonia's central committee to save "the activists of the training-farm population" and transfer them to distant places where they might evade the threat of annihilation or, at the very least, gain some time to consider their next moves. Eventually Geller realized that the Jews living in these seemingly "placid" areas were blinded by an illusion; that the organized Jewish community—including its youth—was not prepared for what awaited it; and that, from an internal viewpoint, the situation was worse than what was happening in Warsaw.

In an unrelated move, on December 10, 1943, the Dror He-Halutz group at the training farm in Czerniakow, on the outskirts of Warsaw, was disbanded by the Germans, and its eighty-three members, who were forced to move back to the ghetto, reinforced the ranks of the Jewish Fighting Organization.[5]

At the end of October, the negotiations between the various political bodies in the ghetto were completed, and the Jewish Fighting Organization was reconstituted in a new format that united the majority of the political forces active in the ghetto underground (with the exception of the Revisionists and the religious factions). As we shall see, the Revisionists established a separate fighting organization, while the religious movements were never integrated as an organized force into either of the frameworks preparing for armed resistance. Members of Agudat Yisrael and Mizrachi could be found within the framework of activities that centered on the Self-Help, and we also know of many instances of resistance expressed through the organized observance of religious commandments, in defiance of explicit orders issued by the occupation regime. Yet the members of these factions did not constitute a distinct unit within the resistance organizations.

At first the formation of the expanded Ż.O.B., the determination of its structure and goals, and the composition of its institutions were plagued by disagreements. Berlinski's memoirs clearly reflect the problems that arose from differences in approach:

> At the end of October 1942 a consultation was held at the Ha-Shomer headquarters at 61 Miła [Street]. Those present were: Ha-Shomer—Mordecai Anielewicz; He-Halutz—Yitzhak Zuckerman; Left Po'alei Zion—Pola, Berlinski, and [H.] Wasser. The agenda: The defense of the ghetto in Warsaw. After a general discussion, in which Pola [Elster], Berlinski, Wasser, Mordecai, and Yitzhak took part, we arrived at a unanimous decision: (1) *To found the Jewish Fighting Organization in order to prepare for the defense of the Warsaw ghetto.* (2) To teach the Jewish Police, the *Werkschutz* and the directors of the "shops," and all kinds of provocateurs a lesson. When we arrived at the major point—the appointment of the leadership—a violent debate broke out. The question was whether one or two institutions should be set up; whether it [the resistance organization] should be solely a military arm or both military and political. The members of Ha-Shomer and He-Halutz spoke out strongly against two authorities, [since that] might lead to arguments and obstruct the work. We would return to the picture before the deportation, when the parties were bogged down in arguments but did not do anything. . . . *One authority or two?*
>
> We of Left Po'alei Zion believe that any armed operation in the ghetto must first be evaluated and carefully considered. We cannot allow for impetuous moves that might lead to the premature destruction of the Warsaw ghetto. A group or organization formed solely for the purpose of fighting trains with weapons and waits for the "felicitous" moment when it can put those weapons to use. We view as an absolutely essential condition the

establishment of another authority that will judge with keen political sense when the time is ripe to debut as an armed force. . . . We do not want someone to place stones on our graves as a result of ill-considered moves. If you do not agree that the political parties will supervise the fighting organization, you are presenting us with an unacceptable condition that will prevent our joining the organization. . . . "We appeal to the delegates of Ha-Shomer and He-Halutz: Don't be obstinate; accept the validity of our position, and that will enable us to establish a joint fighting organization."

I was just about to leave when, to my surprise, I received their agreement. Elated, I rushed to tell my comrades the news. As soon as we reached an agreement on the two authorities—the military and the political—the cornerstone was laid for a joint fighting organization. We decided to expand our operations and to include the Bund.[6]

Berlinski's description indicates that even after the mass deportation, the political parties were not prepared to adopt the stand of the bodies already united in the existing combat organization. And if these were the reservations of the radical Left Po'alei Zion, whose outlook was relatively close to that of the youth movements, how much greater was the hesitation of the other parties in the underground. The differences between the two camps did not essentially focus on the organizational question of two authorities (political and military) or one (exclusively military), for in this case concepts of organizational structure reflected fundamental differences in doctrine.

The unequivocal conclusion arrived at by the founders of the Ż.O.B. was that any attempt to renew the mass deportation from the Warsaw ghetto must be met with armed resistance. And since they had no doubt that the deportation would be resumed, they had in effect decided *a priori* not only that they would fight, but *when* they would take up arms in battle. It is clear from Berlinski's description, however, that the members of Left Po'alei Zion—and therefore, presumably, the other parties as well—disagreed with the Ż.O.B. and wanted a political authority to settle questions of such a decisive nature. Berlinski intimates that the underground parties had the following reservations about the groups already incorporated in the Ż.O.B.: (1) in their haste they might bring about "the premature destruction of the ghetto," and (2) they were based entirely on "the exclusivity of war" and such a position would accelerate the advent of the conflict because for its proponents, "the use of arms" was an overriding value. They therefore viewed it as vital that a general political authority act as a kind of supervisory body to weigh and examine the situation and decide on a course of action based on objective considerations alone.

In the end, the youth movement representatives agreed to the establishment of a political authority. But they were not actually persuaded by the merits of the idea, nor were they forced to bow to the inevitable. In fact, we may even assume that their attitude of contempt toward the parties in the underground, as reported by Berlinski, did not dissolve once this exchange of views had ended. Why, then, did they give in on such a fundamental issue that would affect the very odds of going into battle? Obviously, one of their considerations was tangible fear that negotiations would break down altogether, meaning that they would squander their chance to establish a broad and powerful fighting organization in the ghetto. But there was another consideration of which Berlinski may not have been aware. The representative of the Ż.O.B. on the "Aryan" side, Arie Wilner, was already conducting negotiations with a spokesman of the A.K., Henryk Woliński (Wacław). The A.K. had made it clear that it was not willing to deal with splinter groups, and, just as the Polish underground was united, the Jewish representatives would have to receive authoritative credentials from the entire Jewish underground. The formation of a body that would unite all the political parties in the underground might provide the legitimization necessary in the talks with the Poles. Thus, although the members of the Ż.O.B. opposed the creation of a "supreme political body," which might complicate their mode of operation and even bind their hands at the critical hour, they were nevertheless forced to reckon with the fact that such a political representation might serve to their advantage by advancing their negotiations with the Poles.

At the end of October 1942, the negotiations between the various segments of the underground were completed and the two new authorities were formed: a public-political body known as the Jewish National Committee (*Żydowski Komitet Narodowy* — Ż.K.N.) and the Jewish Fighting Organization in its new format. The youth movements, Po'alei Zion Z.S., Left Po'alei Zion, and the General Zionist Organization, and the Communists all joined the National Jewish Committee, and once it was formed upon this broad base, negotiations proceeded with the Bund, whose inclusion was vital because of both its influence within the Jewish underground and its status and ties with the Polish underground. The Bund agreed at this stage to join the Ż.O.B. but hesitated to become part of a political framework embracing factions to which it had always been vigorously opposed. In addition, adherence to a body with an independent national-Jewish character was contradictory to the basic tenets of the Bund. Yet the Bund — or rather its remaining members — had undergone a fundamental metamorphosis. Some of the party's leaders, including Maurycy Orzech, had fled to the Polish side of Warsaw, and the activists who remained in the ghetto (especially the party's younger members) now backed the idea of negotiations with the other factions of the Jewish underground. The key figure who led his comrades into strong partnerships in both the political and military spheres during this period was Abrasza Blum.

Marek Edelman elaborated on this shift in the Bund's attitude:

> At the beginning of October 1942, discussions were held between the heads of the central committee and the command of the pioneering fighting organization regarding the establishment of a joint organization. The issue had been discussed at length among our members and was finally decided at a meeting of the Warsaw activists on October 15. We decided to form a joint fighting organization with the aim of putting up armed resistance to the Germans in the event that the liquidation *Aktion* is resumed. We understand that only coordinated work and a supreme joint effort will yield any results whatsoever.[7]

In the end, as Edelman indicates, the Bund agreed to join the Ż.O.B. without reservation, while its participation in the Jewish National Committee was limited. The formula finally worked out was that the Bund and the Jewish National Committee would form a kind of federative union known as the Jewish Coordination Committee (*Komisja Koordynacyjna*).

Thus at the conclusion of extended and intricate negotiations, three bodies emerged out of the new organization efforts: (1) the Jewish National Committee, which included the majority of the forces in the underground except for the Bund; (2) the Coordination Committee, which comprised the National Committee and the Bund; and (3) the Jewish Fighting Organization, which embraced all the bodies represented on the National Committee and the Coordination Committee.

According to Yitzhak Zuckerman's report on the Ż.O.B.,

> The members of the board of the Coordination Committee were: Yitzhak Zuckerman, secretary; Menachem Kirschenbaum; and Abrasza Blum. The members of the plenary were: Alexander [a pseudonym, probably A. Fondamiński], Miriam Einsdorf [Heinsdorf], Melech Feinkind, Eliezer Geller, Zivia Lubetkin, and Yohanan Morgenstern. The Jewish National Committee chose the following people for its board: Yitzhak Zuckerman, Menachem Kirshenbaum, and Yohanan Morgenstern.

Berlinski provides the following version:

> The following were on the Coordination Committee: Bund—Blum, Left Po'alei Zion—Melech Asdak (Feinkind), Right Po'alei Zion [Z.S.]—Morgenstern, Ha-Shomer—Mordecai [Anielewicz], He-Halutz—Yitzhak [Zuckerman], Dror—Zivia [Lubetkin], [General] Zionists—Kirschenbaum.[8]

Zuckerman gives the command of the Ż.O.B. as: Mordecai Anielewicz (Ha-Shomer ha-Za'ir), commander—organization division; Yitzhak Zuckerman (Dror He-Halutz), deputy commander—arms; Marek Edelstein (Edelman, Bund)—intelligence; Yohanan Morgenstern (Po'alei Zion Z.S.)—finances; Hirsch Berlinski (Left Po'alei Zion)—planning; Michael Rosenfeld (Communists).

The representation of the Jewish underground on the "Aryan" side was also built along the same lines. Arie Wilner ("Jurek") was the Ż.O.B. spokesman vis-à-vis the military forces in the Polish underground, while Dr. Adolf Berman represented the National Committee before the Polish civilian institutions. In addition, the representation of the Coordination Committee included the Bund's spokesman on the Polish side, Dr. Leon Feiner ("Mikołaj"). Zuckerman's report also includes a list of the Coordination Committee's subcommittees and mentions the establishment of a civilian council that did not include any members of the Coordination Committee (indeed, some of its members did not even belong to a political party). The very establishment and composition of this committee indicate the significant change that took place in the attitude toward armed resistance and the support that the new Ż.O.B. enjoyed among the remnant population of the ghetto. According to Zuckerman, the civilian council "assumed responsibility for obtaining finances (1) for the needs of the military organization; (2) for building shelters and bunkers and disseminating the idea of active resistance among all segments of the population."

The division of functions between the subcommittees and the civilian council sheds light on the character of the political body that ostensibly exercised its authority over the fighting organization but in reality served to promote the concept of resistance among the public and supply the means for arming the Ż.O.B. and building up its strength. The composition of the civilian council is also important, since it included the heads of the JDC, who throughout the entire war had devoted themselves with great dedication to welfare and self-help projects in both legal and clandestine ways. Under the new circumstances, and evidently out of a desire to continue serving the community in their own way, they joined the ranks of those who supported resistance, thereby providing authoritative public backing for the concept of self-defense, as well as actually supplying vital material resources for the purchase of arms and organizational needs.

The status of the Jewish Fighting Organization changed considerably, and it is therefore important to distinguish between the initial structure of the organization (from the end of July 1942) and the expanded, comprehensive Ż.O.B. at the end of October 1942 (see Table 7). As we have seen, in the earlier stage, the organization consisted of a

TABLE 7

THE MILITARY AND CIVILIAN-POLITICAL STRUCTURE OF THE JEWISH FIGHTING ORGANIZATION
(Ż.O.B.) IN WARSAW

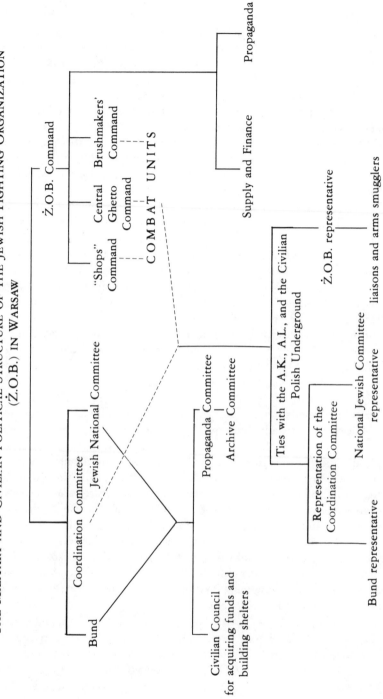

nucleus of about two hundred and fifty youth movement members. The very fact that they had united in preparation to defend themselves — not to mention their plans for armed resistance operations — was then considered by the majority of the ghetto's residents (including a substantial section of the underground) to be a dangerous and daring act that ran contrary to the interests of the endangered Jewish population. Developments following the deportation not only changed the general public mood and the attitude toward the youngsters who had espoused the idea of resistance but also created the opportunity to strengthen the Ż.O.B. and place it on a firm and trusted political base. We can estimate that the youth movements and youth divisions of the parties that now joined the Ż.O.B. comprised about six hundred people, and they were backed by a broader circle of supporters. Thus without forfeiting the hallowed rules of conspiracy, whereby supporters were not permitted to know the organization from the inside or who was active in the combat section — the Ż.O.B. essentially inherited the full backing of the entire ghetto underground. In addition, the quantitative and qualitative changes in the Ż.O.B. now enabled it to deal with the Polish underground on behalf of the very political and communal bodies that had represented Polish Jewry in the Parliament between the two world wars and had led the community's public struggle during the life of the Polish Republic.

The Jewish Military Union (Ż.Z.W.)

Rich and authentic documentary and personal evidence allows us to follow the debates and discussions that preceded the establishment of the Ż.O.B., and even to date its founding with precision to October 20, 1942. We also know which bodies joined it, who its leaders were, the kinds of institutions formed within it, and the goals they set for themselves.

Unfortunately, the same cannot be said of the Revisionist Jewish Military Union (*Żydowski Związek Wojskowy* — Ż.Z.W.), since we lack the kind of authoritative material that would enable us to retrace the steps in its formation. Thus we do not know exactly when it was established and how it was organized. Moreover, the few survivors who might have provided and elucidated these details have not left us with a clear picture of its early stages and development. This is the primary problem in attempting to describe the organization's course and growth in any detail.

The most pressing question in this context is why the Jewish Military Union did not join the Ż.O.B., which at any rate embraced various mutually opposed ideological factions (e.g., in Vilna and at a later stage

in Bialystok). David Wdowiński, the leader of the Revisionists in the
ghetto and by his own testimony the "head of the Jewish Military
Union," provided the following explanation in his memoirs:

> . . . Now the youth decided that in the event of a new "resettlement"
> [deportation] operation, the Germans will have to pay a heavy price for
> Jewish lives. The young will never again agree to be led to Treblinka like
> sheep. This was how the Jewish combat groups—the Jewish Fighting
> Organization and the Jewish Military Union—came into being. From the
> very start, I had hoped that a single fighting organization would arise; but
> after two meetings with Zivia Lubetkin, the representative of the radical
> leftist Zionist party, and Mordechai Anielewicz, the leader of the Jewish
> Fighting Organization, it turned out that the union was not meant to be.
> We Revisionists believed that in order to ensure the maximal effectivenss
> of the revolt, the head of the united fighting front should be the man most
> suited to command from a military viewpoint. The other group insisted
> that a political leader stand at the head of the organization, and naturally
> he was to come from their ranks. Moreover, the others wanted the Betar
> members to join the organization as individuals, rather than as a group.[9]

Adam Halperin, a close supporter of the Jewish Military Union,
also commented on this issue:

> What was the reason for the establishment of another, independent
> fighting organization within the ghetto walls? The blame rests with the
> leadership of the first organization, which was not prepared to accept Betar
> into the ranks of the general organization as a movement. This right, which
> was enjoyed by all the other Jewish organizations, was denied only to Be-
> tar. Betarniks would be allowed to join the organization only as individu-
> als, not as organized and unified body. . . . Obviously the members of
> Betar could not make peace with this arbitrary decision and bow to it, but
> neither could they merely stand on the sidelines at a time when circum-
> stances demanded a response and self-defense. It was therefore decided to
> establish a new fighting organization.[10]

Yitzhak Zuckerman, however, gives a different version of the reasons for the division. He confirms that there were contacts between the
Ż.O.B. and the representatives of the group that eventually founded
the Ż.Z.W. But contrary to Wdowiński's version of events, Zuckerman
claims that the two bodies even reached an agreement that enabled
Betar members to join the Ż.O.B., and a joint organization existed for
a time. The break came, in Zuckerman's telling of it, because of the
following reasons:

1. On their own initiative, Betar members conducted separate
   negotiations with Polish circles.

2. Betar members brought weapons into the ghetto—albeit in small quantities—but when ordered to turn them over to the general headquarters, they refused to do so.
3. Betar members carried on an open propaganda campaign in the ghetto on behalf of the Ż.O.B., while the organization was not willing to expose itself publicly.
4. Betar members, "as the pupils of Jabotinsky," demanded that the commander of the organization come from their ranks.

Each of these problems, and their combined effect—Zuckerman claims—created a situation whereby all the constituent factions of the Ż.O.B. demanded the cessation of the "separatist actions." When their warnings fell on deaf ears, a decision was taken to dismiss the Betar members from the organization.

There is only one point of agreement between the two versions: Betar's insistence that the commander of the Ż.O.B. come from its ranks. On the other hand, Zuckerman does not mention the problem cited by the Betarniks as the reason for the split, i.e., the system by which Betar members were enrolled in the Ż.O.B. Both Wdowiński and Halperin complain that the Betarniks were forced to join as individuals, rather than as an organized body. Halperin is right in calling this a case of discrimination that deviated from the pattern established for the other movements incorporated in the organization, so that the issue deserves careful attention.

The Jewish Fighting Organization was a broad merger of political and ideological factions that bridged varied and often antagonistic philosophies. Even more significant, it was composed of combat groups and cells structured on a movement basis, since the organization had not come into being from scratch but was a union of movements that had already existed in the underground for a long while. This movement-based system of organization, which had been authorized during the earliest stages of the Ż.O.B., was maintained for the most part right through the final uprising. It is therefore difficult to fathom why the Ż.O.B. would even have considered adopting a policy of discrimination against Betar on this issue. After all, such a move would have implied forsaking the principle of movement-based groups and, moreover, would have created difficulties not only for the Betar people (who could not have been expected to accept such a dictate) but for all the other movements, which were no less interested in maintaining their fixed internal structure.

Since some of the Betarniks had undergone military training before the war, had served in the regular Polish army, and had even risen in rank, there were grounds for the proposal (or demand) that the commander of the Ż.O.B. should be a properly qualified member from their ranks. But there is absolutely no basis for the claim that Anielewicz was chosen for his position by virtue of being a political leader or the representative of a particular political faction. It is reasonable to assume that Anielewicz, who lacked any formal military training, was chosen as commander for two reasons: (1) from the very beginning, he and his movement had proposed and demanded armed resistance and had been among the founders of the Ż.O.B. in July 1942; and (2) the members of the underground who knew Anielewicz believed that he possessed the necessary personal traits for the position. Clearly, the various movements amalgamated in the Ż.O.B. viewed the position of commander as more than a military post. To them, the Ż.O.B. was a further evolution of the already existent underground, and they wanted their leader to be a man who had been in on the underground's activities from the start.

It is impossible to provide a precise answer to the question of when the Ż.Z.W. was actually founded. Various publications issued by Betar or its individual members have a tendency to blur the distinction between defined stages and equate the establishment of the Ż.Z.W. with earlier clandestine organizational efforts.

We have no indication as to whether the Revisionist underground and Betar members in the ghetto remained together in one or a number of "shops" during the mass deportation or even whether there was any attempt to maintain a loyal nucleus and plan an organized response when the propitious moment arrived. The resurrection of the movement began after the return of the Betar group from Hrubieszów, where they had been employed on an agricultural farm. They made their way back to Warsaw after an *Aktion* had been carried out in Hrubieszów and its vicinity and they had attempted to take cover in the forests, where they clashed with the Germans. It is therefore clear that the reconsolidation of Betar in Warsaw occurred only after the first deportation, since the *Aktion* in Hrubieszów took place in September 1942. Halperin supports this version of the chronology of events in his comments about the Hrubieszów group: "When they came back to the ghetto and expressed their desire to join the ranks of the general organization [Ż.O.B.]," the conditions that were stipulated prevented their enlistment, and "it was therefore decided to establish a new fighting organization [Ż.Z.W.]."[11]

The exact membership of the Ż.Z.W. at the time of its establishment has not been verified. Wdowiński speaks of 300 members in the early stages, while a document from Polish sources that evidently related to the situation in January 1943 speaks of "approximately 150 young Jews who are prepared for any eventuality and are relatively well equipped."[12] A number of different versions likewise exist about the union's structure, leadership, and various organizational departments, though all agree on the names of the leaders. Dr. Wdowiński noted in his memoirs that the union's political committee comprised three people: Wdowiński himself as chairman; Dr. M. Strykowski, one of the central figures in the Revisionist movement in Poland; and Leon (Arie) Rodal, a journalist. The head of the military command was Pavel Frenkel, whom Wdowiński described as "one of the most beautiful, the most honest, and one of the most modest figures" he had ever met in all of his political life.[13]

Wdowiński does not mention details about any other institutions, while Halperin elaborated on this subject under the subheading "The Administration of the Military Union":

> At the head of the Military Union (Ż.Z.W.) stood the Betarnik P. Frenkel. Under him was the command, composed of Natan Szulc, S. Hazenszprung, Arie Rodal, Eliyahu Albersztein, Yitzhak Bilawski. . . . Dr. David Wdowiński, former head of the Zionist-Revisionist movement, and Dr. Michael Strykowski, who at that time were members of the underground National Committee of the Warsaw ghetto, cooperated with the Ż.Z.W.[14]

In this last remark, Halperin was evidently referring to the membership of the Revisionist movement leaders on the public advisory committee attached to the Self-Help, which he understood to mean representation on the body that, in the course of changes in membership, subsequently became the National Committee. But in fact, the National Committee was a distinct and fundamentally different body.

In addition to the Ż.O.B. and the Ż.Z.W., various other ("wildcat") groups of a different character organized in the ghetto at a later period. We shall discuss the rise of these groups, their organizational format, and their activities further on in this work.

The Jewish Fighting Organization and the Polish Military Underground

As noted earlier, the first attempts by the Ż.O.B. representative on the "Aryan" side, Arie Wilner, to contact the command of the A.K. during the mass deportation were unsuccessful. At the end of September or the beginning of October 1942, however, contact was finally made between Arie Wilner and Henryk Woliński ("Wacław").

In their first meetings, Woliński asked for information on the Ż.O.B., its structure, and its goals and passed it on to his superiors. On October 9 he relayed two declarations of the Jewish National Committee addressed to the civilian and military authorities in the Polish underground. The first requested that the Jews be supplied with arms, while the second, addressed to the Polish civilian institutions, asked that the National Committee be recognized as the authorized representative of the Jewish population vis-à-vis the civilian branches of the Polish underground. "Wacław" passed the two requests on to the "delegate" (the local representative of the Polish government-in-exile). The statement proclaiming the establishment of the Jewish National Committee read:

> As a union of politically conscious circles that constitute Polish Jewry and the focal point for activism during the war, we hereby appeal to you:
> —to recognize the Jewish National Committee as the representative of the Jewish population.
> —The National Jewish Committee hereby declares that it will conduct all aspects of its activities in coordination with the civilian and military authorities of the official Polish underground.[15]

According to Woliński's subsequent report, the supreme commander of the A.K., General Rowecki, sent back a written reply to the Jewish declaration in the form of an order (not in our possession) issued on November 11, 1942: The commander certifies that the declaration has been brought to his attention. He praises the readiness for struggle and recommends that the Jewish Fighting Organization be organized in cells of five members. Other than this noncommittal reply from the Polish military authorities, Woliński reported that the underground civilian authorities did not even answer the declaration addressed to them, though they did acknowledge its receipt verbally.[16]

On December 2 Wilner brought the organization's code of regulations to the attention of the Polish underground. This code was structured in a number of sections. The first was a general introduction—a kind of platform statement—describing the structure of the organization's political institutions. The various factions that constituted the organization were listed in the following order: the General Zionist organizations, Right Po'alei Zion, Left Po'alei Zion, the Revisionist movement, He-Halutz, Ha-Shomer ha-Za'ir, Dror. (The fact that the Revisionists were included in this list evidently indicates that at the beginning of December 1942 they were still considered a component of the Ż.O.B.) For obvious reasons, the General Zionist parties were given prominence, while the Communist faction was ignored altogether. The introduction also explained the relationship with the Bund through the Coordination Committee. Later on in the document, the role of the Coordination Committee was sketched out as follows:

> . . . The purpose of the Coordination Committee is:
> A. Organization of the defense of the ghetto in the event of a renewal of the deportation.

B. Defense of the Jewish masses in the ghetto against the conqueror's agents and collaborators.

C. The Coordination Committee is the founder of the fighting organization, determines its course of action, and supervises it.

D. The Coordination Committee will comprise one representative of each political faction.

The body of the document and its main clauses deal with the Ż.O.B. per se. Its first section, "Structure," states that the basic unit of organization is a "group of six." The second section, "Arms," qualifies the following as weapons: firearms, axes, knives, acids, inflammable materials, etc. The next section, dealing with ground-rules for combat, states that (1) in the event of a further deportation, resistance will be based on the slogan: "We will not give up a single Jew"; (2) terrorist actions will be launched against the Jewish Police, the *"kehillah" (Judenrat)*, and the *Werkshutz*. The fourth section details the "immediate goals," while the last section, "Names," provides a list of the component organizations and institutions.

Finally, the document explains that in order to ensure close ties between the Jewish Fighting Organization and the Coordination Committee, the commander of the fighting organization will take part in all meetings of the latter body. As far as the Polish military underground is concerned, the Ż.O.B. will be represented by a spokesman of the National Jewish Committee, code-named "Jurek" (Arie Wilner), and a representative of the Bund, code-named "Mikołaj" (Dr. Feiner).[17]

The information transmitted to the Polish underground was on the whole quite accurate, except for the fact that the idea of "groups of six" was never implemented by the Ż.O.B. In addition, the only code names revealed to the Poles were those of the Jewish representatives on the "Aryan" side, which were already known to them anyway. Although vague generalities were made about the organization within the "shops," no addresses were listed, nor was so much as a hint supplied as to where the organization's centers of command were located. Woliński appended a memorandum to this detailed document identifying it as the Ż.O.B.'s code of regulations approved in the ghetto on December 2 and passed on to him by "Jurek."

In a subsequent meeting with "Jurek" and "Mikołaj," the spokesman of the Coordination Committee stressed the "imperative of equipping the Jewish Fighting Organization with weapons *without delay*, for they have no supplier whatsoever, the campaign to annihilate the ghetto is not over, and it may be resumed at any moment...." "Mikołaj" and "Jurek" therefore requested:

1. A greater quantity of arms, because the ten revolvers that were received are not sufficient to organize armed resistance or any other campaign of a group or individual nature.

2. The option to purchase arms, since we are examining the possibilities of raising money for this purpose.
3. Instructions and instructors, since the combat element received some paramilitary training in Poland before the war, but the only ones with proper training are serving in the police force and do not enjoy the confidence of the Ż.O.B. members.[18]

In his official summary written in 1944, Woliński stated:

After urgent requests, 10 (ten) revolvers and a small amount of ammunition were turned over to the Jewish Fighting Organization by order of the Supreme Command. The weapons were in a very bad state, and only a few of them were fit for use. The Jewish Fighting Organization saw this gift as satisfying only a fraction of its needs. It therefore demanded considerably more effective aid and offered to set aside a substantial portion of the funds at its disposal for the purchase of weapons. This demand could only be filled to a very small extent. Before January 17, 1943 (the date on which the remnant of the Warsaw ghetto was liquidated—about 50,000 people), the Jewish Fighting Organization received an additional ten revolvers, directives for sabotage actions, a recipe for the manufacture of [Molotov cocktails] and guidance in military actions. In the period up to January 17, 1943, the Jewish Fighting Organization devoted itself to frenzied preparations for the struggle as well as to unrelenting stubborn appeals to the army [A.K.], which reacted to all their appeals with skepticism and with a great measure of reservation.[19]

At this point we should recall the radiogram Rowecki sent to London on January 2, 1943, stating that: "As an experiment I took out a few revolvers . . . [but] I shall not give out any more weapons, for you know that we ourselves have none." Rowecki was indeed consistent on this point, and until the first uprising in the ghetto on January 18, 1943, the Jewish fighters did not receive any further arms from the A.K.

As to the second batch of ten revolvers that Woliński claims were supplied some time prior to January 18, there is no confirmation of this shipment in any Jewish source. In his letter to the "Command of the Armed Forces—A.K.," dated November 26, 1943, Zuckerman wrote: "After we requested arms in November 1942, we received ten revolvers in December; and when we again asked for weapons in January 1943, we received 49 revolvers, 50 hand grenades, and explosives, for which you have our profound gratitude."[20] However, these forty-nine (or fifty, according to Polish sources) revolvers were turned over by the A.K. *after* the January deportation and resistance campaign, so that up to the inception of the second *Aktion* only ten revolvers had been given to the Ż.O.B. Moreover, it is inconceivable that Zuckerman would not have known about a shipment of arms from the A.K., and he certainly could not have understated the total number of weapons in a letter addressed to his benefactors.

As far back as December 1942, the representatives of the Coordination Committee were able to transmit information abroad (by means of the standing services of the *Delegatura*) regarding the formation of defense forces in the ghetto and their need for combat equipment. In addition to Rowecki's radiogram, fragmented information that found its way into one of the overseas reports indicated that "desperate plans to stage resistance are being devised among the Jewish population." The Polish government-in-exile passed on the information—classified as secret—that contact had been established between the military arm of the Polish underground and the Jewish organization deployed for resistance.[21]

Ties far stronger than those established with the A.K. were forged with the Communist faction and its representatives in the Polish underground. We lack information on the concrete aid that the Communists extended to the Ż.O.B. at the time, but it is clear that Arie Wilner, and afterward Yitzhak Zuckerman, maintained close ties with the P.P.R.

The Ż.O.B. from the End of the Mass Deportation to January 17, 1943

The Ż.O.B.'s first operations were directed against the Jewish Police, in retaliation for its diligence and brutality during the mass deportation; senior officials of the *Judenrat* who were known to be on close terms with the Germans; and Jews who had developed a reputation as agents for the various branches of the German police.

The most obvious question that arises in this context is why the Ż.O.B. inflicted its first blows on Jews, of all people. Actually, a number of disparate considerations all seemed to point to the necessity of this step. The primary motivation was a strong urge to retaliate against the commanders of the Jewish Police, who had displayed such fervor and callousness in executing their orders during the deportation. Another major factor was bound up with the Ż.O.B.'s plans for the future. The organization's leaders were convinced that the ghetto could not be set in gear for an armed struggle as long as it contained the equivalent of a "Fifth Column" prepared to collaborate with the Germans by passing on information and even turning people in on request. Furthermore, the Ż.O.B. commanders assumed (correctly, as it turned out) that the Nazis would not bother to intervene in internal vendettas carried out in the ghetto as long as they themselves were not directly affected.

In essence, the attack on Szeryński can be grouped among these actions, even though it was primarily an act of revenge, whereas after the deportation the assassinations were also motivated by considerations related to plans for the future. The first person condemned to death by the Ż.O.B. was Jacob Lejkin, the prime symbol of the Jewish policeman who dedicated himself with "bizarre" devotion to the deportation operation. The hatred of the police, which was a kind of collective response of the remant population of the ghetto and was repeatedly underscored in diaries and memoirs, was first channeled against Lejkin, who was not only an obedient servant of the Germans and unhesitatingly tormented their victims, but even worked out a "philosophy" to justify his work, thereby enabling him to contribute to paralyzing the will of the Jews and the dissemination of false illusions.

The assassination was planned with great care, and the group that accepted the mission consisted of three members of Ha-Shomer ha-Za'ir.[22] Margalit Landau and Mordecai Grobas trailed Lejkin for some time, studying his habits and charting his regular movements and hours of work, while Eliyahu Różański was chosen as the assassin. Toward evening on October 29, Lejkin was shot to death while walking from the police station to his home in Gęsia Street. His aide, Czapliński, who was walking by his side, was injured. The reverberations were felt throughout the ghetto; as Ringelblum described it some time later, "Lejkin, who had allowed power to go to his head and whose dedication to the Germans was boundless, was 'swept out' by the organization to the heartfelt acclamation of the Jewish population."[23]

On the next day, October 30, handbills were posted in a number of spots in the ghetto proclaiming that since the Ż.O.B. had announced the trial of the leaders, officers, and members of the Jewish Police in Warsaw on August 17, the sentence pronounced on the deputy commander of the police, Lejkin, had been carried out. Further on the announcement stated:

> We also hereby inform the population that the following have likewise been convicted:
> (1) The *Judenrat* in Warsaw and its *presidium*, on the grounds of having collaborated with the conqueror in signing the deportation order.
> (2) The managers of the "shops" and members of the *Werkschutz*, due to their cruel treatment of the workers and the "illegal" Jewish population. *Retaliatory measures will be adopted in all their severity.*[24]

Since the verdict against Lejkin and the preparations for implementing it fell into the period prior to the establishment of the expanded Ż.O.B., the operation should essentially be credited to the original, limited organization. This assessment is also fitting in terms of its impact. The long period of impotence and resignation to misery had left its mark, and many could not conceive of the assassins being Jews working on behalf of an underground body in the ghetto. Even Peretz Opoczyński, a member of the "Oneg Shabbat" group that chronicled the history of the ghetto, wrote only that "it is presumed to be a Jewish assault."[25]

The next assassination was directed against Yisrael First, a senior official of the *Judenrat*. First had been one of the directors of the Economic Department, but his influence extended far beyond that sphere. From the earliest days of the *Judenrat*, he had also been the council's liaison officer with various branches of the German police, and he now stood accused of "extending aid to the conqueror during the deportation *Aktion*, maintaining relations with the Germans, and treating the employees of the [*Judenrat*] with cruelty." The verdict against him was carried out on November 28, 1942, by David Shulman of Dror He-Halutz, and Ringelblum counts this assassination among the operations of the Ż.O.B. On November 30, 1942, Levin wrote about the incident at length:

> Yesterday evening there was a political murder in the ghetto: Yisrael First was killed by two bullets on Muranowska Street. He was the director of the Economic Department of the *Judenrat* and close to the "throne" — one of those Jews whom the Germans prized. This Jew did big business in partnership with, and approved by, the Germans. He undoubtedly made a fortune. Who killed him?. . . There are two possibilities. First, the Germans derailed him as they had their other cronies — Kohn, Heller, Ehrlich, and many more. . . . [So] it is possible that First was likewise killed by them. But there is another possibility: It could be that he was brought down by either a Jew or a Pole, killed as a traitor or for selling his soul to the Germans by helping them during the *Aktion*. . . . [26]

Levin's doubts about the perpetrator of the assault confirm again that the population of the ghetto had no idea of or belief in the existence of a Jewish armed resistance.

After the murder, Gerhardt Mende of the local SS office paid a visit to the chairman of the *Judenrat*, Lichtenbaum, and expressed his sorrow at the loss of an "excellent colleague like First." Mende also stated that he knew the perpetrators of the deed were Poles who had been aided by Jews. "The names of the assassins are known to them, and the guilty will not escape punishment," reported the "Oneg Shabbat" publication *Yediot* in December 1942, adding, "with that, the matter was closed."[27] It appears that either the Germans did not wish to admit the existence of an independent resistance force in the ghetto or they simply refused to believe that such a force could possibly arise. In any event, they had no intention of exerting themselves to track down those responsible for the assault and remained content with pretending that the criminals were known to them and the source of the problem was among the Poles.

The internal organization of the Ż.O.B. did not develop very much from September 1942 to January 1943. Most of the fighters were concentrated in the area of the O.B.W. "shop" and the Dror He-Halutz base, which had been moved to Zamenhofa Street. Some groups began to form in the "shops" section, but the shortage of weapons prevented them from being properly equipped or embarking on a plan for widespread resistance. The meager amount of weapons provided by the Poles or purchased with their aid were kept together at the main bases and concealed in special caches. Personal weapons were not yet issued at that time, as the supply of arms was so small that the Ż.O.B. could not even think in such terms. It also appears that a degree of friction existed between the various factions over the division of the few weapons available. While combat units continued to train in the use of revolvers, the Ż.O.B. was in a state of constant tension for fear that a new deportation would begin before the organization had time to decide how it would deploy its forces. A number of times alarms and states of alert were declared, and, of course, the tension always rose as Monday approached.

The Ż.O.B. had planned to hold a public demonstration in the ghetto on January 22 under the banner: "Honor the fallen—half a year of destruction, July 22, 1942–January 22, 1943." Mordecai Anielewicz was to supervise the action, with Berliński and Edelman serving as his deputies. It was scheduled to begin on the evening of January 21 and last for an hour. Berlinski outlined the plan in his memoirs: "The fence on Muranowska Street is to be decorated with wreaths and banners. In the middle of the square, a large fire will be lit. . . . Muranowska and Miła streets are to be taken over by Yellin [Berlinski] and his units; Nalewki, Gęsia, and Zamenhofa by Mordecai and his units." The commanders also planned to detain any policeman who fell into their hands: "The aims of the operation will be explained to him, and he will be marked by the organization as a collaborator with the Germans in executing the mass murder of the Jews."[28] As Edelman elaborated in his report, the small transport of revolvers from the Armia Krajowa "permit[ted] us to plan our first major public step, which we scheduled for January 22 as a retaliation against the Jewish Police."[29]

It was in anticipation of the January 22 operation that the Ż.O.B. published the following manifesto:

> On January 22, 1943, six months will have elapsed since the start of the deportation from Warsaw. We all remember those harrowing days in

which 300,000 of our brothers and sisters were transported to and brutally murdered in the Treblinka death camp. Six months of constant fear of death have passed without our knowing what the next day will bring. We received reports left and right about Jews being killed in the General-gouvernement, Germany, and the occupied countries. As we listened to these terrible tidings, we waited for our own time to come—any day, any moment. Today we must realize that the Hitlerian murders have let us live only to exploit our manpower until the last drop of blood and sweat, until our last breath. We are slaves, and when slaves no longer bring in profits they are killed. Each of us must realize this, and always keep it in mind. . . .

Jewish masses, the hour is drawing near. You must be prepared to resist, not give yourselves up to slaughter like sheep. *Not a single Jew should go to the railroad cars. Those who are unable to put up active resistance should resist passively*, meaning go into hiding. We have just received information from Lvov that the Jewish Police there forcefully executed the deportation of 3,000 Jews. This will not be allowed to happen again in Warsaw. The assassination of Lejkin demonstrates that. Our slogan must be: *All are ready to die as human beings.*[30]

Another poster, found in the second section of the Ringelblum Archive, has been tentatively attributed to the Jewish Military Union and is assumed to be another appeal to the Jews written in January 1943:

We are going out to war! We are among those who have set themselves the goal of rousing the people. We want out people to adopt the slogan: *Rise up and fight! Do not despair of the chance for rescue!* Know that deliverance is not to be found in going to your death impassively, like sheep to the slaughter. It can only be found in something far more noble: War!

He who fights for his life has a chance of being saved: He who rules out resistance from the start is already lost, doomed to a degrading death in the suffocation machine at Treblinka.

Rouse yourselves to war: Find the courage to indulge in acts of madness: Put a stop to the degrading resignation expressed by such statements as: "We are all bound to die." That is a lie: For we have been sentenced to live! We, too, are deserving of life. You merely must know how to fight for it!

. . . In the name of the fight for the lives of the helpless masses, whom we wish to save and whom we must rouse to action, we are rising up in revolt! We do not wish to fight for our own lives alone. We can save ourselves only after we have done out duty! *As long as a Jewish life—even one single, solitary life—is in danger, we must be prepared to fight!*

Our slogan: Not even one single Jew will ever again perish in Treblinka!

Destroy the traitors to the people!

> A war of life or death with the conqueror unto our last breath!
> Prepare for action!
> Be on the alert![31]

If this was indeed an appeal written in January 1943 to express the aims of the Jewish Military Union, it serves to highlight an unequivocal difference between the two combat organizations—not only in terms of emphasis but in fundamental outlook. The Ż.O.B. manifesto makes no reference to the chances of being rescued from death. Its authors promised nothing. On the contrary, their phrasing of the appeal gives reason to believe that the Jews effectively had no chance of escaping death, and the only choice for them was whether to die meekly or in battle—or, in the language of the appeal, "to die as human beings." In contrast, the second proclamation portrays resistance as the only hope of remaining alive. The authors of the Ż.Z.W. appeal note that none can hope to be saved as long as the threat of death hovers over the Jews. Yet rather than equate combat with an honorable death, they offer it as a path that may provide a chance for deliverance. But nowhere in this declaration—so heavily laden with emphatic slogans—do we find so much as a hint of how such deliverance is likely to come about.

Chapter Eleven
The Second *Aktion:*
January 18–22, 1943

The Deportation during the Second *Aktion*

One of the Jews who chronicled the events of the second *Aktion* in January 1943 dubbed the opening day of the operation "the unsuspecting Monday."[1] The ghetto awoke to its usual day of life, as it had been conducted since the mass deportation, and at 6:30 A.M., as on every other day, the *palatzovka* workers reported for duty at the gates of the ghetto in order to be taken to their places of work beyond the walls. But on that morning they found the exits from the ghetto blocked and were instructed to wait nearby. The alerted workers could discern unusual movements on the other side of the wall—the deployment of soldiers and gendarmes—and many of them scattered back to their housing blocks to spread the news that the ghetto was surrounded and a mass deportation was imminent. Close to 7:30 A.M., German units and support troops penetrated the ghetto.

At the beginning of the second *Aktion*—and long after it had ended—the residents of the ghetto believed that the Germans intended to deport all the Jews remaining in Warsaw. But this assumption is not confirmed by any of the German documents at out disposal. We do know that Himmler paid a personal visit to the ghetto on January 9, 1943, and devoted considerable attention to the question of the Jews still living there. Two days later he dispatched a letter to Krieger noting that 40,000 Jews were still living in Warsaw and "8,000 of them will be transported out in the coming days."[2] It therefore appears that upon discovering that his orders regarding the Jews of Warsaw had been ignored, Himmler directed most of his anger at the 8,000 Jews who constituted an "illegal" element, in that they exceeded the quota to be filled by the end of the mass deportation. Upon receiving the general order to liquidate the Jewish community of Warsaw by February 15, 1943, von Sammern, the commander of the SS and the police in the Warsaw District, evidently hoped to quell Himmler's anger by promising to remove the 8,000 without delay. Thus the January deportation was not conceived as the total and final expulsion, though the decision to liquidate the ghetto completely, as well as a timetable for the operation, had already been established by the time the *Aktion* began. The January deportees were transported directly to Treblinka, while most of the "shop" workers were destined to be relocated (at least for a time) in work camps established in the vicinity of Lublin.

Although we lack confirmed data on the identity and number of troops employed in the second *Aktion,* we may assume that von Sammern exploited the presence of the units engaged in rounding up Poles for forced labor in Germany and used them in the ghetto operation. A Polish source notes that the Germans sent two hundred gendarmes, eight hundred Latvians and Lithuanians, and light tanks into the ghetto in response to the incidents of resistance.[3] According to a German source, which is supported by *Wehrmacht* documents, on January 20 (the third day of the *Aktion*) two SS battalions stationed in Lublin surrounded Többens's and Schultz's "shops."[4] What is certain is that the operation was commanded by von Sammern and that the commandant of Treblinka, *Hauptsturmführer* Theodor von Eupen, participated in it.

The second *Aktion* differed from its predecessor in a number of ways, one of them being the Germans' restricted use of the Jewish Police and the *Judenrat* (in comparison to the summer of 1942). The Jewish Police were again forced to serve as guides in the ghetto, but the roundup of deportees and their accompaniment to the *Umschlagplatz* were left in the hands of the Germans and their support troops. The most striking difference between the two operations however, was not in the behavior of the Germans but in the conduct of the Jews.

At the beginning of the *Aktion,* the Germans attempted to round up those who lacked papers—namely, the "illegals" whom Himmler assessed at eight thousand strong. Only after they realized that it would not be possible to snare the Jews they sought did the Germans begin their indiscriminate manhunts in an effort to fill their quota as quickly as possible. But this system of snatching up any Jew who came to hand also met with difficulties. For the Jews had learned from bitter experience, and instead of being taken in by the Germans' assurances or the so-called protection of their work permits, they preferred to go into hiding whenever possible. At any rate, that was the situation in the Central Ghetto (where most of the "wildcat" Jews sought by the Germans were living), and few responded to the German commands to descend to the courtyards for an inspection of papers. It should be pointed out, however, that the leaders of the *Judenrat* still felt obligated to respond to the Germans' dictates and even demanded that their subordinates follow their example. Shmuel Winter, who worked for the Supply Authority, noted in his diary that when the Germans arrived at the authority, respected businessman Abraham Gepner descended first and ordered his assistants to follow him.[5] In contrast to the first deportation, this time the Germans made no dispensation for men of position in the ghetto, and although some members of the *Judenrat* (including Gepner) were released from the *Umschlagplatz,* others (such as Milejkowski, Rosen, and Rozenstadt) were pushed into the freight cars along with the rest of the "catch."[6] Those isolated individuals, like Winter, who did not rely on their "immunity" by virtue of association with the *Judenrat* simply went into hiding.

Among those caught on the first day of the *Aktion* were many of the *palatzovka* workers who had not managed to disperse in time and people who were unaware that the *Aktion* had begun and were surprised on their way to work or inside their apartments before they could manage to hide. Yitzhak Giterman, the JDC director and moving spirit behind the Self-Help in the ghetto, was shot on January 18 while dashing from apartment to apartment in his housing block on Muranowska Street to warn the tenants of the *Aktion.* It was likewise on that first day of the operation that the patients were removed from the ghetto's hospital, which in its final days was located at 6 Gęsia Street.

Most of the residents of the ghetto, however, went into hiding. Stanisław Adler described his escape in January as follows:

> I was awakened from a deep sleep by loud banging on the door of my room. It was close to seven [and] still gray outside. For a long moment I wondered what could be happening. I sprang out of the bed and asked, "Who's there?" "Get up!" . . . "A blockade! Germans in the street! Where is the entrance to the shelter?" . . . We walked past the spot opposite the door leading into the courtyard, which was empty at the moment. Then we went down to the cellar and reached the camouflaged entrance . . . in the meantime some other people joined our group. I stood by the entrance and pushed the people in one by one. I was the last to enter.[7]

Under the title *"Aktion* 2," Yechiel Gorni, who was working in the O.B.W. "shop," kept a journal that was preserved in the second section of the Ringelblum Archive. His description of the first moments of the *Aktion* is as follows:

> The clock reads 5:45 in the morning. Today is January 18, 1943. I get dressed and prepare to go to the shop and, together with the entire group, to move on to 30 Leszno Street. I hear that it must be 6:30 because our

palatzovka, which is working in the court buildings on Leszno Street, is leaving the block. Suddenly a terrified neighbor bursts in: "How come you're still lying around in bed?" she shouts at the other tenants of our room. "The street is surrounded by gendarmes, the *palatzovkas* are not being allowed out of the ghetto, a blockade—it's definitely an *Aktion*." . . . The house dissolves into an uproar—we must hide, and we all crawl into the shelter.[8]

Despite their taking the ghetto by surprise and their indiscriminate roundup of people, the Germans met with far more difficulty than they had expected from their experience during the first deportation. Adler elaborates on this point: "Altogether, about 3,000 were caught on the first day of the *Aktion.* If we take into account the factor of surprise (which was well planned), the radical mode of operation, and the disregard for exemptions, the yield was essentially tiny. The Jewish population can thank the widespread system of hiding places for that result."[9]

The use of armed resistance was an innovation even more radical than the system of shelters. Great importance has been ascribed to the acts of resistance perpetrated on the first day of the January *Aktion,* for the phenomenon of Jews using weapons had a profound effect upon the Germans' conduct. Until that point, the Jews had proved to be passive prey. Thus when the Germans penetrated the ghetto in January, it never occurred to them that they might be up against armed men who were prepared to fight for their lives. That the German command had based the operation on complete surprise leads us to conclude that attempts to hide from the troops had been anticipated. But the structure of the units employed in the second *Aktion* clearly indicates that they were in no way prepared for active resistance, and certainly not for armed resistance. The moment a revolver appeared, the Jew became a human being who had to be reckoned with, and the Germans' scorn and extravagant self-confidence were instantly deflated. Trapped Jews were ordered to keep their hands raised above their heads. The Germans moved around with caution, their glances not only piercing but anxious, and they executed their task without the relish and enthusiasm that had marked their behavior during the initial penetration of the ghetto. In the wake of the gunfire and the losses suffered by the Germans on the first day of the *Aktion,* a striking change took place in their general mode of operation as well. The troops were careful to avoid encounters with armed resisters, and Winter recorded in his diary on January 20 that "thanks to the resistance, during today's *Aktion* there wasn't a single instance of the murderers seeking people out in cellars; they were simply afraid to go down [into them]."[10]

By the second day of the operation, the streets of the ghetto were deserted. On January 18 it had still been possible to trap people taken by surprise or to pull in those who willingly reported for inspection because they trusted the immunity provided by their papers or their places in the "shops" (like the workers from Alexander Landau's factory, who feared failure to report to work as usual would bring about the final liquidation of the "shop").[11] But by the second day of the *Aktion*, everyone had gone into hiding; even though the area of the "shops" was raided on the third and fourth days of the operation as well, those enterprises considered vital to the Germans were hardly affected by the raids. By the fourth day of the *Aktion*, the Germans were reduced to perpetrating a slaughter, shooting wildly and indulging in a frenzy of murder, and January 21 was considered the "Day of Retaliation" for the acts of resistance. It is estimated that during the four days of the January *Aktion*, about one thousand Jews were murdered in the streets of the ghetto.[12]

The hideouts proved to be effective primarily because once the Germans had encountered the demonstrations of resistance on the first day of the *Aktion*, they were afraid to enter them. The truth of the matter is that most of the hideouts used in January were only makeshift shelters. Had the Germans pursued their searches in cellars and attics — despite the danger that might be lurking for them there — they would have had little trouble uncovering the people hiding in them. Thus the success of the hideouts in January was to a large extent related to the armed clashes that occurred during the *Aktion*, although matters had not been planned that way and the causal relationship between the two was merely coincidental.

All in all, approximately 5,000 Jews were removed from the ghetto during the four-day *Aktion* in January (the statistics available on this subject have not been authenticated). An official German document gives the number as 6,500; many Jewish sources cite the figure of 6,500; and some give a total of 5,000.[13] The German estimate is probably deliberately inflated, as von Sammern evidently did not want to admit the failure of the operation, and the number of deportees was far from the quota established by Himmler. In any event, "*Aktion* 2" ended after four days without achieving its aims: the 8,000 Jews to be removed from the ghetto immediately were not rounded up. Even more important, the prospect that the Jews had envisaged with such dread — the final and total annihilation of the ghetto and the Jewish community of Warsaw — did not come to pass. One of the Polish underground newspapers reported that the Germans had filled only half the freight cars waiting to carry off the Jews rounded up during the *Aktion*.[14] Winter noted in his diary that in comparison with the situation during the summer of 1942 the cars left relatively empty, though he credits this fact to the Germans' sadism. During the summer, when the heat was oppressive, he wrote, the Jews were crammed into the cars without mercy, which only intensified the heat and the suffering. During the freezing days of winter, the cars were packed loosely so that the effect of the cold would be heightened inside.[15] Yet it is highly likely that in January it was not the Germans' sadism that decided the density in the freight cars but rather their desire to create an exaggerated impression of the number of Jews transported out of the ghetto.

The Resistance in January   The isolated and unorganized Jews of the ghetto were not the only ones to be caught off guard on January 18, 1943. Even the Jewish Fighting Organization did not expect an *Aktion* to begin on that day and was just as surprised as the rest of the ghetto. Berlinski noted that the command of the Ż.O.B. was scheduled to meet on January 17, and the agenda of the meeting included "approving the defense plan for the ghetto."[16] Paradoxically enough, the inability to convene the Ż.O.B.'s policy-making institutions not only failed to inhibit the acts of resistance in January but probably aided the fighters in their mission. Yitzhak Zuckerman explains this astonishing fact by informing us that a few days before the January *Aktion* began, the National Committee and the Coordination Committee were torn by disagreement over whether to adopt a militant response to the expected deportation, and "the debate was not resolved." He therefore believed that had there been time "to sound out the opinion of our political council, the January revolt in Warsaw would never have taken place." Under the circumstances, not only was it impossible to covene a large body for consultations, but even the various factions within the Ż.O.B. were unable to establish contact with one another. "The He-Halutz combat squads," wrote Zuckerman, "as well as those of Dror—which included members of Gordonia—and Ha-Shomer ha-Za'ir could not make contact with one another; but on the same day, at the same time, each one of them independently decided to fight."[17]

It appears that in January 1943, no decision had yet crystallized within the institutions of the Ż.O.B., and the proposal to initiate hostilities immediately upon the resumption of the *Aktion* still did not have unanimous support. Thus the armed resistance in January was a spontaneous response of individual groups that decided to give battle. Edelman's report states that the January resistance was joined by "only five groups out of the fifty that were prepared. The rest, which were not massed together, were surprised by the *Aktion* and did not manage to get to the arms caches."[18] This version of events gives us reason to believe that many groups (Edelman's reference being primarily to the Bund's combat squads) were not living together, and by the time they realized that the *Aktion* was in progress, it was already too late to assemble the fighters and arm them with weapons.

It therefore becomes evident that only a few of the Ż.O.B. groups fought in January, and these were primarily from the ranks of the movements that had established the original framework at the end of July 1942. Three prerequisites were necessary for self-defense in January: (1) the decision, in principle, to enter combat in response to a resumption of the *Aktion* (which was not agreed upon by all the members of the organization); (2) weapons (which, due to their scarcity, were allocated to only a few groups in the organization); and (3) the concentration or mobilization of the fighters in one place and in a high state of preparedness. Some of the Bund groups that may have had access to quantities of weapons, for example, did not take part in the battle because their members were scattered throughout the ghetto or their fighters and weapons caches were not located in the same place.

The primary battle in January took place in the streets. None of the Jewish participants survived the war, so that all our information on the fighting comes from people who witnessed it from a distance or heard about it from those who took part. The first group involved in the January fighting was a band of Ha-Shomer ha-Za'ir members commanded by Mordecai Anielewicz. Armed with pistols and hand grenades, the group attached itself to a long procession of Jews being led to the *Umschlagplatz*. The fighters dispersed along the length of this march, and each of its members singled out one of the soldiers guarding the line. At a given signal, the fighters sprang out of line and opened fire. A short battle followed, with a number of Germans killed and wounded, while others fled. It is therefore understandable that no account of the battle or the casualties can be found in any German source. Most of the Jewish fighters fell as well. Eliyahu Różański, who had assassinated Lejkin, fought with great valor in this incident, was seriously wounded, and died of his wounds. Margalit Landau, who was also involved in that assassination, likewise fell in this battle.[19] Anielewicz himself fought until his ammunition ran out, then snatched a gun out of the hands of a German soldier and was saved by the intervention of another quick-witted fighter. The remaining Jewish fighters tried to barricade themselves in a small house on Niska Street, but the Germans set fire to the building. Finally, the battle was decided only after German reinforcements had been brought in. Marek Edelman wrote of the incident: "The Ż.O.B. had its baptism by fire in the first substantial street battle on the corner of Miła and Zamenhofa. We lost the cream of our oganization there. The commander of the Ż.O.B., Mordecai

Anielewicz, was saved by a miracle and only thanks to the fortitude of [their] courage."[20] Berlinski described the battle in greater detail:

> Thursday, January 20. Today I am with the Ha-Shomer people again. Mordecai showed me the arms that were taken: a rifle and a Parabellum. The weapons and equipment were stripped off the Germans, and we already know how to use them. Mordecai reported on the battle that took place at the corner of Zamenhofa and Niska when he stood among a group of people who had been caught and took the initiative to open fire. Some of the SS men were killed or wounded; others fled, leaving their hats and even weapons behind. Then the Germans set flame to the house in which Mordecai and his squad were holed up.[21]

Another arena of the resistance struggle in January was inside the ghetto's buildings. The most impressive of these encounters took place at 58 Zamenhofa Street, where a battalion of Dror and Gordonia members, under the command of Yitzhak Zuckerman, was stationed. The accounts we have on this battle come from participants and witnesses alike. Zivia Lubetkin related that forty members of the battalion established themselves in makeshift "positions," and the entire quantity of arms they possessed was four revolvers and four grenades, plus clubs, steel pipes, and sulfuric acid.[22] Tuvia Borzykowski, who was a member of this group, described the course of the battle as follows:

> The door burst open and a group of Germans rushed into the room. The first to confront them were Zecharia Artstein and Hanoch Gutman, who had displayed supreme valor throughout that day. Zecharia sat still and pretended to be reading a book. When the Germans were about to enter the adjoining room, he shot them from behind. One man fell and the rest fled. Gutman and the other comrades with him rushed to the stairs and shot at the Germans outside. A second German tumbled down the stairs. Of our own comrades, Meir Finkelstein was badly wounded and was executed by the Germans the next day.[23]

Additional clashes inside buildings were led by Arie Wilner and Eliezer Geller in other sections of the Central Ghetto, while Yisrael Kanał, who commanded a group that had barricaded itself in the area of Schultz's "shop," shot at the Germans who turned up there on the third day of the *Aktion*.

We also possess reports about physical resistance on the part of unarmed combat groups and resistance displayed by individuals with weapons other than firearms. According to Marek Edelman, for example, an unarmed group of Bund members refused to board the train at the *Umschlagplatz*, and the SS commander, von Eupen, shot and killed sixty of the resisters.[24] On the other hand, we lack any authoritive information on organized resistance actions on the part of the Jewish Military Union (Ż.Z.W.) during the January deportation.

On the evening of January 19, all the groups that had participated in the previous day's skirmishes met at the Ha-Shomer ha-Za'ir headquarters at 61 Miła Street. Despite the Ż.O.B.'s heavy losses, the atmosphere at this meeting was far from despondent, for the events of January 18 had broken through a psychological barrier and dispelled the smothering sense of frustration that had plagued the youth of the underground for so long. Gone was the almost fatalistic sense of helplessness brought on by the conviction that it was impossible to inflict harm—even symbolically—on Germany's might and the manifestations of that power in and around the ghetto. And in its stead came accounts of fleeing Germans, dead Germans, and SS men who walked the streets of the ghetto with caution, fear, and shame. The baptism by fire on January 18 symbolized a break with the past for the Jewish fighters and fostered the yearning and hopes, perhaps no more than the fantasy, that potential had turned into reality.

At the January 19 meeting, the fighters decided to fortify their existing positions, refrain from frontal clashes with the Germans, and concentrate on acquiring arms while awaiting further developments. Thus no further clashes took place in the streets of the Central Ghetto, and operations were limited to attacks on individual soldiers roaming the area in order to strip them of their weapons.[25]

We do not know how many German soldiers were killed and wounded in the January fighting. Neither do we have accurate information on the number of Jewish fighters who were lost or the names of all the fallen. The Polish underground paper *Dzień* (*Day*) of January 29, 1943, described the course of the battle near the *Umschlagplatz* under the headline "How the Warsaw Ghetto Defended Itself." According to this description, the fighters held the street for about fifteen to twenty minutes. "The outcome of the battle: about 12 gendarmes and S.S. men dead and 10 (or more) wounded. The losses among the fighters—9. Three rifles and four revolvers were taken. All during the time, German ambulances drove back and forth between the ghetto and the German hospitals."[26]

The Jewish fighters also learned a good deal about combat tactics from the January battles, and the conclusions they were able to draw from this experience later guided the commanders of the Ż.O.B. in planning their course of action for the April uprising. The battle in the vicinity of the *Umschlagplatz,* led by Mordecai Anielewicz, had major repercussions within the ghetto and beyond it. For over and above permitting the dispersal of hundreds of people being marched to the *Umschlagplatz,* the open, head-on clash proclaimed the existence of an armed Jewish force that was ready and able to fight. Such open battle was costly, however, taking the lives of almost an entire group of select fighters. On the other hand, the partisan struggle within the buildings proved to be effective at the cost of relatively few lives. While the Germans lost much of their confidence in the dark, narrow hallways and the crowded apartments, where hidden dangers lurked for them, the fighters excelled at making their escape over rooftops and through familiar alleyways, far more successfully than in the open streets. Moreover, it was only in closed places that maximum use of the few close-range weapons in the fighters' possession could be made, by exploiting secret lairs and laying ambushes for the Germans.[27] Indeed, the experience gained in January convinced the Ż.O.B. to concentrate on the tactics of fighting in confined areas and from "positions" inside buildings, and the lull between the end of January and April 19, 1943, was used to develop and refine this strategy.

Another important lesson of the January fighting was the imperative of keeping mobilized units concentrated together and ready for action at any moment. The Ż.O.B. realized that an awareness of impending events did not rule out the possibility that the actual initiation of an *Aktion* might come as a surprise. It was now essential to plan for the possibility that an attack on the ghetto might start before the organization would have time to assemble its fighters from their various housing blocks, deal with the allocation of weapons, establish contact with the command, and so forth. The Ż.O.B. would therefore have to shift to a new deployment, based on a system of mobilized units stationed near the place slated to serve as a combat position and weapons store.

In addition to the important gains and the encouraging reversal in the mood of the fighters, the commanders of the Ż.O.B. were also conscious of the weaknesses that had been exposed by the January clashes. The shortage of weapons was now perceived as the most pernicious problem of all, for it left most of the fighters in a state of forced idleness. Also apparent was the need to improve the means of communication between the units and ensure the command's control over its forces. Furthermore, the fighters should not be massed together at any one focal point or area, since the destruction of such a concentrated force might lead to the downfall of Jewish resistance as a whole. It was therefore necessary to scatter the Ż.O.B. units around the ghetto and anchor the resistance in a defined and detailed program that would rule out the kind of impulsive outbursts and responses that characterized the resistance in January.

The Effect of the January Resistance on the Jewish Public

The events in January also engendered a change in the behavior of the Jews remaining in the ghetto and the "shops" and channeled many into a course of concrete action. As stated earlier, after the mass deportation in the summer of 1942, the mood of resistance and disobedience had already made inroads among the Jews of the ghetto. But even those who chided themselves for the passivity during the previous *Aktion* continued to believe that any demonstration of resistance—not to mention an armed struggle—would provoke a murderous German response of unprecedented portions.

From this perspective, the events of January provided the answer to a number of troubling questions—but it was hardly the expected one. First of all, the outcome of the January resistance was interpreted as something of a victory for the Jews. We must remember that Jews of the ghetto took it for granted that a renewal of the *Aktion* would mean the final and total liquidation of the ghetto. Thus the limitation of the operation to four days and the removal of only a few thousand Jews were interpreted as a German retreat and substantiation for the opinion that resistance—both passive (in the form of going into hiding) and active (actual armed fighting)—could repel the Germans. The Jews were not alone in their assessment, for various quarters in the Polish political underground also believed that the Nazis had been forced to halt the *Aktion* because of the resistance they encountered in the ghetto, and this is the way in which the effect of the January fighting was depicted in the Polish underground press.

The definitive change in the prevailing attitude of the ghetto's Jews was particularly noticeable in the writings attributed to Shmuel Winter, which were uncovered in the area of the ghetto after the war. After the first day of the *Aktion*, Winter complained:

> Rumors have reached me that Jews—[members of Ha-Shomer Ha-Za'ir] and [other] pioneering movements—put up a fight on Niska and Zamenhofa streets. They are idealists. What cause are these idealists serving? What evil will they bring down upon us? I believe that from the viewpoint of history, and for the sake of posterity, the work of the historical committee, "Oneg Shabbat," is more important than their Jewish war.

This judgment is followed by the factual comment: "Today 3,000 Jews were removed from the Warsaw ghetto." But on the following day, Winter changed his tone: "Combat groups went out to war again, at Miła 34. Today they took a thousand plus a few hundred more Jews. Blessed be those youngsters." And on the third day he noted: "A few hundred Jews were taken today. The Jews are hiding [and] the Germans are afraid to go into cellars and hideouts." Finally, on the fourth day of the *Aktion*, Winter was prepared to make an entirely new assessment of the resistance: "On the second day of the uprising, the Germans issued an order to abandon the ghetto and assemble together on two streets. The Germans retreated and left the ghetto. I believe that the war of the youngsters forced them to do that. . . ."²⁸

From the perspective of the turn of events within the ghetto, it is not really important whether the Germans halted the *Aktion* because of the unanticipated response from the Jews or because they had always intended to execute only a partial deportation this time. The German documents relating to this subject clearly indicate that the intention was to round up only a portion of the ghetto's Jews in January. But the Jews—who were not privy to authoritative information of any kind and had so often been deceived by the Germans—had learned to evaluate matters solely on the basis of empirical experience: the causes and effects they could perceive with their own eyes. It is therefore only natural that the daily decline in the number of deportees and the cessation of the *Aktion* after four days were taken as proof that the Germans had been confounded. Thus the use of force, as well as the broader concept of passive resistance, had scored a major achievement.

Those who drew a comparison between the conduct of the Jews during the first deportation and that in the January *Aktion* now came to the conclusion that the consistent obedience and lack of opposition to the Germans—and even to the Jewish Police—during the summer had been the downfall of the Jews and had actually broadened the scope of the tragedy. The fact was, they believed, that the number of Jews removed from the ghetto during the four days in January was approximately the average for a single day during the summer *Aktion*. Moreover, most of the January victims were trapped on the first day of the operation, when the effect of the assault had yet to reach its height and before the ghetto's definitive response had had time to crystallize. From the second day onward, the "yield" of the blockades was in steady decline, and the total number of Jews deported during the *Aktion* was a mere fraction of the figure reached during the earlier operation. Thus it was natural to conclude that had similar resistance been in evidence during the summer of 1942, the Germans would have been forced into an extended struggle to trap and deport the Jews, and it is doubtful whether they were prepared for such a difficult and troublesome operation. Yechiel Gorni noted in *"Aktion 2"*:

> Yesterday, on January 22, 1943, I overheard the following stated in a conversation: "If at the beginning of the deportation in July 1942, the Jews had been armed, had attempted to resist, and had killed a number of Ger-

mans and forced the Jewish hooligans [police] to refrain from taking an active role [in the operation], thousands would undoubtedly have been cut down by German bullets, and other Jews would have said: What happened is the fault of their foolish heroism. That such resistance would have slowed down the tempo of the *Aktion* would not have occurred to anyone. Today, when 6,000 Jewish Deportees [cost the lives of] 1,000 Jews and twelve Germans, the public has finally understood the heroism of the "foolish" youngsters." That's how a simple Jew put it in a conversation.[29]

In January the Ż.O.B. revealed its existence as a force devoted to striking back at the Germans and defending the ghetto. For the first time the Jews of Warsaw recognized the path chosen by the underground as an alternative to the policy espoused by the *Judenrat*, and the course of action chosen by the Ż.O.B. stood up to the test and proved itself convincing and effective. Dr. Leńsky, a physician in the ghetto, wrote in his memoirs:

> Unfurling the banner of revolt enhanced the underground's stature in the eyes of the remaining Jews. Many who did not even know that an underground existed now saw concrete proof of its deeds. They sensed that the ghetto has an organized force other than the community council [*Judenrat*]; a moral force that is fed up with the old methods which brought a holocaust down upon the Jews. This organization has chosen a new way of dealing with the Nazis. Hope was revived in the hearts of the doomed. Perhaps the Germans will really not expose their soldiers to danger and will stop sending them to execute operations because the Jews are prepared to resist. . . . [30]

Under the impact of the January resistance, Władysław Szlengel, a Polish-Jewish poet who was living in the area of the Brushmakers' "Shop" at the time, composed a poem called "Counterattack." The following is a translation of a few lines that reflect the feelings expressed by many following the January uprising:

> A gendarme bent over at the gate —
> Stared in astonishment, stood rigid a moment . . .
> Didn't believe —
> Something's awry here . . .
> Blood on Miła Street?
> The gendarme staggered back from the gate trembling
> And aghast: Yes, blood is dripping . . .
> And the guns are already blasting
> On Niska, Dzika, Pawia . . .
> These alleys of Dzika and Ostrowska
> Are like the partisans' forests —

> The block numbers bounce on our chests,
> Like precious ornaments since the War of the Jews,
> A six-lettered outcry is stained in red,
> Its blast like an explosion: Revolt. . . . [31]

It was Yitzhak Zuckerman's assessment that "the January revolt made the April revolt possible." Indeed, an analysis of the course of events leads to the conclusion that the January uprising was an indispensable step that allowed the ghetto to unite and prepare for the April revolt. The ghetto fighters emerged from their experience in January with the feeling that "it is possible to kill Germans and not die; Germans can be defeated."[32] The reluctance and disagreements that still plagued the political cadres united in and around the Ż.O.B. were overshadowed by the fighting in January. And above all, the impact of the January uprising forged a bond of courage between the fighters and the rest of the ghetto's population and a consciousness that rather than bring ruin down on the ghetto, resistance might be the only solution to the existing situation.

The Polish Attitude Toward the January Uprising

The January fighting also had an effect upon the Poles' attitude toward the Jews of the ghetto and particularly the Ż.O.B. Reports of the fighting in the ghetto spread quickly among the Poles and were inflated to fantastic proportions. "Tales of hundreds of German dead [and] the great strength of the Ż.O.B. spread throughout Warsaw," Edelman wrote in his report: "All of underground Poland is full of admiration for us."[33]

The Polish underground press devoted feature articles and commentary to the January uprising in the ghetto. In its January 28, 1943, issue, *Biuletyn Informacyjny*, the official organ of the A.K., followed a detailed description of the clashes with the comment that "the valor of those who have not lost their sense of honor during the saddest moments of Jewish history inspires admiration, and it is a glorious chapter in the history of Polish Jewry."[34] The P.P.R. paper, *Gwardzista*, wrote on February 5, 1943:

> Their *Aktion* is costing the Germans a heavy toll. . . . The population is resisting with desperate courage, using the few firearms and grenades they have plundered from the Germans together with boiling water, blunt instruments, hatchets, and the like. In besieged houses, the Jews pour kerosene or gasoline down the steps and set them aflame the moment the Germans enter. Groups of fighters hide out in deserted buildings and take the Germans by surprise. . . . The battles in the ghetto are the first

[demonstration of] defense of the Jewish population. The Jews have awoken from apathy in a demonstration of resistance worthy of emulation.[35]

At the conclusion of an extensive feature article devoted to the events in the ghetto in its issue of February 28, 1943, the organ of the Peasants' Party, *Przez Walkę do Zwycięstwa*, stated: "Contrary to expectations, the punitive campaign was followed by a temporary lull in which the blockades and deportations ceased. The general assumption was that the cause of the respite was related to the armed resistance put up by the Jews, which made a tremendous overall impression."[36]

One of the activists in the Polish underground, Wacław Zagórski, noted in his journal in January 1943: "The feeling is growing that the only form of self-defense likely to produce results is armed resistance and retaliation. For the first time, the Jews answered the attempt to resume the deportations to the gas chambers of Treblinka with bullets. After three days the Germans halted the *Aktion* and withdrew the police forces from the ghetto."[37]

Finally, the *Delegatura's* official "survey of the situation" during the period of January 1–February 15, 1943, reported on the overall effect of the resistance on the thinking of the Polish public at large:

> The attempt to wipe out the remaining population of the Warsaw ghetto on January 18, 1943, had profound repercussions. It was met by resistance; and whether [the cessation of the *Aktion*] was due to that resistance (fear that the psychosis of resistance would grip the Poles) or because the aims of the liquidation were [from the outset], limited, public opinion, at least, related this fact [the resistance] to the cessation of the alleged liquidation. . . . [38]

How the Germans responded to resistance and the appearance of an armed force was of primary interest to the Poles, since it might enable them to draw conclusions about the likely German reaction to their own eventual fielding of forces. The underground was also curious about the effect of the resistance operations on the Polish public and concerned about the fact that the struggle in the ghetto would engender ferment among the Poles and provoke the demand that armed action be initiated before the time was ripe—from the underground's point of view. Pressure to step up the underground's activities was related less to the notion of assisting the Jews than to the grievance of certain Polish circles—particularly the Communists—that while even the Jews in the ghetto dared to attack the Germans, the Poles and the A.K. contented themselves with minor operations and refused to initiate a formidable armed struggle. This pressure was to become a significant factor in the Poles' relations with the Ż.O.B. and in their readiness to aid the Jews by means of equipment, arms, and coordinated actions.

The Polish public at large, and the underground in particular, had expressed various feelings about the Jewish tragedy: in certain instances sympathy for the Jews, for the most part apathy and disinterest, and in a large number of cases undisguised anti-Semitism. But the events of January and the flood of exaggerated rumors about what had in fact happened inside the ghetto led to a shift in opinion and many expressions of support for the Jews. How is the phenomenon to be understood? It is impossible to believe that the change in mood was a product of astonishment or empathy with the Jews. The Poles had witnessed the long campaign of brutal persecution and the 1942 deportation without showing any inclination to revise their position or institute action. Yet the demonstration of resistance in the ghetto did have an impact upon them and aroused feelings of solidarity and understanding, not to mention its serving as an impetus to take concrete steps.

In his essays on Polish-Jewish relations, Ringelblum noted:

> Polish public opinion was intensely interested in the defense put up by the ghetto. The Underground Press spoke of the heroic attitude of the ghetto with great esteem. January 1943 was compared with July 1942, the passivity of the Warsaw Jews at that time was compared with the active stand they now took after their previous experience. All this, however, brought no change in the attitude of Government elements toward the defense problems of the Jews. In spite of constant appeals on the part of the Jews, arms were supplied only in very small quantities.[39]

It seems to me that Ringelblum's statement is too strong a generalization. It is true that after a short time the government quarters in the underground reverted to their original stand and, for various reasons, stopped providing aid to the Jewish fighters. But the immediate impact of the January uprising yielded concrete results in terms of providing arms and aid in training procedures. It is not by chance that Edelman noted in practically the same breath: "All of underground Poland felt great admiration for us. At the end of January we received fifty large revolvers and fifty grenades from the A.K. command."[40] This delivery, which was the most significant quantity of arms turned over to the Ż.O.B., came on the heels of the combat operations in January and was undoubtedly secured under the impact of the fighting.

The events of January left their mark first and foremost on the military branch of the underground by shattering the commonly held belief (which had served to justify Rowecki's claim that turning equipment and arms over to the Jews was a dubious venture) that the Jews would never fight. In January this allegation was firmly laid to rest.

Moreover, the officers and fighters in the underground were best able to appreciate the amount of effort invested in preparing the uprising and the courage required to act under the existing circumstances. This understanding moved the military underground to make a gesture toward the Jews; but for reasons that will be discussed later on, the willingness to extend active support was quite short-lived.

Chapter Twelve
The Remnant of the Ghetto
from January to April 1943

Changes in the
German Strategy

The interval between January 22 and April 19, 1943—a total of eighty-seven days—was a time of intensive and decisive consolidation for the resistance forces and reinforcement of the combat organizations in anticipation of the final uprising. Curiously enough, the German authorities adopted a moderate stance toward the ghetto during that period, and we are forced to ask ourselves why they opted for restraint following the demonstrations of resistance in January. Is it possible simply to assume that the striking change in the conduct of the Jews was responsible for this modification in German policy? Had it actually forced the Nazis to pursue a less stringent approach?

We have already seen that it is imperative to draw a distinction between the senior echelon of the SS—and particularly Himmler, who kept close tabs on the liquidation process in the ghetto and incessantly prodded his subordinates to execute his fanatic orders—and the operational cadres in the field, who were also subject to pressure from the local *Wehrmacht* authorities over the issue of vital Jewish manpower. Von Sammern, who was having difficulty maintaining control of the undermined security situation throughout Warsaw, naturally tried to keep word of the armed resistance from his superiors. His interests therefore lay in accomplishing the liquidation of the ghetto without resorting to force and provoking more armed clashes, which might further destabilize the area under his jurisdiction.

In order to understand developments in their broader context, as well as the trends that evolved during that period, we must return to survey the main phases in the development of German policy and examine the conflicting positions and contradictory arrangements that were finally arrived at for the Generalgouvernement and Warsaw in particular.

In the course of 1942, the Germans came to realize that the war in the east would be a long one, requiring them both to increase the mobilization of German troops and to heighten their efforts to provide armaments and equipment. One move in this direction, taken in March 1942, was to transfer jurisdiction of the concentration camps to the Management and Economic Authority of the SS. The purpose of this step was to modify the system of humiliating and depleting the strength of the prisoners sentenced to unproductive hard labor and begin exploiting this work force for the benefit of the Reich's war needs — though regarding the Jews of the Generalgouvernement, Himmler stood firm by his rigid policy of "total purification" ("*totale Bereinigung*").

During the second half of 1942 sharp disagreements began to arise between the *Wehrmacht*'s armament and supply authorities in the Generalgouvernement and the commanders of the SS regarding the elimination of Jewish manpower from the area. As a result, a rather paradoxical situation evolved. *Gauleiter* Fritz Sauckel, who was responsible for mobilizing foreign workers for the German economy, pressed for a rise in the quotas governing the transport of Polish slave laborers to Germany. According to official German statistics, in January 1941 there were 798,000 Polish workers in the Reich, and by the middle of 1942, an additional 800,000 Poles had been shipped out of the Generalgouvernement.[1] In light of this massive transfer of Polish workers to Germany, the *Wehrmacht* authorities intended to compensate for their needs within the Generalgouvernement by increasing the number of Jews they employed. Thus as early as May 1942, there was talk of replacing the Poles and Ukrainians employed in the *Wehrmacht* industries with 100,000 skilled Jewish workers. Just as the *Wehrmacht* officers were about to implement their plans, word arrived that Jews were being removed from their enterprises, and that in various places production had actually come to a complete halt. The *Wehrmacht* authorities complained that these indispensable Jewish workers were being extracted without prior warning and that no alternative work force was supplied to replace them. For example, the SS had informed the *Wehrmacht* of the mass deportation from Warsaw only three days before the *Aktion* began,[2] and during the deportation itself the *Kommandos* operating in the ghetto were oblivious to the objections and requests of the *Wehrmacht* representatives.

In July 1942, an agreement was reached between the *Rüstungs-inspektor* in the Generalgouvernement, General Schindler, and the area's *S.S.- und Polizeiführer*, Krieger,[3] whereby the armament factories would be entitled to a fixed and limited number of Jewish workers to be housed in barracks. The SS promised advance coordination of any further deportations from the ghettos, while the armament authorities committed themselves to replacing the Jewish workers gradually with Poles. This agreement was evidently not binding on the branches of the military command in the Generalgouvernement, which were also dependent upon Jews working in enterprises other than the armament factories and maintained both direct and indirect contact with workshops in the ghettos. At the same time, the SS commanders in various districts—and especially Globocnik—totally ignored the agreement, so that the friction was not resolved.

In August 1942 another agreement was reached, whereby the Jews employed in the armament factories would be isolated in a special ghetto. But on September 5, 1942, Field Marshal Keitel, the head of the O.K.W., issued a categorical order—evidently in response to pressures from Himmler—that all the Jews engaged in the production of armaments in the Generalgouvernement were to be replaced by Polish workers,[4] even though no Polish manpower was available to the Germans in that area. Testimony to this dilemma was the fact that on September 19, 1942, the director of the *Arbeitsamt* in Warsaw declared that he was unable to provide even a single Pole for the needs of the *Wehrmacht*.[5] In response to Keitel's order, on September 18, 1942, General C.L. von Gienanth, the commander of the *Wehrmacht* in the Generalgouvernement, sent a comprehensive memorandum to the General Staff, in which he argued that the unforseen removal of Jews led to "a decline in the military potential of the Reich."[6] As to the suggestion that Polish workers be used in place of the Jews, Gienanth stated that the realization of this plan depended upon the relinquishment of 140,000 Polish slave laborers slated for transport to the Reich.

On September 20-22, 1942, when a meeting of senior Nazi officials (including Hitler) took up the issue of labor, a severe confrontation developed between Himmler and Minister for Armaments and Munitions Albert Speer. Their differences centered on the question of prisoners of war and other detainees, but the subject of Jewish workers was also raised in the course of discussion. Fritz Sauckel, the Reich's plenipotentiary-general for manpower, suggested that, for the time being, the skilled Jewish work force be allowed to remain in the Generalgouvernement, and Hitler agreed to his proposal.[7]

Himmler was undoubtedly enraged by Gienanth's memo, but at the same time he could hardly ignore the Führer's will. In a secret directive issued on October 2, he ordered that all Jewish workers employed in factories supplying the needs of the army should be concentrated in camps in Warsaw and Lublin. Since he was prevented from consummating forthwith the total extermination of the Jews in the Generalgouvernement, Himmler decided to imprison the essential Jewish laborers in SS-run concentration camps and maintain the armament factories within the framework of these camps. Thus the new system of concentration camps was conceived as an interim solution to be applied only as long as it proved impossible to relinquish the Jewish workers without causing damage to the war effort. The difficulty that Himmler and his subordinates faced was how to transfer the Jews and the production equipment to these camps and resume work under new conditions without causing a delay in the production schedule, which would be detrimental to the army.

Himmler worked out a program whereby tailors and shoemakers would be concentrated in special camps and the *Wehrmacht* would route its orders through the SS, while the Jews working in armament factories (i.e., plants manufacturing weapons or vehicles) would be grouped together in a separate area of these plants in order to facilitate their removal from the production line in due course.[8] In the meantime, Gienanth had been dismissed from his post and was replaced by General Haenicke, who on October 10 received a second O.K.W. order to remove the Jews from factories producing armaments and support equipment for the army, and to have them replaced by "Aryan forces." Although this order could not be carried out immediately, it signified that *Wehrmacht* intervention in Jewish affairs had come to an end and responsibility for the entire matter — including workers in the *Wehrmacht* enterprises themselves — had been turned over to the SS.[9]

Against the background of these developments and Himmler's unequivocal orders, a new round of negotiations was held between Krieger and the *Wehrmacht* spokesmen in the Generalgouvernement during the latter half of October 1942.[10] The agreement they reached established that the Jewish workers would be subject to another *Selektion* in order to judge which of them were truly indispensable. Work camps set up by the *Wehrmacht* would be transferred to the supervision of the SS, and until these camps were established the Jews were to be kept in barracks in the immediate vicinity of their factories. Moreover, the owners of the plants would be responsible for maintaining the Jewish workers while simultaneously paying out a set fee to the district commanders of the SS in return for the Jewish laborers. The SS affirmed that Jews employed in the factories covered by the agreement would not be deported in the future, but, according to another one of the clauses in the pact, the fundamental principle that Jewish workers must gradually be withdrawn and eliminated from the production process remained in force.

Himmler's orders intimated that those who were attempting to preserve the Jewish work force were concerned not solely with the armament supply but rather with protecting Jewish interests as well — that is, trying to save the Jews doomed to annihilation.[11] Except for a few isolated cases, however, there is no basis to this suggestion that *Wehrmacht* representatives were concerned with aiding the Jews. But they were genuinely alarmed about the labor situation, and even Governor-General Frank, who was a vocal and enthusiastic supporter of the extermination program, complained at a December 9, 1942, meeting of the Generalgouvernement that "a significant work force" was being depleted with the liquidation of the Jews.[12] At one point, Krieger himself was forced to concede that he was aware of the situation and doubted that it was possible to keep up with Himmler's demands. According to the official protocol of a May 1943 meeting of senior members of the Generalgouvernement administration, which was compiled by Himmler's chief lieutenant, Hans Kaltenbrunner, and the head of the Reich Chancery, Hans Lammers, Krieger argued:

> Not long ago, [I] received a reiteration of the order to purify [the area] of Jews as quickly as possible. Jews must be removed even from the armament industry and weapons factories; only Jews serving the most urgent war needs are to remain. After that we placed [the Jews] in large camps, whence they go to the above-cited weapons factories every day. But the *Reichsführer-S.S.* [Himmler] demands that we cease to employ those Jews as well. [I] studied the matter thoroughly with Lieutenant-General Schindler and believe that, in spite of it all, the *Reichsführer*'s order cannot be fulfilled because the Jewish workers include experts, excellent machinists, and experienced artisans in various fields, and it is difficult to find appropriate replacements among the Poles. [I] therefore request that *S.S. Obergruppenführer* Kaltenbrunner explain the situation to the *Reichsführer-S.S.* and ask him to revise his decision concerning the Jewish work force.[13]

We have already noted that Himmler devoted special attention to Warsaw, as evidenced by his personal visit to the city on January 9, 1943. During this visit, Himmler met with *Oberst* Freter, the commander of the *Rüstungskommando* (Armament Command) in Warsaw. Freter wrote up a report on the meeting, which took place on January 9 and was also attended by von Sammern and Himmler's assistant, Wolff. According to Freter's document, Himmler claimed that he had come to Warsaw to confirm whether the Führer's order to liquidate the ghetto by the end of 1942 had been carried out. He discovered that there was indeed foundation to the reports that the ghetto still existed and contained as many as thirty-five thousand Jews, most of whom (twenty thousand) were employed by firms filling orders for the *Rüstung*. Freter was quick to explain that all the arrangements regulating the employment of Jews were in accordance with the agreement reached between Krieger and representatives of the *Rüstung*. But in response, Himmler ordered von Sammern to liquidate the Warsaw ghetto by February 14, 1943, and to transfer the remaining Jews to a concentration camp that the SS had prepared for them in the Lublin District. He also ordered that General Schindler be informed of his "astonishment that his instructions regarding the Jews have not been carried out." Himmler was referring to the fact that machinery had not been confiscated according to the plan suggested by Pohl and that the mode of life in the ghetto did not resemble that of a work camp. The ghetto's factories, which produced clothing, leather and wood products, and brushes, were in Himmler's view no more than "fictitious armament plants." Moreover, they were managed by their German owners with the aid of Jewish foremen and the *Werkschutz* (which was also composed primarily of Jews). Direct SS control over every detail—one of the primary features of a concentration camp—simply did not exist. Finally, Himmler discovered that Warsaw contained not only about six thousand Jews who worked directly for the *Wehrmacht* in *palatzovkas* outside the ghetto, but, most infuriating of all, thousands of people (his estimate was eight thousand) who were not regimented in any defined work battalion (meaning the "wildcats" who had escaped the blockades during the mass deportation). As noted in the previous chapter, von Sammern promised to remove these "illegals" from the ghetto without delay and transport them to death camps, which resulted in the abortive January *Aktion*.

At the same time, Himmler unleashed his wrath on the German businessmen who controlled the enterprises in the ghetto. Following his visit to Warsaw, he demanded that they be removed from their positions at once and be sent directly to the front, while a painstaking examination was to be made of Többens's accounts. In the continuation of his directives, Himmler reiterated his previous written instructions on the desirability of transferring the Jews to Lublin, where they could continue to fill the *Wehrmacht*'s requisitions. Jews who were working in genuine heavy industry should be concentrated together at some location in the Generalgouvernement and be put to work in sections of industrial plants set aside for them alone.[14]

On February 2 von Sammern wrote Himmler a confidential letter to report that the preparations for the resettlement of the ghetto's work force were proceeding well. Globocnik had begun preparing for the transfer of textile factories, and his plan was to be coordinated with the factory owners. This program affected not only the large firms, such as Többens and Schultz, but also six other enterprises. Taken together, the eight "shops" accounted for about twenty thousand Jews, and the transfer to Lublin was to begin on February 3.[15]

Despite these assurances, however, the flow of orders from Himmler regarding the total liquidation of Warsaw's Jewish community did not abate. On February 16, 1943, the *Reichsführer-S.S.* wrote to Pohl that he had issued instructions to establish a concentration camp (*Reichsbetrieb*) in the Warsaw ghetto, meaning that he had ordered the institution of a regimen modeled on a concentration camp. All the Jews were to be moved into the area of this so-called camp, and the private firms in the ghetto would be transferred to its jurisdiction, meaning to the control of the SS. The concentration camp—including both the enterprises and their workers—was to be transported *in toto* to Lublin and the vicinity as soon as possible. But the transfer had to be effected in a way that would avoid delays in production. It follows from Himmler's order that before this mass transfer to the Lublin camps took place, it would be necessary to classify the Jews by work categories.

On exactly the same day, February 16, Himmler sent Krieger a secret dispatch announcing that "for reasons of security" he was ordering the ghetto to be razed after the concentration camp had been transferred out. The concentration camp arrangements and the complete destruction of the ghetto were vital, Himmler believed, if quiet was to be imposed on Warsaw, for "the criminal disorder will never be rooted out as long as the ghetto remains standing. . . ."[16] It is not clear whether this decision to raze the ghetto was in response to the resistance that had emerged during the January deportation (meaning that Himmler knew about the Jewish opposition to the *Aktion*) or was related to a broader notion of constricting the size of Warsaw in an effort to reduce its importance. Yet the explicit stress on the fact that quiet would not be achieved as long as the ghetto remained intact indicates Himmler's belief that the ghetto was in and of itself a focus of security problems.

Himmler's flood of orders and attempts to spur his commanders on stood in sharp contrast to the reality of conditions in Warsaw. Clearly the *Reichsführer-S.S.* wanted to have his cake and eat it too, but the SS commanders in the field lacked the professional qualifications to operate factories producing clothing, shoes, furs, and so forth. Even more problematic was the fact that after revealing their true nature during the two deportations, the SS men in the ghetto could hardly be expected to win the Jews over with their new "image" as the supervisors of camps in which the resettled Jews of Warsaw would be put to work for the needs of the *Wehrmacht*. In light of the January resistance, it should have been clear that any such version of German intentions proffered by the SS would be interpreted as no more than another Nazi ruse to draw the Jews out of the ghetto and send them to their deaths.

Herein lay the essence of the intricate and self-contradictory problem faced by the local SS man. For example, Globocnik, who was renowned as the most zealous and sadistic practitioner of the "Final Solution" in the Generalgouvernement, was metamorphosed into the architect of the camps and production facilities in the Lublin area to be manned by Jews! He suddenly reappeared in Warsaw to open negotiations with the German "shop" owners on the "voluntary" evacuation of their enterprises to the Lublin area. Többens, who more than any other businessman in the ghetto had provoked Himmler's wrath, decided to throw in his lot with Globocnik and was rewarded with the appointment as "*Kommissar* of evacuation affairs" in the ghetto. (In his statements before a German court following the war, Többens claimed that Globocnik had "a constructive approach" and understood the businessmen—in contrast to von Sammern and particularly SS General Stroop, who replaced von Sammern as the *S.S.- und Polizeiführer* of the Warsaw District and whom Többens described as having destructive tendencies.) Yet it turned out that the other factory owners were not enthusiastic about the SS program and, like the Jews themselves, doubted the sincerity of the SS's intentions to establish factories and continue employing Jews. They were therefore reluctant to risk their property by moving it to the Lublin area. In the end, however, essentially for lack of choice, most of the businessmen gave in to SS pressure and coaxing by Többens and Schultz and agreed to the evacuation plan. Eight of the largest "shops" in the Warsaw ghetto were scheduled to be transferred to the Poniatow and Trawniki camps within a set period of time.[17]

In a parallel development, the leaders of the SS and Pohl, as the commander of Management and Economic Authority of the SS, were drawing up plans to establish a holding company that would employ the Jewish work force and exploit the remaining Jewish property to the advantage of the SS's economic power.[18] In January 1943 Pohl sent Dr. Max Horn and some of his aides to Warsaw and Lublin in order to study at firsthand ways to employ the property left behind by the Jewish victims of the "Final Solution" and to evaluate the prospects of extensive economic development under the aegis of the SS. Two months later the Osti (*S.S.-Ostindustrie GmbH*) Company was founded in Berlin, and its tasks were later defined as follows:

1. Exploiting the Jewish work force in the Generalgouvernement through the establishment of enterprises connected with Jewish work camps in the Generalgouvernement.

2. Integration of the economic enterprises managed by the office of the *S.S.- und Polizeiführer* in the Generalgouvernement.
3. Receipt of movable Jewish property, particularly machinery and raw materials. (The machinery was to be operated in the Osti firms, while the raw materials would be used in their production processes.)
4. Exploitation of machinery, tools, and goods that subsequently fell into "Aryan" hands.[19]

This outline clearly indicates that in the final analysis the SS decided to take advantage of the "new course"—an additional transition period allocated for the exploitation of skilled Jewish manpower—to advance its own economic aspirations. Thus the Osti—whose management included Pohl, Krieger, and von Sammern and whose actual directors were the "Engineer" Globocnik and Dr. Horn—would in the course of time have to (1) concentrate in its hands all the Jewish property that was directly confiscated by the SS or had found its way into the hands of the "shop" owners; (2) establish SS industrial enterprises to employ the Jewish work force as long as it could not be spared; and (3) once the Jewish laborers could be dispensed with and annihilated, continue to run these enterprises on the basis of an alternative work force. These plans were expressions of a trend that was provoked by Germany's military reversal on the eastern front and the general deterioration in the Reich's military standing. Clearly the SS intended to build up an independent military and economic instrument powerful enough to influence future political and military developments in the Third Reich.

On January 31, 1943, Globocnik signed a formal contract with Többens.[20] The first clause of this agreement stated that following Himmler's orders, as of February 1, 1943, the *S.S.- und Polizeiführer* of Lublin would assume control of all the armament factories in Warsaw that had been functioning on the basis of Jewish manpower. These enterprises would subsequently be transferred to camps in the Lublin area. At the same time, all the plants producing textiles and leatherwork would be moved to Poniatow, and ten thousand Jews would be added to the fifteen hundred already employed there. The official name of the Poniatow camp was given as "Poniatow Enterprises Inc. in the SS Work Camp at Poniatow." In the contract, Globocnik supposedly affirmed (on behalf of the SS) that the relocated factories would remain under the supervision of the *Rüstung* in the Warsaw area, while Többens (who would take care of the technical-professional management of the plants) would be granted exclusive responsibility for the production process. The other clauses of the agreement established the financial terms for exploiting the Jewish work force, building the camp, and so forth.

At the time this contract was signed, the SS was already determined to assume exclusive control of all the Jewish workers and Jewish
property by eliminating the German factory owners. Yet its representatives had no compunctions about brazenly lying when the contract was
signed—and it seemed to make no difference that the targets of their
deceit were Germans. Moreover, one of the clauses of the contract
stated that the arrangements agreed upon would bind the parties until
the end of the war. Yet the advantages of such a formal, signed agreement were obvious. The SS people needed a contract of this kind as
evidence of their intentions if they were to persuade the Jews to abandon the ghetto peaceably. The "shop" owners were needed to exercise
their influence and intercede among the Jews, as well as provide the
necessary professional expertise during the early stages of running the
plants in the Lublin area. Moreover, the negotiations with the "shop"
owners also served to reassure the *Rüstung* officers, who would otherwise have created formidable obstacles to the SS plans for dealing with
the Jews.

Walter C. Többens, who had made a considerable fortune—first by
purchasing Jewish property in Germany for ridiculous prices and then,
during the war, by engaging in business in the Generalgouvernement
and owning the largest "shop" in the Warsaw ghetto—was, for his part,
willing to sign the contract and to enter into relations with the SS. It
was the only way he could retain his hold on the Jewish property he had
expropriated and extend the time available to realize profits from it. He
assumed that even if the SS commitments could not be taken seriously,
the fact that he had become an official partner in the SS enterprise and
was helping to implement the plan for the ghetto would work to his
advantage and be a profitable venture. He therefore approached his
task of winning over the Jews and effecting the gradual evacuation of
the firms with great energy. At a meeting of Jews who participated in
the management of the "shops," Többens described the work camps as a
means of salvation—a place where the workers and their families could
live in secure and comfortable conditions. He even offered his personal
guarantee that no harm would befall the Jews in their new quarters.[21]

On February 16 the first transport of Jews left for the Trawniki
camp, and on February 23, 850 Jews left the Warsaw ghetto for
Poniatow. Többens dispatched some of the Jews responsible for production in his plant to accompany the machinery to the camps going up
in the Lublin area. When they returned to the ghetto, they readily testified that plants and housing quarters were indeed being prepared for
the arrival of workers.[22]

Yet despite all efforts to calm the Jews living in the area of the
"shops" and cajole them into cooperation, only a relatively small
number stepped forward voluntarily. Most of the "shop" workers, and

even a greater proportion of the Jews living in the Central Ghetto, rejected the credibility of such tempting assurances and firmly refused to leave. Moreover, in a daring move that left no room for misunderstanding, the Ż.O.B. set fire to the factories that were slated to be evacuated first. When Többens reached the conclusion that the Jews were strongly influenced by the fighting organization, he decided to try to compete with the Ż.O.B. Yitzhak Zuckerman stated in his comprehensive report on the organization's activities that on March 14, 1943, the Ż.O.B. put up wall posters "that called for opposition to the Germans' orders, stressing that the 'voluntary relocation' means nothing more than the complete annihilation of the ghetto. On March 20, Többens pasted up his appeals alongside ours, but most of them were confiscated by the Jewish Fighting Organization [as soon as] it discovered [them]."[23]

Többens's appeal read as follows:

To the Jewish *Rüstung* workers in the Jewish residential quarter!

On the night of March 14–15, the *Kommando* of the Jewish Fighting Organization put up posters to which I would like to reply:

1. There was never any intention of executing an evacuation operation (*Aussiedlungsaktion*).
2. Neither Mr. Schultz nor I was forced at gunpoint to carry out the *Aktion*.
3. I hereby affirm that the [Jews in the] last transport were not killed.

It is unfortunate that the armament workers in Schultz's plant did not listen to his well-intended advice. I personally regret that, because I was forced to intervene and had to transfer one of the workshops in order to take advantage of the available transport facilities.

An order has been given to take down the names of the workers who reach Trawniki immediately upon their arrival, and all the baggage will be sent after them. . . .

In Trawniki and Poniatow, each worker received all his baggage and property for his personal disposal.

Jewish armament workers! Do not believe those who are trying to mislead you. They want to incite you so that they can force [upon you] the consequences that will inevitably ensue.

The "shelters" offer no security whatsoever, and life in them is intolerable. The same is true on the "Aryan" side. Doubt alone will consume the armament laborers who are accustomed to working. I ask you: Why are wealthy Jews coming to me, from the "Aryan" side, of their own accord, and asking to be among those shipped out [to Trawiniki]? They have enough money to keep them going on the "Aryan" side, but they couldn't bear it.

With a clear conscience, I can only advise you again: Go to Trawniki, go to Poniatow, for you have a chance to live there; you can sit out the war there! The *Kommando* of the Fighting Organization does you no good, and its promises are meaningless. They will sell you a place in a bunker for a huge sum of money and then throw you out onto the street and abandon you to your fate. You have had enough experience with the symptoms of deception:

Place your faith solely on the heads of the German firms who, together with you, want to transfer the production to Poniatow and Trawniki.

Take your wives and children with you, for they will also be looked after.

Walter C. Többens
Supervisor of the Evacuation of Firms
from the Jewish Quarter of Warsaw

Warsaw, March 20, 1943[24]

As noted above, despite the fact that his appeals were original and were phrased in congenial terms, Többens's efforts at intervention were not very effective, and only a few of the "shop" workers responded to his call to transfer voluntarily to the camps in the Lublin area.[25] Többens was telling the truth about the transports: they were not sent to death camps, and special facilities did indeed exist to integrate the factories. But the resistance and suspicion of the Jews were so strong by then that even the most sophisticated tactics could not overcome them.

The attempt to transfer equipment, raw materials, and workers from the ghetto to Lublin in a gradual, calm, and orderly fashion was thwarted. The Germans attempted to drive a wedge between the relatively few Jews who worked in the munitions field and the rest of the inhabitants of the ghetto, and their unmistakable intention was to follow the evacuation of the factories with an *Aktion* to liquidate the ghetto completely. But the "shop" workers refused to believe in the Nazis' contentions, while the Ż.O.B. resistance operations continued. The SS, which had given Többens and his partners a limited amount of time to prove the effectiveness of their intercession, evidently despaired of winning the ghetto over by persuasion and thus preserving the abandoned Jewish property for its own purposes. Testimony to the extent of their final exasperation came in the form of the assault on the ghetto on April 19, 1943, which was met by a general uprising. It was in anticipation of that final *Aktion* that the irresolute von Sammern was replaced by General Jürgen Stroop, a man with a reputation for being unrelenting and thoroughly experienced in operations against civilian populations.

Chapter Thirteen
The Jewish Fighting Organization Prepares for the Revolt

The Ż.O.B. after January The January trial—the Ż.O.B.'s first serious baptism by fire—initiated a new period of organization and heightened readiness. Two consequences of the January fighting served to strengthen the combat organization. First, there was no longer any doubt among political elements in the ghetto that combat was the proper response. Second, the January fighting had enhanced the status of the Ż.O.B.'s commanders and officers, particularly that of Mordecai Anielewicz, who from then on was the leader of the organization not only by virtue of the internal vote of its membership but also because he had proven his ability to make decisions at critical moments and his personal courage in face-to-face combat.

As noted earlier, however, the incidents in January also highlighted the weak points of the Ż.O.B., namely that the combat squads were not prepared for battle and that the organization could not count upon being warned that an *Aktion* was to begin, which would otherwise allow a certain breathing space for deployment. The Ż.O.B. therefore concluded that its forces must remain mobilized and on an alert footing at all times. Another weakness that stood out in January and heightened the fighters' sense of bitterness and frustration was the severe shortage of weapons. It was impossible to maintain a fighting organization comprising various bodies if the limited number of members who were armed all belonged to specific factions of the broader framework. Future success would depend upon the acquisition of weapons and the arming of all factions within the organization. In addition, the meager

336

quantity of revolvers and grenades allowed for only sporadic attacks that were primarily of a demonstrative nature but could not serve as the basis for a more comprehensive combat strategy. We must also keep in mind that the Jewish attacks in January 1943 had taken the Germans completely by surprise, but the enemy had now been put on notice that an armed organization existed in the ghetto, so that the next confrontation would be under far more trying circumstances. Another important lesson of the January clashes was that Jews armed with small revolvers—not all of which could be relied upon to fire properly—could not pit themselves in open battle against trained German soldiers carrying automatic weapons. It was therefore necessary to devise a set of tactics that would exploit the advantages held by the irregulars: high mobility and familiarity with the territory of the ghetto, which was filled with places to hide in. Instead of an open battle, it was preferable to embark upon a partisan struggle whereby the Jews would set themselves up in fortified positions inside buildings and launch surprise attacks on easy targets while retaining the ability to retreat to other positions without exposing themselves to the enemy.

After January 1943 the Ż.O.B. underwent a rapid process of unification and reorganization. Until then it had been a loose federation of various factions and bodies that were unwilling to relinquish their independence and subject themselves to the unquestioned authority of a single, central body. Tuvia Borzykowski explained in his memoirs that before January, "Formally speaking, all the movements that constituted the National Committee or the Coordination Committee belonged to it [the Ż.O.B.], but in reality there were no combat groups other than those belonging to Dror and Ha-Shomer ha-Za'ir."[1] After January, things changed.

It is true that the Ż.O.B. continued to be made up of squads of fighters grouped according to their movement affiliation, but after January their political or philosophical differences no longer divided them or disrupted the functioning of the organization. Yitzhak Zuckerman explained the logic of the structure based on movements and parties at this late stage of the organization's evolution:

> . . . People asked: Why have this division? What role does movement affiliation play in a fighting organization? We answered: The Jewish Fighting Organization must be composed of combat units in which the ties between members are strong and mutual trust is abundant. We believed that people who had been educated together throughout the war, lived together, and knew each other well would fight more effectively. Perhaps, if we had been preparing this organization for years, we would have structured it along other lines. We might have changed or arranged the makeup of the various units on the basis of different principles. But we knew that

the time available for preparations was short. We knew that if the groups were not loyal to their commanders, and vice versa, they would not fight. We viewed the division along movement lines as a great military advantage. It was for that reason that we founded the organization on a movement basis. This does not mean that all the units were completely homogeneous. . . . We tried to keep members of the Bund together on the assumption that the commander of the Bund would best understand the mentality of his comrades. We also assumed that a commander would be the best judge of his fighters and their strength, of where and how to deploy his men, and of whom to charge [with any specific mission] if he were a member of the same movement. That is why we chose to structure the fighting organization on a movement basis.[2]

We may therefore conclude that it was not the particularistic interests of the various movements or an attempt to perpetuate their cohesiveness that determined the division of the various units along political lines. Even if we assume that the ties of friendship and political partisanship helped to maintain the structure of the individual movements, the leaders of the Ż.O.B. were able to exploit the camaraderie and trust that had developed within the individual frameworks during the course of underground activity to strengthen the cohesion of the larger organization. The movement-based divisions were not hard and fast during the final stage of the organization's development, and most of the squads made up of members of a particular movement also contained individuals from other factions or people who were not affiliated with any movement whatsoever.

Within the new organizational framework, the ghetto was divided into three major combat sectors: (1) the Central Ghetto, under the command of Yisrael Kanał—nine combat units; (2) the "shop" sector (Többens-Schultz), under the command of Yitzhak Zuckerman (replaced close to the start of the revolt by Eliezer Geller)—eight combat units; and (3) the Brushmakers' Area, under the command of Marek Edelman—five combat units. The Ż.O.B. command, which was located in the Central Ghetto, convened to determine the organization's policy, formulate operational defense strategy, and supervise the preparation of the fighting forces. It succeeded in maintaining regular contact with the forces in the Central Ghetto and Brushmakers' Area, but it was far more difficult to maintain contact with the separate "shop" sectors. Decisions of the command were transmitted through the area commanders, who often convened the heads of their squads for consultations and assessments of the situation.

The Ż.O.B.'s overall combat format consisted of twenty-two units, each having from twelve to twenty members. The squads were permanently deployed in residential buildings near their combat positions. This deployment and confinement of the forces was instituted after the

January experience, and from then on only mobilized units were rated as combat squads. Edelman reported that after January, "The fighting forces lived near the operational positions. The method of deployment was designed to prevent a recurrence of being caught off guard when the Germans initiated an *Aktion*, as well as to accustom the people to the spirit of military discipline and constant contact with [their] weapons." Of the twenty-two fighting units, five belonged to the united Dror He-Halutz movement (commanders: Z. Artstein, Y. Blaustein, B. Braudo, H. Gutman, B. Wald); four belonged to Ha-Shomer ha-Za'ir (commanders: M. Growas, S. Winogron, D. Nowodworski, J. Farber); four to the Bund (commanders: J. Blones, L. Gruzalc, D. Hochberg, W. Rozowski); four to the P.P.R.–Communists (commanders: A. Bryskin, J. Grynszpan, H. Zylberberg, H. Kawe); one to Gordonia (commander: J. Fajgenblat); one to Akiva (commander: L. Rotblat); one to Ha-No'ar ha-Ziyyoni (commander: Y. Praszker); one to Po'alei Zion Z.S. (commander: M. Majerowicz); one to Left Po'alei Zion (commander: H. Berlinski).[3]

Most of the members of the combat squads were young—under twenty up to twenty-five. The lifestyle maintained within the squads was based on past ties and the shared experience during the short period of active combat. In their thoughts and conversations, the fighters would turn to memories of the past, or they engaged in reading as an alternate pastime, but their dress, manner of speech, and patterns of behavior were strongly influenced by their new mission and way of life. The operation they had carried out left them with a sense of emotional reawakening, strong impressions, and a desire to share their feelings. A fixed part of every day was devoted to weapons drill. When the doctrine of personal weapons went into effect, the fighters devoted a great deal of time to caring for their personal arms, endlessly dismantling and reconstructing them. The provisions allocated to the units were modest. In the morning and evening, the fighters ate bread with jam and tea sweetened with saccharin. Following the January fighting the Ż.O.B. managed to acquire large sums of money, but the funds acquired or expropriated for armaments were spent almost exclusively on weapons, while the financing of other basic needs was kept to a minimum. The squads were confined to their own quarters and leave to visit their families could only be granted by the commanding officer. Groups situated in close proximity to one another (like those of Zecharia Artstein and Mordecai Growas at 33 and 35 Nalewki Street) would arrange meetings and reciprocal visits. In general, however, the members of each squad were acquainted only with their own commanding officer and knew very little of what was happening in other squads or at the command headquarters.

The day-to-day life of the fighters was not marked by an atmosphere of depression or resignation to their inexorable fate. Execution of the standard tasks and preparations for battle made for a climate of enthusiasm and strong identification with their cause. Though none deceived himself about the outcome of the forthcoming battle, the subject was rarely discussed. The fighters did not wallow in self-pity and sometimes even spoke about their end with a hint of black humor. It was as if the challenge had consumed the man, and he preferred to extract whatever he could from the experience while keeping personal thoughts and fears to himself.

The Ż.O.B.'s activities from January to April focused on a number of clearly defined areas: (1) "purging" the ghetto of dangerous collaborators; (2) obtaining money to purchase arms and cultivating contacts toward that same end; (3) planning the battle and preparing the fighters for combat. It is a sobering fact that during the period under discussion the Ż.O.B. was not especially involved in preparing its own shelters or in attempts to save individuals. Its leaders turned down requests to allocate some of the organization's financial resources to securing hiding places on the "Aryan" side of the city for some of the community's prominent public figures.[4] It was not that the organization denigrated the need to rescue individuals, but it simply viewed its task as first and foremost to prepare for the armed defense of the ghetto and fielding the largest Jewish force possible when the time came to act. The Ż.O.B.'s exclusive concentration on combat needs also stemmed from the fear that any digression from the military goal might arouse false hopes that despite everything, there was still a chance that the fighters might survive. In a meeting with friends after his arrival in Palestine, Yitzhak Zuckerman explained:

> If I had to assess our errors and the things we did right, I would have to say: I am almost positive that we could have gotten many more fighters out of the ghetto. But we were afraid to leave so much as a crack open for retreat. Our fear was that we might arouse the notion that a man could save his life even if he did not fight. It was for that reason alone that we did not prepare any "safe houses" on the "Aryan" side or cars or people who could serve as guides through the sewers. . . . We saw ourselves as a Jewish underground whose fate was a tragic one, as an underground that was not part of the overall war of undergrounds the world over and would have to stand cut off and alone; as a pioneer force not only from the Jewish standpoint but also from the standpoint of the entire embattled world—the first to fight. For our hour had come without any sign of hope or rescue.[5]

The reluctance and failures of the past demanded fanatic devotion to these principles. Indeed, the desire to fight, to enter into and stand up in battle against the Germans became an absolute goal. It was for this reason that the fighters did not prepare bunkers for themselves in the ghetto, did not concern themselves with the question of the destination of their retreat after the battle or prepare tunnels or map out routes through the sewers. As Mordecai Anielewicz wrote in a letter during the uprising, the battle itself was like "a last desire in life."[6]

The first attacks—on Szeryński and Lejkin—were reprisals against men who had served the Germans and inflicted heavy injury on the Jews. After the mass deportation, however, as we have seen, the status of the Jewish Police and the *Judenrat* declined, and it was the informers—Jews who maintained contact with the various branches of the German police—who posed the greatest threat to the Ż.O.B. and the broader resistance movement. Though their number was few—no more than a few dozen—they had the potential to cause tremendous damage.[7] Once the ghetto became a hotbed of illegal activity and prepared for resistance, it became imperative to intensify the sense of mutual trust and eliminate anyone who might divulge the secrets of the resistance. The Ż.O.B.—or, more precisely, the various fighting organizations that existed in the ghetto at the time—struck a mortal blow to these German agents. But their efforts to "clear the air" in the ghetto did not end there. The Ż.O.B.'s goal was to impose its authority over the entire ghetto, so that even if the Germans again intervened in ghetto affairs, the Jewish Police or the *Judenrat* would be incapable of acting in any way that might undermine or thwart the resistance and the armed struggle. The Ż.O.B. wanted it to be clear to every Jew that there was no need to fear the Jewish Police or the *Judenrat*, for they no longer ruled the ghetto.

While living on the "Aryan" side, Ringelblum drew up a "list of people who had been shot to death by order of the Jewish Fighting Organization."[8] This list included a dozen names, and it is doubtful whether it is complete. The figure who evinces the most interest is Dr. Alfred Nossig, who was about eighty years old when he met his tragic end. Nossig was a talented and colorful personality who in his long life had known many radical turnabouts and varied careers as an author, journalist, sculptor, and politician. In his youth he had been associated with assimilationist circles in Galicia. Then he became active in the Zionist movement, subsequently abandoned Zionism, and tried to organize a general association to foster emigration to various parts of the Ottoman Empire—and not necessarily to Palestine. Throughout his organizational and political career, Nossig showed a pronounced bent toward Germany and made a point of demonstrating his identification with German culture. He had lived in Berlin for many years and in the 1920s turned up in Poland, evidently at the invitation of the Polish government, and tried to act as a mediator between the government and the Jewish community in improving the relations between the two parties. Before the outbreak of World War II he returned to Warsaw as a refugee and later became a member of the *Judenrat* on the express order of the SS. As Adam Czerniakow noted in his diary: "I was ordered to accept Dr. Nossig as a member of the *kehillah.*"⁹ From the subsequent entries in Czerniakow's journal, it appears that Nossig kept up special ties with the Germans and enjoyed their patronage. A woman who lived in the same house as Nossig during the last months of the ghetto's existence and was not a member of the underground or the fighting organization wrote in her memoirs: "It was no secret that he belonged to the Gestapo and worked for the Germans," and his association with the Germans was even proclaimed on his front door. Evidently Nossig wrote periodic reports on what was happening in the ghetto. Some of the documents in his possession were confiscated by the Ż.O.B., while the rest were seized by the Gestapo.¹⁰

The Ż.O.B. succeeded in dominating the *Judenrat* and forced the council to follow its orders. It also extracted a quarter of a million zlotys from the *Judenrat* for the purchase of weapons. When the chairman of the *Judenrat*, Marc Lichtenbaum, was threatened that his son would be killed if the money was not paid, the cash was turned over to the Ż.O.B. in three days and the members of the council merely asked that among the reasons given for the payment, the clause reading "a penalty imposed as punishment for services to the Germans" be deleted. Zuckerman commented:

> That was how we overpowered the *Judenrat*. . . . It got to the point where Marc Lichtenbaum did not know whether he should fear the Germans or the Ż.O.B., and he preferred to live in peace with the Ż.O.B. When the Germans approached him and said: "Speak to the Jewish workers [and] organize a quite exit from the ghetto," he replied: "I am not the authority in the ghetto. There is another authority — the Jewish Fighting Organization."¹¹

This is not to say that the *Judenrat* did not try to undermine the hegemony of the Ż.O.B. or damage its most vulnerable relationships. Alfred Sztolcman, who was the strong man in the last incarnation of the *Judenrat*, got through to the institutions of the official Polish underground and complained through an intermediary that the members of the Ż.O.B. were a separatist group that cast terror over the population of the ghetto but did not enjoy the public's support. Woliński relayed news of Sztolcman's contact with the Polish underground back to the Ż.O.B. The Poles did not take the invective of a member of the *Judenrat* seriously, however, and Sztolcman's appeal did not affect the relations between the Polish underground and the Jewish Fighting Organization. Although the Ż.O.B. had decided to retaliate against Sztolcman, the April uprising prevented it from carrying out its resolve.[12]

The Jews of the ghetto now recognized the Ż.O.B.'s authority, sought means to get through to its various bodies, and "turned to [it] in all kinds of matters." The Germans were also well aware that an armed force had established itself within the ghetto and enjoyed growing influence and control over all its affairs, but they did not revise their strategy until the actual outbreak of the uprising. They were determined to remove the Jews, the machinery, and the raw materials from the ghetto—either by persuasion or by deceit—and to avoid intervening in internal Jewish affairs. As we shall see, however, when the casualties were Germans, they responded with a massive counterblow. According to Zuckerman:

> After we "cleared the air" in the ghetto, we knew that a member of the Jewish Fighting Organization could walk around the ghetto safely. From January to April the Germans were forced to walk in numbers. While the fighters of the organization could walk alone, the Germans who had to pass through the ghetto would go in groups or units. You would never see them toward evening. They called the ghetto "Mexico." There was no longer a curfew in the ghetto, and we did not have to be in our homes by eight at night, which had been the rule throughout our life under Nazi domination.[13]

The primary concern of the Ż.O.B. was to arm its forces. As a result of the January resistance, there was a temporary change in the attitude of the Polish underground, and the A.K. sent the Ż.O.B. a shipment of arms that included 49 revolvers, 50 hand grenades, and about 9 pounds of explosives. This shipment was in the nature of a goodwill gesture following the January rebellion. Contact with the Polish armed forces continued, and another, smaller quantity of arms—as well as other types of aid—was obtained from them at a later date. As a rule, however, the Ż.O.B. did not receive substantial aid from this source.

The opportunity to purchase arms grew with the rise in the number of German and allied soldiers passing through Warsaw on their return from the eastern front or visiting the city on short leaves. After the severe setback on the eastern front, they were desperate for cash and even went so far as to sell their weapons. Certain quantities of arms were also purchased from Poles who had owned them since the outbreak of the war or had "liberated" them from ammunition dumps (or armament factories) in the Warsaw area. The weapon most commonly offered for sale was the revolver, which could likewise be smuggled into the ghetto with relative ease. Yet even revolvers were very expensive items, and the cost steadily rose with the incessantly growing demand. The price of a revolver ran between 5,000 and 12,000 zlotys, depending on the caliber and condition of the weapon.

Since the purchase of weapons required substantial sums of money, obtaining such funds became the main challenge facing the Ż.O.B. and its supporters. A certain amount was raised as voluntary donations, but most of the money was extracted under duress. The Ż.O.B. imposed high payment quotas on people who had accumulated their fortunes during the war. For the most part, it stood by its demands forcefully, since the money was slated for the most important cause of all—as the fighters saw it—and were it not for the weapons in the ghetto, all the money and property held by the Jews would at any rate soon fall into German hands. The Ż.O.B.'s supporters engaged in fund-raising, and Shmuel Winter, for example, wrote in his diary that he transferred "Mławski's 5,000 to Mordecai [Anielewicz]."[14] Large sums were collected from the Supply Authority of the *Judenrat* (710,000 zlotys) and from the above-mentioned Mławski family, which dealt in the distribution of food rations to the grocery stores on behalf of the Supply Authority. Compulsory levies—called "Exxes" ("Expropriations")—were sometimes collected in combat-like operations, whereby a group of fighters would take over a building and demand that the tax be paid on the spot. The Ż.O.B. even maintained improvised prisons where the relatives of those who refused to pay could be held until the account had been settled. Edelman noted in his memoirs that in the space of three months, the Ż.O.B. obtained 10 million zlotys.[15]

With the outbreak of the revolt, the armament campaign came to an end and every fighter had been equipped with personal weapons—a revolver with small amounts of ammunition and some hand grenades. The Ż.O.B. had only about ten rifles, so that it was impossible to arm every combat squad with one. Some of these rifles were obtained in armed clashes within the ghetto and some by other means. In the course of time, rifles were offered for sale by various suppliers, primarily Poles, and their price ran from 20,000 to 25,000 zlotys. Yet since the transfer of rifles into the ghetto was especially difficult, the fighters were not able to build up any significant arsenal before the uprising. One group stationed in the Central Ghetto had a submachine gun that had been looted from the Germans. In addition, the Ż.O.B. delegation on the "Aryan" side of the city was active in the purchase and transfer of weapons. Alongside Arie Wilner were Michael Klepfisz, Tosia Altman, Tuvia Szajngut ("Tadek"), Zalman Friedrich ("Zygmunt"), Regina Fuden ("Lilit"), Feigel Peltel ("Władka"), and others. For the most part, the arms purchased on the "Aryan" side were smuggled into the ghetto through the walls.

The local manufacture of weapons (following formulas obtained from the Poles) also contributed substantially to the arming of the Ż.O.B. Michael Klepfisz received special training in a course run by the military section of the P.P.S., and a group of Jews was trained in the use of explosives by the A.K.[16] Once a larger quantity of explosives had been smuggled into the ghetto with the aid of the Poles, the manufacture of incendiary bombs began in special arms workshops. These bombs, which served as a substitute for hand grenades, were put together in a very primitive fashion, but they were adequate for the task and were used very effectively in the April revolt.

As noted earlier, the Ż.O.B.'s struggle against the Germans' objectives called for preventing the evacuation of the "shop" workers to camps in the Lublin area and thwarting the removal of equipment and raw materials from the ghetto. According to Zuckerman, the organization's leadership was well aware of the Nazis' intentions, even when "the respected German factory owner, Többens, came to the ghetto instead of the Gestapo and a civilian came instead of the police. . . ." Although the Ż.O.B. command assumed that the Jews would be granted a stay of a few more months in the camps, it was painfully clear that they were doomed to annihilation in Poniatow and Trawniki as well. The dilemma confronting the organization was whether it had the right to deny the Jews an opportunity to extend their lives for a few more months or the duty to persuade them not to leave and to prevent others from leaving the ghetto. According to Zuckerman, it was obvious that any chance of resistance or rebellion in Poniatow and Trawniki was entirely ruled out, while "the Jews in the Warsaw ghetto were able to revolt." Actually, Többens had also understood the thinking of the Ż.O.B. leadership when he wrote his proclamation (quoted in chapter 12) that the fighters were trying to thwart the evacuation because the removal of the Jews from the ghetto would destroy their basis for action. The members of the Ż.O.B. decided that they were justified in taking steps to prevent the evacuation to the Lublin camps because it did not provide any hope of salvation, while thwarting the evacuation was an essential prerequisite for the revolt. Zuckerman maintains that Többens's proclamation did exactly the opposite of what it was meant to accomplish. The Jews came away with the impression that if Többens found it necessary to counter the claims of the Ż.O.B., the resistance organization must be a force to be reckoned with, and, if anything, Többens's appeal enhanced the Ż.O.B.'s standing in the ghetto.[17]

One of the first factories slated to be dismantled and transferred to Lublin was Hallmann's carpentry "shop," where a significant force of

Ż.O.B. members was active. One night toward the end of February 1943, the squad within Hallmann's area, under the command of Shlomo Winogron, burned the factory's warehouses on Nowolipki Street. According to Edelman, the Germans suffered a million or more zlotys' worth of damage. But the principal German setback only became clear on the morning after the action, when only twenty-five or fifty-five workers showed up instead of the one thousand slated for evacuation. The Nazis suffered a similar or even more serious rebuff when they tried to deport the workers of the Brushmakers' factory. The Ż.O.B. distributed handbills ordering the workers to hide and resist with force rather than obey the evacuation order. On March 6 the warehouse of the *Werterfassung* at 31 Nalewki Street was burned down by the Ż.O.B. This building contained mattresses, beds, and blankets that had belonged to the Jews who had been deported to Treblinka. The Germans called in the fire department to contain the blaze, but it spread throughout the highly inflammable material and could not be brought under control. According to Edelman, after the Ż.O.B. action at Hallmann's "shop," the Germans issued a special bulletin claiming that paratroopers had committed an act of sabotage in the ghetto.

Once the Germans realized that persuasion would not accomplish the evacuation of the ghetto, they tried combining their propaganda campaign with abductions. Armed and uniformed *Werkschutz* units — made up of Ukrainians and mercenaries from the Baltic countries — attempted to trap Jews and detain them at the guard station on one pretext or another, after which they would be sent to the *Umschlagplatz*. The Ż.O.B. command reacted quickly, sending detachments of fighters to attack the guard stations and free the detainees.[18] On March 13 a major clash took place between Ż.O.B. fighters and the German forces. Ukrainians in the *Werkschutz*, who escorted the Jews to work beyond the ghetto walls, systematically maltreated their charges. On the morning of March 13, when Ż.O.B. people turned up to protect the Jewish workers, a skirmish broke out, and in the end it left one member of the *Werkschutz* dead and another wounded. The next day, or perhaps even that same day, a German force managed to capture an armed fighter. A Ż.O.B. unit immediately set out in pursuit of the Germans and succeeded in liberating the prisoner and killing two German soldiers (an unknown number of Jews also fell in that battle). In response, a large SS "punishment detail" broke into the ghetto, surrounded the area where the incident had taken place, and arbitrarily began to remove Jews from all the buildings. According to one source, about 100 Jews were killed in that reprisal action, while another places the number of 210.[19]

The Ż.Z.W and Unaffiliated Fighting Groups in the Ghetto

We will now try, on the basis of reliable sources, to follow the activities of the Ż.Z.W. (Jewish Military Union) from January to April. Thanks to the ties it had forged at an earlier stage, the Ż.Z.W. managed to obtain support from two groups that belonged to the A.K. but retained a certain degree of autonomy within that framework. One was the K.B. (*Korpus Bezpieczeństwa*), a kind of military police responsible for security within the A.K.; the other was the PLAN (*Polska Ludowa Akcja Niepodległościowa*), the armed section of the Democratic Party in the Polish underground. The testimony of Polish activists in these groups (Henryk Iwański, Cezary Ketling, Andrzej Petrykowski) mentions the ties they maintained with the Ż.Z.W. and the aid they tendered to it. Most of their accounts (with the exception of one document) were recorded some time after the war, and the most detailed of them were related years afterward. Undoubtedly they contain a kernel of truth, but they are also riddled with conflicting statements and exaggerated claims that cannot be taken seriously.[20] We will return to discuss the ties between the Poles and the Ż.Z.W. in a later section dealing with the relationship of the Polish underground to the ghetto during the period between January and April 1943.

The Ż.Z.W. was founded as a body within the Revisionist and Betar movements, but it did not maintain its exclusive movement or political character and accepted members who belonged to other political factions or were nonaffiliated (e.g., a group of Communist supporters, including Dr. Richard Walewski, entered the ranks of the Ż.Z.W.).[21] We should mention that one of the issues of contention between the ghetto's two fighting organizations had to do with the structure and size of the resistance movement. The members of the Ż.Z.W. were in favor of opening up the fighting organization to all who expressed a desire to join and of turning it into a mass organization. The Ż.O.B., on the other hand, wanted to maintain its selective character and stringent rules of conspiracy. In the final analysis, neither of the two groups fully realized its philosophy. While the Ż.Z.W. did indeed open up its ranks, it never developed into an open, mass movement. Moreover, it is logical to assume that the integration of new members was conditional upon the preservation of a strong core that provided the organization with its own unique image. The process of consolidation required time, which was clearly not available to the fighters. On the other hand, the Ż.O.B. could not ignore the pressures within the ghetto, and after the January revolt it began forming units of candidates, on the assumption that after a trial period these units could join its ranks.[22]

We lack confirmed information on each organization's exact membership. For the Ż.O.B. it is possible to arrive at estimates that are probably not very far from the actual number. Thus the number of mobilized fighters stood at about 350, to which we must add the members of the command, those who were responsible for the various departments attached to the organization, emissaries to and liaisons with the "Aryan" side of the city, the group of activists that directly supported the organization, and a number of units in training (put together by Lolek Rotblat before April). We can therefore estimate that just before the revolt broke out, the Ż.O.B. numbered between 450 and 500 people. This figure does not include the broad fringe of supporters affiliated with the various parties, the National Committee, and the Coordination Committee.

As mentioned earlier, we lack definitive data upon which to base any estimate of the size of the Ż.Z.W. membership. There are a number of contradictory accounts, with a wide divergence in figures. According to Cezary Ketling, it appears that as of January 1943, the union had about 150 members.[23] Abraham Halperin, who was a supporter of the Ż.Z.W., claims that "there were three fighting sections." The first and undoubtedly the largest and most important of them was located in the Central Ghetto and was made up of three units, each of which numbered about twenty members. Since this principal force was stationed in the heart of the ghetto, we can assume that the other two sections were smaller. In the final version of his book on the Warsaw ghetto uprising, Bernard (Ber) Mark cites the following figures: "At the beginning of the revolt, the Ż.O.B. numbered about 700 people, while the Ż.Z.W. had about 400."[24] Mark does not explain how he arrived at his calculations and estimates. There are also assessments that claim thousands of members for each of the organizations, but they have no basis in reality insofar as they relate to the combat units and groups of activists centered around them rather than to the broad masses on the undisciplined political periphery. We may assume that the Ż.Z.W. had between 200 and 250 fighters just before the revolt broke out.

Like the Ż.O.B., the Ż.Z.W. engaged in reprisals against German agents operating in the ghetto, fund-raising and the acquisition of arms, and preparations for the revolt. The members of the Ż.Z.W. met in a tunnel that had been dug from the organization's headquarters at 7 Muranowska Street to the "Aryan" side of the city, which aided them in maintaining contact and transferring arms into the ghetto. (The tunnel was also to play an important role during the revolt itself, and similar tunnels were dug by different groups of the ghetto population.) The acquisition of arms was accomplished through Polish members of organizations affiliated with the A.K. and purchases made by *palatzovka* workers. We know that the Ż.Z.W. acquired a considerable arsenal of weapons and even obtained a machine gun (which the Ż.O.B. did not have), as well as other automatic weapons, but we do not have exact figures on the quantity of arms in its possession.

The Ż.Z.W. also imposed financial levies and "Exxes," and the very fact that the two organizations independently engaged in raising funds and setting levies on people of means within the ghetto made a clash between them inevitable. Indeed, there were instances in which Jews had no sooner paid a tax to one organization than they were approached with a demand from the other. The relations between the organizations were marked by tension and even intimidation, but eventually the two groups settled their differences, and by the time of the revolt they had devised routine methods of coordinating their maneuvers. In the course of negotiations, the groups arranged to exchange information about operational plans, divide up operational sectors during the revolt, and, according to some sources, even to share arms. As a result of these negotiations, the Ż.Z.W. had essentially subordinated itself to the authority of the Ż.O.B.[25]

Tension was also created by the executions perpetrated by the Ż.Z.W. According to Zuckerman, the Ż.O.B. objected to certain verdicts carried out by the Ż.Z.W. and insisted that the union did not have the right to carry out any sentence without its prior consent. It appears that the Ż.Z.W. bowed to this demand and that an understanding was reached between the two organizations.[26] One of the reports of the Ż.Z.W. command makes mention of an operation against "political informers" that took place on February 21, 1943. Among the important operations credited to the Ż.Z.W. was the attack against the "Żagiew" group, under the leadership of someone known as "Captain Lęcki." The exact nature of this organization is obscure, but it was suspected of being responsible for provocative acts designed to sow confusion and fear within the ghetto. Winter noted in his diary that "the group that published *Żagiew* is very suspicious," and some of its supporters were believed to be Gestapo agents.[27]

In one of his writings, Ringelblum described a visit to the Ż.Z.W. arms cache:

> . . . At the same time I also saw the Ż.Z.W. arsenal. It was situated in an uninhabited, so-called wild block of flats [a building in an area from which Jews had been expelled during the deportation and in which occupancy was no longer permitted]—at 7 Muranowska in a six-room flat on the first floor. There was a first-class radio in the command room, which received news from all over the world, and next to it stood a typewriter. I talked to the people in command for several hours. They were armed with revolvers stuck in their belts. Different kinds of weapons were hung in the

large rooms: light machine guns, rifles, revolvers of different kinds, hand grenades, bags of ammunition, German uniforms, etc., all of which were utilized to the full in the April "action."

In addition to the two organizations that had been established by political bodies, "wildcat" bands also began to make their appearance in the ghetto. These were armed groups that operated under the guise of being underground organizations preparing for an armed struggle. A development of this kind was facilitated by an atmosphere in which the entire ghetto supported the armed struggle, while the combat organizations maintained their secret character. Some of these groups were suspected of theft, which they camouflaged as the actions of a "fighting organization." The Ż.O.B. ambushed and captured a group of this kind in the act of committing a robbery. The fighters confiscated the booty and returned it to its rightful owners, for the fighting organizations were concerned about protecting their reputation.

Nonetheless, these "wildcat" groups should not be regarded merely as gangs of criminals who exploited the chaos solely to rob the population. Some of their members were sincerely interested in preparing for the coming struggle but did not find a way to become part of the organized fighting underground or preferred to operate in a smaller framework of friends and acquaintances. At a later stage, some of these "wildcat" groups (whose identity is unknown) were able to make contact with the fighting organizations, and we know that armed groups of this kind were actively involved in the uprising. Ringelblum mentioned that groups of workers and their foremen armed themselves in a number of "shops," as did porters, wagon drivers, smugglers, *palatzovka* workers, and so on.[28]

The Ghetto's Civilian Population from January to April 1943

Ringelblum characterized the period of the mass deportation as the nadir, the "radical spiritual collapse of the Jews of Warsaw." After the deportation came a period marked by introspection, guilt feelings, and frustration. As mentioned earlier, the anger and desire for revenge during this period found expression in diaries and memoirs but had not yet been translated into concrete forms of action. The call to rise up and resist with whatever came to hand was more in the nature of an enraged outburst than a calculated dictate to the masses. The fact is that during the second deportation, in January 1943, there were hardly any spontaneous acts of resistance on the part of civilians. However, as we have seen, there was a marked rise in the trend to go into hiding—

essentially passive resistance—which testified to a complete lack of faith in the Germans and their promises to honor documents and avoid deporting workers.

Following the January deportation and fighting, the change that came over the population of the ghetto was not restricted to mood alone. This time it also generated action. The experience in January had led to the conclusion that armed resistance, and even passive resistance, were factors that the Germans would not be able to ignore. Active resistance and the refusal to obey the order to report for deportation raised great difficulties for the Germans, forced them to devise new tactics of pacification, and thus postponed the liquidation of the ghetto. These changes in German policy came just at the time when the news arrived of the first significant German defeat (at Stalingrad) and the collapse of the Axis forces in the Middle East. Even though no one really knew how the Jews of the ghetto could be saved, "the news lit a spark of hope among the inhabitants of the ghetto, the remnant of a people," commented Stefan Grajek, a member of the Jewish underground, "and more than one person asked his neighbor: 'Is it possible that some of us will remain alive?'"[29]

Far more important was the sudden burst of activity that overtook the ghetto. In January the Jews had generally concealed themselves in improvised hiding places designed as temporary cover in the event of an *Aktion*. Yet after the January resistance—and the hopes it kindled—a kind of "bunker mania" spread through the ghetto. We are no longer speaking of makeshift cover but of shelters, mainly subterranean, built to sustain people for a lengthy period—which the Jews believed could be the decisive factor in their chances of being saved. In fact, the preparation of sophisticated and well-equipped bunkers became a goal that absolutely preoccupied most of the ghetto's residents. In his reflections on the Warsaw ghetto, Dr. Leński wrote of the bunker campaign as follows:

> One can say without exaggeration that the entire population, from the young to the old, was engaged in preparing hiding places. The ghetto looked like an army camp. In the courtyards, one could see Jews carrying sandbags, bricks, and lime. They worked day and night. Especially industrious were the bakers, because bread was purchased in great quantities for the preparation of rusks. The women worked kneading dough, cutting it into strips, and preparing noodles. . . . No one thought of willingly going to Treblinka. The survivors prepared everything necessary for remaining in hiding for months.[30]

Members of different professions took part in the bunker campaign, planning and executing the camouflage and interior arrangements of the hideouts. In essence, every Jew hoped to find a place in a bunker, and often groups of tenants from various buildings, as well as bands of friends, organized to plan and build a bunker together. The last of the nest eggs that had been saved for the worst were how spent on preparing or buying a place in a bunker. These shelters were of sophisticated design, and much thought was put into camouflaging the entrances. In many cases the Jews did not content themselves with merely converting a cellar, since the building plans stored at the Municipality might give their hideout away. New excavations were dug in courtyards, and in some instances connecting tunnels were dug between bunkers or from houses bordering on the "Aryan" side or no-man's-land to outside the ghetto. Elaborate arrangements were instituted within the bunkers, including the installation of pumps to ensure a supply of water from sources other than the municipal reservoirs and hook-ups to central stations of the city's electricity grid. Wooden bunk beds were installed in many of the bunkers, while enough food was hoarded to last for months. Every bunker also wanted to have a doctor as a permanent resident, and the more sophisticated of them even had a radio. Finally, a substantial number of their inhabitants tried to obtain arms and resolved to resist if they were exposed.

As Alexander Donat related in his memoirs, entitled *The Holocaust Kingdom*,

> Our first thoughts were to upgrade our bunker. We installed electricity, plumbing, and improved the camouflage at the entrance. We set up a special lookout system on constant guard over the steps and the courtyard so that next time no one could surprise us, and we all took part in night duty on two-hour shifts. An alarm system was installed in each apartment, and the signal could be given by pressing a button on the ground floor. The orders were to wake everyone up at the least suspicion. The same was true throughout the ghetto. Shelters were built to stand up to weeks or months [of occupancy], some even until the end of the war. Everyone kept the location of his own shelter and the arrangements at its entrance secret. The majority of these shelters became tombs for the living, but we could not have known that at the time.[31]

Halina Birenbaum wrote in her memoirs:

> Deep under the ground, well-arranged bunkers were built and properly camouflaged hiding places were prepared to facilitate the revenge and resistance. . . . At that very time, joyful news of the massive defeat of the German army on the eastern front passed round by word of mouth. The optimists predicted swift liberation. Even little children in the ghetto knew about the defeat at Stalingrad. They hoped the Germans would be so involved in their own problems that they would leave us alone or wouldn't

have time to carry out their murderous plans. We consoled ourselves with that, but the construction of shelters and bunkers went on as usual. When rumors that the ghetto would be finally annihilated in the spring became increasingly obstinate, Mama obtained a place for us all in the bunker at 3 Miła. She paid for it in dollars (we sold some of the food that my brothers had smuggled over from the "Aryan" side). The bunker was built underneath the cellar and was equipped with various conveniences: a water pump, electricity, fans, bunk beds . . . and wall cupboards for the food stores. All these preparations proved that this was not a temporary hideout in the event of a single *Aktion* or a number of *Aktionen*.[32]

The sophisticated bunkers designed to hold out for an extended period were one aspect of the passive approach to resistance adopted by the ghetto's inhabitants. The fighting organizations were believed to be the moving force behind the change in outlook, and it was assumed that they would defend the bunkers and their inhabitants when the hour arose. In effect, therefore, the bunker system was an integral part of the resistance program, and even though there was no direct connection between the bunker builders and the fighting organizations, both were well aware that they were working toward the realization of a common goal, in which the fighters would play an active role and the residents of the bunkers would be passive partners.

This about-face in outlook and reactions influenced the ghetto's population in other ways as well. Many tried to obtain arms on their own, and the thirst for weapons was particularly strong among young males. Moreover, there was a growing inclination to join one of the fighting organizations, though few found the link that led to one of the combat groups or managed to enter the secret world of the fighters. The organizations did not carry out large-scale enlistment campaigns, since the dearth of weapons and fear of informers—or even those who might unwittingly reveal information out of sheer carelessness—meant that a stringent investigation was required before accepting new members. Expanding at a faster rate was also precluded by the basic aim— especially in the case of the Ż.O.B.—of preserving the organization's elite character as a guarantee that its members would stand up to the challenge before them. We can assume that a portion of the young people who tried to join the fighting organizations at this late stage hoped that the organized resistance movement, which was known to have both material means and resourcefulness, would fight to save the lives of its members. In fact, as mentioned earlier, rescue was not even a secondary goal for the Ż.O.B. Some of those who did not find their way into the Ż.O.B. or the Ż.Z.W. organized into "wildcat" groups or devoted themselves to obtaining arms for their own bunkers. In addition to arms, there was a great demand for poison, especially doses of cyanide, whose fatal effect is instantaneous. For many the cyanide capsule was their last possession, from which they refused to be parted.

The decisive change that overtook the ghetto—identification with the desire to fight and the frantic activity of building shelters—did not totally cancel out the effect of the Germans' conciliatory tactics or the lure of Poniatow and Trawniki. In this context, it is vital to draw a distinction between the Central Ghetto and the area of the "shops." The spirit of resistance was strongest in the Central Ghetto, which contained the headquarters of the fighting organizations and many Jews who lacked an officially recognized status. It was there that the most sophisticated bunkers were built, and almost every Jew in the area found an "address" for himself and his dear ones in one of the underground shelters. It is no exaggeration to state that the network of cells and tunnels resembled a subterranean Jewish city. A bunker had been prepared in almost every house—or "courtyard," as they were known in Warsaw—and many such courtyards (e.g., the one at 30 Franciszkanska Street) had a number of bunkers. The fighting organizations enjoyed maximum popularity and control in this area, and the notion of combat won many faithful disciples.

The situation in the territory of the "shops" was somewhat different, for the workers living there—particularly in the large "shops" run by Többens and Schultz—faced a serious dilemma. As noted earlier, Többens had agreed to send out "spies" in order to prove to their own satisfaction that the camps in the Lublin area were not a trap but a serious, going concern. The vast majority of the workers accepted the Z.O.B.'s interpretation of affairs, but that version did not remove all doubt or serious reservations. At the same time, the work of building bunkers was more difficult to execute in the area of the "shops," because these enclaves were under closer scrutiny by the Germans and the Jews who served them. Többens's efforts (starting early in February 1943) to move the Jews employed in the large "shops" out of Warsaw were a great disappointment to the Germans. Nonetheless, a few thousand Jews—including people close to the management of the plants, favored skilled workers, and volunteers—responded to his appeals and moved out in convoys to the camps in the Lublin area. Többens was given a month to effect the evacuation in his own way. Once that period had passed, the results turned out to be poor, and as time ran out Többens and his aides applied themselves to increasingly stringent methods. The "battle of the posters" between Többens and the Z.O.B. took place in the middle of March. On March 13 Mordecai Anielewicz wrote in a pointed letter to the A.K. that "the situation gets worse from hour to hour. Fifteen hundred men from Schultz's company must leave today. A purge operation is expected in the areas of the ghetto and the 'shops.'" On April 3 German members of the *Werkschutz* surrounded three of Többens's workshops, rounded up their employees (about 400 people), and packed them into railroad cars destined for Poniatow. Between April 6 and 12, 360 workers and 36 "outsiders" were forcibly removed from Többens's "shop."

Following the first wave of the "shop elite," who responded to Többens's appeal out of trust in him and the hope of protecting their preferential status in the plants, came "volunteers" of another kind. At this stage they consisted of the totally destitute, moved by despair and resignation to their fate. However, the number of such "volunteers" was not large.

In March it became clear that *Kommissar* Többens was incapable of executing the task he had taken upon himself within the allotted time. Of the two prevailing approaches—one (represented by Többens and, so he claimed, by Globocnik as well) calling for the transfer of the workers, machinery, and raw materials gradually and by various means, and the other decrying the time wasted on roundabout methods and superfluous persuasion and calling for a decisive and destructive strike—the latter, radical approach soon won out, as demonstrated by the initiation of the final *Aktion* on April 19.

The Poles and the Jewish Resistance Movement from January to April 1943

We have seen that the Poles viewed the armed resistance in January as an awakening from lethargy and capitulation and, characteristically, applauded particularly the display of courage and defense of honor. The admiration expressed by the Polish public at large also led the Polish underground institutions and the fighting organizations subject to them to soften their approach toward the Jews. The Council for Aid to the Jews (*Żegota*), which had been organized at the end of 1942 on the initiative of a group of Poles sympathetic to the plight of the Jews, now received the underground's seal of approval and was allocated a fixed sum by the Polish government in London. Even if we assume that political considerations were involved in this change of heart—i.e., an attempt to refute the charge, voiced abroad, that the Poles were infected by anti-Semitism and remained indifferent in the face of the persecutions and the campaign to annihilate the Jews—and even if the aid was generally extended reluctantly and was minute in comparison to the need, we cannot overlook the fact that the very establishment of a body to offer assistance to the Jews and the patronage extended to this body by the official institutions of the Polish underground were a significant and fruitful step. During the course of time, financial aid channeled through Żegota and help in securing documents and living accommodations evidently touched the lives of thousands of Jews.[33]

The Polish members of Żegota worked together with the Jewish National Committee, and a number of its institutions were set up on a joint basis. The council's chairman was Julian Grobleny ("Trojan"), an activist in the P.P.S., and his deputies were Tadeusz Rek (a member of the Polish Peasants' Party) and Leon Feiner, one of the foremost activists of the Bund. Its dynamic secretary-general was Adolf Berman of Left Po'alei Zion (whose underground code name on the "Aryan" side was "Adam Borowski"). In addition, a number of functionaries from democratic and socialist circles in Poland were active in Żegota's institutions, and for a certain period representatives of the Catholic Movement, including Władysław Bartoszewski ("Ludwik"), belonged to the council. Żegota's aims were to aid Jews who were in hiding and needed help, save children, and organize means to rescue famous Jews, groups of Jewish activists, and party members. The council and its Jewish functionaries (Feiner of the Bund and Berman of the National Committee) reached an agreement on transmitting messages and cables abroad through the communications channels of the Polish underground. Thanks to this agreement, at the beginning of 1943 regular reports and appeals for help from the Jews of Poland began to reach the Jewish representatives in the London-based Polish government-in-exile and Jewish leaders and parties in the United States and Palestine. The council also contributed in no small measure to informing the Polish population of the state of affairs in the ghetto. It called upon the Poles to aid fugitive Jews and to denounce informers and extortionists. Many of Żegota's activists devoted themselves to the Jewish cause with great dedication and placed themselves in mortal danger by carrying out acts of valor. In addition, there can be no doubt that the activities of the council aided the efforts of the ghetto's emissaries on the "Aryan" side of Warsaw.

From October 1942 onward, the contacts between the Ż.O.B. and the A.K. were unbroken, though there were periods of tension and alienation. The Communists on the "Aryan" side were allies of limited power, but within the bounds of their effectiveness they tried to be a faithful source of aid. The Bund's contacts with socialist circles have already been described, and its emissaries even received the support of their socialist comrades for the action undertaken by the Ż.O.B. Another Polish group that proved its loyalty at difficult moments and could be relied upon to exert a certain degree of pressure on the underground section of the Polish government and the resistance movement was the Polish Scouts, which was an ally of the pioneering movements in the ghetto underground. Even Henryk Woliński—the representative of a body that related to the Ż.O.B. and the entire Jewish question with an attitude of detachment—proved that he was personally faithful to the task imposed upon him and tried to persuade his superiors to increase their aid to the Jewish organization. After the January fighting, he dedicated himself to this cause with even greater energy. In his 1944 review, Woliński wrote:

> The liquidation of the ghetto, which was initiated on January 17 [sic], 1943, met with determined armed resistance, which undoubtedly aroused consternation among the German troops and led to the cessation of the Aktion after four days. The Ż.O.B. appreciated its success—for, after all, the final liquidation had been delayed for a while—and continued its preparations for a new struggle with unfettered energy as it urged with ever-increasing vehemence that it be granted aid from the army [the A.K.]. By order of the supreme commander, I held three consultations on this subject with the commander of "Drapacz," Mr. Konar. He agreed to give the Warsaw ghetto material aid and guidance and also mentioned the possibility of outside support from our units. They immediately set to work under the direction of "Chirurg."[34] A link was set up between "Jurek" (of the Ż.O.B.) and our officers. About fifty revolvers, a large quantity of ammunition, 80 kilos [175 pounds] of explosive materials for the manufacture of "bottles" [Molotov cocktails], and a certain quantity of grenades were turned over to the Ż.O.B. A workshop was set into operation in the ghetto to produce "bottles." In addition, the acquisition of arms, which the Ż.O.B. engaged in on its own, was facilitated. A joint plan was formulated for fighting in the ghetto, and the support of our own units was anticipated.[35]

The meager quantity of arms given to the Jews at this late stage was essentially a symbolic gesture of little material significance to the Poles. More than being a substantial contribution that would allow the Jews to engage in true resistance activities, it was evidently calculated as a tactical step to cover up for the Polish underground's indifference and long-standing idleness. The Jewish fighters, who were hungry for arms, rejoiced over every weapon they got. The revolver (one type of weapon that the Polish underground provided, which was also relatively easy to purchase) became the standard personal weapon of the Jewish fighters. Their commanders lacked combat experience and were not familiar with the types of weaponry suitable for street fighting, while the professional Polish officer corps that commanded the A.K. was well grounded in the ways of fighting a battle like the one awaiting the Jews and knew exactly what kind of weapons would enable them to stand up to the enemy. Yet we cannot find any proof—other than their provision of the formula for manufacturing explosives—that the Poles ever gave any thought to the task of defending the ghetto or that they tried to help in overcoming difficulties of a strategic nature. The actual combat value of the revolver was put to the test during the uprising, and only in retrospect—in the course of the battle with the Germans—did the fighters realize that it was not an effective weapon in street fighting. In his last letter to Yitzhak Zuckerman, Mordecai Anielewicz wrote: "And you should know that the revolver is worthless and we hardly used it. What we need is grenades, rifles, machine guns, and explosives."[36]

That the leaders of the Ż.O.B. assessed the posture of the Polish movement realistically is clear from Anielewicz's letter dated March 13, 1943. It was addressed to the representatives of the Coordination Committee on the "Aryan" side and included guidance on how to present their demands to the Poles:

> . . . Please inform the authorities in our name that if massive aid is not forthcoming immediately, we will view [their lack of action] as indifference . . . to the fate of the Jews of Warsaw. Allocating weapons without ammunition impresses [us] as being a bitter mockery of our fate and confirms the assumption that the venom of anti-Semitism continues to permeate the ruling circles of Poland despite the tragic and brutal experience of the last three years. We do not intend to convince anyone of our readiness or ability to fight. Since January 18 the Jewish community in Warsaw has been in a perpetual state of struggle with the conqueror and his lackeys. Whoever denies or doubts that is no more than a spiteful anti-Semite. But we expect the authorities and the representation [of the Polish government] not only to relate to our affairs "with understanding" but to make the murder of the millions of Jewish citizens of Poland a matter of first priority. We sorely regret that we are unable to contact the Allied governments, the government of Poland, and Jewish organizations outside the country directly in order to report on our situation and the attitude of the Polish authorities and public toward us. Gentlemen, please do whatever necessary, without delay, in order to get through to the military authorities and the government's representative. I ask that you read this letter and demand at least 100 grenades, 50 revolvers, 10 rifles, and a few thousand large-caliber bullets, forcefully and immediately. I am ready to supply detailed blueprints of our situation, accompanied by maps, within two days so that the imperative of supplying arms will not be left open to any doubt.[37]

Close to the time that these sharp accusations were delivered against the government institutions in the underground and the A.K. command, an event took place that severely hampered the contact between the Ż.O.B. and the Polish authorities. On March 6, 1943, Arie Wilner ("Jurek") was suddenly arrested on the "Aryan" side of the city and arms were found in his apartment. Wilner's capture was a heavy blow to the Ż.O.B. He had won a solid reputation as a talented and reliable liaison, whose success stemmed from an ability to inspire trust and an unusual gift of persuasion. (As stressed earlier, Henryk Woliński was personally fond of and close to Wilner.) But the damage was not limited to the loss of an effective spokesman, since the ramifications of Wilner's arrest posed a grave danger to the underground. Arie Wilner was one of the few who was thoroughly versed in all the Ż.O.B.'s affairs, and although his staying power could be relied upon, the organization could not afford to underestimate the effectiveness of the Gestapo's methods for breaking a man's will. In addition, the arrest generated a crisis in relations with the Polish underground. According to Woliński, the Poles had warned Wilner that as one who was in on the secrets of the Polish organization and was acquainted with its activists and senior people, he should not be involved in the purchase of arms or keep any incriminating equipment or material in his possession. Woliński mentioned that during one of his visits to Wilner's apartment on Wspólna Street, he noticed arms sticking out from under the bed and upbraided Wilner for dealing in the purchase of weapons. Wilner's reply was that since the Polish underground had denied the Jews arms, he had no other choice.[38]

By Woliński's account, the arrest "curbed the work going on in the sphere of cooperation" between the Ż.O.B. and the Polish representative responsible for the military tie between the ghetto and the A.K. In fact, Wilner's arrest and the attendant complications led to a temporary break in the contacts between the Ż.O.B. and the Polish underground and hindered the planning of support missions in anticipation of the revolt. Woliński related that "more than twenty days after the arrest, I held a discussion with Konar" (General Chruściel). The tension and lost time undoubtedly affected the preparations barely weeks before the uprising was to break out. For a while the Ż.O.B. had no authorized representative on the "Aryan" side, and Yitzhak Zuckerman arrived to replace Wilner just two weeks before the start of the revolt. Naturally, the short time available to him did not allow for resuscitating all the dormant contacts and raising new issues, so that Wilner's arrest had far-reaching consequences.

As later became clear, the Gestapo had not come to arrest Wilner and had no idea who he was even after he had fallen into their hands. Wilner may have been caught as the result of information supplied by an arms dealer, or it may be possible that the previous tenant of his apartment was under surveillance by the Gestapo and Wilner was inadvertently captured in his stead. In any event, the Gestapo believed that it had trapped an active member of the Polish underground. Wilner was kept in prison and subjected to brutal interrogations, accompanied by torture, during which the Gestapo demanded names and details about the structure of the armed Polish underground. At a critical stage of the interrogation, when the pain had become intolerable, he confessed that he was a Jew. Once the Gestapo established that he was telling the truth, their interest in him waned, and he was sent to the Pawiak Prison. Later he was transferred to a labor camp in Rembertow, near Warsaw, where he enlisted the aid of one of the guards in getting a message through to Heniek Grabowski, an associate of the Polish Scout movement who had been the first liaison to reach Vilna. Grabowski checked the accuracy of the information and prepared a plan to liberate Wilner.[39] Shortly before the uprising, a select group of Ż.O.B. activists celebrated the return of a fighter whom they have given up as lost. Wilner's legs were wounded from the torture he had suffered under interrogation and had not fully healed by the time the revolt broke out.

We have few primary sources that relate to the Ż.Z.W.'s ties with the Poles. On the other hand, as stated earlier, some Poles have come forward who claim to have maintained contact with the organization and supplied it with arms and other forms of aid, though their testimony is not confirmed in the memoirs and writings of the Ż.Z.W's members or supporters within the ghetto,[40] and other evidence even casts serious doubt on it. We may therefore assume that a number of the claims regarding aid tendered to the Ż.Z.W. contain self-serving and fabricated information.

At the same time, we can speak of two important facets of the Ż.Z.W.'s network of contacts with the Poles. First, the ties maintained with Polish officers (and especially members of the K.B.) were based on friendships that seem to have gone back to personal relationships from the beginning of the war, that is, before the ghetto was established. Moreover, owing to the character of these ties and the ability to smuggle weapons into the ghetto through a tunnel, the Ż.Z.W. managed to gather together a few heavier weapons (submachine guns and a machine gun) than the Ż.O.B. did, though the Ż.Z.W. also used the revolver as the standard personal weapon.

Postwar Polish assertions emphasize that aid was provided to the Ż.Z.W. on ideological grounds and out of the sense of fraternity common to all fighters. Yet the one original wartime document available on this matter states that Cezary Ketling, a communications officer who commanded PLAN (one of the two organizations that maintained ties with the Ż.Z.W.), conducted the relationship with the union on a commercial basis by supplying weapons in exchange for cash or its equivalent in clothing.[41] We should add, however, that Ketling's testimony indicates that his knowledge of the Ż.Z.W.'s affairs was more than casual: he knew about the size of the union, its structure, the tunnel to the "Aryan" side, and so on. Moreover, his memoirs describe meetings and contacts with members of the Ż.Z.W. and state that the tunnel on Muranowska Street was about 50 meters long and was dug over three months' time (from August to October 1942).

Among those who extended active aid to the Ż.Z.W. was Major Henryk Iwański ("Bystry"), an officer under the command of General Andrzej Petrykowski of the K.B., though the extent of his help is not clear. We do know, however, that Major Iwański collaborated with the Ż.Z.W. during the April fighting.

The Ż.Z.W. evidently obtained most of its weapons through arms dealers and smuggled them into the ghetto. It did not maintain a permanent and official delegation on the "Aryan" side, but it did keep up a secret apartment in the Polish sector of the city used by a number of Jewish girls, including Shoshana ("Emilka") Kossower, to engage in purchasing arms for the union.[42]

Eventually, the arms market moved from the "Aryan" side into the ghetto itself. Like other items that were smuggled in and sold clandestinely, revolvers were spirited into the ghetto at great risk by *palatzovka* workers or transported through secret passages. The purchase and smuggling of weapons was handled mainly by gangs made up of both Poles and Jews. Their motivation was purely commercial, as, in compensation for the high risks involved, arms smuggling guaranteed fat profits. The "wildcat" groups and individuals living in the bunkers usually obtained their weapons from the smugglers and arms dealers operating in the ghetto.

Only obscure hints regarding the existence of a fighting force within the ghetto and its preparations for battle reached the organized Jewish community outside Poland. Reports sent to London by the Polish underground contained only veiled and scant information about the ghetto's preparations for combat. Those relayed by representatives on the National Committee and the Coordination Committee to Jewish organizations and leaders abroad did contain demands for arms, but their emphasis was on appeals for help, the rescue of prominent figures and children, and requests for funds in order to carry out rescue programs.

On April 10, General Rowecki transmitted a message to London reporting on the German plans to liquidate the Warsaw ghetto. His cable states: "According to German plans, 8,000 Jewish metal workers and 3,000 working for the *Werterfassung* are to remain in the Warsaw ghetto. The rest are to be deported or annihilated over a period of two to four weeks. As a result, an atmosphere of tension and depression has overtaken the ghetto." The body of the text mentions nothing whatsoever about Jewish preparations to resist the final liquidation operation.[43]

Beginning in January, the National Committee and Coordination

Committee sent a string of cables and pleas to prominent Jewish figures and organizations abroad. The appeal of the National Committee transmitted on January 13, 1943, was addressed to Stephen Wise, Nahum Goldmann, the Arbeter Ring, and the JDC in the United States. It stated, *inter alia*:

> . . . We hereby inform you of the greatest murder of all time, the murder of more than three million Jews in Poland. In light of the mortal danger to the 400,000 Jews who are still alive, we demand of you:
> (1) revenge against the Germans;
> (2) to force the Hitlerites to halt the murders;
> (3) weapons for the struggle for our lives and honor;
> (4) contact through a liaison in a neutral country;
> (5) the rescue of 10,000 children by [a prisoner] exchange;
> (6) $500,000 for the purpose of resistance and aid.
> Brothers, the remnant of the Jews in Poland live with the knowledge that in the darkest days of our history, you did not offer us aid. Answer us. This is our last call to you.[44]

In the final days of November 1942 Jan Karski, an emissary of the Polish underground, reached London. He had been in the ghetto in August of that year, had spoken with "Mikołaj" Feiner before leaving Warsaw, and now recited a statement that he had committed to memory before leaving the city—a kind of last will and testament of the surviving Jews to their compatriots in the free world. Dr. Ignacy Schwartzbart wrote that Karski was "a rare phenomenon among the Poles. If he thinks as he talks, and if the majority of Poles would act as he says, things would be better."[45] For a long time Karski would not remain silent. He traveled in order to warn Polish, Jewish, British, and American statesmen and public figures of what was happening in Poland. He even met with President Roosevelt and told him details of the fate of Polish Jewry. Karski also transmitted to Shmuel Zygielbojm (who had left Poland at the beginning of the occupation and was the Bund's representative on the Polish National Council in London) a message from the representative of the Bund on the "Aryan" side of the city, Dr. Feiner:

> "Berezowski" [Feiner] told me to transmit to you, Mr. Zygielbojm, and to all the Jews the following things: Tell them that we here feel *hate* for those who were saved there because they are not saving us. . . . They are not doing enough. We know that there, in the humane and free world, it is absolutely impossible to believe what is happening to us here. Let them do something that will force the world to believe. . . . We are all dying; they will also die there. Let them lay siege to Churchill's government and others, proclaim a hunger strike, let them even die of hunger

rather than budge until they believe and take measures to save the last remants who are still alive. We know that no political action, no protests or proclamations of punishment *after* the war will help. None of these make any impression on the Germans. The only thing that could make an impression, and perhaps even save the remnant of the Jews who are still alive, is to execute a number of Germans abroad and state publicly that if the Germans do not stop the slaughter of Polish Jewry, larger numbers of Germans will be shot in public.[46]

When reports of the destruction of Poland's Jews grew increasingly persistent, Zygielbojm was haunted by the nightmare. He lived under great stress and tried to sound the alarm and mobilize aid, but most of his efforts were futile. When the first reports on the final destruction of the ghetto and the uprising of April reached Zygielbojm, he committed suicide on the night of May 12, 1943.[47] He left behind letters to the Polish government and to his surviving friends and acquaintances in the Bund, which stated:

> . . . It has become clear from the information that has reached me from Poland that the Germans are now annihilating the remaining Jews of Poland with terrible cruelty. The last act of a tragedy without precedent in history is now being played out behind the walls of the ghetto. Responsibility for the crime of murdering the entire Jewish population of Poland lies first and foremost with the murderers themselves, but indirectly this responsibility lies with all mankind — the Allied nations and governments who have not yet made any effort toward concrete action to halt the crime. . . . I also wish to declare that even though the Polish government contributed much to awakening world public opinion, it did not do so in an adequate manner. It did nothing befitting the magnitude of the drama now taking place in Poland. . . . I can no longer remain silent. I cannot live when the remnant of the Jewish people in Poland, whom I represent, is being steadily annihilated. My comrades in the Warsaw ghetto fell with weapons in their hands, in the last heroic struggle. I was not fortunate enough to die as they did and together with them. But I belong to them and to their mass graves. By my death I wish to express my vigorous protest against the apathy with which the world regards and resigns itself to the slaughter of the Jewish people.[48]

Chapter Fourteen
Days of Battle

Sources on the Revolt The Jewish sources that relate to the uprising in the Warsaw ghetto consist of official reports of the Jewish Fighting Organization and the Jewish National Committee, which were passed on to London via clandestine channels or published on the "Aryan" side of Warsaw; Mordecai Anielewicz's last letter, written at the height of the revolt; the memoirs of fighters and activists in the Ż.O.B.; and the testimony of survivors who had taken shelter in the bunkers and reported on the uprising from the viewpoint of noncombatants.

The German material, which relates to the preparations for the *Aktion* and provides details on the fighting in the ghetto, includes both official reports and random documents and testimonies. The primary document of relevance to this subject is the report written by *S.S.- und Polizeiführer* Jürgen Stroop, who directed the full-scale German military operation to quash the uprising from 8:00 A.M. on April 19, 1943, until its close on May 16, 1943. Stroop's comprehensive document includes a list of the German forces deployed in the ghetto during the fighting, a summary of the casualties incurred during the operation, daily reports (beginning on April 20), and an overview written for the *S.S.- und Polizeiführer* of the Generalgouvernement, Friedrich Krieger. After the suppression of the revolt and the demolition of the ghetto, Stroop collected his daily reports and overview, added a selection of photographs taken during the fighting, bound them together in an elegant cover, and crowned the entire document with a heading executed in artistic Gothic lettering that read: "The Jewish Residential Quarter Of Warsaw Is No

364

More" ("Es gibt keinen jüdischen Wohnbezirk in Warschau mehr"). Stroop saw to it that his document was duplicated in a number of copies, and one of them was confiscated at his villa in Wiesbaden by an American army unit. It was subsequently presented as evidence for the prosecution at the Nuremberg War Crime Trials, where it made a shocking impression. Since then, the document has been published in a number of editions in various languages.[1] Stroop's trial in Warsaw augmented the material with the protocol of the judicial proceedings and Stroop's answers to the questions posed by investigators and historians.[2] In addition to the reports and Stroop's comments and replies, we have drawn upon the testimony of officers in Stroop's retinue and classified German documents relating to both the revolt and its repercussions within Germany's ruling circles and the senior echelon of the National-Socialist Party.

The Polish sources are a third and independent collection of documents, comprising official surveys and statements of the Polish *Delegatura* (either transmitted to London or published locally); the testimonies and diaries of witnesses to the events; words of admiration and commentary that appeared in the Polish underground press; and the pronouncements of political parties and public bodies both in Poland and abroad, during and immediately after the revolt. To this category of source material we can append the writings of Jews who were on the "Aryan" side of Warsaw—living either under a false identity or in hiding—and who therefore assimilated Polish impressions of the revolt and could describe the prevailing mood of the Polish public.

Since the framework of the various Jewish forces has already been described in earlier chapters, suffice it to say here that the entire array of forces mobilized in the ghetto's fighting organizations stood at approximately 750 fighters (about 500 in the ranks of the Ż.O.B. and 250 in the Ż.Z.W.) divided among three principal fronts: (1) the Central Ghetto, (2) the Brushmakers' Area, and (3) the sector of the large "shops." This total does not include the "wildcat" groups, though what we know of the armed resistance in the ghetto leaves no doubt that these unaffiliated forces also played a role in the combat effort. Unfortunately, we lack official documentation that would allow us to appraise—if only generally—the relative impact of this facet of the resistance and to report on a number of clashes in which they participated.

Detailed data on the deployment of the German forces can be found in Stroop's comprehensive report. In anticipation of the *Aktion* against the ghetto, the Germans massed a force composed of the following units: (1) SS units totaling 821 soldiers and 9 officers; (2) police units for a daily average of 228 patrolmen and 6 officers, plus a few support units; (3) regular army and foreign troops totaling 371 soldiers and 4 officers. Altogether, by Stroop's account, the daily size of the force operating in the ghetto averaged 2,054 soldiers and 36 officers. In the course of his interrogation while under arrest, Stroop stated that the weapons and equipment carried by the units operating in the ghetto were identical to those of parallel units stationed at the fronts. The *Panzer Grenadier* included armored vehicles and some light French tanks, and the arms issued to the German troops—above and beyond standard personal weapons—included cannons, flame-throwers, anti-aircraft weapons, and heavy machine guns.

Exact statistics on the weapons at the disposal of the Jewish organizations have never been uncovered. While it is certain that the fighters were armed with revolvers as their personal weapons, there was no such thing as a standard-issue weapon, meaning that their revolvers were of different makes and various calibers—and some were not even fit for use. According to Marek Edelman, every fighter in the Ż.O.B. received between 10 and 15 bullets and 4 or 5 hand grenades.[3] The total number of hand grenades in the possession of the Ż.O.B. was about 2,000, and we may also assume that the organization had approximately 2,000 Molotov cocktails, a total of about 10 rifles, and one or two submachine guns.

The revolver also served as the personal weapon in the Ż.Z.W., but the union evidently had a larger supply of rifles and submachine guns. Although we have no certified data on this subject and cannot assume that the Ż.Z.W.'s arsenal of heavier weapons was substantial, we do know that the union acquired light machine guns and employed them during the battle. Moreover, since we find no mention of independent arms manufacture by the Ż.Z.W., it is reasonable to assume that the organization possessed some quantity of explosives and Molotov cocktails.

It is impossible to estimate the extent of the weaponry in the hands of individuals and the "wildcat" groups, but at best it must have been no more than one revolver per person and a meager supply of bullets.

Before leaving this subject, we must also take into account the wide disparity in the structure and character of the opposing forces. Irregular groups of youngsters who lacked training and experienced commanders were pitted against regular army troops led by professional officers. Although this placed the Jews at a substantial disadvantage, before the fighting was over it proved to be an even greater embarrassment to the Germans.

The First Day of the Uprising   On Rosh Hashanah, the Jewish
New Year, 1940, the Jewish resi-
dential quarter of Warsaw was subjected to a massive aerial bombardment. From the standpoint of its inhabitants, this was the first
encounter with the might and means of the German enemy. On the eve
of Passover, the festival of freedom, 1943, the Germans opened the
final stage of their campaign to annihilate all trace of the Jewish community of Warsaw. This time, however, the penetration of German
troops into the ghetto did not come as a surprise, for throughout the
month of April persistent rumors had brought "the last stirring of life in
the ghetto" to a halt. "Every day," Tuvia Borzykowski wrote, "and even
a number of times each day, all the Jews would stop whatever they were
doing and dash for shelter."[4] The least suspicion of heightened activity
among the enemy's forces was sufficient to alarm the entire population
and engender a state of alert. Nonetheless, the Jews could not ignore
the approach of the Passover holiday. With a determination that had
characterized the Jews for centuries and a resourcefulness that had
reached unprecedented proportions during the occupation, the surviving remnant of the Warsaw ghetto prepared to celebrate the Passover,
taking care to acquire the ritual Passover foods (matzos and wine) and
cleansing their eating and cooking utensils as prescribed by religious
law.

On April 18, 1943, the ghetto received reports—including authoritative information from the "Aryan" side—that the massing of
troops had been noted in Warsaw and the Germans were evidently
about to initiate the decisive *Aktion* against the ghetto. The lookout
posts that had been set up in buildings throughout the ghetto were now
reinforced, and the night of April 18 was spent watching and waiting.
At 1:00 or 2:00 A.M. came the first reports on the deployment of
enemy forces along the ghetto wall—units of the German gendarmerie
and the Polish Police, who surrounded the ghetto with a cordon of
guards 25 meters apart. Ż.O.B. runners dashed from house to house
alerting the population that an *Aktion* was expected the next morning.
In many cases their warning was superfluous, since the tenants had already received word from the regular lookouts on the rooftops. Many
residents of the ghetto abandoned their festive tables and gathered together in large groups. "No Jew slept that night. Belongings, underwear, bedding, [and] provisions were packed and taken into the
bunkers."

The Ż.O.B. was put in a state of high alert. "At one in the morning," Borzykowski wrote, "the command received the latest reports, on
the basis of which all the groups were mobilized immediately."[5] Edelman noted that the news arrived at 2:00 A.M.: "All the combat groups

were alerted immediately, and at 2:15 — that is, in about fifteen minutes — they had taken up their combat positions."[6] As the forces were mustered, each fighter received a steel combat helmet and a knapsack filled with "underwear, provisions, [and] first-aid materials. In addition to the standard weapons at his disposal, every fighter was now given bombs, Molotov cocktails, etc."[7] Chaim Frimmer described the preparations for battle at the Ż.O.B.'s principal position in the Central Ghetto:

> In the evening a state of alert was proclaimed and the passwords were changed. Now we knew that the Germans were readying themselves for an *Aktion* in the ghetto. A single password was established for the fighters in all the groups — "Jan — Warsaw" — [and] we began fortifying the positions. The approach to the gate of the courtyard was blocked by a wagon that we turned wheels-up. We removed closets and the rest of the heavy furniture from the apartments and stacked them in the gateway. The windows were fortified with sandbags. People were assigned to their various positions. . . . I received an order from Berl Braudo to check the weapons and pass out ammunition to the men. We filled baskets with Molotov cocktails and passed them on to the positions. . . . Mordecai Anielewicz arrived and went into Yisrael [Kanał's] room. After consultation they came out and walked through the rooms and apartments, selecting appropriate spots for positions. People from other groups came to receive provisions, battle rations — rusks, sugar, groats. "Cjank" [doses of cyanide] was passed out to certain people, especially those whose tasks required them to be mobile and heightened their chances of being caught by the Germans and tortured during interrogation.[8]

In his summarizing report on the fighting in the ghetto, General Stroop mentioned the factors that moved the Germans to initiate the final *Aktion* on April 19:

> In January 1943, following his visit to Warsaw, the *Reichsführer-S.S.* [Himmler] ordered the *S.S.- und Polizeiführer* of the Warsaw District [von Sammern] to transfer the equipment and armament plants located in the ghetto, *including their workers and machinery*, to Lublin. The execution of this order became hopelessly bogged down, because both the management of the factories and the Jews resisted the transfer by every means imaginable. As a result, the *S.S.- und Polizeiführer* decided to carry out the transfer of the factories by force in a large operation that was scheduled to last for three days.[9]

In January 1946, Franz Konrad, the SS officer in charge of the *Werterfassung* in von Sammern's headquarters, gave testimony that related to the first day of the April *Aktion*:

A week before Easter 1943—it was a Sunday morning—*S.S.- und Polizeiführer* von Sammern convened a meeting of the heads of the Security Police, *Obersturmbannfüher-S.S.* Hahn, the commanders of the S.S. units in Warsaw, [the commanders] of the cavalry and infantry reserve units, the commanders of the "Sipo" [Security Police] and the "Orpo" [Regular Police], and the officers in his headquarters (myself among them). At this meeting we were notified that on Monday he intended to transfer out the Jews who still remained in the Warsaw ghetto. During the discussion about the appropriate time for sending the various S.S. and police units into action, *Brigadeführer* Jürgen (Josef) Stroop entered and announced that he had been appointed to the post of *S.S.- und Polizeiführer* by order of the *Reichsführer-S.S.*[10]

That same day, April 18, the Polish Police was put under alert (Polish policemen were slated to take part in the encirclement of the ghetto). The declaration of a state of alert was evidently passed on to circles in the Polish underground, who in turn warned the ghetto underground that an *Aktion* might commence the next day.

The question remains whether the Germans were aware of the activities and preparations going on in the ghetto—i.e., that an armed Jewish force was deploying for resistance. It is absolutely certain that the commanders of the SS and the police knew that a resistance force was being organized in the ghetto and that they could expect armed opposition to any forthcoming *Aktion*. After all, the Germans had already experienced combat skirmishes in January. Even though they had experimented with the strategy of a relatively long waiting period and attempted to dismantle the ghetto by means of persuasion—as if disregarding the fact that an underground force was preparing itself to give battle whenever the *Aktion* began—the way in which von Sammern approached the forthcoming *Aktion*—namely his mobilization of an impressive military force and convening of the heads of the commands in Warsaw—indicates that he knew the April *Aktion* would not resemble the previous "resettlement operations," because this time the Jews could resist. All the same, it appears that von Sammern did not appreciate the extent of the resistance or know of the widespread network of bunkers in the ghetto. We may assume that he expected the forthcoming resistance to resemble the street fighting during the January deportation, meaning that the insurgents would try to attack the German troops head on. Von Sammern therefore decided to send in a large force on the first day of the operation in order to break the resistance with a single mighty blow. He likewise accepted as fact Többens's claims that the Ż.O.B. had foiled the peaceful evacuation of the population by pressure and terror tactics and that once the hard core of insurgents had been eliminated, the deportation would go smoothly, since the remainder of the Jews did not support the fighting underground.

The unfolding of events in the ghetto after the mass deportation in the summer of 1942 had undermined von Sammern's credit with Himmler, who decided to place the final task of liquidating the ghetto in the hands of a man who was new to Warsaw but had a reputation as an experienced police commander. Before being posted to Warsaw, Jürgen Stroop had served in the SS and Police Command in eastern Galicia and was regarded as a vigorous man who had proven his abilities and determination in operations against the partisans. Stroop reached Warsaw before the initiation of the *Aktion*, on the evening of April 17. The next day he appeared at the meeting called by von Sammern but did not immediately assume command of the operation, evidently preferring to remain in the position of a supervisor who would be ready to enter into action whenever intervention proved necessary or when the time appreared ripe to assume command. In reply to questions addressed to him after the war, Stroop reported, *inter alia*:

> The German command, and particularly my predecessor as *S.S.- und Polizeiführer*, von Sammern, did not take even the mildest resistance into account. A number of trouble-free deportations had preceded the final *Aktion*, so that Dr. von Sammern assumed that the final deportation would also be executed smoothly. Only on the eve of the *Aktion* did he receive a report that armed resistance could be expected. Of course, he didn't believe it, but for the sake of discipline he passed on the full assessment to Krieger, so that the latter could act accordingly.[11]

It is unreasonable to believe that von Sammern assumed the forthcoming evacuation would resemble the *Aktionen* of the past or that he was surprised to receive a report pointing out the possibility of resistance and personally did not believe it. It is entirely possible, however, that von Sammern did not wish to admit his concern to Stroop or even to brief his successor on the true situation. Confessing to the truth of the matter would not improve his position or personal situation. At the same time, it is imperative to emphasize that the Germans never even imagined the potency of the resistance. General Rowecki, the commander of the A.K., noted in his report on the uprising to the London-based government that "the resistance of groups of Jewish fighters was far beyond all expectations and took the Germans by surprise," and a survey of the Polish underground appraising the situation from May 8 to 14 stated: "The Germans regarded the prolongation of resistance in the ghetto as a stain on their reputation. The oversight that allowed such a line of resistance to come into being cost the commander of the SS and the police in the Warsaw District, von Sammern, his post. Police general Stroop was appointed in his place."[12]

While imprisoned in Poland, Stroop wrote:

> The residents of the ghetto knew about all the moves of the German
> authorities. They were ready for anything and took appropriate counter-
> measures. Thus the building of shelters in cellars, which was done in ac-
> cordance with orders, was exploited for the construction of bunkers to
> defend the ghetto, and this was kept from the German authorities. Col.
> von Sammern told me that despite the secrecy, as early as April 17th [the
> Jews] were informed by telephone of the hour when the operation would
> begin! In my opinion, this was the crucial reason for the failure of the
> operational units under [von Sammern's] command to penetrate [the ghet-
> to] during the morning hours of April 19, 1943! [The Jews] were prepared
> and were not intimidated by the use of armor and half-tracks (they had
> incendiary bottles, powerful homemade bombs, revolvers, low-caliber
> rifles, and even German uniforms). But they underestimated the fighting
> power of the police stationed in Warsaw.[13]

The irony at this stage was that the isolated and doomed Jews were
preparing for the German attack and were forewarned of its immi-
nence, while the omnipotent German regime, backed by secret police
and a network of informers of all kinds and nationalities, knew essentially nothing of what was going on in the ghetto. This important
achievement must be credited to the success of the fighting organizations in the ghetto, particularly the Ż.O.B., in purging the ghetto of
destructive elements and preparing it for the impending trial.

According to Stroop's report for April 20, the "Grand *Aktion*"
commanded by von Sammern began at 3:00 A.M. on April 19 with an
encirclement of the ghetto by reinforced troops. (As we have noted, the
Jewish sources report that the lookouts spotted these forces at 1:00 or
2:00 A.M.) At 6:00 A.M., Stroop's report continues, came "the deployment of *Waffen-S.S.* to the extent of 850/16" (i.e., 850 soldiers and 16
officers). Simha Ratajzer, a Ż.O.B. fighter, subsequently described how
the German forces entering the ghetto appeared from a lookout post in
the Brushmakers' Area:

> At 4:00 in the morning we saw a column of Hitlerites at the Nalewki
> passage moving toward the Central Ghetto. [The column] marched and
> marched without end, a few thousand strong. Behind it came a few tanks,
> armored cars, light cannon, and a few hundred SS troops on motorcycles.
> "They're marching like they're off to war," I commented to Zippora, my
> partner in the position, and suddenly I sensed how weak we were. What
> are we and our force against an armed and equipped army, against tanks
> and armored cars, while we have only revolvers and, at best, grenades in
> our hands. . . . [14]

The German force penetrated the ghetto in two columns. One
marched along Nalewki Street while the second (which had entered the

gate at the corner of Gęsia and Zamenhofa streets) intended to spread out along the other main artery in the Central Ghetto, Zamenhofa-Miła. The Jewish forces in the Central Ghetto were deployed at three points: (1) a force composed of three Ż.O.B. combat squads took up position on the upper floors of the buildings at the corner of Gęsia and Nalewki streets; (2) four Ż.O.B. squads, together with the area headquarters and the general headquarters of the organization, were located in positions at the intersection of Zamenhofa and Gęsia streets; (3) the Ż.Z.W. force in the Central Ghetto, which comprised the union's principal contingent, fortified itself in the sector of Muranowska Square. For months the fighters had been preparing escape routes over the rooftops, so that it would be possible to get from house to house without going out into the streets.

The first armed clash occurred on Nalewki Street, at the corner of Gęsia, where two Ż.O.B. combat squads (under the command of Zecharia Artstein and Lolek Rotblat) came into contact with the Germans. A German column moving up the center of the road while singing boisterously was attacked at the corner by forces positioned in the building at 33 Nalewki Street. The surprise was total and the power of the fire—especially the bombs and hand grenades—inflicted injuries to the enemy and sowed havoc in its ranks, so much so that the Germans retreated and dispersed, leaving their casualties lying on the street. Then the German troops tried to organize a counterattack. This time they no longer exposed themselves in the center of the street but hugged the walls of the buildings and sought shelter in the entrances. The heavy German fire met with only sporadic response from the Jewish side, but the Jews enjoyed a clear advantage: the Germans could not operate without exposing themselves. As one fighter explained in his memoirs, "while we were concealed in our positions," the Germans were easy targets. This second battle likewise ended in a German retreat. There were no casualties to the Jewish side.

While this clash was taking place on the corner of Nalewki and Gęsia, the main battle of April 19 raged at the corner of Zamenhofa and Miła streets. Four squads of Ż.O.B. fighters (under the command of Berl Braudo, Aaron Bryskin, Mordecai Growas, and Leib Gruzalc) positioned themselves around the square that dominated the intersection. Nearby, the Germans had chosen a place to establish an improvised headquarters. The arrival of their equipment—including tables, benches, and communications instruments—was followed by the end of the main German column. Jewish policemen were forced to march at the head of this column to serve as a human wall and protect the German units by absorbing any burst of fire from the Jewish insurgents.

Chaim Frimmer, a fighter in Braudo's squad who viewed the German deployment and subsequent battle from one of the lookout posts, described the events as follows:

> At five in the morning a loud rumble was heard. Suddenly I saw from my lookout on the balcony that cars had come through the ghetto gate. They reached the square, stopped, and soldiers got out and stood to the side. Then a truck arrived carrying tables and benches. The distance between me and the cars was about 200 meters, and since I had good binoculars I could see them clearly. The tables were set up in a D-shape, wires were laid, and telephones were placed on them. Other cars came with soldiers bearing machine guns. Then motorcycle riders arrived [and] some ambulances and light tanks could be seen stopping by the entrance. The Latvians, who had been standing there through the night, were removed and sent *en masse* in the direction of the *Umschlagplatz*. At six a column of infantry entered. One section of the column turned into Wolynska Street and the other remained in place, as if awaiting orders. Before long the Jewish Police came through the gate. They were lined up on both sides of the street and, as ordered, began to advance toward us. I would report everything to a fighter lying down not far from me [who in turn passed word on] to the command room, where Mordecai [Anielewicz], Yisrael [Kanał], and others were seated. When the column of Jewish Police reached our building, I asked how to proceed: Attack or not? The reply was to wait; Germans would surely follow, and the privilege of taking our fire belongs to them. And that's exactly what happened: After the Jewish Police crossed the street, an armed, mobile German column began to move. [I was ordered to wait] until the middle of the column had reached the balcony and then throw a grenade at it, which would serve as a signal to start the action. . . . A mighty blast within the column was the signal to act. Immediately thereafter grenades were thrown at the Germans from all sides, from all the positions on both sides of the street. Above the tumult of explosions and firing, we could hear the sputter of the German Schmeisser [a submachine gun used by the German army] operated by one of our men in the neighboring squad. I myself remained on the balcony and spewed forth fire from my Mauser onto the shocked and confused Germans. . . . The battle lasted for about half an hour. The Germans retreated leaving many dead and wounded in the street. . . . Again my eyes were peeled on the street, and then two tanks came in, followed by an infantry column. When the tank came up to our building, some Molotov cocktails and bombs put together from thick lead pipes were thrown at it. The big tank began to burn and, engulfed in flames, made its way toward the *Umschlagplatz*. The second tank remained in place as fire consumed it from every side.[15]

The first of Stroop's daily reports described the progress of the fighting during the early morning hours of April 19 from the German viewpoint:

As soon as the units deployed, a premeditated attack by the Jews and the bandits; Molotov cocktails were thrown on the tank and on two armored cars. The tank was burning fiercely. At first this attack caused [our] forces to retreat. Our losses in the first action were 12 men (6 SS men, 6 Trawniki men). At close to eight o'clock, the second attack under the command of the undersigned.

It was only after the war, during his trial in Poland, that Stroop added details on what had happened from the moment that the forces under von Sammern's command were repulsed until Stroop assumed command of the operation:

At 6:00 A.M. on April 19, Col. von Sammern initiated the *Aktion*, and he remained in command of it—by mutual agreement—since he had made all the preparations and was familiar with the place. I consented to come to the ghetto, which I had never seen before, at about 9:00 A.M. on April 19. At around 7:30 von Sammern turned up at my lodgings and announced that all was lost, that the forces he had sent into the ghetto had retreated and there were already dead and wounded. I can't remember how many. Von Sammern said that he would call Cracow and request that "Stuka" planes bomb the ghetto to quash the rebellion that had broken out. I told him not to because I wanted to review the situation on the spot. . . . I asked for a map of the ghetto and entered through the gate, while bullets showered down on me incessantly. . . . I handled the forces according to the rules of street fighting, lining stormtroopers along both sides of the main street so that they would not go charging forward blindly, as had evidently happened before. I issued the appropriate orders to the commanders of the units. My intention was to gain control of at least the buildings on the main street.

According to Borzykowski, the battle resumed on Nalewki Street about three hours after the German retreat. The enemy troops removed mattresses from the *Werterfassung* warehouse near the Ż.O.B. positions and constructed a protective barricade as they continued to fire. They operated in groups and were careful not to expose themselves to the snipers firing from the positions. When the barricade was set on fire by Molotov cocktails, the Germans threw their own incendiary bottles into the building at 33 Nalewki Street, where the Ż.O.B. position was located, setting it aflame. The fighters, who were forced to abandon their position and seek cover, evaded the Germans waiting for them in the street by escaping over the rooftops. The positions on Zamenhofa also came under heavy fire, and the order to withdraw was given as a hail of bullets pierced the ceilings of the rooms where the fighters were stationed. Those fighters took shelter in the bunker that housed their headquarters on Zamenhofa Street.

Stroop also reported that at about 7:30 his forces came up against "very strong resistance from a block of buildings, accompanied by machine-gun fire."[16] This is a reference to the battle that broke out in Muranowska Square, where the main contingent of the Ż.Z.W. was located. In the course of the fighting, the Ż.Z.W. unfurled a blue-and-white flag and the national flag of Poland. One of its members reported that on the day of the first battle, a machine gun had reached the union through the tunnel that extended to the "Aryan" side.[17] It was stationed in a position that dominated the entire square and effectively blocked the German advance. Each of the German attacks met with stiff resistance. Edelman noted that during the battle a tank was hit and set aflame, "the second one that day."[18] According to Stroop, "a special combat unit silenced the enemy, penetrated the buildings, [but] did not catch the enemy itself. The Jews and the criminals were fighting everywhere, position by position, and at the last moment they escaped and fled over the rooftops or through underground passages."[19]

On the first day of battle, then, the Jewish fighters attacked from three focal points. In each case, it was the insurgents who opened fire and surprised the enemy. The Germans were forced to withdraw from the ghetto after the first clash, and von Sammern lost his lead when he realized the strength of the Jewish resistance. When Stroop assumed command of the operation, he proceeded cautiously, adopting the tactics of house-to-house fighting. Yet he too was forced into a difficult and drawn-out battle in Muranowska Square. The losses to the Jewish side that day were relatively light. One member of the Ż.O.B. fell (Yechiel from Growas's squad, who fired the submachine gun), while the Ż.Z.W. probably lost a larger number of people.[20] The casualties on the German side (according to Stroop's reports) were one dead and twenty-four wounded, including fourteen SS men, two German gendarmes, six men from the Trawniki unit, and two Polish policemen.[21]

As early as the first day of the uprising, the Germans also met with opposition from a totally unexpected source—i.e., the resistance of the ghetto's population at large, which the Germans dubbed "the battle of the bunkers." Stroop described the nature and significance of this line of resistance in his comprehensive survey: "The number of Jews trapped in and removed from the buildings was very small. It turned out that Jews were hiding in sewers and specially equipped bunkers. During the first few days, only a few bunkers were believed to exist; but as the major operation continued, it became clear that the entire ghetto was systematically equipped with cellars, bunkers, and passages." Stroop's report on the first day of the fighting concludes: "During the search only 200 Jews were caught. Afterward stormtroops were sent into action against the bunkers known to us with orders to bring out their inhabitants and demolish the bunkers themselves. About 380 Jews were caught in this operation. The presence of Jews in the sewers was discovered."[22]

Thus we learn from Stroop's report that as a result of a day of stubborn fighting, which cost the Germans heavy losses, 580 Jews were trapped—about 1 percent of the ghetto's population at the time. According to Stroop, this "accomplishment" was achieved because the Germans knew the location of some of the "shops," and most of the victims of April 19 were trapped in them. On the first day of the operation, then, in addition to the organized and determined armed resistance of the fighting organizations, the Germans came up against the phenomenon of tens of thousands of people fortified below ground.

The Second and Third Days of the Uprising (April 20 and 21) That night the ghetto was free of Germans, which allowed the fighters and civilians to move openly within its walls. The results of the first day of fighting surpassed even the boldest expectations, and a feeling of satisfaction, and even elation, spread among the fighters and many of those holed up in the bunkers. But the commanders of the fighting organizations, who had to plan the continuation of the battle, could not afford to give themselves up to optimism. Even many among the noncombatant population comprehended the lessons of the first day of fighting. The Germans had indeed been defeated in battle and suffered losses in equipment, lives, and—far more serious (from their point of view)—pride and prestige. But the extensive preparation that the Germans had invested, the size of the force they placed in action, and the tactics they adopted clearly indicated that they were determined to liquidate the ghetto and its residents regardless of the cost or the means required to do so. If anyone had deluded himself that the Germans would back down from a fight in a hostile, rebellious city, it soon became clear beyond doubt that such considerations meant nothing to them. By the end of the first day, it was also painfully obvious that the weapons possessed by the fighters, particularly the revolvers, were ineffective at long range. Moreover, the only effective weapons they had—grenades, bombs, and heavy machine guns—were severely limited, and if the scope of the attacks on the first day was indicative of the future, they would last for only a few days. Finally, the shortage of weapons and the limited effectiveness of the revolvers severely reduced the number of fighters who could be sent into action.

On the second day, the fighting took place mainly in the Brushmakers' Area, but April 20 also witnessed a fierce battle in Muranowska

Square, which ended with the destruction of the Z.Z.W.'s main force. (It is not clear whether this battle took place on the second or third day of the uprising. Stroop's comprehensive survey reports it on the second day, while in his daily reports he remarked on the battle on April 22.) Describing the events of April 20, Adam Halperin wrote:

> The Germans heightened their pressure on the Betar fighters. Tanks and armored cars penetrated as far as the approaches to the street and rained hellfire on the Jewish combat group. As the battle grew more heated, the situation of the Betar fighters deteriorated—a problem that was exacerbated by the break in communications with the general fighters' organization [Ż.O.B.]. The Germans began to set fire to the buildings on Muranowska Street, and the Jewish fighters were forced to leave the burning building [and move to] the neighboring building under a hail of German machine-gun fire.[23]

As a consequence of the shooting and the arson, the group of Ż.Z.W. fighters (including some wounded) left the ghetto through the tunnel. Members of the K.B. evidently aided them in organizing their retreat to the "Aryan" side, and they eventually reached a forest between Michalin and Józefów—resort areas in the vicinity of Warsaw—where a Polish policeman informed on them and they came under attack by the Germans.[24] Most of the Ż.Z.W. fighters, headed by Leon Rodal, fell in this clash. The outcome of the skirmish was confirmed in a communiqué of the German gendarmerie, which reported on April 22, 1943, that during a manhunt in Otwock (the area the fighters had reached), the gendarmerie attacked fourteen Jews (eight men and six women). "Some of the Jews had light wounds incurred on the night of April 20/21, 1943, during the incidents in the Warsaw ghetto. The Jews left the ghetto through sewers and underground passages."[25] Another group of Ż.Z.W. fighters, together with a number of civilians, attempted to leave the ghetto at dawn on April 22. They passed through the tunnel and waited for Polish guides in a building at the exit end of the passage. However, they were informed upon —evidently by one of the building's tenants—and German troops and Polish police surrounded the building and trapped the fugitive Jews on the roof.[26]

The main battle on April 20 occurred in the Brushmakers' Area, where five squads of Ż.O.B. fighters (commanded by Berlinski, Blones, Grynszpan, Gutman, and Praszkier) were stationed under area-commander Marek Edelman. A group of Ż.Z.W. fighters under the command of Chaim Łopata was also active there, and there is testimony to the effect that bands of "wildcat" fighters were present in the area.[27] According to Edelman, until 2:00 P.M. on April 20, all was quiet in the Brushmakers' Area. Then a German column advanced toward the gate of the compound, which had earlier been mined by the Ż.O.B. As soon as the Germans were massed in the passage that led into the compound, the mine was set off, and the explosion and attendant casualties led to a disorderly German retreat. After a while the Germans reappeared and advanced toward the area cautiously, while the Jewish fighters opened fire from their positions. The Germans tried to bypass the sources of fire by making their way onto the rooftops, and they succeeded in surprising the insurgents from above. Michael Klepfisz of the Bund (who played an important role in the manufacture of armaments in the ghetto) lost his life in the subsequent hand-to-hand fighting, but the rest of the fighters overcame the Germans and managed a retreat.

At that point three German officers with strips of white cloth attached to their lapels appeared in the street and called for a fifteen-minute truce and negotiations with the command of the area. The fighters believed that the appeal was directed at them and rejected it unequivocally. Other sources suggest that the proposal was addressed not to the fighters but rather to the Jews who supervised the "shop," in the hope that they might now succeed in persuading the residents of the area to surrender and be transferred to Poniatow. This way the Germans hoped to avoid the need to fight and perhaps even salvage the machinery and raw materials in the factory.

The fighters responded to the German proposal with bullets. Stroop reported on this battle and the outcome of the negotiations in his report for April 20:

> At about 1500 hours [3:00 P.M.] I was able to bring about the immediate evacuation of a block of houses occupied by the army's Store Authority containing, as reported, 4,000 Jews. The German supervisor was ordered to demand that the Jewish workers evacuate the place voluntarily. Only twenty-eight Jews responded to this order. I therefore decided to evacuate the block by force or blow it up. The team of three anti-aircraft cannon (2 cm.) put into action here suffered two dead. The Howitzer cannon (10 cm.) drove the gangs out of their strongholds and, as far as it was possible to determine, also inflicted losses on them. We were forced to halt this action because of nightfall. On April 21, 1943, we will return to attack this nest of insurgents, and during the night we will keep it encircled to the best of our ability. . . . In one instance the thugs planted mines.[28]

Thus the Germans' last-ditch attempt to seduce the workers and others living in the area to agree to evacuation was a complete failure. Only twenty-eight people out of four thousand obeyed the order, which indicates that the urge to hide and prepare for the worst, rather than be trapped by the Germans, was characteristic not only of the population of the Central Ghetto but of the workers in the Brushmakers' Area as well.

On April 20, units also went into action in the area of the large "shops" (Többens-Schultz), where eight squads of Ż.O.B. fighters and some units of the Ż.Z.W. were located. The fighters stationed in this sector could not see the Germans entering the Central Ghetto on April 19; they only heard the sounds of battle. Moreover, they were cut off from the Central Ghetto and the Ż.O.B. headquarters there, and their isolation continued throughout the uprising.

The Germans decided to delay their attack on the area of the large "shops" in order to give the German factory owners one last chance to coax their workers into evacuating the "shops" peacefully and to extricate the machinery, raw materials, and finished products. It was for this reason that the German military force was sent into operation in the area of the "shops" only on April 20, although an armed German unit had passed through the sector on its way to the Central Ghetto. The fighters who were deployed for battle in a Ż.O.B. position at 76 Leszno Street attacked that column when it passed the building. Eliezer Geller, the commander of that stretch of street, threw a grenade at it, but the Germans merely evacuated their casualties and continued to advance without stopping or returning the fire. The squad commanded by Benjamin Wald awaited the advancing column in the building at 36 Leszno Street, and here, too, grenades were thrown. This time the Germans returned their fire, but they did not follow up with a general reprisal action. Their restraint evidently stemmed from the assumption that it was best not to fuel the flames of the revolt in the area of the "shops," as they had yet to exhaust their efforts to "move the residents of the Többens-Schultz area to labor camps without a battle." When the German unit moved down Smocza Street, the members of David Nowodworski's squad tried to set off the mine that had been planted there, but it did not explode, because of a defective fuse. Stroop noted in his daily report that a tank was attacked and "two units of stormtroopers overcame nests of insurgents and opened the way for the tank crew" in the area through which the unit passed.[29]

The second day of the uprising also witnessed two abortive "support actions" by the Polish underground. A band of fighters from the A.K. attempted to break through the wall on Bonifraterska Street. This operation, under the command of Major Jozef Pszenny ("Chwacki"), was conceived as a major action in the A.K. plan to aid the ghetto.[30] The Polish unit moved up the wall at six in the evening. Getting there was not difficult, since the Germans did not interfere with the assembly of Poles near the wall. But this very fact, which made it easy for the Poles to reach their objective, ultimately got in the way of the action itself. The commander found it difficult to maintain eye contact with his men, who were dispersed around the area to execute various tasks. In the end, the Poles did not complete their mission, since the Polish Police had them under surveillance and called in the Germans. The one mine activated during the assault tore a crater in the road, but the wall remained intact. In the meantime, shooting had broken out between the Polish fighters and the Germans called to the scene. According to Polish sources, some armed Germans were hit during this clash, while two A.K. fighters (Józef Wilk and Eugeniusz Morawski) fell in the battle and two others were wounded.

The same day a combat group of the People's Army (*Armia Ludowa* — A.L.), under the command of Franciszek Bartoszek ("Jacek") and including the Jewish fighter Niuta Tejtelbaum, attacked a German artillery crew stationed on Nowiniarska Street to shell the Brushmakers' Area. The action began at about seven in the evening. According to the Polish version of events, the German crew (made up of two men) was hit and silenced, while another A.L. group (under the command of Jerzy Lerner — "Mietek") attempted to attack the German sentries at the corner of Gęsia and Okopowa. This latter attack failed, owing to the fact that before the band ever got near the Germans, it encountered a group of Polish hooligans who ganged up on its Jewish commander. The scuffle with the Poles roused the attention of the German force, and the Polish unit dispersed. Lerner was killed by German gunfire.[31]

On the opposite side of the ghetto, a group of Jews (probably ten in number) headed by Jacob Rakower, a porter who had been a sergeant in the Polish army, succeeded in breaking through the siege cordon and reaching the Polish sector of the city via the Jewish cemetery bordering Okopowa Street. It is not clear whether this group received aid from the Poles in organizing its escape and, if so, who its benefactors were. Likewise, we have no details on how the break was organized or effected. The group evidently succeeded in making its way through the streets of the Polish sector and reached the area occupied by the partisans, but all trace of it was lost thereafter.[32]

We learn from Stroop's report for Tuesday, April 20, that the deportation operation did not make much headway that day. During the day's action to quell the uprising in the Central Ghetto, "Nine bunkers were uncovered, the inhabitants who offered resistance were overcome in battle [and] the bunkers were blown up. . . . In an action by nine units of stormtroopers, a total of 505 Jews were caught today, and to the extent that they were fit for work, they were spared in order to be sent to Poniatow."[33] According to Stroop's data, a force of 1,262 soldiers and 31 officers was placed in operation that day. It therefore averages out that two and a half Germans were required to trap a single Jew.

Meanwhile, on the "Aryan" side of the city, the representatives of the Jewish National Committee, the Coordination Committee, and emissaries of the Ż.O.B. began to publicize what was happening in the ghetto. Unfortunately, their situation reports, based on sporadic contact with comrades beleaguered within the ghetto, are not accurate and do not add any meaningful details to the history of the uprising. Yet these communiqués do contain interesting details from the perspective of observers on the Polish side of the city. Situation Report #3, dated Tuesday, April 20, 1943, states:

> . . . The Germans threw strong army units, field guns, tanks, and armored units into the battle. On Tuesday afternoon and evening, the shelling continued without respite. The streets bordering on the ghetto — and especially the vicinity of Bonifraterska, Franciszkańska, and Świętojerska — were occupied by the army and the SS. The Germans set up field cannon on the squares, heavy machine guns on the roofs. At about 5–6 P.M., a heavy bombardment of the ghetto began from that side. The blast of the shells could be heard for tens of kilometers. Many fires broke out and no one extinguished them. Smoke billowed up from the ghetto. In the afternoon the movement of tram cars and pedestrians came to a halt on the streets bordering the ghetto. The tram connection between Warsaw and Żolibórz and Marymont was cut. . . . On Tuesday afternoon the Germans tightened the siege of the ghetto. Electricity, water, and gas were cut off from every street [and] police dogs were brought in to uncover the shelters and hiding places (the "Jewish bunkers"). The outcome of the Jewish fighters' struggle on the first day of the *Aktion* [Monday] is already known: more than 100 Germans killed and wounded and a few dozen Germans relieved of their weapons. . . . [34]

The third day of the uprising, April 21, witnessed a change in the tactics adopted by both sides. For the most part, the fighters were not able to hold on to the static positions prepared on the upper floors of the buildings. At the same time, the Germans no longer came out in large groups, which had proved to be easy targets. Instead, they broke up into small bands that roamed throughout the ghetto, forcing the Jewish fighters to adapt their strategy. Thus the subsequent assaults on the Germans were executed by small, mobile squads that lay in ambush, and although the Germans hunted down their attackers by searching out the vicinity from which the fire had been directed at them, their efforts were usually futile.

The battle in the Brushmakers' Area continued on the third day of the uprising, and General Stroop described the situation as follows:

> Last night it was necessary to halt the limited operation in the eastern half of the military Store Authority's housing block because of nightfall. Therefore a combat unit reinforced by the Engineering Corps and heavy

weapons . . . was again put into action. After combing the large block of houses, in which a considerable number of bunkers and underground passages were uncovered, they caught sixty Jews. Despite all the efforts, [however,] it was impossible to catch any more of the 700–800 Jews in the block. They retreated from shelter to shelter via the underground passages, shooting sporadically. I therefore decided to blow up these passages, insofar as they were known to me, and then to set everything ablaze.

. . . Today the enemy used the same weapons as yesterday, especially homemade explosives. Samples are being kept by the commander of the SS and the police. For the first time members of the Women's Jewish Fighting Organization [the pioneering movements] were sighted. The following were captured: rifles, revolvers, hand grenades, explosives, horses, parts of SS uniforms. Our losses: two policemen (Orpo), two SS men, one man from Trawniki (lightly wounded).[35]

On the same day, smaller armed clashes also broke out in the streets of the Central Ghetto: Franciszkańska, Zamenhofa, Miła, etc. Unaffiliated groups and individuals probably fought alongside the Ż.O.B. in these battles. The material at our disposal contains references—usually reliable—to armed clashes in places where no organized forces were stationed. It is possible that these references are either to actions of the mobile Ż.O.B. squads or to the activities of irregular groups. In either case, both Stroop's report and official Jewish sources make mention of unaffiliated armed individuals opening up fire when the Germans attempted to penetrate bunkers.

The main arena of activity on the third day was the Brushmakers' compound. After the Germans despaired of overcoming the insurgents in combat, they began to set off explosions and fires, and the fighters and many others living in the area were forced to flee. As the fighter Simha Ratajzer ("Kazik") reported, since escape routes had not been prepared in time, squads of fighters tried to break through the German siege.[36] The commander of the area, Marek Edelman, described the retreat:

> The fighters put up such a strong stand that the Germans were finally forced to give up on defeating them by force of arms and found new, presumably more effective means. They set fire to the Brushmakers' Area from every direction. In an instant the flames attacked the entire block. Black smoke chokes the throat, seeping into the eyes. We decide to risk everything on one chance and break through to the Central Ghetto. The fighters do not want to fall to the blaze. On the way, the flames lick at our clothes, which catch fire. The asphalt melts under [our] feet and turns into sticky, black slime. The glass scattered everywhere also turns into ooze and [our] feet stick to it. The heat from the paving stones burns the soles of [our] shoes. One after the other we flee through the flames, from build-

ing to building, yard to yard. There's no air left to breathe; a hundred hammers pound in our heads. Burning wooden beams fall on us. Finally we leave the area of the fire. It is wonderful to stand in a place that is not ablaze. But the most difficult is yet to come. The only way to get to the Central Ghetto is through a small opening in the wall guarded by the gendarmerie, Ukrainians, and the "Blue Police." Twelve men are standing guard over a passage 2 meters wide, and five combat squads must get through there. One after the other, our shoes wrapped in rags to muffle the sound of footsteps, under heavy fire and great tension, Gutman, Berlinski, and Greenbaum's groups make their way through. Jurek Blones' group lags behind. The moment its first members reach the street, the Germans illuminate the spot. It looks as if no one else will be able to get through. Romanowicz douses the spotlight with a single shot. Before the Germans recover their wits, we are already on the other side. Here, having joined up with the local groups, we continue to act.[37]

The strategy by which Stroop hoped to suppress the uprising—i.e., burning down buildings—was vigorously opposed by the "shop" owners, for fear that the conflagration would consume their factories and machinery. They claimed that Globocnik (meaning the SS) had promised them immunity and given assurances that their plants would not be damaged during the *Aktion*. The "shop" owners attempted to negotiate with Stroop, and on April 22 Globocnik himself appeared in Warsaw, this time not to supervise the deportation but to persuade Stroop to spare the property in the industrial plants. During his postwar interrogation, Stroop stated that "General Globocnik came to see me at the beginning of the uprising . . . to notify me that all the warehouses and the expropriation of property in the ghetto had been placed under his jurisdiction by order of the ex-'*Reichsführer*' of the SS, Himmler, and that the transport of the ghetto's inhabitants from the railway station was exclusively his affair."[38] It appears that Stroop was prepared to take Globocnik's claims into consideration, but he refused to give priority to the evacuation of machinery and stock from the "shops." The disagreement between Stroop, on the one hand, and Globocnik and Többens, on the other, was evidently brought before Himmler, who sided with Stroop. On April 24 Krieger received a cable from Himmler (sent on the twenty-second) stating that "the combing of the Warsaw ghetto must be carried out thoroughly, with a hard heart, without mercy. It is best to proceed rigorously. The incidents in Warsaw prove how dangerous these Jews are."[39]

In a statement made after the war, Többens charged that in contrast to Globocnik, who was sympathetic to the interests of the factory owners, Stroop acted without restraint. "He allegedly carried out a war against the Jewish resistance movement," Többens complained, "but in fact he acted against everyone in the ghetto." Globocnik also criticized Stroop's behavior, and in a report on the operations of the "Osti," sent from Trieste in January 1944, he claimed that the liquidation of the Warsaw ghetto "caused substantial damage, and because the gravity of the situation was not properly understood, the liquidation was executed by erroneous means." Többens claimed that at a certain stage of the controversy, Globocnik threatened to seek Göring's intervention.[40] If Többens's statement is true, then the friction must have been considerable indeed, for it was highly unusual for a senior SS officer to think of appealing to a political figure outside the SS, especially since Himmler was known to be fanatic about the discipline and internal unity of the SS and was the final arbiter of all disagreements that arose within its ranks. By the second day of the *Aktion*, however, Stroop had his heart set on evacuating the area of the large "shops." On April 20 he reported:

> I succeeded in readying the firms of W. C. Többens, Schultz and Associates, and Hoffmann—including all their workers—for evacuation starting at 6:00 A.M. on April 21, 1943, so that the intent to purge the ghetto would finally become clear. The supervisor of the Többens factory promised to lead the Jews—about 4,000–5,000 of them—to the appointed place for transport of their own will. If the voluntary evacuation does not succeed, as in the case of the army Store Authority, I shall clean out this part of the ghetto by force.[41]

As soon as the uprising broke out, the owners of the large "shops" initiated an intensive campaign to persuade their workers to leave peacefully. They attempted to draw a distinction between what was taking place in the Central Ghetto—the arena of the uprising—and what they called the "productive" ghetto, which must act with foresight. If the workers acted wisely, they promised, and followed their advice and guidance, they could expect a different fate. Többens, Schultz, and others circulated among the workers, attempting to exploit their influence over their Jewish assistants and claiming that the events in the Central Ghetto had nothing to do with the "shop" area. The fact is, they claimed, that two days of the *Aktion* had already gone by and the SS units had made no effort whatsoever to intervene in the affairs of the area containing the large "shops." Többens also tried to prevent the outbreak of fighting in the Brushmakers' Area—that is, the sector that Stroop referred to as the "army Store Authority"—but failed to do so. He therefore concentrated his efforts on the sector of the main "shops," where his own factory, that of Schultz, and other large enterprises were located. On April 21, in accordance with Stroop's demand, Többens issued a deportation order to the management of the sixteen major "shops." He based this order on the authority he had been given by Globocnik and on Stroop's consent to his measures. The order stated, in part:

> . . . I bring the following to your attention: (1) the transfer of all Jewish manpower will take place on April 21, 1943, at 6:00 A.M.; (2) the shipment of materials and machinery will be carried out according to my orders; . . . I hereby firmly direct the attention of the factory managements to the fact that workers found in the area of the closed quarter after the departure of the transports, unless bearing the special documents mentioned above, will be shot (on the spot) in accordance with wartime law. . . . [42]

In his report for April 21, Stroop noted that "5,200 Jews were captured in the former armaments factories and led under guard to the loading platform of deportation."[43] His use of the term "caught" (*erfasst*) was designed to create the impression that these Jews had been hunted down, which he hoped would compensate for the inability of his troops to trap people in the Central Ghetto. In fact, most of the 5,200 people mentioned in the communiqué reported for deportation, as a result of the coaxing by Többens and his associates, though a good number of them were trapped by means of deception.

The situation in the area of the large "shops" therefore appears to have differed substantially from that in the Central Ghetto and the Brushmakers' Area, principally because a large proportion of the workers responded to the appeals of the "shop" owners. However, we should also note that the network of hiding places was neither widespread nor particularly sophisticated in this area—as it was in the Central Ghetto—so that opportunities to go into hiding for a long period were far more limited. It is also highly probable that the magnitude of the struggle in the Central Ghetto and the strategy adopted by the Germans convinced many of the workers that there was no point in taking shelter in the bunkers, for all their inhabitants were doomed to be wiped out sooner or later. These "shop" workers evidently assumed that while the inhabitants of the Central Ghetto had no way out, they themselves still had a slim chance, and it must be seized. Moreover, the outlook prevailing among many of the workers in the sector of the large "shops" undoubtedly determined the scope of activity undertaken by the combat forces stationed there. Although these squads were prepared for battle and attacked the Germans whenever the opportunity arose, they could not carry on a vigorous and extended campaign. Thus the case of the "shops" proves that the uprising—which did include a number of fierce battles and prolonged resistance—was only possible with the cooperation of the population at large.

At the same time, we have already noted that not all the workers who were deported from the Többens-Schultz area had responded to the appeals of the "shop" owners. The Germans did their best to create the impression that those living in the sector of the large "shops" were free to assemble in the street without interference from the SS. Stefan Grajek related that at first the Germans did not respond to these assemblies, but "when the number of people who came out [into the street] grew, the Germans and their Latvian and Lithuanian helpers surrounded them and led them off to 80 Leszno Street." As mentioned earlier, April 21 was essentially the final deadline Stroop had given the "shop" owners. "From that day," Grajek explained, "the sector of the 'shops' ceased to fall under the protection of the owners of the Többens-Schultz factories and came under the full control of Stroop's soldiers, just like the other sections of the ghetto."[44]

The Turning Point in the Uprising

As we have seen, after the initial days of battle, the German command reached the conclusion that the way to overcome the insurgents was to burn down or demolish the ghetto's buildings, thereby forcing the Jews to come out into the open. On April 26 Stroop reported that "during today's operation many housing blocks were set aflame. This is the only and ultimate way to defeat the rabble and scum of the earth and bring them above ground." His April 22 report illustrated this form of warfare and its results:

> The fire that raged all night drove the Jews who — despite all the search operations — were still hiding under roofs, in cellars, and in other hiding places out of the housing blocks in order to escape the flames in one way or another. Scores of burning Jews — whole families — jumped from windows or tried to slide down sheets that had been tied together, etc. We took pains to ensure that those Jews, as well as others, were wiped out immediately.

Initially the Germans allocated three days for the liquidation of the ghetto. Stroop was naturally interested in accelerating the pace of the operation and evidently thought that the fire and demolition would achieve his aim quickly. On the fifth day of the *Aktion,* April 23, he believed that the revolt had come to an end. He therefore divided the ghetto into twenty-four sectors and ordered his troops, likewise divided into units according to sector, to comb the area in a final search. In his report for April 23, Stroop noted that "the troops were notified that the *Aktion* will end today," but it soon became evident that his announcement was premature, for "the Jews and the hooligans are [still] to be found in a number of blocks."[45]

The principal difficulty confronting Stroop at this stage of the uprising was the "battle of the bunkers," which continued for close to a month and evidently did not end even on May 16, 1943—the day on which he officially pronounced the close of the "Grand *Aktion*" in the ghetto. After the war, during his interrogation, Stroop repeatedly stressed that "We did not find out about all the bunkers and strongholds set up and equipped for the uprising until after the start of the battle!" In each of his daily reports, he spoke of dozens of bunkers being discovered, cleaned out, and blown up. On May 24, 1943, when he replied in writing to questions addressed to him by Krieger, Stroop testified that 631 bunkers were destroyed during the "Grand *Aktion*."

The Germans needed special facilities for their campaign against the bunkers, such as police dogs, special listening devices to detect sounds underground, and poisonous gas for the bunkers whose inhabitants refused to come out. A gas of the chlorine variety was also used to annihilate the inhabitants of the bunkers, since the Germans would not dare to infiltrate the labyrinth of hiding places. Stroop does not mention the use of gas in his reports and would not confess to it even after the war. In both cases, he insisted that only smoke bombs were used to clear out the bunkers, but the truth is that many were killed by the poisonous gases used against these hideouts. In fact, it was the gas, more than anything else, that forced the victims to come out. There were also many cases of delayed complications and respiratory diseases, and people so affected later died in "Revir," the special section for the sick in the Majdanek concentration camp.[46]

All of these measures did little to bring about the swift defeat of the bunkers. On the contrary, the "battle of the bunkers" turned into a drawn-out operation in which the Germans made slow progress. The condition of the bunkers' inhabitants—meaning the entire population of the Central Ghetto, including the fighters—steadily deteriorated until it turned into a state of unrelieved suffering and torture. At the beginning of the uprising, the Germans set fire to individual buildings or housing blocks, but in the course of time the fire spread until it engulfed the entire ghetto. Many bunkers collapsed as a result of the blaze and the consequent buckling of building walls. When only the skeletons of buildings remained, the cellars grew so hot that it was impossible to breathe in them. But the Germans did not content themselves with the results of the fire and went on to blow up what remained of the gutted structures. Bunkers became uninhabitable and were abandoned. Yet even under these circumstances, the population of the bunkers did not give up the struggle, and they began to wander from bunker to bunker or seek cover among the ruins. One memoir described the scene in a central bunker at 30 Franciszkańska Street, where a number of injured Ż.O.B. members found shelter:

I can't think of anything but breathing air. The heat in the bunker is unbearable. [But] it's not only the heat. The steaming walls give off an odor as if the mildew absorbed during decades had suddenly been released by the catalyst of heat. And there's no air. I sit here open-mouthed, as do all those around me, deluding ourselves that we can gulp down some air. There is no talk in the bunker [because] it is more difficult to breathe when you talk. But from time to time shouting [and] scuffles break out; nerves are taut, and for the most part the shouts are over nothing. We haven't eaten for twenty-four hours. Only dry bread is left and the water is more or less fit for drinking. All the food has spoiled. The heat and the odor have tainted it, so that the ample reserves are inedible.[47]

In another memoir, a man who wandered from one hiding place to another described the situation in one of these shelters: "The new hideout was not the most pleasant of places. It was crowded; cold crept through your bones; we had to stand in water above our hips; and the water pipe—which was in contact with the electricity cable—was electrified. . . ."[48] Despite it all, however, the inhabitants of the bunkers refused to surrender. They continued to struggle under great stress and intolerable physical conditions, and every instance of successfully evading the Germans was regarded as deliverance.

In addition to the sophisticated devices for exposing the bunkers, the Germans also employed informers, who were promised their lives in return for revealing the whereabouts of the bunkers' entrances. The Germans hauled these informers along with them, and when the entrance to a bunker was breached, they were ordered to call out in Yiddish for everyone to come out, since the bunker had been exposed and only those who would come out willingly had a chance of saving themselves. The Germans also forced the informers to stand directly in front of the entrance, since the initial response to their call was often a round of gunfire.

The "battle of the bunkers" proved to the Germans that the Jews were determined not to surrender themselves. On April 24 Stroop reported: "From time to time it became clear that despite the terror of the raging fire, the Jews and the hooligans preferred to turn back into the flames rather than fall into our hands." And on May 4 he confessed in his daily battle report: "Uncovering the bunkers becomes more difficult. Often it would be impossible to find [them] were it not for the treachery of other Jews. The command to leave the bunkers voluntarily is almost never obeyed; only the use of smoke bombs forces the Jews to respond to it."

Many bunkers were the strongholds of recalcitrants who not only preferred death by fire or gassing to capture but even fought back. Often they were members of the fighting organizations who had found their way into the bunkers and resisted when the Germans arrived, though it must be added that the armed struggle of individuals and unaffiliated groups focused primarily on the defense of the bunkers. On April 26 Stroop detailed a number of incidents of this nature:

> The entire former Jewish residential quarter was again combed today by the same stormtroopers going over the same sectors. That way I hoped that the commanders would approach as far as the open lines of the housing blocks and courtyards familiar to them so that they could advance further and infiltrate the labyrinth of bunkers and underground passages. Almost all the stormtroopers reported some resistance, but it was broken by firing back or blowing up the bunkers.[49]

The fortified labyrinth of subterranean bunkers and tunnels made the ghetto into a unique partisan fighting ground. Since a substantial portion of the bunkers were not uncovered by the police dogs, listening devices, or informers, the network of shelters that protected the remains of Warsaw's Jewish community posed a serious challenge to the Germans. A clear-cut order demanded that every Jew be trapped and liquidated or sent to a camp. Yet in the heart of a large metropolis, clandestine Jewish life continued to go on below ground, and even after weeks of employing the most radical and brutal tactics, the Germans had difficulty snuffing it out. The "battle of the bunkers" held down German troops and, above all, took time. And that time—the days and weeks—was precisely what discomfited the Germans most. The *Aktion,* conceived as a three-day final purge of the Warsaw ghetto, had turned into a drawn-out and far from routine battle in which German military and police forces were pitted against Jewish civilians holed up in bunkers. In full view of the Polish public, under the curious and mocking gaze of the population of a city that was the focus of constant security problems, the "battle of the bunkers" was regarded as a blot on the Germans' prestige and a serious security risk.

The full-scale battle fought by the members of the combat organizations lasted primarily for the first three days of the uprising. From then on the Germans generally succeeded in overcoming the pockets of resistance, driving the fighters out of their positions, and forcing them to retreat into the bunkers, which thereafter served as bases for the combat forces. Although the network of subterranean shelters had originally been regarded as refuges for the noncombatant population, it now assimilated the fighters as well, allowing them to continue their struggle. It was from these bunkers that bands of fighters went out on raids and attacked the enemy. If the hundreds of fighters had been forced to operate in an unpopulated ghetto, or were opposed by a hostile population, the Germans would probably have suppressed the rebellion during the first days of open combat. While it is true that not all of the bunkers willingly accepted the fighters, for their presence was regarded as an additional risk and provocation of the Germans, most of them welcomed the combatants with open arms and agreed to place the defense of the bunker in their hands. As a rule, therefore, the network of bunkers played an important role in the Warsaw ghetto uprising by considerably extending the life of the revolt. In point of fact, it took the Germans longer to quell the Warsaw ghetto uprising than it had taken them to defeat entire countries. Moreover, the stand of the population in the bunkers accorded the uprising the character of a popular revolt in which thousands of civilians took part. Thus it was to the credit of the bunkers that the outburst of the combat squads developed into a partisan struggle that went on for an extended period of time.

On April 23, Mordecai Anielewicz wrote to his comrade Yitzhak Zuckerman, who was stationed on the "Aryan" side of the city:

> I can't begin to describe the conditions under which the Jews are living. Only an elect few will hold out under them. All the others will perish, sooner or later. Our fate is sealed. In the bunkers where our comrades are hiding, it is not even possible to light a candle at night for lack of air. . . . During the day they sit in the hideouts. Starting in the evening we go over to the partisan method of action. At night six of our companies go out with two tasks before them: armed reconnaissance and the acquisition of arms.[50]

Marek Edelman wrote in A Fighting Ghetto:

> Because conditions had changed so much, the Ż.O.B. revised its tactics [and] attempted to defend larger concentrations of people hiding from the Germans in bunkers. Thus, for example, two Ż.O.B. squads (Hochberg's and Berek's) moved a few hundred people from a shelter that had been blocked on 37 Miła Street to 7 Miła Street in broad daylight. This [latter] position, which contained a few thousand people, was held for over a week. In the meantime, the burning of the ghetto was drawing to a close. Places of shelter are sorely lacking and—even worse—there is a shortage of water. The fighters are going down into the shelters together with the civilian population. There they will continue to fight as best they can. The battles and clashes take place mostly at night now. During the day the ghetto is like a city of the dead. Only on the totally darkened streets do Ż.O.B. squads meet up with German units. Whoever fires first has the advantage. Our units circulate through the entire ghetto, [and] every night many from both sides are killed. The Germans and Ukrainians go out only in large units and more often than not set up ambushes.[51]

Thus even after all hopes of remaining underground for a prolonged period—perhaps even until the end of the war—were dashed, the alliance between the fighters and the many civilians living in the bunkers held fast. Even the bunker housing the Ż.O.B. headquarters at 18 Miła Street, in which the organization's command and principal force found refuge, was not a Ż.O.B. bunker per se but had been set up by a group of hardened smugglers. The fighters, for their part, combined the continuation of the armed struggle with the defense of the bunkers. Yet both the fighters and civilians in the ghetto realized that the situation generated by the resistance could only be temporary.

Stroop's reports reveal that the armed clashes continued, and the troops charged with wiping out the bunkers were forced to operate under combat conditions. On April 23 he reported that "the Jews and the thugs restrained themselves until the last moment in order to pour intense fire on the units." On April 24 he commented that "from time to time the Jews continued to shoot, almost until the end of the operation. . . ." The next day Stroop noted that "today, as well, there was occasional armed resistance, and three revolvers and explosives were captured in one of the bunkers." Three days later he made note of the fact that "the external appearance of the Jews being caught now implies that the turn of the . . . leaders of the rebellion has come. Swearing against Germany and the Führer and cursing the German soldiers, they hurled themselves out of windows and off balconies." His report for April 28 stated that "today, as well, armed resistance was exhibited and broken in a number of places." On May 2 Stroop recorded that "the SS patrols operating at night sometimes met up with armed resistance from the Jews." The next day he elaborated that "in most cases, the Jews fought with weapons before abandoning the bunkers," and "last night shots were aimed at some of the patrols operating in the ghetto." On May 4: "In order to catch the Jews totally off guard, the troops on patrol wrapped their shoes in rags and other materials at night. Thirty Jews were shot to death in clashes with the patrol units." On May 5: "Today, as well, Jews fought in a number of places before being captured." As late as May 13 he wrote:

> While mopping up one of the bunkers, a real battle took place in which Jews not only opened fire with .08-caliber revolvers and Polish Wiss pistols but even tossed oval-shaped, Polish-manufactured hand grenades at the SS men. After a few of the bunker's [fighters] were brought out and stood waiting to be searched, one of the women slipped her hand under her dress in a flash and—as has often happened—pulled a hand grenade out of her underwear, released the cap, and hurled it at the men who were searching her, while she herself jumped back quickly and took cover.[52]

Descriptions of battles in the bunkers were also available from Jewish sources. Marek Edelman described one such battle in a bunker at 30 Franciszkańska Street, a building with a number of courtyards and sophisticated bunkers. One of them had taken in some fighters who had earlier retreated from the Brushmakers' Area:

> ... The shelter on 30 Franciszkańska Street, which housed an operative base of fighters who had broken through from the Brushmakers' Area, was uncovered on May 3. The men fought one of the most outstanding battles from the technical point of view. It lasted for two days, and 50 percent of our men fell. Berek was killed by a grenade. . . . It is difficult to speak of victory when people are fighting for their lives and so many are lost, but one thing can be said of this battle: We did not allow the Germans to execute their plans.[53]

German Losses during the "Grand *Aktion*"

The number of German dead and wounded, according to Stroop's comprehensive and daily reports, is detailed in Table 8. (The main figures come from Stroop's final review, while the figures in parentheses were given in his daily reports.)

Determining the number of German losses in the April uprising is a very complex affair. Jewish sources note hundreds of dead and wounded, while other witnesses speak of thousands of German casualties. (We have come across mention of as many as scores of German dead and wounded in a single battle.)[54] High estimates of the German casualty figures are also given by Polish observers. Even the *Delegatura*, which displayed a pronounced inclination to underplay the scope and impact of the revolt, reported on April 22 that the Germans had suffered 86 dead and 420 wounded.[55] Moreover, the *Delegatura* had access to reliable information from sources who followed developments among the Germans, so that the figures it reported were presented not as generalized estimates but as exact. On the other hand, during his pretrial interrogation, Stroop claimed that the casualty figures he reported were usually double-checked and exacting. There are obvious discrepancies between Stroop's daily reports and his comprehensive survey, but even these differences do not fundamentally change the broader picture, since the gap between Stroop's two versions and the figures cited in Polish and Jewish sources remains substantial.

Which source then, are we to believe? Is it permissible simply to assume that Stroop and Krieger deliberately diminished the number of casualties to underplay the gravity of the uprising and avoid admitting (to internal security circles and the families of the casualties) how many were killed and wounded in battle within the Warsaw ghetto? Although such an assumption is highly probable, we cannot ignore Stroop's ten-

TABLE 8
STROOP'S RECORD OF GERMAN LOSSES

Date	Killed	Wounded	Unspecified Losses*
April 19	1	24	(12)
April 20	3 (2)	10 (9)	
April 21		4 (1)	(4)
April 22	3	(1)	(1)
April 23		3 (3)	
April 24		3 (2)	
April 25		4 (4)	
April 26		1	
April 27		4 (3)	
April 28		3 (3)	
April 30		(1)	
May 1	2 (1)	2	
May 2		1 (7)	
May 3		3 (3)	
May 5		1 (1)	
May 6	2 (1)	1 (2)	
May 7		1 (1)	
May 8	2 (2)	3 (3)	
May 10		4 (3)	
May 11	1	2 (1)	
May 12		1 (1)	
May 13	2 (2)	4 (4)	
May 14		5 (5)	
May 15		1 (1)	
Total	16 (8)	85 (59)	(17)

*Not specified whether dead or wounded

dency to liken the battle in the ghetto to a genuine, full-scale military operation and to depict those who fell in the action as heroes who died "for the Führer and the Motherland" and "will never be forgotten." Stroop also requested that he and his men be awarded medals in recognition of their service and acts of "valor" in the ghetto, and Himmler honored his request. The number cited by Stroop cannot be rejected out of hand, but it is likely that his list was neither complete, free of errors, nor indicative of the German losses throughout the entire period of resistance, that is, until the absolute liquidation of Jewish life in the ghetto. All the same, the German casualty figures cited by the various Jewish sources are probably highly exaggerated. It is easy to understand how the magnitude of the fighting and the fighters' ability to strike at the Germans and paralyze their advance created the impression that the number of casualties was very high. Yet we must consider the fact that the arms wielded by the Jewish fighters were primitive and largely ineffective against the advanced and expedient weaponry used by the Germans. This sharp imbalance meant that the concrete effect of the resistance lagged far behind the dimensions of the uprising and the courage displayed by the Jewish combatants.

We can assume that the principal impact of the Warsaw ghetto uprising lay not in the casualties it caused but in the fact that the Germans were forced to invest a substantial number of men and weapons merely to hold their own in what turned out to be a long struggle under the most disadvantageous conditions—from the viewpoint of both political propaganda and the effect of the fighting upon the non-Jewish population of Poland. The primary repercussions of the revolt stemmed from its character as an open rebellion in which tens of thousands of Jews took part—some actively, others in the battle for the bunkers. Moreover, the fighting itself proved that limited forces armed with little more than great determination to fight were capable of turning an urban area into a partisan battleground.

Stroop's own daily citations of the number of people trapped in the ghetto, as well as his comprehensive interim summaries, make clear both the Germans' objectives and the difficulties they encountered in attempting to achieve them. In his report for April 25, he declared: "Up until today, a total of 27,464 people have been caught in the former Jewish ghetto of Warsaw." On May 1 he recorded that "The total number of Jews caught up until now [has reached] 38,385." The next day the number stated in his report was 44,089; on May 6, 47,068; on May 8, 49,712; and on May 11, 53,667. In the last of his daily reports, for May 16, Stroop declared that "The total number of Jews caught and destroyed, for certain, exceeds 56,065." Finally, in a letter sent to Krieger on May 24, 1943, he explained: "Of the total of 56,065 captured Jews, 7,000 were wiped out in the course of the 'Grand *Aktion*' in the former Jewish quarter itself [and] 6,929 in transports to T II [the death camp at Treblinka]; thus a total of 13,929 Jews were annihilated. Above and beyond those 56,065, some 5,000–6,000 were liquidated in explosions and fires."[56]

If we are to believe this calculation, there were over 60,000 Jews in the ghetto at the start of the final *Aktion*. The figures reported by Stroop are detailed and show that data were collected from the various units operating in the ghetto in order to arrive at as thorough a calculation as possible. But Stroop's calculations and the total arrived at on the basis of these data are exaggerated and unrealistic. The most probable estimate is that following the mass deportation in the summer of 1942, about 55,000 Jews remained in the ghetto, including both the "legitimate" and "wildcat" populations. About 5,000 of them were deported during the January *Aktion*, and approximately 8,000 crossed over to the "Aryan" side of the city between the end of that *Aktion* and the final purge in April. Although some of these fugitives returned to the ghetto because of disappointing experiences on the Polish side, and others came back after the amnesty was proclaimed, there is no reason to assume that the total number who returned exceeded 2,000 people. It likewise makes sense to subtract from the total of 55,000 those who died in the ghetto from September 1942 to April 1943, and we must also consider the Jews who were transferred to Poniatow and Trawniki. After deducting these categories, we can assume with a high degree of probability that the number of Jews present in the Warsaw ghetto during the April uprising did not exceed 40,000. If so, how can we account for Stroop's arriving at a figure that is more than 33 percent higher? There can be no doubt that the units operating in the ghetto deliberately inflated their statistics to prove that they were succeeding in their mission.

The Last Stage of the Uprising One of the battles on which Stroop dwells at length relates to the destruction of the bunker at 18 Miła Street, where the Ż.O.B. command and a large contingent of fighters (about 100 people) were holed up. On May 7 Stroop reported: "The location of the bunker containing the inner 'party leadership,' as it is called, is known to us now. Tomorrow it will be broken into by force."[57] The next day he recorded:

> The work of locating the bunker of the inner "party leadership" . . . continues today as well. We managed to open up the bunker of the party leadership and capture about sixty heavily armed thugs. We succeeded in trapping and wiping out the deputy commander of the Jewish military organization "Z.W.Z." and the so-called head of its command.[58] About 200 Jews were living in this bunker: 60 of them were caught, 140 were destroyed by the smoke bombs and large explosive charges planted at a number of places. . . . Beforehand, the Jews who were brought out [of the bunker] reported many dead from the smoke bombs. If the war against the Jews and thugs was difficult on the first six days, we can now state that the Jews and Jewesses who made war in those days are steadily being captured. Again, no bunker is opened up without the Jews inside fighting back with everything they have—machine guns, revolvers, and hand grenades.[59]

The summary report for that day, May 8, cites two dead and three wounded.

We do not have any firsthand accounts of what took place during those final hours in the Ż.O.B.'s central bunker at 18 Miła Street. Although a group of people, including a few of the central figures in the organization, escaped from the bunker and reached the "Aryan" side, they all perished during the war. The testimony that has come down to us is based upon accounts they related to comrades who did survive the war. When the bunker at 18 Miła was uncovered, its five exits were blocked, the main entrance was broken open, and canisters of poisonous gas were thrown inside. Arie Wilner and Lolek Rotblat called on the fighters to take their own lives rather than surrender to the Germans. Some of the fighters did indeed commit suicide, while others perished from the gas, and a handful succeeded in taking shelter in one of the alcoves and later escaped. It is impossible to know precisely who was captured by the Germans, but the assumption is that the captives were mainly civilian inhabitants of the bunker. We likewise do not know to whom Stroop was referring by the titles "deputy commander and head of the command." Many of the leaders of the Jewish underground and architects of the last battle for Jewish Warsaw, including Mordecai Anielewicz, fell in the bunker at 18 Miła Street. We are unable to reconstruct the last moments of any of them.

In his daily reports, Stroop makes note of the number of weapons captured from the Jews. His style of reporting on this subject indicates that he wanted to play up the size of the arsenal possessed by the Jews in the hope that it would explain the difficulties he faced and justify the time it took for his troops to suppress the revolt. In a letter dated May 24, he replied to Krieger's questions by enumerating the total amount of weapons, ammunition, and combat equipment captured during the *Aktion*: " . . . Seven Polish rifles, one Russian rifle, and one German rifle. Fifty-nine revolvers of various calibers. A few hundred hand grenades, including Polish grenades and homemade ones. Large amounts of explosives; ammunition for firearms of all calibers, including machine guns." Thus the total number of weapons that fell into German hands throughout the uprising was in fact inconsequential. In order to soften the impression created by the small amounts of firearms, Stroop places emphasis on the explosives and homemade grenades. Clearly, the weapons under discussion were technically primitive and of little value in combat (though they were exploited very effectively in battle). Stroop undoubtedly sensed that despite his attempt to magnify the significance of the captured weapons, the total remained amazingly small, so he added the following as an afterthought:

As to the booty of weapons, it is worth remembering that in most cases it was not possible to capture the weapons themselves, since before falling into our hands the thugs and Jews hid them in caches and holes that cannot be located. Throwing smoke bombs into the bunkers also prevented the capture of the weapons, and since it was necessary to blow up the bunkers immediately, there was no sense in taking them afterward.

Yet Stroop's claim is only a half-truth, for while the Germans were prevented from capturing most of the revolvers (we can assume that the fighters abandoned them at the last moment or that they remained in their well-hidden caches), this still does not explain why more weapons were not captured during skirmishes, ambushes, and the purge of the bunkers (even though Stroop comments in his individual reports that the fighters were well armed and a variety of heavy weapons were taken from them). It also does not explain why heavier weapons such as rifles and submachine guns (if there were any)—which could not be dropped at the last moment or easily hidden—did not fall into German hands. The simple truth is that the nine rifles that Stroop captured during the revolt were a large, if not overwhelming, proportion of the few "heavy" weapons in the fighters' possession.

Starting in the first week of May, Stroop repeatedly noted in his reports that the struggle with the hard core of insurgents had begun and that he was engaged in annihilating the focal points of the revolt. On May 15 he reported:

Last night patrol units in the ghetto reported that they did not come up against Jews, except on rare occasions. . . . In the exchange of fire that took place during the afternoon hours—when the thugs again fought with Molotov cocktails, revolvers, and homemade hand grenades—after the gang was destroyed, one of the policemen (Orpo) was wounded by a bullet in his right thigh. The last block that remains intact . . . was searched a second time and then destroyed by a special commando unit. Toward evening the synagogue in the Jewish cemetery, the mortuary room, and all the surrounding buildings were blown up or set to the torch.

It was the destruction of the largest Jewish synagogue in Warsaw—a building of special architectural design located outside the boundaries of the ghetto—that symbolized the "victory" over Warsaw's Jewish community and the end of the fighting in the ghetto. On May 16 Stroop wrote: "One hundred and eighty Jews, thugs, and the scum of humanity were killed. The 'Grand *Aktion*' ended at 2015 [8:15 P.M.] with the demolition of the Warsaw synagogue."

Yet it was clear to Stroop that concluding the operation was not equivalent to wiping out all the bunkers and Jews who had fortified themselves in the ghetto. Despite his firm resolve, Stroop did not succeed in completing the liquidation of the ghetto. On May 13 he reported that he intended to conclude the "Grand *Aktion*" on May 16 "and turn over the task of the forthcoming operations . . . to a police battalion. . . ." Indeed, on May 16 he noted that he would charge said police battalion with "continuing or concluding the actions that have yet to be carried out."[60]

Proof of the fact that the Jewish resistance was not supressed during the four weeks of the "Grand *Aktion*" under Stroop's command can be found in the daily reports of the Polish "Blue Police" that describe the situation after May 16. The report for May 18 states: "Jewish units emerge from underground and attack the Germans by surprise. At night the SS men withdraw to the borders of the ghetto; there is not a single German in the ghetto. SS men claim that thousands of Jews are hiding out among the ruins and in the underground niches." On May 20 the "Blue Police" review noted: " . . . Shots in the ghetto night and day. Sometimes they are accompanied by loud blasts of explosives—the demolition of certain buildings and the tossing of grenades by both sides." On May 21 there was again mention of "shooting in the ghetto from light weapons and both sides throwing grenades." On May 22 and 23:

> . . . Gunfire from light and automatic weapons and the sound of explosions. According to an unconfirmed report, Himmler's visit has made it certain that the area of the ghetto will be attacked and the wall surrounding it will be raised higher because the German police and SS men involved in security work in the ghetto are suffering heavy losses and the number of German functionaries who have fallen is excessive.

The report of May 27–31 states:

> On the 27th, 28th, 29th, and 30th of this month, exchanges of fire day and night, especially during the night of May 30; and during the day of May 31, heavy fighting [raged] on Przejazd and Leszno streets. . . . Jews attempted to break through to the "Aryan" side. On the other hand, during the day the Germans continue to pull Jews out of the bunkers and from under burned-out buildings and shoot them on the spot.

Finally, the last report we have from this source, covering June 1–2, states:

> The situation in the ghetto appears to be deteriorating. . . . Today the borders of the ghetto were surrounded by strong SS units and armored cars penetrated [the area]. We can expect the Germans to take far-reaching steps against the Jews in hiding. According to information from the "G" [probably the Gestapo], the German casualties who have fallen in the course of liquidating the Jews have been very heavy.[61]

Information from reliable Jewish sources also testifies to the presence of people in the ghetto after May 16, the date proclaimed by Stroop as the conclusion of the "Grand *Aktion*." In his book *The Last Ones*, Arie Najberg described the situation in the ghetto between May 19 and May 26:

> The strategy of the operation constantly changed. Up to then they had used armed force aided by technical support—fire, dynamite, listening devices—and sometimes by dogs. But as the *Aktion* progressed, it became more difficult to uncover the remaining bunkers and more difficult still to capture people alive. They therefore turned to ruses. When they entered an area, the German companies would bring along Poles and a Jewish informer. The informer would walk around in the courtyards and call out various names or shout in Yiddish: "Jews come out! The war is over!" The Poles served as "bait": They were supposedly sent from the "Aryan" side to bring help to the Jews. But we who were hiding in the gutted buildings could hear the orders exactly as they were given, and we were not fooled. We also warned all the [other] Jews in our area.

From our point of view, it is interesting to note that Najberg writes of the weeks before and after May 16 as one continuous period. He was totally unaware that Stroop had proclaimed the conclusion of the "Grand *Aktion*," and many other Jews like him—ignorant of how the situation appeared to the Germans or what forces were being used to suppress the uprising and expose the people in hiding—continued to hide and fight. Najberg wrote of meeting hundreds of Jews at night, of battles and skirmishes with Germans and Poles in the area of the ghetto, of the building at 4 Walowa Street, which contained 150 people on June 3, 1943 (the day on which it was destroyed), and was referred to by its inhabitants as a "hotel." He described the residents of the bunkers in June 1943: "Those living in the shelters became harrowingly thin and looked like skeletons. After six weeks in these graves, they looked like ghosts frightened of the living."

Despite everything, groups of the "last survivors" holding out among the ruins or in the bunkers succeeded in making contact with individual Poles who helped them get out of the ghetto and infiltrate the Polish side of the city. Of Najberg's group, which numbered forty-five people living among the ruins, four remained alive on September 26, 1943—more than five months after the outbreak of the revolt—when, still armed, they stole across the border to the "Aryan" side.

According to a Polish source, small mutally isolated groups of totally exhausted Jews remained in the ghetto until October. Individual survivors of these groups, like Najberg's band, succeeded in crossing over to the Polish sector of the city in September and October 1943 via the sewers and other passages.[62] We also know of one bunker that remained populated until January 1944.[63] In September the Germans sent a battalion of Polish laborers into the ghetto and ordered them to demolish the infrastructures and walls that were still standing in the area. Those who still remained in hiding evidently met their deaths during these demolition activities, although a few individuals continued to live in dugouts, totally cut off from nature, light, and human company.

The ghetto was destroyed. Hitler's Third Reich had accomplished its mission. No Jews or Jewish dwellings remained in the Warsaw ghetto.

Chapter Fifteen
Repercussions of the Revolt

The Response of the Polish Population and Underground Press

The attitude of the Poles toward the April revolt must be examined from a number of perspectives, including direct Polish involvement in the uprising, the attitude of the government authorities and various factions in the Polish underground toward the armed resistance of the Jews, and the effect of the revolt on various strata of Polish society. There are three forms that direct Polish intervention might have taken: (1) participation in the fighting within the ghetto; (2) the supply of arms and equipment during the battle; and (3) operations on the "Aryan" side to divert pressure from the ghetto and large-scale rescue actions, i.e., breaching the wall at a number of points and preparing shelters for the fugitive civilians and surviving fighters.

The Germans did their best to foster the impression that the armed struggle in the ghetto was carried out with the active cooperation of Poles and Communists, since widespread participation on the part of Polish citizens would have explained the magnitude of the uprising and the difficulties the German troops faced. Moreover, Nazi pride would have suffered less if the adversary in the ghetto had been Polish, rather than the inferior race of Jews. We must also take note of the Germans' tendency to point to the ghetto as the central base of the Communists in Warsaw and the source of security disturbances throughout the city.

At the same time, we cannot assume that these German claims were aired exclusively in the interests of propaganda. On the contrary, the Germans probably believed quite sincerely that Poles had participated in organizing the revolt and that Polish forces were actively involved in the fighting. Otherwise the Germans would not have been able to comprehend how a population that had been imprisoned and sequestered from the outside world had managed to build up reserves of military hardware and plan a broad-scale military operation suited to local conditions. In the course of time, it appears that Stroop learned the truth. He began to understand that he faced an exclusively Jewish force and had growing doubts whether any Poles whatsoever were prepared to extend aid to or work in concert with the Jews. In reply to questions addressed to him after the war, Stroop explained:

> There were channels of communication with the outside. Some of them were discovered during the purge. But it is impossible to know what was brought in or taken out via these channels. After all, everything needed for the battle was found in the ghetto; perhaps extra ammunition was brought in. Since the Polish population behaved with complete indifference, I suppose that any aid from that quarter was completely inconsequential. There is no doubt that there was a connection with the Polish resistance movement, [but] I don't think it extended any real aid.[1]

The Poles, who were equally surprised by the character of the revolt, likewise assumed that their compatriots had participated in leading the uprising and in the fighting itself. They regarded the outbreak of fighting as a sharp and abrupt *volte-face* from what they viewed as Jewish complacency and resignation during the long period of the deportations. To those who were unaware of the developments taking place in the ghetto, the clashes in January, which were reported in the Polish underground press, were only minor incidents compared with the full-scale military uprising. It was natural for the Poles to explain away this seemingly jarring and inexplicable reversal in Jewish behavior by crediting it to the intervention of "Poles and Communists" who had come over the wall. For many Poles, the turnabout did not accord with the accepted historical image of the Jews, and they had great difficulty admitting that Jews were capable of carrying out an armed struggle and displaying impressive feats of bravery. The claim that outsiders were doing the work of the Jews—or at least leading them in battle—rescued people ingrained with such prejudices from vexing embarrassment.

Even the meticulous Ludwik Landau, a Jew by origin and by Nazi racialist definition, who was affiliated with Polish underground circles, was guilty of this error. That Landau was very impressed by the events in the ghetto can be seen in the feelings he expressed in his diary, which was usually written in a low-key style. On April 20 Landau wrote:

At this very moment a real war—with exchanges of gunfire, fires, and even armored vehicles and cannon—is going on right next to us—a contemporary "War of the Jews" worthy of the pen of a modern-day Josephus Flavius. . . .

The optimists believe that the ghetto will fight for at least a few weeks—and in that case there are evidently people who are prepared to rush out to that front of struggle with the Germans. In fact, there are said to be outside volunteers there even now, as well as . . . German deserters hiding out there.[2]

On April 22 he added: "We cannot know if there is any truth in the rumors about the participation of battalions of "Aryan" workers in the fighting—those no longer permitted to leave the ghetto once the fighting began." And on April 27 he noted that the rumors about what was happening in the ghetto were full of exaggerations:

It is estimated that the number of Jewish fighters there is 7,000, and some Polish group or another—which evidently really exists—is participating in the fighting and has expanded into a unit numbering about 1,500 [people]. What's more, according to other rumors the battlefield in the ghetto is regarded as a training ground for the fight against the Germans, and we will send in relay groups at set periods for "training." The family name of an officer who heads the "reinforcements"—Captain Czarny—is being mentioned. Undoubtedly closer to the truth are the figures commanding the Jewish fighters—at first the military physician Major Dr. Ganc and thereafter, when he was wounded in battle, Colonel Marcus.[3]

The Polish underground knew perfectly well who the fighters in the ghetto were. In fact, the *Delegatura* reported to London on the "war of the Jews against the Germans," noting that "the omniscient Gestapo was unable to obstruct the excellent preparations of the Jewish population for the struggle and self-defense, so much so that the combined forces of the gendarmerie, the SS, and the army have not yet been able to overcome that resistance despite their prolonged assault of six days."[4] This report makes no mention whatsoever of Poles participating in the fighting or of any military operation designed to aid the fighting ghetto. The truth of the matter is that there was not so much as a single Pole inside the ghetto, either in the ranks or in the command of the fighting organizations.

The Polish underground press devoted much space to the battle in the ghetto and showered praise on the Jewish fighters. *Biuletyn Informacyjny*, the A.K. newspaper, which also printed reliable information regarding Jewish affairs, wrote in its April 29 issue:

. . . The second act of the savage annihilation of the Jews of Poland
opened a week ago. The Germans had intended to deport the 40,000 Jews
still remaining in Warsaw, [but] the ghetto responded with armed resistance. The "Jewish Fighting Organization" initiated a war of the weak
against the strong. With meager forces scarcely [armed] with weapons and
ammunition, without water, blinded by the smoke and the fire, the Jewish
fighters defended the streets and individual buildings and silently retreated
one step at a time — more from the fire that engulfed the crowded buildings than from the enemy, who was equipped with the latest instruments
of war. They will consider it a victory if some of those imprisoned in the
ghetto can escape; they will consider it a victory if the enemy's forces are
weakened a bit; and finally, they will consider it a victory if they can die
with weapons in their hands.[5]

Alongside descriptions of the fighting and expressions of surprise
at the development of the battle and the fighters' stand, the underground Polish press wrote at length about the fundamental change in
the Jews' behavior. Its articles are sprinkled with subtle and sometimes
even vulgar reproaches for the resignation and capitulation of the past,
as well as an examination of the reversal in conduct. The April 30 issue
of the underground organ *Myśl Państwowa* (*Government Thinking*) contained an editorial entitled "The Greatest Crime in the World":

Now, when Warsaw is witness to the ultimate act of German bestial-
ity, we cannot overlook the reversal in the attitude of the victims, who are
unable to change their fate but have decided to fall with weapons in their
hands. Their stand, which is understandable to every Pole, changes the
picture completely. From a helpless people, a flock slaughtered by the
German murderers, the Jews have risen to the level of a fighting people.
And even if they do not fight for their existence — which is out of the
question, considering the absolute superiority of the enemy — they have
nonetheless demonstrated their right to national existence. The Polish
public looks upon this phenomenon with unrestrained admiration, affords
it moral support, and hopes that the resistance will continue for as long as
possible.[6]

Another organ, *Tydzień* (*Week*), wrote in an article entitled "The
Ghetto Defends Itself":

The totally passive attitude of the Jews was matched by an unequivocally negative attitude on the part of the Polish public. [But] the
present battle, which has been going on in the streets of the ghetto for ten
days now, is worthy of the full admiration of the Polish public, which
cannot help the Jews in any concrete manner . . . but can extend its moral
support.[7]

A similar attitude was expressed by another underground paper, *Nowa Polska (New Poland)*, in an article entitled "The Fate of the Ghetto is Sealed" (published on May 7, 1943): "Surely the brave resistance of the Jews lifts the stain they brought upon themselves by their capitulation and lethargy in going like sheep to the slaughter rather than defending themselves. This is probably their first show of courage since the days of Bar-Kochba."[8]

In an article entitled "The Jewish-German Battle," the underground organ *Polska (Poland)* wrote that "this time the Jewish stand evokes respect."[9] Another newspaper, *Głos Pracy (The Voice of Labor)*, stated in an article entitled "The Destruction of the Ghetto in Warsaw": "Warsaw watches the humiliation of the degenerate [Germans] with pain and fear. It would like to come to the aid of the Jews in the fight that is so hopeless, but cold reason prevents us from taking that step, which might bring unimaginable consequences in its wake. Our time has not yet come."[10]

In its May 1, 1943, issue, *Walka Ludów (The Peoples' Struggle)* published an aritcle entitled "Flames Over Warsaw" declaring that the German crime cannot be allowed to pass without retribution. A people capable of such crimes must be subdued and disarmed, just as the mentally ill are subdued:

> . . . The [Polish] independence organizations would like to come to the aid of the besieged [Jews]. Unfortunately, that is impossible at present. The P.P.R., as usual, provokes the Polish people to start a general uprising, promising the aid of the Red Army. As far as the uprising in the ghetto is concerned, no such aid has come to date, contrary to expectations. It was assumed that Soviet planes would bomb the German quarter and supply the besieged [Jews] with reinforcements of paratroop units, or at least food and ammunition.[11]

The A.K.'s *Biuletyn Informacyjny*, which held a special position among the underground publications, appraised the significance of the struggle as follows: "The death of the masses of Jews without resistance did not engender any new values and was pointless. [But] dying with weapons in hand might introduce new values into the life of the Jewish people and bestow upon the death of Polish Jews for the Sanctification of the Name the halo of a struggle for the right to life."[12]

Prawda Młodych (The Truth of the Young), the organ of the Catholic youth in the underground, pursued a similar theme in an article entitled "Around the Burning Ghetto":

> The last time the Jews fought was 1800 years ago. With valor, though in vain, they defended Jerusalem against Titus's legions. That was the last

accord for the existence of the state and the honor of the people—the short-lived revolt of Bar-Kochba. . . . The Jews are fighting. Not for their lives, since their war against the Germans is one of desperation and despair; their war is about the price of life. Not in order to rescue themselves from death, but over the manner of death—to die as men and not like worms. For the first time in eighteen centuries, they have risen from their humiliation. This is a momentous time. Who knows whether the spirit of Israel will not rise out of the ashes of Warsaw, out of its ruins and its fallen? Who knows whether the Jews will not emerge from the fire purified; if the wandering, parasitical, dangerous Jews will not return to being a normal people that will embark upon an independent, creative life wherever they may be. The Warsaw ghetto may not be an end but a beginning; whoever dies as a human being has not perished in vain.[13]

Even publications that took note of the fact that the Jews of Warsaw were citizens of Poland fighting on Polish soil qualified their words of admiration by stressing the sharp contrast with the past. The organ *Polska Zwycięży* (*Poland Will Be Victorious*) wrote in its May 10 issue: "Despite the deep sociopolitical differences that have developed in the course of [our] life with the Jews, the entire Polish public stands united before the tragedy that surrounds this battle, fully understanding that it is a part of the broader tragedy of Poland."[14]

Walka (*The Struggle*), the paper of the right-wing Nationalist Party, exploited this subject to advance its own position:

> Even in quarters where Poland was not accorded appropriate understanding and was often slandered—inside the walls of the ghetto—when the final battle came, the Polish flag, a symbol of the struggle against amnesty for the murderers, was hoisted on those walls. For the Jewish fighter understood that even if he were a hundredfold more worthy, his fate could not be other than to shock the world in the name of Poland.[15]

From this review of the relevant literature, we are able to distinguish a number of motifs that appear as standard elements in the attitude of the Polish national underground. Most of the publications praise and encourage the battle taking place in the ghetto and contrast the armed struggle of the Jews with the demeaning passivity of the past. Yet these articles fail to discuss the implications of the struggle being waged under ghetto conditions and evade the question of whether the Jews were provided with the means to defend themselves. Most of the articles suggest—whether outright or in a shrewdly vague manner—that abject passivity befits the Jews, or at least has been characteristic of them since the loss of their independence almost two millennia ago. Resistance, these spokesmen of the Polish underground believe, is closer to the character of the Poles and makes the Jews understandable to the Polish public. Nevertheless, few of these publications are prepared to deal with the question of whether the Polish underground is obliged to come to the aid of the fighters in the ghetto, and the papers that do take up this question content themselves with the arbitrary or sanctimonious statement that the Poles are unable to act. It is, of course, right to help the Jews, but the hour has not yet come for the Poles to make their move. Here and there we find reference to the belief that the courageous war in the ghetto accords the Jews the status of a national entity and perhaps even symbolizes an awakening and turning point in the history of the Jewish people. But even such expressions of recognition for the national rights of the Jews are not free of derogatory comments. Even now, the nationalist press, which had a long tradition of rabid anti-Semitism, did not abandon its notorious libel or refrain from expressing malicious joy over the tragedy of the ghetto.

The underground press of the democratic and leftist factions in Poland adopted a different tone. *Polska Walczy (Fighting Poland)*, for example, wrote in its April 30 issue:

> In the British Isles, the American continent, and countries beyond the German hell, the flames rising above Poland—the symbol of the tortures and suffering of men being abandoned to atrocities—cannot be seen. You beyond that "other shore" *do not see and do not hear,* while every echo that reaches us from the burning ghetto racks our consciences and grieves us. The cup of terrible crimes runneth over. We read bulletins from the fronts—Africa, Russia, China, the Pacific. There too people are dying; there too valor and contempt for death have their place. But *there* fighters are dying under different circumstances. In the battle raging behind the ghetto's walls, people are dying "differently." It is a battle of the hopeless against a berserk beast of prey. A bulletin from this battlefield should be read out on the front of embattled humanity, so that the fighters on that front can take pride in their comrades-in-arms who are dying in the buildings and on the streets of the ghetto with weapons in hand. It cannot be that the clouds of smoke over Warsaw will disperse without trace, because then all that we cherish as valor in life would disappear, together with the abominable deeds of the Germans that cry out for revenge.[16]

Robotnik (The Worker), the newspaper of the Polish Socialists, also addressed itself to the silence and inertia of the Allied Powers in its May 1 issue. But it was not content to place responsibility on the shoulders of the "major powers" and directed its criticism against official quarters in the Polish underground as well:

> Warsaw is waiting expectantly for a retaliatory air attack by the Soviets or the British, which would raise the morale of the Jews fighting in the

ghetto. In the meantime, we have the impression that abroad nothing is known about what is taking place in the Warsaw ghetto. Who is responsible for this? Is it the man who fills the post of the *Delegatura* or the Z.W.Z.?[17] It comes to mind that facts a hundredfold less important are made known to London almost immediately and broadcast to all parts of the world. In contrast, the world was informed of the previous liquidation operation against Polish Jewry, in which more than half a million Jews were lost, only after it was over.[18]

The P.P.R. (Communists) expressed strong admiration for the uprising in the ghetto and tried to depict it as an example worthy of emulation by the Poles. The May 15 issue of its paper *Trybuna Wolności* (*The Platform of Liberty*) states:

> The battles in the ghetto are of tremendous political importance. They are the most impressive display of organized self-defense in the occupied countries . . . [and] prove how fully the public supports the call for active revolt and armed struggle. The Jews, who had been obedient until now, responded with [a show of] resistance that has earned respect and esteem throughout the country and the world. The revolt in the ghetto proves that determined self-defense — especially if organized in time, and even if not properly armed — can strike a smarting blow to the enemy. The commanders of the battle in the ghetto are young men, most of whom never even received training in the Polish army. They are commanders who have emerged from the people in the course of the struggle. The conqueror spreads rumors that the defenders are numerous, well equipped, and led by high-ranking Polish officers, [but] these reports bear no relationship to the truth.[19]

An article entitled "The Fighting Ghetto," published in the newspaper *Gwardzista* (*The Guard*) on May 20, 1943, noted that "the courageous resistance of the Warsaw ghetto has been going on for a month now. It is the strongest and most prolonged act of resistance in the occupied territories."[20]

The Communist press did not devote much attention to the ultimate fate of the fighters, and its articles do not relate to the irksome question of why the Allies, and particularly the Soviet Union — which hoped to agitate the populace and induce it to embark upon combat operations — did not come to the aid of the fighters in the ghetto. Instead the Communist organs placed emphasis on the gains achieved by the fighting and the ability of a small force to hold down a much larger opponent and battle it for a relatively long period. The example set by the fighting ghetto served the Communists primarily as a stimulus to arouse the Poles to an armed struggle, and they identified with this example by expressing admiration and comradely sentiments toward the Jewish fighters.

The attitude of the radically anti-Semitic organs was precisely the opposite. For example, the *Agencja A,* an organ of the intelligence branch of the A.K., commented in a review entitled "The Resistance in the Ghetto in Its Proper Light" (published in its May 15 issue):

> The Jewish resistance at the time of the final liquidation of the Warsaw ghetto was not, as some of the underground press reported it, collective resistance that proved a change in attitude among the surviving Jews. If the overwhelming majority of Europe's Jews were murdered as they remained completely passive, the remnant, in their racial materialism, lacked any motivation to resist. Only a tiny proportion of the few thousand Jews remaining in Warsaw (about 10 percent) engaged in the struggle — and with support from the Communist camp at that. It was the nonregistered Jews who rebelled, the "wildcat" residents in the ghetto. On the other hand, the Jews who were registered and turned up for work did not take part in the action. They capitulated by the hundreds to the Germans, who led them by the [same] old methods to the new place of slaughter, at Majdanek. The resistance and supply of weapons to a public encompassing tens of thousands . . . was organized and effected by the Bund and the Communists. It is precisely among that element that a mood of hostility toward the Poles has been evident throughout the occupation, and they have trained themselves in the framework of Communist organizations for a bloody battle against the Poles during the decisive transition period. According to the Communist program, the ghetto was meant to force a premature uprising, which the P.P.R. wants to provoke. That same ghetto has contained Communist printing presses, weapons arsenals, and the Communist headquarters for a long while now, and it was from there that the Soviet officers commanded the division.[21]

Polska, the right-wing organ of the movement comprising Pilsudski's disciples, which ruled Poland during the last years before the outbreak of World War II, published a report in its April 29 issue under the headline "The Great Week in the Ghetto." It enumerated the various elements that constituted the fighting force in the ghetto:

1. Jewish Bundists and Communists, who had disguised their activities until now, worked in the German armament industry, and readied themselves for sabotage and an armed operation.

2. German-Aryan Communists, who benefited from a lax attitude after the agreement with Russia—though later, after the agreement was broken, they were again subject to severe treatment. They escaped from the Reich to the occupied countries, hid from the police, and found a safe haven among their Jewish "comrades."

3. German-Aryan deserters who fled from the eastern front and could not find shelter among the Polish population, which regarded them with suspicion and feared that *provacateurs* were planted among

them. They were greeted warmly and found understanding in the ghetto.

4. Soviet agents, Jews and Aryans, who parachuted into the ghetto and supplied arms and ammunition in this manner. They are the experts who lead the revolutionary struggle and sabotage operations.

5. Polish soldiers and officers of Jewish origin—many of them converts who had assimilated into Polish society—who were forced into the ghetto and first and foremost seek a way to free themselves.[22]

The Polish right automatically lumped the Jews and Communists together and attempted to depict the uprising in the ghetto as an operation instigated by the Communists and fought by their supporters. These publications would not state that Poles took part in the rebellion, but since it was difficult or embarrassing for them to credit the contemptible Jews with a struggle of such impressive dimension, they invented various kinds of fictitious "Aryans": German Communists, German deserters, Soviet paratroopers, etc. And if Poles were inevitably mixed in with this hodgepodge, they were not "pure" Poles but at best converted Jews. The aim of these publications was twofold: to diminish the impression that genuine Jews had demonstrated the desire and ability to fight, and to disseminate the lie that the ghetto served as a stronghold for Communists and other elements hostile to Poland. It followed that the destruction of the ghetto was for the best, since with its fall a wellspring of danger to the Poles would cease to exist.

We also have in our hands a document composed by the intelligence service of the *Delegatura* and the A.K., that is, a source affiliated with the major official bodies of the Polish underground:

> The ghetto. As a pretext for the current events, its was reported that German intelligence received a tip that on April 20, 1943, a Communist-organized uprising would break out within the borders of the General-gouvernement. Since the headquarters of Communist activity was in the ghetto, it was decided to put a stop to these activities by [taking] counteraction. . . . According to rumor, the Jewish insurgents were led by a Pole, Dr. Adolf Kohn, and a sergeant who had deserted from the German army. The number of Jews who took part in the military action is not known. [Yet] according to the rumor, units of the Polish Communists are fighting alongside the Jews. . . .[23]

The claim that the rebels in the ghetto were Russians and Soviet agents received widespread attention and was to some degree accepted even by the leaders of the Polish government-in-exile. In reply to the vague conjectures from Warsaw, the Polish defense minister, General Marian Kukieł, cabled the commander of the armed forces in the underground to query: ". . . Was the resistance of the Jews of Warsaw during the liquidation of the ghetto really led and organized by Soviet officers and noncommissioned officers parachuted into the ghetto, and were arms, ammunition, and anti-tank guns supplied in the same fashion? . . ."[24]

We shall not deal at length with the attitude of the Polish government-in-exile and its supporters among the Polish émigrés in London. However, it is pertinent to cite Prime Minister Sikorski's May 5 appeal to the population of Poland, which stated: ". . . The greatest crime in human history is being perpetrated. We know that you are helping the tortured Jews as much as you can. I thank you, my countrymen, personally and in the name of the government. I ask you to extend all possible aid and, at the same time, to soften the sting of this terrible brutality."[25] This time Sikorski's appeal includes an explicit plea to come to the aid of the Jews and also hints at taking action to soften the German blows, that is, operations designed to hamper the enemy. At the same time, as has often been noted, this call to aid the Jews essentially came too late: Sikorski's statement was broadcast seventeen days after the outbreak of the revolt—by which time the principal Jewish fighting force had already been neutralized—and three days before the fall of the Ż.O.B. bunker. The socialist leader Adam Ciołkosz, one of the chief statesmen in the London-based government, attempted to justify this belatedness by explaining that the Polish prime minister had been under a great strain at the time and was forced to make momentous decisions regarding Poland's future. Ciołkosz was referring to the fact that the weeks of the uprising coincided with the crisis brought on by the discovery of the graves of thousands of Polish officers at Katyń, the consequent political tension, and the breach between Poland and the Soviet Union.[26] As we have already noted, however, an examination of the official Polish newspaper *Dziennik Polski* reveals that the uprising in the ghetto was not mentioned at all for weeks preceding and following Sikorski's address, even though details of far less important events in Poland were published in its pages during the same period. Thus the government's silence was in no way merely coincidental, and Ciołkosz's efforts to justify it are far from satisfactory.

On the other hand, the underground radio station, Świt, extended broad coverage to the fighting in the ghetto and emphasized the significance of the struggle. Świt claimed that its transmissions originated in Poland, and it steadily responded to events taking place in the occupied country. In point of fact, however, Świt was located in London. It received information from Poland through underground channels and, presenting itself as a local Polish station with transmitters powerful enough to be picked up throughout Poland, broadcast news and commentary. The Świt broadcasts were monitored in the ghetto and served as an encouraging sign that news of the the uprising had reached the outside world.[27]

A wide variety of sources allow us to glean a picture of how the average Pole viewed the uprising in the ghetto. Many residents of Warsaw made their way to the ghetto wall (perhaps out of curiosity) to see for themselves both the fighters engaged in the struggle and the pitiful people in the burning buildings. Even those who did not come to feast their eyes on the sight of fighting could see the pillars of fire and clouds of smoke, hear the echo of shots, blasts, and explosions, and smell the odors that wafted from the direction of the Jewish quarter. Naturally, the revolt—both the Jewish struggle and the Germans' methods of destruction and murder—was the topic on everyone's lips. But reactions were not consistent, ranging from sincere expressions of sorrow to indifference and even hostility. Circles active in *Żegota* tried to help those who had made it past the wall, while bands of extortionists and informers loitered around that same wall hoping to snare whoever managed to escape the burning ghetto.

Emmanuel Ringelblum, who was not an eyewitness to the uprising, collected "some authentic conversations" overheard in the streets of Warsaw during those days:

A God-fearing grandmother: "During Easter week Christ was tortured by the Jews, [and] during Easter week the Jews were tortured by the Germans."

A seventy-year-old priest: "It's a good thing. The Jews had a large military force in the ghetto. If they hadn't turned it on the Germans, they would have turned it on us."

A conversation overheard on the tram: "The little Jews are being burned and the big ones control America and after the war will dominate us."

A middle-class housewife: "It's terrifying to see what's going on in the ghetto. Terrible things. But perhaps it's just as well that it's happened. The Jews suck our blood. They used to say: The streets are yours and the buildings are ours. They used to say to us: You would like Poland without Jews, but what you have is Jews without Poland."

Two merchants from Grzybowska Square: One regrets that because of the fires in the ghetto, much property [relevant to] Poland's future is going to ruin; so much state property has gone up in smoke. His friend replied to that: "Don't be sorry. The ghetto was a stinking neighborhood, and it's better that it's no longer around. We'll build that neighborhood from scratch and it will be nicer, cleaner, and free of Jews, too."

A teacher, an old maid: "A man takes pity on a cat, and a Jew is also a human being, even though he's a Jew." But then, after she received a letter from a relative in the Majdanek camp [claiming] that Jewish prisoners of war behave badly toward Poles, she said: "I pitied those Jews, but now, with their brothers behaving so badly toward our own, I hope the Germans slaughter every last one of them."

A member of the O.N.R.[28] formulated his "credo" regarding the April *Aktion*: "Even if the Jews burn, that's still only a drop of what they deserve." Another cannibal put it even more succinctly: "The bugs are being burned."

Speaking of the aid demanded by the ghetto, the wife of a colonel, who worked as a postal clerk [said]: "The Jews spied for the enemy before the war, and now these criminals are demanding help from us, as if we didn't have [anyone] to shed our blood for."

A member of the P.P.S.: "The party is not prepared for a military move. We sympathize with the Jews in their tragic plight. We should supply them with weapons, but active collaboration is out of the question. All must suffer for the primary goal, for the liberation. The party must choose the most convenient moment to embark upon the struggle and not act according to emotional impulse, even the most virtuous kind. Noble-hearted individuals complained that the great tragedy playing itself out before the eyes of the entire population is met with apathy and indifference: 'We continue to live as if it were yesterday, as if nothing happened. We eat a tasty dinner, then we go out to the balcony and stare at the glow of the fires from the ghetto. We hear the echo of the bombs and explosives demolishing buildings and shelters—and remain silent.'"

These Polish remarks on the events in the ghetto were usually dominated by an overtone of anti-Semitism and satisfaction that Warsaw had finally become *"Judenfrei"* [free of Jews], that the boldest dreams of the Polish anti-Semites had been fulfilled and Warsaw was rid of Jews. Openly or secretly, people expressed their satisfaction that the Germans had done the dirty work of killing Jews. Sympathy was expressed by saying: "It's true that the victims are Jews, but then they are, after all, people." They felt worse about the charred buildings than about the burning of people alive. Only fear of the future and the anxiety that after liquidating the Jews, the Germans might turn against the Poles dampened their joy over the "cleansing" of Warsaw of its Jews. As to Jewish fighters unfurling the Polish flag, the anti-Semites said: "They want to cull favor with the Poles." These anti-Semites could not believe their own eyes, seeing that Jews are able to defend themselves and shoot; that they rebelled against the enemy.

The Polish public was intrigued by the heroic stand of the ghetto. They called it "Little Stalingrad" and compared it to the defense of Westerplatte [a stronghold near Danzig that was defended to the last man at the beginning of the German attack on Poland]. They placed great hopes on the uprising in the ghetto and chose to regard it as primarily a national rebellion that the Jews had sparked off.[29]

Ringelblum's harsh remarks imply that the anti-Semitic sentiment was dominant, even though he wrote this piece while he himself was hiding on the "Aryan" side of the city under the protection of Poles. His perspective and responsibility as an historian were above reproach, but it is entirely possible that the ugly slander pronounced on the streets of Warsaw is what left the most lasting impression on his memory. Ringelblum's description clearly creates the impression that the methodical and sustained destruction of the Jewish population of Warsaw did not fundamentally change the hostile attitude of the Poles. It is true that one could find people with sensitive consciences who were not diehard anti-Semites, and some of them were even moved to place their own lives in danger in order to help Jews. But for all that, there was no perceptible change in the attitude of the population at large. On the contrary, the popular attitude was permeated with deep-seated prejudice that surpassed even the sentiments of the various forces in the underground. The courageous stand of the Jews was impressive, but it did not always lead to a softening of attitude, and in many cases the existent hostility was even bolstered by a new dimension of fear of the Jews' suddenly apparent strength. Occasionally we also detect a tone of rage against the Jews, e.g., for allegedly firing at the tramcars that passed nearby the ghetto during the fighting. Ludwik Landau recorded in his diary on April 21:

> Warsaw continues to be preoccupied with the battle going on nearby, the Jewish-German war, the "third front," as it is called. The emotional attitude toward this struggle varies: While some exhibit a pronounced sense of support for the valiant resistance of Hitler's victims, among others the anti-Semitism that flourishes at such times is especially prominent, whereas the majority is best described as neutral observers. But we find a certain expression of admiration even among the indifferent or hostile, and there is an alert, even tense interest everywhere.[30]

Helena Balicka-Kozłowska, a Polish woman who extended aid to the Jews in the underground, wrote in her memoirs, *The Wall Had Two Sides:*

> After a few days of fighting, the Germans halted the traffic of the tram and pedestrians on Bonifraterska Street, which bordered on the ghetto. They set up a temporary junction for the tram in Krasinskich Square, whence the vehicles carry passengers set out for Żolibórz. The square had the look of a marketplace. People sold water, candies, and cigarettes there; it was filled with loud cries, conversation, laughter. Alongside the commerce and boisterous uproar were field guns. Their crews did not necessarily drive the curious away. Evidently [standing] in a crowd of Poles made them feel safer from the impending Jewish attack.

Thus we can see that even those who viewed events from the Polish side, or from the perspective of the Poles, admit to signs of anti-Semitism. These last pieces are attempts on the part of their writers to present a balanced view of impressions and behavior, but the facts are not distorted. Poles who were sympathetic toward the Jews and sensitive to the repugnant behavior of their countrymen tried to relate this negative phenomenon to the corrupting influence of wartime conditions, which was undoubtedly a valid factor but was only one that operated among many others.

We gain a completely different perspective through examining the feelings and reactions of Jews living on the Polish side of the city disguised as "Aryans." They were plagued by inner torture and a storm of emotions but were forced to conceal any hint of their turmoil from the people around them, even though their isolation and duplicity bore down on them much more now than it had before the outbreak of the revolt. These modern-day "Marranos" were drawn to the arena of the fighting even though their very presence near the walls exposed them to danger. Balicka-Kozłowska wrote of this phenomenon in her book:

> Events in the ghetto drew thousands of people to the vicinity of the walls. As far as one could see, most of them came out of curiosity, assuming that they might be able to watch a part of the battle. . . . The tragedy of the ghetto had a magnetic attraction for many others—Poles and Jews alike—who were driven by despair and could not sit at home when thousands of innocent people were dying close by. It was easy to identify them because they stared at the brick walls of Bonifraterska, Świętojerska, and other streets with their lips pursed in silence. Many Jews who had been hiding out on the "Aryan" side for quite a while [now] fell victim to the extortionists and informers who loitered around the area day and night and occasionally sniffed out new victims.[31]

In his book on Warsaw during the war years, the writer Kazimierz Brandys wrote:

> The memory preserves odd pictures from those spring days. I shuffled for hours along the crowded streets then, but the force that drove me out of my house was not the smell of the flowering pines. Greater things than spring were taking place in the city. I wanted to see them. The people behind the wall chose their own kind of death. I stood rooted by the train station and watched how a thick, black morass burst out of Towarowa Street, where the Germans stole through the cellars like rats to burn the building of a fighting Jew. A group of the ghetto's defenders rose upward, over the city. . . . I wanted to be near them in those days. I was tortured by the reproach of not being together with them. I infiltrated various places where the whistle of bullets and the sound of German shouts could be heard, but I did not see much. The wall always blocked my view. . . . I wanted to be close to them so that the wind would bring me a hint of their war [and I could] glimpse from behind the wall some part of a building in which they chose to die. . . . [32]

Polish Combat and Rescue Actions   We shall now turn to an examination of the plans conceived by the Poles to aid the embattled ghetto and describe the rescue operation mounted during the final stages of the revolt in order to save the last of the insurgents. (We will not consider at this point the subject of operations designed to rescue individuals, though we should note that the number of fugitives who found shelter among the Poles rose during this period.)

As explained in an earlier chapter, the relations between the Ż.O.B. and the fighting Polish underground were severely disrupted by the arrest of Arie Wilner, and the circumstances surrounding his arrest continued to impede the work of both sides even after contact was renewed, when Yitzhak Zuckerman arrived on the "Aryan" side to replace Wilner. More damaging than anything else was the loss of precious time. Zuckerman reached the "Aryan" side on the eve of the revolt and did not have enough time to renew contacts and revitalize the network of relations that had lapsed. As Woliński wrote in his report on the activities of the A.K.'s Jewish Department:

> On March 6, 1943, "Jurek" was arrested (in an apartment on Wspólna Street). This fact hampered the work going on in the field of cooperation between the Jewish Fighting Organization and the "Drapacz." More than ten days after the arrest, I held a conversation with Konar. The subject of the discussion was to define the aim of having our units cooperate with the fighting ghetto. The goal had to be to remove the greatest possible number of Jews from the Warsaw area and to find shelter for them, which I could have done at any moment. This plan was not carried out. No unit left for the sector assigned to it. The Jewish Fighting Organization decided that it was impossible for our people to prepare a route for them over a distance of hundreds of kilometers. On the other hand, Konar gave his consent to organize Jews in unarmed insurgent units. One such unit was established in Warsaw, and an officer of ours was appointed to train it. He reached the training area and set up a meeting, but he did not show up at it. After repeated coaxing he reached the training place a second time, but then he was drunk. Further appeals were useless. The Jewish insurgent unit did not receive any training and ceased to exist.[33]

Woliński's version of events has it that a program was drawn up to move groups of Jewish fighters from Warsaw all the way to Volhynia, in southeast Poland, an area that had been under Soviet domination from September 1939 to June 1941. We may assume that his plan reflected the aim of the A.K., or certain quarters therein, to move the Jews preparing themselves for battle far away from the ghetto, precisely in order to prevent the outbreak of fighting and the attendant complications, which would have been inconvenient for the A.K. and contrary to the policy of the underground sponsored by the London-based government. The assumption that such an explicit aim did in fact exist is supported by the discussions held between the A.K. representatives and Yitzhak Zuckerman.[34] The Ż.O.B. rejected this proposal, which was in total contradiction to its position, and Woliński's report creates the impression that the Jews turned it down because it was not formulated properly or readily implemented. It certainly makes sense that the Ż.O.B. would not be interested in focusing on differences of opinion and preferred to explain its refusal by citing the difficulties involved in implementing the plan. In any case, Woliński's account makes it clear that the members of the A.K. were not willing to absorb Jews into their partisan units in the Warsaw area. It is likewise clear that the officers assigned to train Jews sabotaged their mission. A Jewish source relating to the period in which Wilner was still active on the "Aryan" side of the city also describes how the A.K. officers behaved irresponsibly toward the task of training Jewish groups.[35]

Zuckerman testified that close to the time of his arrival on the "Aryan" side and again after the outbreak of the revolt, he met with a central figure in the A.K., the "head of the all-powerful Polish secret police" who "introduced himself as Grenadier Karol." When Zuckerman demanded immediate aid for the beleaguered ghetto in the form of arms, the Pole replied that he was prepared to spirit combat companies out of the ghetto, to which Zuckerman responded: "The combat companies will not leave the ghetto as long as they have a single bullet left in [their] rifles to shoot themselves with." As the revolt moved toward its second stage—during which the opportunities to resist waned—Zuckerman demanded "that automobiles and people be prepared in time to get the survivors out; that houses [be readied] to take in and conceal the fighters." In reply, the Polish underground spokesman said:

> Actually, I can speak to you frankly: We don't believe you. We believe that the ghetto is no more than a base for Soviet Russia. A plan exists, and [we] Poles know what it is. The Russians were the ones who prepared the revolt in the Warsaw ghetto, and you have far more weapons than you let on; and I am sure that on May 1, 1943 [May Day], they will land Dessant in the Warsaw ghetto.

At the close of the conversation, Zuckerman continued, no arms were received and the aid in saving the last of the fighters after the battle was neither promised nor tendered. The Polish representative merely stated:

> "There is anxiety among the Polish public that the revolt will spread beyond the ghetto and the Poles will rise up [in rebellion], which is what

the A.L. [*Armia Ludowa*, associated with the P.P.R.] wants. So I warn you: If this comes to pass, and if you collaborate with the A.L. and it comes to your aid, we will move against the ghetto!" With that the conversation ended.[36]

Zuckerman also reported that a day or two before the outbreak of the revolt, he talked with Woliński, who said that "we are being asked not to rebel in the ghetto but to go out to the forests." Zuckerman responded that for a long time the Poles had voiced sharp criticism against the Jews for not defending themselves, and now, when there was finally a chance to fight, official quarters in the A.K. were trying to prevent it. "The reply to that was: The command has decided that it is premature to fight in Warsaw. . . . They are willing to do everything necessary to prepare combat bases for us in the forests. My reply was: The battle will be in Warsaw."[37]

Our research has produced a letter written by General Chruściel (known by the code names Konar and Monter), the commander of the Warsaw section of the A.K., on the Home Army's ties with the Jewish Fighting Organization and its activities during the period of the uprising. The letter was written in 1958 (when Chruściel was living in the United States) and states that on the first day of the uprising a meeting of the A.K. command was held with the participation of General Komorowski (General Rowecki's replacement at the time). Komorowski asked "with embarrassment whether we were prepared to extend any aid whatsoever to the Fighting Organization." Chruściel claims to have replied in the affirmative and presented a plan that had been drawn up long before the meeting. He adds that his attitude and readiness to help made a profound impression on those present, for they had never once considered an immediate response to the Jews' appeals.

Chruściel defined the task he had taken upon himself as follows:

> . . . The plan was simple: to breach the ghetto walls and facilitate the escape of those who were able to flee. Toward this end we intended to breach [the wall] at a number of places on the Parysowska and Stawki side to permit movement in the direction of Kampinos Forest. To divert the Germans [we would] attack them first along the entire circumference of the ghetto wall. Those unable to march on foot . . . would be taken out through the sewers.[38]

Even this program described in 1958 does not call for linking up with the fighters or taking part in the battle within the ghetto. Instead, it relates to a comprehensive rescue program, and what is unique is the fact that it was supposedly designed not only to rescue the surviving fighters but also to open an escape route for any Jew willing and able to save himself. In point of fact, however, Chruściel's plan was never executed, nor was there even an attempt to realize it—at least not in the format and dimensions he outlined.

It is therefore fair to assume that the A.K. never had any plan prepared or even displayed any genuine readiness to act in the fashion and scope described by Chruściel. First, any such plan would have required close coordination with the Jewish side, but the Jews were never informed of a broad rescue plan or briefed on the role they would assume in such an operation. As we have already seen, during the uprising A.K. fighters carried out two actions on a limited scale, but they did not succeed in breaching the wall or linking up with the Jewish fighters. We therefore can only conclude that these improvised actions were embarked upon more for the purpose of demonstrating solidarity than to provide concrete aid to the ghetto or to rescue people. At any rate, they cannot be compared with the massive operation described by Chruściel. Moreover, we have already noted that there is no evidence of any discussions with Jewish quarters regarding the implementation of a joint action. Clearly it was impossible to assemble Jews together in broad daylight in the besieged ghetto, and any attempt to do so would have been equivalent to a suicide action. The success of such an operation would depend on a high degree of accuracy, speed, and coordinated action on the part of the armed forces of both sides.[39] Furthermore, there is no evidence of any A.K. preparations for dealing with the Jews who would escape from the ghetto, in terms of leading them to a temporary or more permanent place of refuge.

The *Gwardia Ludowa*, or, as it later came to be known, *Armia Ludowa* (A.L.), namely the armed force of the Communists, was guided by the Communist Party's aim of extending the scope of the uprising. In particular, they hoped to build upon the impetus of the Jewish uprising and have it evolve into a broader insurgency by citing the uprising as proof that even a small, poorly armed force was able to inflict substantial damage on the enemy and hold out for a long period. At the same time, as we have already noted, the direct relationship between the Communist ranks and the Jews in the ghetto was one of sincere comradeship and was free of the reserve and suspicion that marked the ties with the right-wing factions. During the first days of the revolt, the P.P.R. turned twenty rifles over to the Ż.O.B. as a contribution to the battle in the ghetto. Considering the amount of equipment in Jewish hands, this was a significant gesture, but no way could be found to transfer these weapons into the ghetto, and they were not employed in the fighting.

The A.K. actions that we have reviewed were basically of a demonstrative nature. Of course, in addition to serving as an expression of solidarity, the operations mounted by the A.K. and the A.L. added another dimension to the struggle by forcing the Germans to keep reinforced units around the ghetto and to bear in mind the possibility that the uprising might spread to the Polish quarter. At the same time, as Stroop's reports show, the Germans took note of a general decline in harassment actions and in the activities of the armed Polish underground during the period of the ghetto uprising, and they credited this phenomenon to the fact that the Poles had learned a lesson from their rigorous response to the revolt in the ghetto.

The K.B., which maintained ties with the Ż.Z.W., was not a full-scale organization that operated according to clear-cut political or tactical aims. As we have already noted, the nature of the ties between these two organizations was based upon personal relationships—and perhaps on the commercial profits that the Poles hoped to realize. Yet even if some Poles, including members of the underground, profited from the sale of weapons and the supply of vital services, we can assume that their devotion to such dangerous tasks stemmed from more than the profit motive. On the other hand, the claim that people in the ranks of the K.B. participated in the fighting within the ghetto is not confirmed by any Jewish source or responsible Polish institution. According to Adam Halperin, the K.B. extended aid to the Jews only when the first group of fighters left the ghetto. David Wdowiński makes no mention whatsoever of Polish aid during the fighting. A comparison of the details in Stroop's report and Iwański's testimony on the battle of April 27 reveals insoluable contradictions, leaving the degree of Polish participation in this clash and the identity of the Poles involved (if any) surrounded by a cloud of doubt. It is unlikely that there is any chance of lifting that cloud after all these years and arriving at a credible reconstruction of the events.

Quite independent of this subject is the question of the Polish role in rescue operations designed to spirit the last of the Jewish fighters out of the ghetto once the fighting was over. Halperin wrote that at the end of the first day of fighting, a group of Jews made their way through the tunnel on Muranowska Street and Polish liaisons led them to the nearby forests. He does not explicitly state that Ż.Z.W. fighters were in this group, but, according to confirmed information in our hands, we can conclude that some of the union's fighters, as well as members of its command, were indeed among these escapees.[40] We do not know what motivated these Ż.Z.W. fighters to leave the ghetto at the end of the first day of battle. It may be that they remained faithful to the movement's principle that a defensive battle must be fought—to fulfill their obligation to resist and take vengeance on their murderers—but following the battle the movement should concentrate on rescue efforts, which is presumably proof of the conjecture that the Ż.Z.W. regarded resistance as a means of deliverance.[41] Yet since we have no material on the internal debates within the Ż.Z.W., we cannot speak with authority on the attitudes that consolidated within the union regarding this subject. It is certainly possible that this first group included wounded, the weak, and escorts for them, and we should not automatically assume from the fact of their leaving that there were differences of philosophy between the Ż.O.B. and the Ż.Z.W., or parts thereof, regarding the purpose and nature of the resistance.

On April 27 a group of Ż.Z.W. members and civilians left the building at 5 Karmelicka Street, in the sector of the "shops." They were aided by a Pole who was evidently a member of the A.K. The more than thirty people in this group wandered around the sewer system until they exited on Grzybowska Street, on the "Aryan" side, and temporarily established themselves in the building at 13 Grzybowska Street, where the Ż.Z.W. contingent that had left the ghetto on the second day of the revolt was located. The fighters were to wait for Polish guides to take them to the forests, but some of them lost patience and tried to move out on their own. Most of these fell in clashes with the Germans, while the better part of the force, still led by Pavel Frenkel, was discovered on May 11. The fighters were holed up in a bunker attached to the building on Grzybowska Street, and when most of them refused to obey the German order to come out and decided to fight, they were killed in the bunker (three were shot by the Germans).[42]

At dawn on April 30, the major contingent of the Ż.O.B. force that remained in the "shop" area—including the area commander, Eliezer Geller—escaped from the ghetto. The liaisons operating in this area, especially Regina ("Lilit") Fuden, tried to assemble together all the fighters who were capable of making their way out of the area (the members of Shlomo Winogron's squad and most of Wolf Rozowski's squad could not be found). Then a force of forty people entered the sewer system from a house on Leszno Street. One of the survivors who joined in this flight through the sewers described it in his memoirs:

> At nine we descended to the cellar in order to enter the sewer. The passage was very narrow and [we] had to crawl on [our] bellies to get in. The first ones failed to make it: They had entered head first and couldn't jump when they reached the end of the passage, which caused a lot of difficulty. We obviously learned from their experience and entered the narrow passage feet first, so the jump was easy.
> . . . [Our] feet sloshed around in the water and it was very noisy. The water was deeper here than it had been at the spot where we entered, so

we held our weapons [over our heads] to prevent them from getting wet. Then there was an announcement that "Lilit" had arrived and the line began to move forward. It was pitch black so we lit candles. I stayed with the members of our squad. We continued on our way for some time and then suddenly someone shouted that gas was being pumped into the tunnel. Sure enough, at the end of the tunnel we could see some kind of white cloud rising and spreading. . . . There was a great uproar and people began to turn and run back to where we had come from. . . . "Lilit" went out on a patrol again and returned to announce that what we had seen was not gas but the steam from the sewer illuminated by light penetrating an opening at one of the junctions.

. . . We kept going for a long while until we entered the main channel. Here the [radius] of the pipe was [wider] than a man's height, and we could stand up straight. The current was strong and the water deeper. We were ordered to keep an eye on one another so that no one would drown, heaven forbid. An order was given for each one to check his partner, and it was passed from mouth to mouth and strictly followed. We continued walking in the broad channel until we turned into a side channel that was narrower.

. . . And so it went until we reached an intersection, where we were supposed to receive the signal to climb out of the sewer. We stood some distance from the exit, about 25 meters away, and only Eliezer and Lilit approached it and waited for the signal. We stood waiting for a couple of hours. It was night by the time we heard a knocking sound on the manhole cover, and we were told that the vehicle that was supposed to come for us was late for some reason. The food hadn't arrived either. The manhole wasn't opened till two in the morning, when we were told that we were leaving. Our exit from the sewer could not be carried out as originally agreed. According to the plan, a truck was supposed to be waiting to take us out of the city, [but] it didn't show. There was no question of returning to the ghetto, and it was impossible to remain in the sewer for another day. We were hungry, depressed, and exhausted, so an emergency plan was adopted: We would leave the sewer and hide on one of the nearby rooftops.

We exited one by one, helping each other up onto the street. The scene we had imagined to ourselves just the day before, when we were notified of our escape, was so different from the situation we found ourselves in now! . . . Yesterday we envisioned many people armed from head to toe coming to help us, guarding the spot of our exit, giving us something to eat, and a big truck standing by to take us to the forest. What we now saw in the darkness was so pitiful and disappointing—there wasn't a living soul around, a dark night, hunger eating away at our guts, and we're [crowded] in the navel of a street. Not far from here, at the corner of Żelazna-Ogrodowa, German sentries were standing on guard, but they didn't sense our presence. From there our guides led us to the gate of the house at 27 Ogrodowa Street.[43]

"Lilit," one of the experienced liaisons of the underground and later of the Ż.O.B., did not remain with the forces rescued from the ghetto. She decided to return to the area of the "shops" to search out the squads remaining there and try to lead them out by the same route. Later it was reported that she returned to the "shop" area, found the remaining fighters, and was wounded by a German bullet while leading the force out, so that she remained in the ghetto. On April 30 the long-awaited truck arrived at Grzybowska Street with two men—an A.L. officer named Władysław Gajek ("Krzaczek"), who played a major role in the actions designed to rescue the remaining Jewish fighters, and the Ż.O.B. liaison Tuvia ("Tadek") Szajngut. The thirty or so people who mounted the truck were taken to a forest near Warsaw and constituted the core of a partisan unit that was built around the surviving members of the Ż.O.B.

On April 29 Simha Ratajzer ("Kazik") and Zalman ("Zygmunt") Friedrich left the ghetto to establish contact with Yitzhak Zuckerman and organize a campaign to rescue the fighters who remained among the ruins. With the aid of a number of A.L. comrades, and particularly the above-mentioned "Krzaczek," the Ż.O.B. people on the "Aryan" side managed to put together a rescue team. At dawn on May 8 it started to make its way toward the ghetto through the sewer system, but it could not get through and was forced to return to the "Aryan" side. The next day a second team left for the ghetto. The trek through the sewers was led by Polish sewer workers. Simha Ratajzer described that route, which he covered together with Rysiek Moselman, a Jewish fighter in the ranks of the P.P.R.:

> At 10:30 on the night of May 9 we descended into the sewer system, the sewer workers who were guiding us in the lead. . . . After we had gone a few dozen meters they stopped and announced that they would go no further. They were thoroughly drunk. I snapped in a severe tone: "You are under my command. Forward march!" I can't begin to describe that journey with them. Every hundred meters they stopped and demanded whiskey, *kwas* [an intoxicating liquor], and food. No amount of coaxing helped; only my revolver had any effect on them. I left the sewer at two in the morning, at the corner of Stawki and Zamenhofa. Rysiek remained with the sewer workers.

Ratajzer roamed the streets of the ghetto trying to locate the remaining fighters. When he could not find anyone, he returned to the sewer in despair, and the team began to make its way back to the "Aryan" side. While still inside the sewer, however, they came across ten fighters who were trying to escape from the ghetto and described the last days of the uprising and the fall of the bunker at 18 Miła Street.

The rescue team had arrived two days too late. Two of these fighters returned to the ghetto to bring out the remaining survivors. Then they all assembled close to the exit manhole, and it was decided that they would emerge on Prosta Street the next day.

The next morning Ratajzer and Tuvia Szajngut waited for the truck that was supposed to be bringing "Krzaczek." Their plan was to get the people out of the sewer as early as possible, before the street filled with pedestrians and vehicles. But "Krzaczek" was late, and Szajngut, who was a veteran liaison on the "Aryan" side, hoped to get a truck through his own connections. As Ratajzer subsequently related:

> The time was nine in the morning. None of them returned. It was too late to risk getting the comrades out of the sewer. On the other hand, it was clear to me that if we didn't get them out they would perish in there. So I decided that we must move them today, whenever an opportunity arises. It would have been better if we had had an armed guard present when they emerged from there, but unfortunately there was no one. Another hour passed. Suddenly the truck arrived with Kostek ["Krzaczek"] and some good-looking boys: Jurek [Zolotow], Rysiek, and Wacek. We surrounded the manhole with vehicles that had been readied for that purpose beforehand, because a German-Ukrainian guard was standing on the corner of Żelazna Street—the guard over the "Little Ghetto." We opened the manhole cover and the exit began. I didn't recognize anyone, though I knew them all, because they weren't people but ghosts who could barely stand on their feet. A crowd of people gathered around, staring and exclaiming: "The cats are coming out." Suddenly I noticed that the cover was open and no one else was coming out. Kostek was getting nervous, the truck was already full, and a second truck arrived just at that moment. I walked up to Kostek and was told that the second truck wasn't ours. "The truck is already full," I told him. "No one else is coming out. Why are we waiting?" I gave an order to close the manhole and move. Once in the truck, [however], I learned that fifteen people were still in the sewer, in a side channel. We decided that the truck would go back for them after it had deposited the [present] group [at the appointed place]. We traveled to a forest near Łomianki. I stayed behind to lead the comrades to the group from Többens's workshop, which we had moved from Ogrodowa Street two weeks earlier.[44]

Tuvia Borzykowski was among those who escaped that day after meeting Ratajzer in the sewer. He had been part of a reconnaissance group that was making its third attempt to find a route from the ghetto to the "Aryan" side. His account continues the story:

> The exit [from the sewer] had been going on for half an hour. Suddenly word reached us that there were Germans near Prosta Street. Krzaczek started to hurry us up. But the comrades deep in the channel didn't

make it to the manhole in time; even Adolf Hochberg and Szlomo Szuster, who went back to get them, didn't get back in time. We waited for them for a while, but because of the danger of waiting any longer, Krzaczek ordered the driver to move. He intended to come back and get the rest of the people out. The truck sped through the main streets of Warsaw. Sitting there crushed together, we took in the taste of fresh air after so long, and every blossoming pine was like a wonder to us. We were already approaching the roadblock set up by the Germans. Expecting a clash to take place here, Krzaczek ordered the weapons prepared. To tell the truth, if we had had to use them, we wouldn't have accomplished anything, simply because they were wet. But Krzaczek immediately changed his mind, ordered the driver to reverse, and avoided an open clash with the enemy. The truck turned off in another direction, passed through another roadblock without difficulty, and left the city. We reached a thick forest near Łomianki, a few kilometers outside of Warsaw. All subsequent efforts to return and rescue our remaining comrades were futile. A little while afterward, the Germans found out [about the action]. They placed Prosta and the nearby streets under siege, stationing guards around all the sewers and roads leading out of the city and blocking every means of extending aid to our comrades in the sewer. A few days later we received word that they had attempted to leave the sewer on their own, encountered Germans, and engaged them in battle. All of them, each and every one, was lost.[45]

Among the Ż.O.B. fighters who escaped through the sewers were some of the leaders of the Warsaw underground and commanders of the Ż.O.B., including Yisrael Kanał, Marek Edelman, Zivia Lubetkin, Tosia Altman, Yehuda Wengrower, Michael Rosenfeld, Hirsch Berlinski, Eliezer Geller, and Tuvia Borzykowski. Altogether, about eighty Ż.O.B. fighters were rescued. Some of them died in Warsaw (a group hiding out in a celluloid factory was trapped there in a fire), but most of the fighters were taken to the forests around the city and established a unit named in memory of Mordecai Anielewicz. Some fell in clashes with German forces, and many were murdered by Polish partisans. Of the entire Ż.O.B. force in Warsaw, only a dozen or so people lived to witness the liberation of Poland.

A group of activists headed by Yitzhak Zuckerman continued to engage in liaison and rescue operations throughout occupied Poland, in close cooperation with the Jewish National Committee and the Coordination Committee on the "Aryan" side of Warsaw. In addition, a group of Ż.O.B. members took part in the fighting during the Polish uprising in Warsaw in August 1944.

As we have seen, the A.K. did not play a significant role in rescuing either fighters or civilians from the ghetto. The Jews anticipated that they would be received graciously on the "Aryan" side as the survivors of a great battle, but the reality of the situation was quite different.

Although the A.L. extended substantial aid in rescue operations and we find this movement mentioned in connection with all the actions to get the remaining Ż.O.B. groups out of the ghetto, these activities essentially bore a joint nature: Ż.O.B. activists were the instigators and moving spirit behind the rescue activities, and they were aided by members of the A.L. and random Poles who became involved for a handsome fee.

It is not by chance that the Ż.O.B., more than the Ż.Z.W., managed to establish a foothold in the underground on the "Aryan" side. The reason lies in the nature of the ties that the two organizations maintained with various branches of the Polish underground. The contacts nurtured by the Ż.Z.W. were sufficient to get people out of the ghetto but not to ensure refuge on the "Aryan" side. The Ż.O.B. fighters likewise faced great hardship, and most of them were lost, but despite it all members of the Polish underground came to their aid and helped them find cover among the Polish population and even function as a Jewish body in the underground.

German Reactions to the Uprising

The uprising in the Warsaw ghetto, together with the prolonged fighting and attendant complications, came as a complete surprise and quite a shock to the Germans responsible for the government and security of the occupied areas of Poland. Until the revolt broke out, the Germans had hardly considered the possibility that Jews were capable of resisting their operations with force. Random German documents occasionally noted that Jews had escaped from the ghettos and joined up with partisan units, and the Germans evidently assumed that the Jews might cause difficulties after fleeing the ghettos and being absorbed into frameworks commanded by others. But they never imagined that on their own initiative, and under the conditions prevailing within the ghetto, the Jews would be capable of fielding a force that demanded serious attention. As we have already explained, this lack of foresight and contempt for Jewish prowess facilitated the consolidation of the Jewish fighting force and the preparations for armed resistance in Warsaw.

After the Warsaw ghetto revolt, the Germans changed their tactics regarding deportations. They had armed forces ready and available before initiating the *Aktionen* so as to preclude any demonstration of resistance. For example, before sending in their troops, the Germans would use deceptive methods to locate the organized force in a ghetto and seal it off from the Jewish population at large. An analysis of the post–April 1943 deportation strategy employed in various places—Bialystok,

Częstochowa, Zagłębie, etc.—indicates that the Germans had learned from their experience in the Warsaw ghetto and acted with considerable caution in order to prevent an armed clash with the Jews.

We have already noted that General Stroop regarded the suppression of the ghetto uprising as a standard military operation. As a loyal Nazi, he did not refrain from using the accepted derogatory terminology when speaking about the Jews, but we nonetheless get the impression that he was pitted against a resolute, courageous, and resourceful enemy. In his summarizing report, Stroop commented that "the resistance of the Jews and the hooligans could only be broken by the vigorous and incessant action of stormtroops day and night," and, "it was combat units of eighteen- to twenty-five-year-old Jewish boys—each with twenty to thirty or more people, including an appropriate number of women—that sparked off the rebellion and renewed it from time to time. These combat units received the order to resist . . . until the end and to commit suicide if necessary rather than be captured. . . ."[46] On June 18, 1943, Stroop was awarded a Class-A Iron Cross by Field Marshal Keitel in appreciation of his command over the "Grand *Aktion*" in the Warsaw ghetto.

The Warsaw ghetto uprising is mentioned for the most part in official German documents. On April 20, 1943, Frank sent a letter to the director-general of the Chancellor's Office, *Reichsminister* Lammers, which opens as follows:

> The meeting of the Generalgouvernement administration held today in honor of the Führer's birthday was preoccupied by developments in the security situation. As a consequence of various unorthodox conditions, these developments are moving in a most dangerous direction. As of yesterday, we are witness to a well-organized revolt in the Warsaw ghetto, and artillery has already been needed to oppose it . . . [47]

References to the Warsaw ghetto uprising (sometimes as much as whole paragraphs) can also be found in the diary of Joseph Goebbels, the propaganda minister. On April 25, 1943, the first day of Easter, he recorded that "the ghetto is being bombarded with artillery now. In an occupied city, this situation can hardly be considered to fall within the bounds of peace. The time has come to eliminate the Jews from the Generalgouvernement as well, [and] as quickly as possible. . . ." On May 1 Goebbels again turned to this subject in his diary:

> The reports from the conquered territories don't contain any startling news. The only noteworthy item is the very stiff fighting between our police, including to some degree the army, and the insurgent Jews. The Jews have managed to fortify the ghetto for defense. The fighting there is

very bitter, and matters have reached the point where the Jewish high command is issuing daily military communiqués. The joke evidently won't last long, but it is a perfect example of what can be expected of these Jews when they have weapons in their hands. Unfortunately, they also have excellent German weapons, especially machine guns. God in heaven only knows how they got their hands on them.[48]

The uprising in the ghetto was also taken up in the May 31 meeting of the Generalgouvernement administration, which was devoted to security matters. Krieger noted that only the Jews referred to as "Maccabees," who were excellent workers, and Jewish women, who proved themselves to be much stronger than their German counterparts, remained in the industrial enterprises. According to the protocol, he went on to comment: "The same thing aroused attention during the evacuation of the Warsaw ghetto, which was a most trying operation. The losses of the police totalled fifteen dead and eighty-eight wounded. It was established that armed Jewish women also persisted in resisting the *Waffen-S.S.* and police forces until the last breath.[49]

A comprehensive report on the Warsaw ghetto revolt written by Wilhelm Ohlenbusch, who was in charge of propaganda within the Generalgouvernement, was sent on to the Propaganda Ministry of the Reich on May 3, 1943. It states, *inter alia*:

> It has proven impossible to crush the resistance until now except by the use of flamethrowers and heavy infantry weapons against the housing blocks in which many tried to resist, for the resistance of the last groups of fighters is incredibly stubborn. Often the hooligans who burst out of burning buildings or smoke-filled [bunkers turned and] went back into the flames once it became clear to them that they would not be able to break out.

Ohlenbusch concluded his report by noting: "The Poles are saying that the battle for the ghetto has gone on longer than the battle for Poland."[50]

Naturally enough, the radio and press of the Third Reich, both in Germany proper and in the Generalgouvernement, did not report on the uprising in the ghetto or follow the development of the battle. This silence on the part of the media, which usually carried reports and commentary following guidelines established by the Propaganda Ministry, calls for some explanation. We cannot imagine that the ministry merely overlooked the news about the ghetto, since Goebbels himself testified in his diary that the uprising had made a strong impression on him. Thus a deliberate decision must have been made to ignore the events in the ghetto in order to conceal the humiliation of the Reich.

Yet, although the German regime was able to force the media to suppress news of the ghetto uprising, and perhaps even conceal it from the public in Germany and the other occupied countries, it was impossible to suppress knowledge of the revolt in Poland itself. News of the revolt spread throughout the country by word of mouth and through the extensive coverage that the Polish underground press gave to the revolt and its significance. Moreover, as usual in such cases, the rumor mill grossly exaggerated what had actually happened, and the Germans had reason to fear that the effect of the uprising might arouse the Poles to action and further undermine the precarious security situation in the Generalgouvernement. Goebbels noted in his diary on May 7 that the situation in the Generalgouvernement had reached the point where "the governor-general, Dr. Frank, cannot be [allowed to] remain in his post." He also clearly implies that it was the uprising in the ghetto that finally undermined the status of the omnipotent governor-general. Although Stroop believed that the uprising had dissuaded the Poles from embarking on a similar venture, the senior echelons of the Reich probably regarded the Jewish revolt as an ominous sign of the situation in the Generalgouvernement. Even if we take into consideration Goebbels's lack of support for Frank and his interest in accelerating the latter's downfall (while Frank's political status was dependent upon Hitler alone), the very fact that the propaganda minister assumed that the events in the ghetto would finally topple Frank indicates the importance ascribed to the revolt.

In order to temper the effect of the uprising and cool the Poles' eagerness for action, the Germans went out of their way to spread rumors that the revolt was not a Jewish operation but a Communist one. This claim, aired for the benefit of the Poles, had two major purposes: (1) Since most of the Poles were hostile toward Communism and its conspicuous political and territorial aspirations, the Germans hoped that identifying the uprising with the Communists might turn the Poles against it; (2) if the uprising were indeed a Communist operation, there would be nothing particularly surprising about its magnitude. We have aready seen how certain Polish quarters collaborated in spreading this lie, which was in line with their own anti-Semitic attitude and political aims. Moreover, a claim of this sort had good chances of being accepted, since the anti-Semites in Poland had long attempted to equate Jews with Communists and create the impression that the entire Jewish population of the country was infected by Bolshevism. On May 13, 1943, the governor of the Warsaw District, Dr. L. Fischer, published an appeal to the population of Warsaw stating:

> Lately, a number of murderous assaults have been perpetrated in Warsaw. They were committed by the same hand that is responsible for the mass graves of the Polish officers at Katyń. All these Communist hooligans

have found refuge in the former Jewish residential quarter of Warsaw, where they receive generous help and full backing. Thus the Jewish residential quarter has become a nest of all the followers of the Bolshevik ideology, who try to sow disquiet among the population by any means possible. The former Jewish residential quarter is steadily being destroyed, and together with it go the hopes of the Communists. Anyone who continues to deceive himself that the bloody regime of the Bolsheviks will yet arise in this country is making a grave error. Right now it is everyone's duty to prevent the Communist agents and the Jews from carrying out their provocations. Any Jew or Bolshevik who is still free today is the most dangerous enemy of the people. . . . [51]

After the uprising, German orders regarding the security situation in the occupied countries began to stress the "role of the Jewish element" and the danger it presented. For example, Himmler's August 1943 directive to destroy the Jews concentrated in the Lublin camps— including Poniatow and Trawniki (i.e., the remaining Jews of Warsaw)—opened with the words: "The Jewish problem in the Lublin District has grown to dangerous proportions."[52] He was undoubtedly referring to the rebellions in the Sobibor and Treblinka death camps, in particular, but there can be no doubt that his very admission that Jewish attempts at self-defense were of serious consequence is related to the impression created by the Warsaw ghetto uprising.

Naturally, we cannot know whether it was out of fear of rebellions among the Jews and their effects on the broader security situation that the Germans accelerated the liquidation of the ghettos and camps in the eastern sector of the Generalgouvernement. It is fair to assume, however, that the intensified liquidation program was not designed to preempt outbursts from the Jews. Rather, it is far more likely that the danger allegedly embodied by the Jews was merely being seized upon as an excuse to overrule German circles that were still lobbying to preserve the Jewish work force by impeding the progress of the "Final Solution."

As news of the uprising in the Warsaw ghetto spread, it left its mark on three separate parties to the war. First, the Germans became more cautious in their operations and began to take account of the possibility of armed Jewish resistance. Their confidence and prestige had been seriously undermined. Second, the Poles were very impressed by the action, and the Jewish struggle in Warsaw had a stimulating effect upon the Polish underground. Finally, and perhaps most important of all, news of the Warsaw ghetto revolt, which soon grew into a legend, inspired a sense of self-worth among the oppressed Jews of occupied Poland and generated further initiatives in the directions of self-defense and rescue. The uprising constituted a remarkable event not only in Jewish history but in the history of mankind.

NOTES

Introduction

1. Kazimierz Brandys, *Miasto niepokonane* (Warsaw, 1960), p. 5.

Chapter 1: The First Months of the Nazi Occupation

1. Tania Fuchs, *A vanderung iber okupirte gebitn* (*Wanderings through the Occupied Territory*) (Buenos Aires, 1947), pp. 9–10.

2. Chaim A. Kaplan, *Megillat Yissurin: Yoman Getto Varsha* (*Scroll of Agony: A Warsaw Ghetto Diary*) (Tel Aviv–Jerusalem, 1966), p. 3.

3. Ibid., p. 5.

4 Adam Czerniakow, *The Warsaw Diary of Adam Czerniakow: Prelude to Doom*, ed. Raul Hilberg, Stanislaw Staron, and Josef Kermisz (New York, 1979), p. 73.

5. Chaim A. Kaplan, *Scroll of Agony: The Warsaw Diary of Chaim A. Kaplan*, ed. Abraham I. Katsch (London, 1966), p. 30; *Megillat Yissurin*, p. 21.

6. Michael Weichert, *Milhamah-Zikhronot* (*War Memoirs*) (Tel Aviv, 1963), p. 26.

7. Czerniakow, *Warsaw Diary*, p. 75. Emmanuel Ringelblum, *Ktovim fun geto* (*Writings from the Ghetto*), Vol. I (Warsaw, 1961), p. 28.

8. The number of casualties and extent of the damage were never officially determined, and we have come across various estimates and statistics. The last order issued by the Warsaw command stated: "The number of injured, by a count that cannot be considered precise, is as high as 16,000 soldiers and 20,000 civilians." According to figures that were arrived at later on, there were approximately fifty thousand casualties, and this is the figure cited in most Polish publications. The extent of serious damage and physical destruction of buildings was never determined exactly. In the 1947 edition of the official *Warszawa w liczbach* (pp. 21 and 28), it was stated that at the time of the battles in September 1939, Warsaw lost 12 percent of its buildings; 7 percent of its rooms used as living quarters were completely destroyed, and 17 percent were partially damaged.

9. Kaplan, *Scroll of Agony*, p. 41.

10. Kaplan, *Megillat Yissurin*, p. 46.

11. Ibid., p. 43.

12. According to the copy of the manuscript of the diary of Henryk Brysker in the Moreshet Archive; see also *Biuletyn Żydowskiego Instytutu Historycznego* (*B.Ż.I.H.*), 62 (1967), 86.

13. Walter Hofer, *Die Entfesselung des zweiten Weltkrieges, Geheimes Zusatzprotokoll zum deutsch-sowjetischen Nichtangriffsvertrag* (Frankfurt, 1960), pp. 102–103.

14. Ibid., p. 116.

15. *Akten zur deutschen auswärtigen Politik, 1918–1945*, Series D, Vol. 4 (Baden-Baden, 1951), p. 291.

16. Hans Buchheim et al., *Anatomie des SS-Staates*, Vol. II (Munich, 1967), p. 28.

17. Norman H. Baynes, ed., *The Speeches of Adolf Hitler, April 1922 – August 1939*, Vol. I (London, 1942), p. 741.

18. Chaim Szoszkes, *A velt vos iz forbay* (*A World That Has Passed*) (Buenos Aires, 1949, p. 276.

19. [Philip Friedman], "Zagłada Żydów polskich w latach 1939–1945," *Biuletyn Głównej Komisji Badania Zbrodni Hitlerowskich w Polsce*, 1 (1946), 177.

20. On the differences between the *Wehrmacht* and the SS during the early stages of the occupation of Poland, see Czesław Madajczyk, *Polityka III Rzeszy w Okupowanej Polsce*, Vol. I (Warsaw, 1970), pp. 46–59, and Martin Broszat, *Nationalsozialistische Polenpolitik, 1939–1945* (Stuttgart, 1965), pp. 29–36.

21. The official name of the territorial framework was *Generalgouvernement für die besetzten polnischen Gebiete*. This name was dropped on July 8, 1940, and thereafter the area was called solely the Generalgouvernement.

22. Karol M. Pospieszalski, ed., *Hitlerowskie "prawo" okupacyjne w Polsce: Wybór dokumentów* (*Documenta Occupationis*, Vol. VI) (Poznan, 1958), pp. 20–21. (Hereafter *Documenta Occupationis*.)

23. Ibid., p. 18. In 1941, as a result of the German conquests in the war with the Soviet Union, eastern Galicia was added on to the Generalgouvernement. The overall area was thus extended by 54,585 square miles and the overall population rose to 16,800,000.

24. Buchheim et al., *Anatomie*, p. 291.

25. Broszat, *Nationalsozialistische Polenpolitik*, pp. 20–22.

26. See Nuremberg Documents, PS-3363.

27. *Documenta Occupationis*, Vol. VI, pp. 30–31.

28. Stanisław Piotrowski, *Dziennik Hansa Franka* (*The Diary of Hans Frank*) (Warsaw, 1956), pp. 266, 408.

29. Ibid.

30. Philip Friedman estimates that at least three hundred thousand Jews left the areas occupied by the Germans and settled in the territory annexed to the Soviet Union and in the Baltic states. These figures are based on an estimate, and it is impossible to verify their accuracy. See *Biuletyn GKBZNwP*, 1 (1946), 167–68.

31. Apolinary Hartglas, "Ha-Hodashim ha-Rishonim be-Kibush ha-Nazi" ("The First Months of the Nazi Occupation") in Yitzhak Gruenbaum, ed., *Enziklopedya shel Galuyyot* (*Encyclopaedia of the Jewish Diaspora*), Vol. VI, *Warsaw*, Part 2, (Jerusalem, 1959), p. 507.

32. Szoszkes, *A velt vos iz forbay*, pp. 337–38.

33. See the detailed survey of economic activity in the Generalgouvernement in Madajczyk, *Polityka III Rzeszy*, Vol. I, pp. 560–96.

34. Tatiana Berenstein, Artur Eisenbach, and Adam Rutkowski, eds., *Eksterminacja Żydów na ziemiach polskich: Zbiór dokumentów* (Warsaw, 1957), pp. 154–58.

35. Ibid., p. 161.

36. Ibid., pp. 202–203.

37. Tatiana Berenstein, "Praca przymusowa Żydów w Warszawie," *B.Ż.I.H.*, 45–46 (1963), 42–93.

38. Opposition to the policy of the *Judenrat* was expressed in meetings of

the building council representatives. See Ruta Sakowska, "Komitety domowe w getcie warszawskim," *B.Ż.I.H.*, 61 (1967), 59–86.

39. Tatiana Berenstein, "Ceny produktów żywnósowych w warszawie i w getcie warszawskim w Latach okupacji Hitlerowskiej," *B.Ż.I.H.*, 70 (1969), 3–19.

40. Kaplan, *Scroll of Agony*, pp. 105–106.

41. Ibid., pp. 97–98.

42. Details can be found in Ludwik Hirszfeld, *Historia jednego życia* (Warsaw, 1946).

43. Michael Weichert, "Zikhronot al Adam Czerniakow" ("Reminiscences on Adam Czerniakow"), *Molad*, 9:219 (1969), 310–32. See also Benjamin Mintz and Yisrael Klausner, eds., *Sefer ha-Zeva'ot (The Book of Atrocities)* (Jerusalem, 1965), pp. 47, 49.

44. Kaplan, *Scroll of Agony*, p. 114.

45. Emmanuel Ringelblum, *Ktovim fun geto (Writings from the Ghetto)*, Vol. I (Warsaw, 1961), pp. 78–79.

46. Mintz and Klausner, *Sefer ha-Zeva'ot*, pp. 46–48.

47. Ibid., p. 52.

48. Ibid., pp. 52–53.

49. *Documenta Occupationis*, Vol. VI, pp. 536–37.

50. Mintz and Klausner, *Sefer ha-Zeva'ot*, pp. 184–85.

51. According to this order, the following would be considered Jews: (1) anyone who belongs or belonged to the Jewish community; (2) anyone whose father or mother belongs or belonged to the Jewish community. Frank's order defining who was considered a Jew within the boundaries of the General-gouvernement was issued in July 1940. The concept of a Jew here corresponds to the accepted definition in the racist legislation of the Reich. See *Documenta Occupationis*, Vol. VI, pp. 558–59.

52. Ibid., pp. 562–64.

53. Weichert, "Zikhronot al Adam Czerniakow," p. 313.

54. Mintz and Klausner, *Sefer ha-Zeva'ot* (Hartglas's testimony), pp. 5, 32, 42, 54.

55. Ibid., pp. 32, 52.

56. Hirszfeld, *Historia jednego życia*, pp. 189–92.

57. Ibid., p. 191.

58. Ruta Sakowska, "Łączność pocztowa warsawskiego getta," *B.Ż.I.H.*, 78 (1971), 45–46.

59. Hartglas, "Ha-Hodashim ha-Rishonim," p. 497.

60. Czerniakow, *Warsaw Diary*, p. 92. It is not clear from this entry whether the demand for a "contribution" was a consequence of the incident, but subsequent developments leave no doubt that there was a connection between the incident and the blackmail.

61. Ibid., p. 93.

62. Kaplan, *Megillat Yissurin*, pp. 97, 104.

63. For details on this subject, see Adam Rutkowski, "Sprawa Kotta w środowisku żydowskim w Warszawie (Styczeń 1940)," *B.Ż.I.H.*, 62 (1967), 63–75.

64. Ludwik Landau, *Kronika lat wojny i okupacji*, Vol. I (Warsaw, 1962), p. 209.

65. Ringelblum, *Ktovim*, Vol. I, p. 77.

66. A full list of those murdered is appended to Rutkowski, *Sprawa Kotta*.

67. For details on the evacuation of deportees and the state of the refugees in Warsaw, see Ruta Pups-Sakowska, "Opieka nad uchodźcami i przesiedleńcami żydowskimi w Warszawie w latach okupacji hitlerowskiej," B.Ż.I.H., 65–66 (1968), 73–104.
68. Kaplan, *Megillat Yissurin*, p. 221.
69. Kaplan, *Scroll of Agony*, p. 61; *Megillat Yissurin*, pp. 69–70.
70. Kaplan, *Megillat Yissurin*, p. 73.
71. Hartglas, "Ha-Hodashim ha-Rishonim," pp. 490–510.
72. Mintz and Klausner, *Sefer ha-Zeva'ot* (Kerner's testimony), pp. 8–12.
73. Yad Vashem Archive, JM-1112.
74. According to entries from Kaplan's diary that are not included in the published edition of *Megillat Yissurin* and are preserved in the Moreshet Archive. See also fragments in *Yalkut Moreshet*, 4 (December 1964).
75. B.Ż.I.H., 73 (1970), 111; 74: 103–104.
76. Weichert, "Zikhronot al Adam Czerniakow," pp. 51–52.
77. Jonas Turkow, *Hayo Hayta Varsha Yehudit (Jewish Warsaw of Yore)* (Tel Aviv, 1969), p. 20.
78. Weichert, *Milhamah-Zikhronot*, pp. 51–52.
79. Ringelblum, *Ktovim*, Vol. 1, p. 365.
80. Sakowska, "Komitety domowe w getcie warszawskim."
81. During the week of Passover 1941, the chairmen and representatives of the building councils were convened by the *Judenrat* in an attempt to justify its system of mobilization for the labor camps and enlist the aid of the building councils in this campaign. The assembly was marked by outbursts and sharp criticism of the members of the *Judenrat*, and the building councils refused to cooperate in this matter.
82. Czerniakow, *Warsaw Diary*, p. 318.

Chapter 2: The Establishment of the Ghetto

1. The journalist Chaim Szoszkes, who was a member of the first *Judenrat* in Warsaw, related in his memoirs, *Bleter fun a geto togbukh (Pages of a Ghetto Diary)* (New York, 1944), p. 11, that the *Judenrat* was summoned on November 7. According to Hartglas's memoirs, the date was November 4, and this latter date is confirmed authoritatively by the entry in Czerniakow's diary (p. 87).
2. This list of streets was published, *inter alia*, in Yosef Ziemian, *Gevulot Getto Varsha ve-Shinuyehem (The Boundaries of the Warsaw Ghetto and Changes Therein)* (Jerusalem, 1971), pp. 4–5.
3. For details on this incident, see Hartglas, "Ha-Hodashim ha-Rishonim be-Kibush ha-Nazi," and Hartglas's testimony in Mintz and Klausner, *Sefer ha-Zeva'ot*, p. 51. Szoszkes, *Bleter fun a geto togbukh,* pp. 11–12; Czerniakow, pp. 87, 88.
4. Ya'akov S. Hertz, ed., *Zygielbojm-Bukh (Zygielbojm Book)* (New York, 1947), p. 131.
5. Szoszkes suggested in his memoirs that he too was a member of the delegation. Hartglas claims that Szoszkes was indeed supposed to arrive with the others but did not show, and his claim is confirmed by the entries in Czerniakow's diary.
6. Mintz and Klausner, *Sefer ha-Zeva'ot* (Hartglas's testimony), p. 52.

7. Szoszkes, *Bleter fun a geto togbukh*, p. 18.

8. *Documenta Occupationis*, Vol. VI, p. 522.

9. T.B., "Waldemar Schön, organizator Getta w Warszawie," *B.Ż.I.H.*, 49 (1964), 85–90.

10. Szymon Datner, "Działalność Warszwskiej 'Gminy wyzananiowej Żydowskiej' w dokumentach podziemnego archiwum getta warszawskiego," *B.Ż.I.H.*, 74 (1970), 87–136.

11. Czerniakow, *Warsaw Diary*, p. 136.

12. Landau, *Kronika*, Vol. I, pp. 403–404.

13. See parts of Schön's survey in Berenstein, Eisenbach, and Rutkowski, *Eksterminacja Żydów*, pp. 99–108.

14. Ibid., pp. 100–101.

15. Kaplan, *Scroll of Agony*, pp. 207–208.

16. Stanisław Piotrowski, *Misja Odyla Globocnika* (*The Mission of Odilo Globocnik*) (Warsaw, 1970), p. 271.

17. *Okupacja i ruch oporu w dzienniku Hansa Franka, 1939–1945* (*The Nazi Occupation and Resistance in Hans Frank's Diary*), Vol. I (Warsaw, 1972), p. 335. (Hereafter *Okupacja i ruch oporu*.)

18. *Gazeta Żydowska*, 27 (October 21, 1940).

19. Hirszfeld, *Historia jednego życia*, p. 197.

20. These figures are confirmed by Jewish sources, and Ringelblum reports the same numbers (*Ktovim*, Vol. I, p. 159). Kaplan noted that "to a certain degree, the edict caused more harm to the Poles than to the Jews, for the Poles have been ordered and are about to abandon their apartments not just in the Jewish ghetto but in the German quarter as well" (*Megillat Yissurin*, p. 361). Yet all these estimates were made early on, before the area of the ghetto was diminished. The numerical relationship changed substantially, and it became incontrovertibly clear that the edict was meant primarily to injure the Jews.

21. Yad Vashem Archive, O-25/59, *Wiadomości Polskie* (November 5, 1940).

22. Yad Vashem Archive, O-25/20, *Kronika Okupacji* (October 25–November 25).

23. Yad Vashem Archive, O-25/12, *Gwardia* (December 15, 1940).

24. Julian Kulski, *Zarzad Miejski Warszawy, 1939–1944* (*Warsaw's Municipality*) (Warsaw, 1964), p. 134.

25. Yad Vashem Archive, O-25/59, *Wiadomości Polskie* (November 5, 1940).

26. Landau was the editor of the underground Polish newspaper *Kronika Okupacji*, cited above. It is fair to presume that the sad commentary on the state of the Jews, who were uprooted from their natural Polish environment, was written by Landau himself or with his approval. See Landau, *Kronika*, Vol. I, p. 742.

27. Ringelblum, *Ktovim*, Vol. I, p. 189.

28. Kaplan, *Scroll of Agony*, p. 211.

29. Ringelblum, *Ktovim*, Vol. I, pp. 164–65.

30. Ibid., p. 167. Count Ronikier, who had a way with the Germans, was thought of as having an inclination to compromise with them.

31. Czerniakow, *Warsaw Diary*, pp. 208–209.

32. For the German estimate, see Schön's survey in Berenstein, Eisenbach, and Rutkowski, *Eksterminacja Żydów*; for Jewish figures and estimates, see Ziemian, *Gevulot Getto Varsha*.

Chapter 3: The Warsaw Ghetto

1. *Gazeta Żydowska*, 38 (May 13, 1941).
2. Ziemian, *Gevulot Getto Varsha*, p. 25.
3. *Okupacja i ruch oporu*, p. 542.
4. Ringelblum, *Ktovim*, Vol. I, p. 239.
5. Ibid., p. 275.
6. Madaczyk, *Polityka III Rzeszy*, Vol. II, p. 71.
7. Yad Vashem Archive, O-33/258 (Szymkowicz's diary; Polish), p. 90. A questionnaire that was secretly filled out in the Warsaw ghetto established that the daily caloric value of food consumed by the various social strata in the ghetto was as follows: *Judenrat* and Supply Authority officials—1,665 calories; unemployed members of the intelligentsia—1,395; independent craftsmen—1,407; "shop" employees—1,229; wholesale merchants—1,429; street merchants—1,277; wagoners ("rickshaw" drivers)—1,544; doormen—1,300; refugees in hostels—807; street beggars—784; overall population (an attempt to arrive at an average for the ghetto residents)—1,125. Statistics according to the questionnaire on consumption in the ghetto, *Bleter far Geshikhte*, II:1–4 (1949), 277.
8. Henryk Brysker's diary, written during the war on the "Aryan" side of Warsaw, p. 43.
9. M. Passenstein, "Szmugiel w getcie warszawskim," *B.Ż.I.H.*, 26 (1958) 42–72.
10. Ibid.
11. Yad Vashem Archive, O-33/258 (Szymkowicz's diary), p. 103.
12. Passenstein, "Szmugiel w getcie warszawskim."
13. The Polish-Jewish poetess Henryka Łazowert dedicated a poem to the unknown "Little Smuggler." The final stanza reads:

> I shall not return to you again,
> No more a voice from afar,
> The dust of the street is my grave,
> An infant's fate is sealed.
> And on my lips alone,
> A single care is frozen;
> Who, my soul's delight,
> Will bring you a crust tomorrow?

See the full text of the poem in Yitzhak Zuckerman and Moshe Basok, eds., *Sefer Milhamot ha-Getta'ot* (*The Book of the Wars of the Ghettos*) (Tel Aviv, 1947), p. 90.
14. On Leon Berensohn, see Ringelblum, *Ktovim*, Vol. II (Warsaw, 1963), pp. 230–233.
15. Ringelblum, *Ktovim*, Vol. I, p. 350.
16. Yad Vashem Archive O-6/102 (police officer's diary), p. 6.
17. The brave women who engaged in "small-time" smuggling were forced to stop when the executions were instituted as punishment for crossing over to the "Aryan" side. See entries on the Jewish women during the war in the Yad Vashem Archive M-10/Ph-16-2-1, JM/217/4.
18. Kaplan, *Megillat Yissurin*, p. 408.
19. On the edicts regarding limitations on and confiscation of Jewish property, see Berenstein, Eisenbach, and Rutkowski, *Eksterminacja Żydów*, Docu-

ment No. 71; *Documenta Occupationis*, Documents No. 30, 31, 33; Tatiana Berenstein and Adam Rutkowski, "Grabieżcza polityka gospodarcza hitlerowskiej administracji wojskowej w Polsce," *B.Ż.I.H.*, 42 (1962), 61–87; Tatiana Brustin-Berenstein, "O niektórych zagadnieniach gospodarczych w tzw Generalnej Guberni w świetle "dziennika Franka," *B.Ż.I.H.*, 9–10 (1954), 236–87.

20. Yad Vashem Archive, M-2/262 (memorandum by Knoll, undated).

21. Madajczyk claims that in 1940 it was estimated that Jewish craftsmanship accounted for 50 percent of all the crafts in the Warsaw and *Radom distrikt* (p. 581). He determined that in 1939 there was a total of 235,000 workshops in the Generalgouvernement, of which 115,000 were Jewish owned. In that same year, 587,000 people were employed in the crafts, of whom 280,000 were Jews. In 1941, however, 118,000 workshops were registered in the Generalgouvernement, of which only 24,000 were Jewish owned; and a total of 295,000 people were employed in the crafts, of whom 60,000 were Jews. See Madajczyk, *Polityka III Rzeszy*, Vol. I, p. 581; Vol. II, p. 32.

22. On the same occasion, Frank went on to state that the problem could not be solved immediately: "We cannot imbue the Poles with enough energy and talent to enable them to replace the Jews. Thus we are forced to permit Jewish craftsmen to continue their work." *Okupacja i ruch oporu*, pp. 249, 403–404.

23. *Gazeta Żydowska*, 41 (December 13, 1940).

24. Ibid., 61 (July 21, 1941).

25. Ibid., 70 (August 11, 1941).

26. Jerzy Winkler, "Getto walczy z niewolą gospodarczą," *B.Ż.I.H.*, 35 (1960), 55–86.

27. Yad Vashem Archive, O-6/100 (Stanisław Adler's manuscript; Polish), Part I, pp, 106, 152.

28. Brysker's diary, manuscript in the author's possession, pp. 59–60.

29. Yad Vashem Archive, O-6/103 (Ernest's diary), p. 60.

30. Ibid., pp. 74–75.

31. Czerniakow, *Warsaw Diary*, p. 172.

32. Abraham Levin, *Mi-Pinkaso shel ha-More mi-"Yehudiya"* (*The Journal of the Teacher from Yehudiyah*) (Beit Lohamei Ha-Getta'ot, 1969), p. 43.

33. *Gazeta Żydowska*, 46 (December 27, 1940); 21 (March 14, 1941).

34. Ibid., 13 (February 14, 1941).

35. *Gazeta Żydowska*, 32 (November 8, 1940) announced that "the authorities brought it to the attention of the Jewish community in Warsaw that in accordance with regulations published on January 26, 1940, the holding of prayers is forbidden due to the epidemic." In Issue 34 of the same, dated April 29, 1941, we read that "the authorities have given the Jewish Council permission to open three synagogues for the purpose of holding prayers."

36. Czerniakow, *Warsaw Diary*, p. 313.

37. Yad Vashem Archive, O-6/103 (Ernest), p. 7.

38. Yad Vashem Archive, O-6/100 (Adler), p. 103.

39. See the list of taxes and levies in Nachman Blumental, "Getto Varsha ve-Hurbano" ("The Warsaw Ghetto and Its Destruction") in Gruenbaum, *Enziklopedya*, Vol. II, *Warsaw* (Jerusalem, 1953), p. 608.

40. *Gazeta Żydowska*, 15 (September 10, 1940). The paper returned to this subject during the period of the ghetto, when it criticized the autonomous Supply Authority and argued that its board of directors consisted exclusively of

successful merchants and the wealthy, who had never been in touch with the lower classes of Warsaw society. Later on in the article, the paper wrote in relation to taxes: "And in general, the system of indirect taxation has been a blow to the poorest among us, who for the most part must feed especially large families, and a boon to men of means" (42, May 27, 1941).

41. A. Natanblut, "Shuln in varshever geto," *YIVO-Bleter*, 2 (1947). Ruta Sakowska, *Ludzie z dzielnicy zamknietej* (Warsaw, 1975), pp. 187-200.

42. On September 5, 1941, Czerniakow recorded in his diary: "At last permission was given today for opening the elementary schools" (p. 277).

43. See, e.g., Ringelblum's biting piece "Di syne tsu der politsye" ("The Hatred toward the Police"), December 1942, in *Ktovim*, Vol. II, pp. 34-37. Hostility toward and denunciation of the police, against the background of the mass deportation in the summer of 1942, is one of the central motifs found in memoirs. We shall return to this subject at length in the coming chapters.

44. *Gazeta Żydowska*, 40 (December 6, 1940); 45 (December 24, 1940).

45. Yad Vashem Archive, O-6/100 (Adler), p. 91.

46. Yad Vashem Archive, O-6/102 (police officer's diary), p. 5.

47. The "Blue Police," which was built around a nucleus of veteran members of the Polish police force, was reinforced by Poles of German extraction and Polish collaborators. It was thought of as a force that usually received its orders from the Germans and operated among the Polish public. Thus the "Blue Police" excelled all the more in its persecution of the Jews and attempts to profit from the Jewish tragedy. During the existence of the ghetto, its members extorted Jewish money and property by various tactics; afterward the "Blue Police" collaborated in hunting down Jews who were living under cover or in hiding on the "Aryan" side of Warsaw and engaged in both blackmail and turning Jews in to the Germans.

48. Ringelblum, *Ktovim*, Vol. I, pp. 197, 216.

49. Ibid., Vol. II, p. 31.

50. On the prison in the ghetto, see Czerniakow's entries for June 6, 1941; June 10, 1941; July 3, 1941; July 31, 1941; February 23, 1942; March 11, 1942; March 22, 1942. See also Yad Vashem Archive, O-6/100 (Adler).

51. It is interesting that Ringelblum, who found any form of collaboration with the Germans revolting, wrote the following about the execution of Kohn and Heller during the mass deportation from Warsaw in the summer of 1942: "They killed Kohn and Heller and afterward Ehrlich. The reason: their intervention at the *Umschlagplatz* and the release of many people in exchange for money—and not just for money. Many Hasidim were hiding out in their homes. Contact with rabbis" (*Ktovim*, Vol. II, p. 14).

52. Ibid., Vol. I, p. 263.

53. See a description of a rally and the reaction to it in Jonas Turkow, *Azoy iz es geven* (*It Happened Thus*) (Buenos Aires, 1948), p. 87.

54. See the short biographical sketch of Gancwajch in Zuckerman and Basok, *Sefer Milhamot*, pp. 714-15. See also the comprehensive article written by Aaron Weiss, "Group of the 13," *Yalkut Moreshet*, 21 (1976).

55. *Okupacja i ruch oporu*, Vol. I, pp. 210-11.

56. Ibid., p. 215.

57. Ibid., pp. 338, 496, 382, 374. There is no doubt that this announcement of Frank's hints at the beginning of the "Final Solution," as conceived by Hitler on the eve of the war against the Soviet Union. In any case, it is clear that when the *Einsatzgruppen* campaign was being planned, the notion of ex-

tending the "solution" into the bounds of the Generalgouvernement was already under discussion.

58. Characteristic of this concern was the position held by Dr. Bühler, who was Frank's deputy and representative at the Wannsee Conference on January 20, 1942. At this meeting, which dealt with formulating an operative plan for implementing the "Final Solution," Bühler declared that the authority to solve the Jewish problem in the Generalgouvernement had been turned over to the Security Police and the S.D., which would receive the full cooperation of the Generalgouvernement regime in carrying out their tasks. Bühler's special request at the conference was that the Jewish problem be solved in the Generalgouvernement as quickly as possible, i.e., that the area be the first in which the extermination program be put into operation. See Berenstein, Eisenbach, and Rutkowski, *Eksterminacja Żydów*, p. 272.

59. Czerniakow, *Warsaw Diary*, p. 295.

60. This order was issued as a result of discussions held during Frank's visit to Warsaw. Ringelblum recorded that it was issued at the beginning of November, which leads us to understand that it was known to the ghetto population at that time. Ringelblum, *Ktovim*, Vol. I, p. 313.

61. Yad Vashem Archive, Underground Press Division, *El Al*, 4 (November 1941). Under the headline "Nightmare," the paper wrote: "It is inconceivable that the November 17 murder of eight Jews innocent of any sin will ever be forgotten. The murderers—each and every one of them without exception—must pay for their crime." See also *Biuletyn*, 14:24 (December 20, 1941).

62. Yad Vashem Archive, Auerswald-Leist Division, JM/1112.

63. Czerniakow, *Warsaw Diary*, p. 286.

64. See a description of the institution and its staff in Turkow, *Hayo Hayta Varsha Yehudit*, pp. 20–24. See also Nathan Eck, *Ha-To'im be-Darkei ha-Mavet (Wanderers along the Roads to Death)* (Jerusalem, 1960), p. 33.

65. On this subject, see Ringelblum's biographical sketch of Mordecai Anielewicz, *Ktovim*, Vol. II, pp. 141–59.

66. Yad Vashem Archive, M-10/Ph-17–1–1, JM/216/1.

67. In his recent book *American Jewry and the Holocaust* (Detroit, 1981, pp. 94–103), Yehuda Bauer reveals discussions among the leadership of the JDC in New York regarding the question of help for Polish Jews. He explains the reasons for the failures during the crucial years.

68. *Gazeta Żydowska* (second year), 76 (August 25, 1941).

69. Yad Vashem Archive, O-3/714, O-3/618/58.

70. *Gazeta Żydowska*, 49 (June 20, 1941).

71. Kaplan, *Megillat Yissurin*, p. 415.

72. Czerniakow, *Warsaw Diary*, p. 239.

73. Ringelblum, *Ktovim*, Vol. I, p. 241.

74. *Gazeta Żydowska*, 29 (April 11, 1941).

75. See, e.g., Joseph Kermish, "Nigudim Ma'amadi'ym be-Getto Varsha" ("Class Differentiations in the Warsaw Ghetto") in Gruenbaum, *Enziklopedya*, Vol. II (Jerusalem, 1959), pp. 557–86. See also Bernard Mark's definitions in the various editions of his book on the Warsaw ghetto uprising, *Powstanie w getcie warszawskim* (Warsaw, 1963).

76. Ringelblum, *Ktovim*, Vol. I, pp. 288–89.

77. Yad Vashem Archive, O-33/258 (Szymkowicz manuscript), p. 88.

78. On the incidence of disease and the epidemic in the Warsaw ghetto,

see Mordecai Leńsky, *Hayei ha-Yehudim be-Getto Varsha: Zikhronotav shel Rofe* (*Jewish Life in the Warsaw Ghetto: A Doctor's Memoirs*) (Jerusalem, 1961). See also Ryszard Zablotniak, "Epidemia duru plamistego wśrod ludności żydowskiej w Warszawie w latach II wojny światowej," *B.Z.I.H.*, 4:80 (1971), 3-21.

79. Sakowska, "Łączność pocztowa warszawskiego getta."

80. See Czerniakow, *Warsaw Diary*, pp. 274, 286.

81. Berenstein, Eisenbach, and Rutkowski, *Eksterminacja Żydów*, pp. 167-68.

82. Ringelblum, *Ktovim*, Vol. II, pp. 44-46.

83. In his diary, Henryk Brysker listed twenty different armbands (pp. 104-105).

84. Levin, *Mi-Pinkaso*, p. 30.

85. Yad Vashem Archive, O-6/100 (Adler), pp. 38-39.

Chapter 4: The Political Underground in the Warsaw Ghetto

1. Martin Broszat, *Nationalsozialistische Polenpolitik, 1939-1945* (Stuttgart, 1965), pp. 70-72; Czesław Madajczyk, *Polityka III Rzeszy w Okupowanej Polsce* (Warsaw, 1970), pp. 83-123; *Documenta Occupationis*, Vol. VI, pp. 36-41.

2. *Documenta Occupationis*, Vol. VI, pp. 451-54.

3. Ibid., p. 27.

4. Ibid., p. 406.

5. *Okupacja i ruch oporu*, Vol. I, pp. 81-82; *Documenta Occupationis*, Vol. VI, p. 407.

6. See Levi Dror and Yisrael Rosenzweig, eds., *Sefer Ha-Shomer ha-Za'ir* (*The Ha-Shomer ha-Za'ir Book*), Vol. I (Merhavyah, 1956), p. 479. A letter from Vilna dated November 9, 1939, states: " . . . It is imperative to keep in contact with the portion of the movement in Germany [meaning the German-occupied part of Poland], and we also decided that Tosia [Altman] must go there." And in a letter from Vilna to Palestine dated December 7, 1939, we read: " . . . We wrote to you in our last letter that we are about to send people there [the German-occupied sector] to work toward halting the flight of our members from the area."

In an undated postcard sent from Lvov in the area annexed by the Soviet Union, Yitzhak Zuckerman notified his comrades in Palestine that "Soon I will be with Frumka [Płotnicka]," i.e., in Warsaw, and he arrived in Warsaw during the latter half of April 1940. See Yehuda Hellman, "Mikhtavei Pe'ilim ve-Shelihim" ("Letters of Activists and Liaisons"), in *Dappim le-Heker ha-Sho'a ve-ha-Mered* (*Selected Research on the Holocaust and the Revolt*), Second Collection (Beit Lohamei ha-Getta'ot, 1973), pp. 166-67.

7. Hirsch Berlinski, "Zikhronot" ("Memoirs"), *Yalkut Moreshet* 1 (1964), 24-25.

8. Ringelblum, *Ktovim*, Vol. I, entry for December 24-25, 1941, p. 322.

9. Hertz, *Zygielbojm-Bukh*, p. 189.

10. Ringelblum, *Ktovim*, Vol. II, p. 109.

11. Yad Vashem Archive, Underground Press Division, *Bafrayung* (*Liberation*), 1940 (no issue number or date).

12. Yad Vashem Archive, Underground Press Division, *Proletarisher Gedank* (*Proletarian Thought*), 2 (May 1941).

13. Yad Vashem Archive, Underground Press Division, *Yugntruf* (*The Call to Youth*), January 1941.

14. Yad Vashem Archive, Underground Press Division, *Yugntruf*, 2 (October 1941). An article headlined "The Path of Jewish Youth" states: "We must face reality squarely in the eye. Reality demands the forging of a large force of Jewish youth; a force that, when the time comes, will help gain liberty for the entire world and for the Jewish laborers, shoulder to shoulder with the Red Army and the Jewish proletariat." In the January 1941 issue of *Yugntruf* we read: " . . . We . . . Jewish youth do not place our hopes on the victory of either of the imperialist sides. We believe that both of them must vanish from the face of the earth."

15. Yad Vashem Archive, Underground Press Division, *Yugnt-Shtime* (*The Voice of Youth*), 1–2, 4–5 (January–February 1941).

16. Yad Vashem Archive, Underground Press Division, *Yunge Gwardye* (*Young Guard*), 1 (July 1941).

17. Yad Vashem Archive, Underground Press Division, *Tsayt Fragn* (*Questions of the Time*), 2 (November 1941). The December 3, 1941, issue of this paper states: "Do the persecutions strengthen the solidarity of the Jewish public? Presumably yes. Under the terrible blows of Hitlerism, in the atmosphere of the terrible destruction and the threat of death, the sense of mutual responsibility, of common fate, is heightened . . . but that is just a superficial and fleeting phenomenon."

18. Yad Vashem Archive, Underground Press Division, *Bafrayung* (December 1940 is the presumed date of publication).

19. Yad Vashem Archive, Underground Press Division, *Magen David* (*The Shield of David*) (February 1942 is the presumed date of publication).

20. Ringelblum, *Ktovim*, Vol. I, entries for February 27 and 28, 1941, p. 221.

21. Ibid., Vol. II, in the biographical sketch of Menachem Linder, p. 166.

22. Ibid., Vol. I, p. 353.

23. Yitzhak Zuckerman expressed his opinion on this matter at a conference dedicated to Jewish resistance: "I was both a party man and a member of a youth organization. I think that during the period we are discussing the parties excelled in just one thing—social work. In every other field of underground activity that began in 1940, from the underground seminar in Warsaw in the middle of that year to the first appearance of the underground press, the party men were not to be found among the initiators or promoters or operators. In all these things the initiators were the youth movements. I wish to say that had the fate of the Jews in 1942 lain in the hands only of the parties, the revolt would never have taken place." See *Jewish Resistance During the Holocaust: Proceedings of the Conference on Manifestations of Jewish Resistance* (Jerusalem, 1971), p. 150.

24. See *Korespondentzia Penimit* (*Internal Correspondence*), No. 4 (an attempt to summarize the movement's activities from the end of 1939 to the middle of 1942). There is no date on the document, but it surveys, *inter alia*, the meeting held sometime between May 8 and 11, 1942, so that it must have been written after these dates and before July 22, 1942, i.e., the commencement of the mass deportation from Warsaw. It was published in *Dappim le-Heker ha-Sho'a ve-ha-Mered*, 1 (April 1951), 148–56. (Hereafter *Korespondentzia Penimit*.)

25. Ibid.; see the article "Nahshol Anashim Kana'im" ("A Flood of Zealous Men"), movement newspaper, 1942, in Dror and Rosenzweig, *Sefer Ha-Shomer ha-Za'ir*, Vol. I, p. 439.

26. B. Auerbach, "Ha-No'ar ha-Ziyyoni be-Getto Varsha ve-Helko ba-Mered" ("Zionist Youth in the Warsaw Ghetto and its Role in the Revolt"), *Massu'ah (Beacon)*, 2 (1974).

27. See Chaim Lazar, *Mezada shel Varsha: Ha-Irgun ha-Zeva'i ha-Yehudi be-Mered Ghetto Varsha (The Fortress of Warsaw: The Jewish Military Union in the Warsaw Ghetto Uprising)* (Tel Aviv, 1963,), p. 49. Lazar also writes of the census taken among Betar members, in which about two thousand youngsters were counted (p. 55). But he does not state when and how this count was taken or the source of the data.

28. Marek Edelman, *Getto walczy* (Warsaw, 1946), p. 18.

29. Yad Vashem Archive, Underground Press Division, *El Al*, 1 (1941).

30. Yad Vashem Archive, M-20/86 (a letter from Tosia Altman dated March 29, 1940).

31. *Korespondentzia Penimit*; Zionist Archive, S/26/1158 (memorandum of a member of the Central Committee of He-Halutz in Poland).

32. Zionist Archive, S/26/1157 (a letter from Zivia [Lubetkin] to comrades in the United States, dated September 25, 1941); *Korespondentzia Penimit*; Chana Gelbard and Yerahmiel Helfgot, eds., *Mi-Bein Homot Varsha (Within the Walls of Warsaw)* (Ein-Harod, 1944); and the testimony of Hadassah Złotnicka-Talmon, who was a member of the training-farm group at Grochów, solicited by the author in 1975 (author's private file).

33. The Bund's *Yugnt-Shtime*, 3/6 (March 1941) wrote on this question: " . . . As to the edict, at this difficult time, irresponsible parties have associated the tragedy of the 'work camps' with the motto 'agricultural training.' They are preparing to transfer Jewish youth to work voluntarily in the villages [and] on Polish farms. Don't think for a moment that farmers are lacking in the Polish countryside. . . . No, there is no shortage of hands in the Polish countryside; but the German conqueror deports them to Germany, where hands *are* short. . . . The jobs made available by the deportation of the Polish farmer are to be filled by young Jewish *volunteers*. The 'nationalist' circles who support this 'training' have always been alien to the concrete national interests of the Jewish masses in Poland" (Yad Vashem Archive, Underground Press Division). On the influence of groups from the pioneering youth movements on the work camps, see Yad Vashem Archive, M-10/Ph-10–1–8.

34. Lazar, *Mezada shel Varsha*, p. 75, states that: "During the summer more than 600 members of Betar went to Hrubieszów, including all the activists and the command." He does not cite the source on which he bases this figure. Levin speaks in his diary (in the entry for May 23, 1942) of a meeting with his former pupil Hanka T[auber], who was on the farm in Hrubieszów. Levin describes the farm and work conditions there in detail and relates, *inter alia*: "The farm is worked by Ukrainian farmers, and there are many of them. Betar brought youngsters from Warsaw there — boys and girls, all middle-class students — who have been working on the farm from the beginning of last summer to this very day. There are thirty of them. They live in two rooms in a brewery and maintain a cooperative lifestyle modeled on the *kevuzot* [collectives] in Palestine. Three members remain at home every day and prepare meals for the entire group . . ." (p. 48).

35. In addition to Jewish sources on the farm at Czerniakow, we also have a Polish source on the nature of that farm: Helena Balicka-Kozłowska, *Mur miał dwie strony* (Warsaw, 1958).

36. Ringelblum, *Ktovim*, Vol. II, p. 143.

37. Yad Vashem Archive, Underground Press Division, *Yugnt-Shtime*, 11 (September 1941).

38. Yad Vashem Archive, Underground Press Division, *Neged ha-Zerem* (*Against the Current*), 13/2.

39. See Bracha Habas, *Mikhtavim min ha-Getta'ot* (*Letters from the Ghettos*) (Tel Aviv, 1943), p. 15.

40. Yad Vashem Archive, Underground Press Division, *Neged ha-Zerem*, 15/4 (May 1941).

41. Ringelbaum, *Ktovim*, Vol. II, p. 148.

42. Yitzhak Zuckerman, "Mered ha-Yehudim" ("The War of the Jews"), *Mibifnim* (*From Within*), 12:3 (June 1947), 414.

43. See the comments by Hirsch Wasser, the secretary of the "Oneg Shabbat" project, in the *Minutes of the Conference in Memory of Dr. Emmanuel Ringelblum*, Yad Vashem (Jerusalem, March 25, 1964), p. 18.

44. Ibid., pp. 22, 24.

45. Yad Vashem Archive, Underground Press Division, *Biuletyn*, 11 (September 1941).

46. Edelman, *Getto walczy*, p. 21.

47. See, e.g., details on the printing of the Bund underground papers in *In di yoren fun yidishn Khurbn* (*In the Years of the Jewish Catastrophe*) (New York, 1948), pp. 332–34. See also Shalom Grajek, "Itonut ha-Mahteret" ("The Underground Press") in Zuckerman and Basok, *Sefer Milhamot*, pp. 44–48.

48. See the book by the Polish underground activist Wacław Zagórski, *Wolność w niewoli* (*Liberty in Slavery*) (London, 1971), pp. 163–64, 172, 211, 234. A Polish actress associated with Socialist circles and suffering from a terminal disease took it upon herself to smuggle the material. She was caught at Piotorkow-Trebunalski. During a search at the railway station, a suitcase was found to contain the Bund's underground newspapers, and a list of places and addresses to which the forbidden material was destined was uncovered in the actress's lipstick case. The incident is described in a number of sources: Ya'akov Kurtz, *Sefer Edut* (*A Book of Testimony*) (Tel Aviv, 1960), pp. 176–78; *In di yoren fun yidishn Khurbn*, pp. 64, 140; Ya'akov Tselemenski, *Mitn farshnitenem folk* (*With the Destroyed People*) (New York, 1963), pp. 144–52. As a result of the incident, in the summer of 1941 thirteen Bund members, including four members of the local *Judenrat* (one being the chairman), were arrested in Piotorkow. One of the prisoners, Ya'akov Lubliner, had turned himself in when it became clear to him that his failure to do so endangered the Jews of the city. Arrests were also made in Częstochowa, Tomaszów-Mazowiecki, and Cracow. The detainees were tortured, most of them were sent to Auschwitz, and all of them perished.

49. One of these incidents was the arrest and death of a seventeen-year-old Bund member, Yisrael Bas, whom Ya'akov Tselemenski mentions in his memoirs. Bas was caught with a bundle of the Bund's underground youth papers, *Yugnt-Shtime*, in his possession. See Tselemenski, pp. 69–70.

50. Yad Vashem Archive, Underground Press Division, *Yugnt-Shtime*, 1 (December 1940).

51. See, e.g., *Jutrznia*, First Year, No. 5 (March 14, 1942). Yad Vashem Archive, Underground Press Division.

52. Yad Vashem Archive, Underground Press Division, *Yediot*, 8 (June 1942).

Chapter 5: Prelude to the Mass Deportation

1. Kaplan, sections of the diary not included in the published editions, found in the copy in the Moreshet Archive, p. 73.
2. See, e.g., a serious discussion of this subject in Jan M. Ciechanowski, *Powstanie warszawskie* (London, 1971).
3. *Słowo Młodych* (*The Word of Youth*), 5:19 (July 1941), in *Ittonut Gordonya be-Mahteret Getto Varsha* (*The Gordonia Newspapers in the Warsaw Ghetto Underground*) (Hulda, 1966), p. 45.
4. Hans A. Jacobsen, *Der Zweite Weltkrieg* (Frankfurt, 1965), pp. 107–14.
5. Uwe D. Adam, *Judenpolitik im Dritten Reich* (Düsseldorf, 1972).
6. Ibid., p. 305.
7. Szymon Datner, 55 *dni Wermachtu w Polsce* (55 *Days of the Wehrmacht in Poland*) (Warsaw, 1967), p. 619.
8. Madajczyk, *Polityka III Rzeszy*, Vol. I, p. 45.
9. Buchheim et al., *Anatomie des SS-Staates*, Vol. II, p. 302.
10. Ibid., pp. 301–302.
11. "Obóz zagłady Chełmno," *Biuletyn GKBZNwP*, 1 (1946), 147–64.
12. Yad Vashem Archive, Underground Press Division, *Neged ha-Zerem*, 7/8 (18/19).
13. See Rayzl (Różka) Korczak, *Lehavot ba-Efer* (*Flames in Ash*) (Merhavya, 1965), p. 54.
14. Lazar, *Mezada shel Varsha*, p. 84.
15. Mordecai Tenenbaum-Tamarof, *Dappim min ha-Deleka* (*Pages from the Conflagration*) (Beit Lohamei ha-Getta'ot, 1948), p. 8.
16. Yad Vashem Archive, Underground Press Division, *Neged ha-Zerem*, 7/8 (18/19).
17. Ringelblum, *Ktovim*, Vol. II, p. 147.
18. Edelman, *Getto walczy*, pp. 17, 25.
19. Yad Vashem Archive, JM/2713, Ph/27/1–6 (Grojanowski's testimony).
20. News reached Warsaw of two hundred youngsters from the city of Nowogródek who resisted with weapons and perished in battle, along with twenty enemy soldiers. There is no corroboration of this revolt in any official source, and we cannot know how this news reached Warsaw.
21. Yad Vashem Archive, Underground Press Division, lead article in *Jutrznia*, 7 (March 1942).
22. It is not clear what Czerniakow is referring to or from whom or when he received such an announcement, as it is not corroborated in his diary. Edicts referring to the concentration of Jews in a number of central ghettos were issued in November 1942—i.e., after the mass deportation from Warsaw in the summer of 1942—and as far as we can see, their purpose was to seduce the Jews in hiding or roaming about beyond the confines of the ghettos to return to these enclosed areas.
23. David Wdowiński, *And We Are Not Saved* (London, 1964), pp. 54–55. (Translated from *Ve-Anahnu Lo Noshanu*, pp. 92–93.)
24. Ż.O.B. report, which has been published in a number of places. See, e.g., Melekh Neustadt, *Hurban ve-Mered Yehudei Varsha* (*The Destruction and Revolt of the Jews of Warsaw*) (Tel Aviv, 1947). The archive of Kibbutz Lohamei ha-Getta'ot contains the copy of the minutes of the meeting recorded by Eliyahu Gutkowski, a member of the "Oneg Shabbat" team. The copy is damaged and unclear, and one can only make out isolated names and fragments of sentences.

25. Berlinski; the original version in Yiddish was published in Pola Elster, Hirsch Berlinski, and Eliyahu Ehrlich, *Dray* (*Three*) (Tel Aviv, 1966), pp. 157–58.

26. Ibid., p. 158.

27. Edelman, pp. 16–17.

28. Zivia Lubetkin, "Bi-Yemei Kilayon ve-Mered" ("In Days of Annihilation and Revolt") in David Gotesfirch, Haim Hadari, and Aháron Reichman, eds., *Sefer Dror* (*The Book of Dror*) (Tel Aviv, 1947), pp. 470–71.

29. This was the dominant issue in the polemical articles of the Communist press, and evidently this debate influenced the Polish underground's relationship with the defense force in the ghetto.

30. Adolf Abraham Berman, *Mi-Yemei ha-Mahteret* (*From the Days of the Underground*) (Tel Aviv, 1971), p. 45.

31. Ż.O.B. report.

32. Gotesfirch, Hadari, and Reichman, *Sefer Dror*, p. 472.

33. Berman, *Mi-Yemei ha-Mahteret*, p. 46.

34. Ester (Edwarda) Mark, "Pinhas (Pioter) Kartin—'Andrzej Szmidt,'" *Yidishe Shriftn* (*Yiddish Writings*), 1–4 (242–45) (January–April 1968).

35. Zuckerman, "Mered ha-Yehudim." Zuckerman continues there: "After a long period of this ideological war in the ranks of the Anti-Fascist Bloc, it was decided to found a parallel organization within the bloc. It was headed by Mordecai Tenenbaum, who had just come to Warsaw from Vilna-Bialystok and was our representative in the military organization of the Anti-Fascist Bloc, and he was placed at the head of the fighting division in the ghetto" (p. 419).

36. According to Kotlicki's statement; see Bernard Mark, *Walka i zagłada warszawskiego getta* (Warsaw, 1959), pp. 102–103.

37. Wdowiński, *And We Are Not Saved*, pp. 55–56. (Translated from *Ve-Anahnu Lo Noshanu,* pp. 93–94.)

38. Many rumors were afloat about the number of victims and the methods of killing. This is the reason for the disparities between the descriptions in the various sources. Zuckerman states in the general Ż.O.B. report that on the night of April 17, 1942, forty-nine Jews of all classes and public associations were removed from their apartments. Edelman speaks of more than fifty activists being killed that night (p. 24). Mark stated in *Walka i zagłada*, on the basis of material found in the archive of the Jewish Historical Institute in Warsaw, that the number of victims that night was fifty-two (p. 86).

39. Kaplan, *Scroll of Agony*, p. 316.

40. See Zuckerman's introduction to *Dappim min ha-Deleka*, p. 9, and the testimony of Hadassah Zlotnicka-Talmon (author's private file).

41. Bernard Goldstein, *Finef yor in varshever geto* (*Five Years in the Warsaw Ghetto*) (New York, 1947), p. 223.

42. Kaplan, section of the diary in the Moreshet Archive, entry for April 20, 1942.

43. Czerniakow, *Warsaw Diary*, p. 344.

44. Zuckerman's introduction to *Dappim min ha-Deleka*, p. 9.

45. Ringelblum, *Ktovim*, Vol. I, entry for May 12, 1942, p. 354.

46. Goldstein, *Finef Yor*, p. 224.

47. Zuckerman's introduction to *Dappim min ha-Deleka*, p. 9.

48. *Słowo Młodych,* 11 (25), in *Ittonut Gordonya be-Mahteret Getto Varsha,* p. 220.

49. *Tsum tsentn yortog fun oyfshtand in Varshever geto: Dokumentn un materialn.* Gezamelt un mit a forvort un Bamerkungen fun Bernard Mark (*The*

Tenth Anniversary of the Revolt in the Warsaw Ghetto: Documents and Material. Foreword and Commentary by Ber Mark) (Warsaw, 1953), p. 75.

50. Mark, *Powstanie w getcie warszawskim*, pp. 163–64.

51. Yad Vashem Archive, Underground Press Division, *Yediot* (July 1942).

52. Levin, *Mi-Pinkaso*, p. 29.

Chapter 6: The Fateful Deportation

1. A day of fasting and mourning for the Jews. According to Jewish tradition, it was the date of the destruction of the First and Second Temples and of the expulsion of the Jews from Spain.

2. On *Einsatz Reinhardt* and Odilo Globocnik, the *S.S.- und Polizeiführer* of the Lublin District, see Stanisław Piotrowski, *Misja Odyla Globocnika* (Warsaw, 1949). See also Himmler's letter, Nuremberg Documents, NO-5574.

3. In a letter dated July 23, 1942, *SS Oberführer* Brack, a senior official in the Führer's bureau, wrote to Himmler: " . . . *Brigadeführer* Globocnik believes that we must carry out the entire operation against the Jews at a faster pace, for the difficulties that might turn up can freeze the entire operation, and then we will be stuck midway through." See Nuremberg Documents, NO-205.

4. Piotrowski, *Misja Odyla Globocnika*, p. 24.

5. Nuremberg Documents, NO-5574.

6. From the protocol of the *Generalgouvernement* administration meeting of December 16, 1942, *Okupacja i ruch oporu*, Vol. I, p. 416.

7. See the document given as Appendix 80A in *Okupacja i ruch opporu*, Vol. I, pp. 573–76.

8. See Yad Vashem Archive, O-6/102 (police officer's diary), p. 129.

9. Nuremberg Documents, NO-5574.

10. See, e.g., the letter sent by Himmler to Krieger, Pohl, Globocnik, and *Wehrmacht* officers involved in the employment of Jews (October 9, 1942). It ends by stating that even those Jews who remain as a work force under special closed conditions for a defined period of time should just be done away with some day, in accordance with the Führer's will (". . . Jedoch auch dort sollen eines Tages, dem Wunsche des Führers entsprechend, die Juden verschwinden"), Nuremberg Documents, NO-1611.

11. The figures are taken from a lecture by Korherr, the head of the SS Statistics Division, given in March 1943. Nuremberg Documents, NO-5192–4.

12. Levin, *Mi-Pinkaso*, pp. 30–31.

13. Czerniakow, *Warsaw Diary*, entries for April 1, 1942; April 5, 1942; April 16, 1942; April 17, 1942; April 25, 1942; Kaplan, *Megillat Yissurin*, p. 515.

14. Kaplan, *Scroll of Agony*, p. 321.

15. Czerniakow, *Warsaw Diary*, pp. 317, 351, 354, 355.

16. See the full text of the document (in Polish) in *B.Ż.I.H.*, 1 (1951), 63.

17. Czerniakow, *Warsaw Diary*, p. 385.

18. See the full text of the announcement in *B.Ż.I.H.*, 1 (1951), 65–66.

19. The rumors rampant in the ghetto spoke of the impending deportation

of 60,000–70,000 Jews. Such rumors were evidently based on calculations that took into account the categories slated for deportation according to the announcement. See, e.g., Goldstein, *Finef yor*, p. 245.

20. Yad Vashem Archive, TR-10/26 (Többens's statement in the prosecution file).

21. Ibid. About Többens's appearance and activities in the ghetto, see F. Tusk-Scheinwechsler, "Walter C. Többens, Fabryka śmierci w getcie warszawskim" ("The Factory of Death in the Warsaw Ghetto"), *B.Ż.I.H.*, 23 (1957).

22. See, e.g., Levin's entry for August 7, 1942, where he speaks of the "outburst of workers against the intelligentsia. A shocking experience" (p. 98). Eck wrote of the "shop" in which Levin was employed and stated that the workers threatened the "shop" owner when they discovered that many who had found refuge in the plant were activists in the ghetto underground or acquaintances of the owner, rather than skilled workers. See Eck, *Ha-To'im be-Darkei ha-Mavet*, p. 49; Ringelblum, *Ktovim*, Vol. II, p. 29.

23. See the appendixes to Yisrael Gutman's article "Czerniakow—Ha-Ish ve-ha-Yoman" ("Czerniakow—The Man and the Diary"), *Yalkut Moreshet*, 10 (1969), 115–44. On the attitude of the Bund, see Goldstein, *Finef yor*, p. 255.

24. Yitzhak Katzenelson, "Pinkas Vitel" ("The Vitel Notebook") in *Ketavim Aharonim (Last Works)* (Beit Lohamei ha-Getta'ot, 1956), p. 181.

25. On this question, see the diary of Henryk Brysker, Hebrew manuscript in this author's hands, p. 221. See also the report of the Jewish underground on the deportation, *B.Ż.I.H.*, 1 (1951), 74.

26. Yad Vashem Archive, O-6/102. An anonymous police officer recorded in his diary: "During the first week, Ya'akov Zackheim, a policeman, was murdered for carrying out his task in an irresponsible manner. Some were killed for releasing people from the lines (Obczyński, Sterling, Kaplański). . . . It would not be an exaggeration to speak of many of these [Jewish policemen killed by the Germans]. I estimate the number of policemen who were murdered or deported for deeds of this kind [disobeying orders or releasing people who were slated for deportation] at 20–30 people" (pp. 174–75).

27. Yad Vashem Archive, O-4/20(26)–2 (from the indictment against Wolff, No. 300).

28. Yad Vashem Archive, TR-10/26 (Többens's statement in the file of the indictment against him).

29. Yad Vashem Archive, O-6/102 (police officer's diary).

30. A document from the second section of the Ringelblum Archive stated that the number of ration cards on the eve of the deportation was 335,514. See "Struktura demograficzna ludności żydowskiej pozostalej w Warszawie" ("Demographic Structure of the Population Remaining in Warsaw"), *B.Ż.I.H.*, 37 (1961), 98.

31. According to the underground's report on the mass deportation from the Warsaw ghetto, there were approximately 370,000 Jews in the ghetto at the start of the deportation operation. See the table of statistics in the underground report, *B.Ż.I.H.*, 1 (1951), 60.

32. Yad Vashem Archive, M-2/451 (statement by Tokar-Warszawski).

33. Władka—Feigel Peltel-Międzyrzecka, *Mi-Shenei Evrei ha-Homa: Zi-khronot shel Kasharit (From Both Sides of the Wall: The Memoirs of a Liaison)*, Hebrew translation from the Yiddish (Tel Aviv, 1963), p. 14.

34. Yad Vashem Archive, O-6/102 (police officer's diary), p. 135. See also Ringelblum, *Ktovim*, Vol. II, p. 22.

35. Levin, *Mi-Pinkaso*, pp. 94-95, 97, 110-11.

36. Yad Vashem Archive, O-33/79-2 (the memoirs of Mira Piżyc).

37. Ringelblum, *Ktovim*, Vol. II, p. 30. Levin wrote in his diary on July 24: "Fictitious weddings with policemen" (p. 88). See also Halina Szereszewska, *Ha-Perek ha-Aharon (The Last Chapter)* (Tel Aviv, 1968), p. 150.

38. Levin, *Mi-Pinkaso*, p. 103. Yad Vashem Archive, O-6/102 (police officer's diary). See also Ringelblum, *Ktovim*, Vol. II, p. 22.

39. Ringelblum, *Ktovim*, Vol. II, p. 23.

40. Yad Vashem Archive, O-33/79-2 (the memoirs of Mira Piżyc).

41. See the underground's report on the deportation, *B.Ż.I.H.*, 1 (1950), 116.

42. Yad Vashem Archive, O-6/102 (police officer's diary), pp. 190, 239.

43. Turkow, *Azoy iz es geven*, p. 313.

44. For example, Ringelblum states that "the strong and successful resistance, from the psychological point of view, has been proven. No people in the world would persevere so effectively and for so long, from the psychological viewpoint, as the Jews do, and the best proof is the low number of suicides among the Jews of Warsaw. The Germans often expressed their dissatisfaction with Polish Jews on that score. They were even reported to have said that the Jews of Poland have no sense of pride, like the Jews of Germany" (*Ktovim*, Vol. II, p. 55).

45. Levin, *Mi-Pinkaso*, pp. 90, 98.

46. Ringelblum, *Ktovim*, Vol. II, p. 54.

47. Yad Vashem Archive, O-6/103 (Ernest), p. 198.

48. See the underground's report on the deportation, *B.Ż.I.H.*, 1 (1951), 75. On this subject, see also Ringelblum, *Ktovim*, Vol. II, p. 24.

49. Levin, *Mi-Pinkaso*, pp. 94, 97, 105.

50. Yad Vashem Archive, M-2/451 (statement by Tokar-Warszawski).

51. Yad Vashem Archive, Underground Press Division, *Oyf der vakh* (September 20, 1942).

52. See, e.g., Yisrael Gutman, *Mered ha-Nezurim: Mordecai Anielewicz Milhemet Getto Varsha (The Revolt of the Besieged: Mordecai Anielewicz and the War of the Warsaw Ghetto)* (Merhavyah, 1963), pp. 252-45.

53. Ringelblum, *Ktovim*, Vol. II, under the heading "The Ten Tribes," pp. 42-43.

54. Yad Vashem Archive, O-6/103 (Ernest), p. 194.

55. Levin, *Mi-Pinkaso*, pp. 98, 101-102, 115.

56. Goldstein, *Finef yor*, pp. 259-60; Edelman, *Getto walczy*, p. 32; Yad Vashem Archive, Underground Press Division, *Oyf der vakh* (September 20, 1942).

57. Ringelblum, *Ktovim*, Vol. II, "The Ten Tribes," p. 44.

58. Levin, *Mi-Pinkaso*, pp. 99-100.

59. See the breakdown on p. 277.

60. See Philip Friedman, "Hitnagdut Yehudit le-Nazism—Hebetim ve-Zurot" ("Jewish Resistance to Nazism—Facets and Forms"), in *Sho'at Yehudei Europa (The Catastrophe of European Jewry)*, ed. Yisrael Gutman and Livia Rothkirchen (Jerusalem, 1973), p. 365.

61. See Henri Michel, "Jewish Resistance and the European Resistance Movement," *Yad Vashem Studies*, 7 (1968), 7–10.

Chapter 7: The Ghetto Underground during the Deportation

1. Berlinski, "Zikhronot," pp. 9–10.

2. Edelman, *Getto walczy*, p. 30; Goldstein, *Finef yor*, p. 248.

3. Berlinski, "Zikhronot," p. 10.

4. Edelman, *Getto walczy*, pp. 30–31; Goldstein, *Finef yor*, p. 249.

5. With the exception of a group of Jews who were members of the Polish Socialist Party (P.P.S.) and maintained their association with their party even in the ghetto. They even published a journal in the ghetto, *Getto Podziemne (The Ghetto Underground)*, and one issue has been preserved. See the list of underground publications in chapter 4.

6. Anna Duracz, "Ba-Mahteret mi-Shenei Zidei ha-Homa" ("In the Underground on Both Sides of the Wall"), *Yalkut Moreshet*, 15 (1973), 15–16. About the Communists in the ghetto and about Joseph Lewartwoski, see J. Barski, "O niektorych zagadineniach warszawskiego getta" ("About Certain Problems of the Warsaw Ghetto"), *B.Ż.I.H.*, 49 (1964).

7. David Wdowiński, *Ve-Anahnu Lo Noshanu (And We Are Not Saved)* (Tel Aviv, 1970), pp. 99–111.

8. Yad Vashem Archive, M-20/115a (letter signed by Eugeniusz, the *nom de guerre* of Eliezer Geller, dated January 8, 1943).

9. Ż.O.B. report.

10. Goldstein, *Finef yor*, p. 249.

11. Yad Vashem Archive, O-3/443 (testimony of Arie Najberg).

12. Yad Vashem Archive, O-6/102 (police officer's diary), p. 181.

13. Levin, *Mi-Pinkaso*, p. 109.

14. Berman, *Mi-Yemei ha-Mahteret*, pp. 56–57.

15. Levin, *Mi-Pinkaso*, pp. 109, 112–13.

16. Berlinski, "Zikhronot," p. 13.

17. Duracz, "Ba-Mahteret," p. 11.

18. *Dappim min ha-Deleka*, p. 133.

19. Zuckerman and Basok, *Sefer Milhamot*, p. 106.

20. Ibid.

21. Yitzhak Zuckerman, "Yemei September 1942" ("The Days of September 1942"), *Mibifnim*, 16:4 (July 1953), 28; reprinted in *Yalkut Moreshet*, 16 (1973), 28. See also Gutman, *Mered ha-Nezurim*, pp. 253–54; Adam (Zylberstejn), *Getta'ot: Varsha-Częstochowa (Ghettos: Warsaw-Częstochowa)* (Merhavya, 1945), pp. 58–59. On Zeltzer's personality and image during this period, see also Eck, *Ha-To'im be-Darkei ha-Mavet*, pp. 176 ff.

22. Ringelbum, *Ktovim*, Vol. II, p. 11.

23. Zuckerman, "Yemei September 1942," p. 30.

24. Gutman, *Mered ha-Nezurim*, p. 253.

25. Zuckerman, "Yemei September 1942," p. 29.

26. Adam, *Getta'ot*, p. 58.

27. Moreshet Archive, D.2.6 (chapter of the memoirs of Yehuda Engelman, a former policeman who helped the Ż.O.B.).

28. Gutman, *Mered ha-Nezurim*, p. 253.

29. Ibid., pp. 257-58.

30. Zuckerman, "Yemei September 1942," pp. 32-33.

Chapter 8: The Polish Response to the Liquidation of Warsaw Jewry

1. Ringelblum, *Ktovim*, Vol. II, p. 328.

2. See the memorandum by Knol, Yad Vashem Archive, M-2/204, and M-2/189. Ringelblum wrote on this subject: "The middle class as a whole continued to bow down to an anti-Semitic ideology and was glad that the Nazis had solved the Jewish Problem in Poland. Thanks to Hitler, the members of the Polish middle class were rid of the undesirable elements—Jewish bankers and merchants—and as a result of the mass slaughter of Jews, the *numerus nullus* program was realized in industry, the crafts, commerce, and economic life as a whole. Because of the liquidation of the Jews, the 'merchants' (*Kaufmänner*) instantly became the owners of many commercial and industrial enterprises, and people got rid of their Jewish partners. 'Aryan' trustees took control of the goods left in their hands by the Jews."

3. Ringelblum noted " . . . that the German-backed press, supported by the anti-Semitic underground press, aroused strong public reaction. Under the influence of the anti-Semitic incitement published in *Nowy Kurier Warszawski* in April and May of this year [1943], the German-instigated persecution of Jews on the 'Aryan' side received support among the broad masses. When leaving [the ghetto] for the 'Aryan' side, Jewish workers knew *a priori* that in the wake of an anti-Jewish article in the papers, or even in the Readers' Letters, they could expect a difficult day of punches [and] stone-throwing by the rabble, etc." Emmanuel Ringelblum, "Ha-Yehassim Bin ha-polanim ve-ha-Yehudim be-Milhemet ha-'Olam ha-Sheniya" ("Polish-Jewish Relations during the Second World War"), *Yalkut Moreshet*, 1, 36–38.

4. Stefan Korboński, *W imieniu Rzeczypospolitej* (Paris, 1954), pp. 253-54.

5. See note by Schwartzbart dated October 24, 1944, Yad Vashem Archive, Schwartzbart Division, M-2/755.

6. General Stefan Rowecki ("Grot") was the commander in chief of the armed forces in the Polish underground and was subject to the authority of the Polish government-in-exile in London from 1940 until his arrest in the summer of 1943. This clandestine force was known by various names during its existence, but the most common was the A.K., which is used throughout this work.

7. "Wacław," *mom de guerre* of Henryk Woliński, the head of the "Jewish Department" of the A.K. Woliński was devoted to his task and eventually became very active in establishing ties with the Jewish Fighting Organization.

8. Tadeusz Bor-Komorowski, *The Secret Army* (New York, 1951), pp. 99–100.

9. Woliński wrote of his work: "The department was established on February 1, 1942. Its task during its early days was limited to intelligence alone." See Woliński's official survey on his work in *Ha-Meri ve-ha-Mered be-Getto Varsha (Resistance and Revolt in the Warsaw Ghetto)*, ed. Nachman Blumental and Joseph Kermish (Jerusalem, 1965), p. 399. See also Bartoszewski's introduction to *Righteous Among Nations*, ed. Władysław Bartoszewski and Zofia Lewin (London, 1969).

10. It appears that this version of the radiogram was deliberately altered in the People's Republic of Poland. But the change under discussion—"Jews from all kinds of groups, including Communists, have turned to us . . ." rather than "Jews from all kinds of Communist groups . . ."—does not really make any difference regarding the basic attitude. See the version of the radiogram in the Polish Underground Study Trust, London (copy available in the Yad Vashem Archive). As to the alteration of the wording, see Michał Borwicz, "The Relations between the Polish and Jewish Underground," in *Jewish Resistance During the Holocaust*, Proceedings of the Conference on Manifestations of Jewish Resistance (Jerusalem, 1971), p. 348.

11. See Leon Mitkiewicz, "Powstanie warszawskie—Z mojego notatnika w Waszyngtonie," *Zeszyty Historyczne*, 1 ([Paris], 1972), 95–156.

12. See the version of the declaration in Władysław Bartoszewski, *The Bloodshed United Us* (Warsaw, 1970), pp. 50–51.

13. See Ireneusz Caban and Zygmunt Mańkowski, *Związek Walki Zbrojnej I Armia Krajowa w okręgu lubelskim, 1939–1944 (Union for Armed Struggle: Home Army in the Lublin District)*, Vol. II (Warsaw, 1971), p. 60.

14. *Trybuna Chłopska (The Farmers' Platform)*, 6 (August 1942) in *Tsum tsentn yortog*, pp. 90–91.

15. Bartoszewski and Lewin, *Righteous Among Nations*, pp. 767–68.

16. See the Introduction to *Reprezentacja Żydostwa Polskiego—Sprawozdanie z działalności w latach 1940–1945 (Report on the Activities of the Representation of Polish Jewry, 1940–1945)* (stencilled), p. 2. (Hereafter *Representation of Polish Jewry*).

17. Ibid., pp. 43–46. For details on this subject, see Kurtz, *Sefer Edut*.

18. Ibid., p. 53. See the minutes of the meeting with Kot, ibid., pp. 52–57.

19. Ibid., pp. 54, 59.

20. Ibid., the replies of Raczyński and Sikorski, p. 60.

21. See details on the structure of Żegota in Abraham Berman, "Ha-Yehudim ba-Zad ha-Ari" ("Jews on the Aryan Side") in Gruenbaum, *Enziklopedya shel Galuyot*, Vol. I, pp. 685–732. This article is also included in Berman, *Mi-Yemei ha-Mahteret*, pp. 79–155.

22. See, e.g., Ringelblum's entry "Priests Want to Save Jewish Children," Ringelblum, *Ktovim*, Vol. II, December 14, 1942, pp. 40–41.

23. Schwartzbart wrote in his diary on December 11, 1941: " . . . Then he showed me a long cable in which the commander of the Polish army reported on November 17 that the statements of the Polish government regarding the Jewish question—such as the declaration of the government, Sikorski's New

Year's greetings, Schwartzbart's address to the country [Poland]—create among the Polish public a mood of indisposition toward the government. The Polish public, the cable continues, is overwhelmingly disposed toward anti-Semitism, and that is true not only of the *Endeks* and members of the O.N.R. but of members of the Farmers' Party and some of the Socialists. By its declaration in favor of the Jews, the government is subverting its own work, and it must therefore abandon this pro-Jewish policy." See Yad Vashem Archive, Schwartzbart Division, M-2/749.

Chapter 9: The Remnant of the Ghetto until January 1943

1. See Yosef Ziemian, *Gevulot Getto Varsha ve-Shinuyehem* (Jerusalem, 1971), pp. 28–29.

2. See Yad Vashem Archive, Auerswald-Leist Division, JM/1112. In a letter dated September 28, 1942, Auerswald notified Bischoff that in line with the declarations of the *S.S.- und Polizeiführer*, which were known to Bischoff, "the Jewish quarter of Warsaw will be liquidated no later than December 31 of this year." On that date, at the latest, the *Transferstelle* was to cease its activities. See also Bischoff's letter to Auerswald, dated January 7, 1943, in which he reports on developments related to the liquidation of the *Transferstelle*. Even the *Kommissariat* for Jewish Affairs, managed by Auerswald, formally remained in existence until the end of 1942, but in fact this office had no influence whatsoever on events in the ghetto from the inception of the *Aktion* onward. The diary of an anonymous police officer notes that following the deportation, "the *Kommissar* did not reassume control of the Jewish quarter. The lord and master is Brandt; Jews continue to be subject to the exclusive control of the SS." Yad Vashem Archive, O-6/102, p. 200.

3. See the order of the *S.S.- und Polizeiführer* of the Generalgouvernement dated October 28, 1942, in Berenstein, Eisenbach, and Rutkowski, *Eksterminacja Żydów*, pp. 311–13. Opoczyński stated in his entry for November 13, 1942, that the SS general declared an amnesty for all those who escaped to the "Aryan" side. Yad Vashem Archive, M-10/Ph-2–3–1.

4. Yad Vashem Archive, O-6/102 (police officer's diary), p. 207. On this question, see also Opoczyński's entry for November 2, 1942, Yad Vashem Archive, M-10/Ph-2–3–1, and Levin, *Mi-Pinkaso*, entry for November 1, 1942, p. 136.

5. See the report of the governor of the Warsaw District, Dr. Fischer, for August and September 1942 regarding the situation in the Warsaw ghetto following the mass deportation in Berenstein, Eisenbach, and Rutkowski, *Eksterminacja Żydów*, pp. 304–305. Opoczyński reports in his entry for October 18: "Jews are saying today that Krieger is complaining to the SS people in Warsaw about deporting so many of the veteran and good skilled workers and leaving the 'parasites' where they were." Yad Vashem Archive, M-10/Ph-2–3–2.

6. Levin recorded in his diary on October 30, 1942: "And if a man asks in the future: 'By what means and how did an elect individual who survived support himself?' it will be difficult to give a clear and satisfactory answer. [People]

live basically off the sale of belongings, i.e., mostly from this sale of clothing" (p. 134).

7. See Fischer's report in Berenstein, Eisenbach, and Rutkowski, *Eksterminacja Żydów*, pp. 304–305.

8. Yad Vashem Archive, O-6/102 (police officer's diary), p. 202.

9. Ibid., p. 221.

10. See von Sammern's order, Yad Vashem Archive, O-4/20–30–2 (legal file—Heinrich Klostermeyer), pp. 16–17.

11. Levin, *Mi-Pinkaso*, p. 127.

12. Yad Vashem Archive, M-10/Ph-2-2-2.

13. Report of the *Judenrat* for December 1942. Data can be found, *inter alia*, in Yad Vashem Archive, O-4/20–30–2 (Klostermeyer file), p. 18.

14. *Okupacja i ruch oporu*, Vol. II, pp. 48–50.

15. See Pohl's trial, Nuremburg Documents, NO/1257, NO/1882.

16. On November 1, 1942, Levin wrote in his diary: "Even in the Jewish world there was a sense of relief today. The streets filled with strollers. . . . What affected the mood of the Jews? Firstly, the liberation of the children from the *Umschlagplatz*" (p. 135).

17. Levin, *Mi-Pinkaso*, pp. 141–42. See also Opoczyński, entry for November 20, 1942, Yad Vashem Archive, M-10/Ph-2-3-2.

18. Levin, *Mi-Pinkaso*, p. 165. See also Opoczyński's entry for December 6, 1942: "Early this morning a rumor got round that the *palatzovka* workers were not being permitted to leave their residential blocks today, despite the fact that it's Sunday. The news caused great disquiet. And immediately everyone began to say that tomorrow, or at the latest the day after, the final deportation will begin." Yad Vashem Archive, M-10/Ph-2-3-2.

19. Levin, *Mi-Pinkaso*, p. 169. This entry expresses the belief that the Germans had begun to exterminate the Jews of Europe. The conjecture is not the result of any information that reached Levin, who was usually well informed as a member of the group that worked for the "Oneg Shabbat." Levin reached this conclusion on the basis of empirical observation in the ghetto itself.

20. Levin, *Mi-Pinkaso*, p. 171.

21. Cf. Landau, *Kronika*, Vol. II, the entries for January 15–18, pp. 114–22.

Chapter 10: The Movement toward Combat

1. Yad Vashem Archive, O-6/102 (police officer's diary), p. 192.

2. See Opoczyński's entry for December 10, 1942, Yad Vashem Archive, PH/2-3-3.

3. Yad Vashem Archive, O-33/13-2 (Dr. Leńsky's memoirs).

4. Berlinski, "Zikhronot," p. 14.

5. Yad Vashem Archive, Underground Press Division, *Yediot*, 3 (December 23, 1942). See also Levin's entry for December 11, 1942: "Yesterday the members of the He-Halutz who were at the farm near Warsaw—at Czerniakow—as an agricultural group were brought to the ghetto (to the *Judenrat*—19 Zamenhofa)" (p. 157).

6. Berlinski, "Zikhronot," pp. 14–16; Elster, Berlinski, and Ehrlich, *Dray*, pp. 169–71.

7. Edelman, *Getto walczy*, p. 44.

8. Berlinski, "Zikhronot," p. 16.

9. Wdowiński, *Ve-Anahnu Lo Noshanu*, pp. 79–80.

10. See Adam Halperin's entry in *Ha-Emet al ha-Mered be-Getto Varsha* (*The Truth About the Revolt in the Warsaw Ghetto*) (Information Department of Betar, 1946), pp. 13–14.

11. Ibid., p. 14.

12. This document is presented in *Ha-Meri ve-ha-Mered* and the date October 18, 1942, is recorded next to it. The document was taken from Mark's book *Powstanie w getcie warszawskim*, Document No. 15, pp. 193–94. It is a statement by Cezary Ketling, the commander of PLAN (a small underground combat unit affiliated with the A.K.), before an internal court of the A.K. Blumental and Kermish, the editors of *Ha-Meri ve-ha-Mered*, copied the document without checking whether the date noted in the margin was indeed precise. In fact, the document does not relate to October 1942 but to January 1943, and that is the date which appears in other sources. Concrete proof of the January date is provided by Ketling himself in a document that likewise appears in *Ha-Meri ve-ha-Mered*, p. 168.

13. Wdowiński, *Ve-Anahnu Lo Noshanu*, p. 80.

14. Halperin in *Ha-Emet al ha-Mered be-Getto Varsha*, pp. 15–16.

15. See the report on the establishment of the Jewish National Committee in the Underground dated November 9, 1942. See also Document No. 16 in Mark, *Powstanie w getcie warszawskim*, p. 195.

16. See Woliński's report on the activities of the Jewish Department in Blumental and Kermish, *Ha-Meri ve-ha-Mered*, p. 400.

17. Mark, *Powstanie w getcie warszawskim*, pp. 197–98.

18. See Wacław's (Woliński's) memorandum, which includes the Ż.O.B. demands and is addressed to the A.K. authorities and the *Delegatura*, in Blumental and Kermish, *Ha-Meri ve-ha-Mered*, Document No. 18, pp. 199–200.

19. Ibid., pp. 400–401.

20. Ibid., p. 141.

21. See Yad Vashem Archive, M-2/2, a cable sent from London to Rozmaryn, the Polish counsel in Palestine, on April 5, 1943. It states, *inter alia*: "Rozmaryn—For his eyes only. Top secret. The Polish government is in contact with a Jewish organization at home [in Poland]."

22. See Ż.O.B. report; Gutman, *Mered ha-Nezurim*, pp. 281–83.

23. Ringelblum, "Polish-Jewish Relations During the Second World War," *Ktovim*, Vol. II, p. 332.

24. See Blumental and Kermish, *Ha-Meri ve-ha-Mered*, p. 116; the document is from the Ringelblum Archive, Part II.

25. Yad Vashem Archive, M-10/Ph-2–3–1.

26. Levin, *Mi-Pinkaso*, p. 153.

27. Yad Vashem Archive, Underground Press Division, *Yediot*, 3 (December 1942).

28. Berlinski, "Zikhronot," p. 20.

29. Edelman, *Getto walczy*, p. 48.

30. See the text of the manifesto in Blumental and Kermish, *Ha-Meri ve-ha-Mered*, pp. 122–23.

31. Ibid., pp. 151–52.

Chapter 11: The Second *Aktion*

1. Yechiel Gorni, "Aktsiye Nr. 2, 28 Yanuar 1943" (*"Aktion* No. 2, January 28, 1943"), in the Ringelblum Archive, Part II; published in *Bleter far geshikhte*, 4:1 (January–March 1951), 88–91.

2. Pohl trial, Nuremberg Documents, NO-1882.

3. See the article on the *Aktion* in the underground newspaper *Głos Warszawy* (*The Voice of Warsaw*), 5 (January 20, 1943), quoted in Blumental and Kermish, *Ha-Meri ve-ha-Mered*, p. 196. The figures are almost certainly inflated, and the reference to the tanks is not corroborated in any other source.

4. See Hans von Kranhals's brief for Wolff's trial (the material was thoughtfully placed at my disposal by the late Emmanuel Brand of the Yad Vashem Archive), p. 27. (Hereafter von Kranhals.)

5. See selections from Shmuel Winter's diary in Bernard Mark, *Khurves dertseyln* (*Ruins Tell*) (Lodz, 1947), p. 141. Only a few damaged pages remained of Shmuel Winter's diary. Additional selections from it were published in Bernard Mark, "Shmuel Winters Togbukh" ("Shmuel Winter's Diary"), *Bleter far geshikhte*, 3:1–2 (January–June 1950), pp. 29–48.

6. Yad Vashem Archive, O-6/102. The police officer's diary states that among the members of the *Judenrat* taken in January were: Dr. Glücksberg, Dr. Milejkowski, Jaszuński, Horowic, and Rozensztadt and his family; Sztolcman and Gepner were released together with their families (p. 229).

7. Yad Vashem Archive, O-6/101 (Adler's "Four Days"), pp. 19–20.

8. Gorni, "Aktsiye Nr. 2."

9. Yad Vashem Archive, O-6/101 (Adler's "Four Days"), p. 26.

10. See the entry from Shmuel Winter's diary in Mark, *Khurves dertseyln*, p. 141.

11. Gorni, "Aktsiye Nr. 2."

12. On the retaliatory action during the last day of the operation, see the Polish underground paper *Dzień*, 19 (January 28, 1943), quoted in Mark, *Powstanie w getcie warszawskim*, pp. 212–13. The Warsaw *Judenrat* stated in an official report that 1,171 people were shot in the ghetto in January, whereas 65 people were shot in December 1942. Statistics according to Mark, ibid., p. 294.

13. The figure quoted by SS General Jürgen Stroop, who commanded the battle against the Warsaw ghetto uprising in April, is 6,500 people. See Joseph Kermish, ed., *Mered Getto Varsha be-Einei ha-Oyev: Ha-Dohot shel Jürgen Stroop* (*The Warsaw Ghetto Uprising from the Enemy's View: The Reports of Jürgen Stroop*) (Jerusalem, 1966), p. 128. A Polish source, the underground newspaper *Gwardzista*, 12 (February 5, 1942), gives the figure of 5,000 people (see Blumental and Kermish, *Ha-Meri ve-ha-Mered*, p. 197); Maurycy Orzech, one of the leading figures in the Bund, cites the figure of 6,000 people in his cable to London (ibid., p. 195); the anonymous police officer's diary cites the figure of 4,700 (Yad Vashem Archive, O-6/102, p. 231). Ringelblum speaks of 10,000 people deported from Warsaw in January, of whom 1,000 were shot (*Ktovim*, Vol. II). His figure is highly exaggerated, and we can assume that the number of deportees and casualties in January ran between 4,500 and 5,000 people.

14. The *Biuletyn Informacyjny* issue of January 28, 1943, reported that on

Monday and Tuesday no more than 5,000 people were removed from the ghetto, despite the fact that wagons for twice as many had been prepared.

15. See Winter's entry for January 20, 1943, in Mark, *Khurves dertseyln*, p. 142.

16. Berlinski, "Zikhronot," p. 21.

17. Zuckerman, "Mered ha-Yehudim," p. 421.

18. Edelman, *Getto walczy* p. 47.

19. Gorni, "Aktsiye Nr. 2," reports that Margalit Landau fell in a clash on Miła Street, not in this major street battle. However, he was mistaken on this point. Both Margalit Landau and Eliyahu Różański were among those who fell in the battle commanded by Mordecai Anielewicz. See Gutman, *Mered ha-Nezurim*, pp. 294-95.

20. Edelman, *Getto walczy*, pp. 46-47.

21. Berlinski, "Zikhronot," p. 23.

22. Zivia Lubetkin, *Aharonim al ha-Homa* (Ein-Harod, 1947), p. 428.

23. Tuvia Borzykowski, *Bein Kirot Noflim (Among Falling Walls)* (Tel Aviv, 1950), p. 10.

24. Edelman, *Getto walczy*, p. 47.

25. Borzykowski, *Bein Kirot Noflim*, pp. 12-13.

26. See Mark, *Powstanie w getcie warszawskim*, pp. 212-13. The figure of nine fallen fighters recurs in other publications. There are a few versions as to the number of German dead, all evidently based on rumor or conjecture and not corroborated.

27. Edelman wrote: "It turns out that a street battle is too costly for us—we are not prepared for it. We don't have appropriate weapons. We are going over to a partisan struggle" (*Getto walczy*, p. 47).

28. Quoted in Zuckerman, "Mered ha-Yehudim," p. 422. Zuckerman related: "One day after the liberation, we found among the ruins of the ghetto some pages that had been blackened by the wind and rain, cold and heat, and the effects of time—a half-torn notebook. The journal was brought to me and I sat down to read it. I recognized the style, the subjects, the circumstances, and the man. It was the diary of a man well known in Poland in YIVO circles, Winter from Włocławek, a good, loyal Jew who had a feel for national culture and national life and was active in the ghetto. One of the pillars of 'Oneg Shabbat.' . . ." It is a moot question whether Zuckerman's identification of the author was mistaken, because there is a lack of consistency between the selections from Winter's diary that remained hidden and were subsequently published and those quoted by Zuckerman. At any rate, it is clear that the writer quoted by Zuckerman was involved in public affairs and was associated with the underground, and these selections are persuasive evidence of the change in attitude among a certain circle during the January fighting. These same selections are presented in an abbreviated version by the historian Philip Friedman, ed., *Martyrs and Fighters, The Epic of the Warsaw Ghetto* (New York, 1954), p. 221. Following Zuckerman, Friedman assumes that the author of these fragments is Shmuel Winter.

29. Gorni, "Aktsiye Nr. 2."

30. Yad Vashem Archive, O-33/13-2, O-33/257 (Dr. Leńsky's manuscript), p. 116.

31. The original Polish version published in Michał M. Borwicz, *Pieśń ujdzie cało . . . (The Song is the One to Survive)* (Warsaw, 1947), pp. 190-93.

32. Zuckerman, "Mered ha-Yehudim," p. 422.

33. Edelman, *Getto walczy*, p. 48.
34. See *Biuletyn Informacyjny*, 4 (January 28, 1943).
35. *Gwardzista*, 12 (February 5, 1943), quoted in *Tsum tsentn yortog*, pp. 132–33.
36. See Yad Vashem Archive, O-25/43, issue dated February 28, 1943.
37. Zagórski, *Wolność w niewoli*, p. 360.
38. See Yad Vashem Archive, M-10/Ph-2-12, *Delegatura* Internal Division, report on the situation between January 1 and February 15, 1943.
39. Ringelblum, *Ktovim*, Vol. II, p. 335.
40. Edelman, *Getto walczy*, p. 48.

Chapter 12: The Remnant of the Ghetto from January to April 1943

1. Artur Eisenbach, *Hitlerowska polityka eksterminacji Żydów* (*The Nazi Policy of the Jews' Extermination*) (Warsaw, 1953), p. 220.
2. See von Kranhals, p. 11.
3. See copy of the document, Yad Vashem Archive, O-4/4-2.
4. Von Kranhals, O.K.W. order 02533/42, p. 16. See also Buchheim et al., *Anatomie des SS-Staates*, p. 348.
5. See von Kranhals, pp. 12–13.
6. See a copy of the document in the Yad Vashem Archive, O-4/4-2; see also Buchheim et al., *Anatomie des SS-Staates*, pp. 349–51.
7. The minutes of this consultation were presented as evidence for the prosecution in Krupp's trial; see Eisenbach, *Hitlerowska polityka*, p. 248.
8. See von Kranhals, pp. 21–22 (for October 9) and the legal material on the Wolff trial, Yad Vashem Archive, O-4/20(26)-2.
9. Von Kranhals's brief states that we cannot know exactly what happened after General von Gienanth's strongly worded memo was received and passed on to Himmler. We only know that nineteen days later, General von Gienanth was dismissed from his post, and on October 10 his replacement, General Haenicke, again received the O.K.W. order.
10. See Eisenbach, *Hitlerowska polityka*, pp. 273–75.
11. See the letter dated October 2 (according to von Kranhals, October 9) in note 8 above.
12. See Eisenbach, *Hitlerowska polityka*, p. 310. This statement by Frank should not be regarded as a fundamental change in his attitude toward the "Final Solution." It stems from his desire to emphasize the opposition to Himmler and the SS, and it may likewise be an expression of the immediate difficulties felt in the Generalgouvernement as a result of the elimination of the Jews from the economic system. As we have seen, Frank gave his unqualified backing to the extermination program and expressed his support again afterward. See *Okupacja i ruch oporu*, Vol. I, pp. 420–21, Frank's remarks on March 4, 1944, regarding the elimination of the Jews from the Generalgouvernement: "I ask you to imagine to yourselves how the situation in the Generalgouvernement would be now if we still had here—as in 1939—a million and a half to two million Jews. Please remember how difficult, how very difficult, what a task was the solution to the Jewish problem. If some faint-hearted, teary-eyed soul regrets what happened to the Jews and says that what was done to them was a terrible thing, ask him if he feels that way at this very moment. If we had two million fully active Jews in the country now, as opposed to just a handful of us Germans, we wouldn't be able to control the situation any longer."

13. *Okupacja i ruch oporu*, Vol. II, p. 150.
14. Von Kranhals, Himmler's letter to Krieger dated March 11, 1943, p. 24; Nuremberg Documents, NO-1882.
15. Berenstein, Eisenbach, and Rutkowski, *Eksterminacja Żydów*, Document No. 131, p. 249.
16. Ibid., Documents Nos. NO-2514, NO-2494, pp. 323-24.
17. Yad Vashem Archive, TR/10-26 (Többens's file).
18. See Nuremberg Documents, NO-1270, a consultation attended by Pohl on February 13, 1943. The necessary administrative and skilled manpower to establish a combined SS industrial enterprise was not available. Horn, Pohl's right-hand man, suggested "that the Jews concentrated in camps will continue to work in certain trustworthy private enterprises."
19. Stanisław Piotrowski, *Misja Odyla Globocnika* (Warsaw, 1940), pp. 45-52.
20. See Yad Vashem Archive, TR/10-26 (Többens's file).
21. See the statement of David Joselzon, one of the workers in Schultz's "shop," regarding Többens's remarks at a meeting of representatives of the industrial enterprises in the ghetto. Yad Vashem Archive, TR/10-26 (Többens's file).
22. Yad Vashem Archive, TR/10-26 (Többens's file).
23. Ż.O.B. report.
24. A photocopy of the document is in the Yad Vashem Archive, TR/10-26 (Többens's file).
25. According to the Ż.O.B. report, 25 people out of 1,000 workers in Hallmann's plant reported for the first organized deportations, but out of the 3,500 people employed in the Brushmakers' factory, not one man reported for deportation.

Chapter 13: The Jewish Fighting Organization Prepares for the Revolt

1. Borzykowski, *Bein Kirot Noflim*, p. 6.
2. Zuckerman, "Mered ha-Yehudim," p. 428.
3. The number of squads and names of commanders are cited according to Zuckerman's comprehensive Ż.O.B. report.
4. Ringelblum wrote in his biographical sketch of Mordecai Anielewicz: "When the National Committee, of which Mordecai was also a member, decided in February-March 1943 to aid the social and cultural activists in finding shelter on the 'Aryan' side, Mordecai was very cool toward the resolution that was passed. . . . When the time came and it was possible for important figures among the activists to find some arrangement on the 'Aryan' side, Comrade Mordecai did not agree that the money should be taken from another fund [evidently meaning the fund slated for the purchase of arms], over which Comrade Mordecai had control" (*Ktovim*, Vol. II, p. 148).
5. Zuckerman, "Mered ha-Yehudim," p. 429.
6. According to the version given in Dror and Rosenzweig, *Sefer Ha-Shomer ha-Za'ir*, pp. 581-82.
7. Ringelblum wrote on May 18, 1942: " . . . because there's talk of about 400 informers in the ghetto" (*Ktovim*, Vol. 1, p. 356). It is not clear how this number was arrived at; Ringelblum based his figure on rumors or unconfirmed information on this question. It is likewise not clear who was included in the

category of "informers," making their number soar into the hundreds. We may fairly assume that a handful of people had ties with the Germans—probably a dozen or so, and at the very most a few score. It is true that these people were aided by associates and paid lackeys, but even if we take such partners into account, the figure of 400 is probably a gross exaggeration.

8. See Blumental and Kermish, *Ha-Meri ve-ha-Mered*, pp. 146–47.

9. See Czerniakow's entry for December 9, 1939, p. 97.

10. See Zuckerman and Basok, *Sefer Milhamot*, biographical sketch of Nossig, pp. 737–38, and the testimony of Halina Szereszewska, Yad Vashem Archive, O-33/191, p. 29.

11. Zuckerman, "Mered ha-Yehudim," p. 426.

12. Zuckerman in a conversation with the author in July 1974.

13. Zuckerman, "Mered ha-Yehudim," p. 427.

14. See selections from Winter's diary in Blumental and Kermish, *Ha-Meri ve-ha-Mered*, p. 193.

15. Edelman, *Getto walczy*, p. 50.

16. Ibid., p. 51; the memoirs of Guta Wilner in the Moreshet Archive. The biographical sketch of Klepfisz in Zuckerman and Basok, *Sefer Milhamot*, states that "he acquired the formula for producing incendiary bottles" (p. 750).

17. Zuckerman, "Mered ha-Yehudim," p. 424.

18. Edelman, *Getto walczy*, p. 49.

19. *Informacja Bieżąca (Ongoing Information)*, 13 (86) (April 1, 1943). See also Blumental and Kermish, *Ha-Meri ve-ha-Mered*, p. 199.

20. Prominent among these dubious statements are the claims from Polish quarters that the Ż.Z.W. or an armed organization that was the precursor of the Ż.Z.W. was established as early as 1939. Yet no such force is ever mentioned, even in passing, in the chronicles of writers who dealt with all spheres of life in the ghetto, such as Ringelblum's works. It is likewise never mentioned in the memoirs of the leading figures of the Revisionist movement (such as Wdowiński) or in the Revisionist press. Nor can we cite any activity carried out by such a body among the Jews or on their behalf before the establishment of the ghetto or during the existence of the ghetto, until we reach the period during which the Ż.Z.W. was organized. One classic example (among many) of the self-serving nature of such falsehoods is the "revelation" by Tadeusz Bednarczyk that Czerniakow was a member of the Ż.Z.W. and that he (Bednarczyk) met with him in the courthouse on Leszno Street. It is clear to anyone with even the slightest knowledge of the conditions prevailing in the ghetto and of Czerniakow's personality that this story is an easily refutable fabrication. The claim that Czerniakow—who was a well-known figure and was forced to be very circumspect in his movements within the ghetto—met with a person like Bednarczyk in a place where almost anyone would recognize him, and in order to talk about matters related to an armed organization, cannot possibly be taken seriously. See "Dyskusja," *B.Ż.I.H.*, 2–3 (86–87) (April–September 1973), 268–70.

21. See Walewski's statement, *inter alia*, in Lazar, *Mezada shel Varsha*, pp. 226–30.

22. Alexander Donat, *The Holocaust Kingdom* (London, 1965), pp. 128–29.

23. Blumental and Kermish, *Ha-Meri ve-ha-Mered*, p. 151.

24. Mark, *Powstanie w getcie warszawskim*, p. 36.

25. Ringelblum, *Ktovim*, Vol. II, p. 332.

26. Conversation between Zuckerman and the author on July 17, 1974. The agreement between the Ż.O.B. and the Ż.Z.W. was also reported in the testimony given by Walewski, a member of the Ż.Z.W., in Lazar, *Mezada shel Varsha*, p. 229. See also Halperin in *Ha-Emet al ha-Mered be-Getto Varsha*, pp. 19–20.

27. Selections from Winter's diary in Blumental and Kermish, *Ha-Meri ve-ha-Mered*, pp. 193–94. Halperin also speaks of the Ż.Z.W. fight against "attempts at provocation" in *Ha-Emet al ha-Mered be-Getto Varsha*, pp. 18–19. See Ringelblum, *Ktovim*, Vol. II, pp. 332–33.

28. Ringelblum, *Ktovim*, Vol. II, pp. 332–33.

29. Shalom-Stefan Grajek, *Sheloshah Yemei Kerav (Three Days of Battle)* (Tel Aviv, 1972), p. 27.

30. Yad Veshem Archive, O-33/13-2 (Dr. Leńsky's manuscript), p. 120.

31. Donat, *The Holocaust Kingdom*, p. 124.

32. Halina Birenbaum, *Nadzieja umiera ostatnia (Hope Is the Last to Die)* (Warsaw, 1967), pp. 60, 63.

33. A description of Żegota, its activities, and its system of maintaining contact with Jews in hiding is given in Berman, *Mi-Yemei ha-Mahteret*, pp. 79–156; see also the parallel chapters in Bartoszewski and Lewin, *Righteous among Nations*.

34. "Drapacz": the code name for the Warsaw section of the A.K.; "Konar": the *nom de guerre* of General Antoni Chruściel, the commander of the Warsaw section of the A.K.; "Chirurg": the *nom de guerre* of the chief of staff of the Warsaw section of the A.K., Stanisław Weber.

35. For Woliński's report, see Mark, *Powstanie w getcie warszawskim*, p. 342. The report is signed with the name Zakrzewski, one of Woliński's code names. The Hebrew version of the report appears in Blumental and Kermish, *Ha-Meri ve-ha-Mered*.

36. Zuckerman and Basok, *Sefer Milhamot*, p. 158.

37. Blumental and Kermish, *Ha-Meri ve-ha-Mered*, p. 125. Identifying the letter and its author was a complex matter. After the letter (written in Polish) was found, there were attempts to make out the signature. In early publications the author of the letter was given as Kalecki. Only after additional examination did it become clear that the document was signed with a pseudonym, "Malakhi," the *nom de guerre* of Mordecai Anielewicz (the name Anielewicz is derived from the Polish word *anioł*, which in Hebrew is *malakh*).

38. Details supplied by Woliński during a conversation with the author in Woliński's home in Katowice, 1960. See also Gutman, *Mered ha-Nezurim*, p. 326.

39. See a selection from the memoirs of Heniek Grabowski in the newspaper *Mosty* (April 1948).

40. Selections on the Ż.Z.W. in Blumental and Kermish, *Ha-Meri ve-ha-Mered*, pp. 160–74. See also parallel selections in Mark, *Powstanie w getcie warszawskim*, pp. 193–94, 228–31, and the memoirs of Halperin, Wdowiński, Walewski, Korngold, et al. in the Yad Vashem Archive. New light was shed on the events in the Ż.Z.W. bunker connected to the tunnel and on the ties between the union and other Jewish and Polish groups by the memoirs of a member of the Polish underground and an outstanding figure in the A.K. partisan organization. See Michał Jaworski, "Plac Muranowski 7, fragment wspomnień," *B.Ż.I.H.*, 2/90 (1974), 69–89; 3/91 (1974), 59–78.

41. Taken from Ketling's statement; see Blumental and Kermish, *Ha-Meri ve-ha-Mered*, p. 151.

42. Yad Vashem Archive, O-33/50 (memoirs of Shoshana ["Emilka"] Kossower).

43. See Mark, *Powstanie w getcie warszawskim*, Document No. 40, p. 226. The message sent by the A.K. command to London on December 12, 1942 (i.e., before the outbreak of the January resistance), stated: "Public executions and shooting of passersby in the street have again started in the Warsaw ghetto. The small workshops are also being liquidated. Többens' workshops have been totally isolated from the rest of the ghetto. A plan for desperate resistance has been put together by the Jewish population." Ibid., Document No. 21, p. 201. See a Hebrew translation of the message in Blumental and Kermish, *Ha-Meri ve-ha-Mered*, Document No. 35, p. 102.

44. Blumental and Kermish, *Ha-Meri ve-ha-Mered*, Document No. 34, p. 101.

45. Yad Vashem Archive, Schwartzbart Division, M-2/587.

46. See the New York Yiddish monthly *Unzer tsayt* (*Our Time*) (March 1943). Selections also in Hertz, *Zygielbojm-Bukh*, pp. 372–73; Melekh Neustadt, *Khurbn un oyfshtand fun di yidn in Varshe* (*Destruction and Uprising: The Epic of the Jews in Warsaw*) (Tel Aviv, 1946), p. 58.

47. See remarks by Yitzhak Deutscher, who was an associate of Zygielbojm's, on the reasons for the latter's suicide and the man's last days in *Yediot Yad Vashem* (*Yad Vashem News*), 32 (1964).

48. See Hertz, *Zygielbojm-Bukh*, pp. 364–65, a letter written by Zygielbojm before his suicide and addressed to Władysław Raczkiewicz, the president of the Polish Republic (who was in exile in London).

Chapter 14: Days of Battle

1. Jürgen Stroop, *The Report of Jürgen Stroop* (Warsaw, 1958).

2. See the questions addressed to Stroop while he was under detention in a Polish prison in Kermish, *Mered Getto Varsha*. Cf. the protocol of his trial in *Bleter far geshikhte*, 6:1–2 (April 1953); 1:3–4 (1948); and 3:1–2 (1950). A wealth of material on Stroop, his remarks, and his replies to his interrogators and to the questions addressed to him after the war can be found in Josef Wulf, *Das Dritte Reich und seine Vollstrecker, Die Liquidation von 500,000 Juden im Ghetto Warschau* (Berlin, 1961). A Polish writer named Kazimierz Moczarski has recently published reminiscences of Stroop relating to the period of his pretrial imprisonment under the title "Conversations with a Hangman." Moczarski is well acquainted with the documentary material relating to the uprising and the role played by Stroop during the fighting. It is difficult to decide whether we can trust the data and details given by Moczarski, that is, whether we can discriminate between the portion of his writings that reflects Stroop's own comments and the places where the writer lets his imagination take flight in order to round out his portrait of Stroop. The material should therefore be approached with reservation. Kazimierz Moczarski, "Rozmowy z katem," *Odra* (1972–74).

3. Edelman, *Getto walczy*, p. 51.

4. Borzykowski, *Bein Kirot Noflim*, p. 26.

5. Ibid., p. 29.

6. Edelman, *Getto walczy*, pp. 52–53.

7. Borzykowski, *Bein Kirot Noflim*, p. 29.

8. Aharon Carmi and Chaim Frimmer, *Min ha-Deleka ha-Hi (From that Conflagration)* (Tel Aviv, 1961), p. 215 (the memoirs of Chaim Frimmer).

9. See Kermish, *Mered Getto Varsha*, p. 128.

10. See Konrad's statement in Blumental and Kermish, *Ha-Meri ve-ha-Mered*, p. 370. In fact, it was not until June 29, 1943, that Stroop was nominated, by order of Himmler, to the post of "S.S.- *und Polizeiführer* in the District of Warsaw."

11. Kermish, *Mered Getto Varsha*, pp. 189–90.

12. See Mark, *Powstanie w getcie warszawskim*, Document No. 102, pp. 335, 337.

13. Kermish, *Mered Getto Varsha*, p. 206. In the above-mentioned material by Moczarski, Stroop's arrival in Warsaw is described as follows: "On April 15 Stroop, who was at the headquarters of the *S.S.- und Polizeiführer* of Galicia, Katzman, received a telephone call." According to Moczarski, Stroop related in the first person: "Suddenly the telephone rang. . . . I heard an officer ask for me. The next thing I heard was the voice of Heinrich Himmler himself. I sensed that it was something important. The *Reichsführer-S.S.* gave me a brief order, as soldiers are wont to do, to leave for Cracow the next day and consult with Commander Krieger before going on to Warsaw." In the conversation he held with Krieger, Stroop was told that von Sammern was soft-hearted and could not be relied upon. When Stroop reached Warsaw, it turned out that his liaison in his new post was Dr. Ludwig Hahn, the commander of the Security Police in the city. It is pertinent to point out that Hahn has succeeded in evading trial for many years and lives prosperously in the Federal Republic of Germany.

14. See Blumental and Kermish, *Ha-Meri ve-ha-Mered*, p. 249.

15. Carmi and Frimmer, *Min ha-Deleka ha-Hi*, pp. 216–17.

16. Kermish, *Mered Getto Varsha*, pp. 138–39, 211.

17. See the selection from the memoirs of Dr. Walewski in Lazar, *Mezada shel Varsha*, pp. 245–46.

18. Edelman, *Getto walczy*, p. 55.

19. Kermish, *Mered Getto Varsha*, p. 139.

20. According to Halperin, eight members of Betar fell that day, including a member of the command, Eliyahu Halberstein. See *Ha-Emet al ha-Mered be-Getto Varsha*, p. 21.

21. See Stroop's statistics on p. 393. A full list of the wounded and their names appears in Wulf, *Das Dritte Reich,* pp. 65–66.

22. Kermish, *Mered Getto Varsha*, p. 139.

23. *Ha-Emet al ha-Mered be-Getto Varsha*, pp. 22–23.

24. We do not know the precise details of this escape. One source (undated) speaks of Captain Cezary Ketling moving a group of people with the aid of "caravans" (escort vehicles). These people were taken to Michalin, near Warsaw; there is mention of eighteen people being taken out in each transport, with the exit lasting for a week (Lazar, p. 315). Iwański speaks of removing a group of thirty-four people, some of whom also reached Michalin (Blumental and Kermish, *Ha-Meri ve-ha-Mered*, pp. 164–65). These are probably references to two separate actions, since the concentration of such a large number of people (140) in a forest near Warsaw is clearly improbable, and we cannot assume that Captain Ketling had at his disposal the means to organize an action on this scale. Furthermore, this action is not corroborated by any Jewish source.

25. See Mark, *Powstanie w getcie warszawskim*, Document No. 55A, the

report of the gendarmerie on the clash with Jewish groups in the vicinity of Warsaw, p. 260.

26. See Jaworski, "Plac Muranowski 7."

27. Yad Vashem Archive, O-3/443 (testimony of Arie Najberg).

28. Kermish, *Mered Getto Varsha*, p. 142.

29. Ibid., p. 140.

30. See the report of Major Pszenny, who commanded the operation, in Blumental and Kermish, *Ha-Meri ve-ha-Mered*, pp. 404–406. Mark also published a letter he received from General Chruściel in 1958, when the latter was living in exile in the United States (Mark, *Powstanie w getcie warszawskim*, Document No. 65, pp. 272–74). There is also the letter sent by Chruściel to Woliński on April 22, which states that "as a result of our action on Bonifraterska Street, we had many dead and wounded" (Blumental and Kermish, *Ha-Meri ve-ha-Mered*, p. 404). According to this letter, the first action was carried out on April 19.

31. See Mark, *Powstanie w getcie warszawskim*, Document No. 60, pp. 265–66. Mark's version has it that a group "was supposed to attack a guard of the SS and Blue Police at the corner of Okopowa and Gęsia streets. The grenades did not explode. The soldiers of the *Gwardia* began to shoot and the Germans returned a hail of fire. With that the action ended." Lęczyski, an A.K. soldier involved in the action, reported a different version of the event. The commander of the action, Mietek Lerner, was a Jew. On his way to execute the action, he was stopped by a blackmailer and threatened. Lerner took out a revolver and shot the extortionist, and the shot attracted a lot of attention. The members of the group retreated to the Polish sector, and while Lerner ran in the direction of the ghetto, Germans appeared and shot him. See *Wspomnienia warszawskich PPRowców* (*The Recollections of Members of the PPR of Warsaw*) (Warsaw, 1963), p. 52.

32. Mark, *Powstanie w getcie warszawskim*, p. 75. According to Mark there were ten armed people in the group. In his letter to Mark (see note 30), Chruściel states that there were 300 people in this group. His claim is totally unfounded, and the inflation of the figure was designed to enhance the aid tendered by the Poles.

33. Kermish, *Mered Getto Varsha*, pp. 141–42.

34. Blumental and Kermish, *Ha-Meri ve-ha-Mered*, p. 212.

35. Kermish, *Mered Getto Varsha*, pp. 144–45.

36. Yad Vashem Archive, O-3/2511 (testimony of Simha Ratajzer-Rotem).

37. Edelman, *Getto walczy*, pp. 57–58.

38. See Kermish, *Mered Getto Varsha*, p. 202.

39. Blumental and Kermish, *Ha-Meri ve-ha-Mered*, Document No. 130, p. 367.

40. See Yad Vashem Archive, TR-10/26 (Többens's file).

41. Kermish, *Mered Getto Varsha*, p. 142.

42. Blumental and Kermish, *Ha-Meri ve-ha-Mered*, Document No. 126, pp. 349–50.

43. Kermish, *Mered Getto Varsha*, p. 144.

44. Grajek, *Sheloshah Yemei Kerav*, pp. 120–21.

45. Kermish, *Mered Getto Varsha*, p. 149.

46. See Yisrael Gutman, *Anashim va-Efer: Sefer Auschwitz-Birkenau* (*People and Ashes: The Book of Auschwitz-Birkenau*) (Tel Aviv, 1957), pp. 196–97.

47. Gutman, *Mered ha-Nezurim*, p. 362.

48. B. Goldman, "75 Yom be-Getto Varsha ha-Ole be-Lehavot" ("75 Days in the Burning Warsaw Ghetto") in Blumental and Kermish, *Ha-Meri ve-ha-Mered*, p. 281.

49. Kermish, *Mered Gretto Varsha*, pp. 151–52, 156, 171.

50. See Zuckerman and Basok, *Sefer Milhamot*, p. 158.

51. Edelman, *Getto walczy*, p. 61.

52. Kermish, *Mered Getto Varsha*, pp. 149, 152, 154, 159, 161, 170, 172–73, 186. In each case of a reference to Stroop's reports, I refer the reader to the Hebrew translation in Kermish. At the same time, I have checked each translation against the original German and sometimes believe it necessary to render certain corrections; hence the differences between Kermish's version and the English translations given here.

53. Edelman, *Getto walczy* p. 62.

54. Communiqué No. 5 of the Jewish underground on the "Aryan" side of Warsaw, dated April 22, states that "according to interim calculations, the number of German casualties in the first three days of fighting was 200 dead and 400 wounded"; see Zuckerman and Basok, *Sefer Milhamet*, p. 180. Edelman states that "more than 100 SS men were killed by the explosion" of mines in the Brushmakers' Area on April 20; see Edelman, *Getto walczy*, p. 55. Borzykowski states that "according to a lookout, the Germans left behind a few dozen dead and wounded after the first battle on Nalewki" (p. 32). Finally, the Ż.O.B. report has it that 200 Germans fell on the first day in the main battle at the corner of Miła and Zamenhofa.

55. See Blumental and Kermish, *Ha-Meri ve-ha-Mered*, p. 330.

56. Kermish, *Mered Getto Varsha*, pp. 154, 166, 192, 193.

57. Ibid., pp. 176, 231.

58. The Ż.O.B. did not have a chief of staff. Though it is possible to view the commander of the Central Ghetto as a kind of chief of staff, Yisrael Kanał, who was not among the people trapped by Stroop, came closer to fitting this designation. Kanał was in the group that managed to escape the ghetto at the end of the fighting and reach the forest in the Wyszków area. In August 1943 Kanał, now a South American subject, returned to Warsaw and was sent to Bergen-Belsen. In October 1943 he was deported to Auschwitz and perished there. See Zuckerman and Basok, *Sefer Milhamot*, p. 747.

59. Kermish, *Mered Getto Varsha*, pp. 177–78.

60. Ibid., pp. 187, 192.

61. See Blumental and Kermish, *Ha-Meri ve-ha-Mered*, p. 345.

62. Arie Najberg, *Ha-Ahronim: Be-kez ha-Mered shel Getto Varsha (The Last Ones: At the End of the Warsaw Ghetto Uprising)* (Tel Aviv, 1958), pp. 110–11, 133–34, 189–91.

63. Yad Vashem Archive, O-3/714 (testimony of Stefania Fiedelzeid, who lived in a bunker within the area of the ghetto until January 1944).

Chapter 15: Repercussions of the Revolt

1. Kermish, *Mered Getto Varsha*, p. 201; see also pp. 129, 138, 148.

2. Landau, *Kronika*, Vol. II, pp. 335, 358. Landau goes on to state that the rumors and news on the development of the battles raging in the ghetto created the impression that the ghetto was a fortress controlled by its inhabitants.

3. Ibid., pp. 362, 370.

4. Blumental and Kermish, *Ha-Meri ve-ha-Mered*, Document No. 116, p. 333.

5. See Mark, *Powstanie w getcie warszawskim*, p. 312. *Biuletyn Informacyjny* was an organ of the circles within the A.K. and was regarded as an official mouthpiece of the armed underground in Poland. As stated, this paper gave broad coverage to Jewish affairs and received accurate information, as a rule, regarding what was going on in the ghetto. This fact is to be credited to the paper's editor, Aleksander Kamiński, who belonged to the Polish Scouts, which had previously been associated with the Jewish youth movements. Kamiński aided a number of members of the Jewish underground. According to Woliński, it was Kamiński who put Arie Wilner in contact with him.

6. Yad Vashem Archive, O-25/25.

7. Yad Vashem Archive, O-25/140, *Tydzień*, 6 (April 29, 1943).

8. Ibid., *Nowa Polska*, 91 (May 7, 1943).

9. Ibid., *Polska*, 16 (May 6, 1943).

10. Ibid., *Głos Pracy*, 18 (undated). This paper reported that during the first week of fighting in the ghetto, the number of German dead and wounded reached 1,000, and it portrayed "the war of the Germans in the Warsaw ghetto as a fiasco" from the military point of view. See Bartoszewski's article "Hagannat ha-Getto be-Aspeklaryat ha-Itonut ha-Mahtartit" ("The Defense of the Ghetto as Reflected in the Underground Press") in Blumental and Kermish, *Ha-Meri ve-ha-Mered*, p. 438.

11. Yad Vashem Archive, O-25/202-3.

12. See Mark, *Powstanie w getcie warszawskim*, pp. 312–13.

13. *Tsum tsentn yortog, Prawda Młodych* (April–May 1943), pp. 279–80; published by the Catholic youth who established the *Front Odrodzenia Polski* (Front for the Renewal of Poland).

14. Quoted in Bartoszewski, "Hagannat ha-Getto," p. 437.

15. *Tsum tsentn yortog*, pp. 277–78.

16. Bartoszewski, "Hagannat ha-Getto," p. 437.

17. *Związek Walki Zbrojnej*, the name of the movement that was a precursor of the A.K.

18. Yad Vashem Archive, O-25/202-3, *Robotnik*, 113 (May 1, 1943).

19. *Tsum tsentn yortog*, p. 270.

20. Ibid., p. 191.

21. Yad Vashem Archive, O-25/1.

22. Yad Vashem Archive, O-25/35, 15-302 (*Polska*).

23. Mark, *Powstanie w getcie warszawskim*, Document No. 76, pp. 290–91.

24. See the cable from General Kukieł in the Polish Underground Study Trust, London, 06.3.1.1.

25. Sikorski's appeal, which was broadcast over the BBC and addressed to the Polish population, received wide coverage in the underground Polish press. In its wake came the statement by the underground organizations in Poland (the Polish independence organizations). See Blumental and Kermish, *Ha-Meri ve-ha-Mered*, Document No. 140, pp. 392–93.

26. In the middle of April 1943 the Nazis spread reports that the Soviets had murdered thousands of Polish officers who had been taken as prisoners of war in 1939. The Germans claimed that the bodies were found in several mass graves in the Katyń Forest near Smolensk. The Poles demanded that an inquiry be conducted by the International Red Cross. In response, Stalin announced the breaking off of relations with the Polish government-in-exile on April 26,

1943. Today it is generally assumed that the Soviets were responsible for this massacre, an assumption confirmed by substantial documentation.

27. See Ber Mark, *Walka i zagłada warszawskiego getta* (*The Struggle and Destruction of the Warsaw Ghetto*) (Warsaw, 1959), p. 327.

28. The radically nationalist, anti-Semitic wing in Polish politics, *Obóz Narodowo-Radykalny* (Radical Nationalist Camp).

29. Ringelblum, *Ktovim*, Vol. II, pp. 341-42.

30. Landau, *Kronika*, Vol. II, pp. 355, 357.

31. Balicka-Kozłowska, pp. 31-32.

32. Kazimierz Brandys, *Miasto niepokonane* (*The Invincible City*) (Warsaw, 1960), pp. 195-96.

33. Blumental and Kermish, *Ha-Meri ve-ha-Mered*, pp. 399-403.

34. See Zuckerman's remarks on his relationship with the Poles — representatives of the underground at large and A.K. people — at the outbreak of and during the uprising in "Mered ha-Yehudim"; further details on these ties were given by Zuckerman in a meeting of the Moreshet Study Circle held on February 26, 1973, in Tel Aviv (the minutes of which are in the author's possession). At this meeting, Zuckerman spoke about this means of communication with the ghetto until the outbreak of the revolt: "A few words on the means of communication with the ghetto. Jews were working in a printing press on Tłomacka Street, which was outside the ghetto. We had three loyal people in the police, and one of them was an officer. Through them we used to pass my letters to the printing workers, and they would bring them into the ghetto. In the morning I would receive the reply. Another means was by telephone. There were a number of unlisted phones. They could call us, but we couldn't call them. A third means was via the Jewish cemetery, which bordered on the Christian cemetery."

On the same occasion, Zuckerman also stated that in March (the exact date was not given) 1943, "an urgent telephone call came from the A.K. stating that they were prepared to renew contact. . . ." The wording of this urgent announcement was: "If you don't want the salt to follow the food, call immediately," meaning that the contact must be renewed quickly or it might be too late.

35. Moreshet Archive, the memoirs of Guta Wilner (Arie Wilner's sister).

36. See Zuckerman, "Mered ha-Yehudim," p. 430.

37. At the above-cited meeting of the Moreshet Study Circle, Zuckerman again described his meeting with the A.K. intelligence man. " . . . He stated things quite clearly: 'You won't receive aid. We know that the ghetto serves as a base for the Communists.' My reply was that the Jewish Fighting Organization is not a Communist group. It is composed of Jews. The fact that the commander is [from a pioneering movement] and his deputy (that is, myself) is also [from a pioneering movement] speaks for itself. If there are Communists in the ranks of the Jewish Fighting Organization, well, there may also be Communists in the A.K. He repeated his statement that help will not be given in any form whatsoever. They were only willing to do one thing, and that is get people out of the ghetto. I wouldn't agree to that. Only when there is no other choice would they agree to leave. My basic demand: passage [out of the ghetto] and especially a map of the sewer system (it should be noted that a map of this kind is not a secret document in any city). His reply was negative." (Minutes of the meeting in the author's possession.)

38. See Chruściel's letter in Blumental and Kermish, *Ha-Meri ve-ha-Mered*, Document No. 148, pp. 406-408.

39. We have in our hands a letter sent by Chruściel to Woliński on April 22. Written at the height of the uprising, it states: "Your urgent letters reach me without delay. Please, don't be shocked and explain to "Antek" [Zuckerman] that at such a time of emergency, there is no place for personal contact; we must act now." At the meeting of the Moreshet Study Circle, Zuckerman explained that he demanded to meet with the commander of the A.K., but this meeting never took place and the A.K. authorities later claimed that it failed to take place because "Antek" was ill. Zuckerman claims, however, that he was not ill at all, and the only reason the meeting did not take place was because the A.K. did not want it to. Chruściel's letter clearly suggests an attempt to avoid meeting Zuckerman, and it is not at all understandable why an emergency situation would preclude such a meeting with the official representative of the Jewish Fighting Organization. Moreover, it is unthinkable that any effective or significant action—of which Chruściel was supposedly in favor—could have been mounted without such prior contact.

40. See Mark, *Walka i zagłada warszawskiego getta*, pp. 286–87.

41. See the manifesto ascribed to the Ż.Z.W. in Blumental and Kermish, *Ha-Meri ve-ha-Mered*, pp. 151–52.

42. Yad Vashem Archive, O-3/2913 (Simha Korngold's manuscript); Lazar, *Mezada shel Varsha*, p. 314.

43. Carmi's story in Carmi and Frimmer, *Min ha-Deleka ha-Hi*, pp. 149–52.

44. See the testimony of Simha Ratajzer in Blumental and Kermish, *Ha-Meri ve-ha-Mered*, pp. 253–55.

45. Borzykowski, *Bein Kirot Noflim*, pp. 92–93.

46. Kermish, *Mered Getto Varsha*, pp. 133–34.

47. Wulf, *Das Dritte Reich*, pp. 28, 370.

48. *Goebbels' Tagebücher aus den Jahren 1942–43 mit andern Dokumenten*, ed. Louis P. Lochner (Zurich, 1948), pp. 313, 318.

49. *Okupacja i ruch oporu*, Vol. II, p. 150.

50. See Joseph Kermish, "The Warsaw Ghetto Uprising in the Light of a Hitherto Unpublished Official German Report," *Yad Vashem Studies*, 9 (1973), 7–27.

51. Fischer's announcement of May 13, 1943. Hebrew translation in Blumental and Kermish, *Ha-Meri ve-ha-Mered*, p. 368.

52. Piotrowski, *Misja Odyla Globocnika*, pp. 56–57.

SOURCES

I. Archives

A. Yad Vashem Archive

M–1/E	Testimonies and diaries
M–3	JUS Division and JDC material
M–2	Schwartzbart Collection
M–20	"Relico" Division—Silberstein, Geneva
M–10	Ringelblum Archive Division—"Oneg Shabbat"
M–11	Underground Archive of Bialystok Ghetto
O–16	Historical Committee in Poland Collection
O–6	Poland Collection
O–17	YIVO Division
O–25	Zylberberg Collection
O–33	Collection of testimonies and diaries
TR–1	International Nuremberg Trials
TR–2/N–IV	Pohl Case
TR–3	Eichmann Trial
TR–10/26	Többens's Trial
TR–10/475, TR–10/639	Karl Wolff's Trial
TR–548	Klaustermeyer's Trial
TR–10/462	Ernst Brunst's Trial
TR–10/768	Streckenbach's Trial
TR–10/799	Ludwig Hahn's Trial

B. Central Zionist Archive

S–26	Rescue Committee
S–32	Youth and Pioneering Department
S–46	Yitzhak Gruenbaum Division

C. Moreshet Archive

D.1.62	The letters of Mordecai Anielewicz
D.1.33	The Warsaw Ghetto Uprising and the Ż.O.B.
A.262,267	Testimonies on the attitude of the Poles toward the Jews during the occupation
D.2.6	Engleman's memoirs

D. Beit Lohamei ha-Getta'ot Archive

unmarked	Minutes of the meeting of activists in the Warsaw ghetto underground

E. The Polish Institute and Sikorski Museum, London

PRM 57
PRM 142
PRM 24
PRM L
A I

II. Newspapers

A. Underground Jewish Press

Awangarda Młodzieży	*Oyfbroyz*
Bafrayung	*Oyf der vakh*
Biuletyn	*Płomienie*
Der Ruf	*Proletarisher Gedank*
Der Veker	*Przegląd Rolniczy*
Dror	*Słowo Młodych*
El Al	*Tsayt Fragn*
Jutrznia	*Yediot*
Magen David	*Yunge Gwardye*
Morgen-Frayhayt	*Yugntruf*
Neged ha-Zerem	*Yugnt-Shtime*

B. Underground Polish Press

Agencja A	*Nowy Dzień*
Biuletyn Informacyjny	*Polska*
Dzień	*Polska Walczy*
Dzień Warszawy	*Polska Zwycięży*
Dziś i Jutro	*Prawda*
Głos Demokracji	*Prawda Młodych*
Głos Polski	*Przez Walkę do Zwycięstwa*
Głos Pracy	*Robotnik*
Głos Warszawy	*Szaniec*
Gwardia	*Trybuna Wolności*
Gwardia Ludowa	*Walka*
Gwardzista	*Walka Ludu*
Kronika Okupacji	*Walka Młodych*
Myśl Państwowa	*Wiadomości Codzienne*
Nowa Polska	*Wiadomości Polskie*
Nowe Drogi	*WRN*

III. Periodicals, Journals, Miscellaneous

Bleter far geshikhte
Biuletyn Głównej Komisji Badania Zbrodni Niemieckich (Hitlerowskich) w Polsce
Biuletyn Żydowskiego Instytutu Historycznego (B.Ż.I.H.)
Dappim le-Heker ha-Sho'ah ve-ha-Mered
Gazeta Żydowska
The Jewish Quarterly
Jewish Social Studies
Massu'ah
Mi-Bifnim
Molad
Mosty
Odra
Pirsumei Muze'on ha-Lohamim ve-ha-Partizanim
The Wiener Library Bulletin
Yad Vashem: Kovez Mehkarim be-Parshiyot ha-Sho'a ve-ha-Gvura
Yad Vashem Studies

Yalkut Moreshet
Yediot Beit Lohamei ha-Getta'ot
Yediot Yad Vashem
Yidishe Shriftn
YIVO Bleter
Z Pola Walki
Zeszyty Historyczne

BIBLIOGRAPHY

I. Collections of Documents

Apenszlak, Jacob, ed. *The Black Book of Polish Jewry.* New York, 1943.

Arad, Yitzhak; Gutman, Yisrael; and Margaliot, Abraham, eds. *Documents on the Holocaust: Selected Sources on the Destruction of the Jews of Germany and Austria, Poland and the Soviet Union.* Jerusalem, 1981.

Baynes, Norman H., ed. *The Speeches of Adolf Hitler, April 1922–August 1939.* Vols. I–II. London, 1942.

Berenstein, Tatiana; Eisenbach, Artur; and Rutkowski, Adam, eds. *Eksterminacja Żydów na ziemiach polski: Zbiór dokumentów.* Warsaw, 1957.

Blumental, Nachman, and Kermish, Joseph, eds. *Ha-Meri ve-ha-Mered be-Getto Varsha.* Jerusalem, 1965.

Caban, Ireneusz, and Mánkowski, Zygmunt. *Związek Walki Zbrojnej I Armia Krajowa w okregu lubelskim, 1939–1944.* Vol. II. Warsaw, 1971.

Cyprian, Tadeusz, and Sawicki, Jerzy. *Sprawy polskie w procesie norymberskim.* Poznán, 1956.

Dobroszycki, Lucjan, et al., eds. *Cywilna obrona Warszawy we wrześniu 1939: Dokumenty, materiały prasowe i relacje.* Warsaw, 1964.

Domarus, Max. *Hitler-Reden und Proklamationen, 1932–1945.* Vol. II. Bde. Neustadt, 1962–63.

Halder, Franz. *Kriegstagebuch.* Vol. II. Stuttgart, 1952.

Ha-Yo'ez ha-Mishpati la-Memshala Neged Adolf Eichmann–Eduyot. Vols. I–II. Jerusalem, 1963.

Hilberg, Raul, ed. *Documents of Destruction: Germany and Jewry, 1933–1945.* Chicago, 1971.

Hofer, Walter. *Der Nationalsozialismus: Dokumente, 1933–1945.* Frankfurt, 1957.

Ittonut Gordonya be-Mahteret Getto Varsha. Hulda, 1966.

Nazi Conspiracy and Aggression. Washington, D.C., 1946–48.

Okupacja i ruch oporu w dzienniku Hansa Franka, 1939–1945. Vol. I. Warsaw, 1972.

Pospieszalski, Karl M., ed. *Hitlerowskie "prawo" okupacyjne w Polsce: Wybór dokumentów.* (*Documenta Occupationis,* Vol. VI.) Poznán, 1958.

Reprezentacja Żydostwa Polskiego: Sprawozdanja z działalności w Latach 1940–1945. Mimeographed.

Trial of the Major War Criminals Before the International Military Tribunal, 14.XI.1945–1.X.1946. Vols. I–XLII, 1947–49 (PS, NG, NO).

Tsum tsentn yortog fun oyfshtand in Varshever geto: Dokumentn un materialn. Gezamelt un mit a forvort un Bamerkungen fun Ber Mark. Warsaw, 1953.

II. Diaries, Memoirs, Biographies, and Partial Adaptations

Adam (Zylberstejn). *Getta'ot: Varsha-Częstochowa.* Merhavah, 1945.

Auerbach, Rachel. *Be-Huzot Varsha, 1939–1949.* Tel Aviv, 1954.

Balicka-Kozłowska, Helena. *Mur miał dwie strony.* Warsaw, 1958.

Berg, Mary. *Warsaw Ghetto: A Diary by Mary Berg.* Edited by S. L. Schneiderman. New York, 1945.

Berman, Adolf Abraham. *Mi-Yemei ha-Mahteret.* Tel Aviv, 1971.

Berman-Temkin, Batya. *Yoman ba-Mahteret.* Beit Lohamei ha-Getta'ot, 1956.

Birenbaum, Halina. *Nadzieja umiera ostatnia.* Warsaw, 1967.

———. *Hope Is the Last to Die: A Personal Documentation of Nazi Terror.* New York, 1971.

Borwicz, Michael. *Arishe papirn.* Vols. 1–3. Buenos Aires, 1955.

Brandys, Kazimierz. *Miasto niepokonane.* Warsaw, 1960.

Braun, Zvi, and Levin, Dov. *Toldoteha shel Mahteret.* Jerusalem, 1962.

Carmi, Aharon, and Frimmer, Chaim. *Min ha-Deleka ha-Hi.* Tel Aviv, 1961.

Czerniakow, Adam. *The Warsaw Diary of Adam Czerniakow: Prelude to Doom.* Edited by Raul Hilberg, Stanislaw Staron, and Josef Kermisz. New York, 1979.

Donat, Alexander. *The Holocaust Kingdom.* London, 1965.

Dworzecki, Meir. *Yerushalayim de-Lita be-Meri Vashóa.* Tel Aviv, 1951.

Eck, Natan. *Ha-To'im be-Darkei ha-Mavet.* Jerusalem, 1960.

Edelman, Marek. *Getto walczy.* Warsaw, 1946.

Elster, Pola; Berlinski, Hirsch; and Ehrlich, Eliyahu. *Dray.* Tel Aviv, 1966.

Fuchs, Tania. *A vanderung iber okupirte gebitn.* Buenos Aires, 1947.

Gelbard, Chana, and Helfgot, Yerahmiel, eds. *Mi-Bein Homot Varsha.* Ein-Harod, 1944.

Goebbels' Tagebücher aus den Jahren 1942–43 mit andern Dokumenten. Edited by Louis P. Lochner. Zurich, 1948.

Goldkorn, Dorka. *Mayne Zikhroynes fun oyfshtand in varshever geto.* Warsaw, 1948.

Goldstein, Bernard. *Five Years in the Warsaw Ghetto.* New York, 1961.

———. *Finef yor in varshever geto.* New York, 1947.

Grajek, Shalom-Stefan. *Shelosha Yemei Kerav.* Tel Aviv, 1972.

Grossman, Chaika. *Anshei ha-Mahteret.* Merhavyah, 1965.

Grynberg, Henryk. *Wojna żydowska.* Warsaw, 1966.

Gutman, Yisrael. *Mered ha-Nezurim: Mordecai Anielewicz ve-Milhemet Getto Varsha.* Merhavyah, 1963.

Hancze ve-Frumka: Mikhtavim ve-Divrei-Zikkaron. Tel Aviv, 1945.

Hertz, Ya'akov S., ed. *Zygielbojm-Bukh.* New York, 1947.

Hirszfeld, Ludwik. *Historia jednego życia.* Warsaw, 1946.

Huberband, Shimon. *Kiddush ha-Shem.* Tel Aviv, 1969.

Kaplan, Chaim A. *Megillat Yissurin: Yoman Getto Varsha.* Tel Aviv–Jerusalem, 1966.

———. *Scroll of Agony: The Warsaw Diary of Chaim A. Kaplan.* Edited by Abraham I. Katsh. London, 1966.

Karski-Kozielewski, Jan. *Story of a Secret State.* Boston, 1944.

Katzenelson, Yitzhak. *Ketavim Aharonim.* Beit Lohamei ha-Getta'ot, 1956.

Klinger, Chaika. *Mi-Yoman ba-Getto.* Merhavyah, 1959.

Komorowski-Bor, Tadeusz. *The Secret Army.* New York, 1951.

Korboński, Stefan. *W imieniu Rzeczypospolitej.* Paris, 1954.

Korczak, Janusz. *Wybór pism*. Vol. IV. Warsaw, 1958.
Korczak, Rayzl (Rozka). *Lehavot ba-Efer*. Merhavyah, 1965.
Kurtz, Ya'akov. *Sefer Edut*. Tel Aviv, 1944.
Landau, Ludwik. *Kronika lat wojny i okupacji*. Vols. I–III. Warsaw, 1961–62.
Lazar, Chaim. *Mezada shel Varsha: Ha-Irgun ha-Zeva'i ha-Yehudi be-Mered Getto Varsha*. Tel Aviv, 1963.
———. *Muranowska 7: The Warsaw Ghetto Uprising*. Tel Aviv, 1966.
Leńsky, M[ordecai]. *Hayei ha-Yehudim be-Getto Varsha: Zikhronotav shel Rofe*. Jerusalem, 1961.
Levin, Abraham. *Mi-Pinkaso shel ha-More mi-"Yehudiyah."* Beit Lohamei ha-Getta'ot, 1969.
Lubetkin, Zivia. *Aharonim al ha-Homa*. Ein-Harod, 1947.
Mastbaum, Yoel. *Shishim Yom be-Polin shel Hitler*. Tel Aviv, 1940.
Moczarski, Kazimierz. *Rozmowy z Katem*. Warsaw, 1977.
Najberg, Arie. *Ha-Ahronim: Be-Kez ha-Mered shel Getto Varsha*. Tel Aviv, 1958.
Nowodworski, Moshe. *David Nowodworski (1916–1943): Hayav, Po'alo, u-Moto*. Kiryat Yam, 1956 (mimeographed).
Opoczyński, Peretz. *Reshimot*. Beit Lohamei ha-Getta'ot, 1970.
Rowecki, Stefan. *Wspomnienia i notatki, 1939*. Warsaw, 1957.
Ringelblum, Emmanuel. *Notitsn fun varshever geto*. Warsaw, 1952.
———. *Notes from the Warsaw Ghetto: The Journal of Emmanuel Ringelblum*. Edited and translated by Jacob Sloan. New York, 1958.
———. *Ktovim fun geto*. Vols. I–II. Warsaw, 1961.
Rzepecki, Jan. *Wspomnienia i przyczynki historyczne*. Warsaw, 1956.
Smólski, Władysław. *Zaklęte lata*. Warsaw, 1964.
Szereszewska, Halina. *Ha-Perek ha-Aharon*. Tel Aviv, 1968.
———. *Bein ha-Zlav ve-ha-Mezuzah*. Merhavyah, 1969.
Szoszkes, Chaim. *Bleter fun a geto togbukh*. New York, 1944.
———. *A velt vos iz forbay*. Buenos Aires, 1949.
Tenebaum-Tamarof, Mordecai. *Dappim Min ha-Deleka*. Beit Lohamei ha-Getta'ot, 1949.
Tselemenski, Ya'akov. *Mitn farshnitenem folk*. New York, 1963.
Tsveishen Leben un Toit. Warsaw, 1955.
Turkow, Jonas. *Azoy iz es geven*. Buenos Aires, 1948.
———. *Hayo Hayta Varsha Yehudit*. Tel Aviv, 1969.
Wdowiński, David. *Ve-Anahnu Lo Noshanu*. Tel Aviv, 1970.
———. *And We Are Not Saved*. London, 1964.
Weichert, Michael. *Yidishe aleynhilf, 1939–1945*. Tel Aviv, 1962.
———. *Milhamah-Zikhronot*. Tel Aviv, 1963.
Wspomnienia warszawskich peperowców. Warsaw, 1963.
Zagórski, Wacław. *Wolność w niewoli*. London, 1971.
Zeidman, Hillel. *Yoman Getto Varsha*. New York, 1957.
Zonshayn, Moshe. *Yidish Varshe*. Buenos Aires, 1954.

III. Monographs, Reference Works, and Collections

Adam, Uwe D. *Judenpolitik im Dritten Reich*. Düsseldorf, 1972.
Bartoszewski, Władysław, and Lewin, Zofia, eds. *Righteous Among Nations*. London, 1969.

————. *The Samaritans: Heroes of the Holocaust.* New York, 1970.

Bartoszewski, Władysław. *The Bloodshed United Us.* Warsaw, 1970.

Bauer, Yehuda. *American Jewry and the Holocaust: The American Joint Distribution Committee, 1939–1945.* Detroit, 1981.

Borwicz, Michał. *Pieśń ujdzie cało . . .* Warsaw, 1947.

Broszat, Martin. *Nationalsozialistische Polenpolitik, 1939–1945.* Stuttgart, 1965.

Buchheim, Hans, et al. *Anatomy of the S.S. State.* London, 1968.

————. *Anatomie des SS-Staates.* Olten and Freiburg im Breisgau, 1965.

Dawidowicz, Lucy S. *The War Against the Jews, 1933–1945.* New York, 1975.

————, ed. *A Holocaust Reader.* New York, 1976.

Dror, Levi, and Rosenzweig, Yisrael, eds. *Sefer Ha-Shomer ha-Za'ir.* Merhavyah, 1956.

Eisenbach, Artur. *Hitlerowska polityka eksterminacji Żydów.* Warsaw, 1953.

Esh, Shaul, *Iyunim be-Heker ha-Sho'a ve-Yahadut Zemanenu.* Jerusalem, 1973.

Friedman, Philip. *Martyrs and Fighters: The Epic of the Warsaw Ghetto.* New York, 1954.

Georg, Enno. *Die wirtschaftlichen Unternehmungen der SS.* Stuttgart, 1963.

Gotesfirch, David; Hadari, Haim; and Reichman, Aharon, eds. *Sefer Dror.* Tel Aviv, 1947.

Gruenbaum, Yitzhak, ed. *Enziklopedya shel Galuyot.* Vol. I, *Warsaw.* Tel Aviv, 1953. Vol. VI, *Warsaw,* Part 2. Jerusalem, 1959.

Gutman, Yisrael, and Rothkirchen, Livia, eds. *The Catastrophe of European Jewry: Antecedents, History, Reflections.* Jerusalem, 1976.

Gutman, Yisrael, and Zuroff, Efraim, eds. *Rescue Attempts During the Holocaust.* Proceedings of the Second Yad Vashem International Historical Conference, Jerusalem, April 8–11, 1974. Jerusalem, 1977.

Ha-Emet al ha-Mered be-Getto Varsha. N.p., 1946.

Hilberg, Raul. *The Destruction of the European Jews.* London, 1961.

Höhne, Heinz. *The Order of the Death's Head: The Story of Hitler's S.S.* London, 1969.

Iranek-Osmecki, Kazimierz. *He Who Saves One Life.* New York, 1971.

Jacobsen, Hans Adolf. *Der Zweite Weltkrieg.*

Jewish Resistance During the Holocaust. Proceedings of the Conference on Manifestations of Jewish Resistance, Jerusalem, April 7–11, 1968. Jerusalem, 1971.

Kermish, Joseph, ed. *Mered Getto Varsha be-Einei ha-Oyev: Ha-Dohot shel Jürgen Stroop.* Jerusalem, 1966.

Kevuzot Ilit ve-Shekhavot Manhigut be-Toldot Yisrael u-be-Toldot ha-Amim: Kovez Harza'ot she-Hushme'u be-Kenes ha-Asiri le-Iyun be-Historia. Jerusalem, 1967.

Kirchmayer, Jerzy. *Uwagi i Polemiki.* Warsaw, 1958.

Madajczyk, Czesław. *Polityka III Rzeszy w Okupowanej Polsce.* Vols. I–II. Warsaw, 1970.

Mark, Ber. *Khurves dertseyln.* Lodz, 1947.

————. *Walka i Zagłada warszawskiego getta.* Warsaw, 1959.

————. *Powstanie w getcie warszawskim.* Warsaw, 1963.

————. *Uprising in the Warsaw Ghetto.* New York, 1975.

Mintz, Benjamin, and Klausner, Yisrael, eds., *Sefer ha-Zeva'ot.* Vol. I. Jersualem, 1965.

Neustadt, Melekh, ed. *Hurban ve-Mered Yehudei Varsha.* Tel Aviv, 1947.

Pinkas Varshe. Ershter Band. Buenos Aires, 1955.

Piotrowski, Stanisław. *Misja Odyla Globocnika.* Warsaw, 1970.

Porwit, Marian. *Obrona Warszawy, Wrzesień 1939 wspomnienia i fakty.* Warsaw, 1959.

Publicystyka konspiracyjna PPR, 1942–1945: Wybór artykułów. Vols. I–II. Warsaw, 1961.

Sakowska, Ruta. *Ludzie z dzielnicy zamknietej.* Warsaw, 1975.

Sefer ha-Partizanim ha-Yehudim. Vols. 1–2. Merhavyah, 1959.

Stein, A[braham] Sh[emuel]. *Haver Artur: Demuyot u-Perakim mi-Hayei ha-Bund.* Tel Aviv, 1953.

Tenenbaum, Joseph. *Race and Reich.* New York, 1956.

Trunk, Isaiah. *Judenrat: The Jewish Council in Eastern Europe under Nazi Occupation.* New York, 1971.

Understädt, E. R. *18 Tage Weltgeschehen: Der Feldzug gegen Polen.* Berlin, 1940.

Wulf, Josef. *Das Dritte Reich und seine Vollstrecker: Die Liquidation von 500,000 Juden im Ghetto Warschau.* Berlin, 1961.

Yom Iyun le-Zekher Doktor Emmanuel Ringelblum. Jerusalem, 1964.

Ziemian, Yosef. *Gevulot Getto Varsha ve-Shinuyehem.* Jerusalem, 1971.

Zuckerman, Yitzhak, and Basok, Moshe, eds. *Sefer Milhamot ha-Getta'ot.* Tel Aviv, 1947.

INDEX

Names of political parties and movements appear in boldface.

Adam, U. D., 158
Adamowicz, Irena, 137
Adler, Stanisław, 76, 82, 87, 115, 309
Agudat Israel, 37, 81, 230, 287
A. K. (Home Army), 174, 253–59, 289, 297, 298, 300, 301, 304, 320–22, 343, 345, 346, 348, 354, 356–59, 369, 370, 379, 380, 403, 405, 409, 410, 416–20, 425
Akiva, 138, 236, 238, 239
A. L. (People's Army), 380, 418–20, 423
Albersztein, Eliyahu, 297
Altman, Tosia, 136, 236, 243, 344, 425
Alter, Victor, 121
American Red Cross, 41
Anielewicz, Mordecai, 103, 121, 143, 165, 172; messenger to the underground movement in Zagłębie, 287, 290; and establishment of the expanded framework of Ż.O.B., 287, 290; commander of Ż.O.B., 291, 294, 296, 304; in January battle, 313–15; and preparations toward the uprising, 336, 341, 344, 354; commander of the uprising, 364, 368, 373, 396; his last letter, 358, 390; fighting unit in his name, 425
Anti-Fascist Bloc, 152, 169, 170–75, 230, 235, 241, 242, 249
Arlt, Fritz, Dr., 28, 29, 41
Armbands, 26, 29–31
Artstein, Zecharia, 339, 372
Auerswald, Heinz, 68, 71, 80, 82, 85, 94, 96, 97, 99–101, 105, 112, 179, 199, 201–203

Balicka-Kozłowska, Helina, 414, 415
Barash, Ephraim (head of Bialystok *Judenrat*), 82
Bartoszek, Franciszek ("Jacek"), 380
Bartoszewski, Władysław, 256, 356
Bauer, Yehuda, x
Batz, Rudolf, Dr., 48, 49
Będzin, 234, 237
Begin, Menahem, 121
Belzec (extermination camp), 198
Ben-Sasson, Haim-Hillel, x
Berensohn, Leon, 70
Berlin, 10, 16, 38, 341
Berlinski, Hirsch, 121, 168, 169, 229, 231, 241, 286–89, 291, 304, 312, 314, 339, 377, 383, 425
Berman, Abraham-Adolf, xi, 40, 130, 171, 228, 239, 243; spokesman for National Committee on "Aryan" side of Warsaw, 291, 356
Betar, 121, 140, 152, 163, 175; and establishment of Ż.O.B. and Ż.Z.W., 233, 294–96; during the uprising, 377
Bialopolski, Abraham, 121
Bialystok, 82, 157, 163, 219, 237, 294, 426
Bilawski, Yitzhak, 297
Birenbaum, Halina, 352
Blaskowitz, Johannes, 12
Blaustein, Y., 339